Contemporary
Real Estate Law

BUSINESS LAW SERIES

Contemporary Real Estate Law

Second Edition

C. Kerry Fields

Professor of Clinical Finance and Business Economics
Marshall School of Business
University of Southern California

Kevin C. Fields

Assistant Professor of Clinical Finance and Business
Economics
Marshall School of Business
University of Southern California

Wolters Kluwer

1 2 3 4 5 6 7 8 9 0

ISBN 978-1-4548-9627-2

Library of Congress Cataloging-in-Publication Data

Names: Fields, C. Kerry, author. | Fields, Kevin C., author.
Title: Contemporary real estate law / C. Kerry Fields, Professor of Clinical
  Finance and Business Economics, Marshall School of Business, University of
  Southern California; Kevin C. Fields, Assistant Professor of Clinical
  Finance and Business Economics, Marshall School of Business, University of
  Southern California.
Description: Second edition. | New York : Wolters Kluwer, [2018] | Series:
  Business law series | Includes bibliographical references and index.
Identifiers: LCCN 2017055617 | ISBN 9781454896272
Subjects: LCSH: Real property — United States. | Vendors and
  purchasers — United States. | Real estate business — Law and
  legislation — United States.
Classification: LCC KF570 .F54 2018 | DDC 346.7304/3 — dc23 LC record available at https://lccn.loc.gov/2017055617

SUSTAINABLE FORESTRY INITIATIVE   Certified Sourcing
www.sfiprogram.org
SFI-00756

About Wolters Kluwer Legal & Regulatory U.S.

Wolters Kluwer Legal & Regulatory U.S. delivers expert content and solutions in the areas of law, corporate compliance, health compliance, reimbursement, and legal education. Its practical solutions help customers successfully navigate the demands of a changing environment to drive their daily activities, enhance decision quality and inspire confident outcomes.

Serving customers worldwide, its legal and regulatory portfolio includes products under the Aspen Publishers, CCH Incorporated, Kluwer Law International, ftwilliam.com and MediRegs names. They are regarded as exceptional and trusted resources for general legal and practice-specific knowledge, compliance and risk management, dynamic workflow solutions, and expert commentary.

Summary of Contents

Part IV: Special Topics 471

Contents

Part I: Real Property Interests

Chapter 1

Introduction to Real Estate Law   3

Chapter 2

Real Property Rights and Interests   23

Chapter 3

Easements and Other Nonpossessory Rights   53

Chapter 4

Fixtures and Secured Transactions   73

Chapter 5

Real Property Estates and Interests   91

Chapter 6

Land Descriptions   109

Part II: Purchasing, Financing, and Conveying Real Estate

Chapter 7

Agency and Real Estate Brokers   135

Chapter 8

The Purchase Contract   171

Chapter 9

Valuation and Financing of Real Estate   205

Chapter 10

Deeds, Title, and Closing   255

Chapter 11

Defaults, Workouts, and Foreclosures   303

Part III: Owning, Operating, and Insuring Real Estate

Chapter 12

Ownership of Real Property   327

Chapter 13

Multiunit Dwellings and Property Management   353

Chapter 14

Residential and Commercial Leases   373

Chapter 15

Insuring Real Property   411

Chapter 16

Transfers by Operation of Law and Gift   435

Chapter 17

Transfers after Death: Wills, Intestacy, and Probate 453

Part IV: Special Topics

Chapter 18

Zoning and Land Use Issues 473

Chapter 19

Real Estate Taxation   491

Chapter 20

Construction Law, Liens, and Remedies   509

Chapter 21

Bankruptcy and Restructuring Transactions   537

Chapter 22

Environmental Law in Real Estate Transactions   563

About the Authors

C. Kerry Fields

C. Kerry Fields is a Professor of Clinical Finance and Business Economics at the University of Southern California, Marshall School of Business, where he teaches courses in the undergraduate and MBA programs. He is also a practicing attorney who has represented clients in real estate and construction-related disputes for many years. He has received a number of teaching awards and is a frequent media commentator on issues pertaining to business ethics. He is a co-author of two other Wolters Kluwer texts, *Contemporary Employment Law, Third Edition*, and *Essentials of Real Estate*. Professor Fields received his bachelor's degree in business administration from the University of Southern California and his Juris Doctor from Santa Clara University School of Law.

Kevin C. Fields

Kevin C. Fields is an Assistant Professor of Clinical Finance and Business Economics at the University of Southern California, Marshall School of Business, where he teaches courses in the undergraduate and Master of Business for Veterans (MBV) programs in real estate and business law. He also has a legal practice that focuses on real estate and construction-related disputes. He has tried many real estate-related cases in state and federal courts and successfully resolves disputes through alternative dispute resolution. He is also a California licensed real estate broker. He has received several teaching awards at the University of Southern California. In addition to co-authoring the first edition of this text, he is a co-author of one other Wolters Kluwer text, *Essentials of Real Estate*. Professor Fields received his bachelor's degree in business administration from the University of Southern California and his Juris Doctor from Chapman University School of Law.

Preface

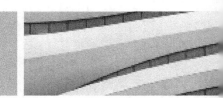

The importance of real estate to the U.S. economy can be recognized by the fact that property is often the single largest component of an individual's wealth. As a result, students should be familiar with a basic understanding of real property laws and their related rules and regulations. Understanding the nature of these interests is the subject of our study.

For the Second Edition of *Contemporary Real Estate*, we spent considerable time trimming material, summarizing concepts, and adding almost 50 new charts, figures, forms, and exhibits to enhance student learning. Three additional chapters were added by separating concepts discussed in existing chapters to make transitions among concepts easier to understand. In this edition, we added a chapter on environmental law to discuss those environmental issues that are frequently encountered in real estate transactions.

As both instructors and practicing attorneys, we know that students want to focus on the practical applications of the material. It is our goal that this text will allow students to recognize potential issues, the competing arguments, and pose fair and equitable solutions to them. We welcome your suggestions to continuously improve this text.

Organization of the Text

This book is written with the student in mind. We have tried to keep legal theory to a minimum and instead introduce the practical applications of concepts in a logical manner. Court cases were carefully screened and concisely edited in a student-friendly manner. To allow the student to grasp the essence of the rules, we have provided many examples that are specially formatted in the text. In addition, a substantial number of the most meaningful terms are defined in chapter margin notes and in a comprehensive glossary at the end of the text.

While the instructor has many choices for their real estate or real property textbook, we believe this text takes a contemporary approach to current real property issues. While all of the traditional topics in a real estate law course are covered, we also include a chapter devoted to defaults, workouts, and foreclosures and a chapter on bankruptcy-related real estate issues. Other unique chapter topics include insuring real property and construction law. In other chapters we discuss construction contracts, defective construction, and mechanic's liens.

The structure of each chapter supports the design of this text. Learning objectives of the most important concepts introduce the subject matter of each chapter. An outline of the significant topics to be discussed follows. Then, an opening scenario invites students to consider how a problem might be solved. This opening prompt is meant to engage the students during the instructor's introduction of chapter material. A summary of terms and concepts keyed to the pages upon which they appear in the text follows. Chapters conclude with a chapter summary and case problems and assignments for discussion or assessment.

The authors' focus on ethics is an important element of this book. Ethical questions are presented with each case and in a variety of boxes throughout the text. Acting upon the challenge to do what is "right" rather than merely what is "permitted" is the character of a great person. We encourage students to make ethical choices in their approach to resolving real estate disputes.

Chapters are structured into four learning units. The first unit begins with real property interests, and six chapters help introduce the student to real property. Students learn the basic rights and interests constituting real property, how they can be possessed, and how those interests may be described.

In the next five chapters, students become familiar with how real estate is purchased, financed, and conveyed. We begin with the law of agency involving real estate professionals. Students will learn how real property is acquired and the elements necessary for an enforceable purchase contract. The legal effects of many of these provisions are carefully explained so that the purchase contract is more readily understood. After that, the student learns how property is valued and financed. The next chapter discusses the different types of deeds, how title is taken to real property, and the closing of a real estate transaction. Once title is taken to real property, a discussion of mortgage defaults, workouts, and foreclosures by a lender is presented.

The next section discusses how real property is owned, operated, insured, and transferred by operation of law, gift, and upon death. The different types of real property ownership begin this part of the book, followed by the different types of multiunit dwellings, including condominiums and cooperatives. Residential and commercial leases and landlord tenant laws are then covered. The types and forms of real property insurance necessary for the use and financing of property is the subject of another chapter. Next, how property is transferred by adverse possession, eminent domain, and gift and then how property is transferred after death through intestate succession, wills, trusts, and probate is discussed.

The last section of the book covers special real estate concepts. Real estate taxation, land use, and zoning, are covered in the first two chapters, followed by construction law and mechanic's liens. We proceed to address the significant bankruptcy aspects involved in real estate transactions and financing and then conclude with a chapter on environmental law in real estate transactions.

Acknowledgments

Although our names appear on the cover of this book, we never would have completed this book without the able assistance of: David Herzig, associate publisher; and Betsy Kenny, developmental editor. We also received the wonderful support of Sarah Hains, project manager for The Froebe Group.

We would especially like to thank Hope Foreman, a third-year student at the Chapman University Dale E. Fowler School of Law, who contributed to the text and ancillary materials.

Special thanks to Donald Mertens and Thomas Propst, both licensed Professional Land Surveyors and instructors at Santiago Canyon College who contributed to the text and many of the figures and exhibits in the Land Descriptions chapter.

Personal Acknowledgments

I dedicate this book to my wife, Patricia, for her years of understanding, love, and support. As to other members of the family, thanks to my son Kevin — my law partner and colleague at the USC Marshall School of Business; my son Brian and his wife, Leigh; my daughter Megan; my daughter-in-law Devon; and the grandkids, who made the family gatherings even more special while writing this.

To the thousands of Trojans we have taught over the years at USC, thank you all. To those whom I have not mentioned by name, the error is mine and unintended.

Fight On!

— C. Kerry Fields

I thank my wife, Devon, and children, Kaitlyn and Ryan, for supporting me and giving me the time to edit this textbook. Your smiles and laughter helped me finish this endeavor.

A special thanks to my co-author and father. Our personal and business relationship working on this project has been one of the most rewarding experiences I have had. You have always been a wonderful mentor and friend. I can't think of a better person with whom I would have wanted to write this book.

Lastly, to the students at the University of Southern California, you motivate me by your spirit and inquisitiveness. Our classroom experiences have helped guide and shape the revisions to this text.

Fight On!

— Kevin C. Fields

Part I
Real Property Interests

Chapter 1
Introduction to Real Estate Law

Property has its duties as well as its rights.
—*Thomas Drummond, British surveyor (1797–1840)*

Learning Objectives

1. Describe what can be considered property.
2. State the differences between real and personal property.
3. List the bundle of rights related to real property.
4. Explain the sources of law governing real property.
5. Discuss the ways to legally resolve a real estate dispute.
6. Identify the advantages and disadvantages of alternative dispute resolution.
7. Recognize the differences between mediation and arbitration.

Chapter Outline

- Introduction
- Nature of Property
- Types of Property

Case 1.1: *In Re Estate of Camas*

- The Law as Rights and Duties
- Property as a Bundle of Rights — The Power to Control
- Sources of Real Estate Law
- Overview of the United States Legal System
- Alternative Dispute Resolution

Case 1.2: *Hall Street Associates, LLC v. Mattel Inc.*

Opening
scenario

The Lobendahns, the sellers, entered into a written contract with the Jacksons, the buyers, to sell their real property located in Utah. The sellers' broker's advertisement of the property included the following provision: "Dispute resolution: this contract will be constructed under Utah law. All controversies arising out of this transaction or this contract or its breach will be settled by binding arbitration in the county where the property is located. The arbitrator may not award any remedy not provided for in this contract."

After closing, the Jacksons visited the property and became concerned that the property included protected wetlands associated with the Great Salt Lake, making the land unusable for the buyer's purposes. The Jacksons filed a lawsuit in Utah state court. The trial court dismissed the case because of the agreement to arbitrate. The Jacksons argued that they should be able to proceed with a lawsuit in state court. Should the Jacksons be compelled to resolve this action in an arbitration proceeding or may they proceed in state court?

Introduction

In this chapter, we begin our study of real estate law. This text deals with the law of real estate with a focus on the practical aspects of that law and not just legal theory. Your understanding of real estate law is important because ownership and use of real property is important to the national economy and personal wealth.

Real estate law involves competing real property interests. For example, open-space preservationists often clash with both developers and urban planners who advocate for increased housing density within urban core communities. When our interest in personal space collides with community planning, the competing policy interests must be considered. This book will cover a wide array of topics and property interests. Understanding the nature of these interests is the focus of our study.

The Importance of Real Estate in Our Economy

In the United States, real property is often the single largest component of individual wealth, and the U.S. Census Bureau reports that more than 63 percent of U.S. householders own their homes.[1] The significant percentage of homeowners in this country means that home ownership plays an important role in, and can significantly impact, our domestic and international economies.

Real estate is the largest personal asset for many Americans and offers security to families. An owner–occupier of real property is motivated to keep it in good repair, as well as to modernize and remodel it. Housing cycles can even affect presidential elections, savings rates, and retirement planning. Undoubtedly, real estate decision-making influences many facets of our economy

Real estate contributes approximately 10 percent of the total output of the U.S. economy, reaching as far as raw material production, manufacturing of finished goods, and construction. A reduction in consumer demand for housing affects consumer demand for other products, such as furniture and home appliances.

Nature of Property

Two theories have been used to define the nature of property. The first is the natural rights doctrine, and the second is the creation of law doctrine.

Natural Rights Doctrine

The **natural rights doctrine** states that certain individual rights are inalienable — that the government cannot take them away from us. This theory underlies many of the duties imposed upon landlords and possessors of property to ensure that real property is maintained in safe and habitable condition.

> *Example:* Building codes require that dwellings be built and maintained in habitable condition, because living in habitable surroundings is an inalienable right.

> *Example:* Federal, state, and local housing discrimination laws and regulations forbid discrimination in the sale, financing, and rental of residential housing; for instance, landlords may not discriminate against an applicant for a rental unit based upon a person's gender.

Natural rights doctrine
Certain individual rights may not be taken away by the government.

These statutes are traceable to this doctrine that the government should neither take nor hinder rights that are essential to an individual's liberty and right to own and control property. This liberty right also protects a landowner from the condemnation of his or her real property by a state highway agency without the receipt of fair compensation for that property. This doctrine appears frequently in the court decisions we will review.

Creation of Law Doctrine

The second theory about the nature of property is the **creation of law doctrine**. Under this rule, property is recognized by government action (whether federal, state, or local), and no person has a particular property right unless the law grants and protects that right. In our study, we will consider many property rights created by the courts and the legislatures.

Creation of law doctrine
Property rights that are created by government action.

> *Example:* The rights and duties of both the lender and the borrower in a residential mortgage transaction are usually defined by state laws and regulations. These laws were created by state statutes and court decisions interpreting those statutes.

Our study of property will involve the rights and duties that flow from these theories. As the law responds to changing societal demands and interests, these theories help frame public debate on various property topics. In our approach, we apply the law in a practical manner as we differentiate between the physical aspects of real property, such as land and buildings, and the legally recognized rights relating to the ownership and use of property, such as the right to develop it.

Types of Property

Property
Anything that can be owned, possessed, controlled, divided, transferred, sold, and made unavailable to others.

Property refers to anything that can be owned, possessed, controlled, divided, transferred, sold, and made unavailable to others. While property may be described and classified in many different ways, property's primary classifications are real property and personal property. Further, within each type of classification, property can be described as either tangible or intangible property.

Real Versus Personal Property

Real property
The earth and all that is permanently attached and connected to the earth.

Real property and personal property classifications have resulted in different rules affecting their ownership and use. **Real property** is characterized as the earth and all that is permanently attached and connected to it.

> *Example:* Land, buildings, landscaping, pools, mineral rights, water rights, and air rights.

We will refer to the term "land" as any unimproved real property. As we will discuss in the next chapter, land ownership includes airspace and subsurface materials and substances, such as water, oil, gas, and geothermal resources.

Personal Property
Property that is movable and not fixed or permanently attached to real property.

Personal property is movable and not fixed or permanently attached to real property. It is sometimes referred to as chattels, goods, or personalty. Generally, anything that is not real property is personal property.

> *Example:* Office chairs, computers, and computer monitors.

The laws of each locality vary greatly as to how personal property is classified. Local laws will often dictate a particular case result, which may vary from the general principles we will study.

> *Example:* Many states will treat a mobile home as personal property. Other states treat them as real property.

Tangible Versus Intangible Property

Tangible property
Property interests that exist in a physical form.

Both real and personal property can be further classified as either tangible or intangible. **Tangible property** interests are those that exist in physical form.

> *Example:* Buildings, landscaping, pools, office chairs, computers, and computer monitors.

Intangible property
Property interests lacking a physical form.

Intangible property is property lacking a physical form.

> *Example:* Air rights, easements, and a copyright held to the building design.

In the following case, the court interpreted the meaning of "personal property" as used in a will.

CASE 1.1

INTENT MAY DETERMINE THE NATURE OF PROPERTY

IN RE ESTATE OF CAMAS
813 N.W.2d 547 (2012)
North Dakota Supreme Court

Eugene Camas died and his son Kevin Camas submitted his will when he filed an application to open probate to have the estate properly distributed. A will provision read in pertinent part, "I hereby leave an undivided one-half ($\frac{1}{2}$) interest in and to the personal property located in my personal residence which I own at the time of my death to my daughter, Sherry." Eugene's daughter Sherry Jensen ("Jensen") was worried her interests would not be protected and filed a motion in probate court requesting the court determine that the term "personal property" should be construed as including both the tangible and intangible property located in Eugene's home. The district court denied the motion, finding that the will unambiguously limited "personal property" to the tangible personal property that was located within the home. Sherry appealed the district court's ruling.

Language of the Court. *Jensen argues the district court erred in denying her motion to construe "personal property" in the will to include intangible property. She asserts the phrase "personal property" must be construed according to its technical meaning under North Dakota statutory law, and, when so construed, the bequest to her includes both tangible and intangible property.*

The intention of a testator as expressed in the testator's will controls the legal effect of the testator's dispositions. From the unambiguous language of the will, it is clear Eugene Camas intended the popular meaning of "personal property" to apply to the bequest to Jensen. Eugene Camas limited the bequest to Jensen to one-half of his personal property "located in my personal residence." By including this qualifying language, Eugene Camas demonstrated his intent to only include personal property that was physically located within his home. Intangible property "lacks a physical existence." Because intangible property cannot be "located" within a home, Jensen is entitled to a one-half interest in the tangible personal property located in Eugene Camas's residence.

Decision. The Supreme Court of North Dakota affirmed the district court's ruling, finding the definition of "personal property" set forth within the will controlled how the court should interpret the will.

FOCUS ON ETHICS

Consider a similar situation in which the court's interpretation of a will is contrary to the expressed intentions of the decedent. Are there occasions when a result required by the law may not agree with one's sense of fairness?

The Law as Rights and Duties

Legal rights and duties must coexist with the other. A **legal right** means an individual interest must be respected by others and is enforced through a legal procedure. Stated differently, legal rights are claims upon persons or property that the state recognizes and enforces. When acting in accordance with the law, the property owner can prevent

Legal right
The ability to have an individual interest respected by others and enforced through court process.

others from interfering with the owner's property interests. For example, if a property owner has the right to build a deck and it interferes with the neighbor's view, the neighbor cannot prohibit the property owner from constructing the deck.

Legal duty
An obligation imposed on an individual either by contract or by applicable law.

A **legal duty** is an obligation imposed on an individual by either a contract or an applicable law. The duty may be a negative duty, such as an obligation not to interfere with the legal rights of another, or it may be an affirmative duty, such as the obligation to conform to local building codes. Sometimes duties are imposed by statutes or local ordinances, while at other times they are imposed by judicial decisions. Property owners are constrained in their use of their real property because society has an interest in ensuring that the property is used for the most beneficial purposes. This principle flows from the creation of law doctrine. Thus, property owners are subject to zoning laws and building codes related to the use and improvement of the real property.

Property as a Bundle of Rights — The Power to Control

An owner may exercise many property rights including the following:

- Ownership (the right to possess and transfer real estate)
- Possession
- Use
- Enjoyment
- Encumbrance (to permit other rights in the property — for example, allowing an adjacent property owner access across the property)
- Disposal (the right to transfer the property's title to another party by sale, gift, abandonment, or destruction of the property).
- Exclusion (the right to exclude others from using the property)

The rights to own and use a property are not absolute. The government may impose regulations upon property owners to ensure that property is used in a manner consistent with greater societal interests. We will study governmental regulation of real property in more detail in chapter 19.

Sources of Real Estate Law

The law of real estate is governed by a complex set of laws, rules, and regulations collectively referred to as the law. The law governs social and economic order among individuals and businesses in society and is generally made and enforced by the government. The sources of law governing real estate ownership and usage are discussed below.

Constitution of the United States

Both our federal and state governments operate through a legal system by which rights are granted to the government by the people. The U.S. Constitution, its amendments, and treaties made pursuant to it are the supreme law of the land. While most real property law is created by the states, several provisions of the U.S. Constitution affect real property.

Fifth Amendment

The **Fifth Amendment** provides that the federal government may not deprive any person of property without due process of law. The U.S. Supreme Court has interpreted the Fifth Amendment's provision to apply to the states under the due process clause of the Fourteenth Amendment. The Fifth Amendment also provides for the government's power to seize private property for public use under the government's eminent domain rights.

Fourteenth Amendment

The **Fourteenth Amendment** is similar to the Fifth Amendment, but it applies to actions by state governments. Two sections of the Fourteenth Amendment are applicable to real property. The first, commonly known as the **equal protection clause**, requires that laws apply to and protect all citizens equally. Under this clause, a law is unconstitutional if it treats persons or classes of persons differently from others. This provision has been used to invalidate discriminatory lending practices.

Another section establishes the **due process clause**. This clause is similar to the equal protection clause, but it prohibits the government from taking a person's life, liberty, or property without due process of the law. This clause requires that procedural safeguards (for example, a court hearing) be followed before the person's life, liberty, or property can be taken by the government or a private party. Lenders must observe due process requirements to foreclose upon a debtor's property.

Treaties

Treaties are agreements with foreign governments. Treaties are negotiated by the executive branch and receive the approval of the Senate.

> **Example:** The U.S. income tax treaty with Denmark allow states to tax income and capital gains associated with real property owned by a resident of a treaty country.[2]

Federal Statutes

The legislative branch of our government creates laws that promote or prohibit conduct. These enactments, known as **statutes**, are contained in the United States Code. These statutes establish laws carrying out the U.S. Constitution and operations of the federal government.

> **Example:** Title VIII of the Civil Rights Act of 1968 (Fair Housing Act); Title II of the Americans with Disabilities Act of 1990, as amended; the Internal Revenue Code.

Federal Administrative Regulations

A governmental agency directs, supervises, and implements every legislative act passed by Congress. Because Congress does not have the resources to manage all societal

Fifth Amendment
No person shall be "deprived of life, liberty, or property, without due process of law; nor shall private property be taken for public use, without just compensation."

Fourteenth Amendment
No State "shall . . . deprive any person of life, liberty, or property, without due process of law; deny to any person within its jurisdiction the equal protection of the laws."

Equal protection clause
Part of the Fourteenth Amendment requiring laws be applied and protect all persons equally.

Due process clause
Part of the Fourteenth Amendment prohibiting the government from taking a person's life, liberty, or property without due process of the law.

Statute
A law enacted by federal or state legislation.

problems, it delegates its authority to administrative agencies. These **administrative agencies** have the power to enact regulations to implement legislative acts creating new law.

Example: The Department of Housing and Urban Development is a federal administrative agency that enforces laws aimed at creating strong, sustainable, inclusive communities and quality affordable housing.

State Constitutions

Each state has adopted its own constitution. Usually, state constitutions are more expansive in their treatment of property rights than is the U.S. Constitution.

Example: Florida's constitution exempts real property used exclusively for educational, literary, scientific, religious, or charitable purposes from taxation.[3]

Example: Texas's constitution provides eminent domain powers of the state and eliminates the state's ability to take property for the primary purpose of economic development or enhancement of tax revenues.[4]

State Statutes

Like the federal government, each state's legislature can enact laws promoting or prohibiting conduct. Many states have adopted the **Uniform Commercial Code** (UCC). The UCC is a uniform set of laws related to the sale of goods that has been adopted by every state except Louisiana. The UCC protects creditors in personal property sales transactions. Because real estate transactions can involve both real and personal property aspects, it is important to understand certain UCC provisions. The UCC is discussed in more detail in chapter 4 related to the subject of fixtures.

Example: A seller of solar panels on credit may require that the panels be used as secured collateral until the debt to the company is paid in full. The solar panels serve as a source of repayment in the event of a default.

State Administrative Regulations

Similar to federal administrative agencies, states have created administrative agencies to regulate real estate matters. Such regulations cover licensing real estate professionals, recording requirements, and the like. These administrative agencies have the power to enact regulations to implement legislative acts creating new law.

Example: The state departments of real estate are examples of state administrative agencies.

Example: The Colorado Division of Real Estate is Colorado's administrative agency governing the licensing of real estate professionals.

Municipal Statutes and Ordinances

Counties, cities, and municipalities can enact their own ordinances promoting or prohibiting conduct.

> ***Example:*** The ordinances of the City of Cambridge, Massachusetts, require that property owners obtain permits from the fire department and the electrical inspector to install or modify any automatic fire protection system.

Contractual Agreements

Contracts between two or more parties (such as between homeowners or a purchaser and seller of real estate) can control real property interests. While these agreements are not law, they generally can establish rights and duties between parties affecting real property.

> ***Example:*** Neighbors may contract to allow one another to hunt on their property. This agreement may take the form of a license (discussed in chapter 3), and the agreement will establish the rights and duties between the parties.

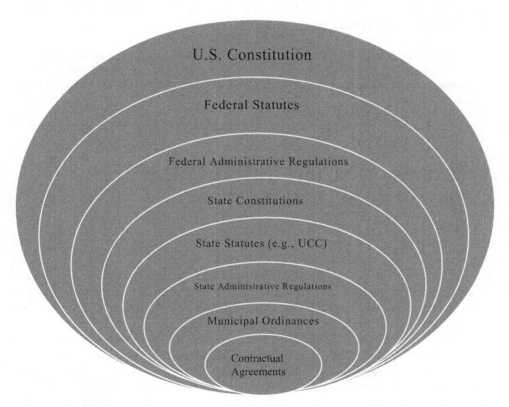

FIGURE 1.1. Sources of Real Estate Law

■ ■ ■ Supremacy Clause

Preemption
A legal doctrine by which the laws of a higher authority displace and control over laws issued by a lower jurisdiction when the lower jurisdiction's laws conflict with those of the higher jurisdiction.

State and local laws, ordinances, and regulations that conflict with the U.S. Constitution are **preempted** (displaced). In terms of priority, treaties are next subordinate to the Constitution, followed by federal statutes and regulations, state constitutions, state statutes and regulations, municipal ordinances, and contractual agreements between parties.

> *Example:* If Congress enacts a law within its power that conflicts with a state law already in place, the federal legislation preempts the conflicting state law. The state would then be required to follow the federal statute.

While most real estate laws are created at the state level, some laws and regulations issued under federal and state laws and local ordinances may apply simultaneously to real estate transactions. While the laws quite often address the same areas of conduct, they are to be reviewed as if they all applied to the same situation. Compliance with one applicable law does not discharge the party's responsibility to comply with the requirements of other applicable laws.

> *Example:* With regard to rental housing, if a local ordinance afforded tenants more protection from discrimination than did state or federal law, such as by prohibiting discrimination based on sexual orientation, the landlord must comply with the more restrictive local ordinance.

Overview of the United States Legal System

Common law
Nonstatutory theories developed by courts covering legal relief for one person against another.

Stare decisis
Latin for "to stand by the decision." A legal principal that requires a court to apply prior appellate case holdings as precedent binding on the court once certain facts have been established.

While there are many federal and state statutes, ordinances, and regulations governing real estate law, many undefined terms and conditions arise that are resolved through common law. **Common law**, which traces its development to the laws of England, is law developed over time by judges who applied common rules to decide cases. These rules became precedent, and later judges used them to decide the cases before them.

In the United States, as the body of court decisions grew, courts adopted a practice known as *stare decisis*. Under this doctrine, lower courts, in considering similar cases, must apply the decision of the highest court in a jurisdiction on the subject at issue. Lower trial courts in both federal and state venues are required to follow *stare decisis* until the higher court reverses or amends its prior decision. Until that point, the decision of the higher court is followed as a precedent binding all lower-level courts in that jurisdiction. *Stare decisis* does not require courts to follow the decisions of equal status (such as two state courts) or in the same state court system (for example, two different counties).

Example: If the U.S. Supreme Court issued a ruling governing eminent domain, due to *stare decisis* all federal and state courts would have to follow that ruling.

Judicial Decisions

Both the federal and state courts issue final decisions that interpret and enforce the law. This process is known as **adjudication**. In this system, a party to a lawsuit files a complaint to commence the proceedings.

Adjudication
The legal process of resolving a dispute.

Jurisdiction

Jurisdiction, as used by the courts and administrative agencies, means the power to hear and determine disputes before the court or the agency. To exercise jurisdiction over a particular dispute, a court or agency must have jurisdiction over the subject matter of the dispute. In disputes involving real property, the state in which the real property is located has jurisdiction to hear the matter.

Jurisdiction
The authority of a court or agency to make a legal determination over the person or property of another.

> *Example:* A state court in Pennsylvania would have jurisdiction to decide a dispute involving real property located in the state of Pennsylvania.

A lack of jurisdiction refers to the absence of the power of a court or an administrative agency to hear or determine a case. The court or administrative agency determines whether it lacks authority over either the subject matter or the parties, or over both. If a court lacks jurisdiction, then any order it may issue is void and unenforceable.

Types of Jurisdiction ■ ■ ■

There are two types of jurisdiction: (1) *in personam* jurisdiction, and (2) *in rem* jurisdiction.

In Personam Jurisdiction

In personam jurisdiction refers to whether the court can exercise jurisdiction over the parties to a controversy. A state court has *in personam* jurisdiction when the party is present in the state when served with a lawsuit, resides in the state, or consents to jurisdiction of the state.

In Rem Jurisdiction

In rem jurisdiction refers to the court's jurisdiction over a particular piece of property. A state has *in rem* jurisdiction in the state in which the property is located.

> *Example:* The state of Texas has *in rem* jurisdiction to hear a dispute over a trespassing claim regarding real property located in the state of Texas.

State Court System

Most real property laws are created by the state, and every state operates a court system to interpret and apply state laws. While many real estate disputes are resolved through alternative dispute resolution, most disputes are resolved through the state court system.

The primary purpose of these courts is to settle disputes through a legal process following federal and state laws. Courts make findings of fact and apply the law to reach a binding decision. The primary trial courts of the state court system are the superior courts. If a party wishes to appeal the decision, most states provide an intermediate appellate court system. Where a party seeks to appeal a ruling from the intermediate appellate court system, the party may appeal to the state's supreme court. The state supreme court will review the decision of the appellate court. In some states, the state's highest court is called the appeals court, and the state's intermediate appellate court is called the supreme court.

Federal Court System

Article III of the U.S. Constitution established the federal court system. The federal courts have the power or jurisdiction to decide those cases that Congress authorizes them to decide. The primary trial courts of the federal court system are the United States District Courts. The decisions of the district courts may be appealed to the United States Court of Appeals. The decisions of the federal courts of appeals serve as the final decision in most federal court litigation and create binding legal precedent for all lower federal courts within that circuit. Lower federal courts must follow the binding precedent under the *stare decisis* doctrine in deciding future similar cases.

The common means for a federal court to hear a real estate matter is premised upon one of couple types of jurisdiction.

Federal Question Jurisdiction

Federal question jurisdiction
A case arising under the U.S. Constitution, treaties, or federal statutes and regulations.

The first is known as **federal question jurisdiction**, in which the federal courts have the authority to decide a dispute arising substantially under federal law (such as the U.S. Constitution, treaties, federal statutes, or federal regulations).

In addition, federal courts have exclusive jurisdiction to hear matters relating to real estate involving federal crimes, antitrust, bankruptcy, lawsuits brought against the United States, or other cases specified by a federal statute. To have exclusive jurisdiction means the federal court is the sole forum for determination for these types of cases.

> *Example:* If a homeowner filed bankruptcy to forestall a mortgage foreclosure, the matter would be heard in a federal court.

Diversity of Citizenship Jurisdiction

Diversity of citizenship jurisdiction
A case where the amount in controversy exceeds $75,000 and all parties to the litigation are citizens of different states, or a citizen of a state and a citizen, or a subject of a foreign country.

The second type is **diversity of citizenship jurisdiction**. For a federal court to hear a case based on diversity of citizenship, two elements are required: (1) the amount in controversy must exceed $75,000, and (2) all parties to the litigation must be diverse in their citizenship. Generally, this last qualification means that the parties (both plaintiffs and defendants) in dispute are citizens of different states, or a citizen of a state and a citizen of a foreign country.

Example: Dwayne, a resident of Illinois, is driving on vacation and is rear-ended by Marcus, a resident of Ohio. The accident occurs in Indiana, and as a result of the accident, Dwayne's car was severely damaged, and Dwayne suffered extensive personal injuries. In total, the cost to repair Dwayne's car and to pay his medical bills amounted to nearly $100,000. If Dwayne sues Marcus for the damages, he could do so in federal court under diversity of citizenship jurisdiction, as Dwayne and Marcus are residents of different states, and the amount in controversy exceeds $75,000.

Ordinarily, the federal courts are not the forum for a typical real estate dispute. Sellers and buyers are often citizens of the same state. As a result, few such disputes are heard in a federal courtroom. Those real estate law disputes that are resolved in the federal courts often involve breaches of federal mortgage regulations or similar federal legislation.

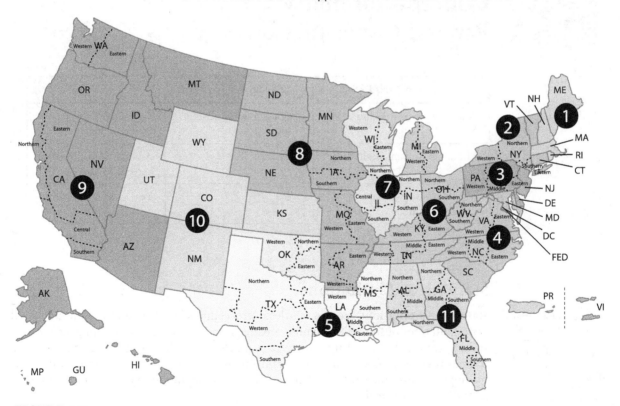

Geographic Boundaries
of United States Courts of Appeals and United States District Courts

FIGURE 1.2.
Source: United States Courts (www.uscourts.gov).

United States Supreme Court

The U.S. Supreme Court accepts approximately 80 cases each year out of the approximately 7,000 to 8,000 cases filed for review in the U.S. Supreme Court. In most instances, a right to appeal to the Supreme Court is not automatic; rather, a party formally petitions the Supreme Court through a **petition for writ of certiorari**. A minimum of four of the nine justices must agree to review the case; if this occurs, the court issues a writ of certiorari and hears the case. If a writ of certiorari is denied by the Supreme Court, the decision of the lower court remains unaffected.

Venue

Venue
The place where a particular case should be filed or administered by a court.

Venue is a different concept from jurisdiction. A venue is the place where a particular case should be filed or administered by a court. Every state has rules that determine the proper venue for different types of lawsuits: It might be the county where the dispute arose, where a defendant resides, or where the real property in dispute is located. A plaintiff may sue in any of the places permitted by state venue law.

Concept Summary
Federal Court Jurisdiction

Basis of Jurisdiction	Federal Question	Diversity
Source of law for dispute	Constitution or federal statute	Federal or state law, common law
Minimum amount in dispute	None	Amount in controversy exceeds $75,000
Must parties be citizens of different states?	No	Yes

Statutes of Limitations

Statute of limitations
The maximum legal period during which a legal proceeding may be initiated, measured from date of occurrence of the event giving rise to the right to pursue the legal claim.

Statutes of limitations require that legal proceedings be commenced within a stated period. Statutes of limitation require a plaintiff to pursue claims in a diligent manner and to give the defendant time to prepare a defense on the merits of the claim. These statutes prevent prosecution of old claims, thereby reducing attempts to conduct proceedings for cases for which evidence has been lost, memories have faded, or witnesses have disappeared or died.

> *Example:* A state might require a plaintiff to file a lawsuit to enforce a real estate contract within four years.

Alternative Dispute Resolution

The real estate industry has embraced **alternative dispute resolution (ADR)**. ADR is a method of resolving legal disputes without using the court system. Most often, ADR occurs through mediation or arbitration. ADR often averts the delay and expense of litigation. Most real estate contracts require ADR before permitting the dispute to be tried in the court system.

> **Example:** Real estate members affiliated with the National Association of Realtors® (NAR) must conduct themselves according to the NAR Code of Ethics. The code requires members to arbitrate disputes to the extent that the dispute arose from a real estate transaction. Additionally, many local real estate associations also require members to arbitrate disputes.

Use of ADR offers several advantages. Resolution of the matter will occur much more quickly than with traditional court methods, and parties can choose professionals and specialists experienced in the subject matter of the litigation to resolve the dispute. Another advantage of ADR proceedings is that they are usually conducted in private. The parties can maintain the results of the proceeding in confidence. In contrast, anyone can enter a public courtroom and hear the evidence being presented, including information formerly held as confidential by a party.

> **Alternative dispute resolution**
> A nonjudicial process that seeks to resolve disputes between parties, such as mediation and arbitration.

Mediation

Mediation is an informal process by which a neutral person, the mediator, assists the parties in reaching a voluntary, negotiated resolution of a dispute. The mediator does not make factual findings or a final binding decision, as could a judge, jury, or arbitrator. Instead, the mediation assists the parties to create, if possible, a settlement agreement among themselves.

No set process exists for mediation, which allows the parties to formulate their own rules. Sometimes the parties, and their lawyers, actively participate in the discussions. Often the parties will bring experts with them to help explain their positions to the other side. The fees of the mediator are usually equally split among the parties. If the mediation is unsuccessful, the parties can still utilize the court system or arbitration to resolve their matter.

> **Mediation**
> A nonjudicial process in which the participants, with the help of a neutral person, attempt to reach an agreement to resolve the dispute.

Arbitration

Arbitration is the process by which parties agree to have one or more neutral third person decide their dispute. Both sides present their evidence to the arbitrator, and after hearing all the evidence, the arbitrator issues an award. Awards are made in writing and may be binding or nonbinding. In binding arbitration, the decision of the arbitrator is final, with limited rights to appeal. In nonbinding arbitration, the decision cannot be enforced against either party.

In nonbinding arbitration, unlike mediation, the arbitrator determines fault and liability; in mediation, the mediator attempts to have parties reach resolution without providing a decision regarding liability.

In the following case, the U.S. Supreme Court considered the reviewability of binding arbitration clauses and the risk that arbitrators may misapply the law.

> **Arbitration**
> A legal proceeding in which disputes are resolved by a neutral third party appointed by the parties to make a (usually) binding and final determination.

CASE 1.2

PARTIES MAY NOT AGREE TO EXPANDED JUDICIAL REVIEW OF AN ARBITRATOR'S AWARD

HALL STREET ASSOCIATES, LLC v. MATTEL INC.

552 U.S. 576 (2008)

United States Supreme Court

The Hall Street case arose out of a real property dispute between a landlord (Hall Street) and its tenant (Mattel). The lease agreement provided that disputes were to be resolved by arbitration. The landlord claimed that Mattel had failed to prevent the contamination of well water on the landlord's property. After the dispute arose, the parties executed a contract providing for limited judicial review by a federal district court of the arbitrator's decision, both to ensure that the award was based on "substantive evidence" and to prevent any contentions that the arbitrator made legal errors in making the award. These grounds for challenging an arbitrator's award were beyond those stated in a New York statute and the Federal Arbitration Act.

Language of the Court. *We do not permit parties to agree by contract to expanded judicial review*

beyond what was stated in the FAA. Any other reading opens the door to the full-bore legal and evidentiary appeals that can render informal arbitration merely a prelude to a more cumbersome and time-consuming judicial review process and bring arbitration theory to grief in post-arbitration process.

Decision. The grounds stated in the FAA were the exclusive grounds for determining whether an arbitration award may be vacated or modified.

FOCUS ON ETHICS

If the parties want to ensure that their arbitration proceeding is fairly administered by allowing for limited judicial review, why shouldn't they be able to knowingly agree to do so?

Key Terms and Concepts

- Natural rights doctrine, page 5
- Creation of law doctrine, page 5
- Property, page 6
- Real property, page 6
- Personal property, page 6
- Tangible property, page 6
- Intangible property, page 6
- Legal right, page 7
- Legal duty, page 8
- Fifth Amendment, page 9
- Fourteenth Amendment, page 9

- Equal protection clause, page 9
- Due process clause, page 9
- Treaties, page 9
- Statute, page 9
- Administrative agencies, page 10
- Uniform Commercial Code, page 10
- Preemption, page 12
- Common law, page 12
- *Stare decisis*, page 12
- Adjudication, page 13
- Jurisdiction, page 13

Chapter Summary

- Two theories define the nature of property. The natural rights doctrine states that certain individual rights are inalienable. The creation of law doctrine states that property is created by government action.

- Property includes anything (tangible or intangible) that can be owned, possessed, controlled, divided, transferred, sold, and made unavailable to others.

- Property consists of real and personal property.

- Real property is characterized as the earth and all that is permanently attached and connected to it.

- Personal property is characterized as property that is moveable and not fixed or permanently attached to real property.

- The law grants legal rights and imposes legal duties upon persons. Some duties are imposed by contract; others are imposed by statutes or regulations.

- Many federal, state, and local sources of law regulate the ownership, use, and taxation of real property. The sources of these laws include the U.S. Constitution, federal laws and administrative regulations, judicial decisions, the UCC, treaties, and contractual agreements between parties. In addition, local jurisdictions issue many rules, regulations, and ordinances with regard to real property.

- Several U.S. Constitutional Amendments affect real property, including the Fifth Amendment and the Fourteenth Amendment.

- Among the functions of courts with regard to real property disputes is deciding the constitutionality of a law, applying laws and deciding those disputes, and issuing orders that enforce their decisions. In real property disputes, courts can issue monetary and equitable relief, including rescission of contracts, specific performance, and injunctions.

- State and local laws, ordinances, and regulations that conflict with the Constitution are preempted.

- American law traces its history to the laws of England, which used the common application of uniform rules known as *common law*.

- American courts adopted a practice known as *stare decisis*, which requires that lower courts, in considering similar cases, apply the decision of the highest court in a jurisdiction on the subject at issue.

- Jurisdiction is the power of a court or administrative agency to hear and decide a dispute.

- Courts have the power to determine whether they have the jurisdiction to settle a dispute. A court must have jurisdiction to decide a dispute. If it lacks jurisdiction, its decision is not binding upon the parties.

- There are two types of jurisdiction. *In personam* jurisdiction states that the court has jurisdiction over the parties to a lawsuit. *In rem* jurisdiction provides the court has jurisdiction over property (real or personal).

- Real property disputes in federal court have jurisdiction commonly through a federal question or diversity of citizenship.

- The U.S. Supreme Court is the supreme court in the land. A party petitions the Supreme Court to hear a case through a petition for writ of certiorari. If the court decides to hear the case, it issues a writ of certiorari.

■ Venue is the place where a particular case should be filed or administered by a court.

■ Statutes of limitations require a person to timely file a lawsuit or else the case will be dismissed. These statutes prompt the timely determination of disputes between parties.

■ Alternative dispute resolution (ADR) provides for the resolution of disputes outside the court system. Mediation and arbitration are the most common forms of ADR.

■ Mediation is an informal process by which a neutral person assists the parties in reaching a voluntary, negotiated resolution of a dispute.

■ Arbitration refers to the process by which parties agree to submit their disputes for resolution by one or more impartial third persons instead of a judge or jury.

Chapter Problems and Assignments

1. For each of the following items, classify the property as either real or personal and as either tangible or intangible property:
   a. Single family home
   b. Sofa
   c. Air conditioning unit attached to a single-family house
   d. Mobile home
   e. Solar easement between neighbors
   f. Gas deposits
   g. Oil deposits

2. Rank in order of priority the following sources of real estate law:
   a. State statutes
   b. Treaties
   c. State constitutions
   d. Federal statutes

3. Compare and contrast the natural rights doctrine from the creation of law doctrine.

4. Vivian owns a residential property and has become delinquent in paying her real property taxes and her mortgage. The mortgage lender files a lawsuit to foreclose on her property, and the lender is required to pay in full the local government's property tax amount because the state supreme court in Vivian's jurisdiction has held that property taxes take precedence over all other types of liens, such as the mortgage lender's lien. When the state court follows the state supreme court's ruling, it did so by applying what doctrine?

5. Amrit is a resident of New York; however, he also owns beachfront property in Florida. He has grown old and wishes to sell the Florida property since he can no longer make the trip down to use it. He sells the property to his friend Ming, who has moved to Florida to escape the harsh New York winters. Amrit knew the property's roof leaked excessively whenever it rained and that Ming would be unable to realize this during an inspection of the property. Months later during a terrible storm, Ming's home was severely damaged due to the leaky roof. Ming wants to sue Amrit for $80,000, but she is unsure where she could file her claim. Advise Ming on all possible jurisdictions in which Amrit can be sued, and explain why each jurisdiction is proper.

6. Construction 'R' Us builds a commercial property and is owed $70,000 after completion of the project. It seeks to file a lawsuit to obtain payment for the balance due and owing. The company's construction colleagues have noted that civil cases, due to a backlog in hearing civil cases, take approximately four to five years to get to trial. Construction 'R' Us wants to file its

lawsuit in federal court. Can Construction 'R' Us file its lawsuit in federal court?

7. Jin had a neighbor who trespassed onto her property. That state required her to file a lawsuit within three years. Jin was on vacation when the three years expired, and immediately upon her return, she filed a lawsuit for trespassing. Her lawsuit was filed at three years and four days. What defense will her neighbor use to prevent Jin proceeding with the lawsuit?

8. Identify and explain the key distinctions between mediation and arbitration.

9. Calvin has a lawsuit that he won at the trial court level; he lost at the appeals level, however, and that ruling was confirmed by the state supreme court. Calvin believes that the state supreme court has not correctly applied the law and wants to go to the U.S. Supreme Court. What must Calvin do to have his case heard at the U.S. Supreme Court? Must the U.S. Supreme Court hear Calvin's lawsuit?

10. Research your state law to determine the applicable statute of limitations for the following:
a. Breach of written contract
b. Property damage from a construction defect

End Notes

1. U.S. Census Bureau News, *Quarterly Residential Vacancies and Homeownership, Second Quarter 2017,* https://www.census.gov/housing/hvs/files/currenthvspress.pdf (released July 27, 2017).

2. Tax Convention with Denmark, January 1, 2001, Art. 13, §1 *et seq.*

3. Florida Const. art. VII, §3(a).

4. Texas Const. art. 1, §17(a)-(b).

Chapter 2
Real Property Rights and Interests

When the well is dry, we know the worth of water.
—Benjamin Franklin (1706–1790), Poor Richard's Almanac, 1746

Learning Objectives

1. Describe air rights and the right to a view.
2. Explain the rights to extract oil and gas deposits.
3. Recognize land issues relating to alternative energy.
4. Understand lateral support rights.
5. Discuss the right to use water.
6. State an owner's right to divert surface water.
7. Explain private and public nuisances.
8. Explain the law relating to trespassers.

Chapter Outline

Opening
scenario

Thirty years ago, James Parker purchased land with views of the Pacific Ocean. The Mancusos purchase property from one of Parker's neighbors and start construction on a two-story property that will partially block Parker's view. Parker has always enjoyed his view, and a real estate appraiser estimated that his property value will decrease significantly if the Mancusos build their two-story home. May Parker preserve his view?

Introduction

The right to own and possess land carries with it certain rights, duties, and liabilities, which we explore in this chapter. While a landowner has the right to use land for profit or pleasure, this right is not absolute. Technological advances in business and transportation have led to legal restrictions on the rights to real property. These limitations apply both above and below the surface of the earth.

Landowners' Rights

A general principle of real property law is that all people may use their own property as they desire, provided this use does not injure others. In turn, landowners have the right to be free of interferences by others to the use and enjoyment of their land. Landowners enjoy many rights to their land:

- Air rights
- Mineral rights, including oil and gas
- Alternative energy resources
- Lateral and subjacent support rights to the land
- Water rights
- Enjoy land free of nuisances
- Exclude trespassers

As is the case with any legal right, there are duties corresponding to the exercise of each of these rights. Statutes and regulations limit the freedom to exercise these rights.

Air Rights

Air rights
The right to develop airspace located above the surface of the earth.

Air rights allow an owner to use and develop the airspace located above the surface of the earth. Most state laws recognize that within limitations the landowner owns the air rights. Absent a restriction, landowners are free to build upon land below navigable airspace as they wish. **Navigable airspace** is the airspace above the minimum safe altitude specified by the Federal Aviation Administration. These rights allow a landowner to construct an antenna, tower, or billboard on its property if it complies with any other restrictions imposed on the land, including zoning ordinances, state statutes, and private-party agreements, such as covenants, conditions, and restrictions. Today, most courts state that the air rights belong to the landowner, with limitations. Pollution, gases, fumes, and foul-smelling odors may invade another's airspace without liability as long as the entry is reasonable and complies with applicable law.

Quite frequently air-right laws are involved between neighbors when tree branches or shrubs overhang onto a neighbor's property. In many states, the remedy for the landowner affected by the overhanging tree branches or shrubs would be to sue for trespass and seek the removal of the branches. Some states allow the homeowner to utilize self-help remedies, such as clipping the tree branches.

Types of Air Interests

Airspace is divided into two areas: the column lot and the air lot. The **column lot** is all airspace from the surface of the earth to an imaginary plane 23 feet above the surface of the earth. The **air lot** is all airspace above the imaginary 23-foot plane.

When property is bought and sold, air rights are usually part of the purchase. However, portions or the entirety of column lot and air lot interests can be sold separately from the ownership of the land. The surface and subsurface rights can also be sold separately.

> *Example:* The sale of a condominium involves the sale of the airspace within that unit, but not the sale of the entire air lot interest.

In urban areas, where land is at a premium, one person may own the subsurface rights (for example, a subterranean parking garage), while others separately own the surface rights (such as a ground lease), portions of the column lot (a two-story structure), and the air lot interests.

Transferability of Air Interests

Through their zoning ordinances, local governments may provide a property owner with the ability to sell the development rights in the property owner's air interests for another owner to utilize. The air interests thus sold are referred to as **transferable development rights (TDRs)**. TDRs were first introduced in New York City, where air interests can be quite valuable.

The sale of air rights involves the sale of unused airspace above existing buildings located near future development sites. Zoning laws often control the amount of air rights that can be transferred as well as the distance allowed between properties for which air rights are sold and bought. Based on the local zoning, landowners can consolidate air interests from several lots to build significantly larger structures.

> *Example:* Donald Trump may be the best-known person to utilize TDRs. When built, Trump World Tower, at 72 stories, was the tallest all-residential tower in the world. It could only be built to that elevation because air interests were acquired from several adjacent properties.

Navigable airspace
The airspace above the minimum safe altitude specified by the Federal Aviation Administration.

Column lot
All airspace from the surface of the earth to an imaginary plane 23 feet above the surface of the earth.

Air lot
All airspace above the imaginary 23-foot plane.

Transferable development rights (TDRs)
The sale or transfer of the right to develop property. Commonly used with the transfer of a right to build within air space.

TDRs may also be used to further public-policy goals, such as preserving historic landmarks, while providing nearby landowners with the benefit of increased density.

> *Example:* Penn Central Railroad in New York City sought to construct a 53-story addition over Grand Central Terminal. The city stopped the development, not wanting to lose the character of the protected landmark. Instead, Penn Central Railroad sold the air rights, which allowed construction of the 59-story MetLife Building.

Rights to Sunlight and Views

Absent an easement (discussed in chapter 3), common law, or a statutory right, a landowner does not have the right to sunlight or views. Thus, property owners can build a structure on their land that casts a large shadow upon an adjacent landowner's property or blocks a neighbor's view, even if the structure was erected partly for spite. The rule is well recognized that, absent a zoning ordinance, owners are free to build on their property and interfere with adjacent owners' sunlight and views.

> *Example:* In the famous case of *Fontainebleau Hotel Corp. v. Forty-Five Twenty-Five, Inc.*, the Fontainebleau Hotel, a luxury beach hotel, constructed a massive addition on its property. The adjacent luxury hotel, the Eden Roc, was adversely affected by the huge shadow cast across its property, including its swimming pool and sunbathing areas, and sought to stop construction of the Fontainebleau addition. The Florida court of appeals declared that where a structure "causes injury to another by cutting off the light and air and interfering with the view that would otherwise be available, it does not give rise to a cause of action."[1] The court held for the Fontainebleau, and the Eden Roc built a second pool away from the Fontainebleau's shadow.

While there is no common law right to sunlight, many states recognize the right to solar energy. Landowners have the right to the full enjoyment of their solar energy system. Owners may sue for damages or seek an injunction against an adjacent landowner who proposes to install a structure substantially impairing or interfering with the solar panel system. Some states limit these rights to the residential setting, excluding commercial buildings.

■ ■ ■   Focus on Ethics: Blocking Views

While there is no right to a view, is it ethical to block a neighbor's view? Within a hillside community in which all homes have ocean views, one owner's addition of a second or third story may block the ocean view for several adjacent homeowners. While adding value to the remodeled home, the value of the adjacent homes will likely significantly decrease because of the lost view. Those homeowners may have paid significant amounts of money for the view in the first place. Is it ethical to "take" the adjacent homeowners' view without compensating them?

In the following case, the Wisconsin Supreme Court applied ordinary nuisance law to a dispute over light.

CASE 2.1

UNREASONABLE INTERFERENCE WITH ACCESS TO SUNLIGHT FOR SOLAR SYSTEM MAY CONSTITUTE A PRIVATE NUISANCE

PRAH v. MARETTI

321 N.W.2d 182 (1982)

Wisconsin Supreme Court

Glen Prah was the owner of a residence in Waukesha County, Wisconsin, and had a rooftop solar energy system used to supply energy for heat and hot water to his home. Richard Maretti purchased a lot adjacent to Prah's house after Prah had completed his solar energy system. When Prah learned of the proposed location of the Maretti's new home construction on Maretti's lot, he advised Maretti that the proposed location would substantially degrade the effectiveness of Prah's solar system. Nevertheless, Maretti began construction. Prah sued to stop the construction of the adjacent residence. The court denied Prah's claim that an unreasonable obstruction of his access to sunlight was a private nuisance. He appealed to the state's supreme court.

Language of the Court. *An owner of land does not have an absolute or unlimited right to use the land in a way that injures the rights of others. The rights of neighboring landowners are relative; the uses by one must not unreasonably impair the uses or enjoyment of the other. When one landowner's use of his or her property unreasonably interferes with another's enjoyment of his or her property, that use is said to be a private nuisance.*

Maretti is asking this court to hold that the private-nuisance doctrine is not applicable in the instant case and that his right to develop his land is a right which is per se *superior to Prah's interest in access to sunlight. However, courts should not implement obsolete policies that have lost their vigor over the course of the years. As we said in Ballstadt v. Pagel, "What is regarded in law as constituting a nuisance in modern times would no doubt have been tolerated without question in former times." That obstruction of access to light might be found to constitute a nuisance in certain circumstances does not mean that it will be or must be found to constitute a nuisance under all circumstances. The result in each case depends on whether the conduct complained of is unreasonable.*

Decision. We hold that Prah, in this case, has stated a claim under which relief can be granted. The judgment of the circuit court is reversed.

FOCUS ON ETHICS

If a homeowner's solar energy system requires large solar arrays that neighboring property owners view as ugly intrusions into a neighborhood, how should these competing interests be weighed?

Common Methods Used to Protect Sunlight or Views

1. Acquire an easement from the adjacent landowner. Easements are discussed in detail in chapter 3. A recorded easement is enforceable against subsequent purchasers.
2. Adopt conditions, covenants, and restrictions recorded on the title to the affected property. These are enforceable against subsequent purchasers.
3. Enter into a contract with the adjacent landowner. The contract is enforceable only between the two parties and is not enforceable against subsequent purchasers.

4. Enact state or local legislation. Such legislation is often created by cities to preserve the character and views of neighborhoods. Legislation can place height restrictions on structures to protect views or sunlight.

Mineral Rights, Including Oil and Gas Rights

Like air rights, a property's subsurface rights can also be sold separately from its surface rights. The most common subsurface rights are oil and gas. Generally, oil and gas deposits are classified as **minerals**, and the surface landowner owns the mineral rights. When they are below the surface, minerals are real property; once extracted, they become personal property. Owners of land may convey the mineral rights to another or reserve them for themselves to convey with the land when it is conveyed. As with air rights, violating a property owner's mineral rights without permission generally constitutes a trespass on that property.

Because oil and gas are not solid, and oil and gas reserves can stretch over several adjacent properties, it is difficult to determine precisely where the oil or gas comes from. The law has created special rules related to these mineral rights.

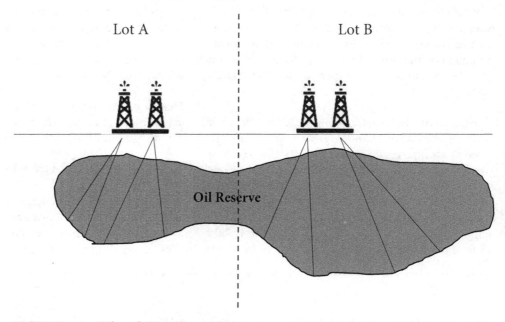

FIGURE 2.1. Oil and Gas Ownership

Rule of Capture

Rule of capture
Entitles an owner to the minerals that are captured and stored from a well on the owner's property, even if the gas and oil flowed to the well from beneath another's property.

The **rule of capture**, the law in the majority of the states, gives an owner title to the gas and oil produced from a well on the owner's property, even if the gas and oil flowed to the well from beneath another's property. The driller of the minerals takes title by capturing the minerals and bringing them to the surface. Once the oil or gas is captured and stored, it cannot be captured by another. The oil and gas belong to the original capturer.

Some oil and gas extraction techniques are not permitted under the rule of capture:

1. No landowner may slant drill. **Slant drilling** is angling and extending the oil or gas drill into another's property. Doing so is a physical trespass and is not protected by the rule of capture.
2. Using enhanced recovery techniques, such as chemical injections or highly pressurized water, to drive oil or gas from another's property is not permitted.
3. Governmental regulations may also affect oil-capture location, amount, or ability, such as by limiting the number of oil wells on a per-acre basis.

Slant drilling
The act of angling and extending the oil or gas drill into another's property.

The public policy goal behind the rule of capture is encouraging the exploration and development of oil and gas reserves. The rule of capture requires that the driller act reasonably and be responsible for all damages caused to the common underground reservoir by negligent operations. As long as the driller is not negligent and does not cause damage to the common pool, the driller may capture all of the oil and gas accessible on a property.

Under the rule of capture, two theories address the rights to the minerals prior to capture.

1. *Ownership Theory.* The first and most popular theory, the **ownership theory**, treats oil and gas deposits in the same manner as other minerals. Oil and gas are owned at the time of the deed and may be severed and sold. However, in an ownership-theory state, the landowner may lose rights to the oil and gas if another person first captures the oil and gas through drilling. Some of the states following the ownership theory are Colorado, Michigan, Ohio, Pennsylvania, and Texas.
2. *Nonownership Theory.* The other theory, the **nonownership theory**, treats oil and gas as migratory and flowing from one parcel of land to another. As migratory items, oil and gas are treated by the courts similarly to wild animals. Under this theory, no landowner owns the oil and gas under the surface until it has been captured. Some states following the nonownership theory include California, New York, and Oklahoma.

Ownership theory
Some states through a deed provide that the owner of property owns the minerals beneath the property but can lose those interests if the minerals are captured through drilling by an adjacent landowner.

Nonownership theory
Some states treat mineral interests as migratory and flowing from one parcel of land to another. The first landowner who captures the mineral interests owns the mineral interest.

As the chart below provides, the key difference between the two theories is the rights prior to capture. Once oil or gas is captured, the rights are identical.

	Ownership Theory	Nonownership Theory
Rights Prior to Capture	Ownership immediate at the time of the deed but can be lost if captured by another first	No ownership of oil or gas rights before capture
Rights Once Captured	Ownership of all oil and gas captured	Ownership of all oil and gas captured

FIGURE 2.2. Rule of Capture Applied to Oil and Gas

Doctrine of Correlative Rights

Doctrine of correlative rights
Doctrine providing landowners a reasonable opportunity to extract a fair and reasonable share of production by preventing the destruction or recovery of mineral interest by an adjacent landowner.

One limitation to the rule of capture is the **doctrine of correlative rights**. Under this doctrine, each landowner has a reasonable opportunity to extract a fair and reasonable share of production. It is unlawful for a landowner to act (or knowingly allow an act to occur) to prevent or destroy the recovery of oil and gas by an adjacent landowner.

Unitization or Pooling

Unitization or pooling
Apportioning the oil and gas extracted between neighboring surface owners.

Due to the rule of capture, neighboring landowners often raced against each other to extract as much of the subsurface resources as quickly as they could. To prevent over-drilling and overexploitation of resources, many states adopted regulations limiting the number of drills on a parcel of land, requiring ownership of a minimum number of acres before a person is entitled to drill, and requiring apportionment of the oil and gas extracted among neighboring surface owners. Known as **unitization** or **pooling**, this limitation prevents drillers from taking disproportionate amounts of the underground resources.

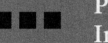

Practice Tip: Interpretation of Interests Conveyed

When conveying mineral interests, it is imperative to articulate clearly what is being transferred in the deed or lease. For example, state supreme courts have ruled differently in various cases addressing whether coal-seam methane gas (a fuel contained within the coal and released by a depressurizing process during mining) is included in deeds or leases containing the words "coal and other minerals." Some courts have interpreted the words to provide for the extraction of coal-seam methane gas, but others have not. A careful deed or lease drafter will provide a detailed list of inclusions or exclusions for what is being leased or conveyed to protect the interests of all parties.

Offshore Oil and Gas Rights

Offshore drilling provides a large percentage of the U.S. oil and gas supply. Generally, states own mineral rights within three nautical miles of the shore. Some states, such as Texas and Florida, own mineral rights within nine nautical miles of shore. Beyond those boundaries, the federal government owns the mineral rights and often enters into mineral leases with oil companies. These mineral leases can be quite profitable for the federal government, providing billions of dollars in mineral-lease royalties.

As environmental and safety concerns increase regarding the effects of offshore drilling, some states, such as California, have created statutes banning new offshore-drilling leases. The environmental and safety concerns over water pollution is discussed in detail in chapter 22.

Concept Summary

Unless oil and gas rights are expressly reserved, the sale of land surface transfers those rights as well. Because these rights can be so valuable, the subsurface rights may be conveyed separately from the surface rights.

Alternative Energy

Generally, **alternative energy** refers to electricity or any fuel other than natural gas or petroleum. Alternative energy accounts for approximately 10 percent of total U.S. energy consumption.[2] Property issues may arise from the right to produce electricity from one of these sources. Examples of common types of alternative energy include the following:

1. *Biomass.* **Biomass** is created by converting energy stored by plants, animals, wood, and solid waste. Biomass may be burned to produce steam that is used to make energy. It may also be converted into usable forms of energy such as methane gas. Biomass currently accounts for approximately 47 percent of alternative energy production.[3]

2. *Hydroelectricity.* **Hydroelectricity** is energy created by moving water. The amount of energy created depends upon the speed at which the water moves. Quickly moving rivers and water descending rapidly from a high point (such as Niagara Falls) can carry a lot of energy. Energy is created by the water flowing through pipes, then pushing against blades that cause a turbine to spin, producing electricity. The natural flow of rivers can produce the needed pressure. In a dam system, water accumulates and is then released as needed to create the pressure necessary to generate electricity. Hydroelectricity is one of the oldest forms of energy and currently the largest producer of renewable energy in the United States. It accounts for approximately 25 percent of alternative energy production.[4]

3. *Wind.* **Wind energy** is created by moving air through wind turbines. Wind flowing through the turbine blades creates lift, causing the blades to turn and thereby creating energy. Wind energy currently accounts for approximately 20 percent of alternative energy production.[5]

4. *Solar.* **Solar energy** is created by capturing the radiant light and heat from the sun. Solar energy is the most popular form of alternative energy used by homeowners. Because the cost of installing solar panels in homes is decreasing and the federal government is providing tax incentives to install them, more and more homeowners are adopting this form of alternative energy. Many states void a deed or covenant restriction prohibiting or unreasonably restricting the installation of solar energy. While solar energy is becoming more popular, with a few homebuilders installing solar power systems as a standard feature in some homes, today it accounts for only approximately 6 percent of alternative energy production.[6]

5. *Geothermal.* **Geothermal energy** is created by capturing the pressurized steam and hot water under the surface of the earth. The steam is used to turn steam turbines, creating electricity. While cost-effective, naturally occurring geothermal vents have historically been limited toc locations near tectonic plate boundaries. (The earth's outer surface layer is broken into seven plates, which are in constant motion in different directions and different speeds.) Geothermal energy accounts for approximately 2 percent of alternative energy production.[7]

Rights to Support of Land

Landowners are entitled to have their land supported in its natural state against damaging action originating on an adjacent landowner's property. Landowners may face liability if, when excavating into soil on their property, damage occurs to an adjacent landowner's property. Two kinds of support are recognized: lateral support and subjacent support.

Lateral Support

Lateral support
A requirement that landowners not damage the support of adjacent land by causing land to slip, cave in, fall, or move.

Lateral support protects a landowner from slippage, cave-in, landslides, and sideways movement on or onto their property caused by others. Landowners are **strictly liable** for damages to a neighbor (or other landowners) whose property is damaged when lateral support is removed, causing the neighbor's (or other landowners') land to slip, cave-in, fall, or move. Strict liability makes landowners responsible for damages regardless of the care with which they performed the activity. There is no defense, even if the excavation was conducted under professional supervision and reasonably performed. Once landowners change the natural conditions of their land and erect structures, such as retaining walls, on that land, they have liability if the changes made cause harm to adjacent properties. Landowners are not liable when the lateral support failure is due to an act of God, such as a flood or earthquake.

> *Example:* Jacqueline owns a home and wants to expand her backyard by cutting into the slope at the rear of her yard and building a retaining wall. Even with proper engineering, the property located at the top of the slope may fail. If the slope fails, causing injury to Jacqueline's neighbor, Jacqueline will be strictly liable for any resulting damage on the neighboring property.

Subjacent Support

Subjacent support
A requirement that adjacent landowners preserve the support of the surface of the earth by not causing the land to subside.

Subjacent support is support from below the surface. It applies when a party mines or extracts minerals or water from below the surface. Often the land surface subsides (sinks or caves in) from the removal of subjacent support. Landowners are strictly liable to a neighbor (or other landowners) whose property is damaged when subjacent support is removed, causing the neighbor's (or other landowners) land to sink or cave-in.

> *Example:* Ellie begins to extract oil from underneath her property. After removing much of the oil deposit, her neighbor's property begins to sink in due to the removal of the subjacent support the oil deposit was providing to the neighbor's property. Ellie will be strictly liable for the harm caused to her neighbor.

Water Rights

Water right
The right to use water.

A **water right** is the right to use water. Water rights, like air rights, are considered real-property interests. Due to the varied local abundance and scarcity of water across the United States, states have adopted different legal approaches to dealing with water rights. The two common law forms of water rights' ownership widely used in the United States are *riparian rights* and *prior appropriation doctrine*. Depending on which law is employed, the rights to own, use, and allocate water differ. However, the modern trend is for states to regulate water rights rather than following one of the two common law methods of water rights discussed below.

Navigable Water

Under American law, bodies of water are distinguished according to their use. **Navigable waters** are those that can be used for navigation. Navigable waters can be used for business or pleasure transportation, but they do not need to be utilized for navigation at all; the name simply means that they *could* be used for this purpose. The Supreme Court established a four-factor test for whether a body of water is navigable: (1) Is the body of water subject to the ebb and flow of the tide? (2) Does it connect with a continuous interstate waterway? (3) Does it have navigable capacity? (4) Is the body of water actually navigable?[8] Under this test, even shallow streams capable of merely floating watercraft have been held to be navigable bodies of water because they can be made navigable through dredging or the installation of locks that increase and regulate the water depth.

> **Navigable waters**
> Bodies of water that can be used for business or transportation purposes.

Generally, the states, as trustees for the public, own navigable waters. The federal government has jurisdiction over navigable waters and can determine how they are used, by whom, and under what conditions. It may alter their course, dam, or dredge them. The expansiveness of federal jurisdiction is realized in several ways through the enforcement powers given to the U.S. Army Corps of Engineers.

The distinction between navigable and nonnavigable water is important for determining the division of ownership of the riverbed. Generally, if the water is navigable, the proper location of the boundary of a navigable river is determined under state law. Depending on the state, the property boundary usually extends to the high-water mark, the low-water mark, or the center of the stream, as determined under state law. If the water is nonnavigable, each abutting landowner owns to the center of the river or streambed. This distinction is important if oil and gas are present, as the payment of royalties from the production of these minerals may be worth millions of dollars, depending on its location.

In most states, nonnavigable waters may be privately owned. By whom and how depend on whether the state follows riparian right or prior appropriation theory.

Riparian Rights

Water rights vary greatly across the United States. The eastern states receive, on average 30 inches or more of rainfall each year, while western states often receive substantially less than that amount. Because of the regional differences in the amount of natural water provided, different rules have developed based on the availability of water.

The eastern states, and a majority of all states, follow the **riparian doctrine**. It provides that water belongs to those who own land bordering the water course. They are known as riparian owners. The ownership of land that borders a river, stream, or other watercourse includes the right to reasonably use that water in common with other landowners who abut the same water source. The rule infers a right to reasonably use and share the water with all riparian owners. When there is not enough water to satisfy the demands of all the adjoining landowners, allocations are made in proportion

> **Riparian doctrine**
> The right of a landowner to the reasonable use of water on, under, or adjacent to his or her property.

to the owners' frontages on the water source. Natural uses of water (such as household drinking water) take priority over artificial uses of water (such as manufacturing and farming). During times of water shortage, all riparians must reduce their usage proportionately.

The riparian rights doctrine applies to natural water sources but not artificial ones, such as man-made lakes. When a landowner's property borders a lake or sea, the landowner has the right to use and enjoy the water touching their land but may not alter the water's position by artificial means. These rights are known as **littoral rights**.

Littoral rights
Waterfront property owners' right to water from an adjacent lake, sea, or ocean.

Prior Appropriation Doctrine

Prior appropriation doctrine
The right of priority acquired on a "first in time, first in right to use water over later users."

The prior appropriation doctrine of water rights has been adopted in many western states where water is scarce. The **prior appropriation doctrine** does not promote equality in water use. Instead, it follows a doctrine of "first in time, first in right to use water over later users." Under this doctrine, water rights are acquired regardless of whether the individual is a riparian owner. To establish the priority needed under this system, the claimant must divert and use the water regularly for domestic, industrial, agricultural, or some other beneficial use. Some states have extended the use to recreational activities as well. Note that the right to prior appropriation extends only to withdrawing and using the water and does not confer a right of private ownership of the watercourse.

> *Example:* Assume that Industrial Manufacturing, Inc., is located ten miles from a water source in a state following the prior appropriation doctrine. If farmland is adjacent to the water source but began using the water after Industrial did, Industrial would have the legal right to utilize all of the water from the source. Under the prior appropriation doctrine, it does not matter that the farmland owner is a riparian.

Riparian Doctrine	Prior Appropriation Doctrine
1. Only riparian owners can acquire water rights.	1. Anyone can acquire water rights.
2. Riparian owners share water rights equally by reasonable use.	2. Acquirer can use all water under the "first in time, first in right to water," with no reasonable-use restrictions.
3. Natural uses of water are distinguished from artificial uses of water in priority allocation.	3. No distinction is made between different types of water uses.
4. Riparian owners gain water rights simply by being riparian owners.	4. The first to divert and use water regularly for beneficial purpose acquires the rights.

FIGURE 2.3. A Few Differences Between the Two Water Theories

As the following case provides, rainfall is a real property right.

CASE 2.2

THE RIGHT TO RECEIVE NATURAL RAINFALL IS A PROPERTY RIGHT

SOUTHWEST WEATHER RESEARCH v. JIM DUNCAN

319 S.W.2d 940 (1958)

Texas Court of Appeals

Southwest Weather Research used airplanes and equipment in connection with a weather-modification program. A Texas trial court found that Southwest's operations that expelled substances into the clouds changed the contents of the clouds. The trial court held that doing so interfered with the ranch owners' property rights because the program decreased rainfall over the ranchers' lands. The trial court ordered the cloud-seeding operations to stop, and Southwest Weather Research appealed.

Language of the Court. *Southwest Weather Research operated their airplanes at various times over portions of lands belonging to ranchers, for the purpose of "cloud seeding." The president of the company stated, "We seeded the clouds to attempt to suppress the hail." Southwest maintains that such an operation does not and cannot decrease either the present or ultimate rainfall from any cloud or clouds so treated. Southwest was hired for a hail-suppression program by a large number of farmers. The farmers' land was frequently ravaged by damaging hail storms.*

The ranchers' testimony, on the other hand, was to the effect that this program of cloud seeding destroyed potential rain clouds over their property.

Considering the property right of every man to the use and enjoyment of his land, and considering the profound effect that natural rainfall has upon the realization of this right, it would appear that the benefits of natural rainfall should come within the scope of judicial protection, and a duty should be imposed on adjoining landowners not to interfere therewith.

Precipitation, like air, oxygen, sunlight, and the soil itself, is essential to many reasonable uses of the land. The plant and animal life on the land are both ultimately dependent upon rainfall. To the extent that rain is important to the use of land, the landowner should be entitled to the natural rainfall.

Decision. The landowner is entitled to such rainfall as may come from clouds over his own property that Nature may provide. The trial court's injunction was affirmed so as to restrain the cloud seeding over the ranchers' lands.

FOCUS ON ETHICS

Is it ethical to divert rainfall to irrigate your property when doing so makes water unavailable to farmers in distant areas?

Related Water Terms

- **Watercourse**: A stream of water flowing in a fixed direction or course in a bed with banks. The term is applied only to inland streams such as rivers, brooks, and creeks, which are distinguished only by the water volume.
- **Accretion**: The process of increasing riparian land, in areas previously covered by water, by the depositing of solid materials, such as mud, sand, or sediment, so that it becomes dry land.

- ■ **Erosion**: The gradual washing away of land bordering a stream or body of water by the water's action.
- ■ **Reliction**: The process of uncovering land by a permanent recession of a body of water rather than a seasonal retreat of water.
- ■ **Avulsion**: The sudden and perceptible loss of or addition to land caused by the action of water or a sudden change in the bed or course of a stream.

These terms are used to determine title issues. Title to land is lost when it is eroded away slowly, while accretion or reliction passes title to the soil added by the river to the upland riparian. If the stream leaves its old bed and forms a new one through avulsion, the boundaries remain unchanged.

Surface Waters

Surface waters
Waters that originate from rain, springs, or melting snow.

Surface waters are waters that originate from rain, springs, or melting snow. They are surface waters because they have not yet reached a natural watercourse (such as a river) or basin. Landowners may be responsible for surface-water runoff.

The modern trend is to allow diversion of surface waters as long as the conduct is "reasonable" under the circumstances. Known as the **reasonable conduct rule**, it requires that each case stand on its own facts because reasonableness is determined by how the parties acted. The majority of states apply the reasonable conduct rule to resolve disputes over streams and lake-water rights. Such water disputes arise in the context of competing demands for irrigation, water power, drinking water, habitats, and recreational uses. The courts will look at all the factors involved in the case, including the benefits accruing to and injuries suffered by each party.

Reasonable conduct rule
The allowance of the diversion of surface waters so long as the conduct is deemed "reasonable" under the circumstances.

Groundwater

Large amounts of water are stored in the ground. Most of the water in the ground comes from precipitation and from melting snow that seeped into the cracks and crevices of the earth. The upper layer of the soil is the *unsaturated zone,* where water is present in varying amounts that change over time, without saturating the soil. Below this layer is the *saturated zone,* where all of the pores, cracks, and spaces between rock particles are saturated with water. The term **groundwater** (or **percolating water**) is used to describe this area. *Aquifer* is another term that can be used to describe groundwater. Groundwater moves slowly and may eventually discharge into streams, lakes, and oceans.

Groundwater
Water that flows underneath the soil and is found in the pores, cracks, and spaces between rock particles.

States differ on the ownership of groundwater. States may allocate the resources through a system similar to that addressing surface waters; other states allocate the resources through a reasonable use rule allowing surface owners to divert, obstruct, or dam groundwater on their land, if it will not unreasonably injure the property of adjacent landowners.

> *Example:* Hugh pumps groundwater through a pumping well to supply water for his family. After several years of pumping groundwater, his neighbor's property develops a sinkhole due to the removal of excessive amounts of groundwater. Hugh will be liable to his neighbor for causing the sinkhole on his neighbor's property.

Nuisance

The term *nuisance* cannot be precisely defined. Many things are embraced within that term. Most courts recognize that a nuisance occurs when someone has created a substantial and unreasonable interference with the use and enjoyment of another's land. Nuisances arise with intangible (that is, not physical) invasions to real property. They can include many things, such as odors, smoke, noise, fumes, liquids, or sounds emanating from one property and affecting another.

Nuisance
A substantial and unreasonable interference with the use and enjoyment of another's land.

Nuisances include everything that endangers life or health, obstructs the reasonable and comfortable use of property, or violates the laws of decency. Thus, business operations that pollute, utilize noisy equipment, or operate illegally can create a nuisance prompting another landowner to sue to stop it from continuing. If a tangible object invades another's land (such as the parking of cars), a trespass claim and not a nuisance claim is pursued.

The two types of nuisance are *private nuisances* and *public nuisances*. The difference between them lies in the scope of their effect. Private nuisances affect one or a limited number of individuals. If the nuisance affects the public at large, it is a public nuisance.

Private Nuisance

Private nuisances are substantial and unreasonable interferences with the use and enjoyment of another's land. To establish a claim for private nuisance, the injured person must show that the interference was substantial and unreasonable, and the interference must be offensive, inconvenient, or annoying to an average person in the community. A person who is unusually sensitive does not have a nuisance claim.

Private nuisance
Substantial and unreasonable interferences with the use and enjoyment of one or a limited number of individuals' land.

> *Example:* Jenkins purchased a home adjacent to a railroad yard. The railroad regularly transported railroad ties that had been treated with creosote (an oily liquid used to preserve wood). Jenkins was unusually sensitive to creosote and began to smell creosote in his house. Because Jenkins was unusually sensitive to creosote, he does not have a nuisance claim.

A primary factor in determining whether a nuisance exists is the unreasonableness of the interference with the neighbor's property rights. A balancing test is used to determine if the defendant's use of the defendant's property is "unreasonable." Plaintiffs have the burden of showing that their enjoyment and use of their land outweighs the utility and necessity of the defendant's use. Conduct undertaken to annoy or harass another has no utility, so it would be unreasonable and thus would constitute grounds for private nuisance. A reasonable fear of continued harm is a significant factor in favor of unreasonableness.

> *Example:* A homeowner allows her teenager to occasionally practice with her band in the garage in the late afternoon for a few hours. While irritating the neighbors, the practice does not create a nuisance. If the teenager played constantly at high volume without relief for prolonged periods of time, the circumstances would be different, and a private nuisance might arise.

In the following case, the court considered whether noise generated from a private wind turbine used in a residential neighborhood could constitute a private nuisance.

CASE 2.3

INCREASED NOISE AND PROPERTY VALUE DIMINUTION CAN CREATE PRIVATE NUSIANCES

SOWERS v. FOREST HILLS SUBDIVISION

294 P.3d 427 (2013)

Nevada Supreme Court

Sowers informed the residents of the Forest Hills Subdivision of his intention to construct a wind turbine on his residential property. Sowers's neighbors, the Halls, along with the Forest Hills Subdivision filed a complaint asserting that a wind turbine would be a nuisance because it would generate a constant noise and obstruct the neighboring properties' views. The Halls and the subdivision sought a permanent injunction of the wind turbine.

A preliminary injunction was granted based upon the testimony that the subdivision was a very quiet area and the turbine would create noise. A specialist testified that the turbine would likely generate noise equivalent to "the hum of a highway." The district court considered the "overwhelming impression of gigantism" created by the turbine when they visited the site as well as the subdivision's panoramic views, which would be obstructed, and the likely decrease of property values in the area should the turbine be constructed. The district court determined that the proposed wind turbine would constitute a nuisance, since the turbine would substantially interfere with the neighbor's quiet enjoyment and use of their property, and it granted a permanent injunction. Sowers appealed to the Supreme Court of Nevada.

Language of the Court. *A nuisance is "anything which is injurious to health, or indecent and offensive to the senses, or an obstruction to the free use of property, so as to interfere with the comfortable enjoyment of life or property." In the small body of national case law regarding wind turbines, noise and diminution of property values are the most universally considered factors in determining whether a private nuisance exists. Some states also consider the presence of shadow flicker in combination with noise and property value reduction.*

Since a renewable energy expert testified that the noise created by the turbine would be similar to that of the hum on a nearby highway, there is some evidence that the quiet would most likely be gone. Based on this evidence, the district court could have determined that the proposed wind turbine constitutes a nuisance as a source of excessive noise.

Decision. We affirm the district court order granting a permanent injunction preventing the construction of the turbine.

FOCUS ON ETHICS

What are the interests at issue in this case? How should we balance environmental matters with aesthetic and livability considerations?

Public Nuisance

Public nuisance
A substantial and unreasonable interference with the health, safety, or morals of the public.

Public nuisances are substantial and unreasonable interferences with the health, safety, or morals of the public in general. A public nuisance does not necessarily need to affect the entire community. A public nuisance may exist where the nuisance affects, unreasonably interferes with, endangers, or injures a substantial or any considerable number of persons, or if it annoys a substantial portion of the community, or endangers or injures the property of a considerable number of persons.

A lawful business may be considered a public nuisance because of the manner in which it operates. For example, an exotic dance club can be considered a public nuisance because it causes negative effects upon the community. Other common examples of public nuisances can include:

1. Criminal activity such as drug dealing, prostitution, gambling, and related crimes.

Example: A city can invoke public nuisance laws to seek an injunction against local street gangs. This can allow a city to fight drug dealing and reduce shootings, robberies, drinking, and urinating in public.

2. Air and water pollution in violation of public statutes and ordinances.
3. Unreasonable use of private property that harms the public.

Example: An industrial business creates a public nuisance when it allows hazardous materials and waste to leach into the town's water aquifer.

Nuisance *Per Se*

Another type of nuisance is known as a **nuisance *per se***, which is an activity, structure, instrument, or occupation that, by its very nature and of itself, is always considered a nuisance. This is true regardless of the time, circumstances, location, surroundings, or care with which it is conducted.[9]

> **Nuisance *per se***
> Negligence arising from the violation of a public duty.

Example: An oil refinery that emits noxious fumes that causes the average person to feel sick is a nuisance per se because it is a violation of the refinery's duty to not make people sick.

Nuisance Defense: Coming to the Nuisance

A defense may be available when the plaintiff knowingly and voluntarily moves into the range of an existing nuisance. Many courts consider the knowledge plaintiffs had with respect to the consequences of their conduct as a determinative factor. If the person was aware or should have been aware of the injury complained of, courts may not grant the relief sought, or they may grant the relief and require the plaintiff to pay for the nuisance-causing defendant's relocation. However, a person who was not aware or would not have reasonably known of the nuisance before acquiring the property will not be barred from a nuisance action.

Frequently, this defense arises when a residential owner moves to a property located near existing industrial properties or an airport from which offending noise, traffic, and odors may be emitted.

Focus on Ethics: Coming to the Nuisance ■ ■ ■

Is it ethical to allow a homeowner who moved next to an industrial plant to be able to shut down its operation or obtain damages because of plant odors? Does it change your opinion if the owner paid less for the property because it was located near the factory, but the owner was still entitled to recover damages against the industrial plant?

As urban development expands, sometimes the courts adopt innovative solutions to nuisance claims that are met with a **coming to the nuisance defense**, as the following case presents.

CASE 2.4

COURTS WILL BALANCE PROPERTY INTERESTS IN APPLYING THE COMING TO THE NUISANCE DEFENSE

SPUR INDUSTRIES INC. v. DEL E. WEBB DEV. CO.

494 P.2d 700 (1972)

Arizona Supreme Court

Spur Industries operated a cattle feedlot in an area located about 15 miles west of downtown Phoenix, Arizona, near Del Webb's retirement community. The area was well suited to cattle feeding, and by 1959 there were 25 cattle-feeding pens and dairy operations within the area. In 1959, Del Webb began to plan the development of a retirement area known as Sun City and purchased land located near the feedlots for substantially less than land located near Phoenix. Following the construction of approximately 500 houses, Del Webb met considerable resistance from potential buyers due to the odor emanating from the Spur feed pens. Del Webb sued Spur, claiming that its feeding operation was a public nuisance because of the flies and odor that were drifting or being blown by prevailing winds toward the development. At the time of the suit, Spur was feeding between 20,000 and 30,000 head of cattle, which resulted in over a million pounds of wet manure per day. The trial court ordered Spur to cease operating the feedlots. On appeal, the Supreme Court of Arizona considered the "coming to the nuisance" defense.

Language of the Court. *The difference between a private nuisance and a public nuisance is generally one of degree. A public nuisance is one affecting the rights enjoyed by citizens as a part of the public. The nuisance must affect a considerable number of people or an entire community or neighborhood. We have no difficulty in agreeing with the conclusion of the trial court that Spur's operation was a public nuisance as far as the people in the southern portion of Del Webb's Sun City were concerned.*

There was no indication at the time Spur moved to western Maricopa County that a new city would spring up alongside the feeding operation and that the developer of that city would ask the court to order Spur to move because of the new city. Spur is required to move not because of any wrongdoing on the part of Spur, but because of a proper and legitimate regard of the courts for the rights and interests of the public. Del Webb is entitled to a permanent injunction, not because Webb is blameless, but because of the damage to the people who have been encouraged to purchase homes in Sun City. It is not equitable that Webb is free of any liability to Spur if Webb has in fact been the cause of the damage Spur has sustained. It does not seem harsh to require a developer, who has taken advantage of the lesser land values in a rural area as well as the availability of large tracts of land on which to build and develop a new town or city in the area, to indemnify [pay compensation for any incurred loss or damage to] those who are forced to leave as a result.

Decision. The decision of the appeals court is affirmed in part and reversed in part. Webb is entitled to the permanent injunction, but Webb must indemnify Spur for a reasonable amount of the cost of moving or shutting down.

FOCUS ON ETHICS

Does it seem fair that the developer must compensate the cattle-feedlot operator?

Remedies for Nuisances

Nuisance remedies involve either monetary damages or equitable relief (through an injunction). The appropriate remedy depends upon the nature of the nuisance. In the usual case, monetary damages and, perhaps, an injunction (if it is continuing) are in order. Nuisance **monetary damages** compensate for the injury or loss suffered by the substantial and unreasonable interference on the use and enjoyment of property. These damages may include medical expenses, lost income from any illness, or compensation for the loss of the use of the property.

> **Monetary damages**
> Money award to compensate for the injury or loss incurred.

> *Example:* A neighbor who has a smelly compost pile may be sued for a private nuisance. The neighbor may seek monetary damages to compensate for the loss of the use of her property because of the smell from the compost pile.

While infrequently granted, a court may also grant an **injunction**. The injunction restrains the nuisance-causing activity. In private nuisances, the injured party may seek either monetary damages or an injunction. In public nuisance situations, the public may only seek an injunction.

> **Injunction**
> An equitable remedy by which the court restrains the nuisance causing activity.

> *Example:* The city of Irwindale, California, sued the maker of sriracha, an Asian chili sauce. The city sued claiming that the odor was a public nuisance and requested a judge to halt production at the factory until the smell could be reduced. In its court filing, the city claimed that it "has received numerous complaints of offensive chili odors or fumes emanating from the Facility causing irritation to residents' eye and throats which make residents cough, have difficulty breathing and suffer headaches, bloody noses and heartburn. These odors and fumes are so offensive and strong as to have caused residents to limit their activities out-doors, move outdoor activities indoors and even to vacate their residences temporarily to seek relief from the odors." The city council considered passing a resolution declaring the hot sauce factory a public nuisance. When the company threatened to move its operations to the Dallas area, the city conceded and dropped its lawsuit.

Remedies for Nuisance	
Private Nuisance	▪ **Monetary Damages** ▪ **Equitable Relief (injunction)**
Public Nuisance	▪ **Equitable Relief (injunction)**

FIGURE 2.4. Remedies for Nuisance

Trespass to Land

Property owners have the right to exclude people from or admit people to their property. **Trespass** is the intentional invasion of an object into another's land without consent. A trespasser is a person who enters another's land without permission. No harm to the plaintiff is required. Reaching over a neighbor's fence, while causing no harm, is still trespass to land. The adjoining landowner is entitled to damages for the trespass.

> **Trespass**
> An intentional invasion of a tangible object into another's land without consent.

Intentional Invasion

The first element of trespass to land is an intentional invasion. This means that someone deliberately did something that resulted in something entering another's land. It does not require that the person knew that they were on the land of another.

> ***Example:*** Kayla is hiking on a trail in the mountains. Unknown to Kayla, the trail she is hiking crosses through Taylor's property. While Kayla believed that she was always on the public trail, she intentionally traveled on what was Taylor's property. Through her actions, Kayla has trespassed on Taylor's property and is liable for damages.

Trespass to land may arise where a person intentionally causes an object to enter another's land.

> ***Example:*** If a neighbor diverted surface waters from their property to that of an adjacent neighbor, a trespass to land would result.

Trespass to land also arises from causing something to occur on the land of another by failing to take required action.

> ***Example:*** Allowing trees to overhang your neighbor's yard is a trespass to land. By failing to trim the branches, you have caused a trespass.

Tangible Object

The second element of trespass requires that a tangible object enter another's land. Water, while it may evaporate, is still a tangible object. It is a trespass if it enters another's property. However, shining a bright light onto a neighbor's property is not a trespass — but it may be a nuisance.

> ***Example:*** A uniquely designed public building caused problems for residential neighbors in Los Angeles. The Frank Gehry–designed Walt Disney Concert Hall was completed to worldwide acclaim citing, among other features, its mirror-like, curving, stainless steel walls. But homeowners in the adjacent Promenade condominiums complained that the reflected sunlight made their properties unlivable because of the increased solar heating and glare. The resulting heat also increased the condominium's air-conditioning costs. In response to the complaints, the offending panels on the building were removed and dulled by lightly sanding them to eliminate the glare.

Courts have consistently ruled that a mistake is not a defense to trespass. Even those who enter another's property without knowing they have done so have committed a trespass.

Defenses to Trespass to Land

Some entries onto another's land are protected and not actionable as a trespass. The most common types of trespass defenses include (1) consent, (2) necessity, and (3) recapture of personal property.

Consent

Entry onto another's land is lawful if consent is given. Consent may be explicit, as in the case of a landlord granting possession to a tenant under a lease, or it may be implied, as in the case of a restaurant that is ready to serve the public. Once consent is given, persons may become trespassers if they exceed the scope of the consent given. For example, trespass occurs when a person enters a restricted area or the landowner has withdrawn consent and the person remains on the land.

Necessity

Necessity may be a privileged trespass. Trespass is permitted if performed in an emergency to protect the community. The trespasser is not liable for any damages resulting from protecting the community.

> *Example:* A fire is racing down a hillside toward many homes. A homeowner may trespass onto a neighbor's yard to assist in combating the approaching blaze.

Where the necessary trespass is done to protect someone's own interest from destruction or injury, the trespasser is liable for actual damages.

> *Example:* A cooking fire erupts, and your kitchen catches fire. If while trespassing onto your neighbors' yard to use their garden hose to suppress the fire you cause damage to the neighbors' property, you will be liable for any of the damages incurred from your trespass.

Recapture of Personal Property

Trespass may also be privileged when recapturing personal property. If the personal property is on the land of another without any fault of the trespasser, the trespass is privileged. If the personal property is on the land of another because of the trespasser's fault, there is no privilege, and the trespasser is liable for damages.

> *Example:* While napping under a shade umbrella on what appeared to be a calm afternoon, the winds pick up, and your umbrella blows onto your neighbor's yard. Your entry upon your neighbor's yard to retrieve the umbrella is privileged.

> *Example:* You threw a football onto your neighbor's yard and trespassed to retrieve it; the trespass is not privileged, and you would be liable for any damages caused by your entry (such as the neighbor's dog escaping from the yard).

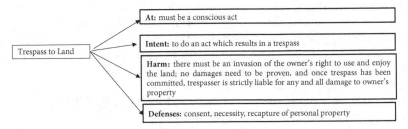

FIGURE 2.5. Elements of a Trespass to Property

When a nuisance case also involves a trespass, can the coming to a nuisance defense be used? That is the subject of the following case.

DEFENSE OF COMING TO A NUISANCE CAN BE DEFEATED WHEN THE COURT FINDS EVIDENCE OF A TRESPASS

AMARAL v. CUPPELS
831 N.E.2d 915 (2005)
Massachusetts Appeals Court

The Cuppelses have owned and operated a private golf course, known as the Middlebrook Country Club, since 1981. In the late 1990s, the Amarals moved into a newly constructed home adjacent to the ninth hole of the golf course. After moving into their home, the Amarals discovered their home was frequently struck by errant golf balls from the neighboring golf course. The parties failed to negotiate a mutually acceptable resolution, and the Amarals filed a complaint for injunctive relief and damages.

At trial, Amaral presented six buckets, containing 300 golf balls each, as evidence of the golf balls' recurrent entry onto her property. Amaral also testified that as a result of the golf balls she had to replace five window screens and one large window. Amaral testified that the fear of being struck by a golf ball had a significant effect on her use and enjoyment of her yard. The Cuppelses testified that upon learning of Amaral's concerns they made several adjustments to the ninth hole, such as eliminating a tee location, placing signs instructing golfers to "aim left," and planting trees along the right side of the fairway. These changes reduced the number of balls entering Amaral's property, although not significantly. The trial judge concluded the operation of the golf course did not constitute a nuisance and dismissed the case. The Amarals appealed.

Language of the Court. *By invoking the plaintiffs' prior awareness of the risk of encroaching golf balls, the defendants wish us assess whether the plaintiff in such circumstances was "coming to a nuisance." However, we need not determine whether the various factors applicable to the plaintiffs' nuisance claim weigh in favor of their request for relief because such* *factors do not affect the right to relief on a claim of trespass. There is, in other words, no cognate notion of "coming to a trespass," and the continuing and frequent invasion of golf balls from the defendants' course onto the plaintiffs' properties, resulting from the ordinary conduct by the defendants' members of the golfing activity for which the defendants intend the course to be used, constitutes a continuing trespass.*

To the extent that the ordinary use of the defendants' golf course requires land beyond the course boundaries to accommodate the travel of errant shots, it is incumbent on the defendants to acquire either the fee in the additional land itself, or the right to use the additional land for that purpose. The defendants assert no claim of right to use, occupy, or propel golf balls onto the plaintiffs' properties, and we accordingly see no reason why the plaintiffs should be required to suffer such intrusion merely because the defendants commenced operation of the course before the plaintiffs arrived on the scene, or because it would be difficult or burdensome for the defendants to confine their use to the boundaries of their own property.

Decision. The judgment of dismissal is reversed. The superior court is to enter a new judgment declaring that the projection of golf balls from the defendant's property onto the plaintiff's properties constituted a trespass.

FOCUS ON ETHICS

Is it ethical to allow the plaintiffs to prevail if the golf course operations were in place before the plaintiffs purchased their home?

Exercise 2.1

Determine whether the action constitutes a nuisance or a trespass under each of the situations identified below. If a nuisance, identify whether it is public or private.

1. A blasting operation that causes shaking on several adjacent properties.
2. A blasting operation that causes debris to land on adjacent properties.
3. A sprinkler system that sprays water onto a neighbor's grass.
4. Neighbors complaining about the smell of a compost pile in an adjacent landowner's backyard.
5. A tree branch that extends into the neighbor's yard.
6. An adult nightclub known for attracting prostitutes.
7. Teenagers who shined high-intensity flashlights into the next-door neighbor's bedroom to awaken the neighbor.
8. A work-from-home employee who is subjected to a neighbor's dog barking for several hours each day.
9. A homeowner inadvertently plants rosebushes two feet beyond the owner's property line and upon the neighbor's property.
10. A private drone flown over a neighbor's yard.

Landowners' Duties to Persons Entering Land

A landowner's right to the use and enjoyment of his property is not absolute. A landowner owes specific duties to others based on the status or category of persons entering the land. These categories include: (1) trespassers, (2) licensees, and (3) invitees. In determining liability and duty, classify the entrant into one of these categories, then apply the applicable rule.

Trespassers

A **trespasser** is a person who enters another's land without permission. Landowner's may not intentionally injure trespassers.

> **Trespasser**
> A person who enters another's land without permission.

> *Example:* A landowner might own many acres of desert property, which is home to many rattlesnakes. The landowner may not be liable for a trespasser's snake bite.

A person also commits trespass by refusing to leave the premises after being notified to leave. Even if the entry onto the premises was with consent, the person becomes a trespasser when that permission to remain on the property is withdrawn. A person ordered to leave must be allowed a reasonable time to exit.

A landowner who anticipates trespassers is forbidden from intentionally injuring any trespasser and must also warn of human-made concealed dangers. Landowners do not have a duty to warn about conditions on the land that a trespasser should be expected to discover (open and obvious conditions) or that occur naturally on the property (waterfalls, deep ravines).

> *Example:* A homeowner who is aware that teenagers climb over her concrete dividing wall to access an adjacent property installs broken glass on top of the wall. She believes the teenagers will stop trespassing on her property as a result of the broken glass. The homeowner will be liable for any resulting harm caused to the teenage trespassers.[10]

Child Trespassers

Attractive nuisance doctrine
Landowners will be liable for injuries caused to trespassing children if they are injured by a hazardous object or condition on the property and they were on the property because of an object or condition likely to attract children.

The **attractive nuisance doctrine** provides that a landowner will be liable for injuries caused to trespassing children if the injury is caused by a hazardous object or condition on the property and the child was on the property because of an object or condition likely to attract children. Children need not have been injured by the condition attracting them onto the property to recover damages.

> *Example:* A house next to a children's playground has a tire swing hanging from a backyard tree. If a child trespasses onto the property to play on the tire swing and is then injured through its use, the owner may be liable for the harm caused to the child because of the attractive nuisance doctrine.

Licensees

Licensee
A person who enters land with permission of the owner.

Licensees are persons who enter land with permission of the owner. Most licensees are invited social guests. Social guests are persons entering the property on a social basis. Emergency personnel (such as firefighters and police officers) have implied permission to enter property in emergencies, and home solicitation salespersons have implied permission to enter land as well.

The landowner's duties owed to licensees are greater than those owed to trespassers. The landowner must not intentionally injure the licensee and must either warn or make safe any known dangers on the property. Common examples of things a landowner must provide warning about include uneven or slick surfaces; dangerous animals or devices; and any defects in construction that may cause injury, such as cracked or missing railings, flooring, and steps.

> *Example:* Zach fails to tell his guests that a floorboard on the stairs is loose. A person coming down the stairs slips and breaks his ankle. Zach is liable for damages for his failure to either fix the floorboard or to warn the guests of the danger.

Invitees

Invitee
Persons who enter land that is generally open to the public or who enter land for a business purpose.

Invitees are people who enter land that is generally open to the public or enter land for a business purpose. For example, a person attending a religious service or entering a park is an invitee. More commonly, invitees are customers visiting a business, but invitees can also be businesses that are called or invited by a homeowner to perform a service. For example, service-repair persons are invitees.

Landowners owe the highest duty of care to invitees. They must not intentionally injure them, and they must warn or make safe known dangers, as is required for trespassers and licensees. However, the landowner also owes invitees the duty to reasonably inspect and discover non-obvious or hidden dangerous conditions and to warn against or make safe those conditions.

Example: Service-repair persons are invitees.

The distinction between licensees and invitees may seem subtle. Social guests, while invited to the premises, are licensees, not invitees, because social guests have no implied assurance of reasonable care. The distinction depends on whether a person receives mere permission (licensee) as opposed to an invitation (invitee) to enter or remain on the property. A person who enters without permission is a trespasser. Once given permission, the person is deemed a licensee, and the status may be altered to that of an invitee by a transaction between the parties after the person is on the premises.

Example: A door-to-door salesperson selling solar energy systems is a licensee. If the homeowner purchases one, the company installers who arrive to install the service are invitees.

Person	Duty
Trespassers	1. Not to intentionally injure
Child trespassers	1. Not to intentionally injure, and 2. Must reasonably protect children from dangers
Licensees	1. Not to intentionally injure, and 2. Must either warn against or make safe any known dangers on the property
Invitees	1. Not to intentionally injure 2. Must either warn against or make safe any known dangers on the property, and 3. Must reasonably inspect and discover nonobvious or hidden dangerous conditions and warn against or make safe those conditions

FIGURE 2.6. Landowner's Duties

Exercise 2.2

Determine the status of each land entrant below. State the landowner's duties owed to each.

1. Customers at a restaurant
2. A door-to-door salesperson
3. Paramedics arriving at an incident
4. Fan at a college football game
5. Guests who attend a party
6. People attending a free lecture at a local library
7. Persons attending a church service
8. A person recovering a baseball thrown into a neighbor's yard

Key Terms and Concepts

Chapter Summary

- Air rights are the rights of an owner to develop the airspace located above the surface of the earth.

- Air rights may be transferred through transferable development rights.

- While the traditional view is that a landowner does not have the right to sunlight, many states recognize the right to solar energy. A landowner may sue for nuisance if the owner's use of a solar energy system is substantially interfered with by adjacent structures.

- The rule of capture provides that a mineral-rights owner has title to the gas and oil produced from a well bottomed on the property, even if the minerals flowed from beneath another's property.

- A limitation on the rule of capture is the doctrine of correlative rights. Each surface owner has a reasonable opportunity to extract a fair and reasonable share of production.

■ In general, the states own mineral rights within three nautical miles of shore. Beyond those boundaries, the federal government owns the mineral rights.

■ Alternative energy is electricity produced by means other than natural gas or petroleum. The most common types of alternative energy in the United States include hydroelectricity, wind, biomass, geothermal, and solar.

■ A landowner is strictly liable to another whose property is damaged when lateral support is removed and the neighbor's land is damaged as a result.

■ Subjacent support refers to the removal of support by the excavation of mineral resources or the pumping of groundwater. The owner of a mineral interest can be liable for the harm caused to an adjacent landowner.

■ Navigable waters can be used for navigation. The states, as trustees for the public, own navigable waters under the jurisdiction of the federal government.

■ The riparian doctrine is utilized primarily in the eastern and central states. Water belongs to those who own land bordering the watercourse. They may reasonably use the water, with natural uses taking priority over artificial uses of water. When the water is from a lake or sea, these rights are known as littoral rights.

■ In the arid parts of the United States, the prior appropriation doctrine is most often followed. Equality of water use is not considered. The first to appropriate the water has priority over later water users.

■ Surface waters originate from rain, springs, or melting snow.

■ Under the reasonable conduct rule, a property owner must act reasonably in diverting water across the owner's property.

■ A nuisance is a substantial and unreasonable interference with another's use and enjoyment of land. The interference can constitute either a private or a public nuisance, based on the scope of the nuisance's effect.

■ An injured party may sue to enjoin the continuing nuisance or pursue a claim for damages.

■ A nuisance *per se* is an activity, act, structure, instrument, or occupation that, by its very nature and of itself, is always considered a nuisance.

■ The "coming to the nuisance" defense may be asserted when a plaintiff knowingly moves to an objectionable activity.

■ Trespass is an intentional invasion of a tangible object onto another's land without consent. No actual harm to the landowner is required.

■ Trespassing entitles the landowner to damages and an injunction, even if harm was not suffered. In contrast, a landowner sued for nuisance must prove significant injury and unreasonable interference with his property interests in order to prevail.

■ Consent, necessity, and recapture of personal property are protected and act as a defense to a trespass action.

■ A trespasser is a person who enters another's land without permission. Landowners must not intentionally injure trespassers.

■ If a landowner is aware of or anticipates trespassers, the landowners must also warn the trespassers of any man-made, concealed dangers.

■ Landowners are liable if children are injured by a hazardous object or condition to which they were drawn onto the property.

■ Licensees are persons who enter land with the owner's permission. Landowners must not intentionally injure them and must either warn or make safe any known dangers on the property.

■ Invitees are people who enter land that is generally open to the public or enter land for a business purpose. Landowners have a duty to not intentionally injure, to either warn against or make safe any known dangers on the property, and to reasonably inspect for and discover non-obvious or hidden dangerous conditions and warn against or make safe those conditions.

Chapter Problems and Assignments

1. A six-year-old child was injured while playing a game of hide-and-seek in a partially constructed home. While playing, he backed into and fell through a hole in the floor where the staircase was going to be built. He was injured as a result of the fall. His mother, on his behalf, wants to sue those responsible under attractive nuisance doctrine. Does it apply?

2. Evea and Bruno are adjacent neighbors. Evea possesses a deed to her property stating the gas deposit under her property belongs to her. However, Bruno captures the gas before Evea may do so. What is the outcome? Does the outcome change based on the state where the properties of Evea and Bruno are located?

3. Tao wishes to install an in-ground swimming pool is his backyard. He hires a professional excavation company to dig the hole for the pool. The excavation process results in damage to lateral support of property owned by his neighbor, Abi. The neighbor sues Tao for the damage to her property. Tao contends he is not liable because the excavation company did not act negligently. Is he liable for damages? Explain why or why not.

4. Determine the law of your state on trespass to land and the use of "no trespassing" signs. What effect do these signs have upon potential trespassing claims?

5. Bonnie owns a home in rural Kansas. When Bonnie purchased the property, she had no neighbors within five miles. Seven years after purchasing the property, Fracking, Inc. built a fracking facility a half-mile away from Bonnie's property. Since the fracking operations began, Bonnie has experienced severe vibrations in her home throughout the day. The vibrations have damaged Bonnie's walls and foundation. Does Bonnie have a nuisance claim against Fracking, Inc.? If so, how would the nuisance be classified?

6. Robert was hiking through the woods when he came upon a beautiful lake. Robert thought a quick swim in the lake would be refreshing. Little did Robert know that the lake was not part of the public hiking trial but the private property of Ines. In Robert's haste to cool off, he failed to notice the sign Ines had posted warning that the water was contaminated. If Robert later becomes sick as a result of the contaminated water, can he sue Ines for his injury?

7. A group of farmers wishes to sue a power company for damages for injuries to their crops and loss of market value of their farmlands. The electrical generation plant emitted sulfur dioxide, causing tangible but minor property damage to each of their homes and farm properties. These damages included rusty screens that became totally unusable within two years, the inability to grow flowers or garden vegetables, and the partial loss of their alfalfa crops. What nuisance remedies should they seek against the power company?

8. The public policy rationale for the rule of capture is to encourage the exploration and development of oil and gas reserves. Some argue, however, that the rule of capture incentivizes the exploitation of resources by encouraging individuals to take possession of more resources than necessary to prevent others from capturing it for themselves. Can a balance be found between encouraging exploration and preventing exploitation?

9. Miguel spent the night at a medical office building operated by a medical group as a participant in a sleep study. The next morning, Miguel left the building at approximately 6:45 a.m. After taking a couple of steps on the sidewalk, Miguel slipped on some ice. He stated that he was looking at the sidewalk as he walked, and it appeared to be clear. He described the ice as "transparent." A sleep technician who accompanied Miguel

outside the building similarly stated that she did not see any ice on the sidewalk before Miguel fell. Did the medical group owe Miguel a duty to provide notice of the icy conditions before Miguel fell?

10. Why is it unnecessary for a trespasser to knowingly enter the land of another for it to be considered "intentional"? Do you think it is fair that a person can be liable for the damages resulting from their unknowing trespass?

End Notes

1. 114 So. 2d 357 (1959).
2. U.S. Energy Information Administration, *Renewable Energy Explained,* https://www.eia.gov/energyexplained/index.cfm?page=renewable_home (last accessed October 26, 2017).
3. *Id.*
4. U.S. Energy Information Administration, *Total Energy, Monthly Energy Review,* https://www.eia.gov/totalenergy/ data/monthly/pdf/sec10_3.pdf (last accessed October 26, 2017).
5. *Id.*
6. *Id.*
7. *Id.*
8. *Kaiser Aetna v. United States,* 444 U.S. 164 (1979).
9. 58 Am Jur 2d Nuisances §16.
10. A true account from a family member of one of the authors.

Chapter 3
Easements and Other Nonpossessory Rights

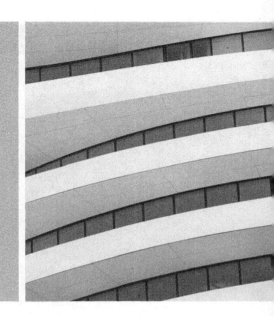

The most common trait of all primitive peoples is a reverence for the life-giving earth, and the Native American shared this elemental ethic: The land was alive to his loving touch, and he, its son, was brother to all creatures.
—Stewart Udall, American politician and Secretary of the Interior (1920–2010)

Learning Objectives

1. Define the rights created by an easement.
2. Describe different ways to create easements.
3. Discuss the transferability of easements.
4. Identify the advantages of granting an easement.
5. Explain how easements may be enforced.
6. Explain the differences between licenses and profits.

Chapter Outline

- Introduction
- Easements

Case 3.1: *Windham v. Riddle*
Case 3.2: *Burnham v. Kwentus*
Case 3.3: *Walsh v. Ellis*

- Conservation Easements
- Profits
- Licenses
- Covenants

Opening
scenario

In 1922, the original landowners granted an easement to Southwest Bell Telephone Company to construct and maintain telephone lines and electrical service on a piece of property. In 1982, Continental Cablevision acquired a license from the telephone company to enter onto these easements to install cable television equipment. The landowners sued in 1983, demanding that the cable company remove the cable system equipment. At trial, both parties agreed that the subject easements were easements in gross — that is, easements that are personal to the holder and not directly related to the ownership of adjacent real property. The landowner argued that the cable company could acquire no rights from the telephone company, because the easements did not mention television cables, and the cable equipment constituted an increase in the burden on the servient estate (the affected land). Should the court permit the scope of the original easement to be expanded to include cable television communication equipment?[1]

Introduction

Nonpossessory interests are valuable real-property rights. A **nonpossessory interest** is an interest in land that constitutes less than full possession or ownership of the land. It provides some right of entry to or use of another's land. Users and owners of land often desire the right to use the land of another owner. This chapter presents an overview of the rights to burden land by offering another party the right or opportunity to use it. These agreements can allow access, the harvesting of timber or crops, recreational opportunities, better land utilization, and a variety of other purposes. Nonpossessory rights can be granted temporarily or permanently and include easements, profits, licenses, and covenants.

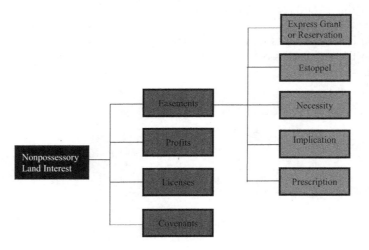

FIGURE 3.1. Types of Nonpossessory Interests

Easements

An **easement** gives its owner the right to use another's land for a specific purpose. When an easement exists, two parties are involved: the holder of the easement and the landowner, whose use of the land is subject to the rights of the easement holder. These two parties may simultaneously make use of the same land.

    Easements are common and are used for such purposes as giving a public utility the right to install and maintain utility services across property boundaries or allowing a neighbor to use a private driveway to gain access to adjacent property. Easements play an important role in the use, development, and taxation of real property.

> **Easement**
> A right of a person to use the land of another for a specific purpose.

Classification of Easements

Appurtenant or in Gross

Easements are also classified as either appurtenant or in gross. An **easement appurtenant** is one that benefits a particular parcel of land, rather than conferring a personal benefit upon the holder of the easement. Easements appurtenant require the existence of at least two parcels of land. The party whose land is benefited is the **dominant estate** or the **dominant tenement**, and the party whose land is burdened by the easement is the **servient estate** or the **servient tenement**.

> **Easement appurtenant**
> An easement that benefits a particular parcel of land, rather than conferring a personal benefit upon the holder of the easement.

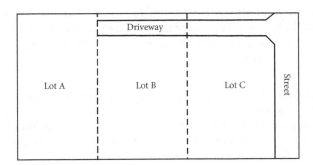

FIGURE 3.2. Easement Appurtenant

> *Example:* In Figure 3.2, assume that the owners of both Lot A and Lot B need access to the street located at the east end of the figure. The driveway is the subject of the easement that grants access to the owners of Lots A and B to cross Lot C to gain access to the street. The owner of Lot A has an easement appurtenant as to Lots B and C.
>
>   Lot A is the dominant estate, and Lots B and C are the servient estates. The owner of Lot B needs an easement appurtenant to cross Lot C. Lot C is a servient estate to both Lot A and Lot B. In this example, Lot B is both a dominant estate and a servient estate to different property owners.

Easement in gross
An easement that benefits a person, regardless of whether that person owns any land at all.

An **easement in gross** delivers a personal benefit to someone. A holder of an easement in gross does not have to own any land. Easements in gross lack a dominant estate. Easements in gross are not attached, or appurtenant, to any parcel of land. The most common examples of easements in gross are utility easements.

> *Example:* Fields Gas & Electric obtains an easement to install utility lines through Austin's front yard. The utility has an easement in gross.

If there is ambiguity as to the easement's type, courts generally hold the easement to be appurtenant. For this reason, easements in gross must be clearly identified. In the example above, if Austin deeds to "his neighbor" the right to park a motor home in his backyard, an easement is created, but it will be an easement appurtenant and will benefit both his neighbors as the current owner and any future owner as well.

Affirmative or Negative

Affirmative easement
An easement that allows the holder or owner of the dominant tenement to use the land of the servient tenement.

Easements are classified as either affirmative or negative. An **affirmative easement** is an interest that allows the holder or owner of the easement to use the land of another. Almost all easements are affirmative in character.

> *Example:* Emily grants an easement to her next-door neighbor Michael to use her driveway for faster access to the street. Michael has an affirmative easement across Emily's property.

Negative easement
An easement that prohibits the servient tenement from some use of the land.

A **negative easement** grants the right to restrain or prevent the use of land owned or possessed by another person. For example, a negative easement could limit the height of trees or improvements on a neighbor's property that would obstruct a view from the easement holder's property.

> *Example:* Chris grants an easement to his next-door neighbor, Tyler, by which Chris agrees to maintain the trees on his hillside property at a height of 25 feet or less to allow Tyler an unobstructed view from Tyler's property. Tyler has a negative easement that prevents Chris from exercising the right to maintain his landscaping in any manner he desires.

Transferability of Easements

Whether an easement can be transferred to another person depends on whether it is an easement appurtenant or an easement in gross.

Transfers of Appurtenant Easement

Run with the land
Once created, easements automatically transfer when the property is transferred, even if the easement is not mentioned in the conveyance.

Easements appurtenant **run with the land**. This means that, once created, the easement automatically transfers when the property is transferred, even if the easement is not mentioned in the conveyance. The new owner is either benefited or burdened by the easement. The person who transfers the dominant estate loses the easement right to the person who acquires the dominant estate, because easements appurtenant are not personal and, instead, transfer with the land. Likewise, a new owner of the servient estate will be burdened by the easement already in existence.

> *Example:* If the owner of a servient estate sold the property and the transfer document included the easement right, but the purchaser of the servient estate did not know the easement existed, the purchaser would still be subject to the easement because of the constructive notice provided in the transfer document.

An exception to appurtenant easement transferring when the property is transferred occurs when a purchaser takes ownership of the property without actual or constructive notice of the easement. In such a case, the purchaser takes the property free of the easement. This rule applies to all easements and all forms of their creation. **Constructive notice** arises when the easement was recorded on title. It creates a presumption of knowledge where a party had the opportunity to make normal and reasonable inquiries about the property.

Constructive notice
A notice given by recording or occupancy.

Transfers of Easements in Gross

Most states have created different rules for easements in gross intended for commercial and noncommercial purposes. **Commercial easements in gross** are those created for a business or another money-making purpose. Commercial easements, unless specifically indicated otherwise, are transferable.

> *Example:* A cable company's easements passing through a neighborhood are transferable upon the sale of the cable company's assets.

Noncommercial easements in gross, or personal easements, are easements granted for the owner's personal use. Because they are treated as a personal right, noncommercial easements are not transferable. Recreational hunting and fishing rights are the most common forms of nontransferable, noncommercial easements in gross.

> *Example:* Cassandra obtained an easement providing her with the right to water-ski on a privately owned lake, but this easement is not transferable by her to another person.

In the following case, neighboring property owners disputed whether an easement was in gross or in appurtenant.

CASE 3.1

ENTERING INTO AN INSTALLMENT LAND CONTRACT DOES NOT CREATE AN EASEMENT APPURTENANT

WINDHAM v. RIDDLE

672 S.E.2d 578 (2009)

South Carolina Supreme Court

The Windhams and the Riddles were adjacent property owners who purchased their property from a common grantor, Danny Covington. In 1992, Covington had divided the property into two tracts, 1-A and 1-B. In November 1992, Covington and Windham entered into an installment land contract for 142.398 acres of tract 1-B. The contract provided that Covington would maintain an easement for the purposes of operating and maintaining an irrigation system, as well as retaining all rights to use the waters in a pond. In 1997, Covington sold the entirety of tract 1-A to the Riddles. The deed stated, "Said conveyance is subject to a 30-foot easement, a 50-foot irrigation easement, a 25-foot access easement along existing woods road and a canal, all as set forth and shown on the above-referenced plat." Windham allowed the Riddles to use the pond for irrigation until November of 2003 when she brought an action for declaratory judgment and injunctive relief against the Riddles. Windham asserted the easement created in the contract of sale and resulting deed was an easement in gross and the Riddles had no right to the easement. By contrast, the Riddles asserted the easement was appurtenant to their tract.

The trial court found that the easements were appurtenant to the Riddle tract and, as a result, passed to the Riddles when Covington conveyed the land to them. Windham appealed. The court of appeals reversed, finding the easement to be in gross and did not pass to the Riddles. The Riddles appealed to the Supreme Court of South Carolina.

Language of the Court. *With an installment land contract, the seller retains legal title until the purchase price is fully paid. Thus, an installment land contract is not, as asserted by the Riddles, tantamountto a conveyance. Pursuant to the Windham sales contract, Covington retained legal title to the Windham tract until 1998, when Windham paid off the purchase price. The 1998 Windham deed stated that it was subject to the easement in favor of Covington, the seller, as set forth in the 1992 sales contract. Because Covington retained legal title to both the Windham tract and the Riddle tract in 1992, an easement could not have been created by the 1992 installment land contract.*

Decision. We agree with the court of appeals that the 1998 Riddle deed did not create an appurtenant easement. An easement in gross was created.

FOCUS ON ETHICS

Is it fair that Windham allowed the Riddles to continue to use the easement for several years before asserting they had no right to use the easement to access the pond?

Creation of Easements

Most easements are created by **grant**, **estoppel**, **necessity**, **implication**, or **prescription**.

Easements by Grant

Easements by grant are those created by express agreement. Most easements are easements by grant created by either a deed or another legal document. When created by grant, the easement must meet the requirements of the state's Statute of Frauds. Most states require that the easement must be in writing, signed by the grantor, and recorded.

Easement by grant
An easement created by an express agreement.

Two types of easements by grant can be created: express grants and express reservations. Most easements are expressly created by a deed or some other type of conveyance (that is, something that transfers title to land). Because it is an interest in land, with some exceptions, its creation must be in a writing signed by the grantor. When created by reservation, a grantor will convey land to another and, in the same deed, "reserve" an easement in favor of the grantor or a third party.

Easement by **express grant** arise when a property owner (the grantor) grants to another the right to use a portion of the grantor's property. The grantor's property is then a servient tenement to the grantee (recipient) of the easement.

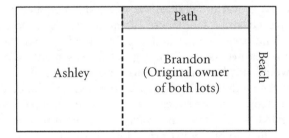

FIGURE 3.3. Easement by Express Grant

> *Example:* In Figure 3.3, assume that Brandon owned a large beachfront property, partitioned it, and then conveyed the back portion to Ashley. Brandon retains the lot with the path to the beach. For Ashley to use the path, Brandon would convey an easement across his property to her.

An easement by **express reservation** occurs when a landowner conveys a portion of the property and expressly reserves (that is, retains) an easement right across the grantee's property. The landowner who conveyed the property has a dominant tenement over the grantee's property.

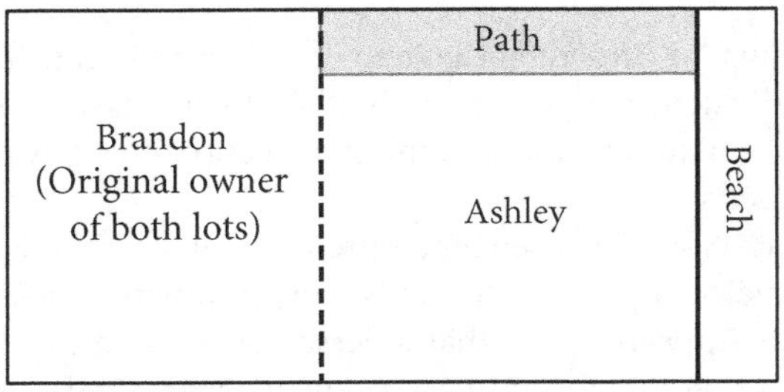

FIGURE 3.4. Easement by Express Reservation

Example: In Figure 3.4, assume that Brandon owned a large beachfront property, partitioned it, and, then, conveyed the beach-fronting portion to Ashley. Ashley owns the lot with an access easement reserved by Brandon for his use. Brandon has expressly reserved the right to cross Ashley's land to access the beach.

Easements Created by Estoppel

Easements by estoppel arise when the conduct (words or actions) of a landowner leads another person to believe that he or she person has an easement. Such easements are created to prevent unfairness to the person who detrimentally relies upon representations made by the owner of the land. Easements by estoppel are referred to as irrevocable licenses in some states. Not all states recognize an easement by estoppel.

Example: An owner shows a prospective buyer a map of undeveloped property. The map shows that a road grants access to the property. If the buyer purchases the property, and the previous owner does not want to grant access using the road, the previous owner would be precluded from asserting the nonexistence of the easement.

Easements by Necessity

Easement by necessity
An easement recognized when an owner conveys land to another but the land conveyed has no access except over the grantor's adjacent property or over the land of strangers.

An **easement by necessity** is recognized when an owner conveys land to another to which the only access is over the grantor's adjacent other property or over the land of strangers: The conveyed land is landlocked (without access). An easement for a right of way between the landlocked parcel and a public road, across the original owner's retained land, becomes necessary. Courts grant an easement because it is assumed that the parties would not have intended to render land unfit for occupancy. Most states require that the landowner burdened by the easement be paid reasonable compensation for the easement. Some states have unique requirements for an easement by necessity to be created. While states may vary on easement by necessity requirements, many states require that a party must prove four elements:

1. Unity of ownership of the dominant and servient estates prior to division of the property
2. Severance or a division and transfer of one of the estates to another person
3. That the easement was *strictly or absolutely necessary* for the benefit of either the parcel transferred or the parcel retained
4. A continuing strict or absolute necessity for an easement

Example: Jon conveys half of his property to Claudia. As Claudia's property was completely landlocked from this transfer, Claudia has an easement by necessity.

The necessity must be present at the time of the original transfer and at the time the easement is asserted. Such an easement ends when the necessity for the easement ends. For example, the easement terminates upon the creation of a new public road servicing the landlocked property.

In the following case, a subsequent purchaser of a property refused to allow a neighbor to continue using a road to access his otherwise landlocked property. The Mississippi Court of Appeals found that a person seeking to establish an easement by necessity must show that the properties were once owned by the same person and that there is no practical access to the property.

AN EASEMENT BY NECESSITY IS CREATED WHEN THE LAND IS LANDLOCKED AND CONTINUES AS LONG AS THE NECESSITY EXISTS

BURNHAM v. KWENTUS

174 So.3d 286 (2015)

Court of Appeals of the State of Mississippi

For over fifty years, Chester Burnham crossed his neighbor's property by use of Ridge Road, a private road that extended from a public road to Burnham's landlocked parcel. Burnham's neighbor at the time had granted him this access out of neighborly courtesy. However, when the neighbor sold this property to Kwentus in 2008, Burnham was instructed to stop using Ridge Road and instead use a newer road. Burnham viewed this newer road as impassable and sued Kwentus, claiming a prescriptive easement across Ridge Road.

At trial, Burnham presented evidence that in 1937, Kwentus's property and an undivided one-third of Burnham's property was owned by Capitol Bank. At that time, Capitol Bank conveyed the one-third interest to Robert F. Young, thereby landlocking the property. When Burnham purchased the property in 1952, he began using Ridge Road across his neighbor's property, as it was his only means of accessing his property. The trial court denied Burnham a prescriptive easement but found that Burnham had an easement by necessity. Both sides appealed to the Court of Appeals of Mississippi.

Language of the Court. Burnham failed to meet the burden for adverse possession. Burnham's use of the road was open, notorious, and visible; continuous and uninterrupted for more than fifty years; and peaceful. And though his use was "actual," it was not hostile. Dr. Brannan and his father had allowed Burnham to use Ridge Road as a gesture of kindness.

To meet his burden for an easement by necessity, Burnham had to show the easement was "continuous, apparent, permanent, and necessary." He had to show that the tract that is blocked in its access to a public road was once joined with the tract over which access is allegedly necessary." Burnham met the first step of showing the two tracts were once joined together by the common ownership of Capitol. And the necessity of the easement arose when Capitol sold its interest to Young, who had no access to his property except by crossing Capitol's property to reach the public road. So just as it was necessary in 1937 for Young to have an easement over Capitol's property to get to the public road, it is still necessary today for Burnham to have that same easement across Kwentus's.

The evidence showed Burnham is the successor to Young's interest in the landlocked property. Thus, Young's implied grant of a right-of-way traveled with Young's interest, so long as the same necessity for access continued. The same necessity that arose in 1937 still exists more than three-quarters of a century later.

Decision. The court of appeals found Burnham had an easement by necessity across Kwentus's property and affirmed the trial court's decision.

FOCUS ON ETHICS

Is it fair that while a newer road existed Burnham still had a right to an easement by necessity?

Easements by Implication

Easement by implication
An easement implied by a prior or preexisting use.

Easements by implication are also known as easements implied by a prior or preexisting use. They arise where, before a unified tract of land was severed into smaller parcels, the landowner used one section of his or her unified tract in a way that benefited another portion of the land. For example, consider the original tract owner who had previously used a portion of the land for a road or pipeline. When a conveyance occurs, the prior particular use placed upon what is now the servient estate is implied. The owner retains a right to use the servient estate not from an express reservation but by implication. This use must be one that has been so long continued and obvious as to show that it was meant to be permanent.

These easements are not granted in writing and do not satisfy the writing requirements of the Statute of Frauds. This statute, adopted in all states, requires certain contracts to be in writing in order to be enforceable. Unlike an express easement, which is clearly stated in a document, these easements arise out of the facts implied from the circumstances.

To establish an easement implied by a prior use of land, a party must prove four elements:

1. Unity of ownership of the dominant and servient estates prior to division of the property
2. Severance or division and transfer of one of the estates to another
3. That the prior use existed at the time of the division of the land. The use was continued and was so obvious to show at the time of conveyance a permanent use was intended.

    At the time the property was divided, the use must have been apparent. This does not necessarily mean that the use was visible. While many uses may be visible, such as roadways, easements by implication can also be created for underground utility lines. While not visible, they are discoverable by detection, and their existence may be inferred by their use.

    Before the unity of ownership was severed, the prior owner must have used the property as if an easement were in place.
4. That the easement was important and *reasonably necessary* at the time of the division of the property for the proper and reasonable enjoyment of the dominant estate

An easement by implication is permanent and continues even if the need for the easement no longer exists. Implied easements are not recorded on titles to real property. They reflect the practical use of the property.

> *Example:* Jon owns a property and conveys half of his property to Claudia with an access road as the boundary line between the properties. The deed did not provide Claudia with ingress and egress through the access road, but Jon had told Claudia she would be entitled to use the road. The court would grant Claudia an easement by implication to use the road.

Comparing Easements by Necessity and Implication		
	Easements by Necessity	**Easements by Implication**
Essential Elements	1. Unity of ownership prior to division of property 2. Severance or division of the property 3. Use of the easement was strictly or absolutely necessary 4. Continuing strict or absolute necessity for an easement	1. Unity of ownership prior to division of property 2. Severance or division of the property 3. Use of the implied easement continued and intention to convey a permanent use after division of title was obvious 4. Easement was reasonably necessary at the time of division of the property
Why created?	Created for public policy reasons; land should not be unfit for use or occupancy due to a lack of access	Implied by a prior or preexisting use
How long does easement last?	Continues as long as the necessity continues	Permanent and continues even if the need for the easement no longer exists

FIGURE 3.5. **Comparing Easements by Necessity and Implication**

Easements by Prescription

Easements may also be created by prescription. This is a concept equivalent to adverse possession: the taking of title to a property interest in the land of another without the consent of the other landowner. Prescriptive easements are available on private property, but they are prohibited on public land. For example, a person may not acquire an easement by prescription in a national park. Easements by prescription require the following elements:

Easement by prescription
An easement created by continuously and in an open, notorious manner utilizing without consent the land of another for a statutorily defined period of time.

1. *Adverse to that of the landowner (that is, without the owner's permission).* The adversity of the claim is measured by what a neutral, third party would think about the use — that is, whether that person would believe the use was permitted by the owner. For example, a trespasser is an adverse user. Permitted use never becomes prescriptive because no matter how long the use continues, it began and continued without any adverse claim being made by a user to the landowner. The continuing use of an easement after the easement has been terminated can create an easement by prescription if the requirements above occur. Note: the adversity does not require that the use be hostile to the owner; it just may not be permissive.

Example: If a person infrequently mowed a strip of lawn and infrequently traveled over and parked on the strip of lawn, the person's use of the strip would be insufficient to make the claim adverse.

2. *Open and notorious.* The use may not be carried on in secret or concealed from observation. An observant landowner should or would know of the use's existence; however, a landowner may not be aware of the use's existence if the landowner lives far away or never inspects the property. Without such awareness, an easement by prescription is not created.
3. *Continuous for the prescriptive period set by law.* The continuous use is consistent with the nature of the claimed easement for the prescriptive period. Continuous use does not mean daily use; the use may even be periodic. The use must be consistent with the nature of the claimed easement.

Example: Cross-country skiers could consistently use a property to access adjacent trails. A prescriptive easement during the winter months might be recognized, even if the trails are not used during other months of the year.

Each state provides a length of time for which the claimant must use the property before an easement by prescription will be created. Generally, the statutory period is tied into the state's statute-of-limitations period for trespassing. The statutory period often ranges from 5 years to 20 years. If the adverse use is interrupted, the prescriptive period restarts.

A prescriptive easement may be claimed against an individual who holds less than a fee simple interest in the land, such as a tenant.

Example: The Gosline family claimed that they had acquired a prescriptive easement over a portion of their neighbor's property. Both the Goslines and their neighbors leased their properties. The Superior Court of New Jersey held that the easement existed and that "an easement by prescription may be obtained against the holder of less than fee interest."[2]

A minority of states require that the adverse use be exclusive (not shared with anyone else).

Example: A property owner in Chicago, Illinois, sued Nick Karris over Karris's claim to have a nonexclusive prescriptive easement over a walkway on the owner's property. The Illinois Court of Appeals held that under its state law a claimant must show that its use of the land was such that the "true owners were deprived of use or possession" of the land. Karris could not prove exclusivity, and his claim failed.[3]

In the following case, the court considered whether a neighbor's continuous use developed into a prescriptive easement.

CASE 3.3
OPEN AND NOTORIOUS ADVERSE USE MUST BE CONTINUOUS

WALSH v. ELLIS

64 A.3d 702 (2009)

New York Supreme Court, Appellate Division

The property in dispute, known as the Walsh lot, was vacant land located in Richmond County, New York. The property was directly to the east of Asharaf Abdelaal's property. Abdelaal had purchased his property in 2002. The trial court held that Abdelaal had acquired an easement by prescription over two driveways that traversed the vacant lot. The testimony presented at trial indicated that Abdelaal, who had previously owned the Walsh lot, had exclusively mowed the grass on the lot. Abdelaal testified that on unspecified occasions in the past, he had cut down two rotting trees, planted two new trees, planted an unknown number of shrubs, and performed maintenance upon a chain-link fence, which was approximately one foot high and ran along the side of the Walsh lot that bordered a roadway.

Language of the Court. *An easement by prescription is generally demonstrated by proof of the adverse, open and notorious, continuous, and uninterrupted use of the subject property for the ten-year* *prescriptive period. Abdelaal testified that he used the circular driveway crossing the Walsh lot on a daily basis. This use manifested a sufficient degree of openness, notoriety, and continuity to give rise to a prescriptive easement. In contrast, his use of the driveway that crossed the northern portion of the Walsh lot was admittedly occasional, and the evidence offered no clear indication of the frequency of use of this driveway by Abdelaal or his guests. This evidence was thus insufficient to establish, by clear and convincing evidence, that his use of the northern driveway was notorious and continuous.*

Decision. The plaintiffs use of the circular driveway traversing the lot on a daily basis created a prescriptive easement over the northern driveway.

FOCUS ON ETHICS

Do you think prescriptive easements reflect ethical conduct? Why does the law allow them?

Expansion of Prescriptive Easements

Courts have been reluctant to permit any expansion of the scope of prescriptive easements to accommodate the changed future needs of the dominant estate.

> **Example:** The Supreme Court of Colorado prevented the expansion of a prescriptive easement. The court considered the scope of an easement for a barely passable roadway that was available for ranching only six months out of the year. The court held that the holder of a prescriptive easement would be allowed to vary the use of the easement to a reasonable extent. However, the flexibility of the use was limited by the concern about how much the variance would further burden the servient estate. The court held that the road had never been used for access to any residence on the affected property in the past and that the prescriptive use could not be expanded to permit access to a residential subdivision.[4]

Scope of Easements

Once an easement is created, two questions arise. First, how extensively and intensively may the holder use the easement? Second, to what extent may the servient estate owner use or interfere with the easement? Courts will look first to the parties' intention in creating the easement. When the intention is not clearly stated, the courts will look to the circumstances to infer the parties' intent. The general rules for interpreting these easement issues are discussed below.

Generally, the scope of an easement by implication is defined by the prior use. Easements by necessity are defined by the necessity and are not expandable beyond that necessity. Easements by prescription are defined by the adverse use by the prescriptive user. Courts are reluctant to permit any expansion of the scope of prescriptive easements to adjust to the increased needs of the dominant estate. Once the location of an easement is fixed, the location is permanent unless the parties agree to change it. Courts do permit modifications to an easement if no additional burden occurs. For example, a water company granted the right to install underground wooden waterlines in the late 1800s would be entitled to replace them now with reinforced concrete pipe.

Use and Intensity Changes

Easement holders may use the easement for what is reasonably convenient or necessary to fully enjoy the purposes of the easement. Normal increases in use are permitted as long as they do not unduly burden the servient estate. Reasonable use is determined at the time the dispute arises and not at the time the easement was created. Courts favor the use of easements that are consistent with current technologies and purposes, even though they may not have been available at the time of the easement's creation.

> *Example:* In 1910, Able granted Baker an easement over Able's unimproved property to reach a public road. At the time, the easement was a dirt road heavily traveled by foot and horse-drawn carriages. A modern court might permit the easement to be used by automobiles as long as the servient estate was not unduly burdened. Other issues to be resolved would include whether Baker's successors could improve the roadbed to better handle vehicular traffic.

Courts often deal with claims that the scope of the easement must be adjusted to conform to changes in the use of the dominant estate. Foreseeable, normal, and reasonable development of the dominant estate is permitted. Thus, a reasonable new use may be permitted, such as the expansion of bike lanes within a pedestrian path.

The holder of an easement obtains rights over the servient estate owner. The servient estate owner loses the ability to have unrestricted use of his property. If the easement is for a particular portion of the servient estate, the servient owner may not force the holder of the easement to use a different portion of the servient estate. For this reason, easements are often carefully drawn to provide the servient estate with rights to adjust the easement and limit its duration.

If a court determines that the servient estate is unduly burdened by the unreasonable use of the easement by the dominant estate, the servient holder has several remedies. The servient estate holder may sue the dominant estate holder to enjoin (prevent) the dominant estate holder from exceeding the scope of the easement. In extreme cases, the servient estate may obtain a court order extinguishing the easement.

Example: Use of easement involving an access road to a remote cabin might increase if the cabin use increased in frequency from the occasional weekend to daily use. However, the increased private use of that road by commercial trucks utilizing the easement to routinely haul crops year-round from other nearby properties would not be considered a reasonable increased use.

Example: A timber-access-road easement was created when horses hauled the timber from the forest. The use of modern commercial trucks to do the same would be a consistent and reasonable use of that easement.

Servient Estate's Use of the Easement

Reasonable use of the easement by the servient estate owner is permitted unless exclusive use of the easement was granted to the dominant estate easement holder. Generally, no use may be made of the easement that is different from that established when the easement was created. The owner of the servient estate retains the right to use the land in any manner that does not unreasonably interfere with the use granted in the easement.

However, the dominant estate holder may sue the servient estate holder for interference with easement rights. For example, a servient estate holder may grow weary of constant traffic across an easement that is an access road and install a locked gate across the road. That interference is a form of trespass, and a court may order the removal of the interfering gate and award damages to the dominant estate easement holder.

Easement Maintenance and Repair

The terms of an express easement often control the duties of repair and maintenance of easements. Without such an agreement or if the agreement is silent, then the holder of the easement (the dominant estate) has an affirmative duty to maintain the easement in good repair. Generally, the servient owner has no duty to contribute toward the costs of maintenance or repair, although the servient estate party must allow reasonable access for the required repairs.

The holder of the easement may make only limited improvements to the easement, consistent with the nature of the easement, and may not materially increase the burden upon the servient estate. For example, the dominant estate may pave a gravel road as an improvement. Moreover, an owner of the servient estate may not unreasonably interfere with use of the easement by its holder.

Termination of Easements

Courts tend to treat easements as continuing forever unless a contrary intent is indicated in the document creating the easement. Even though permanent in nature, an easement can be terminated several ways:

- *Achievement of the purpose or time for their creation.* Easements terminate when their purpose for creation has been completed. They also terminate if they were created for a specific duration of time and that duration has expired.

Example: An easement granted to allow access across a property to construct a building is terminated upon the completion of the construction project.

- *Merger.* When the owner of the dominant estate purchases the servient estate, the easement is terminated.
- *Abandonment.* Clear, conclusive, and unequivocal abandonment of the easement by the dominant estate holder terminates an easement.
- *Incompatible act.* Performance of any incompatible act relative to the nature or exercise of the easement upon either the dominant or the servient estate terminates the easement.

Example: If an easement existed for pedestrian access and the dominant tenement attempts to expand the easement for high-volume commercial hauling.

- *Written release.* The holder of the easement may release or terminate in writing the right to use the easement. The language used should manifest a clear and unequivocal intention to abandon the easement. Mere lack of use is usually insufficient proof of abandonment.
- *Foreclosure of the servient estate.* The foreclosure of a mortgage or deed of trust on a servient estate property terminates an easement that was created after the mortgage or deed of trust was created. In some states, a property tax foreclosure sale terminates easements on a servient estate.

Conservation Easements

Almost all states permit **conservation easements**. These promote the preservation of land and, if properly drawn, can serve as a tax-planning strategy for the grantor. They are negative in nature and do not benefit a dominant estate. They are created in perpetuity for the benefit of ecological conservation. Usually they apply to locations containing natural resources meriting protection, such as watersheds, unimproved forest or desert land, and areas of historical or architectural significance. While these easements can advance public conservation interests, they often reduce public tax rolls by reducing the amount of taxable land.

The decision to place a conservation easement on real property is a voluntary act. The restrictions of a conservation easement run with the land and are binding upon all future owners of the property. The recorded easement protects and restricts the land from certain uses or future development. A conservation easement may not be defeated by adverse possession.

Federal Tax Treatment

Under federal tax law, landowners who donate qualifying land to a qualified land-protection organization for use as a conservation easement may be eligible for federal income tax deductions equal to the value of their donation. Additionally, federal estate taxes may be reduced through the creation of conservation easements. Usually, the property must have an appreciable natural, scenic, historic, scientific, recreational, or open-space value. Several states, including Virginia, Delaware, Colorado, Connecticut, South Carolina, and California, have state tax credits available for such donors.

Enforcement

Conservation easements may only be enforced by the grantor, the grantee (or a permitted assignee), or a public body or nonprofit conservation organization designated in the easement as having enforcement rights. The Nature Conservancy™ is one notable conservation group actively utilizing conservation easements. The organization has been using these easements to protect landscapes from development. They have secured such easements to conserve watersheds and aquifers and to buffer national parks from development and human activity and to promote the protection of the natural resources within and around the parks.

Profits

A **profit** (short for a *profit à prendre*) is the right to enter another's land and take something from it. These rights do not grant the profit holder the right of full possession of the land. The difference between an easement and a profit is that an easement gives the holder the right to use another's land, but a profit gives the holder the right to take something from the land. Easements do not allow the removal of resources. Common examples of profits include the right to remove timber, crops, or sand and gravel.

> **Profit**
> The right to enter another's land and take something from the land.

> *Example:* Helen negotiates the rights to enter Sam's 10 acres of land and remove sand and gravel for her concrete business. Her right to remove the material from Sam's land is a profit.

Profits may be classified as appurtenant or in gross. Like easements, profits appurtenant benefit a particular parcel of land and require the existence of at least two parcels of land. An appurtenant profit has been considered an interest in land required to be in writing. A profit in gross benefits a person, regardless of whether that person owns any land at all. Profits in gross are freely transferable to third parties. The basis for this treatment is that most profits have good economic value to the holder and can be efficiently utilized if they are transferable.

Licenses

A **license** is permission to enter the licensor's property. Unlike easements, licenses are created informally. They are usually temporary and are revocable unless the parties otherwise agree. Licensees do not have possession but only a limited right to use the owner's land for a particular purpose or activity.

> **License**
> The privilege to use the land of another; usually temporary and revocable.

It is a personal, revocable, and unassignable (nontransferable) right. It is not an interest in land, and it does not pass with the title to the property. They may be oral or written. We receive a license when we attend sporting events or use amusement parks, recreational facilities, parking structures, educational facilities, and other places of public accommodation. In exchange for the entry fee, the premise's owner and operator (such as a stadium tenant) can control our behavior and limit his or her liability to us. The next time you enter a public parking lot, review the posted limitations of liability that the owner has imposed upon you.

> *Example:* To enter a stadium parking lot you receive a parking ticket when entering the parking structure. You have been granted a license to park your vehicle.

Exercise 3.1

For each of the following, determine whether an easement, a profit, or a license has been created.

1. Tommy purchases a ticket to attend a college football game at his alma mater.
2. In an unusually dry rainy season, George is granted permission to utilize water from a spring on his neighbor's land.
3. Kevin's neighbor's children have thrown a few toys into his backyard. Kevin grants his neighbor permission to enter his backyard and retrieve the toys.
4. Holiday Tree Company is granted the right to enter Sally's 500 acres to harvest trees to be used during the upcoming holiday season.
5. Jorge purchases a landlocked property. To gain access to the nearest road, Jorge's neighbor grants him permission to travel across her property.

Covenants

Covenant
An unconditional promise to another.

Real property owners and lessees often want to ensure that neighboring property is restricted to uses compatible to those of their own land. In the context of real property, a **covenant** is a contractual promise that binds the current and subsequent owners of the property to the promises made. Covenants must be in writing to be enforceable against subsequent transferees.

Covenants are often created by developers who record a set of covenants, conditions, and restrictions (CC&Rs) on the title to each of the lots to be sold. They may also be created by a homeowners' association or a community association to create and enforce rules binding subsequent transferees of the property. They are often used as a means of preserving and protecting property values, often through the control of neighborhood aesthetics.

> *Example:* A property owner may have the duty to install and maintain landscaping in accordance with a common landscape design for the neighborhood.

> *Example:* A community association may prohibit the possession of more than two pets within a residence.

Key Terms and Concepts

- Nonpossessory interest, page 54
- Easement, page 55
- Easement appurtenant, page 55
- Dominant estate/dominant tenement, page 55
- Servient estate/servient tenement, page 55
- Easement in gross, page 56
- Affirmative easement, page 56
- Negative easement, page 56
- Run with the land, page 56
- Constructive notice, page 57
- Commercial easements in gross, page 57
- Noncommercial easements in gross, page 57

- Easement by grant, page 59
- Express grants, page 59
- Express reservation, page 59
- Easement by estoppel, page 60
- Easement by necessity, page 60
- Easement by implication, page 62
- Easement by prescription, page 63
- Conservation easement, page 68
- Profit, page 69
- License, page 69
- Covenant, page 70

Chapter Summary

- An easement gives the holder the right to use or prevent the use of property the easement owner does not own or possess. It is a nonpossessory interest in the land of another.

- Disputes over easements normally arise in the context of their creation, the scope of their permitted use, and their termination.

- Easements are created by grant, estoppel, implication, necessity, and prescription.

- Easements are classified as either affirmative or negative.

- Every easement must be either appurtenant or in gross.

- An easement appurtenant is one that benefits the owner of another parcel of land. The benefited property is the dominant estate, and the burdened property is the servient estate.

- An easement designed to deliver a personal benefit rather than to benefit a landowner is an easement in gross. Easements in gross are not appurtenant to any parcel of land.

- Easements implied from prior use require the following: that there was common ownership

before the division of the property, that the prior use exists at the time of division, that the use has been apparent so that it could have been reasonably detected or inferred, and that the prior use has been reasonably necessary for the use and enjoyment of the dominant estate.

- Easements by necessity arise in situations of landlocked properties.

- Easements created by prescription arise when the use is adverse to the landowner, open/notorious, and continuous for the statutory period.

- Easements may be terminated by any of the following: achievement of their purpose, destruction of the servient estate, prescription, merger, release or abandonment, and condemnation or eminent-domain seizure.

- Profits are the right to enter another's land and take something from it.

- Licenses are the right to enter the property of another for a delineated purpose. They are freely revocable.

- Covenants are unconditional promises to which subsequent owners must abide.

Chapter Problems and Assignments

1. Explain the differences between affirmative and negative easements.

2. If Kyle wanted to protect his right to a view on his property, why would he want to ensure his easement with his neighbor Xavier was appurtenant rather than in gross?

3. If Chance has an interest in his neighbor's property that allows Chance to use the property for a specific purpose, but does not give him ownership in that property, what type of interest does Chance have?

4. Identify and explain the four elements necessary to prove the presence of an easement by necessity.

5. Taylor's property is only accessible by means of a gravel driveway that runs through a portion of Rebecca's property. The easement that benefits Taylor's property is classified as what type? Would it be appurtenant or in gross?

6. If Suki grants her neighbor, Damion, an easement appurtenant to park his car in her driveway, what will happen to the easement if Damion moves away?

7. Ricardo owns a large beachfront property. Ricardo wishes to split the property into two lots and build another home on the portion farther from the ocean. Ricardo decides he wants to live in the new home because the crashing of the waves keeps him up at night. However, Ricardo still wants to be able to access the beach from the newly built home. Ricardo has agreed to sell the beachfront property to Esther. Advise Ricardo on the appropriate easement to meet his needs.

8. When it is unclear if an easement is appurtenant or in gross, the judicial preference is to find the easement is appurtenant. Why do you believe this preference exists?

9. Identify and explain the differences between an easement and a license.

10. Why would a landowner agree to a covenant that prevents her use of her property in a particular way?

End Notes

1. *Henley v. Continental Cablevision*, 692 S.W.2d 825 (1985).
2. *Ludwig v. Gosline*, 465 A.2d 946 (1983).
3. *Catholic Bishop of Chicago v. Chicago Title & Trust*, 954 N.E.2d 797 (2011).
4. *Wright v. Horse Creek Ranches, Inc.*, 697 P.2d 384 (1985).

Chapter 4
Fixtures and Secured Transactions

Owing money has never concerned me so long as I know where it could be repaid.
—Col. Henry Crown, American industrialist and philanthropist (1896–1990)

Learning Objectives

1. Define what constitutes a fixture.
2. Describe the different types of attachments.
3. Identify the different tests for classifying fixtures.
4. Explain how a creditor can perfect its rights to personal property.

Chapter Outline

- Introduction
- Fixtures

Case 4.1: *In re Ryerson*

Case 4.2: *H. Allen Holmes, Inc. v. Jim Molter, Inc.*

- Attachments
- Creating and Perfecting Creditors' Rights: Secured Transactions

Case 4.3: *In the Matter of United Thrift Stores, Inc., Bankrupt*

Opening scenario

Michael has just sold his home. When he moves, he takes with him several high-end televisions, several satellite television receivers, a wall-mounted 3-D projection television display, and whole-home integrated audio and video equipment. Steven, the new owner, is furious and demands that the items be returned to the home. He contacts the police and files a report claiming Michael has stolen his property. Steven also sues Michael for the value of the goods he allegedly removed from the residence. In his defense, Michael believes the items were personal property, meaning that he could take them when moving. Looking to the law of fixtures, how should the court rule?

Introduction

In chapter 1, we studied the nature of property. This chapter examines how specific types of property, including crops and fixtures, can be viewed as either real or personal, and it covers the classification tests used by courts and real estate professionals. As the opening scenario suggests, seemingly small details in a purchase and sale contract can cause emotions to run high, especially when a detective is involved, and the threat of criminal prosecution looms. A detailed, carefully drafted purchase agreement could have avoided this conflict. Real estate professionals, attorneys, or homeowners may face liability for failing to carefully define what is to be included as a fixture.

Fixtures

Often it is a simple task to determine if property is real or personal property; however, what happens if personal property is difficult to remove from its attachment? Determining when something is no longer considered personal property but rather as real property is known as the law of fixtures.

Fixture
Personal property that has become so attached to the real property that it loses its identity as personal property.

A **fixture** is personal property that has become so attached to the real property that it loses its identity as personal property. As previously discussed, personal property is movable and not fixed or permanently attached to real property. Fixtures pass with the transfer of title to real property, while title to personal property remains in the possession of the holder and does not transfer with the sale or conveyance of real property.

Real property includes not only the land but also any personal property permanently affixed to it (that is, fixtures). In the absence of an agreement between the parties, a fixture is owned by the owner of the land upon which the structure is permanently affixed.

Example: Leo and Elsa purchase lumber and supplies at a home improvement center and construct an attic bedroom. The supplies were personal property when they were transported to their home, but they become a fixture once they are installed.

Fixture Tests

Sometimes an item, such as a refrigerator, may or may not be a fixture depending on the circumstances. Fixture disputes often arise in residential purchase transactions and commercial leases and between secured creditors and third parties. The dispute is triggered when one party seeks to remove what they consider personal property from the premises.

The courts have developed many tests, guidelines, and rules to determine whether something is a fixture, and these tests consider all the particular facts of a given case. It is not unusual for a real estate professional to be perplexed by the conflicting approaches to fixture classification taken by courts and legislatures. Many unsuccessful attempts have been made to find a single definition that clarifies problems involving the rights of parties regarding fixtures. Generally, one or more of the following tests must be satisfied for an item to be considered a fixture:

- Intention (agreement) of the parties
- Character of the property and adaption to use with real property
- Actual or constructive annexation
- Substantial harm caused to the real property by its removal

Intention (Agreement) of the Parties

Where the parties have expressly agreed to the character of property, this intention often controls whether the property is a fixture.

Example: The parties in a residential purchase agreement may agree that an old, rusty jungle gym in the backyard is personal property that must be removed before the close of escrow. The jungle gym could have been considered a fixture that would transfer with the sale of the real property, but the parties expressly agreed that the jungle gym would remain personal property.

As a subset of the intention test, some courts consider the relation of the parties to the transaction. The courts look to what type of relationship the parties to the transaction have. These relationships and preferences are as follows:

- *Between a seller and buyer*: The law favors the buyer as to whatever is essential for the use of the buildings, even if it might be severed without injury at the time of its removal. The general rule in this situation is that fixtures pass with the title to the land unless they are expressly reserved in writing.

Example: A seller of a property located in a hot climate might install expensive canvas awnings over south-facing windows to temper solar heating in the home. The awnings should remain with the real property at the close of the sale.

■ *Between a mortgagor* (property owner) *and mortgagee-beneficiary* (property lender): The law favors the mortgagee-beneficiary.

Example: The owner of an apartment building installed drapes and carpeting, both of which were easily removable, but the owner lost the property to foreclosure. The lender would be able to keep the drapes and carpeting as fixtures.

Some courts consider the assumptions of a reasonable buyer of the land. For instance, would the average purchaser of the real property reasonably expect the personal property to be sold as a part of the real estate?

Example: A bank claims an interest in a farmer's irrigation system. In a bankruptcy proceeding, the bank claimed that the irrigation system was a fixture and not merely movable farm equipment, as the farmer maintained. The bankruptcy court determined that the irrigation system was a fixture.[1]

Character and Adaptation

Courts will also consider the character of the property and its adaptation to the use of the real property. This test considers how integrally connected the property is to the real property. Unique, custom-manufactured goods are often determined to be fixtures, whereas goods that may be used elsewhere may not be fixtures.

Example: A pipe organ installed in a place of worship may be a fixture, whereas one installed at a residence may not be. The pipe organ is a regular component of the music in a worship service, but it would be considered a hobbyist's instrument in a home.

Example: A wood-paneled refrigerator with custom wood paneling made to match the kitchen cabinets is likely to be considered a fixture. The same refrigerator without matching wood paneling would be considered personal property.

In the following case, the court had to determine if the prior owner was permitted to remove a gourmet kitchen stove.

CASE 4.1

DESIGNING A ROOM TO ACCOMMODATE AN APPLIANCE WILL CLASSIFY THE APPLIANCE AS A FIXTURE

IN RE RYERSON

519 B.R. 275 (2014)

United States Bankruptcy Court for the District of Idaho

A bankrupt debtor, Ryerson filed a petition for bankruptcy. Immediately following the foreclosure of Ryerson's luxury custom home, the foreclosing creditor, Anaconda LLC inspected the property. Anaconda agreed that Ryerson was entitled to remove personal property, such as furniture and art, but contended that certain fixtures had been improperly removed. Ten days after the foreclosure, Anaconda sued for over $550,000 worth of fixtures that had been removed from the property and sought to have Ryerson return and pay the reinstallation fees for any fixtures that had been sold or transferred by Ryerson. Ryerson argued that none of the removed property was a fixture. One of the main items of contention was an expensive 65-inch La Cornue gas range stove, a non-standard- sized appliance. Ryerson argued that this item did not qualify as a fixture due to its ease of removal and free-standing characteristics.

Language of the Court. *Whether an item is a fixture is a mixed question of law and fact. To determine whether an item is a fixture, the Court is to apply a three-part test evaluating (1) the annexation of the item to the realty, either actual or constructive, (2) the adaptation or application of the item to the use or purpose to that part of the realty to which it is connected is appropriate, and (3) the intention to make the article a permanent accession to the property. Of these elements, intention is the most signif-*

icant, and the other two assist the fact finder in addressing intent. Intent is objectively evaluated by the circumstances surrounding the disputed item's installation.

The 65" La Cornue gas range was a non-standard size appliance. It was a wedding present from Ryerson to his wife, and was acquired at the La Cornue factory in France. The stove was free-standing on its "legs" and simply connected to a natural gas line and electric outlets. And it was removed without damage. Both of these factors were repeatedly emphasized by Ryersons. However, the kitchen area was custom-designed around the stove's non-standard dimensions, including cabinetry, tiling, and an exhaust hood. The La Cornue stove was "installed" in a manner that speaks objectively to the intent that it be a permanent improvement.

Decision. The stove was a fixture and Ryerson was required to return or pay the fair market value plus installation costs to Anaconda.

FOCUS ON ETHICS

Is it fair the court places more deference to the custom design of the kitchen to accommodate the stove qualifies it as a fixture rather than the fact that freestanding and easily movable?

Actual or Constructive Annexation

Once considered the sole or most important test, actual or constructive annexation no longer carries top status in determining whether something is a fixture. However, it is still an important guideline. Permanency of annexation suggests that the item is a fixture and has become real property. The means of the property's attachment guides the decision. For example, was the property attached with cement, plaster, adhesives, nails, or screws? The degree of difficulty involved in its removal aids in the interpretation of permanency.

> *Example:* A small decorative mirror in a hallway might easily be removed from the wall and considered personal property. A mantel-mounted, large, heavy mirror installed over a fireplace with the aid of several cross-braces, wall reinforcements, and attachments to special casings might be considered a fixture.

Constructive annexation of personal property may result in an item becoming a fixture. Goods not actually annexed or fastened to the land can still be considered real property by association. If an item is not physically attached to the real property but is used in such a way, or so associated with the use of the building, that the nonattached personal property has become part of the realty or would not be adaptable for general use if removed, it is considered a fixture.

> *Example:* While leasing land, a farmer made improvements, including the installation of two water wells. The wells were annexed to real property as fixtures because they are best understood and accepted as annexed to the property.[2]

When the constructive-annexation test applies to machinery in an industrial setting, it is known as the **industrial plant rule**. In such situations, if the machinery is essential to the proper functioning of an industrial facility, then the personal property is deemed a fixture. This rule usually applies in situations with heavy machinery that, although not physically attached to the land, is so heavy that it can no longer be regarded as movable.

Substantial Harm

A few states review the degree of difficulty in the removal and the resulting damage in determining fixture status. When the removal of the property causes substantial harm, the item is a fixture. When it does not, the item is personal property.

Trade Fixtures

Trade fixtures
Personal property installed by a business tenant used in conducting a trade or business on the premises. They are considered personal property and may be removed by the tenant.

Trade fixtures are items installed by a commercial tenant for the purpose of conducting a trade or business on the premises upon which they were installed. Trade fixtures remain the personal property of the tenant. Unlike fixtures arising in a residential context, the tenant may remove trade fixtures at any time during the term of a lease and for a reasonable period following the termination of the lease. Trade fixtures may be removed if they do not cause material or permanent injury to the realty.

> *Example:* A restaurant owner's lease expired. When vacating the premises, the restaurateur may remove the wood flooring, wall paneling and floor displays, lighting, furniture, equipment, and kitchen appliances. The tenant is entitled to do so because the items are trade fixtures.

Even a freestanding building can be deemed a fixture.

Example: A tenant operating a diner placed buildings on land specifically for conducting the diner and restaurant business. The diner was a trade fixture, as the building was designed for purposes of trade, and as so designed, it was a trade fixture and could be removable by the tenant irrespective of other factors.[3]

In the following case, a lease was ambiguous as to whether the tenant was entitled to retain trade fixtures upon the lease's expiration. The tenant sued the landlord for retaining the security deposit to repair damage caused by removal of the fixtures.

CASE 4.2

CONTRACT AMBIGUITIES REGARDING RETENTION OF TRADE FIXTURES FAVOR THE TENANT

H. ALLEN HOLMES, INC. v. JIM MOLTER, INC.

127 So. 3d 695 (2013)

Florida District Court of Appeal

The tenant, an interior designer, removed its trade fixtures and vacated the premises following the expiration of a lease contract. The landlord then retained the tenant's security deposit. This resulted in the tenant suing the landlord for breach of contract for the landlord's improper retention of the security deposit. The landlord then filed claims against the tenant for breach of contract, conversion, and civil theft for the alleged improper removal of the trade fixtures from the premise.

The trial court found the tenant was entitled to retain the trade fixtures and a partial return of its security deposit. In addition, the landlord was entitled to retain a portion of the security deposit to repair the damages the tenant caused to the premises by removing the fixtures. The landlord was not entitled to a judgment on its civil theft claims. Both parties appealed.

Language of the Court. *We conclude that the parties' lease contract was ambiguous as to which party was entitled to retain the trade fixtures when the lease expired. Because the lease contract was ambiguous, we conclude that the tenant was entitled to retain the trade fixtures.*

Where the relationship of landlord-tenant exists, the presumption is in favor of the right of a tenant to remove structures or articles the tenant has placed on the leased property for its own purpose, even in the absence of an express stipulation. Nothing short of the clearest expression of an agreement by the parties to that effect can justify the extension of the grasp of the landlord so as to cover personal property brought upon the premises by the tenant, in pursuance of the business for which the premises were leased. For in the absence of an express contract as to trade fixtures, there is an implied contract permitting the tenant to remove them at the proper time and in a proper manner.

Decision. The court affirmed the trial court's decision. The tenant was entitled to retain the trade fixtures and a partial return of its security deposit.

FOCUS ON ETHICS?

Why does the law favor a commercial tenant in such circumstances?

Wrongful Removal of a Fixture

State statutes may provide that the unauthorized removal of a fixture is a crime subjecting a person who wrongfully removed the fixture to criminal prosecution. Additionally, and more frequently, the wrongful removal is considered waste. **Waste** is the destruction, harm, or injury caused to the use of real property by a person in possession of the property.

When a person without the right to remove a fixture attempts or threatens to do so, the owner of the property may seek an injunction. An **injunction** is an equitable remedy (a nonmonetary remedy that can be used when monetary damages are inadequate) by which the court prevents the party from removing the fixture. If the fixture is removed before an injunction can be issued, the owner may sue to recover the property or to recover damages resulting from the loss of the property.

> *Example:* Included in the purchase and sale agreement of a residential home was a beautiful chandelier. When escrow closed, the purchaser discovered that the seller had removed the chandelier. At this point, the purchaser cannot seek an injunction but may sue the previous owner for waste to recover the chandelier or its value.

Innocent Improver: Right of Removal

Many states provide for a right of removal of fixtures where an innocent improver, acting in good faith, improves the land of another. This right of removal is known as **wrongful or mistaken improver** of real property. Most states require that the innocent improver pay any resulting damages to the owner of the real estate for any harm caused in the removal process.

> *Example:* Fuel Exploration, Inc. mistakenly installed oilfield equipment on the defendant landowner's property instead of the property of an adjacent landowner. The defendant landowners contended that they had become owners of the equipment because the equipment was now a fixture. The company attempted to buy the land on which the equipment sat. The landowners refused to sell, erected a temporary fence around the equipment area, posted No Trespassing signs, maintained a 24-hour guard on the property, and warned the company neither to trespass nor to remove any of the equipment. The company sued under mistaken improver of real property and prevailed.[4]

Whether or not a trespasser who installed fixtures has the right to remove them without the landowner or lender's consent will vary by each state and will depend on the circumstances. The majority of jurisdictions will provide that the trespasser may be able to remove the fixtures under the right of removal if damages are paid.

Fixtures Taxable as Real Property

A local property tax assessor can treat fixtures as permanent improvements and tax them as the real property of the landowner. The intention of the parties for taxation purposes will be determined by objectively reviewing the outward appearances without regard to the agreement or relationship of the parties. Generally, a fixture will be taxable as real property. If it is not attached and can easily be removed without damage to the building, the fixture is not treated as a fixture for real property taxation purposes.

Waste
Destruction, harm, or injury caused to the use of real property by a person in possession of the property.

Fixtures should be distinguished from an improvement to real property, as the terms are not synonymous. A fixture is something that was at one time personal property; however, an improvement to real property more broadly defines everything that is attached permanently to the land and improves the value of the land for its general use.

Example: An aboveground swimming pool may be considered a fixture for real property taxation purposes. On the other hand, an installed belowground swimming pool is an improvement to real property and will also be included in the valuation of the real property for taxation purposes.

Exercise 4.1

Classify the following types of property as personal property, a fixture, or a trade fixture.

1. Office chairs
2. Artwork hanging on a wall of a residence
3. A wireless garage door opener
4. Walk-in freezer, air-conditioning units, shelving and cabinetry securely affixed inside a restaurant tenant's space
5. Chandeliers inside a residence
6. Built-in desk inside a residence
7. Tile flooring inside a restaurant installed by the restaurant tenant
8. Ceiling fans
9. Refrigerator inside a residence
10. Smoke detectors installed inside a single-family residence

Attachments

Attachments are crops, trees, bushes, and grasses attached or affixed to the land. They may be considered real property or personal property, depending upon how they are produced. It is important to distinguish between these types of attachments because, depending on its classification, property will transfer with the sale or conveyance of the real property. Courts have developed special tests to assist in determining whether objects growing on the land pass with the sale of the land. They are as follows:

> **Attachments**
> Crops, trees, bushes, and grasses attached or affixed to the land.

■ *Fructus naturales:* Those things produced primarily by nature, such as forests and shrubbery. They require no annual labor or cultivation and are considered real property. Because these items are real property, title to them will pass with the sale of the land.

■ *Fructus industriales* Those things produced through human effort, such as crops or fruit groves. They require some sort of annual planting or cultivation. They are considered severable from real property and remain personal property with the sale of the land.

A special rule for annual *fructus industriales* applies to tenants. A tenant who grows *fructus industriales* is entitled to the crop's harvest, even if the tenant's right to occupy the land ends before the harvest. **Emblements** are the rights to cultivate and harvest annual crops.

Creating and Perfecting Creditors' Rights: Secured Transactions

Secured transaction
An agreement whereby a lender or seller retains a security interest in personal property of the person who owes payment (i.e., the debtor).

Debtor
The borrower in a credit transaction.

Creditor
The lender in a credit transaction.

Security agreement
An agreement whereby a lender or seller retains a security interest in personal property of the debtor.

When an owner improves real property and borrows money for the improvement, a secured transaction may arise. When the owner installs personal property that become fixtures, the party extending credit wants to make sure it has the ability to obtain the property or have priority of payment over other creditors in the event that the owner is unable to pay for the debt. A **secured transaction** is one that creates rights in the personal property or fixtures of another.

Often where personal property will not be movable and must be installed or affixed to the realty (such as rooftop air conditioning units), the lender requires the borrower to provide written acknowledgment that the item remains personal property. This written acknowledgement is known as a **security agreement**. The lender creates a security agreement to protect itself in the event of default. The right created in the security agreement to the debtor's personal property, fixtures, or other property is known as a security interest. The lender, who has a security interest in the collateral, in such circumstances is known as a **secured creditor** because they have property which secures the debt that they are owed.

The **security interest** secures the payment or performance of an obligation and gives the holder of that security interest the right to repossess, retain, or dispose of the collateral if the person who owes the obligation fails to perform. Whether a transaction creates a security interest is determined by the facts of each case.

The other right that is created under a secured transaction is **priority**. The holder of the security interest has the right to be paid first among all creditors with respect to that collateral in the event of default. Article 9 of the Uniform Commercial Code, which has been adopted by every state, provides for the creation and enforcement of creditors' interests in personal property and fixtures.

Attachment to the Collateral

For a secured transaction to occur, a creditor's security interest must "attach" to the personal property or fixture. Attachment occurs when a security interest attaches to the collateral and becomes enforceable against the debtor with regard to the debtor's collateral. Three things must occur to create a valid security interest:

■ A written agreement recognizing the security interest or the collateral must be in possession of the secured party.

- The value is given to the debtor.
- The debtor must have rights in the collateral.

Security Agreement

A **security agreement** is a contract between a creditor and a debtor that creates or provides for a security interest in personal property or fixtures. Unless the creditor has possession of the collateral, there must be evidence of a record (such as a writing), the agreement must be signed by the debtor, and it must contain a description of the collateral that reasonably identifies the collateral subject to the security agreement. A general description, such as "all of the debtor's personal property," is not a sufficient description. The security agreement is effective between the parties, against purchasers of the collateral, and against creditors. Courts look to the parties' objective actions and statements indicating their intent to create a security interest.

Value Given to the Debtor

The creditor must have given value to the debtor. This is most often met in fixtures by the creditor extending credit (i.e., the loan) to the debtor. However, any form of consideration would constitute value given to the debtor.

Debtor Must Have Rights in the Collateral

The debtor must have rights to some form of ownership interest or right to obtain possession of the collateral. With fixtures, the debtor is usually already in possession of the collateral and provides the fixtures as collateral for the loan.

Perfection

When a security attaches, it will be either perfected or unperfected. The creation of a security interest and the security agreement must be distinguished from the perfection of a security interest. A secured party must look to the collateral to satisfy the debtor's promise or obligation in the event of default. To obtain the maximum protection against the claims of a debtor with many creditors in the debtor's assets, a secured party will perfect the security interest.

To perfect a security interest, the security agreement itself need not be filed to give notice to third parties. A simple notice, known as a **financing statement**, is filed in the public records office, usually at the county level, to notify third parties of a secured party's interest in the described personal property or fixtures. An example of a financing statement is provided as Exhibit 4.1. While perfection can occur through taking possession of goods, filing a financing statement is generally necessary to perfect security interests. Generally, a filed financing statement is effective for five years after the date of filing. The effectiveness of a financing statement will lapse on the expiration of the five years unless a continuation statement is filed at least six months before the expiration of the five-year period. A financing statement must do all of the following:

- Identify the debtor and have the debtor's signature
- Identify the secured party
- State, with sufficient description, the collateral covered by the financing statement

UCC FINANCING STATEMENT
FOLLOW INSTRUCTIONS

A. NAME & PHONE OF CONTACT AT FILER (optional)

B. E-MAIL CONTACT AT FILER (optional)

C. SEND ACKNOWLEDGMENT TO: (Name and Address)

Print	Reset

THE ABOVE SPACE IS FOR FILING OFFICE USE ONLY

1. DEBTOR'S NAME: Provide only <u>one</u> Debtor name (1a or 1b) (use exact, full name; do not omit, modify, or abbreviate any part of the Debtor's name); if any part of the Individual Debtor's name will not fit in line 1b, leave all of item 1 blank, check here ☐ and provide the Individual Debtor information in item 10 of the Financing Statement Addendum (Form UCC1Ad)

1a. ORGANIZATION'S NAME			
1b. INDIVIDUAL'S SURNAME	FIRST PERSONAL NAME	ADDITIONAL NAME(S)/INITIAL(S)	SUFFIX
1c. MAILING ADDRESS	CITY	STATE POSTAL CODE	COUNTRY

2. DEBTOR'S NAME: Provide only <u>one</u> Debtor name (2a or 2b) (use exact, full name; do not omit, modify, or abbreviate any part of the Debtor's name); if any part of the Individual Debtor's name will not fit in line 2b, leave all of item 2 blank, check here ☐ and provide the Individual Debtor information in item 10 of the Financing Statement Addendum (Form UCC1Ad)

2a. ORGANIZATION'S NAME			
2b. INDIVIDUAL'S SURNAME	FIRST PERSONAL NAME	ADDITIONAL NAME(S)/INITIAL(S)	SUFFIX
2c. MAILING ADDRESS	CITY	STATE POSTAL CODE	COUNTRY

3. SECURED PARTY'S NAME (or NAME of ASSIGNEE of ASSIGNOR SECURED PARTY): Provide only <u>one</u> Secured Party name (3a or 3b)

3a. ORGANIZATION'S NAME			
3b. INDIVIDUAL'S SURNAME	FIRST PERSONAL NAME	ADDITIONAL NAME(S)/INITIAL(S)	SUFFIX
3c. MAILING ADDRESS	CITY	STATE POSTAL CODE	COUNTRY

4. COLLATERAL: This financing statement covers the following collateral:

5. Check <u>only</u> if applicable and check <u>only</u> one box: Collateral is ☐ held in a Trust (see UCC1Ad, item 17 and Instructions)   ☐ being administered by a Decedent's Personal Representative

6a. Check <u>only</u> if applicable and check <u>only</u> one box:			6b. Check <u>only</u> if applicable and check <u>only</u> one box:	
☐ Public-Finance Transaction	☐ Manufactured-Home Transaction	☐ A Debtor is a Transmitting Utility	☐ Agricultural Lien	☐ Non-UCC Filing

7. ALTERNATIVE DESIGNATION (if applicable): ☐ Lessee/Lessor   ☐ Consignee/Consignor   ☐ Seller/Buyer   ☐ Bailee/Bailor   ☐ Licensee/Licensor

8. OPTIONAL FILER REFERENCE DATA:

UCC FINANCING STATEMENT (Form UCC1) (Rev. 04/20/11)

Exhibit 4.1. Financing Statement

Does the timing of the filing of a financing statement affect the creditor's rights in the collateral? That was the question presented to the federal court in the following case.

CASE 4.3

A FINANCING STATEMENT MAY BE FILED PRIOR TO THE EXISTENCE OF A SECURITY AGREEMENT

IN THE MATTER OF UNITED THRIFT STORES, INC., BANKRUPT

242 F. Supp. 714 (1965)

United States District Court for the District of New Jersey

United Thrift Stores was a retailer of home appliances to consumers. When United Thrift filed for bankruptcy, Redisco sought to reclaim the assets listed in its security agreement with United Thrift. Redisco had filed a financing statement on March 12, 1963. The financing statement listed Redisco as a secured creditor to the debtor United Thrift. Thereafter, United Thrift executed a security agreement in favor of Redisco. Redisco appealed an order of the bankruptcy court denying that it was a secured creditor that could not reclaim the goods it had identified as collateral for the repayment of its loan. Upon appeal, the court held for the secured creditor.

Language of the Court. *The financing statement in this case between Redisco and United Thrift was executed and filed prior to the making of the security agreements. The Trustee contends that an agreement for the creation of a security interest must be in existence prior to the filing of a financing statement, because under New Jersey state law a security interest cannot attach until there is an agreement that it attaches.*

This Court finds no such requirement in the Code. The New Jersey statute provides that "(a) financing statement may be filed before a security agreement is made or a security interest otherwise attaches." Where the financing statement is filed before the security interest attaches, the security interest is perfected when it does so attach. Thus, the Code clearly contemplates that the financing statement may be filed prior to the making of the security agreement, and that a security interest need not be in existence at the time the financing statement is filed.

Decision. The order denying Redisco's reclamation will be reversed and Redisco is entitled to reclaim the property listed in its security agreement.

FOCUS ON ETHICS

Does this rule adequately protect the interests of the creditor?

Security Agreement and Financing Statement Compared

A security agreement states the agreement of the parties and grants or reserves a security interest in the collateral in favor of the creditor. If the creditor gave value to the debtor and if the debtor has rights in the collateral, a security interest attaches. In contrast, the financing statement is filed to perfect the security interest and generally does not, by itself, create a security interest in the debtor's personal property.

A financing statement is a document filed in a public records office to notify third parties of a secured party's interest in the goods. It identifies the names of the debtor and the secured party, is executed by the debtor, contains the mailing information of the parties, and provides a description of the collateral.

Purchase Money Security Interest (PMSI)

A perfected **purchase money security interest** (PMSI) in personal property or fixtures arises where a supplier of goods (a creditor) advances funds for the purchase of collateral. A PMSI creditor will have priority over a conflicting interest in the same goods if the PMSI is perfected (that is, the financing statement is timely filed) when the debtor receives possession of the collateral or within 20 days thereafter. A holder of a PMSI has priority over another creditor's security interest in the same collateral.

> *Example:* If Home Depot were to finance the installation of kitchen cabinets in a residence and received a security interest in the cabinets as a fixture, and if the homeowner were to obtain another loan for which the cabinets served as collateral, the PMSI creditor Home Depot would have priority. The first-to-file or perfect rule of interests applies. However, if the homeowner purchased the cabinets at Home Depot and financed the kitchen cabinets using a credit card, neither Home Depot nor the credit card company would be PMSI creditors.

Priority

The Uniform Commercial Code (UCC) sets forth the priority rights between secured creditors and between a secured creditor and unsecured creditors with respect to the collateral. An **unsecured creditor** is one that does not have some property or asset serving as collateral (that is security) for the debt.

> *Example:* Legal or medical fees and credit card charges are unsecured creditors. They do not have any property or assets serving as collateral in the event of default.

The UCC also establishes the priorities between a secured creditor and a purchaser of the collateral. Although many exceptions exist and the law of each state should be consulted, some general rules for resolving such disputes follow:

1. A perfected PMSI will take priority over all creditors (perfected secured creditors, secured creditors and unsecured creditors).
2. Perfected secured creditors take priority over unperfected secured creditors. An unperfected secured creditor is one who has not filed a financing statement or taken possession of the collateral.
3. Secured creditors have priority over unsecured creditors.
4. Between two or more unperfected secured creditors the first to attach (create a security agreement) has priority.

In some states, statutes create special priorities with respect to fixtures and creditor rights in real property. Generally, when a security interest attaches to personal property prior to its becoming a fixture, the secured creditor does not lose priority to a subsequent real estate mortgage holder because a mortgage was recorded before the goods became fixtures.

Defaults and Remedies

Upon default by the debtor, the secured party may exercise those rights and remedies available under a state's adoption of the Uniform Commercial Code. These remedies often include the following: (1) reducing the claim to judgment and seeking to recover the debt due, (2) foreclosing or enforcing the rights to repossess or sell the collateral in a commercially reasonable manner, or (3) seeking a deficiency judgment against the debtor if the proceeds from a disposition of the collateral are insufficient to pay the debt owed.

Exercise 4.2

On January 2, Chris obtained a mortgage through First Bank. On February 2, Chris obtained a second mortgage through Second Bank, which recorded its mortgage the same day. On February 4, First Bank recorded its mortgage. On November 1, Chris purchased and had installed a dishwasher through BigMart and obtained financing through BigMart. BigMart filed a financing statement on November 10.

1. Who has priority?
2. Who would have priority if BigMart filed a financing statement on November 30?
3. Who would have priority if First Bank recorded its mortgage on February 1?

Key Terms and Concepts

- Fixture, page 74
- Constructive annexation, page 78
- Industrial plant rule, page 78
- Trade fixtures, page 78
- Waste, page 80
- Injunction, page 80
- Right of removal, page 80
- Wrongful or mistaken improver, page 80
- Attachments, page 81
- *Fructus naturales, page 81*
- *Fructus industriales, page 82*

- Emblements, page 82
- Secured transactions, page 82
- Debtor, page 82
- Creditor, page 82
- Security agreement, page 82
- Secured creditor, page 82
- Security interest, page 82
- Priority, page 82
- Financing statement, page 83
- Purchase money security interest, page 86
- Unsecured creditor, page 86

Chapter Summary

- A fixture is property that is incorporated into or attached to real estate. It is so affixed or attached to the land as to become part of it.

- To determine whether a particular item has become a fixture, the law applies a three-part test: the intention of the parties, the character of the property and its adaption to the use or purpose of the realty, and the actual or constructive annexation of the item to the land.

- The relationship of the parties is an important consideration in deciding whether an item is a fixture. The law favors a buyer and the borrower over a creditor mortgagee.

- A trade fixture is an item installed by a commercial tenant for the purposes of conducting a trade or business on the premises. A commercial tenant may remove trade fixtures at the end of the lease, in the absence of a contrary agreement.

- Security interests in personal property or fixtures can affect real estate transactions. A security interest is created when the debtor's interest in personal property has attached and the debtor executes a written security agreement.

- Perfection of its security interest in the debtor's personal property or fixtures by the creditor is not required to enforce the obligation between the debtor and creditor. Perfection gives notice to potential subsequent lienors that the secured party has an interest in the debtor's collateral.

- In general, a perfected secured party prevails in a conflict over priority of interests in the debtor's personal property or fixtures. A purchase money secured creditor, even if the securing occurred later in time than an earlier recorded mortgage, will have priority as to the personal property or fixtures that it finances if it perfects its interest in the same within twenty days of the property's annexation to the realty.

Chapter Problems and Assignments

1. Haru is a skilled carpenter who built a custom bar for the basement of his home where he throws many parties for his friends. Haru has decided to sell his home, but he has stipulated that the bar is to be considered personal property in a contractual agreement with the buyers of the home. Explain whether the bar is considered a fixture.

2. Carmen owns a high-end clothing store. She decides she needs a bigger store to support the business's popularity. Her current lease expires next month, and Carmen is worried that she won't be able to take her vintage chandelier and custom flooring and shelving. Which, if any, of these items can be removed to her new location?

3. Not long after Billy moved to California from his farm in Iowa, he began craving the farm's sweet corn. Billy decided to plant some corn in the backyard of his rented home. After his lease expired, Billy returned to harvest the sweet corn. Is Billy permitted to do so? Explain.

4. What steps are necessary for a creditor's security interest to attach to personal property or a fixture?

5. Hanna took out a $10,000 loan from Banco on January 26. The loan was secured by a mortgage upon her home. The following month, Hanna went to Lendco and took out a $5,000 loan, which was unsecured, partly because she knew the owner, Meeko, who

knew Hanna would always repay her debts. Then just before the holidays, Hanna went to Loanco and took out a $8,000 loan to buy gifts for all her family and friends. This holiday loan was secured by the title to her car. After the New Year, Hanna was laid off and defaulted on all her loans. Discuss the order in which creditors would be paid if Hanna sold her car and home.

6. Assume the same facts from the previous question, except Hanna has not sold her home or car. Discuss the potential remedies of the creditors. Which remedy do you think would be the most beneficial under these circumstances?

7. Alpha, Inc. finances the purchase and installation of new machinery and equipment in Darren's plant. Alpha receives and timely perfects a security interest in these assets. Darren subsequently borrows from his bank and secures the loan with the machinery and equipment. If Darren were to default in repaying both parties, who would be in a better position to collect? Explain.

8. Constructive annexation and the industrial plant rule can be particularly troublesome to potential sellers of commercial or industrial property. Are these rules fair? Can you think of a better alternative?

9. Research the laws of your state to determine whether a trespasser that installed fixtures has the right to remove them without the landowner's or lender's consent. Do you agree with the law of your state? Why or why not?

10. Do you think it is fair that potential fixtures are subjected to a different test for tax purposes, and that test is administered by objectively reviewing the outward appearances without regard to the agreement or relationship of the parties?

End Notes

1. *In Re: Sand & Sage Farm & Ranch, Inc.,* 266 B.R. 507, 38 Bankr. Ct. Dec. 69 (US Bkcy Ct. D. Ks. [2001]).
2. *Rowan v. Riley,* 72 P.3d 889 (2003).
3. *Butler v. Butler's Diner, Inc.,* 98 A. 2d 875 (R.I. 1953).
4. *Fuel Exploration, Inc. v. Novotry,* 374 N.W.2d 838 (Neb. 1985).

Chapter 5
Real Property Estates and Interests

Among the natural rights of colonists are these: first, a right to life; secondly, to liberty; thirdly, to property; together with the right to support and defend them as best they can.
—Samuel Adams, "The Rights of Colonists"

Learning Objectives

1. State the rules of priority for interests in personal property.
2. Recognize the different types of freehold estates.
3. Identify the different types of future interests that may be created.

Chapter Outline

- Introduction
- Real Property Estates and Interests

Case 5.1: *Allen v. Hall*

Case 5.2: *Rearick v. Sieving*

Opening scenario

Sasha wants to gift real property to a religious institution that she would like to see grow and prosper. She is concerned that this religious institution may not use the gift only for religious instruction, and she would like the option, in the event that the religious institution does not use the real property as originally intended, to obtain title back. As you read this chapter, discuss which of the freehold estates discussed in this chapter can help Sasha accomplish her objective.

Introduction

In this chapter we review the various ways to classify an **interest** in real property. This classification system originated from medieval concepts of land ownership and use, and some forms of it are still used today. These concepts help us recognize and classify legal relationships that arise in many contexts — including real property leases, sales, and purchases — and the rights among owners, creditors, and third parties.

Real Property Estates and Interests

The concept of estates and interests entails an understanding of several concepts and vocabulary terms. An **estate** is an interest in land that has two characteristics: namely, the right to possess the land, and the length of time ownership may last.

An interest in property is classified as either a present interest or a future interest. **Present interests** refer to current ownership in property, while **future interests** refer to an interest requiring a person to wait for some event or time in the future to obtain possession.

Freehold estate
An estate in which the owner has a present possessory interest in the real property.

Traditionally, present-interest estates are divided into two types: freehold and nonfreehold. Today we associate the term **freehold** with an ownership interest in land and **nonfreehold** with something less than an ownership interest. Sometimes, nonfreehold estates are referred to as **leasehold estates**. In this chapter, we will also review the various types of land possession and ownership within the freehold estate system. Nonfreehold estates are discussed in chapter 14.

Freehold Estates

There are several types of freehold estates recognized by American law:

- Fee simple estates (two types)
  - Fee simple absolute, *aka* fee simple

☐ Fee simple defeasible (two types)
 ☐ Fee simple determinable
 ☐ Fee simple subject to a condition subsequent
■ Fee tail
■ Life estate

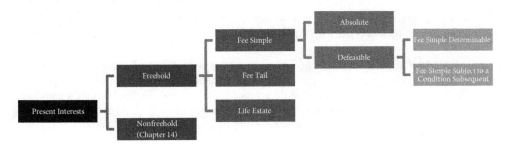

FIGURE 5.1. Present Interests

Fee Simple Absolute

Fee simple absolute, now more commonly known as a **fee simple** or **fee interest** in land, is complete ownership lasting until the end of time; it is subject only to certain limitations, such as contractual limitations between homeowners (such as restrictions placed upon homeowners within a planned unit development) and governmental regulations (such as building and zoning codes). Historically, a fee simple absolute interest was created by a grantor conveying land to "A and his [or her] heirs." Over time, the reference to his or her heirs was viewed as unnecessary and is not required to convey a fee simple absolute interest. Today, the conveyance "to A" is sufficient to convey a fee simple absolute interest to A.

> **Example:** "To A" or "To A and her heirs" create fee simple estates.

A holder of a fee simple absolute interest may sell, gift, or convey the interest during his or her lifetime. If A is deceased at the time of the conveyance, the fee simple absolute interest transfers to A's heirs.

Fee simple (or fee interest)
Ownership that is characterized as complete ownership lasting until the end of time.

Fee Simple Defeasible

Over time, a slight modification occurred to the fee simple absolute interest. Grantors began to restrict the use of or condition the length of the conveyance. **Fee simple defeasible** interests are interests that may be cut short by the occurrence (or non-occurrence) of a condition, limitation, or restriction as to the property. Depending on the type of defeasible fee estate, either the grantee's interest will terminate automatically or the grantor must file an action in court (called a **quiet title action**) to terminate ownership. There are two types of fee simple defeasible interests:

1. Fee simple determinable
2. Fee simple subject to a condition subsequent

Fee simple defeasible
Fee simple interest ownership that may be cut short by the occurrence (or non-occurrence) of a condition, limitation, or restriction.

FEE SIMPLE DETERMINABLE

**Fee simple
determinable**
Ownership interest
that automatically
terminates upon the
occurrence or non-
occurrence of some
condition, limitation,
or restriction.

Fee simple determinable is a fee simple absolute interest that automatically terminates upon the occurrence or non-occurrence of some condition, limitation, or restriction to the property. If the specified event or condition occurs, then the grantor automatically reacquires possession. When the interest ends, the property reverts to the original grantor. If the original grantor is deceased, the property reverts to the grantor's heirs. The usual circumstance is that the grantor intends to prevent the property from being put to a certain use.

> **Example:** The religious beliefs of original settlers from an area prohibited the consumption of alcohol. Subsequent deeds granted by them contain restrictions such as "to A, *so long as* the sale and distribution of alcohol do not occur on the land." A holds a fee simple determinable interest. If the sale or distribution of alcohol occurs on the land deeded, the land will automatically revert back to the original grantor.

The grant of a fee simple determinable uses language indicating that possession may automatically terminate. Typical language utilized with a fee simple determinable includes the words "until," "so long as," "unless," and "for the time that." If the specified event or condition occurs, then the grantor automatically reacquires possession.

> **Example:** A deed issued by a grantor at the end of an earlier century states, "to A, *so long as* the property continues to be used for the raising of livestock." If the area has become urbanized and the continued enforcement of the restriction is incompatible with modern society, a court could order the property free of restrictions. Unlike the public health benefits obtained by lessening the sale and consumption of alcohol, refusing the development of land to continue the nonuse of former pastureland may not advance public interests.

A fee simple determinable estate is characterized by its duration and not by the grantor's motives or intent. If a grantor was less than certain in the grant of the land and merely expressed a desire as to how the property should be used, then the fee is not limited in duration, and it is held as a fee simple absolute.

> **Example:** "To A, with the intention that this property shall be used as a recreational center for underprivileged children." This grant does not limit the use or duration of the fee; instead, it expresses the grantor's interest in how succeeding transferees should put the property to use and conveys a fee simple absolute interest.

FEE SIMPLE DETERMINABLE: THE FUTURE INTEREST

The fee simple determinable interest is a present interest. When the restriction creating the fee simple determinable is not met, the land reverts to the grantor automatically. The grantor has an interest in the property. This interest is known as a future interest. A fee simple determinable's future interest held by the grantor is known as a **possibility of reverter.**

Until the stated event occurs or does not occur, the holder of the fee simple determinable may use the property for all purposes not in conflict with the restriction. Moreover, the fee simple determinable interest can be inherited. Because the estate may last forever, it is a fee interest in land, and because it may end on the occurrence of an event, it is known as a "determinable" (that is, one whose term may come to an end) interest. Some states have abolished the determinable estate.

> **Example:** Beginning in 1983, California legislatively converted all existing fee simple determinable estates to fee simple subject to condition subsequent estates.[1]

What happens when a property subject to a fee simple determinable incurs debt by the new grantee? If the property reverts to the original grantor, is the grantor now liable for the debts incurred by the third party who owned it? That is the subject at issue in the next case.

CASE 5.1

WHEN TITLE REVERTS DUE TO A FEE SIMPLE DETERMINABLE IT IS NOT SUBJECT TO ANY POST-CONVEYANCE INDEBTEDNESS

ALLEN v. HALL

148 P.3d 939 (2006)

Utah Supreme Court

In 1993 as part of her divorce from David Allen, Sarah Satterfield acquired the marital home. However, the title conveyed to Satterfield stated that if she moved more than 50 miles away from Salt Lake City, Utah, before the couple's youngest child turned 18, the residence would revert to Allen. Allen would then be required to sell the home and divide the equity equally with Satterfield.

Satterfield moved to North Carolina when their youngest child was only 14 years old. Prior to her move, Satterfield refinanced the home several times before selling her interest in it to a third party, Thomas Hall. Hall made various improvements to the home. Allen sued to reclaim his interest in the home. Hall counterclaimed seeking to quiet his own title and reimbursement in the event the court sided with Allen. The trial court denied Allen's claim and quieted title to Hall. The trial court found that if Allen were to be awarded title to the property, he would take the property subject to all existing debt, with Hall entitled to reimbursement. Allen appealed. The court of appeals reversed, finding that Allen was entitled to the property, but he was still subject to all existing debts. Allen appealed to the Supreme Court of Utah.

Language of the Court. *Paragraph 10 of the divorce decree states that, in the event Ms. Satterfield moves more than fifty miles from Salt Lake City before the youngest child of the parties turns eighteen years of age, "ownership of the marital residence shall revert to [Mr. Allen]." This is unambiguous language creating a fee simple determinable. This language was repeated in the quit-claim deed through which Mr. Allen conveyed the property to Ms. Satterfield.*

Based on its interpretation of the terms of the decree of divorce, the court of appeals held that Mr. Allen was liable for indebtedness, secured by the property, that was acquired after he conveyed the home to Ms. Satterfield. The court of appeals agreed with the trial court that Mr. Allen's consent to "be responsible for all indebtedness thereon until the house is sold" meant that he would be liable for debt acquired before the property reverted to him by reason of Ms. Satterfield's relocation. This interpretation fails to account for the effect of the reversion on that indebtedness.

The estate that reverted to Mr. Allen was the same estate that he held at the time he conveyed the fee simple determinable interest to Ms. Satterfield. That estate was one unencumbered by any indebtedness acquired after the conveyance. It is the nature of the fee simple determinable property interest created by the terms of the decree of divorce that defines the scope of Mr. Allen's post-reversion debt obligations. Upon the reversion of the property to Mr. Allen, no indebtedness was owed on it, and thus no debt existed for which Mr. Allen was responsible. We hold that Mr. Allen's title is unencumbered by post-conveyance indebtedness.

Decision. The Supreme Court of Utah reversed and the court of appeals and awarded title to Allen. The property was returned to Allen in fee simple absolute and clear of any debt held by the parties.

FOCUS ON ETHICS

Is it fair that Hall will be responsible for debts to a property that he does not own title to anymore?

Creditor's Rights

A mortgage lender should not take as collateral a property held in fee simple determinable or fee simple subject to a condition subsequent. If the grantor or the grantor's heirs gain title as fee simple, the lender will be unsecured (not have any security interest in the property). That result follows from the fact that the holder of the future interest did not mortgage his interest in the property.

Fee Simple Subject to Condition Subsequent

Fee simple subject to a condition subsequent
Ownership interest that is subject to a condition, and the grant generally provides that the grantor may reenter the property (take possession) and terminate the estate.

A **fee simple subject to a condition subsequent** is a fee simple absolute interest that can terminate upon the occurrence or non-occurrence of some condition, limitation, or restriction to the property. While similar to a fee simple determinable, with a fee simple subject to a condition subsequent, the grantor or grantor's heirs (where the grantor has deceased) must actually reenter the estate or bring a lawsuit to restore possession. Until they do so, the holder of the fee simple subject to condition subsequent remains in possession

For this fee to occur, the grantor must state that the fee is subject to a condition. The language commonly found with a fee simple subject to a condition subsequent includes words such as "on the condition that," "but if," or "provided that" to indicate this category of fee. The grantor or grantor's heirs must actually reenter the estate or bring a lawsuit to restore possession. Until they do so, the holder of the fee simple subject to condition subsequent remains in possession.

> *Example:* The religious tenets of original settlers from an area prohibited the consumption of alcohol. The deeds granted by them contain restrictions such as "to A, *on the condition that* the sale and distribution of alcohol do not occur on the land." A holds a fee simple subject to a condition subsequent interest. If the sale or distribution of alcohol occurs on the land deeded, the grantors' heirs have the right to terminate A's estate.
>
> Note that this language differs from the similar example above by the words in italics. The specific words dictate what type of fee simple defeasible is created by the deed.

Fee Simple Subject to Condition Subsequent: The Future Interest

Like a fee simple determinable, a fee simple subject to a condition subsequent has a future interest. If the fee's condition is not met, the grantor holds a **right of reentry**, or, as known in some states, a **power of termination**. This right of reentry is the future interest held by the grantor or the grantor's heirs. If the future interest is held by anyone other than the grantor or the grantor's heirs, the future interest is known as an executory interest, discussed later in this chapter.

While a fee simple determinable reverts automatically to the grantor (or the grantor's heirs), the grantor of a fee simple subject to a condition subsequent has the power to decide what to do with the land, as the land does not revert automatically to the holder of the reversionary interest. The grantor may choose not to terminate the interest and either to work with the present holder of the fee simple subject to a condition subsequent, helping the grantee conform to the conditions placed on the property, or to accept the modified conditions and not terminate the interest.

Exercise 5.1

Determine the type of present and future interest created in the following transfers:

1. "O conveys Blackacre to A."
2. "O conveys Blackacre to A, so long as the property is used for commercial purposes."
3. "O conveys Blackacre to the University, provided that the property be used for educational purposes."
4. "O conveys Blackacre to A and A's heirs, on the condition that alcohol never be sold on the premises."
5. "O conveys Blackacre to A for the time that the land is used for a football stadium."

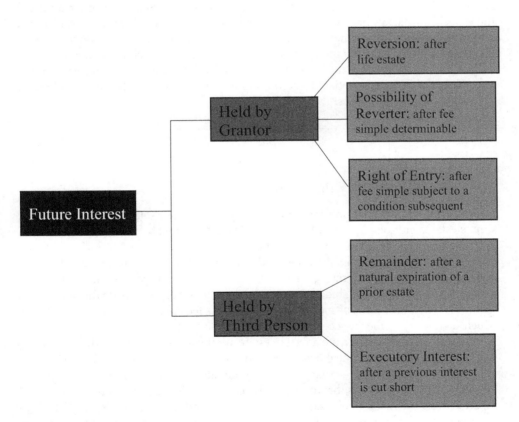

FIGURE 5.2. Future Interests

■ ■ ■   A Fee Simple Determinable and Monkey Business

Joseph Prentice was a teacher, lawyer, shoe salesman, horse trader, orange grower, and eventually a millionaire donor of land to the city of Santa Ana, California, for use as a city zoo. His gift had one catch. The deed to the city required the zoo to keep at least 50 monkeys on display, in "ample accommodations," in the park forever. A zoo is a matter of civic pride, because most communities do not have one, and far fewer have the recognition this zoo eventually earned.

From the zoo's founding in 1949, the city kept the requisite number of monkeys. This situation ended in 2009, when the monkey count dropped to 48. Prentice's great-nephew, his sole heir, demanded immediate repossession of the land from the city. Declaring, "We plan to proceed with our rights under the grant deed to have the property revert back to Mr. Prentice's heirs," the Prentice heir had the law of defeasible estates on his side. In the intervening years, the market value of the 12-acre park had appreciated greatly, and the city had expended substantial funds to improve and staff the zoo. California law had changed in the intervening years as well, and now treated the original fee simple determinable as a fee simple subject to a condition subsequent. That change permitted the city some time to negotiate with the heir before the heir exercised a right of termination as to the future interest held by the family. Not wanting to lose its valuable asset, the city negotiated a resolution of the dispute with the great-nephew, to the satisfaction of all parties.[2]

Fee Tails: Keeping It in the Family

Fee tail
A fee interest in which the estate must be inherited by the lineal descendants of the grantee.

A **fee tail** is a fee interest found rarely, but it does exist in a few states. It is similar to a fee simple estate, with one important exception: The estate must be inherited by the lineal descendants of the grantee. Only in the states of Delaware, Maine, Massachusetts, and Rhode Island is the fee tail still recognized. Under modern land law, a fee tail is converted to a fee simple interest. In essence, the fee tail is a way of ensuring that real property will descend along bloodlines and will not be conveyed outside the family tree. The most well-known line of succession dictated by a fee tail is the English royal family, which dictates the inheritance of the English throne.

The words needed to create a fee tail estate are those indicating that the property is to pass only to the direct lineal descendants of the grantee. This means that those who are not direct descendants — that is, sons and daughters — may not inherit the estate. (Parents, uncles and aunts, brothers and sisters, stepchildren, and nephews may not inherit.) Most often, a fee tail estate is stated as "to A and the heirs of his body." If there are no heirs of the grantee alive to take the gift, then the property reverts to the grantor or the grantor's heirs.

Life Estates

One of the oldest types of freehold estates is the life estate. A **life estate** arises where property is held for a person's lifespan. When the person dies whose life is the measure of the life estate, the life estate terminates. The person holding the life estate interest is the life tenant.

> **Life estate**
> An estate in which the property is held for the duration of a person's lifetime.

> *Example:* "To Charlie for life" is a life estate that will last for Charlie's lifetime.

A **life estate** *pur autre vie* arises when the measuring life is that of someone other than the holder of the life estate.

> *Example:* Rich Uncle grants a life estate in the form of a South Beach mansion to Nephew for the life of Niece, then to Big Bucks College. In this case, Nephew has a life estate *pur autre vie* because the life estate to Nephew will last for the life of Niece.

A life estate allows the grantor of a life estate to control who takes the property at the life tenant's death. The reasons for doing so may be complex or as simple as the grantor's affection for the life tenant and contempt for the life tenant's probable heirs.

> *Example:* A young couple with children may establish a life estate through their estate plan to provide assets to the surviving spouse during the surviving spouse's lifetime, in the event that the grantor dies prematurely, while ensuring that the property passes to the grantor's and the surviving spouse's children. The concern for the grantor is that the surviving spouse will remarry, and the grantor's children may not be treated equitably relative to children from the new marriage.

Estate planners who place property in trusts create life estates. Every life estate is followed by an interest in someone other than a grantor who will receive the property upon the death of the designated life tenant. Life estates have limited value outside of estate planning due to the inflexibility they pose to the changing circumstances of the life tenant and the holder of the future interest. Sometimes life estates are used for family long-term-care planning needs and for making gifts that might later qualify the property owner to receive Medicaid or state medical assistance programs.

Like any other grant of property, life estates may be subject to conditions. Parents and wealthy individuals sometimes wish to influence the behavior of the life tenant, so they will set up an estate in which the life tenant could lose the estate upon the violation of a condition.

> *Example:* A wealthy parent could give their son a life estate to an oceanfront property as long as the son remains an active member of Alcoholics Anonymous.

A life estate is not inheritable because the life tenant's estate does not have any interest in the estate upon death. The holder of the future interest takes the property immediately upon the life tenant's death. In the following case, the parties disputed whether a life estate interest was granted.

CASE 5.2

INTENT IS NECESSARY TO CREATE A LIFE ESTATE

REARICK v. SIEVING
103 So.3d 815 (2012)
Alabama Court of Civil Appeals

In May 2007, Rearick contacted the Sievings and offered to sell them her property for $50,000. The Sievings accepted this offer. On July 31, 2007, the parties met with a real-estate attorney to close on the property. Rearick was very emotional at the closing, as she had lived in the mobile home on the property for a very long time. Following the parties signing the deed to transfer the property in fee simple to the Sievings, the Sievings instructed the attorney to draft an agreement that would allow Rearick to continue to live on the property. About a month after the parties signed the agreement, the Sievings learned that Rearick was allowing family members to reside in the mobile home. The Sievings believed this to be a violation of the agreement and sought to collect rent from the family members. The Sievings then received a letter from an attorney that stated Rearick possessed a life estate; she could therefore allow individuals to live in the mobile home. The Sievings assert they never intended the agreement to convey a life estate to Rearick. The Sievings sent a letter to Rearick stating she had breached the agreement and had 30 days to vacate. The Sievings sued to terminate the agreement and cause Rearick to vacate the property. The trial court entered a judgment in favor of the Sievings, Rearick appealed.

Language of the Court: *Black's Law Dictionary defines a "life estate" as "[a]n estate held only for the duration of a specified person's life, usually the possessor's." A "life tenant" is defined as "a person who, until death, is beneficially entitled to property; the holder of a life estate." In contrast, a "license" is defined as "a permission, usually revocable, to commit some act that would otherwise be unlawful; especially, an agreement (not amounting to a lease or profit a prendre) that it is lawful for the licensee to enter the licensor's land to do some act that would otherwise be illegal, such as hunting game." In the*

agreement, the Sievings "agreed to allow . . . Rearick to live in the present residence" on the property. This language is indicative of a revocable license.

Rearick includes an excerpt from the quote above in her brief — " '[i]f possible, the intent of the parties must be ascertained from the language used in the instrument as a whole.' " We agree. The language in the agreement, when taken as a whole, indicates that the Sievings intended to permit Rearick to continue living in the mobile home, not to convey to her a life estate in the property.

The trial court heard testimony from all the parties and Williams, the drafter of the agreement. The Sievings testified that it was never their intent to convey a life estate to Rearick. In fact, they further testified that the decision to allow Rearick to continue living in the mobile home was made only after they witnessed her emotional state at the real-estate closing. Williams also testified that she did not draft the agreement to convey a life estate. Specifically, she testified that she drafted the agreement separately from the deed so that it would not be mistaken as creating a life estate and, therefore, potentially encumber the title to the property in the future. Based on this evidence, in addition to the plain language of the agreement, the trial court could have determined that the Sievings did not intend to create a life estate in favor of Rearick but, rather, to grant their permission to Rearick to live in the mobile home in the form of a revocable license.

Decision. The court of appeals affirmed the trial court's ruling, finding Rearick only possessed a license, not a life estate.

FOCUS ON ETHICS

Was the appellate ruling fair to the parties?

Remainders and Reversions

If the holder of the future interest following the life estate is the grantor, then the interest is named a **reversion**. If the holder of the future interest is someone other than the grantor, then it is a **remainder**. If the holder of the future interest is deceased at the time of the reversion or remainder, then the heirs to the grantor or other party inherit the property.

> *Example:* Rich Uncle grants a life estate in a South Beach mansion to Nephew for life. Nephew has a life estate. At the end of Nephew's life, the land reverts to Rich Uncle, the grantor. The interest held by Rich Uncle is a reversion.

As discussed above, a remainder is the future interest held in favor of someone other than the grantor. This third party may be a legal entity, but a remainder cannot be created for persons deceased at the time the interest was created.

There are two types of remainders: vested remainders and contingent remainders. These types can be further subdivided into more precise subcategories, but that discussion is beyond the scope of this text. A **vested remainder** is a remainder interest provided to an ascertained or identified person or persons that does not contain a condition.

> *Example:* Rich Uncle grants a life estate in a South Beach mansion to Nephew for life, then to Big Bucks College. Nephew has a life estate. Big Bucks College holds a vested remainder interest. Big Bucks College is ascertainable, and no condition is placed on the remainder interest. Big Bucks College will receive the property in fee simple upon Nephew's death.

A **contingent remainder** is a remainder given to an unascertained or unidentified person or a remainder that is subject to a condition precedent. A **condition precedent** is an event or condition that must occur before the interest becomes vested.

> *Example:* Rich Uncle grants a life estate in a South Beach mansion to Nephew for life, then to Great-Niece if Great-Niece has graduated from medical school. Nephew has a life estate. Great-Niece holds a contingent remainder interest, as there is a condition to her possession of the interest — she must graduate from medical school.

Exercise 5.2

Determine the type of present and future interest created in the following transfers. Where there are remainder interests, classify the remainders as either vested or contingent.

1. "O conveys Old Homestead to A for life, then to B."
2. "O conveys Old Homestead to A for life, then to B's children." B is childless.
3. "O conveys Old Homestead to A for life, then to B's children." B has children.
4. "O conveys Old Homestead to A for life, then, if B survives A, to B."
5. "O conveys Old Homestead to A for life so long as she remains unmarried; if she marries, then to B."
6. "O conveys Old Homestead to A in ten years."
7. "O conveys Old Homestead to A and his bodily heirs."

The holder of the life estate has the right to:

- Undisturbed possession during the life estate.
- Sell (convey), transfer, or convey the life-estate interest to another person. Any conveyance of the property will still be subject to the termination of the life estate at the end of the measuring life. Selling a property subject to a life estate is of dubious value and not worth very much in many cases.
- Lease the life estate interest and retain all the rents, profits, and other income from the property.

The life tenant cannot treat the property in the same manner as the owner of a fee simple interest. The life tenant has the following duties:

- Not committing waste. Waste is committed when the life tenant permanently impairs the property's value. A life tenant may not unreasonably use the property so that its nature, character, and improvements are lost to the holder of the future interest.
- Making ordinary repairs so the property does not fall into disrepair due to neglect. Ordinary repairs include such activities as painting, roof repairing, and window replacement.
- Paying the property taxes.
- Paying interest, but not principal, payments on the mortgage recorded on the title to the property at the time the life tenant takes the estate.

Concept Summary

In classifying the type of estate, students should look for the technical language required and the length of the estate's duration. This method involves the following steps:

1. Classifying the type of interest
2. Identifying whether there is more than a present interest in the grant and who holds those interests

3. Recognizing how the future interest will become possessory
4. Identifying what interest the holder of the future interest has until the event or condition occurs or fails to occur
5. Identifying whether the future interest, if there is one, is vested (i.e., will automatically be received) or contingent

Executory interest
A future interest held by someone other than the grantor or the grantor's heirs that is triggered upon occurrence of some future event.

Executory Interests

An **executory interest** is a future interest similar to a fee simple determinable's possibility of reverter, but arises when the future interest is held by someone other than the grantor (or the grantor's heirs). In a fee simple determinable, the future interest held in the grantor is a possibility of reverter. In a fee simple subject to a condition subsequent, the future interest held in the grantor is known as a right of reentry.

Example: "A grants Blackacre to B for so long as the property is used for educational purposes, then to C." B holds a fee simple determinable. C holds an executory interest. In this example, if the words *then to C* were removed, the grantor, A, would hold a possibility of reverter rather than an executory interest.

Many grantors may use an executory interest to promote certain behavior in a potential third party. The third party can be required to graduate from college, earn a graduate degree, or not have children by a certain age before they are entitled to the estate.

Example: "A grants Blackacre to B, but if B does not graduate from college by the age of twenty-five, then to C." B owns a present estate held as a fee simple subject to a condition subsequent. C holds an executory interest.

Executory interests may also arise where a gap in time is placed between the present interest and the future interest. In these situations, once the time has elapsed, the executory interest "springs" into existence.

Example: Bob conveys title to a mountain château to his son Tom in five years. Tom has an executory interest that becomes effective in five years.

Rules of Contingent Interests

Deriving from England's common law, three rules apply to the interpretation of contingent or uncertain future interests in property: the Rule in Shelley's Case, Doctrine of Worthier Title, and Rule Against Perpetuities. These three ancient rules were intended to prevent the avoidance of death taxes, but they continue to exist to promote the free transferability of land. Many states have abolished the first two rules. However, the third one, the Rule against Perpetuities, survives.

The Rule in Shelley's Case

At common law, the **Rule in Shelley's Case** merges a life estate in the grantee with a remainder in the grantee's heirs. This merger creates a fee simple absolute interest and merges the present and future interest held in the grantee. This rule applies regardless of the grantor's intent.

Example: Suppose a grant reads, "Ozzie grants Baker Street to Abe for life, then to Abe's heirs." The Rule in Shelley's Case would merge Abe's life estate with his contingent remainder (as the heirs are not ascertainable until Abe's death; even if Abe has an heir now, that heir may be dead when Abe dies). Abe would own the interest as a fee simple. Under the Rule in Shelley's Case, the above grant effectively reads, "Ozzie grants Baker Street to Abe."

As noted, the Rule in Shelley's Case has been virtually abolished in the United States. Instead, in this example, Abe would hold a life estate, Abe's yet unknown heirs would hold a contingent remainder, and Ozzie would hold a reversion (since Abe could die with no heirs).

The Doctrine of Worthier Title

The **Doctrine of Worthier Title** provides that when a grant creates a future interest in the heirs of the grantor, the future interest is void, and the grantor has a reversion. In some states, the doctrine has been abolished; in other states, the doctrine still holds.

> ***Example:*** Suppose a grant reads, "Ozzie grants Baker Street to Abe for life, then to Ozzie's heirs." This grant to the heirs is void. Ozzie has a reversion, and the heirs have *no* interest. The problem lies in referring to "heirs" in the grant.

The Rule Against Perpetuities

This is the most important of the three rules. It often receives great attention from parties to real estate and estate-planning transactions. The rule limits the period of time a grantor may control the transfer of title at the time the grant was given. The rule is directed toward those contingent interests that *might vest* in the future.

This rule invalidates future nonvested interests unless it is certain that they will vest or fail to vest within someone's lifetime or no later than 21 years after that person's death. Stated another way, the **Rule Against Perpetuities** holds that all future interests in real property must vest within 21 years after the death of someone who was alive on the effective date of the grant. If the rule is violated, the entire future interest is void, and the grantee holds a fee simple. Courts look to see if it is possible that the rule could be violated at the time the grant was created and determine whether it will vest or fail within the perpetuities period of the rule.

> ***Example:*** O conveys Baker Street to "the first child of my brother Hector to graduate from medical school." If none of Hector's sons or daughters is a medical doctor at the time of the grant, it is possible that the first of Hector's children to graduate from medical school might not occur until after 21 years. Since this might happen, if the occurrence happens at all, the gift is void and never comes into effect.

The Rule Against Perpetuities applies only to executory interests and contingent remainders, not to vested remainders (when the members of the remainder class are identified). The rule does not apply to interests held by the grantor, such as reversion, possibilities of reverter, and rights of termination.

Concept Summary

The following summary presents the possible types of interests in a conditional grant in land:

1. Any interest held by the grantor: reversion
2. A possibility of reverter
3. A right of reentry
4. Interests held by third parties: remainder
5. An executory interest

Summary of the Law of Estates

Fee Simple

Words typically used to create:

"To A," "to A and his/her heirs"

Characteristics:

Absolute ownership. Freely transferable, lasts forever.
Future interest in grantor
None
Future interest in third parties
None

Fee Simple Determinable

Words typically used to create:

To A, "so long as," "until," "for the time that," "while," "unless," or "during" a condition

Characteristics:

Potentially infinite, but will automatically end upon some event, limits duration; lasts as long as the condition is met
Future interest in grantor
Possibility of reverter
Future interest in third parties
Executory interest

Fee Simple on Condition Subsequent

Words typically used to create:

To A, "but if," "on the condition that," or "provided that"

Characteristics:

Potentially infinite. Does not automatically end on the happening of the condition. Grantor has option to terminate through power of reentry.

Future interest in grantor
Right of reentry, aka power of termination
Future interest in third parties
Executory interest

Fee Tail

Words typically used to create:

"To A and the heirs of her/his body (or issue)," "and if A dies without heirs, then to B and his heirs"

Characteristics:

Lasts as long as the grantee or any of grantee's descendants are alive, and the estate is inheritable only by such descendants.
Future interest in grantor
Reversion. A reversion can be created *only* in the grantor's heirs.
Future interest in third parties
Potentially a remainder. If the grantee dies without heirs and the deed states "to A and the heirs of his body, and if A dies without children, then to B," B would have a remainder in fee simple.

Life Estate

Words typically used to create:

"To A for life" or "to A for the life of B"

Characteristics:

Lasts for the duration of the measuring life
Future interest in grantor
Reversion
Future interest in third parties
Remainder or an executory interest

Key Terms and Concepts

Chapter Summary

- The fee simple absolute (fee simple) estate is the greatest or largest of the estates. The law in every grant of real estate presumes this estate unless specific limiting words are included in the grant. The fee simple land interest is subject to the other restrictions, such as zoning ordinances and building codes.

- If a grantor holds less than a fee simple estate, the grantor may convey only that which the grantor owns that is less than a fee.

- A fee simple determinable is a limited fee simple designed to continue until its automatic expiration upon the occurrence of an event. Since the event may never occur, the estate is a fee. When a fee is determinable upon an event that is certain to happen (such as death), the other interest is a reversion. When the event is not certain, it is a possibility of reverter.

- A fee simple subject to a condition subsequent is an absolute grant that is subject to a condition. A grantor uses a fee simple determinable if she intends to give the property only for so long as the property is used for a specific purpose. The grantor will use the fee simple subject to a condition subsequent if she intends to compel compliance with a condition by the penalty of forfeiting title.

- A fee tail is an unconventional form of holding title in which the interest in land is inheritable only by the direct descendants of the grantee. It has been abolished in its original form in all states and exists in only limited circumstances in a few states.

- A life estate is a freehold estate that lasts only for the life of its holder or for some other life. It ends upon the death of the measuring life. Those who hold life estates are life tenants. They cannot commit waste upon the property so that the rights of the holder of the future interest are harmed.

■ Remainders may be vested in someone who will immediately succeed to the rights in the land upon the death of the measuring life.

■ Remainders may be contingent when the identity of the person who will succeed to those rights upon the end of the measuring life is unascertained or subject to a condition precedent. If the contingent remainder fails, the grantor maintains a reversion.

■ A reversion is a future interest held in the grantor following the end of the life estate. A remainder is a future interest held in someone other than the grantor following the end of the life estate or a fee tail.

■ An executory interest is a future interest held by grantees that, to become possessory, must cut short the prior estate or spring out of the grantor later.

■ The Rule in Shelley's Case merges the interest of a holder in a life estate and a contingent remainder in the heirs of the life tenant into a fee interest in the holder of the life estate.

■ The Doctrine of Worthier Title creates a reversion in the grantor, and the grantor's heirs receive nothing unless the grantor dies within the life tenant's lifetime, in which case they receive the grantor's reversion.

■ The Rule Against Perpetuities states that if a contingent interest might (as opposed to will unconditionally) vest in the future, the grant is void.

Chapter Problems and Assignments

1. Determine the type of present and future interest created in the following transfers:
   a. Olivia convey Blackacre to Alden, so long as the property contains a garden with African violets.
   b. Ophelia conveys Blackacre to Aaron and his heirs, on the condition that animals are never housed on the property.
   c. Oliver conveys Blackacre to Alice.
   d. Oakley conveys Blackacre to Anita, for the time that the land is used as a tennis court.
   e. Omari conveys Blackacre to the Foundation, provided the property is used as a recreational area for children.

2. Compare and contrast a fee simple and a fee tail. What are the policy interests that are supported by a fee tail?

3. Harper conveyed her beach house to her son Clifford for the life of her brother Hayden. What type of interest does Clifford have in the beach house?

4. Determine the present and future interest created in the following transfers. Classify any remainders as either vested or contingent if applicable.
   a. Ollie conveys Whiteacre to Ajay for life, then to Bianca's children. Bianca is childless.
   b. Odell conveys Whiteacre to Ana for life, then if Berta survives Ana, to Berta.
   c. Omar conveys Whiteacre to Amelia for life, then to Bai.
   d. Octavia conveys Whiteacre to Abdul for life, then to Blane's children. Blane has two children.

5. Classify the following transfer of property. "Andi conveys Blackacre to Brooklyn for so long as it is used for agricultural purposes, then to Cynthia."

6. Explain the potential issue presented in the following transfer. "Owen conveys Blackacre to 'his first grandchild to graduate from Highbrow University.'" At the time of the conveyance, none of Owen's grandchildren have graduated from Highbrow University.

7. What do you believe is the rationale or purpose is behind the Rule Against Perpetuities?

8. Life tenants are more restricted in terms of what they can do with the property compared to those who hold property in a fee simple. Why do you believe this is? Is it fair?

9. Discuss what happens when a person dies owning property in a fee simple.

10. If the fee's condition is not met, the grantor holds a right of reentry, or, in some states, a power of termination. Research which rule your state follows, and explain why it is or is not better than the alternative.

End Notes

1. Ca. Civil Code Section 885.020.
2. Los Angeles Times, *Land heir rattles a zoo's cage*, January 23, 2009.

Chapter 6
Land Descriptions

Talk of mysteries! Think of our life in nature —daily to be shown matter, to come in contact with it —rocks, trees, wind on our cheeks! The solid earth! The actual world! The common sense! Contact! Contact! Who are we? Where are we? —Henry David Thoreau, The Maine Woods, "Ktaadn" (surveyor and writer)

Learning Objectives

1. Know how land is physically described.
2. Understand the different types of property description systems.
3. Identify property located in a government survey.
4. Identify types of informal property description references.
5. Understand how inconsistencies in property descriptions are resolved.

Chapter Outline

- Introduction
- Surveying
- Land Description Systems
- Case 6.1: *Rivers v. Lozeau*
- Case 6.2: *Sullivan v. Kanable*
- Informal References
- Resolving Disputes
- Case 6.3: *CNX Gas Co. v. Rasnake*

Opening
scenario

The Vavold family owned a parcel of real property totaling more than six acres in Idaho. The owners of the property abutting the western boundary of the property sued the Vavolds. A prior owner of the Vavolds' property had constructed a north-south fence parallel to the property's western boundary but approximately six to ten feet on his side of the boundary. The abutting property owners sued to have the fence declared the boundary line between their properties and the Vavolds' property. Although no dispute existed regarding the true boundary line, the abutting property owners contended that the location of the true boundary had been uncertain and that an implied agreement existed that the fence constituted a boundary-line change. The Vavolds defended their claim on the grounds that no agreement had fixed the fence as the boundary. Should the existing fence determine the boundary line? How should the court rule?[1]

Introduction

Property may be conveyed from one person to another in any fashion that clearly and accurately identifies the land's unique location. Although a street address is sufficient for most purposes in everyday transactions, conveying real property requires accurate descriptions of its location. Those descriptions of the land are referred to as "legal descriptions" because they must be adequate to withstand legal scrutiny. Land is considered unique — so unique that each parcel of land must be described so as to distinguish it from every other parcel. The purpose of a legal land description is to provide the precise boundary lines of a property. When a land description is clear and unambiguous, the description is legally sufficient for conveying the land to another.

Three of the most common methods for describing a land location are: (1) metes and bounds, (2) the Public Land Survey System, and (3) subdivision plats. Any of these methods is sufficient if it identifies the land or furnishes the means of identifying the particular parcel.

Surveys have many uses. Lenders and buyers use them to obtain a visual representation of the property they wish to lend against or purchase. Sellers want to confirm the representations that they make concerning their properties in sales contracts. Property owners obtain them to review encroachments and building site disputes.

Surveying

Surveying is the art and science of measuring and mapping land and its boundaries. Surveys are key to most real estate transactions. Surveyors are professionals with specialized education, training, and licensing. The use of land surveying is traced to the ancient Egyptians, who used surveying to locate the various parcels of land for taxation purposes. Even religious scripture contains verses indicating the importance given to accurate location of land and the protection of boundary evidence.[2] The Industrial Revolution created a demand for public improvements (roads, railroads) and made prominent the importance of exact boundaries and surveying. Today, surveying is utilized to prepare navigational maps, establish land boundaries, and develop engineering data for construction. Of importance to this chapter is the use of surveying in creating legal descriptions of land.

Surveying
The process of measuring and mapping land.

To complete a survey, a surveyor will review deeds, maps, title reports, records, and plans of the property and neighboring properties as well as previous surveys of the property. The surveyor will visit the property site and record field measurements of distance and direction using specially calibrated equipment. The surveyor will then prepare a drawing showing the property boundaries and such other information (such as structures onsite, easements, and utilities) as called for in the surveyor's contract. While the surveying equipment may be carefully calibrated, no measurement is perfect. That drawing is the surveyor's opinion as to where the boundary lines are located, and it is what is usually referred to as the survey.

Why Get a Survey?

A survey gives the user the comfort of knowing that the legal description being used in the legal documents can actually be used to locate the boundaries of the real property. The survey may also show the boundary's relationship with improvements. A survey provides valuable information not covered by a title insurance policy. For example, a survey may provide information concerning the location of improvements, visible evidence of utilities, the relationship of the boundary lines with adjoining lots, and current land use.

Types of Surveys

A surveyor may be asked to prepare various types of surveys. Surveys come in different types, and the terms designating them are not used consistently across the nation. Among two of the most common types of surveys are boundary surveys and as-built surveys. A **boundary survey** is a survey used to identify the boundary lines of a property. An **as-built survey** provides details of the location of the improvements within the property boundaries. Improvements detailed in an as-built survey include buildings, roads, utility installations (such as sewer and electric), and fences. As-built surveys are often requested by mortgage lenders to protect their investment and determine if the property is in conformance with current building regulations (for example, that minimum setbacks of structures from the street were observed) that can affect the value of the property.

Boundary survey
A survey used to identify the boundary lines of a property.

As-built survey
A survey providing the details of the location of improvements located within the property boundaries.

Famous American Land Surveyors

Most people cannot identify any notable Americans who were trained surveyors. Although the following list is incomplete, here are a few names from a far longer list of American surveyors.

- George Washington: At age 17, he was commissioned as the county surveyor of Culpepper County, Virginia.
- Benjamin Banneker: He was self-taught mathematician, astronomer, and surveyor who, at Washington's request, surveyed the area of present-day Washington, D.C.
- Thomas Jefferson: Appointed county surveyor in Albemarle County, Virginia, he was instrumental in the development of the U.S. Survey System, and he also commissioned Lewis and Clark to survey the West.
- Daniel Boone: As a land surveyor, he resolved many Kentucky settlers' boundary conflicts.
- Charles Mason and Jeremiah Dixon: They surveyed the boundary between Maryland and Pennsylvania. Their boundary, commonly known as the Mason-Dixon Line, was used to determine slave-holding and non-slave-holding states prior to the Civil War.
- Abraham Lincoln: He worked as a land surveyor prior to becoming an attorney and being elected to the Illinois legislature.
- John Wesley Powell: Explorer and surveyor of part of the Rocky Mountains, he was the man for whom Lake Powell on the Colorado River is named.

Land Description Systems

The many types of legal descriptions can be broadly sorted into the following three types: metes and bounds, Public Land Survey System, and subdivision maps.

Metes and Bounds

Metes and bounds
A legal description that uses a series of instructions that set forth all boundary lines by describing the length and direction of the boundaries of the property.

Metes and bounds descriptions were the first land description method used in the United States. They were adopted in the original 13 colonies because the method was in use in England. Metes and bounds descriptions are still used extensively in all states today (see Figure 6.1).

A metes and bounds description uses a series of instructions, known as a **call**, describing the length and direction of the boundaries of the property and often calling for monuments at the endpoints. A **boundary** is the dividing line between two parcels of land. The term **metes** refers to the measure of direction and length, and the term **bounds** refers to the direction to follow starting from a point of beginning given in the description. Generally, the description of the boundary lines is given in a consistent manner, either clockwise or counter-clockwise starting from the point of beginning (POB), then following a series of calls, around the perimeter of the property, returning to that point of beginning. However, some types of metes and bounds descriptions do not "close" on themselves, particularly the "centerline" type of metes and bounds description common in describing easements. Those types will begin at some described point and traverse along the proposed centerline to a remote point.

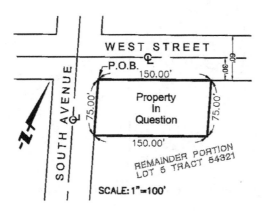

FIGURE 6.1. Metes and Bounds

Example: In Figure 6.1, the metes and bounds description of the property would be as follows: That portion of Lot 5 of Tract 54321, in the city of _____ , County of _____ , State of _____ , described as follows:

Beginning at the southeasterly corner of the intersection of West Street and South Avenue; thence easterly along the southerly right-of-way of West Street 150 feet; thence southerly parallel with South Avenue 75 feet; thence westerly parallel with West Street 150 feet to the easterly right-of-way of South Avenue; thence along said right-of-way northerly 75 feet to the point of beginning.

Describing a Call

Metes and bounds descriptions, while seemingly simple, are the most difficult type to properly create and retrace. Distances are given in feet, usually to the nearest hundredth (1/100) of a foot. Usually, instead of a direction measured out of a 360-degree circle, a bearing, or course bearing, provides the direction of the boundary line. The surveyor divides the circle into four equal 90-degree quadrants (northwest, northeast, southeast, and southwest).

A direction is then given within a quadrant in degrees and in finer gradations of minutes and seconds. A curved boundary line is composed of the arc of a circle. There are 360 degrees (°) in a circle, 60 minutes (′) to each degree, and 60 seconds (″) to each minute. Minutes and second designations are usually impossible to discern on a typical compass; a land surveyor's instruments are necessary to discern these tiny measures.

BEARINGS AS DIRECTIONS

Surveyors use directions as measured from north-south axis. For example, the bearing angle shown in the Southeast Quadrant is 63°06′52″ from the axis and is read as "South 63 degrees, 0-6 minutes, 52 seconds East." Note that the same line could be stated as having an opposite direction of N 63°06′52″ W.

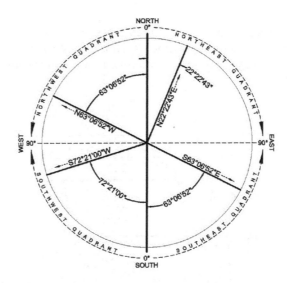

FIGURE 6.2. How Surveyors Use Bearings as Directions

Point of Beginning

Monuments
Objects used to define either the point of beginning or corners of a parcel of land.

A metes and bounds description requires that the point of beginning (i.e., the starting point of the description) be stable and definite. Otherwise, the description lacks the required certainty. **Monuments** are objects that can be used to define either the point of beginning or corners of a parcel. **Natural monuments** can include mountain tops, streams, rivers, watercourses, and trees. **Artificial** or **human-made monuments** may include stakes, roads, fences, walls, buildings, and the like. Not all physical objects are monuments, but a physical object can become a monument when a legal instrument refers to the physical object as a monument

The use of natural and artificial monuments within the metes and bounds description has drawbacks that can create title problems in the future. For example, an old oak tree used as a monument may die or be removed. Streams and river boundaries used as monuments may change courses.

> *Example:* "Begin at the large Moreton fig tree and go north for 250 feet to the large rock. Then turn right and go east for 125 feet to the old oak tree. Then turn right and go south for 250 feet to the creek. Then turn right and go 125 feet west back to the large Moreton fig tree."

The metes and bounds description in the example includes many natural monuments that may have ceased to exist. The Moreton fig tree or oak tree may have been cut down for development or killed by disease. The creek's boundary line may have changed, affecting the metes and bounds description.

Missing descriptors may cause boundary disputes between adjacent property owners. In these situations, a current survey of the property will determine if the property boundaries are locatable based on the description and other evidence the surveyor may uncover. In addition, metes and bounds descriptions are lengthy and detailed, and an error may occur in their preparation. Such an error, unless apparent and corrected, is then often replicated in subsequent transfers of the property. Thus, one error early on could cause problems with the chain of title for many generations.

Curved Boundaries

Many properties cannot be described using only straight lines. When a boundary line is curved, a surveyor must reference a certain number of what are known as the elements of a curve (see Figure 6.3). The arc length is the length of the curved line. The radius is the distance from any point on the curved line to the center of an imaginary circle that would exist if the curved line were formed into a complete circle. The chord distance is the straight-line distance from the starting of the arc to the end of the arc.

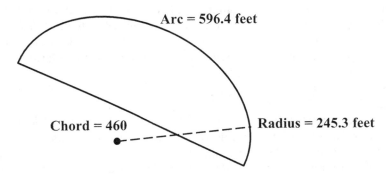

FIGURE 6.3. Curved Property

Units Describing Distance ■ ■ ■

The units used to describe distance have changed over time. In some parts of the country, descriptions from the 1960s and earlier commonly provided units of distance in terms such as chains, rods, and links. These units of measurement can still be found in rural areas.

- ■ 1 mile = 80 chains
- ■ 1 chain = 66 feet (100 links)
- ■ 1 rod = 16.5 feet (25 links)
- ■ 1 link = 0.66 feet (7.92 inches)

When earlier surveyors surveyed properties, others who accompanied them (called "chainmen") would hold the two pole chains and measure distances. Trees, stones, stakes, or other natural monuments were used to mark the corners of the tract. When the field notes were completed, the surveyor would use a compass, protractor, and plotting scales to make a scaled drawing and description of the land. Total acreage was then computed, and the document was dated and signed. The names of the surveyor and crew were also sometimes listed.

The following case recognizes that corners to land boundaries are fixed by the original surveys. Mistakes made during subsequent land surveys do not adjust the land boundaries. The court noted that, as a result of a treaty with Spain in 1819, the United States became the owner of all land now in the state of Florida. The original survey lines cannot be reset, and they control all references to legal descriptions.

CASE 6.1
THE ORIGINAL SURVEY LINES ESTABLISH LAND BOUNDARIES

RIVERS v. LOZEAU
539 So. 2d 1147 (1989)
Florida District Court of Appeal

A dispute arose between adjacent owners of land parcels located in Marion County, Florida. The owners' land bordered land owned by the U.S. government. An earlier property owner of both parcels had hired a surveyor to establish certain land lines for the division of his property. The property was then divided. The boundary line between the two properties was created by reference to a federal government survey monument. Unfortunately, the surveyor incorrectly identified the boundary lines when he placed monuments on the to-be-divided parcel.

The Lozeaus owned the northern half of the property conveyed by the earlier owner, while Rivers owned the southern half of the property. After both the Lozeaus and Rivers had taken ownership of their respective properties, the federal government resurveyed its lands and re-monumented the original positions of the corners of the U.S. government survey. The resurvey resulted in the border of the Lozeaus' land increasing by a little over four feet. The Lozeaus brought suit against Rivers, arguing that they had acquired title to the disputed land through the original deed transfer and that the resurveyed property showed the true location of the government monument. Rivers alleged that the second survey of the land controlled the legal description. The trial court ordered the disputed property to be split, and both parties appealed.

Language of the Court. *Real property descriptions are controlled by the descriptions of their boundary lines, which are themselves controlled by corners as established on the ground by the original surveyor creating those lines.*

The only professional authorized to locate land lines on the ground is a registered land surveyor. However, in the absence of statute, a surveyor has no authority to establish boundaries; he can only state or express his professional opinion as to surveying questions.

Neither title to land nor the boundaries to a deeded parcel move about based on where someone, including a particular surveyor, might erroneously believe the correct location of the true boundary line to be.

Decision. The Florida Court of Appeal found in favor of the Lozeaus finding their survey stated the correct location of the boundary line.

FOCUS ON ETHICS

Is it ethical for the Lozeaus to file a lawsuit against Rivers for the increased land determined by the federal government's resurvey? Should the Lozeaus compensate Rivers for taking this land?

Public Land Survey System
A method of describing property that divides land in the United States into six-mile-square townships.

Public Land Survey System

The government survey system is also known as the GLO (General Land Office) system, the Public Land Survey System (PLSS), the U.S. Survey System, or the rectangular Survey System. The **Public Land Survey System** maps the United States into six-mile-square townships. Townships can then be further divided as discussed below. Congress authorized this system in 1785, after the federal government became the

State	Utilizes	State	Utilizes
Alabama	Public Land	Montana	Public Land
Alaska	Public Land	Nebraska	Public Land
Arizona	Public Land	Nevada	Public Land
Arkansas	Public Land	New Hampshire	*Metes and Bounds*
California	Public Land	New Jersey	*Metes and Bounds*
Colorado	Public Land	New Mexico	Public Land
Connecticut	*Metes and Bounds*	New York	*Metes and Bounds*
Delaware	*Metes and Bounds*	North Carolina	*Metes and Bounds*
Florida	Public Land	North Dakota	Public Land
Georgia	*Metes and Bounds*	Ohio	Public Land
Hawaii	*Metes and Bounds and Unique System*	Oklahoma	Public Land
Idaho	Public Land	Oregon	Public Land
Illinois	Public Land	Pennsylvania	*Metes and Bounds*
Indiana	Public Land	Rhode Island	*Metes and Bounds*
Iowa	Public Land	South Carolina	*Metes and Bounds*
Kansas	Public Land	South Dakota	Public Land
Kentucky	*Metes and Bounds*	Tennessee	*Metes and Bounds*
Louisiana	Public Land	Texas	*Metes and Bounds and Unique System*
Maine	*Metes and Bounds*	Utah	Public Land
Maryland	*Metes and Bounds*	Vermont	*Metes and Bounds*
Massachu-setts	*Metes and Bounds*	Virginia	*Metes and Bounds*
Michigan	Public Land	Washington	Public Land
Minnesota	Public Land	West Virginia	*Metes and Bounds*
Mississippi	Public Land	Wisconsin	Public Land
Missouri	Public Land	Wyoming	Public Land

FIGURE 6.4. State Utilization of Metes and Bounds or Public Land Survey System

holder of large areas of land after the Revolutionary War. The federal government sought to distribute and sell the land to raise money to pay war debts, as well as to reward soldiers for their service. This method is used by more than half of the states, as shown below. Note that Hawaii and Texas entered the Union by treaty and had land systems in place at the time of their entry, so they do not utilize the Public Land System.

■■■ *Land Grants*

Starting in the sixteenth century, European colonizers (including Spain, Portugal, the Netherlands, and Britain) employed the use of land grants. With **land grants**, also called ranchos, land was given to settlers to establish settlements, missions, and farms. The land grantee (a patentee) had to improve the land through cultivation and the construction of improvements on the land; otherwise, it would revert to the government.

From the 1780s to 1821, Spain offered land grants to anyone who settled its colonies. After the Mexican War of Independence ended in 1821, an autonomous Mexico continued to offer land grants. The current states in which Spanish and Mexican land grants were offered include California, Arizona, Colorado, New Mexico, Texas, and Florida. When these lands were transferred to the United States, the treaty included an agreement to honor all valid land grants. Following the Mexican-American War in 1848, hundreds of ranchos and large tracts of land were recognized by the United States.

Land grants are not only historical but also of current interest to local governments seeking modern-day settlers to revitalize the local economy.

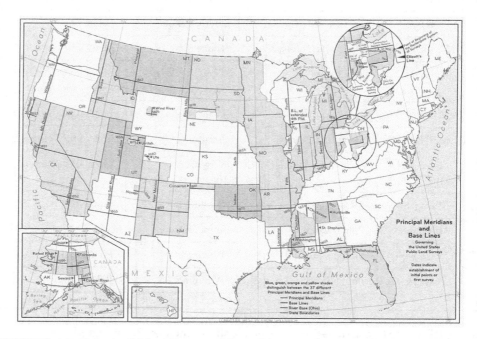

FIGURE 6.5. Principal Meridians and Base Lines in the United States
Source: U.S. Department of the Interior, Bureau of Land Management.

Principal Meridians and Base Lines

The Public Land Survey begins by identifying north-south longitudinal lines called **principal meridians** and east-west latitudinal lines called **base lines**. Where those two lines intersect is referred to as the Initial Point. There are 37 intersecting principal meridians and base lines in the United States.

Guide Meridians and Correction Lines

Between the principal meridian lines and base lines are guide meridians and correction lines. **Guide meridian lines**, running north-south, are placed every 24 miles from the principal meridian. **Correction lines**, running east-west, are placed every 24 miles from the base line. They are labeled "first," "second," and so on from their direction north-south or east-west of the base line or principal meridian, respectively. The guide meridians and correction lines create a 24-mile grid across most of the United States. Each 24-by-24-mile area is called a **check**.

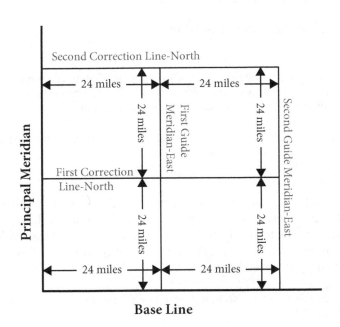

FIGURE 6.6. Checks: Intersection of Guide Meridian Lines and Correction Lines

Range Lines and Township Lines

Range lines run north-south and are established every six miles from the principal meridian. **Township lines** run east-west and are established every six miles from the base line.

The six-mile squares created by the range lines and township lines are known as **townships**. Each township is identified with a township and range designation. Townships are indicated by a location north or south of the baseline, and range designations are indicated by their location east or west of the principal meridian

Range lines
North-south lines placed every six miles from the principal meridian that form the east or west boundary of a township.

Township lines
East-west lines placed every six miles from the base line that form the north or south boundary of a township.

Townships
The six-mile squares created by the intersection of the range lines and township lines.

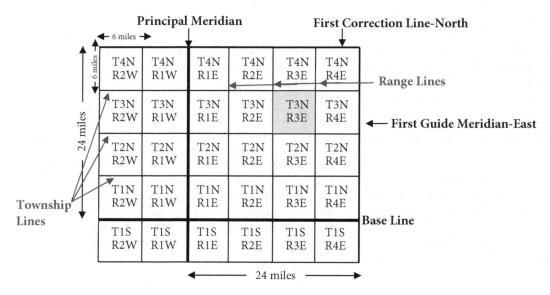

FIGURE 6.7. Range Lines, Township Lines, and Townships

Example: In Figure 6.7, the shaded township is identified as Township 3 North, Range 3 East. This identifies the township as the third row of townships north of the baseline, and in the third column of townships east of a principal meridian

The township numbering system continues to each baseline and principal meridian.

Sections

Section
One square mile containing 640 acres.

Each township is further divided into 36 sections. Each **section** is nominally one square mile, or 640 acres. Sections are numbered in a serpentine fashion starting at the northeast corner of the township and proceeding westerly. Next time you are traveling by air over farmland, you may notice that you can easily see the checkerboard pattern of sections created by farms and roads.

Example: In Figure 6.8, the section in gray would be identified as Section 15, Township 3 North, Range 3 East.

Aliquot Parts

Each section, containing 640 acres, can further be divided into smaller parts. These smaller parts are known as **aliquot parts**. In Public Land Surveys, it refers to halves (1/2), quarters (1/4), sixteenths (generally referred to as "quarter-quarters"), and so forth. Any parcel of land smaller than a full section is identified by its position in the section. The description is created by dividing the section into quarters and halves as shown in the Figure 6.9.

Example: In Figure 6.9, the land highlighted would be identified as SE 1/4 of NE 1/4 of Section 15, Township 3 North, Range 3 East.

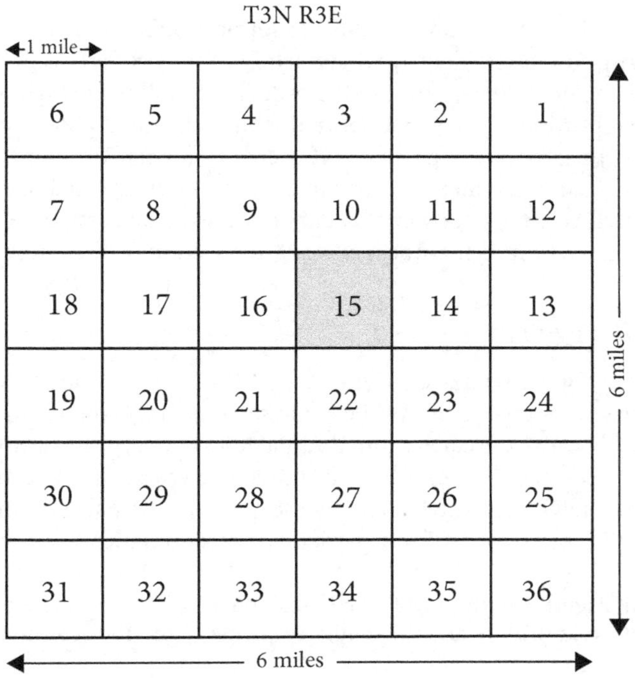

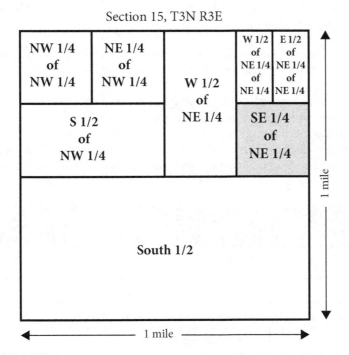

T3N R3E

6	5	4	3	2	1
7	8	9	10	11	12
18	17	16	15	14	13
19	20	21	22	23	24
30	29	28	27	26	25
31	32	33	34	35	36

FIGURE 6.8. Sections in a Township

Section 15, T3N R3E

FIGURE 6.9. Dividing a Section into its Aliquot Parts

When describing or ascertaining the aliquot part, it is often easiest to start at the end of the description. First, identify what portion of the property is in question. In the above example, the northeast quarter of the property contains the highlighted property. Next, divide that portion of the property. In this case, the highlighted portion is located in the southeast quarter of the property. If there are further divisions, those are then ascertained in the same manner. For example, the property located immediately north of the highlighted section is detailed as either the west or east parcel of land of the northeast quarter section of the northeast quarter section of the entire section.

Putting It All Together

One benefit of using government surveys is that the legal description of the parcel of land reveals the size of the parcel. While some sections may contain more or less than 640 acres (either because the earth's longitudinal lines converge towards the North Pole or because of survey errors dating back hundreds of years), most sections nominally contain 640 acres. Dividing the 640 acres by the quarters and halves of the land description yields the number of acres for a particular parcel of land.

> **Example:** In Figure 6.9, the highlighted area contains 40 acres. (The northeast quarter contains 160 acres (640/4), and the southeast quarter of the 160 acres is 40 acres [160/4].)

Legal descriptions using the Public Land Survey System should include the state, principal meridian name, township and range designations, section number, and description within the section, if applicable. Omitting the names of the particular county and state in a description based on the PLSS does not necessarily make a description defective. Their addition to a description, however, makes it easier to identify the location of the property in question and substantially decreases the possibility of ambiguity in the description.

> **Example:** North 1/2 of the Northwest 1/4 of Section 22, Township 4 South, Range 10 West of the San Bernardino Meridian, County of Orange, State of California.

When reading a legal description using this method, it is easier to work backward. Start your review with a larger area and move to the smaller area.

Adding to this maze of geographical terms are the distinct systems rooted in the history of a few states. For example, parts of the state of Ohio were used as a "proving ground" for the early Public Land System, and have their own unique public land survey systems.

■ ■ ■   Measurements to Know

One acre	43,560 square feet (ten square chains)
One section	640 acres (or one square mile)
One mile	5,280 linear feet (80 chains)

Exercise 6.1

Provide the description and the number of acres for each of the identified parcels of land in the following section:

Sec. 9, T3S, R12E

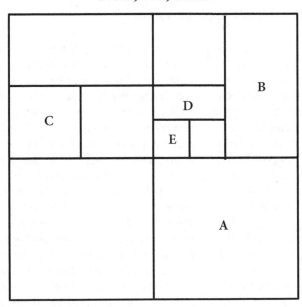

1. A
2. B
3. C
4. D
5. E

In the following case, the Sullivans brought suit against their neighbors, the Kanables, in order to determine the boundary line between the two parcels.

CASE 6.2

SURVEYS REFERENCING A LEGAL DESCRIPTION WILL BE FAVORED OVER THOSE THAT DO NOT

SULLIVAN v. KANABLE

41 N.E.3d 264 (2015)

Illinois Appellate Court

The Sullivans' residential property is located on a lakefront with the Kanables owning lakefront property to the west. The Sullivans sued the Kanables seeking to determine the boundary between the two properties. The Sullivans hired Brian Lee to survey the property, specifically to determine the west boundary line of their property. Upon Lee's survey, he determined the boundary line conforms to that in the legal description. The survey indicated that the iron rod that had been established as a monument by the Kanables' previous surveyor was 19.1 feet onto the Sullivans' property. This led Lee to expand his own survey to include the defendants' property and the two parcels west of the Kanables' property. Lee found that the corner markers on the Kanables' property did not match the legal description for their property. The Kanables' surveyor, Ed Peklay, claimed during his survey he had found no monument at the southeast corner of their property near the lake. He states this was a swampy area, and he believes there might never have been a monument or it had washed away. Peklay claims that his determination of the boundary lines by the use of occupation lines is more correct than Lee's survey that used measurements. The trial court found Lee's survey, based on measurements, was preferable to the occupation lines used by Peklay. The trial court entered a declaratory judgment for the Sullivans that the boundary line between the properties was as shown by Lee's survey. The Kanables appealed.

Language of the Court. *Lee located the boundaries of defendants' property, pursuant to the legal description of the property, with reference to government survey monuments and a properly placed marker for the point of beginning. There is no indication that the boundaries measured in accordance with the legal description conflicted with any occupancy lines on or adjacent to plaintiffs' property. Nor is there any indication that the measurements conflicted with any other controlling element. There is no indication that Lee made any mistake in measuring the distance from the section corner to the place of beginning on the southeast corner of the property. Nor is there any indication that Lee made any mistake in measuring the distance from that point to the southwest corner of the property. As noted, Peklay essentially located the place of beginning without reference to government survey markers, instead placing it at a location that would accommodate the occupation line on the west of the property with the described 400-foot measurement of defendants' south property line. Under the circumstances, this method appears to be arbitrary and inferior to alternative methods of determining the place of beginning of defendants' land.*

Decision. The court of appeal affirmed the trial court's ruling that the boundary line of the properties was shown by the survey obtained by the Sullivans.

FOCUS ON ETHICS

When there are conflicting survey results, what is the fairest way for the court determine which survey to use?

Concept Summary

Government Survey

1. There are 36 intersecting principal meridians and base lines in the United States (see Figure 6.5).
   - Principal meridians are north-south (vertical) longitude lines.
   - Base lines are east-west (horizontal) latitude lines.

2. Checks (see Figure 6.6).
   - Every 24 miles east and west of principal meridians are guide meridians running north-south.
   - Every 24 miles north or south of a base line are correction lines running east-west.

3. Townships (see Figure 6.7).
   - Every six miles east and west of the principal meridian are range lines, running north-south.
   - Every six miles north and south of a base line are township lines, running east-west.

4. Sections (see Figure 6.8).
   - Each township is further divided into 36 sections numbered in a serpentine fashion, starting at the upper right corner of the township and proceeding left.

5. Aliquot parts (see Figure 6.9).
   - Each section can be divided into quarters and halves.

Subdivision Plats or Maps

A third kind and one of the easiest and most convenient methods for describing real property is based on a mapped subdivision of land. It involves the use of plat maps that are approved by a governmental agency as meeting certain requirements for a legal lot capable of being conveyed. A **plat** is a map of a subdivision. In one type of subdivision, the area is divided into units called **blocks**. These blocks are then divided into smaller parcels referred to as lots. Each parcel of land is assigned a unique designator, usually a lot number or letter.

Plat
A plan or map of a subdivision.

The plat provides the size and boundaries of the lots, shows streets and easements serving or encumbering the property, and indicates any restrictive covenants that apply to the subdivision. The exterior boundaries of subdivisions are based on a previous description created by one of our three main types of description: metes and bounds, public land, or subdivision map.

Each subdivision plat or map is recorded in the official records of the local jurisdiction and assigned a book and page reference number. Once the plat has been recorded, usually at the office of the county recorder (or registrar of deeds) where the land is located, the lengthy metes and bounds description is no longer necessary. Reference to the lot and block number, tract name, map book reference, county, and state is sufficient to describe the land legally.

Example: A partial description of the land encompassing Disneyland in California provides, "Parcel 2, in the City of Anaheim, County of Orange, State of California, as per map recorded in Book 78, Page 42 of Parcel Maps, in the office of the County Recorder of Orange County."

Informal References

Informal references such as assessor parcel numbers, street addresses, or popular names may be used to transfer title if the description sufficiently identifies the land so that it cannot be confused with another property. Informal references should be avoided in favor of the three common land description methods to avoid ambiguities, confusion, and possible litigation. The use of proper legal descriptions provides certainty and avoids those shortcomings.

Assessor Parcel Numbers

In addition to official maps, the laws of many jurisdictions allow county land-tax assessors to prepare and file maps that assign an **assessor parcel number** (APN) to each parcel of land in the county. The parcels of land are often designated by numbers or letters. While primarily used to identify property for tax-assessment and collection purposes, the APN is often used to identify properties by real estate agents. If a discrepancy arises between an APN and the legal description in the deed, the stated legal description controls in the event of a problem.

> *Example:* APN: 530-841-10

Street Address

Naming a street and city in an address may be sufficient to pass title if it clearly identifies the property so that it cannot be confused with another property, but it should not be utilized as the sole description of the property. In some locations, the street and city address may describe the location to which mail is delivered, not where the property is located. Additionally, street names and street numbers may change, and mistakes may be made if the indicator of the type of street is not provided.

> *Example:* 16 Pine Avenue may be a completely different property from 16 Pine Terrace, 16 Pine Street, 16 Pine Way, 16 Pine Circle, 16 Pine Lane, or 16 Pine Court.

Popular Name

Early land records often involve large tracts of land described by popular names, such as "the Margaret Murray estate," by which they were known and identified. The advantage of such an informal reference is that it can be easily understood; however, it does not identify precisely the land to be conveyed. If the boundaries of such a description are known, the conveyance by a descriptive name is sufficient. This will rarely be the case in modern practice.

> *Example:* In the western part of the United States, names of well-known Mexican land grants (for example, Rancho Jesús María) were sufficient to transfer title in early-era deeds. Rancho Jesús María encompasses present-day Vandenberg Air Force Base in Santa Barbara County, California.

General Descriptions

Occasionally, a paralegal will encounter a conveyance using a general description, such as "all land of Margaret Murray wherever situated in the county of Blackacre." If the grantor is sufficiently certain and the property is identifiable, the land description will be valid. More likely, however, the description will create confusion or ambiguity and will be inadequate to transfer title.

Example: "All of the land of Kevin Lee wherever situation in the city and county of San Francisco, California" is likely an invalid land description if there is more than one Kevin Lee in San Francisco.

Resolving Disputes

The primary rule in interpreting legal descriptions is to carry out the intention of the parties as to what was being conveyed. Sometimes, even with the best of intentions, ambiguities arise in the description of the property. The ambiguity or mistake may be overcome if enough extrinsic evidence exists to clarify it. **Extrinsic evidence** is evidence not stated within a document but obtainable from reliable outside sources. Such evidence could include:

- The circumstances under which the instrument was executed
- Oral statements the parties made at the time of the execution
- Writings or communications made before or at the time of the execution

Courts strive to determine the intention of the parties involved. When presented with such cases, the courts have developed a set of rules to assist them in interpreting land descriptions in legal documents. A few of these rules of construction are as follows:

1. The grantee (buyer) is preferred in cases of doubt or ambiguity. The result is to benefit the grantee over the grantor, because the grantor should make sure the description is accurate before completing the transaction.
2. Natural monuments control over man-made monuments.

Example: Boundaries established by the edge of a river would be preferred over a road.

3. Specific descriptions of real property control over general descriptions of real property.[3]

Example: Where a dispute arose over whether a conveyance included a water-power plant, canal, basin, and mill race, the language specifically referenced the items controlled over the general conveyance language.[4]

4. Unambiguous descriptions control over ambiguous descriptions in the same document.
5. Fixed lines and monuments generally control over contradictory or conflicting statements of courses, distances, or quantity.

6. References to other portions of the same document, incorporated documents, or other references may be used to explain the description.

Example: The legal description on the deed references Township 2 North, but the title report, purchase contract, and prior deeds of the same property reference Township 3 North. The other documents may be used to explain a typographical error.

A court cures the legal description's ambiguity by exercising its power of reformation. **Reformation** corrects a written legal description to conform to the intent of the original parties to the instrument. Expert testimony is admissible in such proceedings to establish the proper method of surveying a line or locating lost or destroyed monuments.

In the following case, the parties were in dispute regarding ownership of the property's mineral rights.

CASE 6.3

AMBIGUITIES IN A DEED ARE RESOLVED IN FAVOR OF THE GRANTEE

CNX GAS CO. v. RASNAKE

752 S.E.2d 865 (2014)

Virginia Supreme Court

In 1887, the Fullers owned a tract of land spanning 414-1/8 acres located in Virginia. In a deed they conveyed, "all the coal, in, upon, or underlying" the tract to Joseph J. Dorman and W.A. Dick. In 1918, the successor of the Fullers conveyed to Unice Nuckles a 75-acre portion of that tract. The deed included the following language, "This sale is not meant to convey any coals or minerals. The same being sold and deeded to other parties heretofore." CNX claimed the mineral rights, excluding coal in the 75-acre tract as a lessee under the successors to Unice Nuckles. The Rasnakes claimed the same rights as successors in interest to the Fullers. CNX has been producing coal bed methane gas on the property lease for some time. The Rasnakes filed a complaint seeking declaratory judgment of its title to the mineral estate of the 75-acre tract. The lower court found for the Rasnakes, holding they owned the mineral estate. CNX eventually appealed to the state supreme court.

Language of the Court. *Where the language of a deed clearly and unambiguously expresses the inten-*

tion of the parties, no rules of construction should be used to defeat that intention. Where, however, the language is obscure and doubtful, it is frequently helpful to consider the surrounding circumstances and probable motives of the parties.

The disputed language in the 1918 deed is obviously capable of being understood by reasonable persons in more than one way, as demonstrated by the interpretations advanced by Rasnake, CNX, and the opinion of the circuit court.

It is appropriate to go outside the four corners of the deed to consider the existing circumstances, at least to the extent of the fact that coal interests had been conveyed in 1887 but that all other mineral rights remained in the grantors until delivery of the 1918 deed.

When a deed's language is unclear as to the nature and extent of the estate the grantor intended to convey, so strong is the presumption in favor of that interpretation most favorable to the grantee, that we have held that where there is doubt whether one or two parcels of land were intended to be conveyed, the deed will be construed to pass title to both.

So construed, the deed conveys to the grantee in fee simple all of the mineral interests in the land embraced within the deed's metes and bounds description that the grantors were capable of conveying at the time, excluding only the coal, which they no longer owned. Accordingly, we adopt that interpretation and hold that the circuit court erred in construing the disputed language to constitute an unambiguous exception of all coal and other minerals from the conveyance.

Decision. The Supreme Court of Virginia reversed the holding of the lower courts, finding the ambiguities in the deed should be read in favor of the grantee. The Court declared ownership of the mineral estate to CNX.

FOCUS ON ETHICS

Is it fair to construe the title to favor the grantee when the legal description in the deed is ambiguous?

Court Remedies

Disputes over boundaries arise in a variety of contexts. These include governmental taking of private lands in eminent-domain proceedings, trespass action where one party seeks to collect damages from an interfering adjacent property owner, and disputes over title to a particular tract of land.

Disputing claims to the same property can be determined in a **quiet title action**, that is, a lawsuit in which the court establishes who has title to real property against any challenges or claims to ownership of the property.

Similar to a quiet title action, a court can determine ownership of disputed land areas through a proceeding known as an action for a **declaratory judgment**. In this form of civil litigation, the trial court determines the rights and obligations of the parties.

Key Terms and Concepts

- Surveying, page 111
- Boundary survey, page 111
- As-built survey, page 111
- Metes and bounds, page 112
- Call, page 112
- Boundary, page 112
- Monuments, page 114
- Natural monuments, page 114
- Artificial (human-made) monuments, page 114
- Public Land Survey System, page 116
- Land grants, page 118
- Principal meridians, page 119
- Base lines, page 119
- Guide meridian lines, page 119
- Correction lines, page 119
- Check, page 119
- Range lines, page 119
- Township lines, page 119
- Townships, page 119
- Section, page 120
- Aliquot parts, page 120
- Plat, page 125
- Blocks, page 125
- Assessor parcel number, page 126
- Extrinsic evidence, page 127
- Reformation, page 128
- Quiet title action, page 129
- Declaratory judgment, page 129

Chapter Summary

- The purpose of a legal description is to provide the exact boundary lines of a property.

- A boundary is the dividing line between two parcels of land.

- The three legal methods to describe property are metes and bounds, government survey, and subdivision plats.

- A metes and bounds survey describes a parcel's boundary lines in a clockwise manner starting from a point of beginning and returning to the point of beginning.

- A government survey describes a parcel of land by its location within a grid system utilized throughout most of the United States.

- The government survey system begins with 36 intersecting principal meridians and base lines. Guide meridians and correction lines then create a 24-mile grid of checks. These checks are then divided into townships created by range lines and township runs placed every six miles from the principal meridian and baseline. Each township is divided into 36 sections. Each section is then broken down into a description of the acres contained within the section.

- A subdivision plat map is one of the easiest and most convenient methods for describing prop-

erty. It details parcels of property within a subdivision by referring to the parcel's location as a lot number that belongs to a specific book and page number of the plat book.

- Informal references may be used to transfer title if the description sufficiently identifies the land so that it cannot be confused with another property.

- Common informal references include assessor parcel numbers, street addresses, popular names, and general descriptions.

- When resolving inconsistencies in legal descriptions, the intent of the parties as to what is being conveyed controls.

- Courts will allow extrinsic evidence to assist in interpreting the intentions of the parties.

- When faced with extrinsic evidence, courts have adopted rules of construction providing a hierarchy of preference for conflicting evidence.

- A quiet title action is a lawsuit in which the court establishes who has title to real property against any challenges or claims to ownership of the property.

- Declaratory judgment is a form of civil litigation wherein the trial court determines the rights and obligations of the parties.

Chapter Problems and Assignments

1. The following is an example of what kind of description? Start at the large oak tree and go north for 150 feet to the large pine tree. Then turn right and go east for 125 feet to the large rock. Then turn right and go south for 250 feet to the pond. Then turn right and go 125 feet west back to the large oak tree.

2. Parcel 10, in the City of Blight, County of Last Resort, State of Misery, according to the map recorded in Book no. 13, Page 13 of Parcel Maps, in the office of the County Recorder of Last Resort County. This is an example of a land description utilizing which survey method?

3. Determine how many acres are in each of the following parcels:
   a. The S 1/2 of a section
   b. The SE 1/4 of the NE 1/4 of a section
   c. The W 1/2 of the NW 1/4 of a section
   d. The S 1/2 of the SW 1/4 of the NE 1/4 of a section

4. Describe the differences between a boundary survey and an as-built survey.

5. What are monuments, and how do natural monuments differ from artificial or human-made monuments?

6. A deed contained the following description: "All that tract or parcel of land ... in the 13th District of Thomas County, Georgia, and in land lot Number 196, beginning at the northwest corner of said lot and running south about eight chains to a stake; thence running in an easterly course 20 chains to a stake; thence north about six chains to a stake at road; thence west five chains down said road; thence north to the north line of lot running east and west; thence west to starting point, containing 43 acres, more or less. ...." Is this description of land valid to convey title?

7. A.B. Robert owned two parcels of land. The first parcel was a 130-acre farm on which were a number of buildings, including a dwelling. The second parcel was a one-acre piece of land on which was located a remodeled schoolhouse in which Robert lived. Robert sold Wadsworth the farm without the schoolhouse. The legal description named "the A.B. Robert farm in the town of Stanton." Is the legal description adequate to convey title to Wadsworth?

8. The Richardsons own a parcel of land totaling more than five acres in Pennsylvania. Their neighbors to the west of the property threaten to file a lawsuit against the Richardsons because of an encroachment upon what they claim as their property. A prior owner of the Richardsons' property constructed a north-south fence parallel to the property's western boundary but approximately six feet on the neighbor's side of the boundary. The parties dispute where the boundary line is between their respective properties. The Richardsons contend the location of the true boundary had been uncertain and that the fence constituted a boundary-line change. The neighbors deny that an agreement existed that fixed the fence as the boundary. Should the existing fence determine the boundary line?

9. What are the possible remedies that a court might institute in a dispute over the ownership of land?

10. Determine what the nearest principal meridian and base line are from your current location. If you live in a state that does not utilize the Public Lands Survey System, pick a city in a state that does and provide the nearest principal meridian and base line to that city.

End Notes

1. *Downey v. Vavold*, 166 P.3d 382 (Id. 2007).
2. Deuteronomy 19:14 provides, "Thou shalt not remove thy neighbor's landmark, which they of old time have set, in thine inheritance which thou shalt inherit, in the land that Jehovah thy God giveth thee to possess it." Ezekiel 42:16 provides, "He measured on the east side with the measuring reed five hundred reeds, with the measuring reed round about. He measured on the south side five hundred reeds with the measuring reed. He turned about to the west side, and measured five hundred reeds with the measuring reed." Moreover, Zechariah 2:1 provides, "I lifted up mine eyes again, and looked, and behold a man with a measuring line in his hand. Then said I, Whither goest thou? And he said unto me, to measure Jerusalem, to see what is the breadth thereof, and what is the length thereof."
3. *Osteen et al. v Wynn et al.*, 62 S.E. 37 (Ga. 1908).
4. *Nichols v. New England Furniture Co.*, 100 Mich. 230 (Mi. 1894).

Part II
Purchasing, Financing, and Conveying Real Estate

Chapter 7
Agency and Real Estate Brokers

Why has government been instituted at all? Because the passions of man will not conform to the dictates of reason and justice without constraint. —Alexander Hamilton, Statesman and Secretary of the Treasury (1757–1804)

Learning Objectives

1. Define agency.
2. Define the authority of an agent.
3. Differentiate between a broker and a salesperson.
4. State the fiduciary duties of real estate brokers.
5. Identify alternative real estate agency relationships.
6. Recognize the different types of listing agreements.
7. Define when a broker is entitled to be paid.
8. Identify the duties owed by parties to a real estate transaction.
9. Explain the federal laws governing brokers' activities.

Chapter Outline

Opening
scenario

Jacky attends an open house to view a property for sale. The house is perfect for her family, and Jacky decides to purchase the property at the seller's open house. She questions the sales agent about the property and its sales price. She makes a written purchase offer to the real estate agent during the open house. The agent informs the owner of her offer. Does the agent owe Jacky any duties? If so, at what point do they arise? Does Jacky owe any duties to the real estate agent?

Introduction

In this chapter, we study the topics of purchasing, financing, and conveying (that is transferring title) real estate. A **real estate licensee** is a person (broker or salesperson) holding a real estate license granted by a state. All states as well as the District of Columbia regulate the licensure of real estate professionals. States enact professional licensing regulations to protect the public from fraud and incompetent or unethical real estate professionals. Applicants are required to meet certain standards of competency, ethical behavior, and moral character to be licensed and must continue their education to maintain their licenses.

The right to act on behalf of another in a real estate transaction carries great responsibility. Real estate licensees owe specific duties and standards of care imposed on them by law. In this chapter, we discuss the duties of the real estate professional, the types of listing agreements, and the key laws regulating real estate licensees.

Nature of Agency Relationships

Fiduciary relationship
A relationship founded through trust and confidence from one party to another.

The law of agency governs fiduciary relationships existing between real estate brokers and salespersons and their clients. A **fiduciary relationship** is one founded upon trust and confidence between the parties. Real estate brokers and salespersons owe fiduciary duties to their clients, as discussed in this chapter. Students should note the breadth of fiduciary duties create a sizeable percentage of the claims made against licensed real estate professionals.

Agent
An individual who represents another; a principal, in dealings with third parties.

An agency relationship binds the principal in contract with third parties and protects the agent, who is acting on behalf of the principal, from personal liability to third persons. An **agent** is a person who represents another, a principal, in dealings with third parties. In most real estate transactions, the real estate broker or salesperson is the agent of a principal. A **principal** is the person who authorizes another to act on his or her behalf. The buyer and seller in a real estate transaction are principals.

Authority of the Agent

Whether the agent has authority to act on behalf of the principal determines the liability a principal may have for her agent's actions. Generally, the principal is liable to third parties for contracts the agent enters into on the principal's behalf. The agent is not liable on the contract. However, where the agent acts without the principal's authority, the principal is not liable on the contract, but the agent is. An agent may have authority to act on the principal's behalf under one of the following common methods:

1. *Express authority.* **Express authority** arises when a principal expressly agrees, orally or in writing, to authorize the agent to act on his behalf.

   Example: A listing agreement between a seller and a real estate broker or salesperson expressly grants the agent authority to act on the principal's behalf.

   Because the Statute of Frauds requires that real estate contracts be in writing to be enforceable, the **equal dignity rule** requires that the appointment of an agent for a real estate contract also be in writing to be enforceable.

   Equal dignity rule
   Requirement that the appointment of an agent for a real estate contract must be in writing to be enforceable.

   Example: Assume an agent tells a principal that she is an expert in short sales and that the principal states orally that he wants the agent to negotiate a short sale on a certain property. If the agent negotiates the short sale, the principal will not be liable for the transaction because the agency relationship had to be in writing to be enforceable.

2. *Implied authority.* With **implied authority**, the principal has not expressly given authority, but the agent believes that the principal has given the agent authority through the principal's actions or conduct. This authority is implied by the conduct of the parties, customs between the parties, and acts incidental to carrying out the agent's express authority. Express authority given an agent will control over any implied authority.

   Example: Assume that a broker representing the seller is given authority to sell his property to a buyer. The broker will have implied authority to take pictures of the property and market the property to potential buyers.

3. *Apparent authority.* **Apparent authority** arises when an agent does not have authority to act on the principal's behalf, but the principal's words or conduct reasonably imply to a third party that the agent does have this authority. If a third party reasonably relies on that belief, the principal will be liable under apparent authority. The principal will be estopped (prohibited) from claiming that the agent lacked authority to act on his behalf. Apparent authority continues to exist until the third party receives notice of the termination.

   Example: If a buyer learned that the seller had switched brokers, that notice would prevent the former broker from having any power to continue negotiations with the buyer.

4. *Ratification.* **Ratification** occurs when the principal approves unauthorized acts committed by the agent, such as when the agent acts either without

authority or beyond the scope of the authority expressly given by the principal. If a principal ratifies the agent's actions, the principal becomes bound to the terms of the contract. Generally, any words or conduct by the principal showing an intention to adopt the agent's act ratifies the contract.

Example: A broker is given authority to purchase an estate home for $2.5 million. The broker finds the perfect home for the buyer, listed at $2.6 million, and submits an offer on the buyer's behalf. The buyer may ratify the $2.6 million offer made by the agent. Once she does so, the buyer will become bound to the terms of the contract (if the seller accepts the offer).

■ ■ ■ Power of Attorney

A principal grants a **power of attorney** to an agent to authorize the agent to act on the principal's behalf. It is not uncommon to have a power of attorney in real estate transactions. The appointment of the power of attorney must be in writing signed by the principal. The appointed agent is known as an attorney-in-fact, and the person appointing the agent is the principal. While the agent is an attorney-in-fact, that person need not be an attorney. The principal must have legal capacity at the time of executing the power of attorney, and the agent must have the legal capacity to perform the acts authorized on behalf of the principal.

The principal can revoke a power of attorney at any time. The power of attorney is also automatically revoked upon the death of the principal. Additionally, the original power of attorney is revoked when a principal replaces the attorney-in-fact with a new attorney-in-fact. Powers of attorney are also revoked upon the disability or incapacity of the principal, unless the principal expressly granted such continued power of attorney at the time of creation. Where the principal allows a power of attorney to continue upon the principal's disability or incapacity, the power of attorney is called a durable power of attorney.

An attorney-in-fact can only act within the expressly granted power of a power of attorney. There are no implied powers under a power of attorney. Common powers granted under a power of attorney for real estate transactions include the power to sell property, the power to acquire property, and the power to refinance mortgages.

Example: If an attorney-in-fact is given a power of attorney to refinance a piece of real property, he does not have the power to sell that piece of real property.

Partially Disclosed and Undisclosed Principals

Partially disclosed principal
A principal whose existence is known to the third party, but whose identity is not known.

As previously stated, generally the principal, and not the agent, is liable to third parties for contracts entered into by the agent on the principal's behalf. An exception is made when the principal's identity is only partially disclosed or undisclosed. In such cases, both the principal and the agent can be held liable. A **partially disclosed principal** is a person whose existence is known to the third party but whose identity is not known.

With an **undisclosed principal**, the third party is unaware of the existence or identity of the principal. An agent working for an undisclosed principal is called a secret agent. Real estate developers, large corporations, and private and public schools often act as partially disclosed or undisclosed principals. If the identity of the principal were known, third parties might be less willing to sell their property or might seek a higher price, believing that the principal was seeking to secure large amounts of land.

Undisclosed principal
A principal whose existence or identity is unknown to the third party.

In the majority of states, when the identity of a partially disclosed or undisclosed principal is discovered, the third party may choose whether to hold the principal or the agent liable for the performance of the contract. Because agents acting with the authority of principals are not liable for the performance of the contract, they usually enter into indemnity agreements with partially disclosed or undisclosed principals. In an indemnity agreement, the principal agrees to defend the agent and hold the agent harmless from any costs, fees, or damages that may result.

Example: The Walt Disney Company used secret agents to purchase land in Florida to be used for the Walt Disney World theme parks. The company used various non-Disney-named held corporations to acquire approximately 27,443 acres of land in Orange County, Florida. Some of the corporation names, such as "M. T. Lott" and the "Latin American Development and Managers Corporation," are memorialized on the windows above Main Street U.S.A. in the Magic Kingdom. It took several years for the Walt Disney Company to acquire the land needed for the park. Once, before the land purchase was complete, a reporter uncovered that the Walt Disney Company was acquiring the land, and land values increased by almost a thousand times. The first acre for the park was acquired for approximately $80 an acre; the last acre was acquired for approximately $80,000 an acre.

Concept Summary

- The creation of an agency relationship arises when a principal and an agent consent to the relationship. The agent acts on the principal's behalf, under the principal's control.
- An agent's authority to act on the principal's behalf arises through express authority, implied authority, apparent authority, or ratification by the principal. In express authority, implied authority, and ratification, the principal's conduct toward the agent determines the creation of an agency relationship. Apparent authority is created by the principal's conduct toward third parties.

- An agent working with a disclosed principal is not liable for authorized contracts that the agent enters into. The principal is liable for the authorized actions of the agent.
- If a principal is disclosed and the agent makes an unauthorized contract, the agent is liable on the contract. The principal can hold the agent liable for the principal's damages, if any.
- If the principal is partially disclosed or undisclosed, the third party may elect to hold either the principal or the agent liable for the performance of the contract when the identity of the partially disclosed or undisclosed principal is discovered.

Real Estate Brokers and Salespersons

While real estate transactions do not require a real estate agent, the vast majority of property owners still choose to work with a real estate agent. Usually a person selling or buying a home will work with either a real estate broker or a real estate salesperson (often called a sales associate) because of that person's expertise in advertising, finding, and assisting in real estate transactions. Often brokers will specialize in a market. For example, a broker might specialize in a specific geographical location or a specific type of property, such as commercial properties.

Real Estate Brokers

Real estate broker
A state-licensed real estate agent hired for a fee to purchase or sell real estate.

A **real estate broker** is a state-licensed real estate agent hired by a principal for a fee to purchase or sell real estate on the principal's behalf. This agency relationship imposes certain fiduciary duties, discussed later in this chapter. The broker does not have unlimited authority to act for the principal. The principal grants and defines the broker's powers to act on her behalf through a listing agreement.

In most states, to become a licensed broker, the applicant must undertake educational certain coursework and pass a state exam. Many states also require a real estate broker applicant to have been a salesperson under a broker for one or more years.

A real estate broker's activities commonly include any of the following:

1. Listing, negotiating, offering or selling, exchanging, purchasing, renting, or leasing real estate
2. Performing a comparative market analysis (providing an estimate of a real property's value)
3. Advertising the property and finding people and properties for the purposes of securing the sale, exchange, lease, or rental of real estate
4. Assisting with and coordinating aspects of the closing process, including facilitating the property's inspections, surveys, title examinations, and any financing appraisal

Real Estate Salespersons

Real estate salesperson
A state-licensed real estate agent who assists a broker in a real estate transaction.

A **real estate salesperson** is a state-licensed agent who assists a broker in real estate transactions. Salespersons are required to work under the supervision of a real estate broker and may not independently perform any of the activities for which a broker's license is required.

Supervision and Liability

The broker is required to supervise the salespersons and establish policies and procedures to manage and review their activities, including ensuring the rights of parties to a transaction, the handling of trust funds, and advertising of properties.

The broker will be liable for the acts and omissions of a salesperson. Under both common law and state statutes, brokers are liable for the torts (such as civil wrongs, which include negligent acts and omissions) committed by their salespersons within the course and scope of their agency. This is true whether the person is classified as an employee or as an independent contractor. The broker must indemnify parties who are injured by the torts of the salesperson acting on behalf of the broker.

Real Estate Agency Relationships

Brokers can represent both buyers and sellers of property. The same broker can also represent both the buyer and the seller of the property at the same time (a dual agent). The different types of agency are discussed below.

Listing Agent

A listing agent is the most common type of real estate agent. **Listing agents** work with the seller of the property. They are responsible for listing, advertising, and selling the property on the owner's behalf. While listing agents have contact with prospective buyers (that is, through open houses and showings), they do not represent them. When visiting an open house, prospective buyers should keep in mind that the listing agent represents the seller *only*. The fiduciary duties discussed below apply to the seller, not to the prospective buyer.

Listing agent
A real estate agent who represents the seller of a property.

Buyer Agent

While not as common as listing agents, **buyer agents** are brokers who enter into a contract to represent a buyer. The broker owes the buyer fiduciary duties discussed later in this chapter. A conflict of interest may arise because the buyer agent is usually paid a commission based on the final selling price. The higher the selling price, the higher the buyer agent's commission; however, the buyer would prefer to have the selling price as low as possible.

Buyer agent
A real estate agent who represents the buyer of a property.

Dual Agent

Dual agency arises when a broker represents both the buyer and the seller in a transaction. Many states allow dual agency if both the buyer and the seller have full knowledge of the situation and agree to have the broker act on their mutual behalf. Because brokers owe fiduciary duties to their clients, they often do not act as the representative of both sides to a transaction.

Dual agents cannot function as true advocates for their clients' positions because they represent both sides. Instead, they must remain neutral and impartial. The advantage to the broker is that she does not have to share the commission with another broker representing the other party. A broker acting as a dual agent may be liable for damages to one of the parties to the transaction if the broker breaches fiduciary duties and commits negligent acts.

Dual agent
A real estate agent who represents both the buyer and the seller in a real estate transaction.

Designated Agent

Designated agency occurs when different agents within the same firm represent a buyer and a seller. The broker for the firm appoints a salesperson within the same firm to represent the seller and buyer separately. The broker acts as a dual agent because the broker supervises both the seller's agent and the buyer's agent. Information specific to each client is kept separate so that confidential information is protected.

Nonagent Brokers

Nonagent broker
A person who assists buyers and sellers in administrative acts to close the real estate transaction without representing either the buyer or the seller.

A **nonagent broker** represents neither the buyer nor the seller as an agent. Instead, the nonagent broker assists buyers and sellers in administrative acts to close the real estate transaction without representing, as an agent, either side. Because the nonagent broker is not an agent, he or she owes no fiduciary duties to the buyer or seller. States have created different names and duties for these nonagent brokers, including intermediaries, limited agents, and transaction brokers. States that allow nonagent brokers often limit the scope of the disclosures that can be made.

> *Example:* A nonagent may be forbidden to disclose that the seller is willing to accept less than the stated asking price or that the buyer is willing to pay more than the stated asking price.

Retaining the Broker

Real estate brokers are retained through written contracts known as **listing agreements**. These contracts create an agency relationship and set forth the terms of the employment, commission, rights, and duties of the parties. In many states, the **Statute of Frauds** requires that the contract with the broker be in writing in order for the broker to be compensated for the work performed.

Statute of Frauds
A state requirement that certain types of contracts be in writing to be enforceable.

While each state's listing agreement requirements are slightly different, most require that the following elements be present in the written contract:

1. Identification of the type of listing agreement for which the broker and seller are contracting (discussed below).
2. List price and terms. The price the property is listed for, as well as the property's description and location, should be stated.
3. Duration of listing agreement. Most states require listing agreements to have a defined listing duration. When the duration of the listing ends, the broker's authority to act on behalf of the seller terminates.
4. Broker's compensation. The listing agreement should state the amount of a broker's compensation. A broker is often paid a percentage of the selling price of the property. The agreement should also provide when the commission becomes due and is owed to the broker. Additionally, most listing agreements entitle the broker to a commission for a period of time

after the listing agreement has expired or has been terminated (discussed below).

5. Description of the broker's and seller's obligations and duties (discussed below).
6. The seller's signature.

Types of Listings

To whom a commission is owed depends on the type of listing agreement. A seller can enter into several different types of listing agreement with a broker. The three most common types of listing agreements are open listing, exclusive agency, and the exclusive right to sell.

Open Listing

In an **open listing**, the owner can employ more than one broker to sell the same property. The first broker to obtain a buyer earns the commission. The owner of the property may also sell the property. If the owner sells the property, none of the brokers hired is entitled to a commission. Open listings are rarely used in residential-property sales. When used with residential properties, open listings are often utilized to sell large tracts of rural land or very expensive homes. With these types of properties, contracting with brokers from different states (and countries) may be necessary to sell the property.

Exclusive Agency

In an **exclusive agency** listing, the broker is the exclusive agent of the seller, and the broker is entitled to a commission. If the owner hires an additional broker and that broker is able to sell the property, the original broker is still entitled to a commission. In those situations, the owner can be liable to two brokers for a commission on the property. An owner does not owe a commission to a broker if the owner sells the property without the assistance of the broker.

Exclusive Right to Sell

In an **exclusive right to sell** listing, the owner hires a broker to exclusively sell the property. The broker is entitled to a commission regardless of who finds a buyer, including if the owner finds the buyer. While this listing is the least friendly to the property owner, it is the most favorable to brokers because they will receive a commission if the property is sold during the listing period. It is also the most commonly used type of listing in the real estate industry because agents who belong to a multiple-listing service are required to have exclusive right to sell listings.

Under an exclusive right to sell listing, a seller can be held liable for two commissions on the same sale if they employ another broker who finds the buyer during the listing period with the first hired broker.

Listing Agreement	Original Broker Finds Buyer	Subsequent Broker Finds Buyer	Owner Sells Property
Open Listing	Commission owed to original broker	Commission owed to subsequent broker	No commission owed
Exclusive Agency	Commission owed to original broker	Commission owed to both brokers	No commission owed
Exclusive Right to Sell	Commission owed to original broker	Commission owed to both brokers	Commission owed to original broker

FIGURE 7.1. Commission Liability by Listing Agreement Type

Advertising the Listing

Brokers often join trade associations to promote the sale or lease of listed properties and further their educational efforts. The National Association of Realtors (NAR)® is the nation's largest real estate association. While brokers and salespersons are not required to join a trade association, they cannot advertise themselves as Realtors® without joining the association and paying the association's dues.

The trade associations offer a variety of products and services to their members, including contract forms, free software, referral programs, publications, legal information, conventions, lobbying, social functions, and often access to multiple-listing services (MLS).

Multiple Listing Services

Multiple Listing Services (MLS)
A network of real estate listings that provide listing brokers a larger market to advertise their listings.

The **Multiple Listing Services (MLS)** is a network of real estate listings that provide listing brokers a larger market in which to advertise their listings. Each MLS is tailored to a specific geographic market area of properties. In most real estate markets, a single MLS provides the only available comprehensive compilation of listings. Often, several trade associations form together to pool their properties to create a large MLS.

> ***Example:*** The My Florida Regional MLS located in central and southwest Florida includes 14 trade associations: Bartow Board of Realtors™, East Polk County Association of Realtors™, Englewood Area Board of Realtors™, Greater Tampa Association of Realtors™, Lakeland Association of Realtors™, Orlando Regional Realtor Association®, Osceola County Association of Realtors™, Pinellas Realtor Organization™, Punta Gorda-Port Charlotte-North Port Association of Realtors™, Realtors Association of Lake & Sumter Counties™, The Realtor Association of Sarasota & Manatee™, Venice Area Board of Realtors™, West Pasco Board of Realtors™, and West Volusia Association of Realtors™.

In most real estate markets, a single MLS provides the only available comprehensive compilation of listings. Brokers often believe they must participate in the MLS operating in their local market to adequately serve their customers and compete with other brokers.

A listing on the MLS gives brokers more knowledge of available properties. MLS collects and lists detailed information about nearly all properties available for sale. They provide a better understanding of current market prices and demand and allow brokers and consumers to compare prices.

There have been many challenges to the constitutionality of the MLS structure, as the following case discusses. In this case, a broker claimed that the operation of the MLS violated antitrust laws as a restraint of trade.

CASE 7.1

REQUIRING MEMBERSHIP IN A TRADE ASSOCIATION TO ACCESS THE MLS MAY BE LAWFUL

REIFERT v. SOUTH CENTRAL WISCONSIN MLS

450 F.3d 312 (2006)

United States Court of Appeals for the Seventh Circuit

Jay Reifert, a real estate broker, alleged that the local real estate trade association violated the Sherman Antitrust Act. He claimed that it was unlawful to tie access to the board's multiple-listing service to membership on the board. The federal district court granted a judgment in favor of the MLS, and Reifert appealed.

Language of the Court. *The SCWMLS is a computerized database of homes and properties listed for sale by participants in south-central Wisconsin. Access to this multiple listing service is a necessity for real estate agents and appraisers in this area. Virtually all active residential real estate agents in the region subscribe to SCWMLS. Users are charged a quarterly fee to gain access to the full database and must be a member of a Realtors Association affiliated with NAR. The Realtors Association membership requirement has existed for more than fifty years. Generally, any licensed real estate professional who agrees to abide by the NAR Code of Ethics and pays the applicable fees is admitted.*

Article 16 of NAR's Code of Ethics contains a non-solicitation rule that prohibits members from inducing sellers to breach listing contracts, advising sellers of superior services or prices during the time they are under contract with another Realtor, and using information received through a multiple listing service to target clients of other Realtors.

There are no exclusionary conditions attached to Realtor board membership, and there is no contention that the cost is prohibitively high. In this case, no licensed real estate agent was denied access to SCWMLS because of an anticompetitive measure.

Reifert claims that Article 16 of the Code of Ethics of NAR is anticompetitive and violates Section I of the Sherman Act. Article 16 prohibits members of the National Association of Realtors from interfering with the exclusive agreements other members have established with clients.

Reifert's allegations concerning the anticompetitive effects of Article 16, however, are overly broad. Article 16's purpose is to prevent the targeted solicitation of individuals who have exclusively listed their property with another agent and to prevent agents from improperly using multiple listing services as a databank of potential customers. If agents were reluctant to post their listings for fear that other agents would steal their clients, the market would become less transparent and less efficient. Article 16 aids competition and fulfills the purposes of the Sherman Act by providing a more transparent marketplace.

Decision. The Court of Appeals affirmed the judgment in favor of the MLS.

FOCUS ON ETHICS

Is it fair that a broker is compelled to join the MLS in order to effectively assist parties to a residential real estate transaction?

Internet Listing Services

Internet listing services are popular. With an Internet listing service, a broker does not maintain a traditional office and places all listings on a website. This approach reduces the overhead cost to a broker, yielding savings that can be passed on to a buyer or seller of real property in the form of reduced commissions.

These services allow the broker's customers who visit the website to see properties listed for sale. The details provided can include pictures, descriptions, and property comments, viewable at any time or place, so long as a person has a device that can connect to the Internet. This setup allows prospective homebuyers the opportunity to look at homes online, narrow down a list of homes, and then employ a real estate professional to visit the homes and close the deal to purchase them.

Commercial Property Advertising

While commercial properties are also often advertised on the local MLS, the search for commercial property sales, purchases, and leasing is conducted differently than is a search for residential property. Commercial property listings are fewer in number than those of residential properties. In urban areas, commercial listings are most frequently maintained by brokerage firms specializing in buying and selling commercial properties. One national firm, CoStar Group®, provides Internet listing information to its paid subscribers.

Compensating the Broker

Commission
Compensation to a broker given by a percentage of the selling price.

Brokers are compensated by either a commission or a net listing agreement. Brokers are most often paid a **commission** on the property's selling price instead of a salary. Usually, a commission is between 2 and 3 percent of the selling price, but commissions are negotiable, so they may be higher or lower, depending on the circumstances and type of property for sale. Generally, commissions are paid after the closing of the transaction when the seller has received the purchase price.

> *Example:* A homeowner who is moving out of state and wants to sell a property quickly may agree to pay a higher percentage commission to incentivize a broker to make selling their home a priority.

Real estate transactions completed through the use of the MLS often involve two brokers, a listing broker and a cooperating broker. The cooperating broker represents the buyer. The listing broker usually splits the commission equally ("50-50") with the cooperating broker. The amount of commission a cooperating broker will receive is

Ready, willing, and able buyer
A buyer who can purchase the property at the price stated in the listing agreement and under the terms and conditions of the listing agreement.

noted in the MLS listing.

Compensation Entitlement

In most jurisdictions, brokers are entitled to compensation when they present a ready, willing, and able buyer. A **ready, willing, and able buyer** is one who can purchase the property at the price stated in the listing agreement and under the terms and conditions of the listing agreement, unless the parties agree to changes in such terms and conditions. If the transaction does not close (for instance, if the seller breaches the agreement or refuses or is unable to perform the agreement), the brokers are still entitled to the commission.

> *Example:* If the seller is unable to clear a title problem with the property prior to closing and the deal does not close, the broker would still be entitled to a commission, even though no closing occurred.

In a minority of jurisdictions the deal must close before a broker is entitled to a commission. Further, even where a broker is entitled to a commission for presenting a ready, willing, and able buyer, a contract may require the deal to close before a broker is entitled to a commission. To do so, sellers insert a **no deal, no commission clause** into the listing agreement, making the closing of the real estate deal a **condition precedent** (an event or requirement that must be met) to a commission.

In the following case, a broker who assisted the vendor in an unsuccessful attempt to sell a farm brought a claim against the vendor seeking the unpaid commission.

CASE 7.2

BROKERS AGREEING TO BE PAID FROM THE PROCEEDS OF A TRANSACTION ARE NOT ENTITLED TO A COMMISSION IF THE TRANSACTION DOES NOT CLOSE

TRANSNATIONAL VENTURES, INC. v. DERR PLANTATION, INC.

187 So.3d 185 (2016)

Mississippi Court of Appeals

In 2002, the president of Transnational Ventures, Inc. ("Transnational") and a licensed real estate broker, Paul Pillat ("Pillat"), received an offer to purchase a farm owned by Herman Derr ("Derr"), the president of Derr Plantation, Inc. Pillat sent the offer to Derr. Derr responded in a letter stating he would be willing to sell the farm for $10.5 million, less a $500,000 commission to Pillat out of the gross sales proceeds. However, the farm was not sold at that time. A few years later, Pillat alleges Derr asked Pillat to help him sell the farm. At that time, Pillat informed Derr his minimum commission would be 5 percent, and Derr agreed with the commission paid from the gross sales proceeds. Pillat met with a prospective buyer, who offered to buy the farm for $6 million. Pillat sent Derr a letter about the potential buyer, but no deal was reached by the parties. Transnational filed a lawsuit on behalf of Pillat alleging it was entitled to a commission of $500,000 because Pillat provided a buyer that was "ready, willing, and able" to purchase the farm. At trial, the court ruled against Transnational. Transnational appealed.

Language of the Court. *A broker who agreed to be paid from the proceeds of a transaction was not entitled to a commission if the transaction was not consummated, regardless of whether he presented his principal with a "ready, willing, and able" counterparty.*

If Pillat wanted his commission contingent on procuring a buyer ready, willing, and able to consummate the transaction, he very easily could have contracted for as much. With this not being the case, he is not entitled to a commission.

Under longstanding precedent, this means that he was entitled to a commission only upon a successful sale of the farm.

Decision. The court affirmed the decision of the trial court. It held the broker was only entitled to a commission in the event of a sale in accordance with the broker's retention.

FOCUS ON ETHICS

Is it fair that Pillat is not entitled to any commission even though he provided potential buyers who were ready, willing, and able to close the sale?

Procuring Cause

Occasionally, particularly when an open listing and exclusive agency listing are used, a broker may dispute who is entitled to the commission. In those situations, the broker who is the procuring cause will be entitled to a commission. The **procuring cause** is the broker who, through his or her efforts, laid the foundation for the negotiations resulting in a sale.[1]

> *Example:* Broker A shows Brett a home. Brett loves the home but is unsure about purchasing it. A week later, after thinking about the home, Brett contracts with Broker B to purchase it. Broker A may allege that she is the procuring cause and is entitled to a commission on the property.

The National Association of Realtors™ provides a list of factors to consider and questions to ask in determining who is the procuring cause. Examples include:

1. Who first introduced the buyer to the property?
2. When and how was the first introduction made?
3. Did the broker who made the initial introduction to the property engage in conduct (or fail to take action in some way) that caused the buyer to utilize the services of another broker?
4. What length of time elapsed between the broker's efforts and the final sales agreement?
5. Did the broker who made the initial introduction to the property maintain contact with the buyer?
6. Did the buyer make the decision to buy independently of the broker's efforts/information?

One way brokers can show that they were the procuring cause in transactions is to create sign-in sheets. Sign-in sheets are especially prevalent in open houses. While some may view signing in as becoming part of the real estate agent's marketing pool, the main reason for the sign-in sheet is to assist the real estate agent in determining whether his open house is the procuring cause for a buyer to purchase the property.

These issues are less common in an exclusive right to sell listing because the broker earns a commission regardless of who is the procuring cause. Whether a broker is the procuring cause is a question of fact in each case.

Example: Mr. and Mrs. Striklin enter into an exclusive right to sell a listing with Broker. The Striklins spend the next several weekends visiting open houses without the assistance of their real estate agent. On the fourth weekend, they find a property for sale by owner that they decide to purchase. Broker is entitled to a commission, even though she was not the procuring cause of the sale, because of the exclusive right to sell listing.

Net Listing

A second method of compensating a broker is through a net listing. In a **net listing**, the broker and owner enter into one of the three types of listing agreements noted previously. The seller does not pay a percentage of the selling price to the broker; instead, the broker must sell the property above a price set by the seller to receive any commission. Any money above this price is the broker's commission. If the property is sold less than this price, the broker does not earn a commission.

The price set will account for the expenses of the sale and includes mortgage payoff, closing costs, and any cash amount the owner wishes to receive at closing.

Example: An owner enters into an exclusive right to sell agency listing with a broker. The seller wants to receive $50,000 in cash at closing. The closing costs will be $5,000, and the seller has a mortgage on the property of $195,000. The broker will receive a commission for any amount above $250,000 ($195,000 mortgage + $50,000 cash seller wants + $5,000 closing costs).

Expired Listing Commissions

Brokers will often insert a clause in the listing agreement providing that the broker is entitled to a commission if the property is sold within a specified time period after the listing expires to a prospective buyer identified by the broker. These prospective buyers often include persons who physically entered the property during the listing period (such as at an open house). Some states require that the broker provide to the seller a list of all prospective buyers within a certain period of time after the listing period expires to be entitled to any post-expiration commission.

Real Estate Licensing

States regulate the licensure of real estate professionals to protect the public from fraud in its dealings with real estate agents and protect consumers from incompetent or unethical real estate professionals. Licensees are required to meet certain levels of competency, ethics, and moral character to become real estate agents and must continue their education to maintain a license.

An administrative agency within each state regulates the real estate community. To obtain a real estate license, brokers and sales agents are required to pass an examination. Applicants must also meet educational and industry-experience requirements. The applicant must pass a background screening to reveal past business activities and any criminal history. A corporation can also maintain a real estate license. The corporation is licensed through a designated officer who holds a broker's license.

> *Example:* If Victory Realty desired to be a licensed real estate entity, it would need a person holding a broker's license to act as the corporation's designated officer.

While each state's laws vary as to the requirements for a real estate license, they generally require the following to obtain a real estate broker's license:

1. *Minimum age.* The minimum age is the age of majority (18 years or more).
2. *Residency.* Most states require applicants to be residents of the United States. Some states require brokers to have been residents of the state for a period of time (often 30 to 90 days) before the application to the state can be made.
3. *Moral character.* Many states require applicants to be of sound moral character, including honesty, trustworthiness, and integrity.
4. *Examination.* States require both brokers and salespersons to pass a written examination. The level of proficiency required to pass the broker examination is often more stringent than the salesperson examination.
5. *Professional experience.* To become a licensed broker, states require the broker to have a minimum period of experience as a licensed salesperson. The experience requirement is often two or more years of supervision by a real estate broker.
6. *Educational experience.* Most states require license applicants to possess education on real estate subject matter selected by the state. These subjects can be taught at colleges and universities, adult-education facilities, or private real estate schools approved by the state. Some states require applicants to have a college degree.
7. *Fingerprints.* Many states require applicants to establish their identity through fingerprints.
8. *Convictions.* States often check for criminal convictions. While having a criminal conviction may not bar an applicant from becoming licensed, failing to disclose the criminal conviction is considered more serious, as it is a sign the person lacks moral character.

Continuing Education

States require that licensees continue their education after receiving a license. Each licensee must provide proof of having completed state-approved continuing education courses. These classes cover a variety of topics, including the duties of brokers and agents, ethics, handling trust funds, changes in real estate laws, and regulations and taxation. The number of continuing education hours required and the frequency with which licensees must provide proof of completion vary by state.

Exemptions from Licensing Requirements

State laws permit individuals to engage in certain real estate activities without a real estate license. Each state provides its own specific exemptions. Examples of these exemptions include the following:

- Property owners selling their own properties (such as sale by owner) do not need to be licensed.
- Persons holding a power of attorney from the owner of the real property with respect to which the acts are authorized may sell or lease the property.
- Licensed attorneys may be authorized to sell and purchase real estate without a real estate license.

Unlicensed Activities

By law, people required to be licensed as brokers must have the license at the time they perform the act for which they need the license. In many states, it is illegal to act without a real estate license when one is required, and the person doing so may be subject to criminal penalties, including fines and possible imprisonment. Some jurisdictions void any contract entered into by an unlicensed broker or salesperson (that is, courts will not enforce the contract). Additionally, persons acting without a required license are not permitted to collect a commission or compensation.

Finders

Unlicensed brokers often argue that they are acting in the capacity of finders or middlemen. A **finder** is an intermediary who brings together parties for a business opportunity or real estate transaction. The finder may or may not be licensed. The finder locates and introduces the parties, whereas a broker attempts to bring the parties to an agreement. Generally, finders do not (or legally cannot) negotiate transactions to earn their compensation. In interpreting what may be an exception to the state's licensing laws, courts require that the finder must only introduce the parties and do nothing more. However, the laws of each state are unique in their requirements for licenses in these non-licensee transactions.

Finder
A person who brings together the buyer and seller in a real estate transaction.

> *Example:* Franklin, who does not hold a real estate license, is aware of a large tract of property available for sale. At a cocktail party, he meets Brian, a person interested in purchasing ranching land. Franklin may introduce Brian to the owner of the property and receive a finder's fee, so long as his involvement is limited to bringing the two parties together to negotiate a deal. If he assists in the negotiation of the deal between the parties, he has acted without a license and is not permitted to receive any compensation.

■ ■ ■
Tips to Maintain Finder Status

1. No agreement should involve any language implying or creating an agency relationship.
2. The finder's compensation should be tied strictly to bringing the two parties together.
3. The parties should negotiate their own contract, and the finder should not be involved in the negotiation.
4. The finder should not negotiate with either party or have any power to bind either party to a transaction.

Brokers' Fiduciary Duties

A broker owes several duties to the principal. The listing agreement creates certain duties and liabilities for the broker because of the express agency relationship created from the listing agreement. Those duties are identified by the express terms of the agreement. In addition, the law imposes fiduciary duties upon the broker because of the relationship the broker has to the principal. A **fiduciary duty** is a duty to act in the principal's best interest and not advance the broker's own interests. The broker's fiduciary duties generally begin at the time of retention by the client. They exist even in the absence of a written agreement with the client. The main fiduciary duties a broker owes to the client include the duty of care, the duty of loyalty, duty of obedience, and the duty of accounting.

Duty of Care

Duty of care
A fiduciary duty that requires a broker to act as a reasonably competent real estate broker would act under similar circumstances.

The **duty of care** requires that a broker act as a reasonably competent real estate broker would act under similar circumstances. Because the broker possesses a real estate license, the broker is considered to have expertise in real estate matters and is held to a higher level of expertise than would be the average person. The reasonable care requirements that a broker must follow include:

■ *Exercise due diligence and pricing.* The broker is required to exercise due diligence and obtain the best bargain possible under the circumstances for the client.

Example: A listing broker has violated the duty of care if, despite being certain that he can increase the selling price of a property by $5,000 by hosting an open house, he instead pressures the seller to accept an offer without having an open house so that the broker can quickly collect a commission and move on to the next sale.

■ *Investigate.* Some states require a broker to inspect the property and disclose any defects discovered. Where a duty to investigate exists, the duty is usually limited to the physical attributes of the property.

Example: Homeowners in Texas who noticed that the subdivision's levels were different and that their home showed differences in level between the entry door, den, and garage filed suit against the broker. The Texas court held that the broker was required to investigate whether the property was located near an earthquake fault line and was held negligent for violating the duty of care.[2]

- *Communicate.* A broker must communicate reasonably and keep the client informed in a timely manner. A broker must present all offers and assist the principal in evaluating each offer presented.
- *Explain real estate customs and practices.* A broker may explain the customs and practices used in the real estate industry but must not explain the law. Customs and practices often include closing processes, the amount of earnest money used, and so on. Because brokers are not licensed attorneys, they may not give legal advice. Brokers who give legal advice without a legal license may have their broker's licenses suspended or revoked.

Unauthorized Practice of Law

The distinction between practicing law and explaining customs and practices may seem like a fine line in some situations. Generally, the practice of law includes conveyancing, preparing legal documents, and providing opinions related to holding title, zoning, encumbrances, and so on. Because brokers are not licensed attorneys, they may not give legal advice. Brokers who give legal advice without a legal license may have their broker's licenses suspended or revoked.

For example, a broker who has been in the real estate industry for decades and experienced hundreds of transactions still may not give advice to a prospective homeowner regarding the manner in which the homeowner should hold title to the real property to avoid estate taxes or probate. The broker's best response is, "Please see an attorney."

When a broker fails to exercise reasonable care, he may be sued for **negligence** if that failure caused harm to the principal or third party. Brokers cannot limit the responsibilities of the duty of care through contract clauses in a listing agreement or other contract.

Example: A real estate broker who did not visually inspect the property and did not disclose to his buyers a potential construction defect in the foundation of the property could be sued for negligence in a state that requires brokers to investigate the property.

Duty of Loyalty

The duty of loyalty is one of the most fundamental duties a broker owes to a principal. The **duty of loyalty** requires the broker to act in good faith and employ fair dealing with regard to the client. This requires that the broker act in the best interest of the client, even at the expense of the broker. Brokers may be found to have violated the duty of loyalty if they:

Duty of loyalty
A fiduciary duty owed by an agent not to act adversely to the principal's interest.

■ *Make a secret (undisclosed) profit.* Brokers must not profit from the agency relationship without the informed consent of the client. A secret profit includes kickbacks, referral fees, and other unearned fees from title companies, escrow holders, and other brokers. It does not matter that the transaction is otherwise fair to the client. The client is entitled to all such profits made by the broker.

Example: If a broker uses her favorite title company because it provides a $25 gift certificate to her each time she uses it, this is a secret profit.

■ *Disclose confidential information.* A broker may not disclose confidential information about the client. Confidential information includes any information that could weaken the client's bargaining position. This would include information that a seller may sell at less than the listed price or any motivations behind why a seller desires to sell the property.

Example: A listing broker who discloses that the seller has already accepted a job offer in another state and desperately needs to sell the property has violated the duty of loyalty to the client.

■ *Withhold material facts.* A broker cannot withhold any material facts to the client that relate to the property and the transaction. A **material fact** is one that a reasonable person would consider important in making a decision. It includes any facts that affect the value or desirability of the property.

Example: A broker must disclose all offers presented to a seller.

■ *Act as a dual agent without informed consent.* If state law allows for dual agency, the broker must have the informed consent of both the buyer and the seller to represent both sides of the transaction.

Dual agency creates a unique problem in that a broker cannot act in the best interest of each principal because doing so would be adverse to the other principal represented. Many states provide that dual agents must act neutrally toward both principals. Commonly, states require that dual agents not disclose (1) whether the seller is willing to sell the property for less than the listing price, (2) whether the buyer is willing to pay more than the offered listing price, or (3) any motivation or urgency related to either party seeking to purchase or sell the property.

Duty of Obedience

Duty of obedience
A fiduciary duty requiring a broker to obey and follow all lawful instructions and demands of the client.

The **duty of obedience** requires that a broker obey and follow all lawful instructions and demands of the client. A broker is not required to obey instructions that are unlawful, such as misrepresenting the school district the property is located. This duty requires brokers to obey the client's desires, even when they may not be in the best interests of the client.

Example: If a seller is presented with an offer to purchase a home for $275,000 cash and another offer to purchase for $285,000 cash, and the seller desires to sell to the $275,000 buyer, the broker must obey the seller's desires even though the seller is not accepting the highest offer.

Duty of Accounting

Under the duty of accounting, a broker is required to safeguard and account for all money, documents, and deeds that the broker receives or that come into the broker's possession that belong to the client.

> *Example:* If a listing broker receives a down payment deposit from a buyer, the broker cannot deposit the payment into the broker's personal checking account.

Trust Accounts

State laws require that a broker who handles money for other persons acts as a fiduciary. Depositing the principal's money in the broker's personal account is a violation of the licensee's statutory duties to clients. Brokers may not commingle clients' funds with their own but must deposit them in separate, segregated trust accounts. **Commingling** occurs when the funds of a client are mixed with the licensee's personal funds.

Deposits received by a broker may be handled in one of several ways, depending on the agreement between the seller and the buyer. The funds may be deposited into a trust account, given to the principal, or deposited directly into an escrow account. A broker may not disburse trust funds without ensuring that all deposits have cleared the bank.

Brokers' Duties to Third Parties

Generally, brokers do not owe any duties to third parties. Their duty is to their clients and is created through the agency relationship. In some situations, a broker may be exposed to liability for acts or omissions made to third parties. A broker's liability to third parties is most commonly found in instances of misrepresentation, intentional nondisclosure, and failure to provide state-mandated disclosures.

Misrepresentation

Misrepresentation arises when a broker either intentionally or negligently misrepresents a material fact to the third party. Third parties who deal with brokers rely on the statements that a broker makes. These misrepresentations often arise from the property listing, advertisements, fliers, and statements made by the broker at open houses.

A broker **intentionally misrepresents** a third party when she or he is aware of a material fact and either intentionally misstates the fact or knowingly fails to disclose it to a third party, and the third party justifiably relies on the misrepresentation.

> *Example:* A broker who knowingly misrepresents to a third party that a home is inside the boundaries of a top-performing school district when in fact the home is located within a below-average school district has committed a misrepresentation.

Misrepresentation
When a broker either intentionally or negligently misrepresents a material fact to a third party.

A broker may be found liable for negligent misrepresentation if he or she makes a statement of material fact without any reasonable knowledge of its truthfulness and the third party justifiably relies on the statement.

> *Example:* A broker is asked at an open house if the surround-sound system works. If the broker does not know the answer to this question but tells the third party that the system performs adequately, the broker has made a negligent misrepresentation.

Sales Puffing

Sales puffing is a statement of opinion describing the greatness of a property. These statements involve exaggerated expressions such as "a kitchen to die for," "the ultimate ocean view," and "perfectly landscaped yard." Sales puffing does not create liability to the broker; however, when the broker crosses the line and uses sales puffing to misrepresent the truth, she or he can be liable for misrepresentation.

> *Example:* A broker who states that the house is maintenance-free when she knows that the roof will need to be replaced in the next year or so has made a misrepresentation.

Intentional Nondisclosure

Many states require a broker to disclose known material facts concerning a property that the buyer is not likely to observe or discover prior to sale. **Intentional nondisclosure** arises when the broker remains silent when having a duty to disclose the known material facts. The disclosure of these conditions allows the third party to either back out of the deal or make provisions in the deal to address the problems or defects. A broker who fails to disclose the known defective conditions of a property can be held liable for the purchaser's subsequent damages.

> *Example:* If a broker is aware that the owner installed electrical wiring poorly and in violation of electrical building code, the broker has a duty to disclose the information.

Brokers should be aware that when they show a property they may be held liable to prospective buyers or lessors, because the broker has had the opportunity to inspect the property and identify potential dangerous conditions.

> *Example:* Christine fell on a temporary step and hit her head while looking at a house that was under construction and listed for sale with McColly Realtors. She sued McColly for failing to warn her of the defective step. The court found that McColly had a duty to warn a prospective buyer of a hidden defect of which the broker was aware.[3]

Some of the common types of nondisclosure include:

1. Mechanical, electrical, and plumbing system issues
2. Cosmetically covered cracks in the foundation or walls
3. Septic-system problems or defects
4. The existence of mold or other hazardous materials
5. Illegal or nonpermitted additions to, buildings on, and modifications to the property
6. Areas that leak water or flood

In the following case, after purchasing a vacant lot, the buyer was informed of subsurface conditions that would greatly increase the cost of construction. The buyer sued the seller and the seller's broker for breach of their duty to disclose.

CASE 7.3

EVIDENCE DEMONSTRATING SELLER'S ACTUAL KNOWLEDGE OF A DEFECT IS REQUIRED TO SHOW A BREACH OF SELLER'S DUTY TO DISCLOSE

EIMAN v. SULLIVAN
173 So.3d 994 (2015)
Florida District Court of Appeal

In 2005, the Eimans purchased a vacant waterfront lot that was to be the site of their future home. The Eimans were informed that before they could obtain a building permit an invasive species of tree on the southern border had to be removed and the land stabilized to prevent erosion. A third party was hired to remove the trees and stabilize the ground with fill dirt. The Eimans never conducted construction or assessments to determine the suitability of the property for building. Instead they decided to purchase a home already constructed in a different area. The next year, the Sullivans purchased the vacant lot from the Eimans to build their own home. The sales contract indicated the Sullivans were purchasing the property "as is" and stipulated a period of time during which the Sullivans could conduct any assessments they believed were "appropriate to determine the Property's suitability for the Buyer's intended use."

The Sullivans never performed any assessments. Following the closing, the Sullivans' builders performed a subsurface investigation to obtain a building permit from the county. The investigation revealed the presence of subsurface conditions consisting of muck, which would increase the construction estimate by $65,000. The Sullivans abandoned construction and sued the Eimans and the Eimans' real estate broker alleging that the parties breached their duty by failing to disclose a not readily observable defect that materially affected the value of the property. The trial court did not find the broker liable but did rule in favor of the Sullivans, awarding them $65,000 in damages. The Eimans appealed.

Language of the Court. *Even if the presence of the muck under the filled-in portion of the property could be considered a material defect, the Sullivans presented no evidence that the Eimans had actual knowledge of this defect. To hold the seller liable the buyer must prove the seller's actual knowledge of an undisclosed material defect.*

The Sullivans argue that the fact that the Eimans removed Brazilian pepper trees and added fill to stabilize the land where the trees were located is evidence of the Eimans' actual knowledge of the subsurface conditions. However, the Sullivans presented no evidence that the Eimans ever actually observed or assessed the subsurface conditions or knew that the conditions would require increased construction costs.

Because the Sullivans failed to present any evidence that the Eimans had actual knowledge of the subsurface conditions of the property, the trial court erred in finding for the Eimans.

Decision. The court of appeal reversed the trial court ruling. The court found no evidence that the Eimans had actual knowledge of the condition of the soil and could not have known it would materially affect the value of the property.

FOCUS ON ETHICS

Is it fair that it is the burden of the buyer to demonstrate the seller had knowledge of the material defect's presence on the property?

Mandatory Disclosures Required by States

Many states require that certain disclosures be made to buyers. Generally, these statutes apply to the sale of residential property sold through the use of a broker and not to commercial properties or properties sold by an owner. Examples of required disclosures may include:

- *Association assessments.* If the property is part of a homeowner association (HOA), the name and amount of the current HOA dues are often required.
- *Death.* If a person has died on the property within the last three years, it must be disclosed to the buyer.
- *Hazard disclosure.* A natural-hazard disclosure states whether the property is in a special hazard zone (flood-zone area, fire hazards, earthquake fault zone, or seismic hazard zone).
- *Insulation.* Disclosure of the type, thickness, and R-value of insulation.
- *Special tax district.* For homes in a special tax assessment district known as Mello-Roos (discussed in chapter 19), the amount of the assessments must be disclosed.
- *Toxic mold.* If toxic mold is present, its existence must be disclosed.

Selling a Property "As Is"

As is
When a property is sold with all known and unknown faults and defects.

When a property is sold **as is**, it means that the seller is offering to sell the property in its current condition without agreeing to correct any known defects. Most bank-owned properties sold after a foreclosure or trustee sale are sold as is.

Latent defects
Defects that are not easily discoverable by reasonable inspection of the property.

Patent defect
A defect that is obvious and apparent or could be discovered upon a reasonable inspection of the property.

Historically, buyers found themselves victimized by buying a defective property that had **latent defects** (defects not discoverable by reasonable inspection of the property) or buying a property for which a broker was aware of material defects and did not have to disclose them because of the "as is" clause. To reduce this problem, brokers now have a much more substantial duty to provide full disclosure to all parties to the transaction. In most states, for residential purchases the courts will uphold an "as is" clause only if the condition was obvious and apparent or the buyer could learn of the defect upon inspection (a **patent defect**). "As is" clauses will not protect the seller or real estate agent for latent defects that the buyer would not reasonably discover. Brokers can still be held liable for misrepresentation and non-disclosure if they fail to provide material information on latent defects on the property.

> *Example:* Assume a property sold as is has a septic tank that routinely clogs and requires repair. If the broker is aware of this issue and does not inform a potential buyer, she may be liable for not disclosing the septic tank issue, even though the property was sold as is.

Exercise 7.1

In each of the following situations, determine whether a fiduciary duty has been breached. If so, state why this is the case.

1. Sally uses Bob, her broker, to sell her property. Bob sells the property to his brother-in-law and fails to disclose his relationship with the buyer to Sally.
2. Broker Bob has secured a listing agreement with Sally. Bob has received three offers on the property. Two offers are above the asking price and have no contingencies to close. One is significantly below the asking price and has several financial contingencies, making it very unlikely that the person will be able to purchase the property. Bob only shows Sally the two offers that are above the asking price on the property.
3. At Broker Bob's open house, Broker Bob hears a couple who are really interested in the property talking about the great school district in which this property is located. Broker Bob is aware that the school-district boundary the couple is referring to ends across the street. The home is within a completely different school-district boundary. Bob says nothing.
4. Broker Bob is asked why the color of the stucco on a house changes in an exterior location near the foundation. Broker Bob is aware that the foundation has had a few recent issues, but he doesn't want to lose a potential sale in the tight real estate market and answers with "I don't know."
5. Broker Bob sells a property to Peter. Bob fails to disclose to Peter that a child had drowned in the pool a few weeks ago and the homeowners were putting the house on the market for this reason.
6. A prospective buyer asks Broker Bob if she would be able to tear down the one-story home and build a two-story home similar to the other homes on the street. Bob responds that local zoning permits the construction of a two-story structure, so the prospective buyer should not have any problems.
7. At an open house, Broker Bob tells a prospective buyer that he should put an offer on the house quickly or risk losing out on the property to other potential buyers. In reality, Bob has no other offers on the property.

Duties of the Client to the Broker

As brokers are required to act in good faith toward their clients, clients have certain duties they owe their broker. A client's duties to the real estate broker often include the duty to compensate, reimburse, and indemnify. Thus, the client has a duty to compensate the broker for services rendered in accordance with the listing agreement. The duty to reimburse requires that the broker be paid for authorized payments and expenses incurred on behalf of the client.

> **Example:** If the broker incurs costs related to staging a home, the broker should be reimbursed for those costs. Staging a home relates to removing clutter or furniture and bringing in different furniture, plants, or property in order to make the home as appealing as possible to the greatest number of prospective buyers.

In many listing agreements, the client also agrees to indemnify the broker for losses suffered if the seller fails to disclose to the broker any material facts and the broker is sued as a result, or in situations where the broker acted lawfully as directed by the client.

The seller's duties to disclose defects in the condition of the property are the same as those of the broker. Generally, the broker and the seller will be jointly and severally liable (the person harmed can sue either or both parties for the entire harm caused) for any misrepresentations a broker makes to a buyer. If a broker relays a misrepresentation from the seller to the buyer, the broker may not be liable for fraud, but he or she could be liable for negligence to the buyer. The seller would be liable to the buyer for fraud.

> **Example:** If a seller deliberately misstated to the broker the status of repairs to the condition of the property, and the broker relayed that information to a buyer, the broker might, in a lawsuit brought by the buyer for misrepresentation, seek indemnification from the seller under the listing agreement.

The client does not owe any fiduciary duties to the broker. In the ordinary case, the client is not required to act with trust and confidence toward the broker as the broker must to the client.

> **Example:** A Virginia real estate broker contended that the seller wrongfully prevented the sale closing so that the broker would not receive a commission. When the Virginia Supreme Court compared the terms and conditions upon which the seller had agreed to sell and those upon which the buyer procured by the broker presented, the court concluded that they were materially different. The seller had no duty to protect the commission of his broker.[4]

Disciplinary Matters and Recovery Funds

State real estate commissions supervise licensees' actions. Real estate transactions are so commonplace that strong public policies have developed to ensure that the licensees act in accordance with state laws and regulations. The purpose of these statutes is to protect the public from unfair and unscrupulous actions. Depending upon the nature of the licensing-statute violation, the licensee can face a range of discipline methods, including private reprimand, license suspension, license revocation, and possible civil lawsuits for damages and criminal prosecutions.

While not universal throughout the states, the following actions often result in license suspension or revocation.

1. *Breach of a fiduciary duty.* Licensees who breach their fiduciary duties to a principal or engage in unethical conduct may have their license suspended.

Continued breaches or an egregious breach may cause the license to be revoked.

2. *Discriminatory practices.* Licensees who discriminate in showing, selling, or transacting property in a discriminatory manner may face discipline by the licensing agency.
3. *Failing to comply with continuing education requirements.* Real estate licensees who do not comply with the state's licensing requirements often have their licenses suspended.
4. *Failing to pay license fee.* If a real estate licensee does not pay the current licensing fee, the license will be suspended until payment is received.
5. *Felony conviction.* While a felony conviction may not prevent a license applicant from becoming a real estate licensee, a felony conviction while licensed may result in the revocation of a real estate license.
6. *Misappropriating funds.* Licensees who commingle funds, split commissions with a non–real estate agent, or secretly profit from a real estate transaction may face discipline from the licensing agency.
7. *Misleading advertising.* Licensees who use misleading or inaccurate advertisements regarding a property may face discipline.
8. *Unauthorized practice of law.* Licensees who practice law without a license may be disciplined by the state licensing agency and by the state bar (the state licensing agency for attorneys).

Due to the risk of litigation, most broker associations offer group errors and omissions (malpractice) insurance for their members at a minimal cost. **Errors and omissions insurance** provides insurance coverage for a broker if she or he is sued for breach of a fiduciary duty, negligence, misrepresentation, and other covered claims. Known as *E&O policies*, these policies do not cover the licensee's intentional conduct, punitive damages, or errors and omissions arising from the licensee's own real estate transactions.

In the following case, a real estate broker's license was revoked following his felony convictions for child abuse.

Errors and omissions insurance
Insurance provided to a broker insuring the broker for breaches of fiduciary duty, negligence, misrepresentation, and other covered claims.

CASE 7.4

PRIOR CONVICTIONS MAY WARRANT TERMINATION OF REAL ESTATE LICENSE EVEN IF THE CONVICTION IS NOT DIRECTLY RELATED

PAUTSCH v. MARYLAND REAL ESTATE COMMISSION
31 A.3d 489 (2011)
Maryland Court of Appeals

Pautsch, a real estate licensee, pled guilty to felony charges of Sex Abuse with a Minor and Child Abuse by Parent. In addition to his criminal sentencing, the Maryland Real Estate Commission revoked his real estate license. The Commission held a hearing regarding the issue. At this hearing a judge was presented with various exhibits, including reports from law enforcement's investigation of Pautsch and witnesses who testified as to Pautsch's character, professionalism, and post-conviction rehabilitation. Based on these findings, the Commission revoked Pautsch's license.

This lead Pautsch to seek judicial review from the Circuit Court of Baltimore City, which affirmed the revocation on the grounds that there was, "competent, material, and substantial evidence to support" the revocation. The Court of Special Appeals affirmed, finding Pautsch did not demonstrate any factual or legal error in the Commission's decision. Pautsch appealed, asserting that to revoke his license the committee must show a relationship between his previous conviction and his specific occupational license.

Language of the Court. *In deriving a nexus between Mr. Pautsch's convictions and the activities engendered under his real estate license, the Commission found convincing the fact that Mr. Pautsch's real estate licenses allow "access to private homes, and to the residents of those homes" by virtue of a "lock box" system:*

Because a real estate license allows an individual access to private homes, and to the residents of those homes, the Commission must take an especially close look at licensees who have been convicted of crimes related to children. Although Pautsch was convicted of crimes involving family members, the Commission is nonetheless cognizant of the fact that Pautsch may come into contact with unsupervised children during the course of activities authorized by a real estate license such as use of the "lock box" system.

With respect to the issue of nexus, the Commission also found that Mr. Pautsch's child abuse convictions negatively impacted Mr. Pautsch's fitness to be a real estate professional.

Based upon the testimony and the exhibits before it, the Commission found that Mr. Pautsch had been engaged in sexually abusive behavior towards minor children throughout a "fifteen-year period," and that, according to the Commission, showed a lack of responsibility, maturity, and trustworthiness on the part of Mr. Pautsch, as a real estate professional, which prevents a finding that the Commission's sanction was arbitrary or capricious.

Decision. The court of appeals affirmed the decision finding that Pautsch failed to present evidence that demonstrated a lack relationship between his convictions and his duties as a real estate broker. Further, he failed to demonstrate that the Commission's decision was arbitrary.

FOCUS ON ETHICS

Should any felony conviction cause the revocation of a real estate license?

Damages Against a Broker

If a broker breaches the contract with the client, the broker is liable for the resulting damages. The injured party will be compensated for the difference between the value of what was promised to that party and the value of what they received.

In addition, other remedies may allow an injured party to sue a broker for:

- *Broker's breach of fiduciary duty.* Damages will be calculated at the amount needed to compensate the injured party for all the harm caused by the breach.
- *Recovery of secret profits earned by the broker.* Brokers who do not fully disclose a financial interest in a transaction are prohibited from profiting from that nondisclosure.
- *Recovery of the broker's commission.* A party may sue to recover the commission paid to a broker in some cases, such as upon the discovery that the broker was not licensed during the transaction, breached a fiduciary duty, or acted as a dual agent without informed consent.

■ *Punitive damages.* If a broker's misconduct was oppressive, fraudulent, or malicious, punitive damages may be awarded. In almost all states, punitive damages are not available in breach-of-contract actions. Punitive damages often arise in real estate litigation over egregious breaches of fiduciary duties.

In the following case, the court addresses the question of whether a principal must sustain monetary loss from the broker's breach of a fiduciary duty to recover the commission paid to the broker.

CASE 7.5

A BROKER WHO BREACHES A FIDUCIARY DUTY IS NOT ENTITLED TO RETAIN ANY PART OF THE COMMISSION

MOORE AND CO. v. T-A-L-L, INC.

792 P.2d 794 (1990)

Colorado Supreme Court

T-A-L-L, Inc. (TALL) entered into an exclusive listing agreement with Moore & Co. (Moore), a real estate company. The agreement called for TALL to pay Moore a commission of 10 percent of the purchase price for the sale of approximately eighty acres of undeveloped land in Adams County, Colorado. Richison, a licensed real estate broker with Moore, handled the listing agreement for TALL.

On March 1, 1982, Tall accepted an offer from Newcomb-Weidner Company (N-W) for $1.4 million. The sale contract expressly provided that the 10 percent commission to be paid by TALL would be divided equally between Moore and N-W, the purchaser.

On March 5, 1982, DG Shelter Products Co. (DG Shelter) submitted an offer to Richison to purchase the property for $1.6 million. Richison stated that the property was under contract with N-W. Two days later, Richison, without the consent of TALL, contacted an officer of N-W and told him that DG Shelter had made an offer of $1.6 million. Richison thereafter had a meeting with N-W and disclosed the terms of DG Shelter's offer to N-W. Shortly thereafter, N-W assigned its contract to purchase the property to DG Shelter for $300,000. At closing, TALL conveyed the property to DG Shelter pursuant to the assignment.

TALL sued Moore for the commission paid because of its agent's (Richison's) breach of fiduciary duty to TALL in disclosing material confidential information to DG Shelter without TALL's knowledge or consent. The trial court held in favor of TALL, stating that Moore's commission should be returned in full. The court of appeals affirmed, and Moore appealed to the Supreme Court of Colorado.

Language of the Court. *A real estate broker, as agent, owes a fiduciary duty to the seller, as principal. The fiduciary duty owed includes the duty to act with good faith and loyalty in all dealings with the seller and to use reasonable care in carrying out the agency agreement. The broker must make a full and complete disclosure of all facts relative to the subject of his agency which it may be material to the principal to know.*

Where the agency agreement expressly authorizes the broker to sell the property, the broker's fiduciary obligation does not end with the execution of a contract of sale but continues up to and through the closing.

Moore's concealment from TALL of information that bears upon the transaction in question will defeat Moore's claim for compensation. The fact that TALL may not sustain an actual monetary loss as a result of Moore's breach of fiduciary duty to TALL will not serve to exonerate Moore. An agent is entitled to no compensation for conduct that is a breach of his duty of loyalty.

Decision. The Colorado Supreme Court affirmed the decision, holding that Moore's breach of

fiduciary duty to TALL resulted in a forfeiture of Moore's right to a commission.

FOCUS ON ETHICS

Should a client have to prove monetary damages in order to recover a commission paid to a broker?

Federal Laws Regulating Brokers

Housing Discrimination

Real estate licensees who participate in certain discriminatory practices may violate federal or state law. The Fair Housing Act (FHA) and the Civil Rights Act of 1964, as amended, prohibit discriminatory practices in the sale or rental of residences and provide the basis for holding real estate licensees liable for participating in discriminatory practices.

Fair Housing Act

The **Fair Housing Act (FHA)** provides everyone an equal opportunity to buy, rent, sell, and live in residential properties. The act prohibits discrimination on the basis of race, color, religion, sex, handicap, familial status, or national origin. Handicap includes discrimination based on a person's physical or mental impairments (sight, mobility, hearing, HIV/AIDS status). Familial status relates to the type of household in which a person resides (such as married, children, senior housing).

> ***Example:*** It is unlawful to refuse to rent to families with children or to charge families extra if they have children.

States may also expand the list of protected classes. The act applies to sellers, real estate agents, lenders, insurers, and appraisers. Prohibited actions that fall under the act include:

1. Refusing to rent, sell, negotiate, or make housing available
2. Providing different access or services to, or denying access to or services in, a membership group or facility
3. Setting different terms, conditions, or privileges for sale or rental
4. Falsely denying that housing is available for inspection, sale, or rental
5. Racial steering or blockbusting (discussed below)[5]

Certain exemptions exist to the FHA. The following are not subject to the FHA requirements and prohibitions:

1. Sale or rental of a single-family home by an owner if (1) no real estate agent is used, (2) the owner currently owns three or fewer single-family homes, and (3) no discriminatory advertising was used
2. Rental of an owner-occupied residential dwelling containing four or fewer units
3. Religious organizations and private clubs limiting sale or rental to members of the same religion or club, unless membership in such religion or club is restricted on account of race, color, or national origin
4. Qualified housing for seniors

Racial Steering

Racial steering is a prohibited form of housing discrimination under the FHA in which real estate agents guide buyers toward or away from properties in neighborhoods based on the neighborhood's racial, ethnic, or religious demographics. Steering may occur directly or through a broker's actions that influence the buyer's choice of location.

Racial steering
Illegal practice of directing minorities to particular areas.

Blockbusting

Blockbusting is another prohibited form of housing discrimination under the FHA in which homeowners are told to sell their homes because people of a particular race, religion, or national origin are moving into the area and housing prices will likely decline because of their presence. Blockbusting is usually accompanied by scare tactics to force current owners to sell their homes at depressed prices.

Blockbusting
The illegal procedure of inducing panic among owners because of fear of minority groups moving into the neighborhood.

> **Example:** A broker might suggest that, with a change in the characteristics of the neighborhood, resale prices will drop precipitously. The broker can then arrange to purchase the homes at reduced prices.

Fair Housing Act Penalties

FHA violations are enforced through civil court actions in federal or state courts (for damages) or by filing a complaint with the state agency or the U.S. Department of Housing and Urban Development (HUD), a federal agency responsible for enforcing fair housing laws.

If a person files a civil suit in either federal or state court, the remedies available to the plaintiff may include the awarding of damages, penalties, an injunction to halt the activity, and possibly punitive damages. HUD can also initiate a lawsuit on behalf of the injured person.

USA Patriot Act

Section 352(a) of the **USA Patriot Act**[6] may require brokers, attorneys, and other real estate professionals to establish anti-money-laundering programs. The act was created to help intercept and obstruct terrorism. Due to the size of real estate transactions, real estate closings have been used to launder money for terrorist organizations.

Specifically, the act requires establishing minimum standards for financial institutions to verify the identity of a customer and requires financial institutions to develop internal policies, procedures, and controls regarding the source and use of real estate funds. Additionally, the program must be independently audited, a compliance officer must be designated, and employees must have ongoing training. Real estate brokers and attorneys are currently exempt from complying with this part of the act while the Department of the Treasury develops regulations.

Key Terms and Concepts

- Real estate licensee, page 136
- Fiduciary relationship, page 136
- Agent, page 136
- Principal, page 136
- Express authority, page 137
- Equal dignity rule, page 137
- Implied authority, page 137
- Apparent authority, page 137
- Ratification, page 137
- Power of attorney, page 138
- Partially disclosed principal, page 138
- Undisclosed principal, page 139
- Real estate broker, page 140
- Real estate salesperson, page 140
- Listing agent, page 141
- Buyer agent, page 141
- Dual agent, page 141
- Designated agency, page 142
- Nonagent broker, page 142
- Listing agreements, page 142
- Statute of Frauds, page 142
- Open listing, page 143
- Exclusive agency, page 143
- Exclusive right to sell, page 143
- Multiple Listing Services (MLS), page 144
- Internet listing services, page 146

- Commission, page 146
- Ready, willing, and able buyer, page 146
- No deal, no commission clause, page 147
- Condition precedent, page 147
- Procuring cause, page 148
- Net listing, page 149
- Finder, page 151
- Fiduciary duty, page 152
- Duty of care, page 152
- Negligence, page 153
- Duty of loyalty, page 153
- Material fact, page 154
- Duty of obedience, page 154
- Commingling, page 155
- Misrepresentation, page 155
- Intentionally misrepresents, page 155
- Sales puffing, page 156
- Intentional nondisclosure, page 156
- As is, page 158
- Latent defects, page 158
- Patent defect, page 158
- Errors and omissions insurance, page 161
- Fair Housing Act (FHA), page 164
- Racial steering, page 165
- Blockbusting, page 165
- USA Patriot Act, page 165

Chapter Summary

- Agency relationships are created when the principal consents to the relationship and has control over the agent. The agent must act on behalf of the principal.

- Three types of agency relationships may be created: general agency, special agency, or universal agency.

- The principal can grant authority to the agent in several ways: through express authority, implied authority, apparent authority, or ratification.

- Generally the principal, and not the agent, is liable to third parties for contracts entered into by the agent on the principal's behalf.

- A real estate broker is a state-licensed special agent hired by a principal, for a fee, to purchase or sell real estate on the principal's behalf.

- A real estate salesperson is a state-licensed special agent who assists a broker in real estate transactions.

- Three main types of real estate agency relationships exist: listing agency, buyer agency, and dual agency. A listing agent works with the seller of the property. A buyer agent is a broker who enters into an agreement with a buyer. Dual agency arises when a broker represents both the buyer and the seller in a transaction.

- Designated agency occurs when different agents within the same firm represent a buyer and a seller. A nonagent broker is a person who represents neither the buyer nor the seller as an agent. The transaction broker is licensed as a facilitator to the closing of the transaction. An intermediary is employed to negotiate a transaction between the parties.

- The listing agreement is the written contract that establishes the agency agreement between the seller and the broker. The types of listing agreements include (1) open listing, (2) exclusive agency, and (3) exclusive right to sell.

- The MLS is a network of exclusive-right-to-sell listings that provides the listing broker with a larger market in which to advertise their listings. Each MLS is tailored to a specific geographic market area of properties.

- In the majority of jurisdictions, brokers are entitled to compensation when a broker presents a ready, willing, and able prospect to the listing seller under the terms and at the price stated in the listing agreement.

- All states and the District of Columbia regulate the licensure of real estate professionals. States create licensing regulations to protect the public from fraud in its dealings with real estate agents and to protect consumers from incompetent or unethical real estate professionals.

- State laws permit individuals to engage in certain activities without requiring a real estate license.

- In many states, acting without a real estate license when a license is required is illegal and may subject the person to criminal penalties, including fines and possible imprisonment.

- A "finder" is an intermediary who brings together parties for a business opportunity or real estate transaction.

- A fiduciary duty is a duty to act in the principal's best interest and not advance the broker's own interests. The broker's fiduciary duties generally begin at the time of retention by the client.

- The duty of care requires that a broker act as a reasonably competent real estate broker would act under similar circumstances. The standard of care for competency is higher than that for the average person.

- The duty of loyalty requires the broker to act in good faith and engage in fair dealing with regard to the principal.

- Brokers generally do not owe a duty to third parties. A broker's liability to third parties is most commonly found in instances of misrepresentation, intentional nondisclosure, and failure to provide state-mandated disclosures.

- Many states require that various disclosures be made to buyers. These statutes, often called Residential Property Disclosure Acts, generally apply to the sale of residential property sold through the use of a broker.

- When a property is sold "as is," it means that the seller is offering to sell the property in its current condition without agreeing to correct any known defects to the property.

- Most broker associations offer group errors and omissions (malpractice) insurance for their members at a minimal cost. Errors and omissions insurance provides insurance coverage for a broker in the event the broker is sued for breaching a fiduciary duty, negligence, misrepresentation, or other covered claims.

- A principal's duties to the real estate broker often include the duty to compensate, reimburse, and indemnify.

- If a broker breaches the contract with the principal, the broker is liable under contract law for the resulting damages.

- The Fair Housing Act (FHA) and the Civil Rights Act of 1964, as amended, prohibit discriminatory practices in the sale or rental of residences and provide the basis on which to hold real estate licensees liable for participating in discriminatory practices.

- Racial steering is a form of housing discrimination prohibited under the FHA in which real estate agents guide buyers toward or away from properties in neighborhoods based on their race.

- Blockbusting is another form of housing discrimination under the FHA in which homeowners are told to sell their homes because people of a particular race, religion, or national original are moving into the area and housing prices will likely decline because of their presence.

- The USA Patriot Act may require brokers, attorneys, and other real estate professionals to establish anti-money-laundering programs.

Chapter Problems and Assignments

1. Benny Buyer employs Ronald Realtor to assist him in the purchase of a home. Ronald is a licensed real estate salesperson who serves a variety of clients. One day, Benny finds a property that he wishes to purchase. However, it just so happens that Ronald's brother wants to purchase the same property. Ronald's brother is not his client, but he has discussed his interest in the property with Ronald. After finding out Benny intended to submit an offer, Ronald called his brother to submit a higher offer before Benny. How would you classify the relationship between the parties?

2. Identify the type of authority the agent in the following scenarios.
   a. Dawn enters into a listing agreement with Taryn, a real estate broker, to sell her commercial building.
   b. Jamal is an up and coming hip-hop artist. Because of his recent success, he is now in the market for a home. Jamal instructs his manager to go out and search for properties that are within 10 miles of his recording studio. His agent finds several different properties of various amounts and of different styles to present to Jamal.
   c. Assuming the same facts from b, except Jamal gave his manager a price range of $5 million dollars and wanted a modern style home and his agent presents him such homes.
   d. Zander is a professional athlete who has a hired a real estate agent to find him a property in a wealthy neighborhood for $8.7 million. The real estate agent finds a property just outside of the neighborhood that is otherwise perfect. The agent submits an offer on behalf of Zander. Although the property is outside the neighborhood Zander wanted, he loves the property so much he doesn't say anything to the agent.

3. Under what circumstances can/will a power of attorney be revoked?

4. In what situation would a principal not be solely liable to third parties for contracts entered into by the agent on the principal's behalf? In these situations, who is held liable?

5. Anthony is a real estate broker for Realty Inc. Breanne is a real estate salesperson who assists Anthony in his transactions. Breanne is required to do a visual inspection of the property. Upon her inspection she finds a small section of mold on the wall. In fear of losing the sale, Breanne covers the mold with picture. On the forms Breanne submits to the buyer, she does not disclose the mold. After closing, the buyer discovers the home's mold problem has become severe and sues Breanne and Anthony. Who would be liable under the circumstances?

6. What potential problems might arise when a broker acts as a dual agent? What do you think are the benefits of being a dual agent?

7. If a broker has many agents located in different areas, is it fair to impose liability on brokers even though their agents act as independent contractors and generate their own leads and clients?

8. Because of the overwhelming number of realtors, it is often difficult for homeowners to distinguish the good ones from the bad. Are there any safeguards in place to ensure that these agents and brokers are in fact acting in the best interest of their clients? Are there any additional safeguards you think should be implemented? Why?

9. A typical real estate transaction contains many pages of preprinted forms, most of which aim to prevent liability for the broker. Do you think it is better practice to continue using these preprinted forms or to allow the parties to contract as they please? What are the pros and cons of both options?

10. Research your state law to determine what mandatory disclosures are required in your state for residential transactions of real property.

End Notes

1. *Mohamed v. Robbins*, 23 Ariz. App. 195, 531 p.2d 928, 930.
2. *Hagans v. Woodruff*, 830 S.W. 2d 732 (Tex. 1992).
3. *Masick v. McColly Realtors, Inc.*, 858 N.E.2d 682 (2006).
4. *Campbell v. Sickels*, 89 S.E.2d 14 (1955).
5. U.S. Department of Housing and Urban Development, *Fair Housing — It's Your Right*, https://portal.hud.gov/hudportal/HUD?src=/program_offices/fair_housing_equal_opp/FHLaws/yourrights (last accessed October 26, 2017).
6. Pub L 107-56, 115 Stat 272.

Chapter 8
The Purchase Contract

[W]hen I was six years old, my father said to me, "Son, stocks may rise and fall, utilities and transportation systems may collapse. People are no damn good. But they will always need land, and they'll pay through the nose to get it. Remember," my father said, "land." – Lex Luthor, Superman (1978)

Learning Objectives

1. State the requirements to form a binding contract.
2. Analyze offers and acceptances.
3. Recognize common terms in real estate agreements.
4. Understand how contracts are interpreted.
5. Explain the importance of the Statute of Frauds.
6. Understand the defenses to the enforcement of a contract.
7. Describe the remedies to enforce a contract.

Chapter Outline

- Introduction
- Contract Formation
- Case 8.1: *Crow v. Crow's Sports Center*
- Case 8.2: *Simek v. Tate*
- Essential and Important Terms of a Real Estate Contract
- Case 8.3: *Humbert v. Allen*
- Interpretation of Contracts
- Performance
- Remedies for Breach of Contract
- Case 8.4: *Uzan v. 845 UN Limited Partnership*
- Case 8.5: *Stambovsky v. Ackley*
- Defenses to the Enforcement of Contracts
- Raw Land Sales: Interstate Land Sales Full Disclosure Act

Opening scenario

The Delgados bought a home "as is" from National Bank. The bank's real estate agent represented to the Delgados that the home was fundamentally sound and had no structural defects. The Delgados inspected the home and found no obvious defects. Following closing, the Delgados discovered significant structural defects and sued the bank for the cost of fixing the defects. The bank denied knowledge of the real estate agent's representations and denied that it had been aware of the home's condition. The bank asserted that a property sold "as is" meant that the bank made "no express or implied warranties of any kind" to the buyers. Should the bank be held liable for the costs of fixing the home's defects?

Introduction

Real estate transactions are completed in two steps. First, a contract is formed. In this chapter, we introduce contract law and discuss what is necessary to create a real estate contract, how to resolve ambiguities that arise, and what remedies are available for breaches of contracts. Second, the property is financed and insured, and the deed or other instrument of conveyance is given to the buyer. This second step is the topic of chapters 9 and 10.

The study of contracts is important in real estate because contracts provide the terms that bind the two parties in real estate transactions. Most people consult attorneys after a contract has been executed rather than before. However, once a contract has been executed, there is little an attorney can do to change its terms. It is during contract negotiation and execution that a party can receive the most value from an attorney's services. With that in mind, this chapter aims to inform students about contracts so that they can avoid having to pay attorneys significant amounts of money to fix avoidable contract problems.

Contract Formation

Contract
An agreement enforceable by law.

A **contract** is a legally enforceable promise. One of the basic principles regarding contract law is the freedom to contract. The parties voluntarily enter into a contract, and the courts do not look at a contract's fairness to each party. Absent fraud, courts usually will not remake or reform a contract solely based on the fact that a party made a poor bargain, such as a buyer substantially overpaid for a property.

The following elements are required for parties to create a valid real estate contract:

1. Agreement (offer and acceptance)
2. Consideration

3. Legal capacity of the parties
4. Legal purpose
5. Satisfaction of the Statute of Frauds (writing or evidence of record)

Agreement

The first element, agreement, requires the parties' mutual consent. Mutual consent occurs when an offer is made and an acceptance is issued. The mutual consent must be freely made by both parties and communicated to the other party. An **offer** expresses the intent to enter into a binding and enforceable contract. That intent may be stated orally, in writing, or by inference from the participants' conduct. In real estate transactions, the prospective buyer is usually the party who makes the first offer to the seller. The **offeror** is the person who makes the offer, and the **offeree** is the person who receives it.

No unique words or phrases (such as "I offer") are required to create an offer, but an offer must meet three elements: (1) there must be an objective intent to be bound by the offer, (2) the terms of the offer must be expressed definitely and with reasonable certainty, and (3) the offer must be communicated to the other party.

Offeror
The person who makes an offer to enter into a contract.

Offeree
The person who receives an offer to enter into a contract.

Objective intent
A theory of contract law providing that the intent to be bound by an offer is determined by using a reasonable person standard and not by the party's subjective intent.

1. *Objective intent.* In order for a court to determine whether the party had an **objective intent** to be bound by the offer, it must determine whether a reasonable person, viewing the circumstances, would conclude that the party intended to engage in a contract.

   Many factors are considered in determining an objective intent, including the extent to which agreement has been reached on all the offer's terms, whether it is the type of contract that must be in writing to be enforced, the significance of the contract, and the circumstances surrounding the offer (for example, was it written on a napkin in a bar over several drinks?).

   If the offer is made in jest, anger, or great excitement, no objective intent to make the offer exists.

   Example: After finding yet another crack in the stucco of the house with a fair market value of $350,000, the angry homeowner shouts, "I hate all the problems this house has! I'd sell this house for $100 just to get rid of it." A nearby neighbor, hearing this statement, would not be able to accept this offer because it cannot be taken seriously.

   Example: Using the preceding example, if the homeowner, while speaking to a neighbor, complains about all of the issues of the house and, wearing a serious facial expression, states, "I'd sell this house for $300,000 just to get rid of it," the homeowner has created a valid offer.

   In the above examples, the court would look to the circumstances to determine whether there was an objective intent to be bound.

   In addition, communications using language or conduct that consist of preliminary negotiations or invitations to bargain are not offers. Statements such as, "Would you consider ...," "If I bought this, I would like to pay no more than ...," "I couldn't sell this house for less than $125,000," and, "Are you interested in selling this for $50,000 less?" do not constitute offers. General advertisements and mailings are invitations to make an offer; therefore, the listings on an MLS® are not offers to purchase a home but are invitations to make an offer to purchase one.

2. *Definite and reasonably certain terms.* The offer must be clear enough so that the party can decide whether to accept or reject the offer's terms. In real estate transactions, the identity of the parties, the price, a property description, and a time for performance are commonly required terms.

Example: If a homeowner placed a sign on her front lawn that stated, "For Sale by Owner, $200,000 cash, as is, 30 days to close escrow," that promise, although not made to a specific person, would be sufficiently definite to be enforced.

3. *Communicating the offer to the offeree.* To create an offer, the offer must be communicated to the offeree. The communication can be oral, in writing, or made through any means of nonverbal communication.

Most real estate transactions occur utilizing standard purchase-agreement forms that abide by the above requirements to present an offer.

■ ■ ■ Contract Negotiated in a Foreign Language

In most states, if a contract is orally negotiated in a foreign language, the contract must be written in the same language, or a translation of the contract must be furnished in the language in which the contract was negotiated.

Termination of Offers

An offer, once made, does not last in perpetuity. An offer can be terminated, and once that happens, the offer cannot thereafter be accepted. If an acceptance is attempted after an offer has expired, it is treated as an offer, and the other party can choose whether to accept or reject the offer. The most common means by which an offer can be terminated for a real estate transaction include the following:

1. *Lapse of time.* Many standard real estate contracts provide for the offer to be valid for three calendar days after the offer is made. If the contract does not provide for a specific date of termination, a reasonable amount of time is allowed to accept the offer, given the property's circumstances and location of the property. After that time, the offer terminates.
2. *Rejected.* An offer may be rejected. If the offeree rejects the offer, it is terminated and cannot thereafter be accepted.
Counteroffer
A response to an offer containing terms that does not match the original offer.
3. *Counteroffer.* A **counteroffer** arises when the offeree's response contains terms or conditions differing from the original offer. Any change to the offer, even one that is seemingly minor, creates a counteroffer. Counteroffers terminate the original offer and create a new offer that can be accepted, rejected, or replaced by a new counteroffer.

Example: Simon offers to sell Bryshawn one acre of land for $10,000. Bryshawn responds with a counteroffer that he will pay $9,500 for the acre of land. If Simon rejects the counteroffer of $9,500, Bryshawn cannot accept the offer of $10,000 because Bryshawn's counteroffer terminated it.

4. *Revoked.* An offer may be revoked or withdrawn at any time prior to its acceptance, even if the offeror has promised to keep it open for a certain period of time, unless a valid option contract has been created (see discussion below). The offer is not revoked until the offeree has notice of the revocation. Until that time, the offeree may still accept the offer.

Example: Sam lists a home for $175,000. Brian submits an offer to purchase Sam's home for $175,000. However, before Sam accepts Brian's offer, Brian finds another home for sale by Sarah for $150,000. Brian can revoke his offer to Sam any time prior to Sam's acceptance of Brian's offer.

Example: Sean lists a home for sale. Brittany tours his home at 9:00 a.m. and is quite interested in it. If Sean gives Brittany a one-week exclusive option to purchase the home, Sean can still revoke the option at any time. (Note, in this example, Brittany did not pay Sean for the option.)

5. *Death or incompetency of either the offeror or the offeree terminates the offer, effective immediately.* However, some states hold that the death of either party does not terminate the contract and instead makes the contract binding upon the decedent's estate.
6. *Destruction of the subject matter of the contract prior to acceptance.* Many states provide that, if the property is destroyed prior to acceptance, the offer is terminated. Once the contract has been accepted, the risk of destruction falls on the seller (that is why the seller should maintain property insurance until title to the property has transferred).

Option Contracts: Limiting the Right to Revoke

Some real estate transactions require considerable due diligence and time to complete the transaction. For example, a buyer may wish to investigate the property's condition and review the condition of the property's title or zoning for a specified period of time prior to closing. An option period arises if the seller promises not to revoke the offer during this time.

During the option period, the offeror could still revoke the offer at any time prior to the offeree's acceptance. However, if the offeree provides consideration (that is monetary compensation) to the offeror to keep the offer open for the option period, an **option contract** is created. The offeror cannot revoke the offer. No specific amount of consideration is required; the key is that some sort of consideration was given. An option with consideration creates a contract to keep the offer open during the option period. Even if the offeror revokes the option after consideration has been paid, the offeree may still accept the offer and create a contract.

Option contract
A contract created when an optionee provides consideration to the optionor to keep an offer open for an agreed-upon time. This type of contract prevents the optionor from revoking the offer during the option period.

Example: Sean lists a home for sale. Brittany sees the home at 9:00 a.m. and is quite interested in it. If Sean gives Brittany a one-week exclusive option to purchase the home, and Brittany gives Sean $100 to keep the option open for the week, Sean cannot revoke the option during the one-week option period.

Unlike typical offers, when an option has been given, the death of either the offeror or the offeree does not terminate the offer. If the offeree dies, the decedent's estate has the power to exercise the option. If the offeror dies, the estate will be required to honor the offeree's acceptance of the option.

In the following case, a lessee brought action against the lessor, seeking specific performance (that is, forcing the sale) of an option to purchase agreement between the parties.

CASE 8.1

AN OPTION TO PURCHASE AGREEMENT MUST PROVIDE THE METHOD TO DETERMINE THE PURCHASE PRICE

CROW v. CROW'S SPORTS CENTER

119 So.3d 352 (2012)

Mississippi Court of Appeals

In May 2005, Martha Crow and her husband entered into a "Second Amended Lease Agreement" with the Lynn and Rhonda Lambert. The agreement included an option to purchase stating that at the end of the term or upon the death of Mary or her husband, the Lamberts had the option to purchase the property for a fair market value as determined by a licensed real estate appraiser. The option required the Lamberts to provide written notice to the succeeding lessors with proof of the appraisal and evidence of the ability to purchase within 60 days of the option becoming operative.

Crow's husband passed away on April 5, 2010. By means of a letter dated May 25, 2010, the Lamberts informed Crow of their decision to exercise the option to purchase. With their letter the Lamberts included an appraisal of the property for $47,000 and evidence of their ability to purchase. Crow denied their purchase offer, as the property was appraised on July 18, 2007, for $110,000, and the Crows had the property reappraised on June 23, 2010, for $105,000. The Lamberts filed suit against Crow because she had refused to accept their offer to purchase. The trial court found that the Lamberts had complied with the provision of the Second Amended Lease and were entitled to purchase the property for $47,000. Crow appealed.

Language of the Court. *A contract's terms must be definite, and "without some written evidence of purchase price or a method of determining a purchase price," the contract is a mere "memorandum of intent." In this case, the option to purchase provision states that the Lamberts "have the option to purchase said property for a fair market value as determined by appraisal by a licensed real estate appraiser. . . ."*

Here, there was no stated purchase price, but there was a clear method of determining one. The contract states that the option to purchase the property is for the fair market value. However, the court did not follow the proper method of determining the purchase price. Instead, he arbitrarily found that the lowest appraised price of $47,000 submitted by the Lamberts was the fair market value, even though two other appraisals found the property to be worth $110,000 in 2007 and $105,000 in 2010, both more than twice the appraisal submitted by the Lamberts.

The intent of the parties is clear. They intended to sell and purchase the property for the fair market value as determined by a licensed real-estate appraiser. In this case, two appraisals are more than twice the amount of the third. One would think that qualified licensed professionals would not be so far apart on the valuation of property. Otherwise, the implication is that the appraisers have submitted appraisals that favor their respective clients, as opposed to a true fair market value.

Decision. The court of appeals reversed the trial court and ordered an independent appraisal to determine the property's fair market value. The court held that the trial court erred in allowing the Lamberts to purchase the property for $47,000 when there was so clearly a discrepancy in fair market value.

FOCUS ON ETHICS

How often would appraisers favor the party who hired them? Does using three appraisers unduly increase the cost of the transaction?

Acceptance

Once an offer has been made, **acceptance** is the manifestation of the offeree's approval of the offer's terms. Only a person to whom the offer has been made can accept an offer. A third party who overhears the offer and wants to accept it cannot.

In real estate transactions, the **mirror image rule** requires that the acceptance must be in the same terms and conditions as the offer. The addition or deletion of terms in an acceptance creates a counteroffer.

A grumbling acceptance of "I accept, but I wish the price were $10,000 less" is still an acceptance. However, other terms cannot be added or omitted to create a valid acceptance. If additional terms are added or terms are omitted, the acceptance is treated as a counteroffer.

> *Example:* If the offeror states, "I will sell you my vacant land for $25,000," and the offeree responds, "I accept so long as we can complete the transaction within 30 days," then the offeree's response is not in the exact same terms as the offer and is treated as a counteroffer and not as an acceptance.

The offeree must also communicate the acceptance to the offeror. If the offer requires acceptance to be communicated in a particular manner (as an example, via personal delivery), the acceptance must be communicated in that manner to be valid. If the offer requires a particular manner of acceptance and that requirement is not observed, the acceptance is treated as a counteroffer. If the offer does not specify any particular means of acceptance, then acceptance may be made by any reasonable means.

Mirror image rule
A rule in contract law requiring the offeree to accept the terms as stated in the offer.

Timing of Acceptance and Revocation

Under what is commonly known as the **mailbox rule**, acceptance is effective upon dispatch, if the requested manner of acceptance delivery was used. If other means of acceptance were used (for example, standard-mail delivery instead of overnight delivery), acceptance is effective upon receipt. An offer can require that acceptance be effective upon receipt. Once dispatched, the contract is created. For example, if a seller states that all offers must be received by the seller's broker by 5:00 p.m., an offer received thereafter is untimely and does not have to be accepted by the offeror-seller.

A revocation is effective when received by the offeree. To be effective, the revocation of an offer must be communicated to the offeree prior to the offeree's acceptance.

Mailbox rule
A rule in contract law that provides an acceptance is effective upon dispatch, if the requested manner of acceptance delivery was used, even if it was lost in transmission.

Example: Henry submits a written offer to purchase a home for $250,000. Later, Henry decides to revoke the offer and sends a written revocation to the seller. After Henry sends the written revocation but before it has been received, the seller calls Henry to accept the offer. Henry has entered into a contract to purchase the home because the seller accepted the offer prior to her receipt of the revocation.

The mailbox rule becomes very important when a seller receives multiple offers. If the seller enters into negotiations with multiple potential buyers by submitting counter-offers to more than one prospective buyer, the seller may become liable under two (or more) contracts to sell the home if multiple buyers accept the offer before the seller can revoke the offers to the other buyers. A seller could face legal action for breach of contract by both of the buyers.

Consideration

Consideration
A rule of contract law requiring an exchange of value between the parties.

Consideration is the bargained-for exchange given by both parties in a transaction. If only one party provides consideration and the other side does not, a contract has not been formed. In most real estate transactions, the consideration for the transaction is the transfer of title to the property and the payment of the purchase price. Many states allow the real estate contract to simply provide a recital of consideration, which is a written statement identifying valid consideration in the transaction

Consideration need not involve money. Two parties could agree to exchange promises to each other to refrain from building structures, or both parties could exchange properties. Both of those situations are supported by consideration.

Courts allow parties the freedom to contract and generally avoid determining the adequacy of the amount of consideration given by either party. Absent fraud, courts will usually not remake or reform a contract solely because a party made a poor bargain, such as a buyer substantially overpaying for property.

Example: Sarah, currently living in Portland, Oregon, has inherited a property in South Dakota from her mother. Sarah has no desire to live on the property and lists it for sale. She accepts an offer to sell the property for $50,000. If Sarah later discovers that the property was worth significantly more and wants to rescind the contract because the consideration paid was too low, a court would not set it aside because of the failure to price it at fair market value.

Illusory promise
A promise which is not binding on a party. The party can elect to perform or not perform the promise. The resulting contract lacks consideration and is not enforceable.

Not all promises are valid consideration. An **illusory promise** is a promise in which one or both parties can elect not to perform. An illusory promise is not consideration.

Example: If a homeowner tells his neighbor that he will sell his house for $175,000 unless he changes his mind, the promise is illusory. Because the homeowner can elect not to perform, the promise is illusory and not valid consideration.

Capacity of the Parties

To enforce a contract, all parties must have the capacity to enter into a valid agreement. Some persons are not competent to understand the nature and consequences of such an agreement. The law presumes certain classes of persons to be incompetent:

■ *Minors* (under the age of majority, 18 years, unless legally emancipated). A contract made by a person under the age of 18 is voidable at the minor's option. **Voidable** means the person can elect to perform or not perform the contract. The minor can choose whether to enforce the contract or not. The other contracting party does not have such a choice; only the minor has the choice. In other states, such a contract would be void, meaning it never came into existence.

■ Persons under a *conservatorship* or *guardianship*.

■ Persons declared by a court to be *legally incompetent*. Persons who are of unsound mind or who have been declared incompetent by a court may not make a valid contract. They lack the ability to manage their legal affairs, and the court will treat the contract as if it never came into existence. A person will be legally incompetent if she is incapable of understanding or comprehending the nature of the transaction. A failure to read or to understand complex terms in an agreement is not enough to be declared legally incompetent. Contracts entered into by legally incompetent people are void. **Void** contracts are considered as having no legal affect and cannot be enforced.

> *Example:* If an elderly person has dementia affecting his ability to understand or comprehend that he is selling real estate or the value of that real estate, a contract entered into by that person will be void.

■ *Intoxicated persons.* Persons who are under the influence of drugs or alcohol at the time of entering into a contract are entitled to have the contract set aside by a court. They must be so intoxicated that that they are incapable of understanding or comprehending the nature of the transaction.

Legal Purpose

Contracts must also have a lawful purpose. Contracts violating the law are unenforceable.

> *Example:* If a real estate developer bribed public officials in connection with a proposed development, the resulting benefits obtained by the developer would be illegal.

The Statute of Frauds

The **Statute of Frauds** requires that certain contracts must be evidenced by a writing, or have been evidenced by some note or memorandum, to be enforceable. The writing requirement is satisfied by anything that evidences a writing, so long as the terms are certain and definite as to the parties, property, consideration, subject matter, and time of performance.

With a few exceptions (such as in the case of wills and testamentary trusts), the use of electronic signatures and electronic records in commerce have the same legal effect, validity, and enforceability as a "wet ink" signature. In real estate transactions, DocuSign®, an electronic signature technology service, is frequently used to collect electronic signatures from the parties to a real estate transaction. The individual needing to sign a document receives an email, follows the directions to electronically sign their name, and the system completes the rest. Signatures are obtained much faster electronically than through previous methods.

Voidable
Where a person can elect to perform or not perform the contract.

Void
Contracts that have no legal affect and cannot be enforced.

Statute of Frauds
A rule of contract law requiring certain contracts to be in writing to be enforceable.

The Statute of Frauds was intended to eliminate uncertainty, prevent fraud, and prevent continuing disputes involving alleged oral agreements over important matters. Each state has adopted a form of the Statute of Frauds. As the Statute of Frauds pertains to real estate transactions, the following contracts must be in writing or evidenced by a writing to be enforceable:

- Contracts involving a transfer or conveyance of an interest in land

  Example: Deeds, mortgages, easements, liens, or agreements affecting the use of real property must be in writing.

- Contracts for a lease of real property for longer than a year

  Example: A month-to-month lease does not need to be in writing to be enforceable; however, a lease longer than a year must be in writing to be enforceable.

- Contracts that cannot be possibly performed within one year from the date of the contract

Both parties do not necessarily have to execute (sign) the writing. Any agreement that is subject to the Statute of Frauds requires that the writing must be signed by the party against whom enforcement is sought. If the party against whom a person seeks to enforce the writing has not signed the agreement, the agreement cannot be enforced against that party.

> *Example:* Sarah orally agrees to sell Braxton a commercial property. Braxton drafts a written contract and signs his name, but Sarah never signs the contract. The contract cannot be enforced against Sarah because she has not signed the agreement; however, if Sarah wanted to proceed with the transaction, she could enforce the contract against Braxton because he signed it.

A contract may be created by piecing together several agreements that, when construed together, create a contract. These agreements may be assembled from faxes, e-mails, and written correspondence between the parties.

Strict application of the Statute of Frauds may not always lead to fair and equitable results. If a contract has been fully performed, a party cannot thereafter attempt to rescind or cancel it because it does not satisfy the Statute of Frauds since there is no prejudice to either party, as both have performed their apparent agreement.

Part Performance Exception

While full performance satisfies the Statute of Frauds, in real estate transactions, courts have also created a part performance exception for oral contracts that would otherwise violate the Statute of Frauds. While states may have unique requirements, generally the **part performance exception** allows oral real estate contracts to be enforceable if any two of the following three elements are met: (1) the purchase price has been fully or partially paid, (2) the party has received possession of the property, and (3) valuable improvements have been made to the property.

Example: Jacob enters into an oral agreement to sell his home to Jennifer. Jennifer pays Jacob $150,000 for the property, and Jacob gives Jennifer the keys to the property and allows her to take possession of it. This is an oral contract satisfying the part performance exception to the Statute of Frauds.

In a few states, however, part performance of an oral contract is not recognized. In the following case, the parties disagreed as to which settlement agreement was to be enforced. The seller argued that the actions of the parties demonstrated partial performance of the latter settlement agreement, which should therefore be enforced.

CASE 8.2

PARTIAL PERFORMANCE MAY BE SUFFICIENT CONSIDERATION FOR AN ORAL REAL ESTATE AGREEMENT

SIMEK v. TATE
231 P.3d 891 (2010)
Wyoming Supreme Court

Simek purchased property from Carol Brehm in Wyoming. Brehm gave Simek the "first right to purchase" the property if Brehm decided to sell it. Brehm died the following year and gave no indication of her desire to sell the property prior to her death. Simek filed a lawsuit against Brehm's estate, alleging Brehm had breached the sales contract and sought specific performance of the purchase option. The district court dismissed the case because the purchase option was specifically conditioned upon Brehm's desire to sell the property, and that she had not indicated she wanted to do so.

After the district court ruling, Brehm and Simek reached a settlement that provided for Simek's purchase of Brehm's residential property. The court rejected the settlement. In response, Brehm and Simek continued to negotiate the terms of the sale.

They reached a new agreement, but Simek never signed the agreement. As part of this agreement Simek was given a key to the property. Simek used this key to access the property to secure contractor bids for possible renovations to the property. Simek sought to purchase the property at a reduced price, and the case proceeded to trial. The trial court held that there was partial performance of the agreement and enforced it against Simek at the higher sales price. Simek appealed.

Language of the Court. *In the instant case, the trial court concluded that the parties intended for their agreement to be effective upon its oral consummation. Simek accepted and took possession of the premises before the agreement was reduced to writing. Simek retained possession of the premises for several months despite not having executed the written agreement. Simek utilized his possession of the premises to bring in contractors for remodeling assessments, which was in furtherance of the oral agreement.*

We cannot say in the present case that the district court erred as a matter of law. If we consider the factors mentioned to do other than what the district court did in this case would be to return these parties to a seemingly never-ending dispute.

Decision. The Supreme Court of Wyoming affirmed the trial court's decision that the partial performance of the agreement was sufficient to establish an oral agreement between the parties.

FOCUS ON ETHICS

Should a court enforce an oral agreement when one of the parties seeks to change the purchase price?

Equal Dignity Rule

A related rule to the Statute of Frauds is the **equal dignity rule**, which requires that if a contract must be in writing to be enforceable, then the appointment of an agent with regard to that agreement must also be in writing. Thus an agreement to retain a real estate broker or salesperson must be in writing to be enforceable.

These written contracts are important to real estate brokers and salespersons because a person who performs services without obtaining a statutorily required license (such as a real estate broker's license) is often unable to collect a fee for the services rendered.

Exercise 8.1

In each of the following situations, identify if a contract exists. If a contract does not exist, describe the element of contract formation or enforcement that is missing.

1. Jayden submitted an offer to purchase a single-family home. Prior to acceptance, a tornado destroyed this home. Immediately after the tornado and before Jayden had a chance to revoke the offer, the seller accepted Jayden's offer.

2. Olivia, not thinking that Noah had the funds to purchase a home, offered to sell her home to him for $150,000 with closing to occur in 30 days. Noah, believing this to be a great bargain, immediately accepted Olivia's offer. The home had a fair market value of $190,000, and Olivia never intended to sell Noah the home. She wanted Noah to admit that he could not afford to purchase the home.

3. Logan is interested in purchasing Isabella's condominium for $90,000; however, Logan needs a week to make sure that he can qualify for a loan amount required to purchase it. On Monday, Logan gives Isabella $500 to keep the offer open for one week, and Isabella accepts. On Wednesday, Isabella decides not to sell her condominium and calls Logan, telling him she is not interested in selling anymore. On Thursday, after receiving confirmation that he can qualify for the loan, Logan calls Isabella and accepts the offer to purchase the condominium for $90,000.

4. While at an open house, Mia becomes very interested in a property. The real estate agent says the property is offered as is for $375,000 with closing to occur in 45 days. Mia knows that the seller has already moved from the home, and she is very interested in purchasing it. Mia decides to accept the offer but adds a condition that closing is to occur in 30, not 45, days.

5. Upon reaching the age of 17, Natalie is entitled to a distribution from her trust fund. At that time, she decides she should invest in real estate. She submits an offer on a home, which is accepted.

6. Mackenzie orally agrees to purchase a home from Elizabeth for $275,000. Mackenzie and Elizabeth are friends and don't think they need the formalities of employing a real estate agent or having their agreement in writing. Mackenzie provides Elizabeth a $50,000 deposit toward the purchase price of the home and has a contractor begin installing landscaping in the backyard. After seeing how attractive the property will be with the landscaping Mackenzie is installing, Elizabeth tells Mackenzie that she cannot purchase his home because the agreement was not in writing. Mackenzie is furious and wants to proceed with closing of the sale.

Essential and Important Terms of a Real Estate Contract

Once the buyer and seller have reached an agreement, the Statute of Frauds requires real estate contracts to be in writing (unless the part performance exception applies). It is important to be familiar with the common terms used in them.

Identification of the Parties

Real estate transactions must identify the parties who hold an ownership interest in the property at issue in the transaction. For example, the names of the buyer and the seller must be provided in the contract. They are usually provided near the beginning of the contract. Each party signing the contract and their capacity (that is the buyer, seller, and broker) should be specified. The address, telephone number, and e-mail addresses of the parties should be provided as well.

The seller's status and how the seller currently holds title and the buyer's status and how the buyer wants to hold title should also be identified. A **natural person** may be married but may desire to purchase the property as his or her separate property.

Natural person
A living human being.

> *Example:* This Agreement for the Sale of Commercial Real Estate ("Agreement") is made by and between Kevin Fields, a married man, as his sole and separate property ("Seller"), and Devon Fields, a married woman, as her sole and separate property ("Buyer").

Where a legal entity (known as an **artificial person**) will hold title to real property, the identity of the legal entity as well as the identity of the representative signing the contract and the representative's corporate authority (such as the president) to enter into the contract should be provided.

Artificial person
A legal entity that is not a human being but is recognized in law as having legal rights and duties (such as a corporation, limited liability company, or partnership).

Property Description

Real estate contracts must adequately describe the real property. In most states, a property description is sufficient if it identifies the parcel of land sought to be transferred without using external evidence. Commonly, real estate transactions will use a common address (that is a street number and name, city, county, and state). If a full legal description of the property (such as using metes and bounds, government survey description, or a subdivision plat map, all of which are discussed in chapter 6) is available, it is preferable to use such description, often by referencing the recorded document, but many states do not require it. If a property description does not sufficiently identify the real property, the contract is not enforceable.

Fixtures and Personal Property

As discussed in chapter 4, fixtures often transfer with title to real property. One of the tests that must be satisfied for an item to be considered a fixture is the intention of the parties. Many real estate contracts list the items to be specifically either included or excluded as a fixture to the real estate contract. This avoids any ambiguity related to whether a specific item will transfer with title to the real property.

> *Example:* Included in this sale are all existing fixtures and fittings permanently attached to the property, including existing electrical, mechanical, lighting (including chandeliers and ceiling fans), plumbing, and heating fixtures; HVAC equipment; gas logs and grates; built-in appliances; satellite dishes; garage door openers/remote controls. Also included as a fixture is the kitchen refrigerator. Items that are specifically excluded from sale as a fixture include the children's playset in the backyard.

Broker Relationship

If a licensed real estate broker represents the buyer or seller of the property, then that relationship should be identified. If a broker is representing one or both parties, the broker's name, company name, address, phone number, e-mail address, and other related contact information should be provided. If the broker is acting as a dual agent, both parties should acknowledge and provide informed, written consent to the broker representing both the buyer and the seller of the property. The real estate contract may include a provision covering the broker's compensation.

> *Example:* Broker shall be entitled to a commission of 2.5 percent of the acquisition price. Broker shall be entitled to the commission if the buyer enters into a contract to acquire property on terms acceptable to the buyer. Said commission is conditioned upon the Seller completing the transaction.

Purchase Price and Payment

The contract must indicate the property's purchase price. The price is often provided as a fixed sum; however, the parties can set the price based upon its size, such as a price per acre determined by a survey.

Once the parties determine a purchase price, the method of payment should be identified in the purchase contract. If a buyer cannot pay for the entire property in cash, the property must have some form of financing, which can be determined by taking the purchase price and reducing it by any deposits made on the property. The most common methods of acquiring real property include (1) by cash purchase; (2) by the buyer securing a new loan from a lender; or (3) by the purchaser assuming an existing mortgage or taking subject to an existing mortgage. Chapter 9 discusses the details related to these financing mechanisms.

Deposit

A buyer should also indicate the amount of earnest money deposit. **Earnest money** is the buyer's initial deposit. A deposit is not required to purchase property, but it assures the seller that the buyer is interested in purchasing the property. The buyer may also deposit additional sums of money after execution of the agreement as a further incentive for the seller to sell the property to the prospective buyer. Deposits, if used, reduce the financing or cash required to purchase the property. If a buyer breaches a contract before the sale has closed, the law usually entitles the seller to keep the earnest money deposit as liquidated damages.

> *Example:* Deposits, regardless of the form of payment and the person designated as payee, will be paid in U.S. dollars to the broker, who will retain deposits for the seller in an escrow account in conformity with all applicable laws and regulations until consummation or termination of this agreement. The law requires only real estate brokers to hold deposits in accordance with the rules and regulations of the state real estate commission. Checks tendered as deposit monies may be held uncashed, pending the execution of this agreement.

Earnest money
A buyer's initial deposit, which is often damages the seller may keep should the buyer breach the contract before the sale has closed.

Quality of Title

A contract for the sale of real property usually requires the seller to provide evidence of marketable title as a condition of completing the sale. Marketable title is title free from any encumbrances or liens (except those the buyer is aware of and has agreed to accept in the sales contract) and free from reasonable doubt that the seller owns title. With marketable title, a reasonably prudent person, if aware of all the facts, would accept title to the property. Chapter 10 discusses title and title insurance.

> *Example:* The property will be conveyed with good and marketable title that is insurable by a reputable title insurance company at the regular rates, free and clear of all liens, encumbrances, and easements, excepting, however, the following: existing deed restrictions; historic perseveration restrictions or ordinances; building restrictions; ordinances; easements of roads; easements visible upon the ground; easements of record; and privileges or rights of public service companies, if any.

Possession of the Property

Usually a buyer will take possession of the property immediately after the closing or settlement date; however, a buyer can take possession of property either before or after such date. In commercial properties, it may be common for a buyer to take possession before closing to begin tenant improvements. In residential properties, it is common to take possession after the closing to allow the seller to move out of the property once closing has occurred — up to three days is common. If possession occurs on a day other than the closing date, the parties should negotiate the terms of liability, insurance, maintenance, and any expenses that will need to be paid prorated on a daily basis (such as current taxes, interest on mortgages, and homeowner association fees).

> *Example:* Possession is to be delivered by deed, existing keys, and physical possession to a vacant property free of debris, with all structures broom-cleaned, at the day and time of settlement.

Example: Possession shall be delivered to Buyer at 5:00 p.m. on the date of the close of escrow.

Allocation of Costs and Apportionment

The parties will incur expenses in transferring real property. A contract should identity which party is responsible for the specific costs, and if the parties will share any costs, the agreement should provide the percentage of contribution. Expenses incurred in closing often include natural hazard disclosure report fees, inspection reports, escrow fees, title insurance, transfer taxes, recording fees, surveys, homeowner association fees, home warranty plans, and appraisal fees.

Example: Seller shall pay for a natural hazard zone disclosure report.

Example: Buyer will pay for the following: (1) title search, title insurance, or any fee for cancellation; (2) flood insurance, fire insurance, hazard insurance, or any fee for cancellation; (3) appraisal fees and charges paid in advance to the mortgage lender; and (4) buyer's customary settlement costs.

Certain costs may be apportioned between the parties at the time of closing. Commonly apportioned costs include real property taxes and assessments, interest on mortgages being assumed by the buyer, rents (for income-producing properties), homeowner association dues, and insurance premiums. Apportioning the expenses holds a buyer and seller responsible for their fair share of costs based on when they take possession of the property.

Example: The following items shall be prorated between buyer and seller on the basis of a 30-day month as of the closing date: real property taxes relating to the property, insurance premiums relating to the property, and rents collected relating to the property together with the balance of any security deposits paid by each tenant.

Closing or Settlement Date

Closing
The completion of all conditions in a real estate transaction necessary to convey title between the parties.

The **closing** date is the date on which the buyer and seller agree to complete the transaction. Some states refer to this as settlement. The closing is the goal of a real estate transaction. At the closing, the buyer receives a deed, and the seller receives payment for the property. The date of closing should be indicated in the contract. It is often listed as either a set date in the future or as a specified number of days after the contract's formation.

Example: Close of escrow shall occur 45 days after acceptance.

Closing Documents

A contract may provide the documents that must be delivered or executed at closing. A list of closing documents is more common in commercial real estate transactions. The documents to be delivered and executed at closing often include the deed to transfer title, certificate of nonforeign status complying with Internal Revenue Code §1445, promissory notes, mortgages, assignments of leases affecting the property, assignments of all guaranties and warranties relating to the property, and a bill of sale of any equipment and fixtures on the property.

> *Example:* At the close of escrow, seller shall deliver to buyer the following documents, which shall be in a form satisfactory to buyer: (a) a special warranty deed conveying the property to buyer; (b) all leases affecting the property and an assignment of them to buyer; (c) assignments of leases signed by tenants of the property; (d) an assignment of all guaranties and warranties relating to the property; and (e) a bill of sale of the equipment and fixtures on the property.

Buyer's Inspection of Property

In all real estate transactions, sellers are required to make certain disclosures, as required by law. For example, sellers must disclose any known facts that would materially affect the value or desirability of the property when that information is unlikely to be discovered by a buyer performing a diligent search. Even though a seller has provided for such disclosures, real estate contracts often provide a buyer the right to inspect the property before closing.

While many buyers will perform a visual inspection before placing an offer, buyers usually have a contingency on the enforceability of a contract based on the receipt of satisfactory inspection reports. Common inspections that buyers will perform include wood destroying pest inspections, mold inspections, natural hazard reports, soil reports, surveys, and any other inspections a buyer may desire. After such inspections, the buyer often requests the seller to perform repairs. While a seller is usually not required to perform such repairs, sellers commonly perform reasonable repairs.

> *Example:* Buyer shall have the right, at buyer's expense unless otherwise agreed, to conduct inspections, tests, surveys, investigations, and other studies within twenty (20) days after the parties have executed the contract. Buyer has permission to enter on the property to make tests, surveys, or other studies of the Property, provided that no invasive or destructive investigations occur. Buyer shall give the seller, at no cost, copies of all Buyer's reports.

The contract will provide a time frame in which the buyer has to perform inspections and make a request for repairs to the seller. Often during this time, the buyer can cancel the contract, without any liability, if the buyer is not satisfied with the inspection reports.

Statutory Disclosures

Many states require specific disclosures be made to the buyer. These disclosures often pertain to the presence of hazardous substances including asbestos, hazardous waste, lead, toxic mold, radon, and natural hazards.

As Is Provision

Real estate, especially where a lender is selling the property, is sold "as is." An **"as is" clause** is inserted by sellers into real estate contracts to avoid making a misrepresentation to the buyer regarding a property's condition. Note that even with an "as is" provision, the seller is still obligated to disclose latent defects known by the seller.

Latent defect
A defect not readily observable or perceived. Frequently, a defect that is hidden.

A **latent defect** is one that cannot be observed upon ordinary inspection, is not readily apparent, or is hidden or concealed. Most courts would hold that the seller owes a duty of full disclosure in cases of latent defects because the purchaser would not have the means to discover the true facts prior to closing. The presence of an "as is" contract means the seller does not need to make any repairs for apparent defects in the property.

Example: Buyer acknowledges and agrees that: (i) buyer has been given the opportunity to inspect the property; (ii) buyer will accept the property in its "AS IS CONDITION WITH ALL FAULTS" as of closing; and (iii) buyer is relying solely on its inspections and not on any statement, information, and/or other material from seller with respect to the property.

Risk of Loss

Problems can arise if a property is damaged or destroyed through no fault of either party, such as by a hurricane, tornado, earthquake, flood, fire, or vandalism, before closing occurs. Risk of loss clauses indicate which party, after the contract has been entered into, bears the risk for property damaged or destroyed through neither party's fault.

In most states, the risk of loss falls on the buyer once the contract has been executed. While the seller will maintain property insurance until closing, buyers should secure insurance on the property once the property comes under contract, even though they do not yet have title to it. In other states, the risk of loss is on the seller until the buyer takes possession of the property.

Example: If any damage to any portion or destruction of the property occurs before the closing, the seller must elect either (a) to give buyer a credit for the entire amount of such loss and assign to buyer the right to collect any insurance proceeds with respect to such loss, or (b) to terminate this Agreement. If any damage to or destruction of the property occurs, the closing date will be extended until the amount of the insurance proceeds is determined and seller has made any election permitted under this paragraph.

Contingencies

The parties may also place contingencies into the contract. A **contingency** is an event that *may* occur. Contingencies are placed in a contract to protect a party. If a contingency is not met, the party is not obligated to complete performance of the contract, unless the party voluntarily waives the contingency. A buyer may place an offer to purchase a new home contingent on selling his current home, securing a mortgage with an interest rate below a certain percentage, having the home appraised for at least the purchase price, or having the home pass inspections that the buyer will perform. A seller may accept an offer contingent on finding a replacement home within a certain number of days.

Example: Obtaining the loan below is a contingency of this Agreement. Buyer shall act in good faith and expeditiously to obtain the designated loan terms. Obtaining a deposit, down payment, and closing costs are not a contingency. The offer is contingent on Buyer obtaining a first loan in the amount of [the purchase price less any deposits] at a maximum interest rate of 6.0% fixed rate, balance due in 30 years, amortized over 30 years. Buyer shall pay loan fees/points not to exceed 1.0.

The following case discusses whether a contingency in a purchase and sale agreement must be strictly met or if financing in excess of the purchase price satisfies the condition required in the agreement.

CASE 8.3

A MORTGAGE CONTINGENCY IS SATISFIED IF THE OFFER OF FINANCING EXCEEDS THE PURCHASE PRICE

HUMBERT v. ALLEN

89 A.D.3d 804 (2011)

New York Supreme Court, Appellate Division

Mr. and Mrs. Allen entered into a contract to purchase a condominium unit from Christine O'Keeffe Humbert in Nassau County, New York, for a purchase price of $475,000. Upon executing the contract, the Allens deposited a down payment of $47,500 into an escrow account managed by their lawyer. The contract of sale contained a mortgage contingency clause that entitled the Allens to a refund of their down payment if they could not secure a commitment for a mortgage loan in the amount of $427,500.

The Allens applied for a mortgage loan in a far greater amount, intending to purchase another condominium unit in addition to the unit owned by the plaintiff. Although the Allens received a commitment from a bank for a loan in the amount of $846,000, they instructed their lawyer to cancel the contract of sale with Ms. Humbert in accordance with the mortgage contingency clause. Ms. Humbert sued the Allens and their lawyers for breach of contract and sought to retain the down payment as liquidated damages.

Language of the Court. *The Allens did not establish that they would have been entitled to the return of their down payment. As the record indicates, and the Allens do not dispute, they applied for a mortgage loan in an amount far greater than that which was specified under the express terms of the mortgage contingency clause, and they received a commitment from a lender for a loan in an amount almost double that which they needed to secure pursuant to the terms of the contract of sale. Under these circumstances, the Allens did not have grounds to cancel the contract of sale pursuant to the terms of the mortgage contingency clause.*

Decision. The court affirmed the lower court's ruling. The Allens did not meet the express terms of the contingency clause and were not entitled to the return of the $47,500 down payment.

FOCUS ON ETHICS

Can an intentional breach of contract be considered acting ethically?

Execution

As the Statute of Frauds provides, real estate contracts require the evidence of a writing that includes the essential terms and conditions of the transaction. The parties should **execute** the contract in their representative capacities. Failure to provide that a signor is executing a document in a representative capacity may make the signor personally liable for the duties and obligations contained in the contract.

Execute
To sign a legal document.

Example: [Signature for corporation]
Buyer, Inc., a Pennsylvania corporation

By: _____
Its:

[Signature for partnership]
Buyer Partnership

By: _____
Name: _____
Its: General Partner

[Signature for trust]
Buyer Trust Name

By: _____
Name: _____
Trustee of Buyer Trust Name, u/t/d [date of trust]

■ ■ ■   Example of a Purchase and Sale Process

Pre-purchase	Seller employs a real estate broker.
	Property is advertised for sale, often through the use of MLS® and open houses.
	A prospective buyer views the property and makes an offer to the seller to purchase the property.
	Buyer and seller negotiate any terms and conditions of the property through counteroffers.
Purchase	Written contract signed by the parties.
	A closing agent is identified or escrow is opened.
Due diligence	Buyer investigates the condition of the property; the seller, if required, provides a property-condition disclosure statement.
	Experts are retained to inspect the premises to determine the actual condition.
	An appraisal is performed on the property.
	Contingencies are removed from the property (such as financing and the correction and repair of any defects discovered during inspection).
	Preliminary title report is provided to the buyer.
Closing	Once all contingencies have been removed and the seller provides a marketable title, the money is exchanged, and title transfers from seller to buyer.
Recordation	The deed is recorded along with any mortgage or deed of trust.

Interpretation of Contracts

Contracts are interpreted in a manner consistent with the mutual intentions of the parties at the time of contracting. When a contract is clear and unambiguous, the plain meaning of the contract governs its interpretation. However, when an ambiguity exists, courts apply certain rules to interpret the contract and may reference extraneous documents to explain the ambiguity. These rules promote the uniform treatment of contracts so that parties can rely upon them to predict how an agreement will be performed or a remedy applied in the event of a contract's breach. Ambiguities in a contract are resolved as follows:

1. A clear and unambiguous written contract controls over any negotiation or alleged intent of either party.
2. Handwritten words prevail over both preprinted and typed words.
3. Typed words prevail over preprinted words.
4. Ambiguities are resolved against the party that drafted the contract.
5. When words conflict with figures or numerals, the words control.

Example: The preprinted text of a purchase and sale contract may have a provision of items included in the sale. This provision may include in the sale, for example, "fireplace inserts, gas logs, and grates." If the seller wanted to keep the gas logs, she might submit a counteroffer to a prospective buyer and strike through the term *gas logs*, then write in, "Gas logs are excluded from sale." In such a case, the gas logs would be excluded because the written words prevail over the preprinted words.

When interpreting a contract, courts also have certain rules with which they interpret a contract. These rules include the following:

1. When a time for performance is unstated, a reasonable time is implied.
2. The ordinary meanings of words are interpreted as a reasonable person would interpret them. If the word has a special meaning as used in a customary trade or business practice, the special meaning is used.
3. A court may not make a new contract for the parties or rewrite their contract. However, a court may recognize that mere inadvertence or obviousness may have caused the parties not to supply a term. The court may imply a term to carry out the reasonable intentions of the parties.
4. Generally, the word *shall* is mandatory and *may* is permissive.

Parol Evidence Rule

The **parol evidence rule** prohibits the admission of evidence of any prior or contemporaneous oral or written negotiations or agreements that contradict, modify, or vary the terms of a contract intended to be the complete and final expression between the parties. The parol evidence rule was developed to help create finality with agreements and to reduce fraudulent claims made after a contract has been executed; allegations of

Parol evidence rule
A rule used in interpreting written contracts preventing any oral or written statements that alter, contradict, or are in addition to the terms of a written contract.

other oral or written side agreements or terms that vary from the terms of the contract will be ignored.

A **merger clause** or **integration clause** is often used to help strengthen the argument that the writing is intended to be the final and complete expression between the parties. These clauses often specifically note that the agreement is full and complete and that any evidence, oral or written, that contradicts the agreement is prohibited.

> *Example:* A merger clause might state, "This agreement encompasses the entire agreement between the parties and supersedes all previous understandings and agreements between the parties, whether oral or written."

The parol evidence rule applies to written contracts only. The rule is especially important to real estate contracts because of the Statute of Frauds' requirement for a writing.

Parol evidence is permissible for a few exceptions and may be used in the following circumstances:

1. To establish a defense to the enforcement of the contract (that is, to show that the contract was entered into as a result of misrepresentation, fraud, duress, undue influence, or when consideration is lacking for the contract).
2. To explain and interpret existing ambiguous language or terms.

> *Example:* Tina purchases a home from Jordan. During the negotiation, Tina asks Jordan if any issues have occurred with the swimming pool equipment. Jordan states that the pool equipment is "as good as new," but she is aware that the equipment needs significant servicing to fix several major repairs that would not be discovered during a reasonable inspection. The exception to the parol evidence rule would allow for the admission of Jordan's oral statement to Tina in a suit against Jordan for the misrepresentation.

Performance

Performing a contract means carrying out the purposes the parties intended to result from their agreement. When a contract is fully performed, nothing remains to be done by either party, and the parties are discharged from further obligations to each other. Until the parties are discharged, both parties are obligated to complete performance.

Novation: Substituting a Party to a Contract

Sometimes a party who has entered into an enforceable contract does not want to continue performing the contract. Rather than terminating the contract with the other party and thereby subjecting themselves to possible damages, the first party may instead seek a novation of the contract.

Novation
A substitution of a new agreement or party for an existing one.

Novation is the creation of a new contract in which a third party is substituted for one or more of the existing parties to the contract. With a novation, the contract obligations of the party substituted out are terminated. A novation requires the existence of a valid contract, agreement to the substitution by all parties to the original contract, and the creation of a new and enforceable contract.

Remedies for Breach of Contract

A **breach** occurs when a contract is not fully performed. When a party has not fully performed his obligations, the innocent or nonbreaching party is entitled to relief from the other party's breach of contract. The typical remedies available when a party has breached a contract include: (1) specific performance, (2) liquidated damages, (3) monetary damages, or (4) rescission of the contract.

Specific Performance

By ordering the **specific performance** of a contract, a court can compel a party to perform its terms. A court may order specific performance where monetary damages are not an adequate remedy to the nonbreaching party. As a general rule, real property is considered unique; when a seller breaches a contract but is able to perform the contract, specific performance allows the buyer to sue to force the seller to sell the property according to the terms of the contract. As noted, the breaching party must be able to perform the contract for the court to grant specific performance. If it is impossible to perform a contract, such as if the seller does not actually own title to the real property, the court will not order specific performance of the contract.

When a buyer breaches a contract by refusing to purchase the property, a court requires the buyer to pay the agreed-upon purchase price. In such case, the buyer then receives title to the real property.

Liquidated Damages

Many residential real estate contracts provide for liquidated damages. With **liquidated damages**, the parties agree at the time of the contract's formation what the damages will be in the event of a breach. Where a liquidated damages clause exists, it is the exclusive remedy for damages. For the liquidated damages clause to be enforceable, the damages must have been difficult to determine at the time of entering into the contract, and the amount identified as liquidated damages must have been reasonable at the time of entering into the contract.

> **Liquidated damages**
> A contract provision whereby the parties agree at the time of entering into the contract what the amount of damages will be in the event of a breach of contract.

Many residential listing agreements provide that the earnest money deposit (down payment) be awarded as a valid liquidated damages clause. Some states limit the amount of earnest money that can be used as liquidated damages, with any amount over a certain percentage of the purchase price or total monetary amount deemed a penalty and unenforceable.

Liquidated damages may not be used as a penalty. Where damages are punitive or the amount of damages is unconscionable, the liquidated damages will be considered a penalty and is unenforceable

> **Example:** If Buyer fails to complete this purchase because of Buyer's default, Seller shall retain, as liquidated damages, the earnest money deposit. The amount retained as liquidated damages shall be no more than 3 percent of the purchase price. Any excess shall be returned to Buyer.

The following case discusses the enforceability of a liquidated damages clause involving a sale in a high-rise building in New York City.

CASE 8.4

A LIQUIDATED DAMAGES CLAUSE IS ENFORCEABLE EVEN IF THE AMOUNT SEEMS EXCESSIVE AT THE TIME OF THE BREACH

UZAN v. 845 UN LIMITED PARTNERSHIP
778 N.Y.S. 2d 171 (2004)
New York Supreme Court

In October 1998, 845 UN Limited Partnership ("845 UN") began to sell apartments at the Trump World Tower, a luxury condominium building to be constructed at 845 United Nations Plaza. Donald Trump was the managing general partner of 845 UN. Cem Uzan and Hakan Uzan, two Turkish billionaire brothers, sought to purchase multiple units in the building. The Uzan brothers entered into contracts to purchase seven apartments at Trump World Tower. Two penthouse units on the 90th floor and two penthouse units on the 89th floor were subject to this litigation. The contract provided that, in the event of default not cured within 30 days, 845 UN was entitled to keep as liquidated damages the down payment and any interest earned on the down payment at the time of the default.

On September 11, 2001, terrorists attacked New York City by flying two planes into the World Trade Center, the city's two tallest buildings, killing thousands of people. The Uzan brothers, concerned about future terrorist attacks, defaulted in closing on the penthouse units. 845 UN sent a notice to the brothers to cure the default, which they failed to do. Thereafter, 845 UN kept the 25 percent down payment, totaling $8 million, in an escrow account. The Uzan brothers filed suit, alleging that the 25 percent down payment of $8 million was an unenforceable penalty.

Language of the Court. *Donald Trump stated that he sought 25% down payments from preconstruction purchasers at the Trump World Tower because of*

the substantial length of time between contract signing and closing, during which period 845 UN had to keep the units off the market. Trump also stated that down payments in the range of 20 to 25 percent are standard practice in the new-construction luxury-condominium submarket in New York City.

Marilyn Weitzman, president of a nationwide real estate consulting firm headquartered in New York City, echoed Trump's opinion that 20 to 25 percent down payments are customary in New York City for new-construction condominium apartments because of the volatility of the market. Weitzman also noted that the demographic profile for potential purchasers in the luxury-condominium submarket includes many foreign nationals, who are inherently high-risk purchasers because their incomes and assets are often difficult both to measure and to reach.

Real estate down payments have been subject to limited supervision. They have only been refunded upon a showing of disparity of bargaining power between the parties, duress, fraud, illegality, or mutual mistake. It is clear that the Uzan brothers are not entitled to a return of any portion of their down payment. Here the 25% down payment was a specifically negotiated element of the contracts. There is no question that this was an arm's-length transaction. The parties were sophisticated business-people, represented by counsel, who spent two months at the bargaining table before executing the amended purchase agreements. Further, the record evidences that it is customary in the precon-struction luxury condominium industry for parties to price the risk of default at 25% of the purchase price. Finally, there was no evidence of a disparity of bargaining power, or of duress, fraud, illegality, or mutual mistake by the parties in drafting the down payment clause of the purchase agreements.

Decision. The court dismissed the complaint. 845 UN was entitled to retain the $8 million as liquidated damages.

Monetary Damages

If the contract does not provide a liquidated damages clause and specific performance is not required (that is, monetary damages would be sufficient), the nonbreaching party is entitled to monetary damages. **Damages** are designed to compensate the nonbreaching party by placing them in a position equivalent to the one that would have resulted if the contract had been performed.

> *Example:* If a buyer breaches the contract to purchase a property for $350,000 and the seller can resell the property at $325,000, the seller is entitled to damages of $25,000 (that is, the difference in price between that stated in the original contract and the price at which the seller was able to resell the property).

A nonbreaching party will only be compensated for damages that the nonbreaching party incurred because the contract was not performed. The party cannot be placed in a better position because of the breach.

> *Example:* If a buyer breaches the contract to purchase a property for $350,000, and the seller can resell the property at $375,000, the seller is not entitled to any damages.

Damages may also include any incidental costs resulting from the breach. Incidental costs may include the costs such as a title report or property appraisal. In the case of rental property, a breach may also result in lost profits from renting the property, which can also be recovered.

Damages
Compensation for the nonbreaching party by placing the nonbreaching party in a position equivalent to the one that would have resulted if the contract had been performed.

Rescission

Rescission is an action to cancel a contract. Instead of providing a nonbreaching party with monetary damages or requiring the contract to be performed, the parties undo the transaction. The remedy of rescission is invoked in cases of misrepresentation, fraud, or duress.

> *Example:* After purchasing a property, the buyer determines that the foundation has many structural defects yet the seller represented in the sale documents that the foundation was structurally sound. Instead of suing for the damages for the cost of repairing the foundation, the buyers may seek to rescind the contract.

Rescission
Cancellation of a contract. It places the parties in their original positions prior to contract.

Restitution
Restoration of both parties to their original positions prior to the formation of the contract.

When a party seeks to rescind the contract, both parties are required to make restitution. By returning any benefits that were conferred, **restitution** returns the parties to their original positions: it is as if the contract had not been performed. On breach by the seller, the buyer may rescind the contract and recover the earnest money (down payment) deposit. On breach by the buyer, the seller can rescind the contract and recover any out-of-pocket expenses incurred. Rescission and restitution should not place a party in a better position than the party would have been in if the contract had been fully performed.

> *Example:* After two parties enter into a purchase and sale contract, they agree to rescind the contract. At the time of the rescission, the buyer has incurred $100 for a termite report and $500 for an appraisal. The parties can rescind the contract, and the seller will pay the buyer $600 in restitution.

Contract Remedies	
Specific Performance	Court compels a party to perform the terms of the contract.
Liquidated Damages	The parties agree at the time of the contract's formation what the damages will be in the event of a breach.
Monetary Damages	Absent a liquidated damages provision, a party will seek money damages. The amount will be equal to the harm suffered.
Rescission	The contract is cancelled. Rescission places parties as they were before the contract was entered into.

Figure 8.1. Contract Remedies

In the following case, the buyer brought action against the seller and the seller's real estate agent for rescission of the purchase contract. The buyer claimed that the seller and his agent knew the house was haunted when the property was sold, but they failed to disclose this information to the buyer.

CASE 8.5

SELLER'S FAILURE TO DISCLOSE HOUSE MAY BE HAUNTED WAS SUFFICIENT TO WARRANT RESCISSION OF A CONTRACT

STAMBOVSKY v. ACKLEY

169 A.D.2d 254 (1991)

New York Supreme Court, Appellate Division

Stambovsky moved to Nyack, a small suburb of New York City, near Sleepy Hollow, of Headless Horseman fame. He purchased a house from Ackley. At the time of the sale, Ackley and his real estate agent knew the house they had just sold to Stambovsky was haunted by poltergeists (ghosts). It was a widely held belief in the community that the house was haunted by ghosts. This was even reported as fact in local and national publications. Unfortunately, Stambovsky, the buyer, was unaware that the house was believed to be haunted.

After Stambovsky moved in, he learned of the reports that the house was haunted. He was told that the seller and members of her family had on numerous occasions over the last nine years seen the ghosts. Stambovsky sued for rescission of the contract. The trial court dismissed his complaint, stating there was no legal remedy for his claim. Stambovsky appealed.

Language of the Court. *From the perspective of a person in the position of Stambovsky, a very practical problem arises with respect to the discovery of a paranormal phenomenon: "Who you gonna' call?" as the title song to the movie "Ghostbusters" asks. Applying the strict rule of caveat emptor to a contract involving a house possessed by poltergeists conjures up visions of a psychic or medium routinely accompanying the structural engineer and Terminix man on an inspection of every home subject to a contract of sale.*

The notion that a haunting is a condition which can and should be ascertained upon reasonable inspection of the premises is a hobgoblin which should be exorcised from the body of legal precedent and laid quietly to rest.

In this instance, Stambovsky met his obligation to conduct an inspection of the premises and a search of available public records with respect to title. It should be apparent, however, that the most meticulous inspection and the search would not reveal the presence of poltergeists at the premises or unearth the property's ghoulish reputation in the community. There is no sound policy reason to deny plaintiff relief for failing to discover a state of affairs which the most prudent purchaser would not be expected to even contemplate.

Where a condition which has been created by the seller materially impairs the value of the contract and is peculiarly within the knowledge of the seller or unlikely to be discovered by a prudent purchaser exercising due care with respect to the subject transaction, nondisclosure constitutes a basis for rescission as a matter of equity. Any other outcome places upon the buyer not merely the obligation to exercise care in his purchase but rather to be omniscient with respect to any fact which may affect the bargain. No practical purpose is served by imposing such a burden upon a purchaser. To the contrary, it encourages predatory business practice and offends the principle that equity will suffer no wrong to be without a remedy.

Decision. The court modified the trial court's dismissal of the complaint and allowed for the rescission of the contract.

FOCUS ON ETHICS

Should a buyer have a duty to review local and national publications regarding a property before purchasing?

Defenses to the Enforcement of Contracts

In some situations, an otherwise enforceable contract may be held voidable (that is, the party harmed may affirm or reject the contract). The usual defenses to the enforcement of real estate contracts are:

1. Misrepresentation (fraud)
2. Duress
3. Undue influence

Misrepresentation

Misrepresentation
A form of fraud arising
from an intentional
false representation of
a material fact to
another person upon
which reasonable
reliance is placed to
that party's detriment.

Misrepresentation arises when a party intentionally misleads another party into entering into a contract. Unfortunately, misrepresentations occur frequently in real estate transactions. A seller may deliberately misrepresent the condition of the property or other facts relating to the property that would materially affect the buyer's decision to enter into the agreement or to complete the transaction. The elements necessary to establish misrepresentation vary under state law, but generally they include:

1. Misrepresentation of a material fact (one that is important to the reasons for entering into a contract)
2. Misrepresentation made with the intent to deceive
3. A situation in which an innocent party reasonably and justifiably relied upon the misrepresentation

As previously discussed, misrepresentation can involve the intentional nondisclosure or concealment of material facts from the other party (such as the condition of the property or pending lawsuits relating to the property). In addition, negligent misrepresentation can occur when a party states a material fact without any reasonable knowledge of its truthfulness and another party justifiably relies on the statement.

Duress

Duress
A defense asserted to
the enforcement of a
contract because a
party was subjected to
unlawful pressure or
coercion to enter into
the contract.

Duress occurs when one party, by means of wrongful threats or force, induces the other party to consent to a contract out of the other party's fear or apprehension. Duress can include physical or psychological threats or threats of severe economic harm that will occur unless one party's wishes are obeyed by the other.

Undue Influence

Undue influence
A defense asserted to
the enforcement of a
contract arising from
the misuse of a
fiduciary relationship.

Undue influence arises when a person in a dominant position takes advantage of another person's mental, emotional, or physical weakness and persuades that person to enter into a contract. In other words, it arises when a fiduciary (person owing utmost care to another) misuses that position to gain personal advantage.

> *Example:* A conservator is a person appointed to supervise another person's financial affairs, the conservatee. A conservator may not cause persuade the conservatee to sell property to the conservator or others below market value or upon unreasonable and unfair terms.

Raw Land Sales: Interstate Land Sales Full Disclosure Act

Congress passed the Interstate Land Sales Full Disclosure Act (ILSFDA) to protect consumers from fraud and abuse in the sale or lease of unimproved land sold through interstate commerce (commerce crossing over state lines). Although once used to seek rescission of contracts with unsavory developers, recently federal courts have expanded the act to include preconstruction sales of condominium units sold through interstate commerce. The ILSFDA has helped to curb abuse and fraud created by common promotional-purchase schemes for properties that offered little disclosure regarding the status and cost of road and utility installation. Too many people were being duped into buying retirement or vacation "dream lots," only to discover that the lots were not what had been advertised.

The act is frequently used to rescind contracts in areas affected by natural disasters (such as hurricanes and floods) or during times of financial crisis (after the "Great Recession"). During these times, the act has been a popular means by which purchasers can avoid buying a property or can rescind a dissatisfying purchase.

To Whom the Act Applies

The ILSFDA applies only to the sellers or lessors of 100 or more lots or parcels of subdivided land who sell these lots by using the U.S. mail or any other instrument of interstate commerce (such as through television advertising, e-mail, websites, and national publications).

The act includes several important exemptions in which such sales and leases do not need to comply with the ILSFDA. Some of these exemptions include:

- Lots in a subdivision with fewer than 25 lots
- Lots in a subdivision of 20 acres or more in size
- Sales of securities by a real estate investment trust (REIT)
- Land owned by the government
- Cemetery lots

The act also provides exceptions for intrastate land developers (advertising and selling within the same state only). Generally, for an intrastate land developer to be exempt from complying with the ILSFDA, it must:

- Provide for a personal on-the-lot inspection of the lot purchased or leased
- Disclose to the buyer who has responsibility for building and maintaining roads, water, and sewer utilities, and when they will be completed
- Provide that the agreement may be revoked within seven days of its execution

Because the act defines a "developer" as "any person who, directly or indirectly, sells or leases, or offers to sell or lease, or advertises for sale or lease any lots in a subdivision," real estate brokers who actively promote the sale of lots in any unregistered subdivision could be regarded as sharing the owner's responsibility to comply with the act.

Requirements of the Act

The ILSFDA requires developers to file a statement of record with the Consumer Financial Protection Bureau (CFPB) before offering to sell or lease any unimproved lot. The statement of record requires the disclosure of such items as legal descriptions; range of selling prices or rents; availability of sewer and other public utilities, including water, electric, gas, and telephone; and the proximity of the subdivision to nearby municipalities.

In addition, a developer must provide the prospective purchaser with an approved property report, and any advertising or promotional material must be consistent with the information required to be disclosed in the property report. The property report provides the buyer with the information required in the statement of record, usually in a more user-friendly format.

Penalties for Violating the ILSFDA

Rescission Rights

A buyer who has received the property report required under the act is given seven days to rescind the agreement after its execution. If a developer fails to comply with the disclosure requirements, a buyer has two years after its execution to rescind the contract. Once a rescission occurs, the developer must refund the purchase price of the lot; the developer may also be required to pay the reasonable costs of all improvements made by the buyer on the lot. Once a developer is faced with repurchasing numerous properties, bankruptcy filing by the developer is a clear possibility.

Civil and Criminal Penalties

In addition to the possible rescission of the contract, developers who fail to comply with ILSFDA can be subject to both civil and criminal penalties. Civil penalties range from $1,000 to $1,000,000. Criminal penalties may arise for willful violations, subjecting the developer to fines of up to $10,000 and/or up to five years imprisonment.

Key Terms and Concepts

- Contract, page 172
- Offer, page 173
- Offeror, page 173
- Offeree, page 173
- Objective intent, page 173
- Counteroffer, page 174
- Option contract, page 175
- Acceptance, page 177
- Mirror image rule, page 177
- Mailbox rule, page 177
- Consideration, page 178
- Illusory promise, page 178
- Voidable, page 179
- Void, page 179
- Statute of Frauds, page 179
- Part performance exception, page 180
- Equal dignity rule, page 182
- Natural person, page 183
- Artificial person, page 183

- Earnest money, page 185
- Closing, page 186
- As is clause, page 187
- Latent defect, page 188
- Contingency, page 188
- Execute, page 189
- Parol evidence rule, page 191
- Merger clause, page 192
- Integration clause, page 192
- Novation, page 192
- Breach, page 193
- Specific performance, page 193
- Liquidated damages, page 193
- Damages, page 195
- Rescission, page 195
- Restitution, page 196
- Misrepresentation, page 198
- Duress, page 198
- Undue influence, page 198

Chapter Summary

- Contracts are legally enforceable promises.

- The following five elements are required to form a valid real estate contract: (1) agreement (offer and acceptance), (2) consideration, (3) legal capacity of the parties, (4) legal purpose, and (5) satisfaction of the Statute of Frauds requirement of writing or evidence of one.

- Offers express an intent to enter into a binding and enforceable contract. To create an offer, three elements are necessary: (1) an objective intent to be bound by the offer, (2) definite and reasonably certain offer terms, and (3) communication of the offer to the other party.

- An offer may be terminated by the lapse of time, it may be rejected, a counteroffer may be made, or the offer may be revoked. The death of either the offeror or the offeree terminates the offer. The subject matter of the contract may be destroyed prior to acceptance, terminating the offer.

- Generally, offers may be revoked at any time, even if the offer states that it is irrevocable. Revocation can occur any time prior to acceptance.

- If an offer is supported by separate consideration, it is an option and cannot be revoked.

- Acceptance manifests the offeree's approval of the terms of the offer.

- Acceptances must be communicated to be effective. If the offer specifies a specific type of acceptance, no other form is allowed; otherwise, any reasonable means of acceptance is allowable.

- Acceptance is effective upon dispatch, while a revocation is effective upon receipt.

- Every contract must be supported by legal consideration.

- Contracts must have a legal purpose to be enforceable.

- The parties to a contract must have the legal capacity to enter into the contract.

- Unless an exception applies, the Statute of Frauds requires that contracts for the transfer of an interest in real property must be in writing to be enforceable.

- An exception to the Statute of Frauds requirement for real estate transactions is part performance. Oral contracts for the sale of real estate are enforceable if any two of the following three requirements are met: (1) full or partial payment of the purchase price has occurred; (2) the party has received possession of the property; or (3) valuable improvements have been made to the property.

- The parol evidence rule prohibits the admission of evidence of any prior or contemporaneous oral or written negotiations or agreements that contradict, modify, or vary the terms of a contract intended to be the complete and final expression between the parties.

- When the parties have fully performed their contractual obligations, they are discharged from further performance.

- Subject to the provisions of state law, both the seller and the buyer are entitled to the remedies of rescission, specific performance, and damages arising from a breach of their agreement.

- Many real estate contracts provide for liquidated damages. When the clause exists, it is the exclusive remedy for damages.

- In the event of misrepresentation, mutual mistake, duress, and undue influence, a party may void an otherwise enforceable contract.

- ILSFDA regulates the disclosure of important information to interstate buyers of unimproved land and preconstruction sales of condominiums.

Chapter Problems and Assignments

1. Identify, define, and explain the various elements of a valid contract, giving an example for each.

2. Buyer offers to purchase Seller's commercial property for $1,250,000. Seller rejects the offer and offers to sell the property for $1,500,000. Buyer believes the price is too high and offers to purchase the property for $1,350,000. Seller accepts and adds that closing must occur within 45 days. Is there an enforceable contract between the parties?

3. The Oyers bought a home "as is" from American Bank. The bank's real estate agent represented to the Oyers that the home was fundamentally sound and had no structural defects. The Oyers inspected the home and found no obvious defects. Following closing, the Oyers discovered significant structural defects and sued the bank for the cost of fixing the defects. The bank denied knowledge of the real estate agent's representations and denied that it had been aware of the home's condition. The bank asserted that a property sold "as is" meant that the bank made "no express or implied warranties of any kind" to the buyers. Should the bank be held liable for the costs of fixing the home's defects?

4. Texas Incorporated listed a hotel to sell. Ramirez entered into a purchase agreement for hotel at $800,000. Ramirez paid $25,000 in earnest money. The agreement provided for liquidated damages if the purchaser for any reason failed or refused to complete the purchase. Ramirez included a financing contingency that the agreement was conditioned upon Ramirez finding satisfactory financing. Ramirez was not able to obtain satisfactory financing and decided not to purchase the hotel. Texas Incorporated demanded that Ramirez relinquish the earnest money deposit.

Is Ramirez required to pay the liquidated damages?

5. Assume the following scenarios and calculate the amount of monetary damages the designated party would be entitled to receive:
   a. Buyer enters into a contract with seller to purchase a property for $300,000. Buyer breaches the contract, and seller is able to sell the property to a new purchaser for $290,000. What monetary damages may the seller seek against the buyer?
   b. Buyer enters into a contract with seller to purchase a property for $320,000. Buyer breaches the contract, and seller sells the property to a new purchaser for $325,000. What monetary damages may the seller seek against the buyer?
   c. Buyer enters into a contract with seller to purchase a property for $300,000. Buyer breaches the contract, and seller sells the property to a new purchaser for $300,000. The contract contained a liquidated damages clause equal to the earnest money. Buyer put an initial deposit of $10,000 down on the property. What damages may the seller seek against the buyer?

6. Sophia submits a written offer to purchase a real estate property for $500,000. A few days later, Sophia decides to revoke the offer by sending a written revocation letter. After Sophia sends the written revocation, but prior to it being received, the seller of the property calls Sophia to accept the offer. Has Sophia entered into a contract to purchase the property? Why or why not?

7. Explain why the Statute of Frauds is required for some contracts but not others. Should all contracts be required to be in writing to be enforceable?

8. Determine if a defense to the enforcement of the following contracts exists. If so, identify the available defense to the enforcement of the contract.

   a. Sean finds a beautiful home and submits an offer to purchase. The seller accepts Sean's offer. Unbeknownst to Sean, the structural support beams in the attic had significant termite damage, and the seller concealed the damage by applying wood putty and painting over it. After Sean moved in, part of the attic collapsed due to the termite damage. Sean seeks to rescind the contract, but the seller says it's too late to rescind.

   b. Peggy is an elderly grandmother. All of her faculties are intact; however, she is very lonely, as her grandson is the only one who visits her. During one of the visits, Peggy's grandson tells her that he will stop visiting her unless she conveys a portion of her home to him for his time spent visiting her. Peggy, not wanting to be alone, agrees and conveys to her grandson 50 percent of the title to her home. Peggy's children and other grandchildren are upset by this conveyance and want it set aside.

9. Research the disclosures that a seller is required to make to a buyer in a residential transaction in your state. Complete a similar exercise for a commercial transaction in your state.

10. Research the laws of your state to determine who bears the risk of loss once the contract has been executed. Discuss the potential advantages and disadvantages of the law of your state.

Chapter 9
Valuation and Financing of Real Estate

Thieves respect property. They merely wish the property to become their property, that they may more perfectly respect it. —G. K. Chesterton, English writer (1874–1936)

Learning Objectives

1. Differentiate between the different appraisal valuation methods.
2. Explain the professional qualifications of appraisers.
3. Describe the differences between security interests such as mortgages and deeds of trust.
4. Define the essential terms of notes and mortgages.
5. Differentiate between the different types of loans.
6. Understand the differences between taking subject to and assuming a mortgage.
7. Discuss recent federal lending laws relating to residential mortgages.

Chapter Outline

- Introduction
- Property Appraisals
- Introduction to Mortgages
- The Mortgage Process
- Ownership of Mortgaged Property
- Mortgage Creation and Terms
- Types of Loans

Case 9.1: *Commonwealth v. Fremont Investment & Loan*

- Types of Loan Payments
- Taking Subject to and Assuming Mortgages
- Deeds of Trust
- Regulation of Home Mortgage Lending

Case 9.2: *Gancedo v. Del Carpio*

- Construction Loans
- Installment Land Sale Contracts

Case 9.3: *Bean v. Walker*

Opening
scenario

River East Plaza, LLC, a real estate developer, had worked with another party to develop a large retail store on the north side of Chicago. Another developer offered to sell its share of the project to River East. River East shopped around for a loan to allow it to buy out the other developer's share. The loan included a prepayment penalty. When the borrower sold the property and prepaid the loan, it balked at paying a "prepayment fee" according to the terms of the note. What arguments would you make on behalf of the lender that the prepayment clause in the mortgage should be enforced?[1]

Introduction

After the parties to a real estate transaction have executed a purchase contract, the property is then valued and financed. We begin this chapter's discussion with an overview of the appraisal process, followed by a discussion of financing real property. Unless a buyer purchases a property using cash, a lender will be required to extend credit to the borrower to provide financing for the purchase. This process involves creation of a mortgage, deed of trust, or land sale installment contract, which are discussed in this chapter. Chapter 10 discusses the transfer of title and closing, which occur after valuation and financing have taken place.

Property Appraisals

Appraise
To give an estimate of the current market value.

Market value
The price agreed upon by a willing buyer and seller.

To **appraise** real estate means to estimate its current market value. **Market value** refers to the price an informed buyer would pay to purchase the property. Property appraisals are important to lenders because lenders often limit the amount of money they are willing to loan based on a certain percentage of the property's value. In lending to a commercial borrower, lenders often limit commercial loans to a certain percentage of the property's income. If a property is attractive to commercial tenants, the property will generate more income, and that increased income stream will affect the property's value.

Factors Influencing Valuation

Once an appraiser has been employed, her or his duty is to estimate the property's market value. Generally, four elements affect the value of real estate:

1. *Utility*. The higher the property's useful purpose, the higher the market value.
2. *Scarcity*. The relative scarcity of similar properties on the market affects value. The fewer similar properties are on the market, the higher the market value.
3. *Demand*. The demand for the property by those who can afford to buy it affects the price. If demand is low, prices are generally lower. When demand for a property is high, the price is generally higher.
4. *Transferability*. The ease of obtaining and transferring title to the property will affect the price. Where property can be easily transferred, it has more value. Properties that cannot be transferred or that have requirements or regulations that make it difficult to transfer will have a decreased value.

Appraisal Valuation Methods

Three approaches to appraising property exist: (1) the market or sales comparison approach, (2) the cost approach, and (3) the income approach.

Market Approach (Sales Comparison Approach)

The first approach to appraising property is the **market approach**, also known as the **sales comparison approach**. This method of valuation is most often used in single-family residential appraisals and is one of the oldest appraisal methods. Under this approach, the value of the subject property is determined by comparing the selling price of similar properties and making adjustments for the differences among them (such as the presence or absence of amenities and other factors compared to the property being appraised). In setting the appraisal value, the appraiser considers several factors:

Market Approach
An appraisal method in which valuation is based on sale prices of similar properties.

- The real property interests conveyed (such as a fee, leasehold, or life estate)
- The date of the sale
- The financing terms
- The location and features of the property (for example, views, a gated-community setting)
- The characteristics of the property, including lot size, gross living area, number of rooms, age of structure, quality of construction, unique design features, and any improvements (such as upgraded kitchen or renovated bathrooms)

This approach is best used when comparable properties have been sold recently, such as in the last six months. Usually, three to five comparable properties are sufficient to establish a basis for residential appraisals.

Property Characteristics Used for Appraisals

Several physical characteristics are considered when appraising a property in connection with property financing.

- *Square footage.* Both the lot size and the gross square feet of the living area are important to appraising a property's value.
- *Number of rooms.* Appraisers consider the number of total rooms, bedrooms, and bathrooms in calculating the appraisal amount.
- *Quality of construction.* Appraisers consider the building materials used and the quality of construction when valuing a property.
- *Improvements and amenities.* Property improvements and amenities — including swimming pools, spas, kitchens, bathrooms, neighborhood-association common area facilities, and landscaping — can increase a property's appraised value.
- *Energy efficiency.* Frequently, the energy efficiency of a home (for example, installed solar panels) impacts appraisal value.
- *Location near disaster-prone areas.* An appraisal value can be decreased if the property is located near special hazards or disaster-prone areas (such as near a hazardous-waste site, earthquake fault lines, areas prone to volcanic eruptions, high fire-hazard zones, or areas of unstable soil). Appraisal value can also be decreased if the property's condition violates zoning ordinances.
- *Age of the property.* The age of the property can impact the appraisal amount. While some neighborhoods maintain their desirability despite their age because of their prime locations, older houses will require more maintenance, which can decrease the appraisal amount.
- *Paved streets and utilities.* An appraisal value can be decreased if a property lacks street paving or adequate sewer and water facilities.

Competitive market analysis (CMA)
An analysis used to estimate the sale price by adjusting the price paid for comparable properties.

Similar to the market or sales comparison approach is the **competitive market analysis** (CMA). A CMA is usually prepared to assist real estate professionals in determining the price at which to list a property. The agent reviews information taken from the multiple-listing service (MLS) and compares the subject property to properties against which that property may be compared from the MLS sales records. The CMA is not an appraisal, but it uses a method similar to the market or sales comparison approach.

Item	Subject Property	Comparable Sale 1		Comparable Sale 2		Comparable Sale 3	
		Description	+(−) $ Adjustments	Description	+(−) $ Adjustments	Description	+(−) $ Adjustments
Sale Price	$255,000		$280,000		$240,000		$275,000
Financing	Conventional 1st	Conventional 1st		Conventional 1st		Conventional 1st	
Location	Gated project	Gated project		Non-Gated	+ 12,000	Gated project	
Leasehold/Interest	Fee Simple	Fee Simple		Fee Simple		Fee Simple	
Lot Size	3,315 sq. ft.	4,000 sq. ft.	−2,000	4,000 sq. ft.	−2,000	4,528 sq. ft.	−3,000
View	None	None		None		None	
Design	Tract Built	Tract Built		Tract Built		Tract Built	
Quality of Construction	Good	Good		Good		Good	
Condition	Good	Superior	−7,000	Good		Superior	−7,000
Gross Living Area	2,166 sq ft	2,300 sq ft	−2,600	2,100 sq. ft	+ 1,200	2,300 sq. ft	−2,600
Kitchen/Bath	Upgraded Kit/Ba	Superior Kit/Ba	−2,000	Upgraded Kit/Ba		Superior Kit/Ba	−2,000
Net Adjustment (Total)			−13,600		11,200		−14,600
Adjusted Sale Price			$266,400		$251,200		$260,400

FIGURE 9.1. Sample CMA

Cost Approach

The second approach is the cost approach. The **cost approach** estimates the value of the completed project and the cost of building a comparable project. The appraiser does not try to determine a cost of creating an exact replica because construction methods and building codes may have changed, and the original materials may have become obsolete in new construction.

1. Calculates the cost of reproducing the building and other improvements with a comparable design and materials.
2. The value of the land is then added.
3. Depreciation is then subtracted from the value to reflect the age and decreased useful life of the existing project.

The cost approach is most applicable when appraising new or relatively newly constructed projects. It is also used when comparable properties are available. Such a situation often occurs when a property is unique or highly specialized.

Example: Shoe store tycoon Mahlon Haines built a home in Pennsylvania shaped like a boot.[2] For a unique property such as this one, the market comparison approach is not helpful, as no similar properties are available with which to compare it. An appraiser might use the cost approach to value this property if it were for sale.

Income Approach

The third common appraisal approach is the **income approach**, which determines the appraised property value based on the property's ability to generate income or potential income. The income approach is most often used for purchases of commercial or investment property. With this approach, appraisers often consider the property's highest and best use. Highest and best use is defined as use that is legally permissible, physically and financially feasible, and yields the best benefit to the landowner.

Exercise 9.1

For each of the different types of properties identified below, provide the best appraisal valuation method to use to most accurately value the property.

1. A 50-unit apartment complex
2. A condominium located in a suburban development
3. A historical home listed on the national register of historical places
4. An amusement park
5. A newly constructed custom-built home located adjacent to the ocean with panoramic ocean views
6. A single-family home used as a rental

A completed appraisal will contain the following information:

- Property identification.
- Dates of the evaluation of the property and the date the appraisal was completed.
- Appraisal valuation method used.
- Assumptions made and conditions noted by the appraiser. These may include the appraiser's assessment of a property's location near positive or negative influencers of value (such as a property located next to a forested area or a busy highway).
- Supporting data. The report will contain data supporting the appraiser's evaluation. Such data will include photographs of the property and those of comparable properties; preliminary title report information; the history of the property; market space; abstracts of leases; building specifications; income and expense reports; cost estimates; sales and listings for comparable properties; real property taxes and assessments; conformity of the property to the surrounding area; access to other resources such as public transportation; proximity to schools, parks, and social services; population trends; vacancies; rent levels; new construction and development activities in the area; and other beneficial or detrimental influences in the evaluation of the property.
- Appraiser's qualification. The report will indicate the appraiser's qualifications and will reference any associations, standards, and practices that the appraiser has followed.

The appraised value is then stated.

Licensing and Certification

In response to the savings-and-loan crisis of the 1980s, Congress passed the Financial Institutions Reform, Recovery and Enforcement Act (FIRREA).[3] This act requires states to establish requirements for licensing and certifying real estate appraisers, and it applies to both residential and commercial loans. All loans insured by a federal agency (commonly known as Fannie Mae or Freddie Mac) must utilize appraisers who meet the certification requirements. Real estate transactions that involve loans not insured by a federal agency do not require a certified appraiser, but they do require a licensed appraiser.

Appraisal Licensing Categories

Under FIRREA, appraiser qualification requirements are met through state licensing and certification programs for real estate appraisers. At a minimum, licensed appraisers must satisfy the qualifications set forth by the FIRREA appraisal subcommittee. States may also require additional requirements beyond those discussed below. Four categories of appraisers exist:

1. **Trainee appraiser**. A trainee appraiser needs no experience but must be supervised by a certified residential real property appraiser or a certified general appraiser in good standing. Trainee appraisers may work only on appraisals for properties that their supervising appraisers are permitted to appraise. Applicants must complete education hours and pass a core curriculum examination.

2. **Licensed residential appraiser**. This appraiser is qualified to appraise one- to four-unit noncomplex residential properties having a transaction value of up to $1,000,000 and complex one- to four-unit residential units if the value is at or below $250,000. The term *complex* is difficult to define but is usually characterized as a property that is atypical for its surroundings. A licensed residential appraiser must complete education and experience requirements.
3. **Certified residential appraiser**. This appraiser can evaluate one to four residential units without regard to value or the complexity of the transaction. The appraiser must complete education and experience requirements and pass the appraisal exam.
4. **Certified general appraiser**. This appraiser may evaluate all types of real property (residential and commercial) regardless of value or complexity. The appraiser must complete education and experience requirements.

Appraisers' Ethics

Generally, it is considered unethical for an appraiser to:

- Pay a fee for a referral
- Appraise a property in which the appraiser has an undisclosed interest
- Share the appraisal information with anyone other than the principal who ordered the appraisal, unless the principal gives permission for its disclosure
- Charge a fee based on a percentage of the appraisal amount

Appraiser Liability

Appraisers who negligently value a property may be liable to those who suffer damages in relying upon the evaluation, such as lenders who lend money based upon an inadequate appraisal. The appraiser must act with the same degree of skill, prudence, and diligence as real estate appraisers of ordinary skill commonly possess and exercise in the performance of those tasks.

Those appraisers designated by a lender to value a borrower's property owe a duty of care to the lender *and not to the borrower*. A mortgage loan broker owes a fiduciary duty to both the borrower and the third-party investors who purchase the loan.

Uniform Residential Appraisal Report   File

The purpose of this summary appraisal report is to provide the lender/client with an accurate, and adequately supported, opinion of the market value of the subject property.

SUBJECT

Property Address		City		State	Zip Code
Borrower		Owner of Public Record		County	

Legal Description

Assessor's Parcel #		Tax Year	R.E. Taxes $
Neighborhood Name		Map Reference	Census Tract

Occupant ☐ Owner ☐ Tenant ☐ Vacant   Special Assessments $ ☐ PUD   HOA $ ☐ per year ☐ per month

Property Rights Appraised ☐ Fee Simple ☐ Leasehold ☐ Other (describe)

Assignment Type ☐ Purchase Transaction ☐ Refinance Transaction ☐ Other (describe)

Lender/Client   Address

Is the subject property currently offered for sale or has it been offered for sale in the twelve months prior to the effective date of this appraisal? ☐ Yes ☐ No

Report data source(s) used, offering price(s), and date(s).

CONTRACT

I ☐ did ☐ did not analyze the contract for sale for the subject purchase transaction. Explain the results of the analysis of the contract for sale or why the analysis was not performed.

Contract Price $ Date of Contract   Is the property seller the owner of public record? ☐ Yes ☐ No   Data Source(s)

Is there any financial assistance (loan charges, sale concessions, gift or downpayment assistance, etc.) to be paid by any party on behalf of the borrower? ☐ Yes ☐ No
If Yes, report the total dollar amount and describe the items to be paid.

NEIGHBORHOOD

Note: Race and the racial composition of the neighborhood are not appraisal factors.

Neighborhood Characteristics				One-Unit Housing Trends				One-Unit Housing		Present Land Use %	
Location ☐ Urban	☐ Suburban	☐ Rural	Property Values ☐ Increasing		☐ Stable	☐ Declining		PRICE	AGE	One-Unit	%
Built-Up ☐ Over 75%	☐ 25–75%	☐ Under 25%	Demand/Supply ☐ Shortage		☐ In Balance	☐ Over Supply		$ (000)	(yrs)	2-4 Unit	%
Growth ☐ Rapid	☐ Stable	☐ Slow	Marketing Time ☐ Under 3 mths		☐ 3–6 mths	☐ Over 6 mths		Low		Multi-Family	%
Neighborhood Boundaries								High		Commercial	%
								Pred.		Other	%

Neighborhood Description

Market Conditions (including support for the above conclusions)

SITE

Dimensions	Area	Shape	View

Specific Zoning Classification   Zoning Description

Zoning Compliance ☐ Legal ☐ Legal Nonconforming (Grandfathered Use) ☐ No Zoning ☐ Illegal (describe)

Is the highest and best use of the subject property as improved (or as proposed per plans and specifications) the present use? ☐ Yes ☐ No If No, describe

Utilities	Public	Other (describe)		Public	Other (describe)	Off-site Improvements—Type	Public	Private
Electricity	☐	☐	Water	☐	☐	Street	☐	☐
Gas	☐	☐	Sanitary Sewer	☐	☐	Alley	☐	☐

FEMA Special Flood Hazard Area ☐ Yes ☐ No FEMA Flood Zone   FEMA Map #   FEMA Map Date

Are the utilities and off-site improvements typical for the market area? ☐ Yes ☐ No If No, describe

Are there any adverse site conditions or external factors (easements, encroachments, environmental conditions, land uses, etc.)? ☐ Yes ☐ No If Yes, describe

IMPROVEMENTS

General Description		Foundation		Exterior Description	materials/condition	Interior	materials/condition
Units ☐ One ☐ One with Accessory Unit		☐ Concrete Slab ☐ Crawl Space		Foundation Walls		Floors	
# of Stories		☐ Full Basement ☐ Partial Basement		Exterior Walls		Walls	
Type ☐ Det. ☐ Att. ☐ S-Det./End Unit		Basement Area sq. ft.		Roof Surface		Trim/Finish	
☐ Existing ☐ Proposed ☐ Under Const.		Basement Finish %		Gutters & Downspouts		Bath Floor	
Design (Style)		☐ Outside Entry/Exit ☐ Sump Pump		Window Type		Bath Wainscot	
Year Built		Evidence of ☐ Infestation		Storm Sash/Insulated		Car Storage ☐ None	
Effective Age (Yrs)		☐ Dampness ☐ Settlement		Screens		☐ Driveway # of Cars	
Attic ☐ None		Heating ☐ FWA ☐ HWBB ☐ Radiant		Amenities ☐ Woodstove(s) #		Driveway Surface	
☐ Drop Stair ☐ Stairs		☐ Other Fuel		☐ Fireplace(s) # ☐ Fence		☐ Garage # of Cars	
☐ Floor ☐ Scuttle		Cooling ☐ Central Air Conditioning		☐ Patio/Deck ☐ Porch		☐ Carport # of Cars	
☐ Finished ☐ Heated		☐ Individual ☐ Other		☐ Pool ☐ Other		☐ Att. ☐ Det. ☐ Built-in	

Appliances ☐ Refrigerator ☐ Range/Oven ☐ Dishwasher ☐ Disposal ☐ Microwave ☐ Washer/Dryer ☐ Other (describe)

Finished area **above** grade contains: Rooms   Bedrooms   Bath(s)   Square Feet of Gross Living Area Above Grade

Additional features (special energy efficient items, etc.)

Describe the condition of the property (including needed repairs, deterioration, renovations, remodeling, etc.).

Are there any physical deficiencies or adverse conditions that affect the livability, soundness, or structural integrity of the property? ☐ Yes ☐ No If Yes, describe

Does the property generally conform to the neighborhood (functional utility, style, condition, use, construction, etc.)? ☐ Yes ☐ No If No, describe

Freddie Mac Form 70 March 2005   Page 1 of 6   Fannie Mae Form 1004 March 2005

Exhibit 9.1. Uniform Residential Appraisal Report[4]

Uniform Residential Appraisal Report
File #

There are _____ comparable properties currently offered for sale in the subject neighborhood ranging in price from $ _____ to $ _____.

There are _____ comparable sales in the subject neighborhood within the past twelve months ranging in sale price from $ _____ to $ _____.

FEATURE	SUBJECT		COMPARABLE SALE # 1		COMPARABLE SALE # 2		COMPARABLE SALE # 3	
Address								
Proximity to Subject								
Sale Price	$			$		$		$
Sale Price/Gross Liv. Area	$	sq. ft.	$	sq. ft.		sq. ft.	$	sq. ft.
Data Source(s)								
Verification Source(s)								
VALUE ADJUSTMENTS	DESCRIPTION		DESCRIPTION	+(-) $ Adjustment	DESCRIPTION	+(-) $ Adjustment	DESCRIPTION	+(-) $ Adjustment
Sale or Financing Concessions								
Date of Sale/Time								
Location								
Leasehold/Fee Simple								
Site								
View								
Design (Style)								
Quality of Construction								
Actual Age								
Condition								
Above Grade	Total Bdrms. Baths		Total Bdrms. Baths		Total Bdrms. Baths		Total Bdrms. Baths	
Room Count								
Gross Living Area	sq. ft.		sq. ft.		sq. ft.		sq. ft.	
Basement & Finished Rooms Below Grade								
Functional Utility								
Heating/Cooling								
Energy Efficient Items								
Garage/Carport								
Porch/Patio/Deck								
Net Adjustment (Total)			☐ + ☐ -	$	☐ + ☐ -	$	☐ + ☐ -	$
Adjusted Sale Price of Comparables			Net Adj. _____ % Gross Adj. _____ %	$	Net Adj. _____ % Gross Adj. _____ %	$	Net Adj. _____ % Gross Adj. _____ %	$

I ☐ did ☐ did not research the sale or transfer history of the subject property and comparable sales. If not, explain

My research ☐ did ☐ did not reveal any prior sales or transfers of the subject property for the three years prior to the effective date of this appraisal.

Data source(s)

My research ☐ did ☐ did not reveal any prior sales or transfers of the comparable sales for the year prior to the date of sale of the comparable sale.

Data source(s)

Report the results of the research and analysis of the prior sale or transfer history of the subject property and comparable sales (report additional prior sales on page 3).

ITEM	SUBJECT	COMPARABLE SALE # 1	COMPARABLE SALE # 2	COMPARABLE SALE # 3
Date of Prior Sale/Transfer				
Price of Prior Sale/Transfer				
Data Source(s)				
Effective Date of Data Source(s)				

Analysis of prior sale or transfer history of the subject property and comparable sales

Summary of Sales Comparison Approach

Indicated Value by Sales Comparison Approach $ _____

Indicated Value by: Sales Comparison Approach $ _____   Cost Approach (if developed) $ _____   Income Approach (if developed) $ _____

This appraisal is made ☐ "as is", ☐ subject to completion per plans and specifications on the basis of a hypothetical condition that the improvements have been completed, ☐ subject to the following repairs or alterations on the basis of a hypothetical condition that the repairs or alterations have been completed, or ☐ subject to the following required inspection based on the extraordinary assumption that the condition or deficiency does not require alteration or repair:

Based on a complete visual inspection of the interior and exterior areas of the subject property, defined scope of work, statement of assumptions and limiting conditions, and appraiser's certification, my (our) opinion of the market value, as defined, of the real property that is the subject of this report is $ _____, as of _____, which is the date of inspection and the effective date of this appraisal.

Exhibit 9.1. Uniform Residential Appraisal Report (*Continued*)

Uniform Residential Appraisal Report

File #

ADDITIONAL COMMENTS

COST APPROACH TO VALUE (not required by Fannie Mae)

Provide adequate information for the lender/client to replicate the below cost figures and calculations.

Support for the opinion of site value (summary of comparable land sales or other methods for estimating site value)

ESTIMATED ☐ REPRODUCTION OR ☐ REPLACEMENT COST NEW	OPINION OF SITE VALUE		.... = $
Source of cost data	Dwelling	Sq. Ft. @ $	.... =$
Quality rating from cost service Effective date of cost data		Sq. Ft. @ $	.... =$
Comments on Cost Approach (gross living area calculations, depreciation, etc.)	Garage/Carport	Sq. Ft. @ $	.... =$
	Total Estimate of Cost-New		.... = $
	Less Physical	Functional	External
	Depreciation		=$( )
	Depreciated Cost of Improvements.....................................		=$
	"As-is" Value of Site Improvements................................		=$
Estimated Remaining Economic Life (HUD and VA only) Years	Indicated Value By Cost Approach		=$

INCOME APPROACH TO VALUE (not required by Fannie Mae)

Estimated Monthly Market Rent $ X Gross Rent Multiplier   = $ Indicated Value by Income Approach

Summary of Income Approach (including support for market rent and GRM)

PROJECT INFORMATION FOR PUDs (if applicable)

Is the developer/builder in control of the Homeowners' Association (HOA)? ☐ Yes ☐ No   Unit type(s) ☐ Detached ☐ Attached

Provide the following information for PUDs ONLY if the developer/builder is in control of the HOA and the subject property is an attached dwelling unit.

Legal name of project

Total number of phases   Total number of units   Total number of units sold

Total number of units rented   Total number of units for sale   Data source(s)

Was the project created by the conversion of an existing building(s) into a PUD? ☐ Yes ☐ No   If Yes, date of conversion

Does the project contain any multi-dwelling units? ☐ Yes ☐ No   Data source(s)

Are the units, common elements, and recreation facilities complete? ☐ Yes ☐ No   If No, describe the status of completion.

Are the common elements leased to or by the Homeowners' Association? ☐ Yes ☐ No   If Yes, describe the rental terms and options.

Describe common elements and recreational facilities

Exhibit 9.1. Uniform Residential Appraisal Report (*Continued*)

Uniform Residential Appraisal Report

File #

This report form is designed to report an appraisal of a one-unit property or a one-unit property with an accessory unit; including a unit in a planned unit development (PUD). This report form is not designed to report an appraisal of a manufactured home or a unit in a condominium or cooperative project.

This appraisal report is subject to the following scope of work, intended use, intended user, definition of market value, statement of assumptions and limiting conditions, and certifications. Modifications, additions, or deletions to the intended use, intended user, definition of market value, or assumptions and limiting conditions are not permitted. The appraiser may expand the scope of work to include any additional research or analysis necessary based on the complexity of this appraisal assignment. Modifications or deletions to the certifications are also not permitted. However, additional certifications that do not constitute material alterations to this appraisal report, such as those required by law or those related to the appraiser's continuing education or membership in an appraisal organization, are permitted.

SCOPE OF WORK: The scope of work for this appraisal is defined by the complexity of this appraisal assignment and the reporting requirements of this appraisal report form, including the following definition of market value, statement of assumptions and limiting conditions, and certifications. The appraiser must, at a minimum: (1) perform a complete visual inspection of the interior and exterior areas of the subject property, (2) inspect the neighborhood, (3) inspect each of the comparable sales from at least the street, (4) research, verify, and analyze data from reliable public and/or private sources, and (5) report his or her analysis, opinions, and conclusions in this appraisal report.

INTENDED USE: The intended use of this appraisal report is for the lender/client to evaluate the property that is the subject of this appraisal for a mortgage finance transaction.

INTENDED USER: The intended user of this appraisal report is the lender/client.

DEFINITION OF MARKET VALUE: The most probable price which a property should bring in a competitive and open market under all conditions requisite to a fair sale, the buyer and seller, each acting prudently, knowledgeably and assuming the price is not affected by undue stimulus. Implicit in this definition is the consummation of a sale as of a specified date and the passing of title from seller to buyer under conditions whereby: (1) buyer and seller are typically motivated; (2) both parties are well informed or well advised, and each acting in what he or she considers his or her own best interest; (3) a reasonable time is allowed for exposure in the open market; (4) payment is made in terms of cash in U. S. dollars or in terms of financial arrangements comparable thereto; and (5) the price represents the normal consideration for the property sold unaffected by special or creative financing or sales concessions* granted by anyone associated with the sale.

*Adjustments to the comparables must be made for special or creative financing or sales concessions. No adjustments are necessary for those costs which are normally paid by sellers as a result of tradition or law in a market area; these costs are readily identifiable since the seller pays these costs in virtually all sales transactions. Special or creative financing adjustments can be made to the comparable property by comparisons to financing terms offered by a third party institutional lender that is not already involved in the property or transaction. Any adjustment should not be calculated on a mechanical dollar for dollar cost of the financing or concession but the dollar amount of any adjustment should approximate the market's reaction to the financing or concessions based on the appraiser's judgment.

STATEMENT OF ASSUMPTIONS AND LIMITING CONDITIONS: The appraiser's certification in this report is subject to the following assumptions and limiting conditions:

1. The appraiser will not be responsible for matters of a legal nature that affect either the property being appraised or the title to it, except for information that he or she became aware of during the research involved in performing this appraisal. The appraiser assumes that the title is good and marketable and will not render any opinions about the title.

2. The appraiser has provided a sketch in this appraisal report to show the approximate dimensions of the improvements. The sketch is included only to assist the reader in visualizing the property and understanding the appraiser's determination of its size.

3. The appraiser has examined the available flood maps that are provided by the Federal Emergency Management Agency (or other data sources) and has noted in this appraisal report whether any portion of the subject site is located in an identified Special Flood Hazard Area. Because the appraiser is not a surveyor, he or she makes no guarantees, express or implied, regarding this determination.

4. The appraiser will not give testimony or appear in court because he or she made an appraisal of the property in question, unless specific arrangements to do so have been made beforehand, or as otherwise required by law.

5. The appraiser has noted in this appraisal report any adverse conditions (such as needed repairs, deterioration, the presence of hazardous wastes, toxic substances, etc.) observed during the inspection of the subject property or that he or she became aware of during the research involved in performing this appraisal. Unless otherwise stated in this appraisal report, the appraiser has no knowledge of any hidden or unapparent physical deficiencies or adverse conditions of the property (such as, but not limited to, needed repairs, deterioration, the presence of hazardous wastes, toxic substances, adverse environmental conditions, etc.) that would make the property less valuable, and has assumed that there are no such conditions and makes no guarantees or warranties, express or implied. The appraiser will not be responsible for any such conditions that do exist or for any engineering or testing that might be required to discover whether such conditions exist. Because the appraiser is not an expert in the field of environmental hazards, this appraisal report must not be considered as an environmental assessment of the property.

6. The appraiser has based his or her appraisal report and valuation conclusion for an appraisal that is subject to satisfactory completion, repairs, or alterations on the assumption that the completion, repairs, or alterations of the subject property will be performed in a professional manner.

Exhibit 9.1. Uniform Residential Appraisal Report (*Continued*)

Uniform Residential Appraisal Report   File

APPRAISER'S CERTIFICATION: The Appraiser certifies and agrees that:

1. I have, at a minimum, developed and reported this appraisal in accordance with the scope of work requirements stated in this appraisal report.

2. I performed a complete visual inspection of the interior and exterior areas of the subject property. I reported the condition of the improvements in factual, specific terms. I identified and reported the physical deficiencies that could affect the livability, soundness, or structural integrity of the property.

3. I performed this appraisal in accordance with the requirements of the Uniform Standards of Professional Appraisal Practice that were adopted and promulgated by the Appraisal Standards Board of The Appraisal Foundation and that were in place at the time this appraisal report was prepared.

4. I developed my opinion of the market value of the real property that is the subject of this report based on the sales comparison approach to value. I have adequate comparable market data to develop a reliable sales comparison approach for this appraisal assignment. I further certify that I considered the cost and income approaches to value but did not develop them, unless otherwise indicated in this report.

5. I researched, verified, analyzed, and reported on any current agreement for sale for the subject property, any offering for sale of the subject property in the twelve months prior to the effective date of this appraisal, and the prior sales of the subject property for a minimum of three years prior to the effective date of this appraisal, unless otherwise indicated in this report.

6. I researched, verified, analyzed, and reported on the prior sales of the comparable sales for a minimum of one year prior to the date of sale of the comparable sale, unless otherwise indicated in this report.

7. I selected and used comparable sales that are locationally, physically, and functionally the most similar to the subject property.

8. I have not used comparable sales that were the result of combining a land sale with the contract purchase price of a home that has been built or will be built on the land.

9. I have reported adjustments to the comparable sales that reflect the market's reaction to the differences between the subject property and the comparable sales.

10. I verified, from a disinterested source, all information in this report that was provided by parties who have a financial interest in the sale or financing of the subject property.

11. I have knowledge and experience in appraising this type of property in this market area.

12. I am aware of, and have access to, the necessary and appropriate public and private data sources, such as multiple listing services, tax assessment records, public land records and other such data sources for the area in which the property is located.

13. I obtained the information, estimates, and opinions furnished by other parties and expressed in this appraisal report from reliable sources that I believe to be true and correct.

14. I have taken into consideration the factors that have an impact on value with respect to the subject neighborhood, subject property, and the proximity of the subject property to adverse influences in the development of my opinion of market value. I have noted in this appraisal report any adverse conditions (such as, but not limited to, needed repairs, deterioration, the presence of hazardous wastes, toxic substances, adverse environmental conditions, etc.) observed during the inspection of the subject property or that I became aware of during the research involved in performing this appraisal. I have considered these adverse conditions in my analysis of the property value, and have reported on the effect of the conditions on the value and marketability of the subject property.

15. I have not knowingly withheld any significant information from this appraisal report and, to the best of my knowledge, all statements and information in this appraisal report are true and correct.

16. I stated in this appraisal report my own personal, unbiased, and professional analysis, opinions, and conclusions, which are subject only to the assumptions and limiting conditions in this appraisal report.

17. I have no present or prospective interest in the property that is the subject of this report, and I have no present or prospective personal interest or bias with respect to the participants in the transaction. I did not base, either partially or completely, my analysis and/or opinion of market value in this appraisal report on the race, color, religion, sex, age, marital status, handicap, familial status, or national origin of either the prospective owners or occupants of the subject property or of the present owners or occupants of the properties in the vicinity of the subject property or on any other basis prohibited by law.

18. My employment and/or compensation for performing this appraisal or any future or anticipated appraisals was not conditioned on any agreement or understanding, written or otherwise, that I would report (or present analysis supporting) a predetermined specific value, a predetermined minimum value, a range or direction in value, a value that favors the cause of any party, or the attainment of a specific result or occurrence of a specific subsequent event (such as approval of a pending mortgage loan application).

19. I personally prepared all conclusions and opinions about the real estate that were set forth in this appraisal report. If I relied on significant real property appraisal assistance from any individual or individuals in the performance of this appraisal or the preparation of this appraisal report, I have named such individual(s) and disclosed the specific tasks performed in this appraisal report. I certify that any individual so named is qualified to perform the tasks. I have not authorized anyone to make a change to any item in this appraisal report; therefore, any change made to this appraisal is unauthorized and I will take no responsibility for it.

20. I identified the lender/client in this appraisal report who is the individual, organization, or agent for the organization that ordered and will receive this appraisal report.

Exhibit 9.1. Uniform Residential Appraisal Report (*Continued*)

Uniform Residential Appraisal Report   File

21. The lender/client may disclose or distribute this appraisal report to: the borrower; another lender at the request of the borrower; the mortgagee or its successors and assigns; mortgage insurers; government sponsored enterprises; other secondary market participants; data collection or reporting services; professional appraisal organizations; any department, agency, or instrumentality of the United States; and any state, the District of Columbia, or other jurisdictions; without having to obtain the appraiser's or supervisory appraiser's (if applicable) consent. Such consent must be obtained before this appraisal report may be disclosed or distributed to any other party (including, but not limited to, the public through advertising, public relations, news, sales, or other media).

22. I am aware that any disclosure or distribution of this appraisal report by me or the lender/client may be subject to certain laws and regulations. Further, I am also subject to the provisions of the Uniform Standards of Professional Appraisal Practice that pertain to disclosure or distribution by me.

23. The borrower, another lender at the request of the borrower, the mortgagee or its successors and assigns, mortgage insurers, government sponsored enterprises, and other secondary market participants may rely on this appraisal report as part of any mortgage finance transaction that involves any one or more of these parties.

24. If this appraisal report was transmitted as an "electronic record" containing my "electronic signature," as those terms are defined in applicable federal and/or state laws (excluding audio and video recordings), or a facsimile transmission of this appraisal report containing a copy or representation of my signature, the appraisal report shall be as effective, enforceable and valid as if a paper version of this appraisal report were delivered containing my original hand written signature.

25. Any intentional or negligent misrepresentation(s) contained in this appraisal report may result in civil liability and/or criminal penalties including, but not limited to, fine or imprisonment or both under the provisions of Title 18, United States Code, Section 1001, et seq., or similar state laws.

SUPERVISORY APPRAISER'S CERTIFICATION: The Supervisory Appraiser certifies and agrees that:

1. I directly supervised the appraiser for this appraisal assignment, have read the appraisal report, and agree with the appraiser's analysis, opinions, statements, conclusions, and the appraiser's certification.

2. I accept full responsibility for the contents of this appraisal report including, but not limited to, the appraiser's analysis, opinions, statements, conclusions, and the appraiser's certification.

3. The appraiser identified in this appraisal report is either a sub-contractor or an employee of the supervisory appraiser (or the appraisal firm), is qualified to perform this appraisal, and is acceptable to perform this appraisal under the applicable state law.

4. This appraisal report complies with the Uniform Standards of Professional Appraisal Practice that were adopted and promulgated by the Appraisal Standards Board of The Appraisal Foundation and that were in place at the time this appraisal report was prepared.

5. If this appraisal report was transmitted as an "electronic record" containing my "electronic signature," as those terms are defined in applicable federal and/or state laws (excluding audio and video recordings), or a facsimile transmission of this appraisal report containing a copy or representation of my signature, the appraisal report shall be as effective, enforceable and valid as if a paper version of this appraisal report were delivered containing my original hand written signature.

APPRAISER

Signature_____

Name _____

Company Name _____

Company Address_____

_____

Telephone Number _____

Email Address _____

Date of Signature and Report_____

Effective Date of Appraisal _____

State Certification #_____

or State License # _____

or Other (describe) _____ State # _____

State _____

Expiration Date of Certification or License _____

ADDRESS OF PROPERTY APPRAISED

_____

_____

APPRAISED VALUE OF SUBJECT PROPERTY $ _____

LENDER/CLIENT

Name _____

Company Name _____

Company Address_____

_____

Email Address_____

SUPERVISORY APPRAISER (ONLY IF REQUIRED)

Signature_____

Name_____

Company Name _____

Company Address_____

_____

Telephone Number _____

Email Address _____

Date of Signature _____

State Certification #_____

or State License # _____

State _____

Expiration Date of Certification or License _____

SUBJECT PROPERTY

☐ Did not inspect subject property

☐ Did inspect exterior of subject property from street
     Date of Inspection _____

☐ Did inspect interior and exterior of subject property
     Date of Inspection _____

COMPARABLE SALES

☐ Did not inspect exterior of comparable sales from street

☐ Did inspect exterior of comparable sales from street
     Date of Inspection _____

Exhibit 9.1. Uniform Residential Appraisal Report (*Continued*)

Introduction to Mortgages

Where a party does not purchase a property using all cash, it must borrow all or a portion of the purchase price. A **mortgage** is a two-party instrument financing arrangement in which one person, usually the purchaser, borrows money from a creditor. It creates a lien on the borrower's property. Mortgages are an important concept in real estate, as most homeowners will have a mortgage at some point in their lives. Most states use mortgages to secure a real estate loan; however, some states may create their own unique requirements for a mortgage's creation and enforcement. States may also use other instruments in lieu of a mortgage, such as a deed of trust. A deed of trust is briefly discussed in this chapter.

When real property is subject to a mortgage, it is **hypothecated**. That means the property is pledged as security to guarantee the repayment of the loan. The borrower retains possession of the property during the mortgage term. The owner-borrower is the **mortgagor**, and the lender or creditor is the **mortgagee**. If the borrower defaults on the loan, the lender can foreclose on the property and sell it at a public auction.

Mortgage
A real estate security instrument. Borrower retains title but gives a lien interest and note to the lender. Also known as hypothecation.

Hypothecated
To pledge (give as collateral) real property as security without giving up possession to guarantee the repayment of the loan.

Mortgagor
The owner-borrower in a mortgage agreement.

Mortgagee
The lender or creditor in a mortgage agreement.

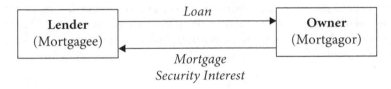

FIGURE 9.2. Mortgage

The Mortgage Process

Obtaining a mortgage can be painless, exceptionally time consuming, or somewhere in the middle. Current market conditions, available financing, and the applicant's financial position affect the experience.

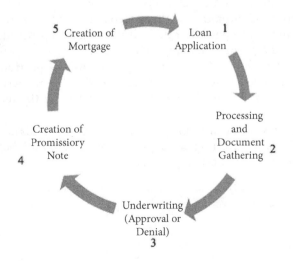

FIGURE 9.3. The Mortgage Process

Loan Application

The first step in obtaining a mortgage loan is the application. Many people utilize mortgage bankers, who are also known as mortgage loan originators (MLOs), loan officers, or loan specialists. **Mortgage bankers** do not lend money directly; they act as intermediaries, gathering the applicant's information and shopping the applicant to potential lenders. The mortgage banker then provides the applicant with a list of potential lenders who would agree to provide a loan to the applicant, as well as those lenders' financing terms.

Mortgage banker
A person who establishes a relationship with multiple lenders to offer different lending products to the mortgage banker's customers. Individuals employed as a mortgage banker are also known as mortgage loan originators.

Once a lender is selected, the mortgage banker submits the loan application to the lender and facilitates the funding and closing of the transaction. One of the benefits of using a mortgage banker is the access to potentially lower interest rates. Rather than utilizing a mortgage broker, an applicant can also apply for a loan directly with a bank, credit union, or other financial institution

> *Example:* Bank A may provide an interest rate of 5.5 percent to an applicant who comes in directly to the bank to apply for a loan. However, Bank A may provide a wholesale rate of 5.25 percent that is available only to mortgage brokers.

Many people prefer to use a bank or credit union directly because they have an established relationship with the bank or credit union, feel a sense of trust, or prefer the ease of gathering documentation if the business holds the applicant's checking, savings, or other investment accounts.

■ ■ ■ Other Sources of Mortgage Loans

Savings and Loan Association. Savings and loan associations (also known as thrift institutions) are federally chartered institutions that function similarly to commercial banks and credit unions. They provide residential, long-term loans to their members. As a result, depositors and borrowers can influence the financial and managerial decisions of the association. This ownership may provide slightly more competitive lending rates to borrowers than commercial banks.

Life Insurance Companies. After receiving premiums from their policyholders, insurance companies often invest these proceeds in long-term commercial and industrial financing. These mortgage loans often amount to a significant part of a life insurance company's investment portfolio. Life insurance companies may also decide to acquire or actively develop real estate projects. This activity allows the insurers to share in the appreciation of the market value of the real property.

Pension Funds. Like life insurance companies, pension funds have diversified their investment portfolios by investing in real estate projects. They will both make mortgage loans as well as own the real estate projects.

Processing and Document Gathering

Lenders often require applicants to provide supporting documentation to obtain a mortgage loan. Applicants must verify income by submitting W-2 federal tax forms, recent pay stubs, or offer-of-employment contracts. Applicants who are self-employed often are required to provide several years of business and personal tax returns to apply.

Underwriting

The lender's process of analyzing documentation, assessing the value of the real property, and approving the loan is called **underwriting**. In underwriting, the borrower's creditworthiness; the property's condition, location, and current use; other relevant economic influences; and the laws pertaining to the foreclosure procedures available to the lender become part of the decision to make the loan.

Underwriting
The lender's process of evaluating the credit worthiness of the prospective borrower and the suitability of the collateral.

Approval or Denial

Once underwriting has been completed, the loan is either approved or denied. Federal law requires the lender to disclose the specific reasons for a loan's denial. If the loan has been approved, a promissory note and its security instrument (such as a mortgage or deed of trust) are issued.

Sale in Secondary Market

Once a loan has been issued, it can be sold to investors. The mortgage loan market has two aspects. The first is the **primary market**, in which loans are originated, either through a broker or directly with the lender. The second is the **secondary market**, in which investors purchase loans made by others. These investors can consist of mutual funds, life insurance companies, pension companies, and others who desire a predictable rate of return from secured real property loans.

Primary market
Market where loans are originated, either through a broker or directly with the lender.

Among the most well-known secondary market organizations are the Federal National Mortgage Association (commonly known as Fannie Mae) and the Federal Home Loan Mortgage Corporation (known as Freddie Mac).

Fannie Mae was originally a government agency but was converted to a private profit-making corporation. Its purpose is to sell commitments to lenders pledging to buy specific dollar amounts of mortgage loans within certain durations. Loans must be made in conformity with Fannie Mae's loan approval criteria and using its approved forms.

Secondary market
Market where investors (such as mutual funds or life insurance companies) purchase loans made by others.

Freddie Mac issues its own securities against its own mortgage pools. Freddie Mac guarantees that principal and interest on the mortgages within its pools are repaid in full and on time, even if the underlying mortgages are in default.

Ownership of Mortgaged Property

For the most part, states have adopted two competing theories concerning the legal ownership of mortgaged real property. The mortgage is either a conveyance of a legal interest to the lender or a lien to secure the repayment of the debt.

Lien theory, used in most states, provides that a mortgage does not transfer legal title to the lender; instead, the lender has a lien on the property to secure repayment of the debt. Under this theory, the lender has legal title and the borrower has equitable title to the property. In the event of a default, the lender must foreclose to take possession of the property. The borrower retains possession until foreclosure has been completed.

Title theory, used in a minority of states, provides that a mortgage is a transfer of property title to the lender for security purposes. The lender has legal title to the mortgaged property until the borrower repays the debt. The borrower has the right to possession during the mortgage, but the lender may take possession of the property upon the borrower's default. When the borrower defaults, the lender remains in possession during the foreclosure proceedings. This approach allows the creditor to protect the property from deterioration while managing the property.

Lien theory
A legal rule recognizing that the buyer holds title to the deed of the property but gives a security interest in the real property to a secured lender.

Title theory
A legal rule recognizing that the buyer transfers title to the real property lender during the term of the loan. Title is restored to the buyer-borrower when the obligation is paid in full.

Mortgage Creation and Terms

Two documents exist with nearly every mortgage. The first is the promissory note, and the second is the mortgage.

Creation of a Promissory Note

The **promissory note** is the borrower's promise to repay the money borrowed. A borrower who defaults in the repayment may be personally liable for the debt owed. The promissory note is the contract between the parties to repay the obligation. The person who borrows money and enters into the promissory note is called the **maker** or the **debtor**. The person who provided the financing is known as the **payee**. The note may or may not be secured by a mortgage or deed of trust.

The note does not create an interest in land, but it serves the important function of showing that the borrower is indebted to the creditor. The promissory note, because it contains a fixed, determinable date of payment, is a negotiable instrument. As negotiable instruments, promissory notes can be sold, transferred, or conveyed to another.

Promissory note
An executed (signed) instrument acknowledging a debt and promising to pay a creditor.

Debtor
A person who executes (signs) a note or contract and is primarily liable for repayment.

Payee
A person who receives payment under a note or negotiable instrument (such as a check).

Exhibit 9.2. Promissory Note

Secured Promissory Note

$_____   [Date]_____

FOR VALUE RECEIVED, _____(hereinafter "Borrower"), promises to pay to _____ (hereinafter "Lender") at the following address at _____, or at such place as Lender may from time to time designate in writing, in legal tender of the United States of America, the unpaid principal amount _____($_____), together with interest on the unpaid principal balance from time to time outstanding at the rate of _____ (_____%) per annum, simple interest accruing monthly (hereinafter "Note").

This Note shall be subject to the following additional provisions:

1. *Payment of Principal and Interest.* Principal and interest shall be payable in consecutive monthly installments of _____ dollars ($_____) or more on the first day of each month beginning _____. Such payments shall continue until the entire indebtedness evidenced by this Note and all accrued and unpaid interest is fully paid, with any unpaid principal and interest due and payable on _____ (the Maturity Date).

   Each payment under this Note shall be credited in the following order: (a) costs, fees, charges, and advances paid or incurred by Lender or payable to Lender and interest under any provision of this Note in such order as Lender, in its sole and absolute discretion, elects, (b) interest payable under the Note, and (c) principal under the Note

2. *Prepayment.* Prepayment in whole or part may occur at any time hereunder without penalty; and provided further that any such partial prepayment shall not operate to postpone or suspend the obligation to make, and shall not have the effect of altering the time for payment of the remaining balance of the Note as provided for above, unless and until the entire obligation is paid in full. All payments received hereunder shall be applied, first, to any costs or expenses incurred by Lender in collecting such payment or to any other unpaid charges or expenses due hereunder; second, to accrued interest; and third, to principal.

3. *Default and Acceleration.* On (a) Borrower's failure to pay any installment or other sum due under this Note when due and payable (whether by extension, acceleration, or otherwise), or (b) any breach of any other promise or obligation in this Note or in any other instrument now or hereafter securing the indebtedness evidenced by this Note, then, and in any such event, Lender may, at its option, declare this Note (including, without limitation, all accrued interest) due and payable immediately regardless of the Maturity Date. Borrower expressly waives notice of the exercise of this option.

4. *Late Charge.* Borrower acknowledges that default in the payment of any sum due under this Note will result in losses and additional expenses to Lender in servicing the indebtedness evidenced by this Note, handling such delinquent

payments, and meeting its other financial obligations. Borrower further acknowledges that the extent of such loss and additional expenses is extremely difficult and impractical to ascertain. Borrower agrees that, if any payment due under this Note is not made within _____ days when due, a charge of _____ cents ($0.__) for each dollar ($1.00) that is not paid when due would be a reasonable estimate of expenses so incurred (the Late Charge).

5. *Interest on Interest.* If any interest payment under this Note is not paid when due, the unpaid interest shall be added to the principal of this Note, shall become and be treated as principal, and shall thereafter bear like interest.

6. *Notice.* Any notice or demand to be given to the parties hereunder shall be deemed to have been given to and received by them and shall be effective when personally delivered or when deposited in the U.S. mail, certified or registered mail, return receipt requested, postage prepaid, and addressed to the party at the addresses set forth above, or at such other address as the one of the parties may hereafter designate in writing to the other party.

7. *Waiver.* The Borrower, endorsers, and all other persons liable or to become liable on this Note, waive presentment for payment, protest, demand, notice of protest, notice of dishonor, and notice of nonpayment, and expressly agree that this Note, or any payment hereunder, may be extended from time to time by the Lender without in any way affecting its liability hereunder.

8. *Miscellaneous.* This Note shall be governed and construed in accordance with the Laws of the State of _____. This Note shall bind and inure to the benefit of Borrower's and Lender's successors and assigns. Time is of the essence for every obligation under this Note. If any court of competent jurisdiction holds any provision of this Note to be illegal, unenforceable, or invalid in whole or in part for any reason, the validity and enforceability of the remaining provisions, or portions of them, will not be affected. Any rule of construction to the effect that ambiguities are to be resolved against the drafting party shall not apply in interpreting this Note. In the event any action is required to enforce the terms of this Promissory Note, the prevailing party is entitled to recover his reasonable attorney fees, costs, and expenses in such collection action.

EXECUTED as of the date first written above.

Borrower:

By: _____
Its: _____

Terms in a Promissory Note

The following terms commonly appear in the promissory note:

1. *Loan amount.* The loan amount or principal is the total amount financed in the transaction. The loan amount is not necessarily the purchase price because purchasers may put an earnest-money deposit down on the property or pay a portion of the purchase price with cash.

2. *Maturity date.* The maturity date is the date on which the loan must be repaid. The maturity date for residential properties is often 30 years, while 20 years is frequently

the standard for commercial properties. The term may be as short as 10 years or as long as 40 years. Generally, the longer the term, the higher the interest rate.

3. *Interest rate.* The rate of interest at which the debtor agrees to pay the payee must be stated. Related to interest rates is the concept of usury. All state laws regulate the interest rates that may be charged by noninstitutional lenders (lenders that do not take deposits from the general public, such as individuals, pension funds, mortgage companies, and brokers). **Usury** occurs when a noninstitutional lender charges in excess of the state-allowed interest rate maximum. The penalties for violating usury laws can be severe. States may allow the borrower to recover amounts paid over a certain period of the loan and damages for amounts paid (including potentially punitive damages). Often the borrower can obtain a judgment canceling all future interest payments over the remainder of the loan.

Usury
A rate of interest above the maximum permitted by state or federal law.

4. *Prepayment penalties.* Prepayment penalties are fines assessed to the borrower if he wishes to pay the loan balance before the loan's maturity date. The penalty assists the lender in recovering a portion of the interest payments the lender would have recovered had the loan not been paid before its maturity. Prepayment penalties are common in commercial and industrial loans.

Example: If any prepayment is made within five (5) years from the date of the Note, there shall be a prepayment penalty equal to five percent (5%) of the principal so prepaid.

Prepayment penalties are prohibited on Federal Housing Administration loans, Veteran's Administration loans, and loans sold to Fannie Mae or Freddie Mac. Most residential lenders do not charge prepayment penalties. In some states, prepayment penalties are unlawful.

Example: Right to Prepay. Borrower may prepay the principal amount outstanding in whole or in part at any time without charge.

5. *Late fee clause.* The monthly (or other periodic date) payment due date is normally stated. Often, lenders provide a grace period in which no penalties or fees apply if the payment is received during this time. Late payment fees may be assessed if payment is made after the grace period; the customary late fee is 5 percent of the payment amount. However, Federal Housing Administration or Veteran's Administration loans cannot charge more than 4 percent of each payment for payments that are more than 15 days late.[5]

Example: Borrower acknowledges that default in the payment of any sum due under this Note will result in losses and additional expenses to Lender in servicing the indebtedness evidenced by this Note, handling such delinquent payments, and meeting its other financial obligations. Borrower further acknowledges that the extent of such loss and additional expenses is extremely difficult and impractical to ascertain. Borrower agrees that, if any payment due under this Note is not made within fifteen (15) days when due, a charge of five cents ($0.05) for each dollar ($1.00) that is not paid when due would be a reasonable estimate of expenses so incurred (the Late Charge).

6. *Acceleration clause.* On payment default or other breach of the agreement, this provision permits the lender the option to declare the entire amount of outstanding principal and interest immediately due and payable. Often, the acceleration is triggered by one of the following: the borrower's default in the payment of principal, interest, taxes, insurance, or other sums to be paid. Most promissory notes contain an acceleration clause, because without such a clause,

a lender could sue only for the unpaid balance of each periodic payment (usually monthly) in default.

Example: On default or any breach of any other promise or obligation in this Note or in any other instrument now or hereafter securing the indebtedness evidenced by this Note, then, and in any such event, Lender may, at its option, declare this Note (including, without limitation, all accrued interest) due and payable immediately regardless of the Maturity Date.

7. *Due-on-sale clause.* A due-on-sale clause is a form of an acceleration clause. When the borrower sells, transfers, or conveys its interest in the property, the lender has the right to accelerate and declare the entire unpaid balance of the loan due on the sale of the property.

Example: If Borrower sells, contracts to sell, gives an option to purchase, conveys, leases with an option to purchase, then Lender, at Lender's option, may, without prior notice, declare all sums secured by this Note due and payable immediately regardless of the Maturity Date.

8. *Guaranty.* A lender may require that an additional party, other than the borrower, guarantee the repayment and performance on the promissory note. Personal guarantees are common when the borrower to a promissory note is a corporation or limited liability company. With a corporation or limited liability entity, the lender may require the shareholders or members, respectively, to personally guarantee the debt. The guarantee provides the lender the right to sue the guarantors in the event the business entity is unable to pay the debt.

Example: The undersigned, in consideration of the extension of credit by Lender to Borrower, unconditionally personally guarantees the full and faithful payment of all amounts owed and performance of each and every one of the obligations, responsibilities, and undertakings to be carried out, performed, or observed by Borrower under the Note to Lender or Lender's successors and assigns. The undersigned consents to any extensions that may be made from time to time between Borrower and Lender, and consents to the release or substitution of any collateral.

■ ■ ■ Checklist for Drafting a Promissory Note

- ■ Parties
  - ☐ Maker (borrower)
  - ☐ Holder or payee (lender)
  - ☐ Guarantor(s), if any
- ■ Caption details
  - ☐ Amount of the note
  - ☐ Date
  - ☐ City and state in which note is made

- Interest rate
  - ☐ Fixed rate
  - ☐ Adjustable rate
  - ☐ Adjustment period
  - ☐ Index or reference rate identified
  - ☐ Maximum and/or minimum rates provided
  - ☐ Usury savings clause
- Payment
  - ☐ Time and manner of payment
  - ☐ Amount of payment
  - ☐ What is included in each payment (principal/interest and so on)
- Prepayment rights
  - ☐ No prepayment allowed
  - ☐ Prepayment allowed
    - ☐ Notice required
    - ☐ Prepayment fee
- Failure to pay
  - ☐ Late charges
    - ☐ Is there a grace period?
    - ☐ Amount and calculation of late charge
  - ☐ Default
    - ☐ Is there a grace period?
    - ☐ Notice required
    - ☐ Waiver of notice of default
    - ☐ Forbearance not a waiver
    - ☐ Acceleration of note on default
    - ☐ Court costs and expenses
    - ☐ Attorney fees
    - ☐ Default interest rate
  - ☐ Cross-default with other loans by lender to borrower
  - ☐ Waiver of homestead or other debtor's rights
  - ☐ Joint and several liability
- Security given for note
  - ☐ Mortgage or deed of trust
  - ☐ Assignment of leases and rents
  - ☐ Security agreement
- Guaranty
  - ☐ Personal guaranty
- Signatures
  - ☐ Maker signature
  - ☐ Holder signature
  - ☐ Guarantor signature
- Miscellaneous
  - ☐ Choice of law
  - ☐ Time is of the essence
  - ☐ Waiver of jury trial

Creation of a Mortgage

The mortgage is a document that gives the lender the right to have the property sold to repay the loan (the promissory note) if the borrower defaults under the terms of the note. The mortgage is recorded on the title to the property and creates an interest in land. Because a mortgage affects an interest in land, the Statute of Frauds requires that it be evidenced by a writing to be enforceable.

With a promissory note and mortgage, a lender can, subject to purchase money mortgage exceptions (discussed later in this chapter), sue a borrower to collect against the promissory note and foreclose on the property that secures the mortgage. This provides the lender with a higher degree of protection in lending money.

Mortgage Terms

While most lenders provide mortgages in a standardized form, a mortgage requires an expression of intent by the parties to create a security interest in the property pledged as collateral for a promissory note. Because mortgages are subject to state law, states may impose additional requirements and terms for a valid mortgage. Generally, the mortgage includes the following terms:

1. *Identification of parties.* The borrower and lender are identified.
2. *Property description.* The mortgaged property will be described unambiguously, usually with the legal description and a description of all personal property that is included as collateral for the loan.
3. *Promissory note terms and conditions.* Mortgages often include all the same provisions found in the promissory note including loan amounts, maturity dates, interest rates, prepayment charges and penalties, late fees, acceleration charges, and due on sale provision.
4. *Property insurance.* The lender will usually require the borrower to obtain property insurance to protect the lender's interest in the property in the event of a fire, earthquake, or flood. Where a borrower fails to maintain insurance, the lender often has a right to purchase the insurance on the borrower's behalf and charge the borrower for the cost of insurance.
5. *Maintenance and protection of the property.* The lender will require the borrower not to destroy, damage, or impair the property or allow the property to deteriorate or commit waste on the property. The lender is often provided the right to inspect the property (often annually in commercial mortgages) and make any necessary or reasonable repairs to maintain the property. By maintaining the property, the lender can maximize a return in the event the property needs to be sold.

Impound account
An account kept by a lender on behalf of a borrower to pay for insurance and property taxes.

6. *Impound Account.* The borrower is responsible for paying property taxes and insurance costs. Property taxes are usually paid annually or twice a year, and a homeowner's insurance fee is often paid once a year. To alleviate the financial burden these large payments can have on homeowners' cash flow, lenders can provide, and in some cases require, an impound, escrow, or reserve account. An impound account is an account in which the borrower prepays for the insurance and property taxes. These prepayments are paid monthly, along with the mortgage payment. The lender then pays the property taxes and insurance when due.
7. *Assignment-of-rents clause.* This clause is common in commercial mortgages. It entitles the lender to any rents or profits generated from the property in the event of default. This enables the lender potentially to recover proceeds during the debtor's default.

8. *Cross-collateralization and cross-default clauses.* Cross-collateralization refers to situations in which a lender makes multiple loans to a single borrower and provides that each piece of collateral is security for each and every loan. In the event of a default of one of the loans, the collateral from all of the loans may be used to pay the lender.

A cross-default provision makes a default under any one loan a default under the other loans. Cross-default provisions are important if borrowers who have little or no equity in one particular property may desire to stop making payments under that loan. With the cross-default provision, the borrower cannot stop payments on one loan without risking foreclosure on all loans.

> *Example:* Any default by Borrower as to any other loan or loans by Lender to Borrower shall, at Lender's option, constitute a default under this Note.

First and Second Mortgages

The same piece of real property can be used as collateral for more than one loan. The **first mortgage** is the one that is recorded first in time. The **second mortgage** is the mortgage recorded next in time. It is possible to have additional mortgages — third mortgages, fourth mortgages, and so on — but they do not occur in most circumstances. Second mortgages have a "junior" position behind the first mortgage. If the first mortgage lender foreclosures its lien, the second mortgage lien is terminated at the foreclosure sale (but not the related debt owing to the lender). Compared to first mortgages, second mortgages (and third mortgages, fourth mortgages, and so on) are usually offered for shorter periods of time and have higher interest rates than first mortgages to compensate for the increased risk.

First mortgage
The mortgage that is recorded first in time.

Second mortgage
The mortgage recorded next in time after a first mortgage is recorded.

Purchase Money Mortgage

A **purchase money mortgage** is a mortgage financing the purchase of a one- to four-unit residential property. A mortgage to purchase a commercial or residential property containing five or more units is not a purchase money mortgage. This mortgage can be for a partial or full purchase price amount. Whether a mortgage is considered, purchase money has significant consequences to a borrower following foreclosure. (We discuss deficiency judgments in chapter 11.)

Purchase money mortgage
A mortgage financing the purchase of a one- to four-unit residential property.

Checklist for Drafting a Mortgage/Deed of Trust

■ ■ ■

- ■ Date
- ■ Parties
  - ☐ Mortgage
    - ☐ Mortgagor (borrower)
    - ☐ Mortgagee (lender)

☐ Deed of trust
   ☐ Trustor (borrower)
   ☐ Beneficiary (lender)
   ☐ Trustee (party holding title)
☐ Guarantor(s)
■ Description of the property
   ☐ Legal description of the real property
   ☐ Description of any included personal property serving as collateral
■ Description of debt
   ☐ Miscellaneous terms and covenants
   ☐ Expression of intent by the parties to create a security interest
   ☐ Property insurance
   ☐ Maintenance and protection of the property
   ☐ Right to inspection of property
   ☐ Impound account for taxes and insurance
   ☐ Default provisions
   ☐ Choice of law
   ☐ Time is of the essence
   ☐ Assignment of leases and rents (commercial property)
   ☐ Cross-default and cross-collateralization
■ Signatures
   ☐ Mortgagor/trustor signature
   ☐ Guarantor signature
   ☐ Witnessed and notarized signatures
■ Mortgage/deed of trust recorded

Types of Loans

Conforming Versus Nonconforming Loans

Conforming loan
A loan that meets
Fannie Mae and
Freddie Mac purchase
criteria in the
secondary market.

Loans can be classified as either conforming or nonconforming (also known as jumbo loans). **Conforming loans** are loans for which the loan amounts are less than or equal to the maximum amount Congress has authorized Fannie Mae and Freddie Mac to purchase from lenders in the secondary market. A loan amount that exceeds the conforming Fannie Mae and Freddie Mac maximum loan limit is a **nonconforming loan**.

Nonconforming loan
A loan that fails to
meet Fannie Mae and
Freddie Mac purchase
criteria.

Government Insured Versus Conventional Mortgages

Loans are either government backed, which means they are insured or guaranteed by a government agency, or conventional, which means they are not insured by a government agency. The government does not act as a lender with government loans; instead, it insures or guarantees to the lender the loan balance, or the percentage of the loan balance, outstanding in the event of a default. As will be discussed, the government limits the amount of the loan balance it will insure. A conventional loan offers no governmental guarantee of repayment if a borrower defaults. With conventional loans, lenders may require a borrower to obtain private mortgage insurance (PMI). PMI is discussed below.

Government Sponsored Mortgage Programs

There are two primary government backed mortgage programs: Federal Housing Administration (FHA) loans and Veterans Administration loans.

FHA Insured Loans

The **Federal Housing Administration** (FHA) is a federal agency within the Department of Housing and Urban Development (HUD). The FHA is not a mortgage lender and does not make loans; instead, mortgage companies, savings banks, and commercial banks make the loans. The FHA offers insurance to these lenders against the total loss arising from a foreclosure. Its primary objective is to assist lenders in providing housing loans or lending opportunities for low- to moderate-income families.

An FHA loan is appropriate for a borrower who may not qualify for conventional financing because the qualifications for an FHA loan are less restrictive than conventional qualifications, allowing more people to qualify for these types of loans. The FHA will insure one- to four-unit properties, the **loans are assumable,** and the FHA allows for down payments of as little as 3.5 percent, depending on the applicant's credit score. The FHA sets a maximum loan amount it will guarantee. This amount can change from time to time and varies depending on whether the property is located in a high cost area.

Assumable loan
A loan where a person takes over the loan obligation and agrees to perform those obligations.

Because borrowers pose a higher risk and the FHA insures the loans, FHA loans often have higher fees. For example, FHA loans require an up-front insurance premium, and an annual **mortgage insurance premium** (MIP) is charged for a minimum of five years, regardless of the down payment amount.

VA Guaranteed Home Loans

The Department of Veteran Affairs (VA) provides a benefit for veterans and members of the National Guard. As with FHA loans, the VA is not a mortgage lender; instead, mortgage companies, savings banks, and commercial banks make the loans. However, unlike FHA loans, VA loans do not impose a maximum loan amount and are not insured. Instead, the VA guarantees a percentage of the loan (for most loans, the guarantee cannot exceed 25 percent) up to a certain limit. The limit is based on the county in which the property is located, and the percentage guaranteed by the federal government is based on the loan amount. The advantage of a VA loan is that it allows 100 percent financing (such as 0 percent down) and does not require any type of mortgage insurance premium.

Unlike FHA loans, VA loans are subject to eligibility requirements based on years of service. To secure a VA loan, the veteran must obtain a certificate of eligibility from the VA. Once a veteran uses the eligibility certificate, he may not qualify for another VA loan unless his eligibility is restored.

> *Example:* If a veteran sells the property and pays off the VA loan, he would need another certificate to purchase a new home.

Lenders may charge a funding fee similar to the FHA's insurance premium. VA loans, like FHA loans, are assumable and may be assumed by nonveterans.

Conventional Loans

Conventional loan
A loan made by an institutional lender that is neither guaranteed nor insured by the federal government.

Conventional loans are not insured or guaranteed by the federal government and are made by institutional lenders. **Institutional lenders**, such as commercial banks and savings and loan banks, take deposits from the general public. Because conventional lenders are not insured or guaranteed by the federal government, they are not subject to requirements like those of the FHA and VA loan programs. As noted above, the same bank can offer FHA, VA, and conventional loans. Most loans originated on one- to four-unit residential dwellings are conventional loans.

Institutional lender
A lender that makes loans to borrowers from its own sources or those that it manages for others.

In addition, conventional loans do not have the loan-maximum requirements placed on them by FHA programs. Lenders reduce their risk by requiring borrowers to provide a higher down payment (thereby reducing the loan amounts) for conventional loans. The ratio of debt to the value of the loan is known as the loan-to-value ratio. Loans that have a lower loan-to-value ratio are less risky to a lender because there is more equity in the property, reducing the risk to a lender in the event of a default. Lenders may also require borrowers to purchase private mortgage insurance if these borrowers seek to purchase a high-priced property with a low down payment (that is, a high loan-to-value ratio).

> **Example:** If a borrower seeks to purchase a $500,000 home and is able to contribute $100,000 as a down payment, the loan-to-value ratio is 80 percent.

Private Mortgage Insurance

Private mortgage insurance (PMI) insures lenders against foreclosure losses. Most lenders require PMI if the purchaser's down payment is less than 20 percent of the purchase price. If the borrower defaults, the mortgage insurer buys the loan from the lender and then enforces the debt obligations against the borrower. Premiums for PMI vary and are based on the loan-to-equity ratio of the property. Usually, they average about one-half of a percent. PMI insures only the amount financed in excess of 80 percent of the purchase price.

> **Example:** A borrower purchased a $400,000 home and financed 90 percent of the purchase price. The lender required PMI. In the event of a default, the mortgage insurer's risk is 10 percent of the purchase price ($40,000). This is the amount financed in excess of 80 percent of the purchase price.

The federal Homeowner's Protection Act[6] requires lenders to cancel the PMI once a loan reaches 78 percent of the property's original value. Lenders can refuse to cancel the insurance if the borrower has not been compliant with the loan terms (for example, if the borrower failed to make timely payments). Borrowers should note carefully the equity in their homes and demand that the lender cancel the PMI once 20 percent equity is reached so as to avoid paying PMI as soon as possible. Otherwise, the borrower will wait until the lender is required under the federal Homeowner's Protection Act to cancel the PMI insurance.

Other Types of Loans

A **subprime loan** is a loan made to a borrower who could not qualify for a loan from a conventional, FHA, or VA lender. Such borrowers typically have lower credit scores. Because their credit scores are less than ideal, they will pay higher interest rates and costs for a subprime loan. Foreclosure rates are higher for subprime loans than for other types of mortgage programs.

Subprime lending was one of the forces that resulted in the real estate collapse of 2007 and 2008. This crisis was caused by prolonged periods of easy credit, lending to unqualified buyers, the use of financial instruments that were complex and opaque, and a lack of effective regulatory oversight. One of the types of easy credit loans offered was an adjustable-rate loan with a low initial rate that borrowers could afford only as long as the rate stayed in effect. Once rates increased, borrowers were unable to continue making mortgage payments at the higher rates.

As a result, Congress passed several acts to reduce the likelihood of a similar situation occurring in the future. One such act, the Secure and Fair Enforcement for Mortgage Licensing Act (SAFE Act), was enacted to enhance consumer protection and reduce fraud by establishing minimum standards for the licensing and registration of *residential* state-licensed mortgage loan brokers. All residential mortgage loan originators must be either state licensed or federally registered.

Predatory Lending

Predatory lending is the term used to characterize unfair and deceptive mortgage practices directed at consumers by unscrupulous lenders who prey upon the poor, the undereducated, and the naïve. Often these practices are fraudulent and involved subprime loans. The following are some, but not all, of the practices considered predatory by the Mortgage Bankers Association:

Predatory lending
A term used to describe illegal and abusive lending practices (such as refinancing without any benefit to the borrower or making loans to borrowers who cannot repay the loan).

- Steering borrowers to high-rate lenders
- Structuring high-cost loans with payments the borrower cannot afford
- Falsifying loan documents
- Making loans to those lacking mental capacity
- Forging signatures on loan documents
- Making adverse changes to the loan terms at closing
- Falsely identifying the loan as a line of credit or open-end mortgage
- Charging excessive prepayment penalties or excessive charges for preparing loan releases
- Failing to provide accurate loan balance and payoff amounts, including failing to respond promptly to an inquiry for a loan payoff

In the following case, a lender made more than half of its loans to subprime borrowers. The Massachusetts attorney general sued the lender, alleging that it had acted unfairly and deceptively, in violation of the state's consumer protection statute. Shortly after this decision was issued, the lender's assets were sold to a third party, and the lender filed for bankruptcy protection.

COMMONWEALTH v. FREMONT INVESTMENT & LOAN

897 N.E.2d 548 (2008)

Massachusetts Supreme Judicial Court

Fremont was a bank that made 50 to 60 percent of its loans to subprime borrowers. After funding its loans, Fremont sold them on the secondary market. The Massachusetts Attorney General sued Fremont for violating the state's consumer protection statute. The Attorney General provided four characteristics that made it almost certain that borrowers would not be able to make the loan payments, leading to defaults and foreclosures. These factors were as follows: (1) the loans were adjustable, with an initial rate that applied for only three years; (2) the initial rate was three points lower than the usual mortgage rate on 30 year loans; (3) the debt-to-income ratio would exceed 50 percent after the initial period expired; and, (4) the loan-to-value ratio was 100 percent.

The trial judge stated that Fremont, as a lender, should have recognized that loans with the first three characteristics described were doomed to foreclosure unless the borrower could refinance the loan at or near the end of the introductory rate period and obtain in the process a new low introductory rate. The judge granted the injunction against Fremont. Fremont appealed the decision.

Language of the Court. *The record suggests that Fremont made no effort to determine whether borrowers could make the scheduled payments under the terms of the loan. Rather, loans were made with the understanding that they would have to be refinanced before the end of the introductory period. Fremont suggested that the loans were underwritten*

in the expectation, reasonable at the time, that housing prices would improve during the introductory loan term, and thus could be refinanced before the higher payments began. However, it was unreasonable, and unfair to the borrower, for Fremont to structure its loans on such unsupportable optimism. As a bank and mortgage lender, Fremont had been warned repeatedly (in the context of guidance on loan safety and soundness) that it needed to consider the performance of its loans in declining markets. Fremont cannot now claim that it was taken by surprise by the effects of an economic decline, or that it should not be held responsible.

The fact that the FDIC ordered Fremont to cease and desist from the use of almost precisely the loan features included in the judge's list of presumptively unfair characteristics indicates that the FDIC considered that, under established mortgage lending standards, marketing loans with these features constituted unsafe and unsound banking practice with clearly harmful consequences for borrowers. Such unsafe and unsound conduct on the part of a lender, insofar as it leads directly to injury for consumers, qualifies as unfair.

Decision. The court affirmed the trial court's decision to prohibit Fremont's lending practices.

FOCUS ON ETHICS

Is it ethical for lenders to issue subprime loans?

Types of Loan Payments

The following types of loan payments have been commonly used in the real estate industry. These loans may be available for either government backed or conventional loans.

Fixed-Rate Mortgages (Amortized Loans)

Fixed-rate mortgages, also known as **amortized loans**, have a fixed interest rate for the life of the loan. Most residential mortgages in the United States are amortized (repaid in regular payments over a given time) for the life of the loan, often with 30-year fixed rates, but it is common to find 15-, 20-, and 40-year maturity dates. Usually, the shorter the maturity date, the lower the interest rate charged. With fixed-rate mortgages, the monthly payment remains the same throughout the duration of the loan. The monthly payment pays both interest and principal throughout the duration of the loan.

To help lower the monthly payment amount, lenders can create loans in which the monthly payments during the fixed maturity are not sufficient to pay off the principal balance owed. This leaves a principal balance due (often referred to as a **balloon payment**) at the time of the loan's maturity. Balloon mortgage payments are often used in commercial lending transactions.

Balloon payment
A loan in which a balance remains due at the time of the loan's maturity.

> *Example:* A borrower obtains a $250,000, 30-year fixed mortgage at 5.5 percent. The lender and borrower agree that at the maturity date, a balloon payment of $50,000 is due. The balloon payment helps reduce the monthly payment the borrower needs to pay monthly but requires the borrower to pay $50,000 at the maturity of the loan.

Adjustable-Rate Mortgages

Adjustable-rate mortgages (ARMs) are mortgages in which the interest rate and the monthly payments may be adjusted periodically. The interest rate is tied to an agreed upon lending index at the time the loan is made.

> *Example:* The London Interbank Offered Rate (LIBOR) tracks the rate international banks charge each other for large loans in the London interbank market.

These loans may be adjusted monthly, quarterly, biannually, or annually. They include a fixed-rate component for a set period of time and then adjust as agreed.

> *Example:* A borrower may obtain a 30-year 7/1 ARM at 4.75 percent. This means the principal and interest are paid over a 30-year term. The 7/1 means the loan is fixed at 4.75 percent for the first seven years and then adjusts to a new interest rate at the end of each year thereafter until the loan is paid in full.

The loans have interest rate caps. The caps can limit the maximum interest rate increase in any one period or can cap the total amount that the interest rate may increase to over the life of the loan. These amounts are stated in the promissory note. Regulation Z (discussed later in this chapter) requires ARM lenders to make specific disclosures to borrowers before making adjustable-rate loans.

As an incentive for consumers to utilize adjustable-rate mortgages, lenders offer lower interest rates than fixed-rate mortgages at the onset of the mortgage. However, as the interest rates adjust, the risk to a borrower is that interest rates will rise in the future, making the adjustable-rate mortgage more expensive over time than the fixed-rate mortgage.

Interest-Only Mortgages (Straight Loans)

Straight loans, commonly known as **interest-only loans**, are loans in which the borrower pays only interest during the loan period, which is usually three to five years. No principal is paid during the loan period; instead, either the loan with principal and interest is amortized over the remaining loan term (often 25 to 27 years), or the principal balance is due at the end of the loan period (a balloon payment).

Piggyback Mortgages

With a **piggyback mortgage**, a borrower takes out two mortgages for the property at the same time. Usually the first mortgage is taken out at 80 percent of the purchase price so that the borrower does not have to pay PMI. At the same time, the borrower takes out a second mortgage on the property to cover the balance of the purchase price or a portion of the purchase price, with the remainder being a cash payment. The second mortgage's interest rate is usually higher than that of the first mortgage.

A common piggyback mortgage is an 80-10-10: the borrower takes out an 80 percent first mortgage, the second mortgage covers the next 10 percent of the purchase price, and the borrower pays 10 percent down on the home to cover the balance of the purchase price.

Reverse Mortgages (Home Equity Conversion Mortgages)

Reverse mortgage
A type of mortgage for people aged 62 or older whereby the mortgagor borrows against his or her equity by receiving monthly payments.

A **reverse mortgage**, or home equity conversion mortgage, is a type of mortgage for people aged 62 or older that allows homeowners to convert the equity in their home into cash. Reverse mortgages are available with owner-occupied family dwellings, condominiums, one- to four-dwelling-unit apartment buildings, and manufactured homes on separate lots. The borrower can take out the equity in the home as a loan in the form of either monthly payments to the borrower or a lump sum payment. No repayment of the mortgage is made until the borrower dies, the borrower vacates the home for more than one year, or the home is sold. The transaction is structured so that the loan amount will not exceed the value of the home over the term of the loan.

The guidelines for reverse mortgages are complex, and not all lenders offer them. Reverse mortgages often require up-front fees that can equal as much as 5 percent of the home's value. In addition, the interest on the mortgage is compounded, and the borrower must pay an annual insurance premium. These factors reduce the equity and potential wealth transfer to the next generation.

Home Equity Loans

A **home equity loan** is a type of second mortgage in which the borrower is able to obtain a second mortgage on the property based on the property's equity (by a down payment amount or appreciation in property value). Lenders often require the borrower to have obtained 20 percent equity in the property before they will grant a home equity loan. The property is pledged as collateral toward the repayment of the loan.

A **home equity line of credit** (HELOC) is similar, but unlike a home equity loan, in which the loan amount is distributed immediately to the borrower, a HELOC allows the borrower to draw against the line of credit as the borrower desires, up to a maximum amount set by the lender. The borrower thereafter repays the HELOC, usually monthly, as required by the lender. HELOCs have higher interest rates than first mortgages.

> **Home Equity Line of Credit (HELOC)**
> A type of loan allowing the borrower to draw against a line of credit secured by the equity in the borrower's property.

Other Types of Loan Payments

Sale Leaseback

A **sale leaseback** is a transaction in which a property owner sells the property to an investor, who then immediately leases the property back to the seller. This type of transaction is used in commercial transactions in which the seller wants to free up invested capital while retaining possession and control of the property under the lease. The investor is provided a prearranged return on the investment over the lease period. The investor also obtains the income tax benefits of ownership and retains the security of the title in its name.

Wraparound Mortgages (Subordinate Loans)

In a **wraparound mortgage** or subordinate loan, the seller keeps the existing mortgage on the property and extends to the buyer a junior mortgage that wraps around and exists in addition to a senior mortgage. The buyer has no liability on the original loan made between the seller and the lender. The junior mortgage amount is for the principal amount due on the underlying mortgage (mortgage between seller and lender), plus an

Buyer makes payment made to Seller

```
┌─────────────────────────────────────────────────────┐
│              Wraparound Mortgage                     │
│               (Buyer of Property)                    │
│  (New note to seller is subordinate (junior to       │
│   Original Loan)                                     │
│  $200,000 – Note and mortgage to seller              │
│  20 year mortgage @ 6.5 % fixed                      │
│  $1,491 – Monthly Payment                            │
│                                                      │
│        ┌──────────────────────────────────┐          │
│        │          Original Loan           │          │
│        │        (Seller of Property)      │          │
│        │  $150,000 – Principal balance     │          │
│        │  owing                           │          │
│        │  20 years to maturity (30 year    │          │
│        │  loan @ 5% fixed)                 │          │
│        │  $805 - Monthly Payment          │          │
│        └──────────────────────────────────┘          │
└─────────────────────────────────────────────────────┘
```

FIGURE 9.4. Wraparound Mortgage

additional amount representing the purchase price in excess of the underlying debt. The buyer makes monthly payments to the seller, who is responsible for making payments on the senior mortgage.

Upon default by the wraparound mortgagor (buyer), the wraparound mortgagee can foreclose for the entire amount due under the wraparound mortgage, including the amount due under the senior mortgage. Wraparound mortgages can only be used when there is no due-on-sale clause in an existing mortgage loan on the property; otherwise, the sale of the property to a buyer would trigger the due-on-sale clause.

Taking Subject to and Assuming Mortgages

At times, a property is sold without paying the balance due on the existing mortgage. This occurs when the purchaser takes "subject to the mortgage" or when the purchaser assumes the mortgage.

Taking Subject to a Mortgage

Taking subject to a mortgage
When a purchaser buys real estate aware of a mortgage and makes payments on the mortgage but does not agree to become personally liable to repay the mortgage debt.

If an existing mortgage does not contain a due-on-sale clause, a buyer may purchase a home subject to the mortgage. When **taking subject to a mortgage**, the buyer takes title to the property but is not personally liable for payment of the mortgage debt. The seller remains liable for the payments on the mortgage. If the mortgage goes into default, the lender may foreclose. The lender may enforce payment only against the original owner. Purchasing a property subject to a mortgage may be desirable when the seller's interest rate on the mortgage is lower than the rate currently available for new loans.

> *Example:* George purchased a home and secured a 30-year mortgage at a fixed rate of 3.75 percent. Ten years later, after interest rates had risen to 8 percent, George sold the home to William, who purchased the home subject to George's existing mortgage. George will still be liable to the original lender if William defaults with regard to the terms of the mortgage.

Assuming an Existing Mortgage

Assume an existing mortgage
When a purchaser agrees to become personally liable for an existing mortgage obligation in a real estate purchase.

Instead of purchasing a home subject to a mortgage, a new purchaser might **assume an existing mortgage**. When assuming a mortgage, the buyer takes over an existing mortgage from the seller. The buyer becomes personally liable for the mortgage payments, while the original owner remains liable for the repayment of the loan. This allows the lender two people (original owner and purchaser) to seek repayment of the loan. If the lender forecloses, the original owner can sue the assuming purchaser.

The original owner may have the lender consent to a release of liability and may request that the lender substitute the new purchaser in place of the original mortgagor. This is known as **novation**. Under a novation, the original owner is no longer liable on the property, while the new purchaser is personally liable. This is the safest approach for a seller who does not desire to remain liable on the loan after transfer of the title to the buyer.

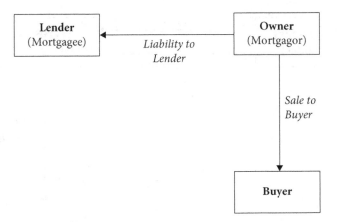

FIGURE 9.5. Taking Subject to a Mortgage

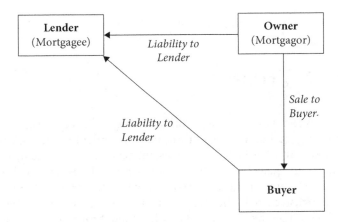

FIGURE 9.6. Assuming an Existing Mortgage

Concept Summary

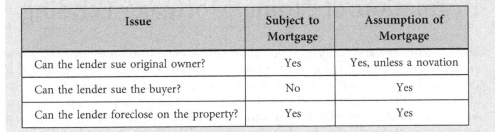

Issue	Subject to Mortgage	Assumption of Mortgage
Can the lender sue original owner?	Yes	Yes, unless a novation
Can the lender sue the buyer?	No	Yes
Can the lender foreclose on the property?	Yes	Yes

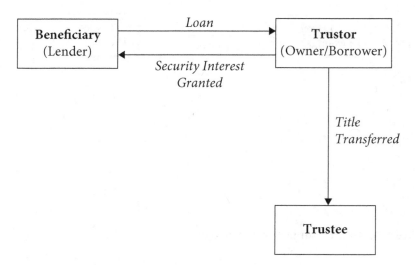

FIGURE 9.7. Deed of Trust

Deeds of Trust

Deed of trust
A three-party instrument financing arrangement that involves a beneficiary, a trustor, and a trustee.

Beneficiary
The lender identified in a deed of trust.

Trustor
The property owner or party to a deed of trust.

Trustee
The party to a deed of trust who holds (equitable) title until the underlying obligation is paid in full. Responds to demands of the beneficiary regarding enforcement of the deed of trust.

Some jurisdictions allow the use of a promissory note and deed of trust. A **deed of trust** is similar to a mortgage, but it involves three parties. Under the deed of trust, the lender is called the **beneficiary**. The beneficiary does not have actual ownership of the property but instead has a lien against it. The borrower or property owner is called the **trustor**. The trustor conveys title to a third party known as the **trustee** (usually a financial institution). The trustee holds the deed of trust for the beneficiary's benefit until the underlying obligation on the note is paid in full. When the loan is paid, the trustee files a written reconveyance with the local public recorder's office; this returns the title to the trustor.

Lenders benefit from deeds of trust because, compared to the traditional mortgage foreclosure process, such a setup enables a swift, inexpensive sale of the property in the event of a default (discussed in chapter 11).

Regulation of Home Mortgage Lending

Many federal laws and regulations govern the financing of real property, especially in the area of residential lending. Among them are the Equal Credit Opportunity Act of 1974, the Truth-in-Lending Act, the Real Estate Settlement Procedures Act of 1974 (discussed in the next chapter), the Community Reinvestment Act, Homeowner's Protection Act (HPA), Home Ownership and Equity Protection Act (HOEPA), Mortgage Assistance Relief Services Rule, and the Dodd-Frank Wall Street Reform and Consumer Protection Act. Several of these regulations are discussed below.

Mortgages vs. Deed of Trust		
	Mortgage	**Deed of Trust**
Parties Involved	Mortgagor – Borrower Mortgagee – Lender	Trustor – Borrower Beneficiary – Lender Trustee – Disinterested third party
Foreclosure Method	Judicial (court action is required)	Judicial or non-judicial means
Benefits	Right to deficiency judgments against borrower	Quicker and cheaper to obtain title than through mortgage foreclosure process
Detriments	Costlier and more time consuming than non-judicial foreclosures	Usually no right to deficiency judgment when non-judicial foreclosure is used

FIGURE 9.8. Mortgages v. Deed of Trust

Equal Credit Opportunity Act of 1974

The Equal Credit Opportunity Act of 1974 makes it unlawful for any lender to discriminate, with respect to any aspect of a lending transaction, on the basis of race, color, religion, national origin, sex, marital status, age, or because any part of the applicant's income derives from a public-assistance program. If a loan is denied, the lender must provide the specific reason for the denial.

Truth-in-Lending Act

The **Truth-in-Lending Act** (TILA) requires disclosures to consumers about the terms and costs of loans. TILA's purpose is to require uniform disclosures of terms and costs by lenders; this provides consumers the opportunity to compare lenders by the costs and credit terms provided. Consumers are also provided the right to cancel certain credit transactions. The regulations that implemented the Act are known collectively as **Regulation Z**, which is intended to provide borrowers with uniform disclosure of important information. TILA does not apply to the following transaction types:

1. Business transactions (including rental housing)
2. Commercial transactions
3. Agricultural transactions
4. Organizational credit transactions

Under the Dodd-Frank Wall Street Reform and Consumer Protection Act (Dodd-Frank Act), which is discussed below, the Consumer Financial Protection Bureau (CFPB) integrated two forms required by the two federal statutes (the initial Truth-in-Lending statement and the Good Faith Estimate). The integrated forms are known as the **TILA-RESPA Integrated Disclosure rule (TRID)**. The integrated disclosure, given near the loan application, is known as the **Loan Estimate**.

Truth in Lending Act
Federal law requiring disclosures to consumers allowing consumers to compare loan terms and conditions by various lenders.

Regulation Z
Federal Reserve regulations implementing the Truth-in-Lending Act.

Organizational credit transactions
Loans not made to natural persons, such as loans to corporations, partnerships, churches, unions, or fraternal organizations.

TILA-RESPA Integrated Disclosure rule
CFPB rule requiring specific loan disclosures to consumer borrowers

Loan Estimate
Disclosures provided no later than three business days after consumer submits a loan application providing key features, costs, and risks of the mortgage for which they are applying.

FICUS BANK

4321 Random Boulevard • Somecity, ST 12340

Save this Loan Estimate to compare with your Closing Disclosure.

Loan Estimate

		LOAN TERM	30 years
		PURPOSE	Purchase
DATE ISSUED	2/15/2013	PRODUCT	5 Year Interest Only, 5/3 Adjustable Rate
APPLICANTS	Michael Jones and Mary Stone	LOAN TYPE	☒ Conventional ☐ FHA ☐ VA ☐ _____
	123 Anywhere Street	LOAN ID #	123456789
	Anytown, ST 12345	RATE LOCK	☐ NO ☒ YES, until 4/16/2013 at 5:00 p.m. EDT
PROPERTY	456 Somewhere Avenue		*Before closing, your interest rate, points, and lender credits can*
	Anytown, ST 12345		*change unless you lock the interest rate. All other estimated*
SALE PRICE	$240,000		*closing costs expire on 3/4/2013 at 5:00 p.m. EDT*

Loan Terms

		Can this amount increase after closing?
Loan Amount	$211,000	**NO**
Interest Rate	4%	**YES** • Adjusts **every 3 years** starting in year 6 • Can go **as high as 12%** in year 15 • See **AIR Table on page 2** for details
Monthly Principal & Interest *See Projected Payments below for your Estimated Total Monthly Payment*	$703.33	**YES** • Adjusts **every 3 years** starting in year 6 • Can go **as high as $2,068** in year 15 • Includes **only interest** and **no principal** until year 6 • See **AP Table on page 2** for details
		Does the loan have these features?
Prepayment Penalty		**NO**
Balloon Payment		**NO**

Projected Payments

Payment Calculation	Years 1-5	Years 6-8	Years 9-11	Years 12-30
Principal & Interest	$703.33 *only interest*	$1,028 min $1,359 max	$1,028 min $1,604 max	$1,028 min $2,068 max
Mortgage Insurance	+ 109	+ 109	+ 109	+ —
Estimated Escrow *Amount can increase over time*	+ 0	+ 0	+ 0	+ 0
Estimated Total Monthly Payment	**$812**	**$1,137–$1,468**	**$1,137–$1,713**	**$1,028–$2,068**

Estimated Taxes, Insurance & Assessments *Amount can increase over time*	$533 a month	This estimate includes ☒ Property Taxes ☒ Homeowner's Insurance ☐ Other: *See Section G on page 2 for escrowed property costs. You must pay for other property costs separately.*	In escrow? NO NO

Costs at Closing

Estimated Closing Costs	$8,791	Includes $5,851 in Loan Costs + $2,940 in Other Costs – $0 in Lender Credits. *See page 2 for details.*
Estimated Cash to Close	$27,791	Includes Closing Costs. *See Calculating Cash to Close on page 2 for details.*

Visit **www.consumerfinance.gov/mortgage-estimate** for general information and tools.

Exhibit 9.3. Loan Estimate

Closing Cost Details

Loan Costs

A. Origination Charges	$3,110
1 % of Loan Amount (Points)	$2,110
Application Fee	$500
Processing Fee	$500

B. Services You Cannot Shop For	$820
Appraisal Fee	$305
Credit Report Fee	$30
Flood Determination Fee	$35
Lender's Attorney Fee	$400
Tax Status Research Fee	$50

C. Services You Can Shop For	$1,921
Pest Inspection Fee	$125
Survey Fee	$150
Title – Courier Fee	$32
Title – Lender's Title Policy	$665
Title – Settlement Agent Fee	$325
Title – Title Search	$624

D. TOTAL LOAN COSTS (A + B + C)	$5,851

Other Costs

E. Taxes and Other Government Fees	$152
Recording Fees and Other Taxes	$152
Transfer Taxes	

F. Prepaids	$1,352
Homeowner's Insurance Premium (12 months)	$1,000
Mortgage Insurance Premium (months)	
Prepaid Interest ($23.44 per day for 15 days @ 4.00%)	$352
Property Taxes (months)	

G. Initial Escrow Payment at Closing			
Homeowner's Insurance	per month for	mo.	
Mortgage Insurance	per month for	mo.	
Property Taxes	per month for	mo.	

H. Other	$1,436
Title – Owner's Title Policy (optional)	$1,436

I. TOTAL OTHER COSTS (E + F + G + H)	$2,940

J. TOTAL CLOSING COSTS	$8,791
D + I	$8,791
Lender Credits	

Calculating Cash to Close

Total Closing Costs (J)	$8,791
Closing Costs Financed (Paid from your Loan Amount)	$0
Down Payment/Funds from Borrower	$29,000
Deposit	– $10,000
Funds for Borrower	$0
Seller Credits	$0
Adjustments and Other Credits	$0
Estimated Cash to Close	$27,791

Adjustable Payment (AP) Table

Interest Only Payments?	YES for your first 60 payments
Optional Payments?	NO
Step Payments?	NO
Seasonal Payments?	NO
Monthly Principal and Interest Payments	
First Change/Amount	$1,028 – $1,359 at 61st payment
Subsequent Changes	Every three years
Maximum Payment	$2,068 starting at 169th payment

Adjustable Interest Rate (AIR) Table

Index + Margin	MTA + 4%
Initial Interest Rate	4%
Minimum/Maximum Interest Rate	3.25%/12%
Change Frequency	
First Change	Beginning of 61st month
Subsequent Changes	Every 36th month after first change
Limits on Interest Rate Changes	
First Change	2%
Subsequent Changes	2%

Exhibit 9.3. Loan Estimate (*Continued*)

Additional Information About This Loan

LENDER	Ficus Bank	**MORTGAGE BROKER**	
NMLS/__ LICENSE ID		**NMLS/__ LICENSE ID**	
LOAN OFFICER	Joe Smith	**LOAN OFFICER**	
NMLS/__ LICENSE ID	12345	**NMLS/__ LICENSE ID**	
EMAIL	joesmith@ficusbank.com	**EMAIL**	
PHONE	123-456-7890	**PHONE**	

Comparisons	Use these measures to compare this loan with other loans.	
In 5 Years	$54,944	Total you will have paid in principal, interest, mortgage insurance, and loan costs.
	$0	Principal you will have paid off.
Annual Percentage Rate (APR)	4.617%	Your costs over the loan term expressed as a rate. This is not your interest rate.
Total Interest Percentage (TIP)	81.18%	The total amount of interest that you will pay over the loan term as a percentage of your loan amount.

Other Considerations	
Appraisal	We may order an appraisal to determine the property's value and charge you for this appraisal. We will promptly give you a copy of any appraisal, even if your loan does not close. You can pay for an additional appraisal for your own use at your own cost.
Assumption	If you sell or transfer this property to another person, we ☐ will allow, under certain conditions, this person to assume this loan on the original terms. ☒ will not allow assumption of this loan on the original terms.
Homeowner's Insurance	This loan requires homeowner's insurance on the property, which you may obtain from a company of your choice that we find acceptable.
Late Payment	If your payment is more than *15* days late, we will charge a late fee of *5% of the monthly principal and interest payment.*
Refinance	Refinancing this loan will depend on your future financial situation, the property value, and market conditions. You may not be able to refinance this loan.
Servicing	We intend ☐ to service your loan. If so, you will make your payments to us. ☒ to transfer servicing of your loan.

Confirm Receipt

By signing, you are only confirming that you have received this form. You do not have to accept this loan because you have signed or received this form.

_____   _____   _____   _____
Applicant Signature   Date   Co-Applicant Signature   Date

Exhibit 9.3. Loan Estimate (*Continued*)

TILA-RESPA Integrated Disclosure Rule Coverage

TRID applies to most closed-end consumer credit transactions secured by real property. A closed-end transaction is one in which the full amount owed (principal, interest, and finance charges) must be paid back by the borrower by a set point in time. Consumer credit means credit offered or extended to a consumer primarily for personal, family, or household purposes. The residential property must be either a one- to four-unit family structure or a manufactured home (mobile home). The Act covers first and second mortgages, refinancing, construction-only loans, loans secured by vacant land, and loans secured by 25 or more acres.

TRID does not apply to:

- Home equity lines of credit (HELOC)
- Reverse mortgages
- Mortgages secured by a mobile home
- Mortgages secured by a dwelling that is not attached to real property (that is, land)

Where TRID does not apply, the borrower will receive a Truth-in-Lending disclosure.

Loan Estimate Timing

Borrowers subject to a Loan Estimate must receive the Loan Estimate no later than the third business day after the lender receives the consumer's application. The Loan Estimate must also be delivered or placed in the mail no later than the seventh business day before the transaction is completed. The Loan Estimate provides disclosures in an easy to understand format that provides the key features, costs, and risks of the mortgage loan for which consumers are applying.

Contents of the Loan Estimate

The Loan Estimate is composed of three pages. Page 1 includes the name and address of the lender and a Loan Terms table with descriptions of applicable information about the loan, including the loan amount, interest rate, monthly principal and interest payment, any prepayment penalties, any required balloon payment, and the estimated costs at closing.

Page 2 includes four main categories of charges: (1) a good faith itemization of the loan costs, taxes, insurance, and other costs associated with the closing; (2) a calculation of the amount of cash needed at closing; (3) for transactions with adjustable monthly payments, an Adjustable Payment Table with relevant information about how the monthly payments will change; and (4) for transactions with adjustable interest rates, an Adjustable Interest Rate Table with relevant information about how the interest rate will change.

Page 3 includes the contact information for the lender; an easy-to-use comparison table that allows the consumer to compare the cost of the loan offer against other loan offers from different lenders; and other considerations the borrower should take into account regarding the loan, such as late payment charges and whether the lender intends to service the loan (that is, whether payments will be made to the lender).

Special Information Booklet

In addition, at the time of the loan application, or no later than three business days after receiving the loan application, lenders must provide borrowers with a "special information booklet" entitled "Your Home Loan Toolkit: A Step-by-Step Guide." The booklet is designed to inform consumers of the steps they need to take to get the best mortgage for their individual situation, to help consumers understand their closing costs and what it takes to buy a home, and to give consumers tips on how to be a successful homeowner.

Right of Rescission

If the borrower is applying for a second mortgage or a home equity line of credit on a residential property, the borrower is given three business days to cancel the agreement. The three-day clock does not start until all three of the following events have happened: (1) the borrower signs the credit contract (usually known as the Promissory Note); (2) the borrower receives a Truth-in-Lending disclosure (in most circumstances, this will be the Closing Disclosure form); and (3) the borrower receives two copies of a notice explaining the borrower's right to rescind. The right to rescission does not apply to first mortgages.

In addition, if a lender fails to provide any of the required disclosures, the borrower is entitled to a three-year right of rescission on all types of residential mortgages (including first mortgages).

In the following case, a husband obtained a loan and placed a second mortgage on his home. At the time the mortgage was executed, neither the husband nor his wife were provided with the appropriate disclosures required by law. Over a year later, the wife sought to rescind the second mortgage.

CASE 9.2

ABSENCE OF DISCLOSURES TO SPOUSE MAY LEAD TO RELEASE OF LIABILITY TO LENDER

GANCEDO v. DEL CARPIO

17 So.3d 843 (2009)

Florida District Court of Appeal

Gancedo loaned $60,000 to Rafel Del Carpio ("Rafel"). To secure the loan, Rafel gave Gancedo a second mortgage on his home that was solely in Rafel's name and not in that of his wife, Sylvia. Both Rafel and Sylvia signed the mortgage; however, the promissory note was only signed by Rafel. Gancedo did not provide either Rafel or Sylvia with disclosures required by the Truth in Lending Act (TILA). Rafel defaulted on the promissory note and mortgage, and Gancedo filed an action to foreclosure on the property. However, Sylvia exercised her right to cancel the transaction within three years from the date of the mortgage under the TILA due to Gancedo's failure to provide the required TILA disclosures. Gancedo argued that Sylvia was not entitled to the disclosures because she had no ownership interest in the property at the time the mortgage was executed and the three-year time period extension did not apply.

Language of the Court. *TILA's purpose is to promote the informed use of credit by "consumers." Through its enactment, Congress sought to assure a meaningful disclosure of credit terms so that the "consumer" would be able to compare more readily the various credit terms available and avoid the uninformed use of credit.*

A natural person to whom consumer credit is offered or extended is a consumer. However, for purposes of rescission of consumer loan, the term also includes a natural person in whose principal dwelling a security interest is or will be retained or acquired, if that person's ownership interest in the dwelling is or will be subject to the security interest.

Sylvia asserts that she had an "ownership interest" in the home, which would bring her within the definition of the term "consumer." The record is clear that the Del Carpios were married at the time that the subject mortgage loan transaction was entered into. As such, Sylvia had homestead rights in the property.

Decision. The Court of Appeal of Florida affirmed the lower court's ruling. It held that Sylvia had an ownership interest in the home at the time the mortgage was executed. She was entitled to TILA disclosures and allowed to cancellation her liability under the loan during the three-year cancellation period.

FOCUS ON ETHICS

Is this a fair decision to both the lender and the borrower?

Advertising

To promote accurate advertisements, if a lender uses certain language, called triggering terms, in the advertisement, Regulation Z requires that certain disclosures also be made to the consumer. A triggering term includes a reference to the amount or number of monthly payments, the cash amount or percentage of down payment required, the length of the loan, or the amount of finance charges. If a triggering term is used, then lenders must disclose the amounts for all the triggering terms, as well as the APR. Note that the use of an APR in an advertisement is not by itself a triggering term requiring disclosure of the other terms.

Exercise 9.2

In each of the following advertisements, determine if triggering terms are used that require Regulation Z disclosure.

1. Rates as low as 5 percent down.
2. Thirty-year fixed loans with rates as low as 5 percent.
3. Condominium for sale with monthly payments of $1,000.
4. Great financing deals available with monthly payments tailored to fit your budget.
5. Single-family home for sale with no down payment required.

Community Reinvestment Act (CRA)

The Community Reinvestment Act (CRA)[7] requires all federally supervised financial institutions to disclose their lending data in their front lobbies and elsewhere. Financial institutions are required to report data regarding the race, gender, income, and census tract of people to whom they lend money. The government grades each institution on the group's efforts to inform the community of available credit and make such loans.

Dodd-Frank Wall Street Reform and Consumer Protection Act

The Dodd-Frank Wall Street Reform and Consumer Protection Act (Dodd-Frank) is a federal statute that covers the reform of financial institutions. It is the most significant change in financial regulation in the United States to have taken place since the reforms after the Great Depression in the 1930s. The Act created several federal agencies, including the Bureau of Consumer Financial Protection (the Bureau).

The Bureau has the power to supervise all participants in the consumer-finance and mortgage arenas. It regulates depository institutions such as commercial and savings banks, as well as nondepositories such as insurance companies, mortgage brokers, credit-counseling firms, debt collection firms, and debt buyers. The Bureau regulates unfair, deceptive, or abusive acts or practices in consumer products and services, and it has broad authority over all forms of consumer transactions. Dodd-Frank broadens the disclosures that must be made to consumers. In addition, it disallows balloon payments and prepayment penalties for certain high-cost mortgages. If a lender violates the law, a borrower may raise these violations as a foreclosure defense.

Construction Loans

A **construction loan** provides the financing to pay for the cost of developing and constructing an improvement on real property. Construction loans often include a sum allowing the borrower to purchase the land. The borrower's funds are used to develop the property and pay for the cost of engineering, architectural, and construction work.

Construction loans are short-term loans by which the borrower pays interest only on the outstanding balance. Once construction is completed, the construction loan is repaid in full by a permanent loan. The construction loan lasts for the period of construction, which usually runs less than 24 months.

Loan Commitment

Loan commitment
A lender's promise to make a loan upon the occurrence of certain conditions.

Negotiating a construction loan begins with a construction loan commitment. The **loan commitment** describes the major loan terms that will be incorporated into the final documents, provides for the conditions required to close the construction loan, and documents the rights and duties of both the lender and the developer of the real property from the time of the commitment until the construction loan closes. The loan commitment also allows both parties to the loan instrument to conduct further due diligence.

As part of the due diligence, the lender will require evidence that the property is properly zoned for its intended use and that all governmental approvals and permits required for the construction project have been or will be obtained. In addition, the lender will require the borrower to provide environmental, seismic, soils, and flood-plain reports. The lender will order its own property appraisal and require that a property survey be conducted and updated upon the project's completion.

Construction Loan Agreement

Once the parties have completed their due diligence regarding the loan commitment, a construction loan agreement is created. This agreement describes the loan fees the borrower will pay to the lender. The fees are usually nonrefundable, even if the loan does not close. The fees are negotiated and paid for during the formation of the loan commitment. Typical loan terms in a construction loan commitment include the following:

- Maximum value of the construction loan amount.
- The commencement and completion dates for the project. The commitment will also state whether a right exists to extend the loan's maturity date, as well as the cost for doing so.
- The amount of equity the borrower must have invested in the project.
- The reserve amount set aside within the loan to pay for interest accruing during the loan's duration.
- Any preleasing or presales requirements. This requirement is important for multiunit construction but is not required for single-family residential construction.

As part of the construction loan package, the lender will have the option, upon the occurrence of certain default events, to complete the construction and recover from the borrower (and any guarantors) the cost of the work required to complete the improvements.

Disbursement of Loan Proceeds

The lender disburses the construction loan proceeds throughout the course of construction in accordance with the loan terms. Usually, the funds are disbursed upon the achievement of certain milestones. Often, these milestones relate to the percentage of project completion. The lender will require an inspector or architect to approve the contractor's progress billings.

Installment Land Sale Contracts

As an alternative to a mortgage or deed of trust, property may also be bought under an installment land sale contract, also known as a contract for deed arrangement. In an **installment land sale contract**, the seller provides the financing to the buyer. The seller retains title to the property as security until the final payment is received. Payments are allocated to principal and interest similar to the allocation used for amortized mortgage payments; alternatively, the contract may involve a balloon payment. The buyer is entitled to possession of the land during the repayment period. Once the buyer has paid the seller all, or substantially all, of the purchase price agreed to in the contract, the buyer receives title to the property.

Installment land sale contracts are widely used in real estate transactions, including those relating to low-cost housing and vacation lots. No bank loan is necessary, the down payment can be small, and the seller may be willing to sell to persons who would not qualify for a conventional loan.

Risks to the Buyer

The lack of a legal title poses some risks for the buyer. If a long period of time elapses between the contract's execution and the time the seller delivers the deed, many things may occur to cause litigation between the seller and the buyer: The seller may die or become bankrupt or incompetent. Moreover, the installment land sale contract could trigger a due-on-sale clause within the seller's existing property financing.

Advantages to the Seller

An advantage to the installment land sale process is that the seller does not have to pursue foreclosure proceedings. The seller can exercise contractual remedies to declare the purchase contract forfeited. Some jurisdictions provide that a buyer forfeits all principal and interest payments made to the seller in the event of a default. However, some jurisdictions hold that if the buyer has paid a substantial portion of the purchase price to the seller, the seller would be unjustly enriched by complete forfeiture; in these jurisdictions, the seller is required to pursue foreclosure proceedings similar to those used for a mortgage.

In the following case, a buyer agreed to purchase the seller's home using an installment land sale contract. The contract provided only a 30-day period to cure a default before the seller could terminate the contract, take possession, and retain all payments made. The New York court held that the installment sales contract was a financing device, placing the buyer in the same position as a mortgagor. Not all states treat installment land sale contracts as a financing device, and the contract can be enforced to cut off the buyer's rights. That was the issue in this case.

CASE 9.3

INSTALLMENT LAND SALE CONTRACTS MAY BE TREATED AS EQUITY

BEAN v. WALKER
95 A.D. 2d 70 (1983)
New York Supreme Court, Appellate Division

In 1973, Carl Walker agreed to buy a home in Syracuse, New York, from Franklin Bean for $15,000. The installment land sale contract stated that the sum would be paid in monthly installments over a 15-year period at 5 percent interest. Bean

retained legal title until he was paid in full. The contract provided that if Walker defaulted in making payments and failed to cure the default within 30 days, Bean could elect to call the remaining balance immediately due or elect to declare the contract terminated and repossess the house. If Bean were to choose the second option, he could retain all the money paid under the contract as liquidated damages. After falling upon hard times owing to an injury, Walker defaulted on the contract, having paid over $12,000 in principal and interest and having made substantial improvements to the house. Bean gave the 30-day notice and filed suit to eject Walker and have Bean declared the lawful owner of the property. The trial court granted summary judgment for Bean. Walker appealed.

Language of the Court. *Certain general principles may be observed. It is well settled that the owner of the real estate, from the time of the execution of a valid contract for its sale, is to be treated as the owner of the purchase money, and the purchaser of the land is to be treated as the equitable owner thereof. The purchase money becomes personal property. Thus, notwithstanding the words of the contract and implications that may arise therefrom, the law of property declares that, upon the execution of a contract for sale of land, the buyer acquires equitable title. The seller holds the legal title in trust for the buyer and has an equitable lien for the payment of the purchase price. The buyer in possession, for all practical purposes, is the owner of the property with all the rights of an owner, subject only to the terms of the contract.*

The effect of the judgment granted by the trial court is that Bean would have the property with improvements made over the years by Walker, along with over $7,000 in principal payments on a purchase price of $15,000, and over $4,000 in interest. The basic inequity of such a result requires no further comment. If a forfeiture would result in the inequitable disposition of property and an exorbitant monetary loss, equity can and should intervene.

Decision. The judgment was reversed. Bean as the seller must foreclose upon Walker's interest or file a lawsuit seeking to recover the purchase price.

FOCUS ON ETHICS

Should state law permit a forfeiture of all principal and interest payments made to the seller in the event of a default?

Key Terms and Concepts

Chapter Summary

- To appraise real estate means to estimate its current market value.

- Three approaches are used to estimate the value of property. The market approach (sales comparison approach) is determined by prices paid for similar properties in the neighborhood. The cost approach estimates the value of the completed project and the cost to build a comparable project. With the income approach, the appraisal value is determined based upon the property's ability to generate income or potential income.

- The Financial Institutions Reform, Recovery and Enforcement Act (FIRREA) requires states to establish requirements for the licensing and certification of real estate appraisers.

- There are four common categories of appraisers: (1) trainee appraiser, (2) licensed residential appraiser, (3) certified residential appraiser, and (4) certified general appraiser.

- A mortgage is a security interest in real property. The mortgagors convey the mortgage to the mortgagee, who is the creditor or lender. Generally, every transfer of an interest in real property that is made to secure the performance of another act is considered to be a mortgage.

- The promissory note is the buyer's personal promise to make the payments. The mortgage causes the property to serve as collateral for the repayment of the note.

- Real estate lending begins with the application and continues with processing and document gathering, followed by underwriting.

- A mortgage loan originator is someone who, for compensation, takes residential loan applications and offers or negotiates residential mortgage loan terms.

- It is the underwriter's task to determine the magnitude of the risk presented by the borrower and the secured property and to compensate for them in the terms and conditions of the loan.

- Under the lien theory, the mortgage is only a lien on the property to secure payment of the debt.

- Under the title theory, a mortgage is a transfer of property, even though it is only to secure the repayment of the debt.

- The mortgage must comply with common law and statutory requirements, including the state Statute of Frauds.

- A purchase money mortgage is granted by a purchase or property to secure payment of the purchase price. It must be granted at the same time the deed is delivered.

- The following types of loan payments have been commonly used in the real estate industry: fixed-rate mortgages, adjustable-rate mortgages, straight loans, piggyback mortgages, reverse mortgages, and home equity loans

- A wraparound mortgage is a form of second mortgage. The face amount of the note is the sum of the existing balance owed on the first mortgage plus the amount of credit extended by the second mortgage.

- If the purchaser takes subject to the mortgage, he is not personally liable for payment of the mortgage debt. If the new buyer assumes payment of the mortgage, she is liable, both to the original mortgagor and to the mortgagee, for repayment of the mortgage loan.

- Under a deed of trust, the debtor transfers title in the real property to a trustee to be held in trust for the benefit of the beneficiary. The title held by the beneficiary is not a true ownership interest and is limited to the rights given under the deed of trust.

- Under an installment land sale contract, the purchaser takes possession and the seller contracts to convey title to the purchaser when he has paid the purchase price in regular installments over a fixed period of time. Financing is provided by the seller.

Chapter Problems and Assignments

1. Sarah lives in a unique home with an Old West theme. The home contains a saloon with working animatronics, a working miniature railroad and track, and similar Old West–theming throughout the interior and exterior of the property. No similar homes exist in the area. When Sarah sells the property, what method is an appraiser likely to use?

2. BigMart, a corporation, has obtained a loan to assist in purchasing real property for its expansion efforts. The company has dealt directly with BigMoney Lending, a lender. In the past, Big-Money Lending has provided BigMart many other loans, which are secured by different parcels of land as collateral. BigMoney Lending is concerned that BigMart's expansion efforts may not be successful. BigMoney Lending wants to protect its interests by requiring that, in the event of a default under one of BigMart's loans, all loans will be in default. In addition, BigMoney Lending wants to make sure that all the collateral BigMart has provided can be used to satisfy a default under any of the loans. What type of provision should BigMoney Lending use in its mortgage with BigMart?

3. A mortgage loan has a principal balance of $250,000. The interest rate is fixed for five years and then every six months thereafter will adjust to the LIBOR rate plus 2 percent. What type of mortgage loan is this?

4. The Greens obtained a mortgage from First Home Savings and Loan. The mortgage contained a clause that stated, "[T]his mortgage shall become due and payable forthwith at the option of the mortgagee if the mortgagor shall convey away said premises or if the title thereto shall become vested in any other person or persons in any manner whatsoever." What type of promissory note clause is this?

5. Mr. Oyer purchased a home from Mr. and Mrs. Richards. He took the property "subject to" a mortgage that the Richards had secured on the property. Oyer never agreed to "assume" the mortgage. Oyer defaulted in making payments to the mortgage holder. The holders of the note and mortgage sued Oyer and the Richards. Who is liable to the mortgage holder?

6. Explain how a mortgage differs from a deed of trust.

7. Ariel obtains a purchase money mortgage to purchase a home. He takes out a $375,000 mortgage. After two years living in the home, an economic recession leaves Ariel without a job. He is unable to pay his mortgage, and unfortunately his home has decreased in value to $350,000. At that time, he owes the bank $365,000 on the mortgage. The lender forecloses on his property. Will Ariel owe the bank the $15,000 difference? Are there any protections available to Ariel?

8. Dora is negotiating the sale of her home to Brittany. Dora will lend the purchase price to Brittany since Brittany has poor credit. Brittany will pay the debt to Dora in monthly payments over the next fifteen years. The parties are debating how to structure the transaction: with a mortgage or through an installment land sale contract. Which form will Brittany likely prefer and why? Which form will Dora likely prefer and why?

9. Research your state law to determine if it permits the use of a trust to purchase a home.

10. Research the laws of your state to determine what remedies are available when default occurs under an installment land sale contract.

End Notes

1. *River East Plaza v. Variable Annuity*, 498 F.3d 718 (7th Cir. 2007).
2. https://maps.google.com/maps?q=197+Shoe+House+Rd+++++++++Hellam,+PA+17406&ll=39.998957,-76.637012&spn=0.001184,0.002551&hnear=197+Shoe+House+Rd,+Borough+of+Hallam,+Pennsylvania+17406&t=h&z=19.
3. Pub.L. 101-73, 103 Stat. 183.
4. https://www.fanniemae.com/content/guide_form/1004.pdf.
5. 24 C.F.R. §203.25.
6. Pub. L. No. 105-216, 112 Stat. 897.
7. Pub.L. 95-128, 12 U.S.C. §2901.

Chapter 10
Deeds, Title, and Closing

Eden is that old-fashioned House
We dwell in every day,
Without suspecting our abode
Until we drive away.
—Emily Dickinson, poet (1830–1836)

Learning Objectives

1. Define the term *title* and explain how ownership is verified.
2. Explain the promises made when a deed is delivered.
3. State the differences among the types of recording statutes.
4. Understand the concept of marketable title.
5. Explain the various ways to provide title assurance.
6. Recognize what actions occur in title and escrow closings.

Chapter Outline

- Introduction
- Deeds
- Requirements for a Deed

Case 10.1: *Rosengrant v. Rosengrant*

- Title Assurance
- Types of Deeds
- Special Purpose Deeds
- Merger of Contract

Case 10.2: *Crystal v. PSA*

- Recording

Case 10.3: *Argent Mortgage v. Wachovia Bank*

- Marketable Title
- Proof of Marketable Title

Case 10.4: *Davis v. Ivey*

- Closing or Settlement
- Real Estate Settlement Procedures Act (RESPA)

Case 10.5: *Freeman v. Quicken Loans, Inc.*

Opening scenario

Prior to the sale of a warehouse, the sellers' contractor failed to obtain the certificate of occupancy (a requirement for the building to be lawfully occupied) when he performed new construction work. The sellers sold the warehouse to two buyers in "as is" condition and "with all faults." The sales contract did not contain any representation as to whether a certificate of occupancy had been issued; however, the sales contract did state that the sellers represented the property as compliant with all local building codes.

Following the closing of the sale, the buyers discovered the lack of a certificate of occupancy and sued the sellers for breach of contract. The trial court held for the sellers, finding that the contract did not state that the provisions relating to code compliance upon which the buyers relied would "survive" the closing (that is, that they would still be effective after the transaction was concluded); further, the court held that the contract merged into the deed given to the buyers, as it was the final expression of the parties' agreement. On appeal, what arguments would you make for the sellers and the buyers?[1]

Introduction

Previous chapters discussed the process of utilizing a real estate agent to find a property, entering into a purchase contract for the real property, and finally valuing and financing the property. This chapter covers the final step in the purchase of real property: the transfer of title at closing. Title is transferred by a deed, and the type of deed provided is important to understanding what, if any, warranties the deed provides.

Title
Evidence of ownership of land passed by a deed or court order.

Title is the ownership of land. When title is known, the ownership of real property allows a person to transfer title of an estate from one person to another. The transfer usually takes one of several forms: sale, gift, testamentary transfer (a transfer pursuant to the owner's will or by operation of law on the owner's death), or adverse possession.

Deeds

Deeds
Written instruments used to convey (transfer) real property.

Deeds are written instruments used to transfer real property from one person, the **grantor** (seller or donor), to another person, the **grantee** (buyer or recipient). This chapter will review the most common forms of deeds.

Grantor
The seller or donor.

While no deed can convey more than what a grantor possesses, the extent of the interests conveyed can vary. Such a transfer can be a fee simple interest or an estate less extensive than a fee simple, such as a life estate. The deed may also "carve out" the rights conveyed so that some are retained by the grantor or place restrictions on the use of the property.

Grantee
The buyer or recipient.

Example: A deed may provide that the grantor retain the right to extract oil and gas from the property.

Requirements for a Deed

All states set minimum requirements that must be met before a deed has any legal significance. While some states impose additional requirements, such as necessitating that a deed contain a seal, the following requirements are generally included:

1. The deed must be in writing and signed by the grantor.
2. The grantor and grantee must be clearly identified.
3. The grantor must have legal capacity.
4. The property must be adequately described.
5. The deed must express the intent to immediately convey a property interest to the grantee.
6. The deed must specify the type of interest and rights given to the grantee.
7. The deed must be acknowledged.
8. The deed must be delivered by the grantor and accepted by the grantee.

Generally, consideration is not necessary for a voluntary transfer; however, most deed forms do state that the deed is given for consideration, although the amount of consideration need not be stated.

Example: A deed may state, "For valuable consideration, receipt of which is hereby acknowledged."

The Deed Must Be in Writing and Signed by the Grantor

To transfer an interest in land, the Statute of Frauds requires an evidence of a writing. The writing is usually in the form of a deed and must have the grantor's signature. It is not necessary for the grantee to execute the deed.

Example: An unsigned deed is not a valid legal document.

Another person may sign a deed on behalf of a grantor if the deed is signed in the grantor's presence and with the grantor's request and authorization. The third party signs the deed on behalf of the grantor through a power of attorney (previously discussed). The power of attorney is usually recorded with the deed.

Example: A person with a physical impairment that impedes his ability to sign could have another person sign the deed on his behalf. The signature on the deed should conform exactly to the name shown as grantor.

Where two or more persons hold title to the property, all persons holding title must sign the deed. If the grantor is married but title is held as separate property, the deed should state that the grantor owns the property separately. Even if the property is held

Dower and curtesy rights
The right of a surviving spouse to receive a portion of the deceased spouse's estate. Dower provides a right to a surviving wife, and curtesy provides a right to a surviving husband.

as separate property by a married person, it is good practice to have both spouses execute the deed. This tactic removes any concern related to community property interests or to **dower and curtesy rights** that could be asserted in the future. These concepts are discussed in chapter 12.

When a business entity (a corporation, LLC, or partnership) holds title to a property, an authorized person must sign on behalf of the business entity and fulfill any additional state requirements (such as placing a corporate seal on the deed). In addition, title companies often require a resolution by the company authorizing the conveyance, such as a resolution by a corporation's board of directors authorizing the purchase or sale of property.

Grantor Signature Types

If the grantor is an individual, the individual will need to sign the deed. The signature can appear as follows:

_____
Kevin C. Fields

If the grantor is a corporation, a duly authorized officer of the corporation will need to sign the deed. The signature can appear as follows:

SCion Properties, Inc.,a Florida corporation

_____
Kevin C. Fields President

If the grantor is a limited liability company, the manager (in a manager managed LLC) or authorized member (in a member managed LLC) will need to sign the deed. The signature can appear as follows:

SCion Properties, LLC,a Georgia limited liability company

_____
Kevin C. Fields, Manager

OR

SCion Properties, LLC,a Georgia limited liability company

_____
Kevin C. Fields, authorized Member

If the grantor is a general partnership, the signature of all general partners is required. The signature can appear as follows:

> SCion Properties, GP, a Delaware general partnership
>
> _____
>
> Kevin C. Fields, General Partner
>
> _____
>
> C. Kerry Fields, General Partner

If the grantor is a limited partnership, the signature of the general partner is required. The signature can appear as follows:

> SCion Properties, LP, a Nevada limited partnership
>
> _____
>
> Kevin C. Fields, General Partner

If the grantor is a limited liability partnership, the signature of the general partner is required. The signature can appear as follows:

> SCion Properties, LLP, a California limited liability partnership
>
> _____
>
> Kevin C. Fields, General Partner

If the grantor is a trust, the trustee(s) will sign the deed. The signature can appear as follows:

> _____
>
> Kevin C. Fields, trustee of the Fields Family Trust dated [date]

If the person signing is an executor (the person died with a will), the signature block of the deed can appear as follows:

> _____
>
> Kevin C. Fields as executor of the will of William Harold, deceased

If the person signing is an administrator of an estate (there was not a valid will), the signature block of the deed can appear as follows:

_____

Kevin C. Fields, administrator of the
estate of William Harold, who
died intestate

If the person signing on behalf of the grantor is the grantor's guardian or conservator, the signature block of the deed can appear as follows:

_____

Kevin C. Fields as guardian of Kaitlyn
Fields, a minor

If the person signing is acting as an attorney-in-fact under a power of attorney, the attorney-in-fact will sign the principal's name, note that he is acting as an attorney-in-fact under a power of attorney, and sign his own name.

[attorney-in-fact signs principal's name]
Kevin C. Fields

_____

Kevin C. Fields under power of attorney
dated [date]

The Grantor and Grantee Must Be Clearly Identified

Both the grantor and the grantee must be clearly identified in the deed. They are identified in the preamble section of the deed, discussed below. A misspelled name or missing middle names or initials may still suffice if the name can be easily identified. Title companies can record a statement of identity to clarify that the same person is known with or without a middle initial or colloquial use of names.

Example: If James A. Richards, Jim A. Richards, James Richards, and Jim Richards are the same person, the title company's identity statement would indicate that the names all refer to the same person.

Example: James A. Richards, also known as Jim A. Richards, also known as James Richards, and also known as Jim Richards.

If the grantor or grantee is an individual, that person should be labeled as such in the preamble.

Example: Charles G. Richards, an individual.

If the grantor or grantee is married but title is (or will be) held as separate property, the deed should state that the grantor or grantee owns (or will own) the property as separate property.

Example: James A. Richards, a married man as his sole and separate property.

If the grantor or grantee is a business entity, the name of the entity as well as the place of incorporation or organization should be stated in the preamble.

Example: SCion Properties, Inc., a Nevada corporation.

Example: SCion Properties, LLC, a Washington limited liability company.

When a grantor's name was misspelled in the original deed, often a title company's identity statement can clarify the single identity linked to variously spelled names; however, the grantor can transfer title in the deed by using the name in the deed with which she originally received title (that is, the name used when the grantor was the grantee).

Example: Devon A. Richards, being the same person who acquired title as Devon A. Richard.

When a grantor has changed their name after receiving title (such as a name change after marriage), the preamble should indicate the grantor's current name and the name of the grantor when they originally received title.

Example: Devon A. Fields, who acquired title to the property described below under her former name of Devon A. Richards.

If the grantees will hold title in disproportionate shares (as may occur with tenants in common), the preamble should state the fractional shares held by each person. If the deed does not contain any fractional-share language, the presumption is that the deed conveys equal shares between or among the grantees.

Example: Devon A. Fields, a sixty percent (60%) interest and Kevin C. Fields, a forty percent (40%) interest as tenants in common.

The Grantor Must Have Legal Capacity

The grantor should have legal capacity to execute the deed. Recall from chapter 8 that capacity is a necessary element to form a valid agreement. Minors, persons under a conservatorship or guardianship, persons declared to be legally incompetent, and intoxicated persons lack capacity. Many states provide that a deed transferred by a person who lacks capacity is void (that is, it is as if the deed never came into existence). Many states provide that the grantee does not need to have legal capacity.

> *Example:* In many states a minor can receive title to real property through a deed, but the minor would be unable to transfer title to a third person until he reached the age of majority (usually 18 years old).

The Property Must Be Adequately Described

The property must be described clearly so that it can be identified. If the property intended to be conveyed cannot be ascertained, the deed can be voided. Usually, errors in the description and other errors in the conveyance are interpreted in favor of the grantee. It is common for lengthy property descriptions that may not fit into the space provided in a deed to be attached as an exhibit to a deed with a reference to see the attached exhibit.

> *Example:* A property description may state the following: As described in attached Exhibit A.

As discussed in chapter 6, property can be described by metes and bounds, reference to a government survey, a recorded plat, a common street address, or the special name of the property.

The Deed Must Express the Intent to Immediately Convey a Property Interest to the Grantee

The deed must express the present intention to convey a property interest to the grantee. This clause is known as a granting clause. While no specific words are required, suitable words of conveyance include *I give*, *grant*, *bargain and sell*, *convey*, *quitclaim*, or *assign*. The type of words used to convey property can provide or limit warranties to title.

> *Example:* "I hereby convey" expresses an intent to presently convey property.

The Deed Must Specify the Type of Interest and Rights Given to the Grantee

Habendum clause
Clause in a deed which sets forth the extent of ownership and any exceptions or reservations to ownership.

The **habendum** clause specifies the type of interest and rights given to the grantee (fee simple, fee simple determinable, life estate, express easement). If the grantor desires to place a restriction in the deed (such as a fee simple determinable), the restriction must be stated in the *habendum* clause. A conveyance of real property passes fee simple unless it appears from the deed that a lesser estate was intended.

The Deed Must Be Acknowledged

The deed must be acknowledged (that is, executed before a notary public or attested by witnesses) before it can be recorded. **Acknowledgment** is a declaration that the person executing the deed is actually the person executing it. The acknowledgment assists in authenticating that the proper parties conveyed the deed.

Acknowledgment
A declaration made before a notary public.

The Deed Must Be Delivered by the Grantor and Accepted by the Grantee

To be effective, the deed must also be delivered by the grantor and accepted by the grantee. Once the grantee accepts a deed, any covenants or restrictions (such as those contained in the deed's *habendum* clause) become effective.

Delivery of the deed may be accomplished by either actually delivering it or by constructively delivering it to the grantee. Actual delivery occurs when the grantor physically hands the deed to the grantee. **Constructive delivery** occurs when the grantor releases all control of the deed. If the grantor retains the right to recall the deed, no delivery has occurred because the grantor has not intended immediately to convey a property interest to the grantee.

Constructive delivery
A type of delivery that is inferred from the conduct of the parties, even if the physical delivery did not take place.

Courts presume that a deed has been delivered if:

- The deed is physically handed to the grantee,
- The deed is acknowledged by the grantor before a notary, or
- The deed has been recorded.

No delivery is presumed if the grantor retains possession of the deed. Each of these presumptions is rebuttable based on evidence presented.

> **Example:** Tony Sr. had three adult children, none of whom got along. During his lifetime, Tony Sr. told his son Anthony in confidence, "I will give you the office building upon my death, but I don't want your sisters knowing about it. If they learn that I favored you with this gift, they will complain. When I am dead, I will not have to hear them complain to me." Tony Sr. placed the deed he had executed before a notary in his desk drawer and said to Anthony, "After I die, record the deed." At the wake for Tony Sr., the sisters demanded to go over the details of the estate with Anthony, who informed them of the just-recorded deed. The sisters sued to set aside the deed to Anthony. The trial court held that no delivery of the deed to Anthony had occurred, because Tony Sr. could have retrieved the deed at any time prior to his death.[2]

In the above example, the grantor did not intend the deed to be effective until his death; the deed was not delivered to Anthony during Tony Sr.'s lifetime and did not meet the requirements of a valid deed.

In the following case, the Oklahoma Court of Appeals had to determine whether delivery of the deed had occurred. The court held that the deed had, in fact, been retrievable at any time by the grantor before his death.

ROSENGRANT v. ROSENGRANT

629 P.2d 800 (1981)

Oklahoma Court of Civil Appeals

Harold and Mildred Rosengrant had six nieces and nephews. One of them was Jay Rosengrant. When Mildred contracted cancer, she called Jay and asked him to meet her and Harold at a bank. Upon meeting their banker, Jay witnessed Harold and Mildred execute a deed to their farm, which the banker had prepared according to their instructions. They informed Jay that they were going to give him their farm, but they wanted Jay to leave the deed at the bank, and they wanted Jay to record it when "something happened" to them. Harold personally handed the deed to Jay to "make this legal." Jay accepted the deed and then handed it back to the banker, who told him he would keep it in the vault until Jay called for it. The deed was contained in an envelope, on which was typed "Jay or Harold Rosengrant." Mildred died, and Harold continued to possess the farm until his own death. When Harold and Mildred had both died, Jay recorded the deed; then his siblings sued to cancel the deed. The trial court held that no delivery had occurred.

Language of the Court. *Jay Rosengrant confuses the issues involved by relying upon Harold and Mildred's goodwill toward him and his wife as if it were a controlling factor. From a fair review of the record, it is apparent that Jay and his wife were attentive, kind, and helpful to this elderly couple. The donative intent on the part of grantors is undeniable. We believe that they fully intended to reward Jay and his wife for their kindness.*

Nevertheless, where a grantor delivers a deed under which he reserves a right of retrieval and attaches to that delivery the condition that the deed is to become operative only after the death of the grantors, and where a grantor continues to use the property as if no transfer had occurred, the grantor's actions are nothing more than an attempt to employ the deed as if it were a will. Under Oklahoma law, this cannot be done.

The ritualistic delivery of the deed to the grantee and his redelivery of the deed to a third party for safekeeping created, under these circumstances, only a symbolic delivery. It amounted to a pro forma *attempt to comply with the legal aspects of delivery. Based on all the facts and circumstances, the true intent of the parties is expressed by the notation on the envelope and by the later conduct of the parties in relation to the land. Legal delivery is not just a symbolic gesture. It necessarily carries all the force and consequence of absolute, outright ownership at the time of delivery, or it is no delivery at all. In this case, the clear implication is that the grantor intended to continue to exercise control over the property, and that the grant was not to take effect until such time as both he and his wife had died and the deed had been recorded.*

Decision. The trial court's judgment was affirmed because there was no delivery of the deed.

FOCUS ON ETHICS

If Jay Rosengrant had been the only sibling to provide elder care for his aunt and uncle until their deaths, do you think that it would have been ethical for his brothers and sisters to sue him as they did? Would you have sued your brother for an interest in the farm?

Acceptance

The law presumes that the grantee has accepted the conveyance. However, a proposed grantee may refuse the conveyance. That refusal may occur when the grantee knows of the delivery and refrains from acting as if acceptance has occurred.

> **Example:** Many universities conduct a thorough due diligence into the condition of properties donated to them by benefactors before accepting the gifts; this is to ensure that the properties have marketable title and are suitable for university ownership (such as determining if they are free of hazardous waste).

Title Assurance

Persons purchasing property want to have assurances that they will obtain the title to that property. **Title assurance** means a person is recognized as having evidence of title in real property. Title-assurance issues arise when the landowner conveys the property to one person and later conveys the same property to another person. These circumstances put the grantees and their mortgage lenders in jeopardy. How do buyers and lenders protect themselves against a title defect that is discovered after the purchase or loan transaction? Four methods of assuring the buyer of title are discussed in this chapter:

Title assurance
A third party's promise to an owner that the owner holds legal title to the property. Most commonly, a title insurance company makes this promise to a purchaser or lender.

1. The six covenants of title arising from a general or special warranty deed
2. A system of recording land titles
3. Title registration (sometimes called the Torrens system)
4. Title insurance

Types of Deeds

State laws recognize different types of deeds. These deeds provide differing covenants and warranties and protection to the grantees. The most commonly used types of deeds include the following:

1. General warranty deed
2. Special warranty deed
3. Grant deed
4. Deed of bargain and sale
5. Quitclaim deed
6. Special purpose deed

General Warranty Deed

General warranty deed
A deed containing a full warranty and set of promises by the grantor to the grantee.

A **general warranty deed** contains a full warranty and set of legal promises by the grantor to the grantee. In some jurisdictions, it is known as the *full covenant and* *warranty deed.* A general warranty deed gives the highest level of protection to the grantee and provides six covenants (warranties) to the grantee. These six covenants are separated by three present covenants of title and three future covenants of title. Present covenants arise when the land is sold, while future covenants arise and could be breached in the future once the property is conveyed. An example of a general warranty deed is provided as Exhibit 10.1 below. The six title covenants, subdivided into present and future, are as follows:

Present Covenants

1. *Seisin.* At the time the deed is delivered to the grantee, the grantor covenants that he or she owns the interest conveyed to the grantee. This covenant is breached if the grantor does not own the interest conveyed.
2. *The right to convey.* The grantor warrants that she or he has the legal right and the power to convey title. With this covenant, a grantor would warrant that she or he is an authorized corporate officer, the trustee of a trust, and so on, with the power to convey the property.
3. *Covenant against encumbrances.* The grantor promises that the property has no undisclosed encumbrances (easements, mortgages, liens, unpaid taxes, etc.). This covenant relates to private encumbrances on title such as those mentioned. It is not breached by the presence of public land-use ordinances and building codes or by an encumbrance on the property to which the grantor accepts title.

Future Covenants

4. *Covenant of warranty.* With this covenant, the grantor promises to defend and compensate the grantee for any losses suffered from all claims that might arise from a defect in the grantor's purported title (undisclosed easements, undisclosed leases, etc.).
5. *Covenant of quiet enjoyment.* The covenant of quiet enjoyment is similar to the covenant of warranty. The grantor promises that the grantee will not be disturbed in possession or enjoyment by a third party asserting a claim of superior title.
6. *Covenant of further assurances.* The grantor promises to perform whatever acts are reasonably necessary to cure a defect in (perfect) the grantee's title. This covenant is often utilized to require the execution of corrective conveyancing documents without having to compensate the grantor.

Warranty Period

The covenants contained in general warranty deeds are not limited to the time during which the grantor owned the real property interest; they relate back to the creation of the property interest. Thus, the future covenants contained in a general warranty deed extend to future grantees of the property, allowing a future owner of the property to sue for a breach of a future covenant.

RECORDING REQUESTED BY AND
WHEN RECORDED MAIL THIS DEED
AND, UNLESS OTHERWISE SHOWN
BELOW, MAIL TAX STATEMENTS TO:

[Name]
[Address]
[Address]

(Space above line for Recorder's use)

GENERAL WARRANTY DEED

The undersigned grantor(s) declare(s):

THIS GENERAL WARRANTY DEED, executed this [Date], by [grantor(s)], whose address is [Address], Grantor, to [grantee(s)], whose address is [Address], Grantee:

WITNESSETH that, the Grantor, for and in consideration of the sum of [amount of consideration, if any] paid by the Grantee, and other good and valuable consideration, receipt of which is hereby acknowledged, does hereby grant and release to Grantee and assigns forever, the following real property situated in the City of [City Name], County of [County Name], [State], described as follows:

[Property Description]

And Grantor covenants as follows:

1. That Grantor is seized of said premises in fee simple.
2. That Grantor has good right and lawful authority to convey said premises.
3. That Grantee shall quietly enjoy the said premises.
4. That the said premises are free from encumbrances.
5. That the Grantor will execute or procure any further necessary assurance of the title to said premises.
6. That Grantor will forever warrant the title to said premises.

IN WTINESS WHEREOF, Grantor has executed this deed.

Dated: _____

_____
[Grantor's name]

- -

STATE OF [STATE]   )
)
County of [County]   )

On [Date], before me, [Notary public name], Notary Public, personally appeared [grantor's name and title], who proved to me on the basis of satisfactory evidence to be the person(s) whose name(s) is/are subscribed to the within instrument and acknowledged to me that he/she/they executed the same in his/her/their authorized capacity(ies), and that by his/her/their signature(s) on the instrument the person(s), or the entity upon behalf of which the person(s) acted, executed the instrument.

I certify under PENALTY OF PERJURY under the laws of the state of [State] that the foregoing paragraph is true and correct.

WITNESS my hand and official seal.

_____
NOTARY PUBLIC

[Notary Seal]

Exhibit 10.1.   General Warranty Deed

Damages

If one of the covenants is breached, the grantee or his or her successors can recover monetary damages for the breach. To avoid relying upon the financial strength of the grantor (because the grantor may, for example, be insolvent), the grantee should obtain title insurance to protect the grantee's interest.

Special Warranty Deed

The **special warranty deed** contains the same warranties as a general warranty deed, with one major difference regarding the covenant period. In a special warranty deed, the grantor warrants that he has not caused any defects in the title during his period of owning the property. In a general warranty deed, the grantor warrants that no one has ever caused any defects in the title.

> **Example:** If there were preexisting easements, liens, and mortgages on the property when the seller received title, the seller would not be liable to the buyer for them under a special warranty deed. However, the seller *would* be liable under a general warranty deed.

Grant Deed

Some states use a form of the warranty deed known as the grant deed. A **grant deed** implies two covenants:

1. The grantor has not previously conveyed the same estate to anyone other than the grantee.
2. The property is free of encumbrances placed on it or permitted by the grantor. A conveyance passes all easements related to it, even if they are not expressly included in the grant.

In those states where warranty deeds are uncommon, the grant deed, combined with a title insurance policy, generally is sufficient to protect grantees.

Deed of Bargain and Sale

A **deed of bargain and sale** used to convey real property implies that the grantor has a claim of ownership in the property, but the grantor makes no other covenants to the grantee. Sometimes a deed of bargain and sale is referred to as an "as is" deed. States may allow a grantor to provide for warranties in the deed.

Quitclaim Deed

A **quitclaim deed** is a deed in which the grantor conveys what interest, if any, she or he has in a specific piece of property. In essence, the grantor states, "If I hold an interest, and I may in fact own no interest in the property, I am conveying whatever it is I do own to you." With a quitclaim deed, the grantee receives no protections and no warranties regarding title to the property.

Upon acceptance of a quitclaim deed, the grantee holds whatever interest the grantor had in the real property. If the grantor holds no interest at all, no interest passes. This is the weakest form of deed and is used as a means of removing any ambiguities in the record of title.

> *Example:* If an ex-wife received title to the property and wanted to sell it, a buyer might require a quitclaim deed from the ex-husband if there was an ambiguity about whether the ex-wife obtained fee simple title. If the ex-husband had no interest in the property, no interest would pass, but if he did still retain an interest in the property, the purchaser would obtain that interest.

Special Purpose Deeds

Judicial or Sheriff's Deed

A **judicial deed**, sometimes called a sheriff's deed, is a deed issued as a result of a judicial foreclosure proceedings. Judicial deeds are quitclaim deeds and do not provide any warranty of title to the grantees.

Trustee Deed

Property can be placed into a trust. In a trust, the owner of the property conveys title to a trustee until the owner has paid the financial obligation to a third party (the beneficiary). When the beneficiary is not paid and the owner defaults, the trustee has the power to sell the trust property through a trustee deed. **Trustee deeds** are quitclaim deeds that do not usually provide any warranty of title to the grantees.

Types of Deeds	
General warranty deed	Grantor guarantees that he holds clear title to the property and has the right to sell it. Includes six convenants and gives highest level of protection.
Special warranty deed	Provides the same warranties as a general deed and also warrants the grantor has not caused any defects in title of the property; however, these warranties are only for the time period in which the grantor owned the property.
Grant deed	Aussures only that the grantor has not previously conveyed the property to anyone else and that the property is free of encumbrances.
Quitclaim deed	Grantor conveys whatever interest she or he has in the property.
Deed of bargain and sale	Only assures that the grantor has a claim of ownership in the property. "As is" deed.
Special purpose deeds	Judicial deeds arise out of foreclosure proceedings. Trustee deeds place the property into a trust.

FIGURE 10.1. Types of Deeds

Merger of Contract

Once the parties have entered into a purchase and sale agreement, the agreement may provide for certain warranties and promises. Once the transaction has closed and the deed has been exchanged, the promises and warranties made in the purchase and sale agreement are extinguished. Acceptance of the deed discharges the seller from liability for any promises or warranties contained in the contract. This concept is known as the **merger doctrine**. The buyer must look to the covenants contained in the deed, because the warranties and promises made in the purchase and sale contract do not survive closing. The rationale for this rule is that the buyer accepts the deed because it is assumed that the seller has complied with the sales contract.

In the following case, the buyer did not obtain from the seller a promise regarding the condition of the property that would survive the closing. At its peril, the buyer relied upon the seller's representation of the property's condition at the time of closing.

Merger doctrine
A legal rule providing that the deed replaces all promises made between the buyer and seller in their purchase agreement.

CASE 10.2

PROMISES MADE IN THE SALES CONTRACT DO NOT SURVIVE CLOSING

CRYSTAL v. PSA
850 N.Y.S.2d 497 (2008)
New York Supreme Court, Appellate Division

The Novelty Crystal Corporation ("Novelty Crystal") bought real property from PSA Institutional Partners, L.P. ("PSA"). Following the closing of the sales transaction, Novelty Crystal discovered that PSA, as the seller, had failed to deliver the premises in "vacant and clean" condition, as required by the sales contract. Novelty Crystal did not raise the issue of the condition of the property prior to closing. After spending $17,000 to remove the items left by PSA, Novelty Crystal sued PSA for breach of contract. The trial court granted Novelty Crystal's motion for summary judgment on damages. PSA appealed.

Language of the Court. *The principal issue presented by this appeal is whether a purchaser of real property can maintain an action after the closing of title, in either contract or tort, to recover damages for the seller's failure to deliver the premises vacant and clean, as required by the contract. We conclude that the purchaser may not do so where, as here, the terms of the contract do not provide for the survival of such a claim.*

The rule of law applicable to such disputes is that generally, the obligations and provisions of a contract for the sale of land are merged in the deed and, as a result, are extinguished upon the closing of title. However, this rule does not apply where the parties evidence a clear intent that a particular provision of the contract of sale shall survive delivery of the deed.

The contract provides that, upon closing, Novelty would accept the premises "as is" and with all of its faults. In addition, Novelty, upon closing, was deemed to have waived, relinquished, and released PSA "from and against any and all claims, demands, and causes of action (including causes of action in tort) which Novelty might have asserted or alleged against PSA arising out of any physical or environmental conditions and any and all other acts, omissions, events, circumstances, or matters regarding the premises."

Next, the contract provides that the acceptance of the deed shall be deemed to be full performance of, and discharge of, every agreement and obligation on PSA's part to be performed under this contract, except for those that this contract specifically provides shall survive the closing. Finally, the contract provides that the parties each agree to "do such other and further acts and things, and to execute and deliver such instruments and documents, which may be reasonably requested from time to time, whether at or after the closing, in furtherance of the purposes of this contract, and that this provision shall survive the closing."

With the exception of the last-quoted provision, the words used in the contract with respect to survivability are susceptible of no interpretation other than that any such claims, whether in tort or contract, are barred. The obligation to deliver the premises vacant and clean, however, is not an "other and further act [or] thing." It is, rather, an explicit obligation of the seller under the contract to be performed at or prior to the closing of title. As such, it is neither "other" nor "further" and, therefore, does not on that basis fall within the category of obligations that survive the closing of title pursuant to this contract provision.

Decision. The court reversed the trial court's ruling. The court held once a contract has been completed, a party cannot sue under breach of contract unless the provision at issue survives the sale.

FOCUS ON ETHICS

Did the application of the merger doctrine lead to a fair result in this case? If you disagree, what rule of law would you put in its place?

Recording

All states have enacted a **recording statute**. These statutes are intended to protect title by preventing fraud. Recorded deeds can be searched by prospective purchasers or lenders to determine what type of title, if any, is owned by the prospective seller or prospective debtor. Recording statutes are also used to establish the priority of rights between and among conflicting deeds on a particular property. These statutes are important in clarifying title in situations of the "double dealer."

Recording statute
A state statute providing constructive notice is deemed to have been given to third parties by virtue of filing a document in the public domain.

> *Example:* Ryan purchases an unimproved lot from Glen. Ryan takes title but does not record the deed. Unknown to Ryan, Glen sells the same property to Kathy, who is unaware that Glen has already sold the property to Ryan. Kathy records the deed.

In this example, either Ryan or Kathy will have title to the property, depending upon the type of recording statute the state has enacted. The different recording statutes are discussed below.

What Documents Can Be Recorded

All states provide that instruments affecting title to land may be recorded, including purchase contracts, leases, mortgages, deeds of trust, liens, judgments, and financing statements.

Where Documents Are Recorded

Each county, parish, or township maintains an office for the recording of instruments affecting title. A county recorder, clerk of the court, or registrar of deeds is the public official charged with operating the office in accordance with state law.

Many states have adopted the Real Property Electronic Recording Act. The purpose of the act is to provide legal authority to county clerks and recorders to electronically receive and record real property documents. The act also establishes minimum standards a recording office must follow.

How Real Estate Records Are Maintained

Records relating to real estate are maintained using either the grantor-grantee index or a tract index system. Most frequently, a grantor-grantee index is used. Under the **grantor-grantee index system**, records are indexed and maintained alphabetically by the grantor's or the grantee's respective names. Along with the grantor's or the grantee's information, the index will contain a date and time, the type of document indexed (such as deed, mortgage, or easement), a short legal description, and a reference to the page and book in the public records where a copy is filed, along with the grantee's or the grantor's name. A title searcher begins the search with the current owner in the grantee index and then searches back in time. All referenced documents are read, and a report is made. The grantor-grantee index is subject to inherent problems in tracing back title when people change names or use a different name in transferring the property.

To alleviate some of these concerns, several states use a tract index system to maintain records. With a **tract index system**, instead of tracing title back through each successive conveyance from grantor to grantee, the county, parish, or township is divided into parcels of land. All documents affecting title to the parcel of land are indexed and summarized on a page for that parcel. Tracing the history of title begins with identifying the appropriate tract index for the parcel. All conveyances affecting title to the parcel will be summarized on the parcel page. While the tract index system makes it easier to find a title's history, most states are reluctant to change to this system because (1) human error will inevitably occur during the reindexing of properties, and (2) it would cost money to change from one index system to another.

Recording Statutes

Title claims are determined by one of three types of recording statutes. Each state has adopted one of these three types: (1) race statute, (2) notice statute, or (3) race-notice statute.

Race Statute (Pure Race)

Race statute
A recording statute that provides title to the first party to record, even if the first to record obtained his or her interest later in time.

Under a **race statute** (also known as a pure race statute), the first party to record takes title to the property, even if the first to record obtained his or her interest later in time. Priority is determined by who wins the race to the recording office. Very few states follow a race statute.[3] In this system, actual notice of other potentially senior interests is irrelevant: The winner of the race prevails.

Example: Day 1: O (Grantor) conveys Blackacre to A
　　　　　 Day 2: O (Grantor) conveys Blackacre to B
　　　　　 Day 3: O (Grantor) conveys Blackacre to C
　　　　　 Day 4: B records
　　　　　 Day 5: A records

In a race jurisdiction, B has title to the property because B is the first to record. It is irrelevant that A received title first or that A recorded title. B was the first to record and is awarded title. C is not recognized as having an ownership interest because of B's recordation.

Notice Statute

Under a **notice statute**, the *last* bona fide purchaser takes title to the property. This is the most common form of recording statute. A **bona fide purchaser** (BFP) is a good faith purchaser who takes title to the property without notice of a prior sale by the grantor. The good faith purchaser must pay some consideration for the property. While the purchaser does not have to pay fair market value of the property to be BFP, the BFP cannot receive property by a gift or through an inheritance.

Notice may be actual, constructive, or inquiry in type. **Actual notice** occurs when the prospective purchaser has actual knowledge of a title defect (for example, that the property has already been sold to another). In most cases, a party to a real estate transaction lacks personal knowledge of the preexisting interests in the real property. **Constructive notice** arises when a search of the title records would have revealed a defect in title (such as, another owner has recorded a deed to that property). All persons are deemed to have notice of what has been made part of the public records, even if they did not search for that information. **Inquiry notice** arises when a party becomes aware, or should have become aware, of certain facts that, if investigated, would reveal the claim of another. Inquiry notice imputes knowledge where the circumstances are such that they would have aroused the suspicions of an ordinary purchaser (for example, a neighbor indicates that the grantor just sold the property to another person). Once a duty to inquire arises, the purchaser will be charged with all knowledge that a reasonable investigation would have revealed.

> **Notice statute**
> A recording statute that provides title to the last bona fide purchaser.

> **Bona fide purchaser (BFP)**
> A good faith purchaser who purchases real property without notice of any prior sale by the grantor.

Example: Day 1: O (Grantor) conveys Blackacre to A (a BFP)
　　　　　 Day 2: O (Grantor) conveys Blackacre to B (a BFP)
　　　　　 Day 3: O (Grantor) conveys Blackacre to C (a BFP)
　　　　　 Day 4: A records
　　　　　 Day 5: C records

In a notice jurisdiction, C has title to the property because C is the last bona fide purchaser. It is irrelevant that A recorded first in this case. Note that on day 1, A owns title to the property because A was the last BFP. On day 2, B owns title to the property because B is the last BFP. On day 3, C owns title to the property because C is the last BFP. Because A and C have recorded title, constructive notice is provided to future grantees.

While the last bona fide purchaser does not need to record to obtain title to the property, she should do so to protect her title from a subsequent bona fide purchaser. Recall that once title is recorded, it provides constructive notice, thereby making the person to record the *last* bona fide purchaser of the property.

Example: Day 1 — O (Grantor) conveys Blackacre to A (a BFP)
Day 2 — O (Grantor) conveys Blackacre to B (a BFP)
Day 3 — B records
Day 4 — O (Grantor) conveys Blackacre to C (*is C a BFP?*)

In a notice jurisdiction, B has title to the property. C cannot be a bona fide purchaser because B recorded title to the property and provided constructive notice. B is the last bona fide purchaser.

Race-Notice Statute

Race-notice statute
A recording statute that states that the first bona fide purchaser to record keeps title to the property.

Finally, with a **race-notice statute**, the *first* BFP to record keeps title to the property. This statute has two requirements: a grantee who records first and is without notice of prior conflicting interests in the property.

Example: Day 1: O (Grantor) conveys Blackacre to A (a BFP)
Day 2: O (Grantor) conveys Blackacre to B (a BFP)
Day 3: O (Grantor) conveys Blackacre to C (a BFP)
Day 4: A records
Day 5: C records

In a race-notice jurisdiction, A obtains title to the property. A is the first BFP to record.

Consider the discussion of these statutes by a decision of the District Court of Appeal of Florida. In this case, the appellate court acknowledged that determining priority between conflicting claims could be difficult. Two lenders disputed whether the Florida statute was a notice statute or a race-notice statute.

CASE 10.3

RECORDING STATUTES DETERMINE PRIORITY BETWEEN MORTGAGES

ARGENT MORTGAGE v. WACHOVIA BANK
52 So.3d 796 (2010)
Florida District Court of Appeal

On August 31, 2004, Gene and Ann Burkes borrowed money on their home and secured the $90,000 loan with a mortgage through Olympus Mortgage Company. The mortgage was recorded on January 5, 2005. The mortgage was subsequently assigned to Wachovia Bank. On December 10, 2004, the Burkes borrowed $65,000 from Argent Mortgage and gave it a mortgage to secure the debt. The Argent Mortgage was recorded on January 31, 2005. Eventually, both mortgages went into default, and Wachovia sued in a Florida trial court. It sought foreclosure and named Argent Mortgage

as a defendant because it might claim some interest in the property due to its recorded mortgage. Both lenders claimed that they had priority over the other due to confusion over the Florida statutes on recordation. The trial court found that the Olympus mortgage prevailed over the Argent mortgage after determining that Florida followed a race-notice statute. Argent appealed.

Language of the Court. *It bears explaining that recording statutes are classified into three categories:*

race, notice, and *race-notice. These can generally be described as follows:*

> *Under a race recording statute, a subsequent mortgagee of real property will prevail against a prior mortgagee of the said real property if the subsequent mortgage is recorded before the prior mortgage.*

> *Under a notice recording statute, a subsequent mortgagee of real property for value and without notice (actual and constructive) of a prior mortgage of the said real property will prevail against the prior mortgagee.*

> *Under a race-notice recording statute, a subsequent mortgagee of real property for value and without notice (actual and constructive) of a prior mortgage of the said real property will prevail against the prior mortgagee if the subsequent mortgage is recorded before the prior mortgage. Importantly, under either a notice or a race-notice recording statute, the subsequent mortgagee cannot be without constructive notice if the prior mortgage has been recorded as of the time of execution of the subsequent mortgage.*

> *Application of each type of recording statute to the undisputed facts here yields the following results:*

>> *Wachovia prevails under a race recording statute because the Olympus Mortgage was recorded before the Argent Mortgage;*
>> *Argent prevails under a notice recording statute because it is a subsequent mortgagee*

for value and did not have notice of the Olympus Mortgage at the time of execution of the Argent Mortgage; and

>> *Wachovia prevails under a race-notice recording statute because, although Argent is a subsequent mortgagee for value and did not have notice of the Olympus Mortgage at the time of execution of the Argent Mortgage, the Olympus Mortgage was recorded before the Argent Mortgage.*

Florida courts over time have described and applied Florida's recording statute in a manner that is consistent with a "notice" type of recording statute. We conclude that Florida is, and remains, a "notice" jurisdiction, and that notice controls the issue of priority. Since Argent is a subsequent mortgagee for value and did not have notice of the Olympus Mortgage at the time of execution of the Argent Mortgage, the Argent Mortgage has priority over the Olympus Mortgage.

Decision. The trial court erred by entering partial summary final judgment in favor of Wachovia on the issue of priority. Wachovia did not have priority.

FOCUS ON ETHICS

Should anything be done to reverse prior transactions that have been affected by the confusion over what recordation statute applies?

Types of Recording Statutes	
Pure Race	First to record is recognized as the true owner.
Notice	Last bona-fide purchaser holds title. An unrecorded conveyance is invalid against a subsequent purchaser who had no notice, regardless of who records first.
Race-Notice	First bona-fide purchaser holds title. Whoever records first is recognized as the true owner, unless they had notice of a prior conveyance.

FIGURE 10.2. Types of Recording Statutes

Exercise 10.1

Assume the following series of events has taken place:

Day 1: O (Grantor) conveys Blackacre to A (a BFP)
Day 2: O (Grantor) conveys Blackacre to B (a BFP)
Day 3: O (Grantor) conveys Blackacre to C
Day 4: C records
Day 5: A records

1. Under a race statute, who owns Blackacre?
2. Under a notice statute, who owns Blackacre?
3. Under a race-notice statute, who owns Blackacre?

■ ■ ■ ■   Torrens System: Title Registration

Torrens title system
System in which a certificate and deed identify who owns the title.

The Torrens title system is an alternative to a recording system. Once used in many states, it is now used in only a few.[4] The system was developed by Sir Robert Torrens in Australia in 1858 and is based upon an Australian ship registry system whereby each ship owner was issued a certificate of title; upon the sale of that ship, the new owner received an ownership certificate. The concept was developed to simplify the transfer of title.

In the **Torrens title system**, a certificate and deed identify who owns the title. The certificate is considered title (not an evidence of title, as the recording system provides) and notes any encumbrances on the property. A subsequent grantee acquires title by requesting the grantor to surrender to the recorder the grantor's certificate of title, along with a deed to the property. The recorder cancels the certificate in the official records and registers a new certificate in favor of the grantee. The recorder gives the grantee a new duplicate certificate and retains a copy in the recorder's records.

Example: Kaitlyn has title to Blackacre registered in her name. Kaitlyn's certificate of title shows that she is the fee owner and lists all the mortgages, liens, easements, and other encumbrances. Kaitlyn decides to sell her property to Ryan. Kaitlyn submits her certificate to the recorder, along with a new deed naming Ryan as the grantee. The recorder cancels the certificate on its books, registers a new certificate in favor of Ryan, and gives Ryan a new certificate of title. If Ryan later mortgages the property, he would submit his certificate, and the recorder would issue a new certificate showing the lender's mortgage.

The Torrens registration system requires a judicial proceeding to remove all past claims to title and obtain a court order defining the present status of title. After notice is given to all parties interested in the title to the property, and following a hearing, the court issues a certificate of title, which is recorded in the tract index in the local recorder's office. One copy of the certificate is given to the owner.

Marketable Title

A contract for the sale of real property usually requires the seller to provide evidence of marketable title (or good title) as a condition of completing the sale. **Marketable title** is title that is free from any encumbrances, defects, claims, or liens (except those the buyer is aware of and has agreed to accept) and free from reasonable doubt that the seller owns title. A prudent buyer or lender, if aware of all facts, would accept the title's condition. It also means that title is free from reasonable doubt that the seller owns title to the property.

Marketable title is necessary at closing and requires that the title's condition does not unreasonably expose the purchaser to litigation following closing. This compels the seller to correct any defects in title or purchase title insurance to insure title to the property before the close of escrow.

Most undisclosed or unrecorded easements or liens make title unmarketable. However, zoning laws, subdivision restrictions (such as conditions, covenants, and restrictions), and visible easements have no effect on marketable title. In addition, the buyer may agree to encumbrances or liens stated in the purchase contract. These agreements would all make title marketable to the encumbrances or liens identified.

Marketable title
A title that is free from any unknown encumbrances or liens. Only agreed-upon encumbrances (such as real property taxes) may exist when title is conveyed, subject to certain exceptions.

Concept Summary

Marketable title *is* affected by:

- Liens (tax liens, judicial liens)
- Leases
- Mortgages
- Recorded and unrecorded easements unless they are visible
- Adverse possessors
- Water rights
- Pending litigation affecting title to the property (constructive notice is given by the recording of a notice of pending action — also known as a *lis pendens* — on the title)

Marketable title *is not* affected by:

- Visible easements
- Covenants, conditions, and restrictions on the use of the property (as long as the buyer's use is consistent with them)
- Zoning and local land-use ordinances

Proof of Marketable Title

The three most common methods of providing proof of marketable title to the buyer are:

1. Abstract of title with an attorney's opinion
2. A policy of title insurance
3. The use of the Torrens system of title registration (discussed previously)

Abstract of Title

To obtain an abstract of title with an attorney's opinion, a title examination must be ordered. The result is a written report (also known as an abstract of title) informing the parties if the property being conveyed or financed is free and clear of any liens, encumbrances, or judgments that arose during the property's prior ownership.

After ordering a title examination, the next step is to prepare a chain of title. The **chain of title** is the chronological history of title on property. It begins with the original owner of title on the property and then tracks each successive owner of the property until it reaches the current owner. Tracking each successive owner creates a "chain" that links the original and current owners through the chronological transfers of title.

Conceivably, every real property transaction could require searching prior title transactions for hundreds of years to get to the original owner of the property. In actual practice, many states set a required date determining the extent of a title examination. Statutes often limit this examination period to 40 to 50 years. These statutes have been adopted in many states and are known as **marketable record title acts**. They require an examination of the records within the required time for the chain of title. Defects in title occurring outside that period have no effect upon the transaction's current owner or buyer. Thus, a deed missing the name of a spouse from a century before will not impact a current transaction. If the title-ownership chain is unbroken, and the title is clear from encumbrances or liens, a marketable title exists.

The **title abstract** provides a condensed chronological summary of the title's history. The title abstract contains a legal description of the property and summarizes every related instrument in chronological order. Because many of the transfer documents may require an interpretation regarding whether a person had legal authority to transfer title (such as a trustee transferring title on behalf of a deceased heir), a title opinion rendered by a title attorney is obtained.

The **title opinion** is a written opinion by an attorney describing who owns the real estate, the quality of title, and exceptions, if any, to clear title for the transaction. The title opinion is not a guarantee that title is marketable. It is the opinion of an attorney, upon review of the chain of title, that determines whether the title is marketable.

Title Insurance

Title insurance is another form of assurance designed to protect buyers and lenders from title defects. Because title examinations are not always perfect and occasionally fraudulently recorded, **title insurance** helps to protect parties to a real estate transaction against damages that arise from purchasing or financing of real property.

Title insurance protects the insured by eliminating risk at the time the policy is issued. It is unlike other forms of insurance, which cover risk for events that may occur *after* the policy is issued, such as an automobile accident or a residential burglary. Title insurance gives parties to a real estate transaction some comfort. It assures them that the title should be clear and not subject to risks of adverse claims and that, if claims do arise, the insurance carrier will pay or be responsible for the loss or injury caused, including attorney fees. Title insurance requires a one-time premium payment. Generally, the cost of title insurance is a few dollars per each $1,000 of coverage.

A title insurance policy does not guarantee good title to the buyer or lender. It is not a representation that the title is in any sort of condition, good or bad, or free from any type of defect or encumbrance. It is simply a promise to pay the insured for damages

---

Chain of title
A recorded instrument found through generally accepted title searching methods. To establish constructive notice, an instrument may be required in the chain.

Marketable record title acts
State laws that limit the look-back period for examination of the public records. These acts clear the title of old defects and reduce the number of required title searches.

Title abstract
A condensed chronological summary of the title's history that follows a chain of title search.

Title opinion
A written certificate of title opinion as to who owns the real estate, the quality of title, and exceptions, if any, to clear title for the transaction.

Title insurance
A policy insuring against loss incurred as the result of defective title.

suffered or to take steps to remedy a defect that should have been disclosed by the insurer when the policy was issued.

Title insurance protects just the title or legal interests in the real property. It does not insure for representations and warranties the seller made to the buyer that do not relate solely to the title. For example, if the seller represented to the buyer in the purchase agreement that the property was free of construction defects, and that statement was untrue, the buyer would sue the seller for the repair costs. The seller would not have coverage for these claims under the title policy.

When a claim is made under a title policy, the insurer may hire lawyers to defend or negotiate the claim. The title company may obtain quitclaim deeds from these adverse claim holders to eliminate clouds on title. A **cloud on title** is a defect or potential defect in the owner's title arising from a lien, easement, or court order.

Cloud on title
A defect or potential defect in the owner's title arising from a lien, easement, or court order.

Reasons for Title Insurance

Like a title opinion, title insurance addresses the same types of issues that arise *after* a transaction has closed. Title insurance provides coverage against loss or damage:

1. Caused by a matter (that is, a cloud on title) in existence when the policy was issued,
2. That affects title to the property, and,
3. That was not excluded from policy coverage.

Matters insured against by a standard title insurance policy include the following:

- Defects in the title (the title is not marketable)
- The validity of the owner's title

> *Example:* The owner of property received title through a forged signature on a quitclaim deed.

The validity, enforceability, and priority of a lender's lien (mortgage or deed of trust)

> *Example:* A mechanic's lien attaches to the title before the current transaction closes, but a claim of lien is recorded after the policy is issued.

Lack of legal right to access to the land

> *Example:* The land is landlocked, and the owner does not have an easement right or access to the street without trespassing onto an adjacent property owner's land.

Endorsements

An **endorsement** provides additional insurance under the policy for risks that would otherwise not be covered under the policy (such as zoning laws). A standard title insurance policy insures the title to the land and does not insure the physical condition of the land. However, endorsements (amendments) insuring against land-related risks

Endorsement
A written amendment to a title insurance policy modifying the policy. It may alter, enlarge, or reduce coverage.

may be purchased from the insurer. These may include endorsements for types of improvements, location of structures, boundaries, encroachments and minerals, as well as physical access. Some endorsements are issued without cost; other endorsements increase the cost of the base policy. The types of endorsements available and modifications made through endorsements are regulated by each state.

Rights and Interests That May Be Insured by Title Insurance

A title insurer can insure any real property interest in which it is legally authorized to conduct business. The following interests are potentially insurable:

- Fee simple interests (whether fee simple absolute, fee simple determinable, or fee simple subject to a condition subsequent)
- An estate for years (a possessor interest of substantial duration is frequently insured)
- Life estates (although rarely insured)
- Easements (whether appurtenant or in gross)
- Profits (*profits a prendre*)
- Some licenses
- Surface and subsurface rights
- Air rights
- Mineral rights
- Liens (such as mortgages and deeds of trust)

In about half of the states, title insurance also may insure security interests and other rights in a borrower's personal property.

Air rights
Rights, which can be easements or in fee, in vertical space above the ground surface and below navigable airspace.

Owner's Policy

Owners and lenders have separate interests to protect in a real estate transaction. Each has a separate insurable interest with regard to title, and either's title insurance will protect the other's title interests. Quite often, a seller pays for an **owner's policy** for the buyer. A commonly used owner's policy form is the ALTA Owner's Policy, discussed later in this chapter.

The policy may be an ALTA Owner's Policy or the ALTA Homeowner's Policy. The second policy provides substantial additional coverage that many purchasers would require.

Owner's policy
Title insurance that insures an owner's land interest against defects, liens, and encumbrances.

Purchasing Title Insurance

Selecting a financially solvent insurer is an important decision for a buyer and lender. After the execution of the purchase contract, the closing agent or escrow agent will order title insurance. A title company will then conduct a title search of the public records. This review process is similar to the one completed with an abstract of title. The title insurer then issues a preliminary report. The **preliminary report** informs the prospective buyer, lender, or tenant of any liens, defects, or encumbrances that will be shown as exceptions to coverage in the title insurance policy issued at closing. The preliminary report reflects what the insurer would include in a title policy if it issued a

Preliminary report
A report prepared prior to issuing a policy of title insurance showing the owner of a parcel of land, along with the liens and encumbrances on title.

policy as of the preliminary report's effective date. This report allows the parties to consider the risks of the stated defects and seek to remove them.

Once the preliminary report has been prepared, reviewed, and evaluated, the title company issues a title commitment. A **title commitment** is an agreement by a title insurance company to issue a policy in favor of the proposed insured at the time the transaction closes. Commitments may be requested in place of or in addition to a preliminary report. They are most often used in commercial transactions and seldom used in residential transactions.

In the following case, the court had to determine whether a provision allowing 15 days to inspect title of a property was a material part of the contract.

Title commitment
An agreement by a title insurance company to issue a policy in favor of the proposed insured at the time the transaction closes. It does not represent the state of title.

CASE 10.4

PROVISIONS REGARDING BUYER'S RIGHT TO REVIEW TITLE ARE MATERIAL TO REAL ESTATE CONTRACTS

DAVIS v. IVEY

984 So. 2d 571 (2008)

Florida District Court of Appeal

Davis and his wife ("Davis") entered into a contract with Ivey for the sale and purchase of Ivey's property located in Orange County, Florida. The contract stated prior to the Closing Date, Ivey would provide Davis a title insurance commitment and that within 15 days from receipt of the evidence of title, the Davis would deliver written notice to Ivey of any title defects.

One day prior to the scheduled closing, Ivey finally provided title insurance commitment to the Davis. On the scheduled closing date, Davis sought to delay the closing; however, Ivey was unwilling to do so. The same day, Davis's counsel advised Ivey of a potential encroachment that had been discovered on the property, and there could be no closing until this title effect was resolved. A week later, Davis informed Ivey in writing that they were satisfied with the title despite not having obtained a current survey, and they were prepared to close, several days before the end of the 15-day period allowed for the purposes of title review. Ivey did not respond to this letter, and no closing occurred.

Davis filed suit seeking specific performance of the sales contract.

The trial court found Davis was not ready, willing, and able to close finding the letter from Davis's attorney to Ivey regarding the potential encroachment to be a delay tactic. Davis appealed.

Language of the Court. *The court must read the provisions of a contract harmoniously in order to give effect to all of its provisions. Every provision should be given meaning and effect and apparent inconsistencies reconciled if possible. Under the plain terms of the contract the Buyers were allowed fifteen days to examine the evidence of title, the title insurance commitment. Within that time frame, the Buyers had the option to either accept the evidence of title or give notice of any title defects. The Seller could then either cure the defect, or, if the Seller believed the defect could not be cured, give notice to the Buyers of his inability to cure. The Buyers then had ten days to terminate the contract or accept the title subject to the existing defect.*

The fundamental problem with the Seller's interpretation of the contract is that it ignores and renders meaningless the contractual provision allowing a fifteen-day title examination period. It effectively precludes the Buyers from any meaningful opportunity to review the title insurance commitment. It is clear from a reading of the contractual provisions that the Buyers should have been allowed 15 days after receiving evidence of title to close. Their motivation for exercising this contractual right is immaterial. The contract allowed the Buyers fifteen days to examine the *title evidence, and the trial court erred in not giving effect to this provision.*

Decision. The court of appeal reversed and found Davis was entitled to specific performance regarding the closing of the property.

FOCUS ON ETHICS

Does this decision appeal to your common sense? Why do you believe the court came to the conclusion it did?

Damages

When the insurer indemnifies the policyholder, it pays compensation, up to the amount indicated in the policy, for damages resulting from a title defect plus the costs of litigation. Those damages can be measured using a variety of methods, including the loss of fair market value or the cost of removing the defect from the title. The measure of damages could equal the amount the title insurer must spend to remove an undisclosed lien or mortgage, or it could equal the amount of a mortgage eliminated by the foreclosure of a senior lien.

When a person publishes a statement that is false and disparages another party's title in such a way that it causes damages (for example, making the title unmarketable), the property owner can sue under **slander of title**.

> *Example:* If a person were to deliberately record a false instrument on another's title, that action could cause damages to the owner. This can arise when someone makes a false accusation regarding having an ownership interest in the property of another.

This recording of a false instrument places a cloud on title. If the recordation affects the behavior of prospective purchasers, lessees, and others who might deal with the title (such as a lender), this wrongful conduct affects the salability of the property. The resulting harm suffered by the owner will allow the owner to claim damages for this conduct.

ALTA Policy

The ATLA is a national trade association representing thousands of title insurance companies. Since its founding in 1907, the ALTA has created standard form title insurance policies that its member institutions use. Over time, these forms have become the standard forms used by title insurance companies throughout the United States.

ALTA Owner's Policy

The most commonly purchased policy is an ALTA Owner's Policy. This type of policy protects the insured from defects in title. The lender will protect its interest in title defects by obtaining a loan policy (discussed later in this chapter). The Owner's Policy insures the owner of the property against loss or damage. The Owner's Policy is broken down into several parts. First, it introduces the risks that are covered by the title insurance policy; Schedule A then identifies many policy attributes; Schedule B then identifies the policy exclusions; and the policy then concludes by discussing the conditions of the title insurance policy. Some of the protections described in the policy include:

1. *Proper vesting of title.* The most important provision title insurance protects is the proper vesting of title. The title insurance company will protect that the insured owns the property.
2. *Defects, liens, or encumbrances on title.* This provision protects against any defects, liens, or encumbrances to the title not disclosed in the policy (such as unpaid real estate taxes and assessments), except for those the title insurance company has excepted from coverage in Schedule B. Additionally, a few of the examples of title insurance protection include defects resulting from forgery, fraud, undue influence, duress, incompetency, incapacity, impersonation, execution by a person lacking authority, and execution under an invalid power of attorney.
3. *Marketable title.* The title insurance company insures that title is free from any encumbrances (except those the buyer is aware of and has agreed to accept in the purchase and sale contract) and free from reasonable doubt that the seller owns title.
4. *Access.* The insured will have a right of access to and from public roads to the property.

Exclusions from Coverage

Certain types of losses are excluded from the standard ALTA Owner's Policy. The standard ALTA Owner's Policy does not insure against the following title defects:

- Liens imposed by law that are not shown on public records (such as unpaid property taxes).
- Claims made by parties in possession of the property, such as tenants and adverse possessors.
- Boundary disputes (because the title insurer does not inspect or survey the property). The standard policy does not insure against encroachments and inaccurate boundary lines and boundary disputes that would be disclosed by an accurate survey or physical inspection of the property. Minor encroachment issues (for example, fences, garage eaves, decks, and misaligned driveways) are similarly excluded from coverage.
- Nonrecorded easements and servitudes, such as easements by implication, necessity, or prescription that would be disclosed by inspection and survey.
- Zoning or building ordinances.
- Hazardous waste that might exist on the property.

Closing or Settlement

The title closing is the goal of a real estate transaction. A **closing** is the completion or settlement of a real estate transaction. The closing of title is also called a "settlement" and is completed when the performance of the parties has been rendered. That means the contract is executed and there is nothing further for the parties to perform regarding the transaction.

Preparation for Closing

When the buyer signs an offer to purchase real estate, normally the broker receives the buyer's earnest money deposit. This deposit becomes part of the consideration paid by the buyer to the seller as part of the selling price. The seller accepts the offer, and the fully signed document forms the contract of purchase and sale.

With a sales contract, the expenses are normally allocated between the buyer and seller. If instructions are not stated in the agreement, the closing agent or escrow agent will have his own set of written instructions that are signed by the seller and buyer so that the closing can occur. If not agreed upon in advance, the closing expenses are allocated according to the custom and practice of the local real estate industry. A **closing statement** is prepared in advance of the closing, stating the distribution of monies that will occur at the time of closing. These closing charges vary widely across the United States but often include the following:

- Points (the money paid the mortgage company to secure a lower interest rate; 1 percent equals one point)
- Mortgage application and processing (underwriting) fees
- Costs of appraising the property for lending purposes
- Costs of inspections required by law, the lender, or the buyer
- Survey fees, if necessary
- Title-search fee (to verify the evidence of title)
- Title insurance premiums
- Recording fees
- Local transfer taxes upon the sale of property

Example: New York State collects a 1 percent tax from buyers who purchase a one-, two-, or three-family home or an individual condominium or cooperative unit for $1 million or more (the Mansion Tax).[5]

- Flood certification fees
- Loan-processing fee (similar to the underwriting fee, it covers the expense of processing the mortgage loan)
- Prepaid association and/or property insurance fees
- Pro rata share of property taxes. (An adjustment to ensure that the buyer and seller pay their proportionate share of the annual property tax. Property taxes are paid in arrears or after the tax year. They are allocated on the basis of the percentage of ownership of the property during the year.)

- Pro rata interest on the buyer's loan for the number of days between the closing date and the date the first payment is due to the lender

During the preclosing phase of the transaction, several activities occur, including the following:

- Inspection of the property by property inspectors and others
- Appraisal of the property
- Securing a title commitment
- Securing a commitment for homeowner's insurance

The buyer's walk through of the property allows the buyer to confirm the condition of the property prior to closing and verify that contingencies have been satisfied.

At the closing, the parties execute the transfer documents (including the deeds and seller's disclosure statement, if that has already not occurred); the parties then pay their share of the closing costs and escrow expenses. Following the closing or settlement meeting, funds held by the escrow, such as the mortgage lender's funds, monies for the broker's commissions, and monies owed the homeowner's association, lien claimants, the seller, and others are disbursed after the mortgage and deed are recorded. Once this has occurred, the keys to the premises are given to the buyer.

Types of Closings

During the negotiations, the seller and the buyer agree upon the date for the closing. Closing procedures vary between states and localities. Generally, closings occur by one of two methods throughout the United States.

Settlement Process or Table Closing

The first method is used primarily in the Eastern, Southeastern, and Midwestern portions of the United States. It is known as the **settlement process** or "table closing." In this closing method, the parties and other interested individuals meet in person on an agreed date and time. The parties will often meet at a settlement company (often a division of a lender or title insurer). However, the closing location can be the lender's office, the office of one of the party's attorneys, the title company's facility, or the local recorder's office. Each jurisdiction has its own practices.

At the meeting the parties will review the closing documents, sign the documents, pay and receive consideration for the property (most often, money), and receive title to the real estate. Buyers, sellers, their attorneys and real estate agents, and lender representatives will attend the title closing. The closing is presided over or supervised by a **settlement agent**, who will cause all of the conveyance documents (such as deeds, assignments of leases, and easements and the like), mortgages, notes, and monies to be exchanged between the buyer and seller and ensures that the lender's funds are properly disbursed.

The settlement agent can be a lender, a real estate broker, a title company, an attorney, or a company specializing in this work, known as an escrow company. Settlement activities can play an important part in the real estate practices of many law firms.

Settlement process
A method of closing in which both the buyer and the seller exchange documents in person.

Settlement agent
A person who supervises the exchange of documents, mortgages, notes, and monies between the buyer and the seller.

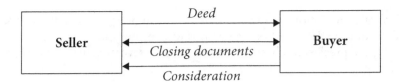

FIGURE 10.3. Eastern, Southeastern, and Midwestern Closing Method

Escrow

Escrow
A method of closing in which both the buyer and the seller deliver documents to an escrow agent, who holds the documents in trust for the parties until all conditions for closing are met.

Escrow agent
A person who facilitates the closing of a transaction and holds a deed in escrow until all the terms and conditions between the buyer and seller are met.

The second method, used primarily in the Western United States, uses an escrow for closing. In an **escrow**, both the buyer and the seller deliver documents to an escrow agent, who holds the documents in trust until all parties meet the closing conditions. The parties do not meet to sign documents or exchange consideration. Instead, at the time of entering into the contract of sale, they sign an escrow agreement, which requires the deposit of documents and funds with the escrow agent within agreed timelines.

The escrow holder is responsible for meeting the agreement's requirements. The **escrow agent** facilitates the efforts of the parties to close the transaction. The escrow process is a mechanism to close both the title and the mortgage transaction simultaneously. Closing occurs at the moment when the seller is paid the purchase price, existing liens against the property are satisfied, the conveyance to the grantee is recorded, and the mortgage lender's mortgage or deed of trust is recorded.

Unlike in the settlement method, when an escrow is used, the escrow company supervises virtually all the steps necessary to satisfy the conditions of closing. When the final steps are to be taken, the check for the purchase price is cleared, the deed is delivered to the buyer, and the escrow holder distributes the proceeds of the sale to those who must be paid to clear title. These parties would include persons holding mortgages and liens authorized to be paid at closing. The balance of the purchase price is then paid to the seller.

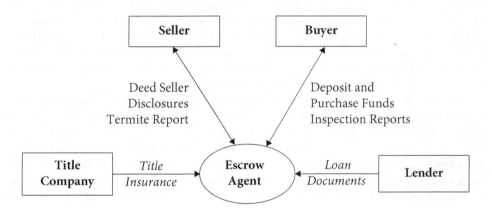

FIGURE 10.4. Simplified Western Closing Method

Throughout the United States, commercial property transactions are conducted primarily using an escrow, often with the title company intimately involved in the closing mechanics. Unlike residential transactions, in commercial transactions the parties' attorneys participate actively in the closings.

Duties Common to Both Settlement Agents and Escrow Holders

■ ■ ■

In acting as a neutral third party, the settlement agent or escrow holder performs the following tasks:

- Acts as the impartial "stakeholder" or depository of documents and funds.
- Processes and coordinates the flow of documents and funds.
- Communicates the status of conditions to closing to all those involved.
- Receives and responds to the lender's requirements.
- Orders the title insurance policy(ies) required for closing.
- If necessary, obtains approval of prospective purchaser from the property owners' association (especially needed for the purchase and sale of a unit within a building owned and operated by a cooperative).
- Obtains approvals of inspection reports and public information reports and documents from the parties.
- Performs the prorating and adjustment of monies due for insurance, taxes, and rents (more fully discussed in chapter 11).
- Records the deed and loan documents.
- Provides a final accounting of monies received and disbursed during the closing (discussed in the next chapter).

Duties of the Settlement Agent or Escrow Holder

Generally, the duties of the settlement agent or escrow holder are straightforward; the agent must strictly follow the instructions of the parties to the transactions and applicable law. They are not required to render services that are not required by those instructions or the law. The standard of care for which they are held accountable is that they must perform their duties with ordinary skill and diligence and follow the parties' instructions given to them. In addition, they are obligated to follow the closing instructions of the buyer's lender or a refinance lender. The settlement agent or escrow holder may incur liability for breach of contract or negligence if the escrow holder fails to follow the parties' or the lender's closing instructions.

Occasionally, the settlement agent or escrow holder may agree to record a document (one not prepared by either of them) on behalf of a party to the escrow without assuming any liability for its consequences. This is referred to as an accommodation recording. The document can be a payoff to an unsecured creditor or, on behalf of a potential tenant, a memorandum of a proposed lease not yet executed for the real property being sold. This is not a recommended practice because it can create liability for the agent or holder for the tort of slander of title. If not recorded by the settlement agent or escrow holder, liability can be incurred by the recording party.

Slander of title occurs when one falsely claims an interest in the ownership of another's property. That is, the party who recorded a document on the title to the property did not have a privilege to do so. Some states follow common law definitions of slander of title and others have defined it in their statutes. The damages to be assessed would include the amount the plaintiff needs to repair the defect of title, including attorney fees, as well as damages caused by the slander, including the loss of the value of the property or the loss of a sale of the property. Many states also permit punitive damages in slander of title claims. Punitive damages are those based on the relative wealth of the defendant and are designed to punish intentional wrongdoing

Documents Exchanged at Closing

Some of the tasks and documents addressed by the settlement agent or escrow holder are listed below. The list is not comprehensive, and not all of these items are involved in every closing:

- Surveys if required by the buyer or the buyer's lender
- Broker's commission statement
- IRS Form 1099-S (Proceeds from Sale of Real Estate Property)
- A closing or settlement statement or a Closing Disclosure
- Tax reporting forms as required by federal, state, and local laws and ordinances
- Deed to the buyer prepared in recordable form
- Seller's disclosure statement, if required
- Inspection reports (as required by law and the purchase and sale agreement)
- Insurance certificates (fire, natural hazard, etc.)
- Leases for delivery to the purchaser at the time of closing, along with assignments to purchaser
- Note and mortgage or deed of trust (or installment land contract)
- Final Truth-In-Lending Act statement
- Title assurance documents
- Foreign Investment in Real Property Tax Act (FIRPTA) certificate

   FIRPTA requires that a capital gains tax be imposed upon foreign persons deriving income on the sale of real property located in the United States. The seller must deliver a FIRPTA certificate to the buyer. The buyer must withhold 10 percent of the purchase price at closing and pay it directly to the Internal Revenue Service. If a real estate broker is aware that the seller is giving a false FIRPTA certificate, the broker is personally liable for the unpaid tax.

The closing process takes 30 to 60 days in an ordinary residential sales transaction, but it can take far longer to close the sale of a commercial or industrial property. The closing may be delayed if conditions for closing do not occur as anticipated. For example, if the seller agrees that the buyer can wait to close until the buyer's current home is sold, substantial delays may occur.

How Long Does It Take to Close?

For the most part, the closing involves the review and signing of numerous documents, most of which relate to the mortgage. The settlement agent will explain the nature and purpose of each one and give the parties the opportunity to read them before signing. In a typical purchase or refinance residential transaction with a traditional mortgage lender (such as a bank or savings and loan), the closing will take approximately one hour. If the closing is funded with the buyer's cash, the closing can occur in much less time.

Several hours will be required for commercial closings to ensure that all the documentation is present for signing, the documents are properly executed, and that a fully executed "closing set" of documents is or will become available for all parties to the transaction.

Real Estate Settlement Procedures Act (RESPA)

The **Real Estate Settlement Procedures Act (RESPA)**[6] is a federal act administered by the federal Consumer Financial Protection Bureau. RESPA ensures that consumers are provided with information about the cost of their mortgages and closings. This information protects consumers from unnecessarily high settlement charges caused by abusive financing and closing practices.

RESPA
Federal law administered by the Consumer Financial Protection Bureau aimed at ensuring that consumers receive information about the cost of their mortgages and closings.

Integrated Disclosure

Chapter 9 discussed how the **Consumer Financial Protection Bureau (CFPB)** integrated two forms related to initial financing disclosures. In addition to the integration of those forms, the CFPB examined the closing and settlement process regulated by the RESPA in conjunction with other financial statutes and regulations. After the review, the CFPB merged the Truth-in-Lending Act (TILA) disclosure form (Regulation Z) with RESPA's HUD-1 Settlement Statement (Regulation X) for most residential transactions covered by RESPA.

CFPB
Federal agency having primary regulatory authority over consumer lending.

The integrated forms are known as the **TILA-RESPA Integrated Disclosure (TRID) rule**. These disclosures are intended to protect the consumer-buyer in residential mortgage transactions. By requiring use of the forms, CSFP intended to obtain clarity and transparency in defining the elements of the mortgage obligation.

TILA-RESPA Integrated Disclosure rule
CFPB rule requiring specific loan disclosures to consumer borrowers.

TRID Rule Coverage

Recall from chapter 9 that the TRID rule applies to most closed-end consumer credit transactions secured by real property. A closed-end transaction is one in which the full amount owed (principal, interest, and finance charges) must be paid back by the borrower by a set point in time. Consumer credit means credit offered or extended to a consumer primarily for personal, family, or household purposes. The residential property must be either a one- to four-unit family structure or a manufactured home (mobile home). The act covers first and second mortgages, refinancing, construction-only loans, loans secured by vacant land, and loans secured by 25 or more acres.

The TRID rule does not apply to the following:

- Home equity lines of credit (HELOC)
- Reverse mortgages
- Mortgages secured by a mobile home
- Mortgages secured by a dwelling that is not attached to real property (that is, land)

TRID Rule Terminology

Those who are involved with residential real estate transactions should be aware of the following relevant terminology used in residential mortgage lending:

Terminology Used in TRID	Definition
Creditor	Lender
Consumer	Borrower
Consummation	The date on which the consumer becomes legally obligated on the loan documents. Consummation commonly occurs at the same time as closing/settlement.
Loan Estimate	Disclosure document provided no later than three business days after consumer submits a loan application. It provides key features, costs, and risks of the mortgage for which they are applying.
Closing Disclosure	Disclosure provided at least three business days prior to consummation. It provides the actual terms and costs of the transaction.

Closing Disclosures

Closing disclosure
Lender's disclosure to
consumer of
anticipated costs and
disbursements at
closing.

For loans that require a Loan Estimate and that proceed to closing, creditors must provide a new final disclosure reflecting the actual terms of the transaction, called the **closing disclosure**. It is designed to provide disclosures that will be helpful to consumers in understanding all costs of the transaction.

Contents of the Closing Disclosure

The closing disclosure is composed of five pages. Page 1 is almost identical to the Loan Estimate discussed in chapter 9. It includes the name and address of the lender and a Loan Terms table with descriptions of applicable information about the loan, including the loan amount, interest rate, monthly principal and interest payment, existence of any prepayment penalties or balloon payments, and the estimated costs at closing will be.

Pages 2 and 3 provide details on the closing costs. It breaks down the costs paid by the borrower, seller, and third parties for costs due either at closing or before closing. The costs details include: (1) an itemization of the loan costs, taxes, insurance, and other costs associated with the closing; (2) a calculation of the amount of cash needed at closing; (3) summaries of the transactions for both the borrower and the seller and how much cash from the borrower is needed to close the transaction and how much cash the seller will receive at closing.

Page 4 provides additional information about the loan, including whether the lender will allow assumption of the loan, whether the loan has a negative amortization feature, if the lender will accept partial payments, and escrow account information.

Page 5 includes a summary of the total amount of payments, finance charges, and amount financed for the loan and provides the contact information for the lender, mortgage broker, real estate brokers, and settlement agents.

Closing Disclosure

This form is a statement of final loan terms and closing costs. Compare this document with your Loan Estimate.

Closing Information

Date Issued	4/15/2013
Closing Date	4/15/2013
Disbursement Date	4/15/2013
Settlement Agent	Epsilon Title Co.
File #	12-3456
Property	456 Somewhere Ave Anytown, ST 12345
Sale Price	$180,000

Transaction Information

Borrower	Michael Jones and Mary Stone 123 Anywhere Street Anytown, ST 12345
Seller	Steve Cole and Amy Doe 321 Somewhere Drive Anytown, ST 12345
Lender	Ficus Bank

Loan Information

Loan Term	30 years
Purpose	Purchase
Product	Fixed Rate
Loan Type	☒ Conventional ☐ FHA ☐ VA ☐ _____
Loan ID #	123456789
MIC #	000654321

Loan Terms

		Can this amount increase after closing?
Loan Amount	$162,000	**NO**
Interest Rate	3.875%	**NO**
Monthly Principal & Interest *See Projected Payments below for your Estimated Total Monthly Payment*	$761.78	**NO**
		Does the loan have these features?
Prepayment Penalty		**YES** • As high as $3,240 if you pay off the loan during the first 2 years
Balloon Payment		**NO**

Projected Payments

Payment Calculation	Years 1-7	Years 8-30
Principal & Interest	$761.78	$761.78
Mortgage Insurance	+ 82.35	+ —
Estimated Escrow *Amount can increase over time*	+ 206.13	+ 206.13
Estimated Total Monthly Payment	**$1,050.26**	**$967.91**

Estimated Taxes, Insurance & Assessments *Amount can increase over time* *See page 4 for details*	$356.13 a month	**This estimate includes** ☒ Property Taxes ☒ Homeowner's Insurance ☒ Other: Homeowner's Association Dues *See Escrow Account on page 4 for details. You must pay for other property costs separately.*	**In escrow?** YES YES NO

Costs at Closing

Closing Costs	$9,712.10	Includes $4,694.05 in Loan Costs + $5,018.05 in Other Costs – $0 in Lender Credits. *See page 2 for details.*
Cash to Close	$14,147.26	Includes Closing Costs. *See Calculating Cash to Close on page 3 for details.*

Exhibit 10.2. Closing Disclosure

Closing Cost Details

Loan Costs		Borrower-Paid		Seller-Paid		Paid by Others
		At Closing	Before Closing	At Closing	Before Closing	
A. Origination Charges		**$1,802.00**				
01 0.25 % of Loan Amount (Points)		$405.00				
02 Application Fee		$300.00				
03 Underwriting Fee		$1,097.00				
04						
05						
06						
07						
08						
B. Services Borrower Did Not Shop For		**$236.55**				
01 Appraisal Fee	to John Smith Appraisers Inc.					$405.00
02 Credit Report Fee	to Information Inc.		$29.80			
03 Flood Determination Fee	to Info Co.	$20.00				
04 Flood Monitoring Fee	to Info Co.	$31.75				
05 Tax Monitoring Fee	to Info Co.	$75.00				
06 Tax Status Research Fee	to Info Co.	$80.00				
07						
08						
09						
10						
C. Services Borrower Did Shop For		**$2,655.50**				
01 Pest Inspection Fee	to Pests Co.	$120.50				
02 Survey Fee	to Surveys Co.	$85.00				
03 Title – Insurance Binder	to Epsilon Title Co.	$650.00				
04 Title – Lender's Title Insurance	to Epsilon Title Co.	$500.00				
05 Title – Settlement Agent Fee	to Epsilon Title Co.	$500.00				
06 Title – Title Search	to Epsilon Title Co.	$800.00				
07						
08						
D. TOTAL LOAN COSTS (Borrower-Paid)		**$4,694.05**				
Loan Costs Subtotals (A + B + C)		$4,664.25	$29.80			

Other Costs						
E. Taxes and Other Government Fees		**$85.00**				
01 Recording Fees	Deed: $40.00 Mortgage: $45.00	$85.00				
02 Transfer Tax	to Any State			$950.00		
F. Prepaids		**$2,120.80**				
01 Homeowner's Insurance Premium (12 mo.) to Insurance Co.		$1,209.96				
02 Mortgage Insurance Premium (mo.)						
03 Prepaid Interest ($17.44 per day from 4/15/13 to 5/1/13)		$279.04				
04 Property Taxes (6 mo.) to Any County USA		$631.80				
05						
G. Initial Escrow Payment at Closing		**$412.25**				
01 Homeowner's Insurance $100.83 per month for 2 mo.		$201.66				
02 Mortgage Insurance per month for mo.						
03 Property Taxes $105.30 per month for 2 mo.		$210.60				
04						
05						
06						
07						
08 Aggregate Adjustment		– 0.01				
H. Other		**$2,400.00**				
01 HOA Capital Contribution	to HOA Acre Inc.	$500.00				
02 HOA Processing Fee	to HOA Acre Inc.	$150.00				
03 Home Inspection Fee	to Engineers Inc.	$750.00			$750.00	
04 Home Warranty Fee	to XYZ Warranty Inc.			$450.00		
05 Real Estate Commission	to Alpha Real Estate Broker			$5,700.00		
06 Real Estate Commission	to Omega Real Estate Broker			$5,700.00		
07 Title – Owner's Title Insurance (optional) to Epsilon Title Co.		$1,000.00				
08						
I. TOTAL OTHER COSTS (Borrower-Paid)		**$5,018.05**				
Other Costs Subtotals (E + F + G + H)		$5,018.05				

J. TOTAL CLOSING COSTS (Borrower-Paid)		**$9,712.10**				
Closing Costs Subtotals (D + I)		$9,682.30	$29.80	$12,800.00	$750.00	$405.00
Lender Credits						

Exhibit 10.2. Closing Disclosure (*Continued*)

Calculating Cash to Close

Use this table to see what has changed from your Loan Estimate.

	Loan Estimate	Final	Did this change?
Total Closing Costs (J)	$8,054.00	$9,712.10	**YES** • See **Total Loan Costs (D)** and **Total Other Costs (I)**
Closing Costs Paid Before Closing	$0	− $29.80	**YES** • You paid these Closing Costs **before closing**
Closing Costs Financed (Paid from your Loan Amount)	$0	$0	**NO**
Down Payment/Funds from Borrower	$18,000.00	$18,000.00	**NO**
Deposit	− $10,000.00	− $10,000.00	**NO**
Funds for Borrower	$0	$0	**NO**
Seller Credits	$0	− $2,500.00	**YES** • See Seller Credits in **Section L**
Adjustments and Other Credits	$0	− $1,035.04	**YES** • See details in **Sections K and L**
Cash to Close	$16,054.00	$14,147.26	

Summaries of Transactions

Use this table to see a summary of your transaction.

BORROWER'S TRANSACTION

K. Due from Borrower at Closing	$189,762.30
01 Sale Price of Property	$180,000.00
02 Sale Price of Any Personal Property Included in Sale	
03 Closing Costs Paid at Closing (J)	$9,682.30
04	
Adjustments	
05	
06	
07	
Adjustments for Items Paid by Seller in Advance	
08 City/Town Taxes to	
09 County Taxes to	
10 Assessments to	
11 HOA Dues 4/15/13 to 4/30/13	$80.00
12	
13	
14	
15	

L. Paid Already by or on Behalf of Borrower at Closing	$175,615.04
01 Deposit	$10,000.00
02 Loan Amount	$162,000.00
03 Existing Loan(s) Assumed or Taken Subject to	
04	
05 Seller Credit	$2,500.00
Other Credits	
06 Rebate from Epsilon Title Co.	$750.00
07	
Adjustments	
08	
09	
10	
11	
Adjustments for Items Unpaid by Seller	
12 City/Town Taxes 1/1/13 to 4/14/13	$365.04
13 County Taxes to	
14 Assessments to	
15	
16	
17	

CALCULATION	
Total Due from Borrower at Closing (K)	$189,762.30
Total Paid Already by or on Behalf of Borrower at Closing (L)	− $175,615.04
Cash to Close ☒ **From** ☐ **To Borrower**	**$14,147.26**

SELLER'S TRANSACTION

M. Due to Seller at Closing	$180,080.00
01 Sale Price of Property	$180,000.00
02 Sale Price of Any Personal Property Included in Sale	
03	
04	
05	
06	
07	
08	
Adjustments for Items Paid by Seller in Advance	
09 City/Town Taxes to	
10 County Taxes to	
11 Assessments to	
12 HOA Dues 4/15/13 to 4/30/13	$80.00
13	
14	
15	
16	

N. Due from Seller at Closing	$115,665.04
01 Excess Deposit	
02 Closing Costs Paid at Closing (J)	$12,800.00
03 Existing Loan(s) Assumed or Taken Subject to	
04 Payoff of First Mortgage Loan	$100,000.00
05 Payoff of Second Mortgage Loan	
06	
07	
08 Seller Credit	$2,500.00
09	
10	
11	
12	
13	
Adjustments for Items Unpaid by Seller	
14 City/Town Taxes 1/1/13 to 4/14/13	$365.04
15 County Taxes to	
16 Assessments to	
17	
18	
19	

CALCULATION	
Total Due to Seller at Closing (M)	$180,080.00
Total Due from Seller at Closing (N)	− $115,665.04
Cash ☐ **From** ☒ **To Seller**	**$64,414.96**

CLOSING DISCLOSURE

Exhibit 10.2. Closing Disclosure (*Continued*)

Additional Information About This Loan

Loan Disclosures

Assumption

If you sell or transfer this property to another person, your lender

☐ will allow, under certain conditions, this person to assume this loan on the original terms.

☒ will not allow assumption of this loan on the original terms.

Demand Feature

Your loan

☐ has a demand feature, which permits your lender to require early repayment of the loan. You should review your note for details.

☒ does not have a demand feature.

Late Payment

If your payment is more than *15* days late, your lender will charge a late fee of *5% of the monthly principal and interest payment.*

Negative Amortization (Increase in Loan Amount)

Under your loan terms, you

☐ are scheduled to make monthly payments that do not pay all of the interest due that month. As a result, your loan amount will increase (negatively amortize), and your loan amount will likely become larger than your original loan amount. Increases in your loan amount lower the equity you have in this property.

☐ may have monthly payments that do not pay all of the interest due that month. If you do, your loan amount will increase (negatively amortize), and, as a result, your loan amount may become larger than your original loan amount. Increases in your loan amount lower the equity you have in this property.

☒ do not have a negative amortization feature.

Partial Payments

Your lender

☒ may accept payments that are less than the full amount due (partial payments) and apply them to your loan.

☐ may hold them in a separate account until you pay the rest of the payment, and then apply the full payment to your loan.

☐ does not accept any partial payments.

If this loan is sold, your new lender may have a different policy.

Security Interest

You are granting a security interest in
456 Somewhere Ave., Anytown, ST 12345

You may lose this property if you do not make your payments or satisfy other obligations for this loan.

Escrow Account

For now, your loan

☒ will have an escrow account (also called an "impound" or "trust" account) to pay the property costs listed below. Without an escrow account, you would pay them directly, possibly in one or two large payments a year. Your lender may be liable for penalties and interest for failing to make a payment.

Escrow		
Escrowed Property Costs over Year 1	$2,473.56	Estimated total amount over year 1 for your escrowed property costs: *Homeowner's Insurance Property Taxes*
Non-Escrowed Property Costs over Year 1	$1,800.00	Estimated total amount over year 1 for your non-escrowed property costs: *Homeowner's Association Dues* You may have other property costs.
Initial Escrow Payment	$412.25	A cushion for the escrow account you pay at closing. See Section G on page 2.
Monthly Escrow Payment	$206.13	The amount included in your total monthly payment.

☐ will not have an escrow account because ☐ you declined it ☐ your lender does not offer one. You must directly pay your property costs, such as taxes and homeowner's insurance. Contact your lender to ask if your loan can have an escrow account.

No Escrow		
Estimated Property Costs over Year 1		Estimated total amount over year 1. You must pay these costs directly, possibly in one or two large payments a year.
Escrow Waiver Fee		

In the future,

Your property costs may change and, as a result, your escrow payment may change. You may be able to cancel your escrow account, but if you do, you must pay your property costs directly. If you fail to pay your property taxes, your state or local government may (1) **impose fines and penalties or (2) place a tax lien on this property. If** you fail to pay any of your property costs, your lender may (1) add the amounts to your loan balance, (2) add an escrow account to your loan, or (3) require you to pay for property insurance that the lender buys on your behalf, which likely would cost more and provide fewer benefits than what you could buy on your own.

Exhibit 10.2. Closing Disclosure (*Continued*)

Loan Calculations

Total of Payments. Total you will have paid after you make all payments of principal, interest, mortgage insurance, and loan costs, as scheduled.	$285,803.36
Finance Charge. The dollar amount the loan will cost you.	$118,830.27
Amount Financed. The loan amount available after paying your upfront finance charge.	$162,000.00
Annual Percentage Rate (APR). Your costs over the loan term expressed as a rate. This is not your interest rate.	4.174%
Total Interest Percentage (TIP). The total amount of interest that you will pay over the loan term as a percentage of your loan amount.	69.46%

Questions? If you have questions about the loan terms or costs on this form, use the contact information below. To get more information or make a complaint, contact the Consumer Financial Protection Bureau at **www.consumerfinance.gov/mortgage-closing**

Other Disclosures

Appraisal
If the property was appraised for your loan, your lender is required to give you a copy at no additional cost at least 3 days before closing. If you have not yet received it, please contact your lender at the information listed below.

Contract Details
See your note and security instrument for information about
- what happens if you fail to make your payments,
- what is a default on the loan,
- situations in which your lender can require early repayment of the loan, and
- the rules for making payments before they are due.

Liability after Foreclosure
If your lender forecloses on this property and the foreclosure does not cover the amount of unpaid balance on this loan,

☒ state law may protect you from liability for the unpaid balance. If you refinance or take on any additional debt on this property, you may lose this protection and have to pay any debt remaining even after foreclosure. You may want to consult a lawyer for more information.

☐ state law does not protect you from liability for the unpaid balance.

Refinance
Refinancing this loan will depend on your future financial situation, the property value, and market conditions. You may not be able to refinance this loan.

Tax Deductions
If you borrow more than this property is worth, the interest on the loan amount above this property's fair market value is not deductible from your federal income taxes. You should consult a tax advisor for more information.

Contact Information

	Lender	Mortgage Broker	Real Estate Broker (B)	Real Estate Broker (S)	Settlement Agent
Name	Ficus Bank		Omega Real Estate Broker Inc.	Alpha Real Estate Broker Co.	Epsilon Title Co.
Address	4321 Random Blvd. Somecity, ST 12340		789 Local Lane Sometown, ST 12345	987 Suburb Ct. Someplace, ST 12340	123 Commerce Pl. Somecity, ST 12344
NMLS ID					
ST License ID			Z765416	Z61456	Z61616
Contact	Joe Smith		Samuel Green	Joseph Cain	Sarah Arnold
Contact NMLS ID	12345				
Contact ST License ID			P16415	P51461	PT1234
Email	joesmith@ ficusbank.com		sam@omegare.biz	joe@alphare.biz	sarah@ epsilontitle.com
Phone	123-456-7890		123-555-1717	321-555-7171	987-555-4321

Confirm Receipt

By signing, you are only confirming that you have received this form. You do not have to accept this loan because you have signed or received this form.

_____   _____   _____   _____
Applicant Signature   Date   Co-Applicant Signature   Date

CLOSING DISCLOSURE

PAGE 5 OF 5 • LOAN ID # 123456789

Exhibit 10.2. Closing Disclosure (*Continued*)

Timing of Closing Disclosure

The CFPB requires the consumer to receive the closing disclosure at least three business days prior to **consummation**. Consummation is the date on which the consumer becomes legally obligated on the loan documents. It commonly occurs at the same time as closing/settlement. Consumers may waive or modify the three-business-day period if the consumer has received the closing disclosure and given a written statement of a case of a bona fide personal financial emergency (such as where loan proceeds are needed by consumer to void a foreclosure sale).

If the creditor provides a corrected disclosure, it may also be required to provide the consumer with an additional three-business-day waiting period prior to consummation.

Mortgage Servicing Disclosure

After closing, a mortgage servicing disclosure statement will be distributed to the borrower. This statement discloses to the borrower whether the lender intends to service the loan or transfer it to another lender.

RESPA Prohibited Conduct

RESPA prohibits a person from giving or accepting kickbacks or unearned fees. RESPA defines a **kickback** as anything of value (such as payments, commissions, fees, gifts, and special privileges) received for referrals of settlement-service business. The unearned fee provision prohibits a person from giving or accepting any part of a charge for services that are not performed. RESPA also prohibits home sellers from requiring homebuyers to purchase title insurance from a particular title insurance company.

Penalties for Prohibited Conduct

Violations of the anti-kickback, referral, and unearned fee provisions of RESPA can result in both criminal and civil penalties. In a criminal case, a violator may be fined up to $10,000 and/or imprisoned for up to one year. In a civil lawsuit, a violator may be liable for an amount equal to three times that of the unlawful charges, plus court costs and attorney fees.

> *Example:* A mortgage lender charges customers $20 for a flood-hazard report, but the firm providing that information charged the bank only $15. This is a violation of RESPA.

Requiring the use of a particular title company incurs a penalty of up to three times the amount charged for title insurance, plus court costs and attorney fees.

In the following case, the U.S. Supreme Court considered whether consumers could sue a lender under RESPA for retaining an unearned fee. The Supreme Court considered whether keeping that fee could be considered an unlawful kickback. The controversy arose because the Department of Housing and Urban Development had issued a policy statement that retaining such unearned fees was a violation of RESPA.

CASE 10.5
UNDER RESPA A KICKBACK REQUIRES THAT A FEE BE SPLIT, NOT MERELY THAT AN UNEARNED FEE BE RETAINED

FREEMAN v. QUICKEN LOANS, INC.

566 U.S. 624 (2012)

United States Supreme Court

Tammy Freeman and two other couples who obtained home mortgage loans from Quicken Loans sued the lender under RESPA. They alleged that Quicken Loans charged them fees for which no services were provided in return. The lender argued that because the unearned fees were not split with another party, Freeman and the others could not recover damages under RESPA. The federal district court granted summary judgment in favor of the lender, and the Fifth Circuit Court of Appeals affirmed. The Supreme Court granted a writ of certiorari.

Language of the Court. *Enacted in 1974, RESPA regulates the market for real estate "settlement services," a term defined by statute to include any service provided in connection with a real estate settlement, such as title searches, title insurance, services rendered by an attorney, the preparation of documents, property surveys, the rendering of credit reports or appraisals, services rendered by a real estate agent or broker, the origination of a federal real estate mortgage loan, the handling of the processing, and closing or settlement. Among RESPA's consumer-protection provisions is one which provides that no person shall give and no person shall accept any fee, kickback, or thing of value pursuant to any agreement or understanding, oral or otherwise, from business incident to or a part of a real estate settlement service involving a federally related mortgage loan that shall be referred to any person.*

The act adds the following: no person shall give and no person shall accept any portion, split, or percentage of any charge made or received for the rendering of a real estate settlement service in connection with a transaction involving a federally related mortgage loan, other than for services actually performed.

In order to establish a violation of RESPA, a plaintiff must demonstrate that a charge for settlement services was divided between two or more persons. Because petitioners Freeman do not contend that respondent Quicken split the challenged charges with anyone else, summary judgment was properly granted in favor of Quicken.

Decision. The Supreme Court affirmed finding Freeman failed to demonstrate that Quicken violated RESPA.

FOCUS ON ETHICS

Do you think that Congress should include unearned settlement fees within the prohibition of RESPA? Do you think it was ethical for Quicken to claim that it was allowed to keep them?

Key Terms and Concepts

- Title, page 256
- Deeds, page 256
- Grantor, page 256
- Grantee, page 256
- Dower and curtesy rights, page 258
- *Habendum clause*, page 262
- Acknowledgment, page 263
- Constructive delivery, page 263
- Title assurance, page 265
- General warranty deed, page 265
- Special warranty deed, page 268
- Grant deed, page 268
- Deed of bargain and sale, page 268
- Quitclaim deed, page 268
- Judicial deed, page 269
- Trustee deed, page 269
- Merger doctrine, page 270
- Recording statute, page 271
- Grantor-grantee index system, page 272
- Tract index system, page 272
- Race statute, page 272
- Notice statute, page 273
- Bona fide purchaser, page 273
- Actual notice, page 273
- Constructive notice, page 273
- Inquiry notice, page 273
- Race-notice statute, page 274
- Torrens title system, page 276

- Marketable title, page 277
- Chain of title, page 278
- Marketable record title acts, page 278
- Title abstract, page 278
- Title opinion, page 278
- Title insurance, page 278
- Cloud on title, page 279
- Endorsement, page 279
- Air rights, page 280
- Owner's policy, page 280
- Preliminary report, page 280
- Title commitment, page 281
- Slander of title, page 282
- Closing, page 284
- Closing statement, page 284
- Settlement process, page 285
- Settlement agent, page 285
- Escrow, page 286
- Escrow agent, page 286
- Slander of title, page 288
- RESPA, page 289
- CFPB, page 289
- TILA-RESPA Integrated Disclosure (TRID) rule, page 289
- Closing disclosures, page 290
- Consummation, page 291
- Kickback, page 291

Chapter Summary

- Title is the ownership of land. When title is known, the ownership of real property allows a person to transfer title of an estate from one person to another.

- Deeds are written instruments used to convey (transfer) real property. The grantor is the seller or donor, and the grantee is the buyer or recipient, of the deed.

- To convey effectively all of the interests in the property, a deed must fulfill eight requirements.

- Delivery of the deed may be accomplished by either actually delivering it or constructively delivering it to the grantee. Actual delivery occurs when the grantor physically hands the deed to the grantee. Constructive delivery occurs when the grantor delivers the deed to a third party for the benefit of the grantee (often through escrow).

- Title assurance is the recognition of having evidence of title.

- State laws recognize different types of deeds. The most common types are (1) general warranty deed, (2) grant deed, (3) special warranty deed, (4) deed of bargain and sale, and (5) quitclaim deeds.

- A general warranty deed contains a full set of legal promises by the grantor to the grantee. The deed provides six warranties or promises to the grantee following the delivery of the deed to the grantee.

- A special warranty deed is one in which the same covenants are made as in the general warranty deed, but they are restricted to the period of time of the grantor's ownership.

- A grant deed is a limited form of a warranty deed.

- A deed of bargain and sale is one in which a claim of ownership is made but is not accompanied by any other warranties.

- A quitclaim deed is one in which the grantor conveys whatever interest the grantor owns but makes no warranty or promise to the grantee.

- There are several specific purpose type deeds that can be used. They include corrective deeds, sheriff's deeds, trustee deeds, and fiduciary deeds.

- The merger doctrine provides that upon the closing of the transaction, in the absence of contrary language in the sales contract, the agreements and promises made in the contract are no longer enforceable. The deed represents the final expression of the parties' intentions.

- The merger doctrine provides that upon the closing of the transaction, in the absence of contrary language in the sales contract, the agreements and promises made in the contract are no longer enforceable. The deed represents the final expression of the parties' intentions.

- A recording system allows all persons to be informed of the condition of the title to real property.

- Title claims are determined by one of three types of recording statutes. Each state has adopted one of these: (1) race statute, (2) notice statute, or (3) race-notice statute.

- Marketable title is the condition of title that a prudent buyer or lender would accept with full knowledge of the condition of the title. Marketable record title acts define the length of the examination period for prior title transactions.

- Marketable title begins with a title search, which is the examination of the public title records. The grantor-grantee indexes are reviewed, and a chain of title is prepared.

- An abstract of title is a condensed history of the title to the land. It states in addition all liens, charges, or liabilities to which the land may be subject that may be material in the purchase of the land.

- The title opinion is a written certificate describing who owns the real estate, the quality of title, and exceptions, if any, to clear title for the transaction. It is the opinion of an attorney upon review of the chain of title that determines whether the title is marketable.

- Title insurance insures against many matters not discoverable by a search and examination of the record title.

- An endorsement provides additional insurance under the policy for risks that would otherwise not be covered under the policy.

- A closing is the completion or settlement of a real estate transaction. The closing of title is also called a settlement.

- Closing procedures vary between states and localities. Generally, closings occur by one of two methods throughout the United States. The first method is used primarily in the Eastern, Southeastern, and Midwestern portions of the United States. It is known as the settlement process or "table closing." The second method, used primarily in the Western United States, uses an escrow for closing.

- In the table closing, the parties and other interested individuals meet in person on an agreed date and time. At the meeting, the parties will review the closing documents, sign the documents, pay and receive consideration for the property (usually, money), and receive title to the real estate.

- In an escrow, both the buyer and the seller deliver documents to an escrow agent, who holds the documents in trust until all parties meet the closing conditions. The parties do not meet to sign documents or exchange consideration.

- The Real Estate Settlement Procedures Act (RESPA) is a federal act administered by the federal Consumer Financial Protection Bureau. The act ensures that consumers are provided with information about the cost of their mortgages and closings.

- The CFPB requires the consumer to receive the closing disclosure at least three business days prior to consummation.

- RESPA prohibits a person from giving or accepting kickbacks or unearned fees.

Chapter Problems and Assignments

1. What are the common types of deeds?

2. What are the different ways in which a person may have notice of a prior sale?

3. Assume the following series of events has taken place:

   Day 1: O (Grantor) conveys Blackacre to A (a BFP)

   Day 2: O (Grantor) conveys Blackacre to B

   Day 3: O (Grantor) conveys Blackacre to C (a BFP)

   Day 4: A records

   Day 5: B records

   Under a race statute, who owns Blackacre?
   Under a notice statute, who owns Blackacre?
   Under a race-notice statute, who owns Blackacre?

4. Tana conveys her property to Declan on January 5. She offers to sell the same property to Zaiden on January 10. The next day Zaiden is at the grocery store when he overhears a conversation nearby, "Did you hear Tana sold her house to Declan last week?" Zaiden quickly leaves and heads to Tana's to accept the offer and pay in cash; he then goes straight to the recorder's office and records his conveyance. Declan finally makes it to the recorder's office a week later and records his conveyance. If this occurs in a jurisdiction where a race-notice statute controls, who has title to the property?

5. The Meadows purchased property in Texas. The land the Meadows purchased stretched over two adjacent counties. When they purchased the property, the property was subject to an oil and gas drilling lease. The lease was recorded in only one of the two counties in which the property was located. The Meadows only checked one of the county records, which did not show the oil and gas drilling lease. Do the Meadows have constructive notice of the oil and gas drilling lease?

6. Aguilar was sued by a neighbor alleging that Aguilar's improvements trespassed onto the neighbor's property. Aguilar demanded that the title insurer defend the case, but the title insurer refused. The title insurance policy contained an exclusion precluding coverage for defects known to the insured on the date of policy and not shown by the public records. Aguilar knew of the boundary question with his neighbor seven years before the policy had been issued, while the dispute was not shown in any public records. Aguilar argued that the title insurance company exclusion did not apply. Does the title insurer have a duty to defend Aguilar?

7. Zachary purchased a warehouse. He was not provided a closing disclosure and believes he was entitled to one. Is Zachary entitled to a closing disclosure under the TILA-RESPA Integrated Disclosure (TRID) rule?

8. Amanda works for a title company. The title company has been around for 25 years and has a good relationship with many real estate agents. The title company has decided that, as a way of thanking the real estate agents who have referred business to the title company, it will hold a monthly dinner and reception for the real estate agents. Will the monthly dinner and reception violate RESPA?

9. You are assisting in a residential real estate transaction with an expected closing of July 10 (a Wednesday). On July 8, the lender sends a closing disclosure that matches the Loan Estimate. Will the closing still occur on July 10? If not, when will closing occur?

10. Research the minimum requirements that must be met for a deed to have legal significance in your state. If applicable, explain how those requirements differ from those listed in the chapter.

11. Research your state's recording statute. What type of recording act does your state follow?

12. Following your research into this law, describe what your state requires for acknowledgement of a deed.

End Notes

1. *Biro v. Maz*, 132 Conn. App. 272 (2011).
2. From the authors' case files.
3. Only Delaware, Louisiana, and North Carolina have race statutes.
4. Colorado, Georgia, Hawaii, Massachusetts, Minnesota, New York, North Carolina, Ohio, and Washington currently provide for the Torrens system.
5. New York State Tax 1402-a; §575.1. *New York State Real Estate Transfer Tax Regulations.*
6. P.L. 93-533, 88 Stat. 1724.

Chapter 11
Defaults, Workouts, and Foreclosures

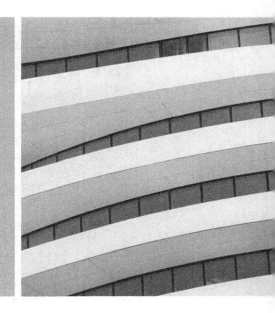

Be not one of those who give their hand in pledge, of those who become surety for debts; for if you have not the means to pay, your bed will be taken from under you.
—Proverbs 22:26–27

Learning Objectives

1. Discuss what events can cause a loan default.
2. Understand the lender's options in the event of a default.
3. Explain what occurs in a loan workout.
4. Recognize the most common forms of loan workouts.
5. Describe the methods of foreclosure.
6. State the rights of junior lienors following foreclosure.

Chapter Outline

Opening
scenario

Jasleen and Justin purchased a home and financed it with a $350,000 mortgage. Subsequently, Jasleen's substantial medical expenses exhausted their savings. The family is unable to pay the monthly mortgage payments. They wish to reside on the property, but they need some time to get their finances in order. They need any help the mortgage lender can provide. What suggestions can you make to them?

Introduction

Unfortunately, not everyone is able to abide by the terms of a loan. This chapter discusses what happens once default has occurred on a loan secured by real property. Preforeclosure workouts and related strategies are explained, as well as the different types and processes of foreclosure and what happens once a foreclosure has occurred.

When Things Go Wrong

If the borrower (that is, the mortgagor) defaults under the terms of the borrower's loan, the lender (the mortgagee) can pursue a variety of options. These options are provided in terms of the mortgage (or deed of trust) and state law. The preforeclosure remedies of a lender are different for residential and commercial loans. Both the remedy pursued and the harm that the borrower may suffer depend on the degree of seriousness of the default. Minor defaults will not trigger legal action, but they will obligate the borrower to the lender in some other manner.

> *Example:* If the borrower fails to maintain required insurance coverage on the property, the residential or commercial lender may secure insurance to protect its interest with regard to the secured property, after giving notice to the borrower. The lender will bill the borrower for the cost of the insurance. This is considered a minor breach. However, failure to pay the mortgage payments is treated as a material breach of the note and mortgage and will likely trigger legal action against the borrower, including the foreclosure of the mortgage.

Default

In addition to making timely payments to the mortgagee or beneficiary, a borrower also has other duties imposed by a typical mortgage or deed of trust.

Example: The borrower will be required to maintain certain types of insurance on the property, timely pay the real property taxes and assessments on the property, keep the title to the property free of adverse claims (such as tax and judgment liens), and pay the indebtedness in full upon certain conditions (such as the sale or transfer of the property).

Lenders usually consider delinquent payments overdue for 90 days or more to be serious breaches of the loan. A **default** occurs when the borrower fails to observe these duties and promises. If a default occurs, most mortgages and deeds of trust contain an acceleration clause requiring the borrower to pay all the unpaid balance due under the promissory note. Even after the default occurs, the loan documents (the note and mortgage or deed of trust) will give the borrower the right to be notified of and have the opportunity to cure the default.

> **Default**
> A material breach in the borrower's promise to the lender.

Choosing the Remedy for Loans in Default

A **secured creditor** has several alternatives to pursue against a borrower who has defaulted on the terms of the loan. The lender has four basic collection strategies:

> **Secured creditor**
> A creditor whose loan has collateral (for example, real property) used to secure the repayment of the debt in the event of a default.

■ Collection methods

 Example: The borrower and lender may work out and compromise their respective positions. The lender may also sue for damages for the amount due under the promissory note and not foreclose on the property. This would be beneficial if the borrower has substantial assets that can satisfy a judgment.

■ Judicial foreclosure
■ Non-judicial foreclosure (trustee's sale under a deed of trust)
■ Lender takes over the operations of the property (receivership)

Workouts

A **workout** is a nonforeclosure response to the default. The term "workout" describes a situation in which the borrower restructures its loan with the lender. In a workout, the parties renegotiate the terms and conditions of the loan as an alternative to the lender filing for foreclosure, the borrower filing for bankruptcy, or the parties engaging in litigation. In practice, many loan workouts are negotiated in the context of the borrower's desperate financial condition, often when the borrower is considering filing bankruptcy.

> **Workout**
> An agreement to restructure a loan.

First Steps for Workouts

One of the first steps in the workout process is for the lender and borrower to gather all the documents related to the original loan transaction. For residential loan transactions, the following documents should be obtained:

■ The promissory note

- The mortgage or deed of trust
- Any modifications or amendments to the note and deed of trust, including partial releases of property securing the repayment
- All notices, real estate title documents, and correspondence

Commercial loans require more documentation than residential transactions. While the list below is not complete, to consider a loan modification, many lenders require full and complete copies of the following documents:

- All subordination agreements. A subordination agreement is an agreement in which a lien holder agrees to the priority of its claim to title.
- All personal guaranties made by the borrower.
- Current income and expense statements for income-producing properties. This information would include a rent roll and accounting of tenant security deposits.
- The lender's title abstract with opinion or insurance policy and any subsequent title guaranties, endorsements, or reports.
- All communications relating to the loan, including those indicating whether the lender and borrower agree on the outstanding loan balance.
- Appraisal, environmental, engineering, zoning, or other third-party reports obtained by the lender.
- Insurance policies required by the loan documents.

Review of Loan Documents

Workouts involve the review of every document related to the loan. If a violation of the Truth in Lending Act (TILA)[1] has occurred, the borrower may be eligible for a loan rescission, which may include crediting back to the borrower all interest collected by the lender on the loan, loan origination fees, broker fees, lender fees, statutory penalties, and attorney fees. As an alternative, when a borrow makes a TILA claim, lenders are often willing to compromise with a loan modification that meets the needs of the borrower.

Common Law Remedies

The workout investigation will also determine whether the borrower has any legal remedies. The following causes of action are the most relevant legal remedies available in residential loan claims.

1. *Fraud.* A fraud claim may exist if the loan broker or lender failed to disclose any material facts relating to the terms of the loan. A fraud claim may also arise if the lender or loan broker made any representations or promises to the borrower that contradicted the terms of the loan documents.
2. *Negligence or duress.* When a lender or its representative makes errors that a reasonably diligent mortgage professional would not have made, a negligence claim for damages might be made.
3. *Breach of contract.* The loan documents are a contract. The loan broker who usually prepares the documents must ensure consistency between the loan

documents and required disclosures, such as in the way the interest is calculated and the penalties the lender assesses. The lender may have breached the contract if it failed to comply with the contract after the loan closed.

4. *Fraud or negligence claims relating to loan assignments and loan servicing.* Loan servicers may have falsified documents by backdating them or had persons without proper authority execute agreements to authorize acts on behalf of mortgage investors. These acts may permit the assignment to be set aside by the borrower.

5. *Bad faith in negotiating loan modification.* Sometimes a borrower may contact a loan servicer or other lending representative about a loan modification and be told that a modification is possible only if the borrower defaults. If the borrower defaults, but would otherwise have continued making payments while attempting a modification, this advice may be the basis for a lawsuit against the lender for bad faith, fraud, or other statutory claims, such as one alleging an unfair business practice.

Types of Preforeclosure Workout Plans

The terms of an existing loan agreement can be modified in many ways that will satisfy both the lender and the borrower. The most common forms of a workout include the following:

1. Modification of the terms of the loan
2. Loan reinstatement (the borrower cures the default)
3. Voluntary conveyance to the lender (deed-in-lieu of foreclosure)
4. Sale to third party (such as a short sale whereby the lender accepts less than what is owed in full satisfaction of the debt)
5. Lender takes over the property

Modification of the Terms of the Loan

Before a lender will agree to negotiate the terms of the loan with a borrower, the lender and the borrower will execute a **pre-workout agreement**. This agreement protects the right the lender has obtained due to the borrower's default. For example, the lender would want to protect its right to foreclose on the collateral if the negotiations break down. Statements made by the lender during the negotiations will be privileged and cannot be used in other legal proceedings; otherwise, the lender is exposed to the risk that the borrower will use them to argue that the lender has waived rights relating to the default.

To modify the terms of the loan, a lender may temporarily reduce or even suspend payments, extend the maturity date, or eliminate accrued interest on the loan. Lenders may be reluctant to reset the terms of a mortgage because it can create serious consequences for them.

Pre-workout agreement
A written agreement between the lender and borrower to permit negotiation of the loan terms while preserving the rights and remedies of each party.

Example: If the lender, through a loan modification, creates a new security interest on the secured real property, the lender may jeopardize its priority among the secured claims recorded on the property. The lender may move from a first-priority position to a second- (or lower-) priority position.

Loan Reinstatement (the Borrower Cures the Default)

One workout method (not available to borrowers who lack access to adequate funds) is to cure the default. Borrowers who are delinquent on mortgage payments can cure the default by paying the lender all delinquent payments, along with any interest and penalties that have accrued. In lieu of foreclosing because of the default, the lender may reinstate the loan.

Voluntary Conveyance to the Lender (Deed-in-Lieu of Foreclosure)

Deed-in-lieu of foreclosure
A deed given by the borrower transferring title to the lender to satisfy a loan default.

The lender may accept a deed-in-lieu of foreclosure, also known as a "deed-in-lieu." A **deed-in-lieu of foreclosure** is a borrower's transfer of title to the lender to satisfy a loan default. The deed-in-lieu avoids foreclosure proceedings initiated by the lender to whom the title was transferred. The lender must accept the deed for it to be effective. The borrower-debtor cannot force the lender to accept the deed. Usually the parties cancel both the promissory note and the mortgage or deed of trust once title has been transferred in a deed-in-lieu of foreclosure. This approach is faster than foreclosure, less costly, and takes less of an emotional toll on the borrower.

While a deed-in-lieu transaction may appeal to both the lender and the creditor, it is not without its risks. Title insurers may charge the lender more for obtaining title through deed-in-lieu conveyances than if title was acquired through a foreclosure sale, because foreclosure sales eliminate all junior lien holders (such as mortgages), while deeds-in-lieu do not. A deed-in-lieu passes title subject to all existing liens. A lender must search the title records to ensure that no junior liens exist that might be promoted to a new and senior position if the transaction is completed. A foreclosure of the mortgage or trust deed may give the lender better title than accepting a deed in this situation.

The documents relating to the deed-in-lieu of foreclosure should require and state that the mortgagor sought the advice of legal counsel or had the reasonable opportunity to consult with counsel prior to delivering the deed and preparing and executing the documents. These recitals will help reduce post-transaction borrower claims of duress, misrepresentation, coercion, or undue influence.

Whenever the terms of the loan are modified, the income tax results to both the lender and the borrower must be considered. Tax law may recognize income to the borrower resulting from the cancellation of indebtedness. (Individuals may be relieved of the duty to recognize income for tax purposes, but business entities may not.) Additionally, a lender faces certain risks in accepting a deed-in-lieu. A bankruptcy court may regard the deed as an act of bad faith, fraudulent conveyance, or a preference.

Sale to Third Party

Unlike a deed-in-lieu, a short sale is designed so that the lender does not take title to the property. Borrowers use the **short sale** to avoid foreclosure by selling their mortgaged property, with the lender's consent, for a price less than the amount owing on the loan. In a short sale, the lender releases its security interest in the property. As with a deed-in-lieu, the lender is incentivized to cooperate to avoid the costs, delays, and uncertainties regarding the market value of foreclosure proceedings. Many lenders prefer to use short sales when dealing with delinquent residential loans.

Short sale
A sale that occurs when a lender allows a property to be sold for less than the current amount owed to the lender under the note and secured by a mortgage or deed of trust.

In a short sale, a commission is paid to both the selling (listing) and procuring (cooperating) sales agents out of the sale's proceeds. Many lenders require that the agents reduce their commissions to below-average market commission rates for short-sale properties. Before a buyer's offer is accepted, the seller's broker must disclose the following to the buyer: the sale is a short sale, the amount owing on the loan secured by the loan agreement, and the buyer's need to obtain lender and lien holder approval of the transaction.

Lender Takes Over the Property

Selling the property may not result in the highest return to the lender, especially when property values are depressed. A **receivership** offers the lender more flexibility and advantages than a foreclosure proceeding. It is most often used in commercial loan settings. It may not be economical for a lender to foreclose when the proceeds from the sale of the subject property will not pay the debt owed the lender. A **receiver** is a person who, for a fee, takes possession of mortgaged property at the lender's request. The receiver acts as the lender's agent to protect the lender's interests in the real property.

Receivership
A legal proceeding whereby a third party is assigned to preserve or manage assets.

Receiver
A person appointed by the court or the parties to preserve or manage assets in a receivership.

Appointing a receiver requires court action. To grant a receivership, many courts require that a material default exist, as well as a demonstrated need for the receivership. A showing of good cause is usually required, such as a material default or that the lender is no longer fully secured by the value of the property. The primary functions of the receiver are to maintain the property, pay the taxes and insurance, and make payments on any senior liens while foreclosure is pending.

The receiver may also be appointed to collect rents and manage the property. The scope of managing the property involves activities that are greater than maintaining it. For example, managing the property often requires the receiver to advertise and negotiate leases with prospective tenants, while maintaining the property entails collecting rents from those leases.

A receiver may be appointed during a foreclosure. This is often the case in judicial foreclosures involving commercial properties, such as office buildings and shopping centers. The lender seeks the court appointment of a receiver to preserve and manage the property. Appointment of a receiver is commonly stated in the terms of the loan documents. In addition to the loan document provisions, state law will govern the appointment of receivers.

■ ■ ■ Servicemembers Civil Relief Act

Servicemembers Civil Relief Act (SCRA)
Federal statute that suspends temporarily judicial and administrative proceedings and transactions against servicemembers during their military service

The **Servicemembers Civil Relief Act** (SCRA) offers protection for consumer loans that were obtained prior to entering into military service so that the interest rates are reduced during the period of military service and one year thereafter. Mortgage lenders must obtain a court order before they can foreclose on a home during any period of military service and for nine months thereafter. Portions of the act also provide an extension of rights and protections to those serving in Reserve units who are ordered to report for military service.

Foreclosure

Foreclosure
A procedure following a default, in which property serving as security for the loan is sold with proceeds applied to retire the debt.

Foreclosure is the legal process of terminating the borrower's claims of ownership in the real property. If lenders do not wish to work out the debt with the borrower through one of the methods discussed above, they may foreclose on the property after default occurs. Only a lender whose loan is in default can foreclose. Foreclosures eliminate all junior-priority liens, enabling the lender to sell the property free and clear of liens to recover the outstanding indebtedness owed to it. While a junior lien holder may have its secured interest terminated, the junior lender still has the right to collect on the unpaid balance due it under the borrower's promissory note.

While a junior-priority lender may wish to join a foreclosure proceeding to avoid having its debt eliminated, it cannot do so unless its debt is in default as well. Buyers who purchase property at a foreclosure sale take title to the property free of any liens, except for those that are not dischargeable (such as certain tax liens). They also take the property in "as is" condition. An exception exists where the *borrower* purchases the property in the foreclosure sale. If the borrower buys the property at the sale, unpaid junior liens are revived.

The lender cannot file a lawsuit to collect money on the promissory note and at the same time seek to foreclose on the mortgage. The lender must elect which action to pursue. If the lender elects to foreclose, two methods of foreclosure are available: (1) judicial foreclosure and (2) foreclosure by power of sales (trustee sale). A few states also use a process known as strict foreclosure.

A pending proposal by the Uniform Law Commission will affect residential foreclosures. This is model legislation that has been proposed for congressional or administrative regulatory action. As it is currently termed, The Home Foreclosure Procedures Act would apply only to residential mortgages and would operate as an overlay to, rather than a replacement of, existing state legislation governing trustee sales. In addition to this proposal, many states have passed laws limiting a lender's right to foreclose residential mortgages.

The Process of Foreclosure ▪ ▪ ▪

On completion of the foreclosure process, the following will have occurred:

1. The debtor's rights in the property are terminated (that is, foreclosed).
2. The property is sold to the highest bidder at a public auction.
3. The buyer at the sale owns the property free and clear of the claims of the former debtor, the foreclosing creditor, and those whose interests are junior (that is, subordinate) in priority to that of the foreclosing creditor.

The creditor receives as much of the sales proceeds as are needed to satisfy the debt, and any surplus passes to those holding other foreclosed interests in their order of priority.

Judicial Foreclosure

Judicial foreclosure is available in all states and is the exclusive method of foreclosure in about two dozen states. Several steps must be followed to judicially foreclose on a property.

File and Serve Complaint

Judicial foreclosure begins with the filing and serving of a complaint against all persons who have an interest in the real property. A title search will reveal the persons who have such an interest. During a judicial foreclosure in some states, the court appoints appraisal agents. These agents fix a minimum value for the property that must be reached in the bidding before the court will confirm the sale.

> *Example:* Persons having an interest in the real property include the present owners, those having possession of the premises, and any lien holders. These persons would include spouses of borrowers.

A **notice of pending action,** also known as a *lis pendens,* is recorded on the title to the property at the time of filing the summons and complaint for foreclosure.

Mortgage Electronic Registration Systems (MERS)

The **Mortgage Electronic Registration Systems** (MERS) is a private land-title registration system created by mortgage banking companies to expedite the transfer and securitization of mortgage loans. Securitization starts when a mortgage originator sells a

Notice of pending action (aka *lis pendens*)
A written notice that a lawsuit has been filed concerning real estate, involving either the title to the property or a claimed ownership interest in it. The notice is usually recorded in the land records of the county in which the property is located.

mortgage and its note to a buyer. The buyers are often a subsidiary of an investment bank. The bank bundles multiple mortgages purchased into a trust and sells income rights to other investors. A pooling and servicing agreement creates two entities that maintain the trust: a trustee, who manages the loan assets, and a servicer, who communicates with and collects monthly payments from the mortgagors.

MERS does not "own" the mortgage and is not a necessary party to a foreclosure proceeding because it is not the lender. MERS does not have a right to the payments from the borrower, nor does it act as the loan servicer. Instead, MERS acts as an agent of the lender, thus eliminating the need to prepare and record assignments when trading residential and commercial mortgage loans. The mission of MERS is to register every mortgage loan in the United States on its system; it is intended to eliminate the need for new recordings when mortgages are transferred. In theory, a person requesting information regarding the ownership of a mortgage need only look to the MERS system and not to the local recording office. Nearly two-thirds of all newly originated residential loans in the United States name MERS as the nominal mortgagee.

Trial and Order of Foreclosure Sale

If any of the parties with an interest in the real property oppose the lender's complaint, a trial will be held to determine the lender's right to foreclose. If the court finds that the lender may foreclose on the property, it will then order a foreclosure sale. When this happens, the local sheriff will publish a notice of the foreclosure for a statutory period. The notice will identify the property and the date, time, and place of the sheriff's sale. In addition, a copy of the judgment will be served upon the lender, and the notice of sale will be posted for a period of time. At the sale, the sheriff will sell the property only to cash bidders (except for the lender, which can bid the amount of the total debt owed to it). The laws of some states require that the sale price be at least one-half of the property's appraised value.

Equity Redemption Rights

Equity of redemption
The right of a borrower to redeem (retain) the mortgaged property before a foreclosure sale occurs.

A borrower may be able to stop the foreclosure sale by satisfying the debt. This process is commonly known as **equity of redemption**. It is the mortgagor's right to pay the indebtedness *before* the foreclosure sale occurs and thereby redeem the property. This right to reinstate the mortgage or deed of trust is guaranteed under most state laws.

Under equity of redemption, the borrower or trustor pays the amount in default at the time the foreclosure proceedings commence, plus all foreclosure costs and the trustee or attorney fees. When payment is made, the loan is considered current from the lender's perspective and is then reinstated. When a mortgage or deed of trust is reinstated, the mortgage foreclosure proceedings are canceled. The lender must cooperate with the borrower or trustor in providing the current payoff amount and all other amounts due to reinstate the mortgage or deed of trust. Failure to cooperate with the borrower will result in the foreclosure sale's postponement.

Foreclosure Sale and Statutory Redemption Rights

Following the foreclosure sale, the sheriff reports the result to the court, which can then confirm the sale. Once the court has confirmed the sale, some states give the borrower an additional right to redeem the property, called a **statutory redemption period**. During this time, the debtor has a right to repurchase the property *after* the foreclosure sale by paying the amount of money for which the property was sold, interest from the sale date at the mortgage's interest rate, and other costs allowed by statute. These other costs can include taxes and assessments paid by the purchaser since the sale date. After the expiration period for redemption, the borrower's rights in the property are terminated.

The redemption period varies by state and is commonly between three months and one year. Many states extend the redemption period if the sale proceeds do not cover the debt owed to the lender.

> *Example:* A state may provide for a three-month redemption period if the sale proceeds cover the lender's debts but provide for a one-year redemption period if the sale proceeds do not cover the debt owed to the lender.

Setting Aside Foreclosures

All states have adopted the rule that foreclosure sale prices below the debt owed do not invalidate a sale. However, in the case of fraud or some material irregularity in the sale, the courts may exercise their discretion to set aside the sale. Courts have developed two standards for setting sales aside: (1) the **shock the conscience standard**, which infers some fraud that should cause the sale to be set aside, and (2) the **gross inadequacy standard**, which is the subject of the following case.

Statutory redemption period
The right of a borrower to redeem (retain) the mortgaged property after a foreclosure sale occurs within a time period established by state law.

Shock the conscience standard
As used in real estate, a manifestly and grossly unjust sales price.

Gross inadequacy standard
Standard that infers the inadequacy of price should be gross and the result of any mistake, accident, surprise, fraud, misconduct, or irregularity for the sale to be set aside.

CASE 11.1

GROSS INADEQUACY OF A SALE PRICE IS GROUNDS FOR SETTING ASIDE A JUDICIAL SALE

LONG BEACH MORTGAGE v. BEBBLE

985 So. 2d 611 (2008)

Florida District Court of Appeal

Long Beach Mortgage Corporation ("Long Beach") foreclosed on a mortgage it held on Florida real property. Long Beach secured a judicial foreclosure in the amount of $716,139.60 plus interest and set a foreclosure sale date. At the foreclosure sale, no one placed a bid on behalf of Long Beach, and the property was sold to Aqua-Terra, Inc. ("Aqua-Terra") on its bid of $1,000. The property was appraised at $500,000. Three days after the sale, Long Beach moved to set aside the sale to Aqua-Terra on the grounds of its own inadvertence, mistake, or accident, as well as that of its attorneys, in failing to attend the sale. At a hearing on the motion, Long Beach presented a scenario of miscommunications and mishaps. The trial judge found that the problem at the sale was not the fault of the purchaser. The trial judge exercised his discretion and denied the motion to vacate. Long Beach appealed.

Language of the Court. *The general rule is that mere inadequacy of price is not a ground for setting aside a judicial sale. But where the inadequacy is gross and is shown to result from any mistake, accident, surprise, fraud, misconduct, or irregularity upon the part of either the purchaser or any other person connected with the sale, with resulting injustice to the complaining party, equity will act to prevent the wrong result.*

This rule is consistent with the view that a judge considering whether to set aside a foreclosure sale has a large discretion that will only be interfered with by the appellate court in a clear case of injustice. The policy behind this standard of review is to ensure a competitive market in the foreclosure sale process. Bidders and buyers at such sales usually bid and buy to make a profit.

To establish a precedent that encourages the easy setting aside of foreclosure sales would be to destroy the incentive that prompts bidding at a sale and thereby work a hardship on both debtors and creditors. However, Long Beach was the innocent victim of the mistakes of its attorneys and agents. The property was sold for $1,000, .02% of its value. Long Beach acted promptly to set aside the sale by filing its motion three days later. The

purpose of the law in this area is to promote the viability of the foreclosure-sale process and to encourage good-faith offers for foreclosed properties, not to protect outrageous windfalls to buyers who make de minimis *bids. Finally, judicial economy favors resolving a case so that a fair sale price is realized in this proceeding, instead of inviting a second lawsuit to allocate the losses between Long Beach and its attorneys.*

Decision. The trial court's decision is reversed and the foreclosure sale is set aside.

FOCUS ON ETHICS

What should the lender have done to cause a higher bid to be received at the time of the sale?

Certificate of sale
Document given to purchaser at a foreclosure sale certifying that, after the redemption period passed, holder received title to foreclosed property.

Sheriff's deed
Deed without warranties issued to purchaser following foreclosure or tax sale.

At the foreclosure sale, the purchaser receives only a **certificate of sale**, not a deed. If the property is not redeemed during the redemption period, then the sheriff issues a deed (sheriff's deed) to the purchaser. A **sheriff's deed** is made without any representation or warranties concerning the quality of the title the purchaser receives. Any title defects that existed prior to the foreclosure sale will pass to the purchaser.

Example: If a creditor who has obtained a lien attaching to the real property that was foreclosed on was not properly named or served in the foreclosure proceedings, the creditor's interest in the real property may remain. The sheriff's deed would not warrant against this encumbrance on title.

Despite the cost and time involved, a judicial foreclosure may be the preferred method of foreclosing on real property in some situations. For example, the mortgage may misidentify the real property, and the creditor may need the court to reform the legal description to permit foreclosure. In other situations, a dispute may occur among lien claimants as to the priority of the mortgage that is being foreclosed, and a court may need to determine the order of priority. Additionally, while a judicial foreclosure allows the lender to receive a deficiency judgment (discussed later in this chapter), some jurisdictions do not allow the lender to receive a deficiency judgment under non-judicial foreclosure methods.

Foreclosure by Power of Sale (Trustee Sale)

State law must be consulted with respect to certain residential loans. Several states allow a lender or a trustee, under a deed of trust (discussed in chapter 9), to exercise a non-judicial foreclosure remedy if the right is stated in the mortgage or deed of trust. This non-judicial foreclosure remedy is known as **foreclosure by power of sale**. It is also known as a trustee sale or a foreclosure by advertisement. The foreclosure occurs without court involvement if the lender properly and timely gives notice of the foreclosure for the statutory periods of time.

Notice of Default

The first step in a foreclosure by power of sale is for the lender or trustee to record a notice of default. A company specializing in the foreclosure process usually handles the foreclosure.

Serve Foreclosure Notices

In some states, a power of attorney will be executed by the mortgage holder prior to the notice of sale being served. A foreclosure company or a law firm representing the lender will then handle the foreclosure. If required by state law, foreclosure prevention and counseling notices will be served upon the borrower.

Set Sale Date

The next step in the process of foreclosure by power of sale is for the trustee to set the date of sale. The notice must be published as required by law. In most cases, it must be published for several weeks in a newspaper of general circulation. The notice of default is also sent to those who are required by law to receive a copy. These recipients include lien holders junior to the foreclosing lien. Often, state laws require that the notice of sale also be physically posted on the property. In addition, the notice is recorded on the title to the property. Notice of sale will be given to the Internal Revenue Service for federal tax liens or to the state official responsible for state tax liens.

Trustee Sale

The final step in foreclosure by power of sale is the trustee's sale. State laws vary greatly with regard to the requirements of the public sale. Generally, the property is sold at public auction to the highest bidder. Each person who bids must bid with cash or an equivalent to cash. Often, state laws will allow the foreclosing lender to bid the amount of its loan (called a **credit bid**). The full amount due is almost always the amount bid. Junior lien holders cannot credit bid the amount due them because the sale is occurring because of what is owed to the senior lien holders.

Redemption Rights

Most states provide a right of redemption for a trustee sale; however, the right of redemption often extends only up to several days before the sale date. Usually no postsale rights of redemption exist in a trustee sale.

Foreclosure by power of sale
A foreclosure that occurs without court involvement if the lender properly and timely gives notice of the foreclosure for the statutory periods of time.

Credit bid
Right of secured creditor to bid the amount owed to the creditor at the time of the foreclosure sale.

Trustee Sale Foreclosure Process

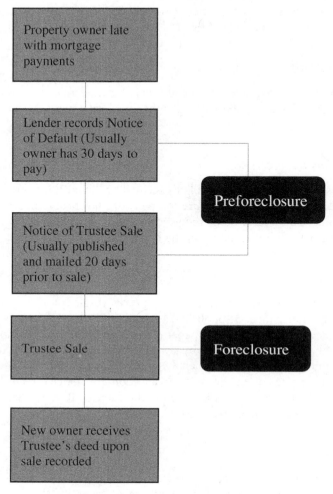

FIGURE 11.1. Trustee Sale Foreclosure Process

Benefits of Trustee Sales

Lenders who have the right to use a trustee sale under a deed of trust prefer to use the deed of trust rather than the mortgage instrument. The procedure for trustee sales is more straightforward than that of judicial foreclosure — less time is required to fore-close, and court delays and attorney fees are avoided.

Detriments of Trustee Sales

If lenders use a trustee sale instead of judicial foreclosure, many states do not allow them to obtain a deficiency judgment. Additionally, the non-judicial sale must be held in a commercially reasonable manner to maximize the sale price. If lenders do not do so, they may be liable to the borrower for the lost equity not realized from the sale. State laws require that the lender not act in a manner that harms the borrower.

Strict Foreclosure

In a few states, strict foreclosure can be used.[2] With **strict foreclosure**, a court orders the borrower to pay the debt owed by a certain date. If the borrower is unable to pay the debt by that date, the borrower loses the right to equitable redemption of the property; the lender automatically takes title of the property and does not need to sell the property following the borrower's default. Where allowed, strict foreclosure is often used when a borrower is insolvent (unable to pay debts), has little or no equity in the property, or has abandoned the property.

Strict foreclosure
A foreclosure where, if the borrower does not pay within the court-designated time, the title to the property vests in the lender without any sale of the property.

Disbursement of Sale Proceeds

Sale proceeds are disbursed by absolute priority. With the **absolute priority rule**, the first-priority debts (those that have the highest seniority) are paid in full before any second-tier debts (junior liens) are paid. The time of recording determines the priority of mortgages, liens, and other encumbrances. The sale proceeds are disbursed in the following order:

Absolute priority rule
Rule stipulating the order of payment wherein the first-priority debts are paid in full before any second-tier debts are paid.

1. Property tax liens
2. Expenses and costs of the foreclosure (court costs, publication, and recording costs)
3. Payment to the first-priority debt (senior lien), including accrued interest and principal
4. Payment to the second-priority debt (junior lien) and any additional junior liens, in order of priority
5. Balance of any surplus sale proceeds (very unlikely) goes to the borrower (mortgagor or trustor)

Deficiency Judgment

If the proceeds of the resulting sale exceed the amount of the debt, the surplus is given to the mortgagor. If the proceeds are insufficient, in some states the lender may proceed against the borrower in an action to collect the remaining balance, called a deficiency judgment. A **deficiency judgment** is a money judgment against a borrower whose foreclosed property was sold but yielded insufficient sale proceeds to pay the loan in full. Only the party foreclosing is entitled, if available, to a deficiency judgment. Deficiency judgments are available for judicial foreclosures but not for non-judicial foreclosures. Thus, the method of foreclosure used makes a big difference to both the lender and the borrower.

Deficiency judgment
A money judgment obtained by the creditor against the borrower when the foreclosure sale does not satisfy the entire debt.

Purchase Money Mortgages

Whether a deficiency judgment is available to a lender depends upon state law. In some states, antideficiency laws exist that provide that a deficiency judgment is not allowed

Purchase money mortgage
A loan by a lender or seller to finance all or a portion of the purchase price of a property.

for purchase money mortgages. Recall from our discussion in chapter 9 that a **purchase money mortgage** is one in which the borrower's funds are used to finance the purchase of a one- to four-unit residential property. These laws were intended to protect homeowners and buyers who purchased overvalued properties secured by a mortgage or deed of trust.

A refinance is not a purchase money mortgage, and in states allowing deficiency judgment following foreclosure, they expose the borrower to that risk. In addition, Federal Housing Administration (FHA) and Veterans Administration (VA) loans are subject to deficiency judgments, even if they are considered purchase money mortgages. In those states permitting a deficiency judgment following a foreclosure sale, only the original borrower is liable, not the purchaser at the foreclosure sale.

Nonrecourse obligations
A secured obligation or debt that is secured by a pledge of collateral, typically real property, but for which the borrower is not personally liable. Following the sale of the collateral due to default, the lender's payment is limited to the proceeds of the sale of collateral.

Purchase money mortgages are considered **nonrecourse obligations**. Nonrecourse means the borrower is not liable to the lender for any deficiency following a foreclosure sale. The lender's recourse is limited to the amount realized from the sale of the real property. Lenders operating in nonrecourse states are exposed to more risk and may require stricter loan underwriting, higher loan-to-value ratios, and higher interest rates. Many states limit the application of nonrecourse debt only to purchase money mortgages.

Example: A homeowner purchases a property for $350,000. The home was purchased with 90 percent financing and a 10 percent down payment. Within three years, the home is worth $175,000, and the borrower is unable to make the monthly payments required under the loan. The bank forecloses and seeks a deficiency judgment. In states providing for a purchase money mortgage exception, the homeowner would not be liable for a deficiency judgment.

Concept Summary

Mortgage foreclosure is costly and time consuming. A lawsuit must be filed, the property must be sold at a public auction, and a redemption period must elapse.

The difference between a mortgage and a deed of trust lies in the handling of the foreclosure process. After the buyer receives title, the trust deed transfers the title from the seller to a trustee who holds it on behalf of the lender (known as the beneficiary). Upon default and upon the instruction of the lender, the trustee sells the property and pays the lender the amount of the sales proceeds, less the costs of sale, up to the amount owed to the lender. The balance, if any, is paid to junior lienholders and then to the debtor. The sale occurs outside of court supervision and can occur more quickly and economically than a judicial foreclosure.

The seller is the lender in a land sale contract. The seller retains the deed and legal title until the last installment payment is received from the buyer. Upon default, some states permit the eviction of the debtor, forfeiture of equity, and resolution to occur more quickly than is permitted under a judicial or nonjudicial foreclosure.

Tax Sales

Borrowers have the obligation to pay their property taxes. These taxes are a prior lien with regard to a mortgage (they are a superior lien to a mortgage). Because they are a lien superior to that of the mortgagee, the mortgagee will often pay the taxes to avoid the high rates of interest and fees assessed as to them. When a tax assessor pursues a tax-sale foreclosure, the procedure is much like that involved in the foreclosure of mortgages.

At the time of the tax sale, the purchaser receives a tax certificate, which is then subject to a statutory right of redemption. If the property is not redeemed within the allotted time period, the purchaser will receive a deed. This deed is without any warranty and may have many defects as to the quality of the title. In the absence of a bidder at the time of sale, the property is deeded to the governmental authority that assessed the tax.

In the following case, the parties disputed whether adequate notice was given to the trustee of the property. The trustee argued that adequate notice was not given, and the tax sale violated due process.

CASE 11.2

SUBSTANTIAL COMPLIANCE WITH SALE NOTICE MAY SATISFY APPLICABLE RULES

FIRST BANK OF WHITING v. 524, LLC

39 N.E.3d 698 (2015)

Indiana Court of Appeals

The ownership of two parcels of land located in Indiana were transferred to First Bank of Whiting as trustee of a trust. In July of 1990, an address change for the bank was correctly entered as 2135 Westchester Boulevard, Westchester, Illinois 60154. The parcels were scheduled to be sold at a tax sale on August 27, 2012, and the foreclosure company served the pre-sale notices to the trustee at four different addresses, including 2135 Westchester Boulevard, and a receipt showed the notices were received.

In August 2012, 524, LLC purchased the two parcels of property at a tax sale. After the sale, notices of the right of redemption were sent to the same four addresses, but this time the one sent to 2135 Westchester Boulevard and another location were not delivered. Following the expiration of the redemption period, 524, LLC sent notices for application for deed to the same four

addresses, and once again they were received and signed for at all addresses but the one for 2135 Westchester Boulevard. Following state law, 524, LLC then appealed to the court for issuance of a deed.

The First Bank of Whiting, as Trustee for the prior owner, filed an objection to 524, LLC's petition for failure to serve notices to all persons and entities. The trial judge held that all notices required by law were given and received. The trial court entered in favor of 524, LLC and directed that tax deeds should be issued to 524, LLC for both parcels. First Bank of Whiting appealed.

Language of the Court. *The Trust contends that 524, LLC did not comply with the requirements in that it did not serve notice to the property owner and to all persons and entities with a substantial interest of public record pursuant to those provisions. The*

Trust contends that the failure to receive proper notice violated its due process rights, and the issuance of tax deeds to the Parcels must be reversed.

The notices in question must be reasonably calculated, under all the circumstances, to apprise any interested parties of the pendency of the action and must afford them an opportunity to present objections.

For purposes of substantial compliance, it is of no moment that less than all four copies of the notices that were sent out during the course of these proceedings reached the intended recipient. The presale notices mailed to the Trustee at 2135 Westchester Blvd., Westchester, IL 60154 were received and signed for at that address. Copies of the notice of right of redemption were sent to four different addresses and two of those four were received and signed for via certified mail on behalf of the Trustee. The notice was also published in the Lowell Tribune. *Finally, copies of the notice of application for issuance of deeds were sent to four different addresses, and the representative of the Trustee received and signed for the certified mailing at three of those four addresses and also the notice was published in the* Lowell Tribune.

Under these circumstances, we conclude that the various notices substantially complied with the applicable rules and the Trust's due process rights were not violated.

Decision. The court of appeals affirmed the trial court's ruling, finding that adequate notice had been given and the sale remained valid.

FOCUS ON ETHICS

Is a rule of substantial, as opposed to absolute, compliance with foreclosure statutes fair to apply in this case?

Mortgage Guaranty Insurance

Mortgage lenders can obtain insurance against loss from foreclosure. This insurance is available through public and private mortgage insurance programs. Some of these programs were discussed in chapter 9.

Federal Housing Administration (FHA)

The Federal Housing Administration (FHA) is not the lender but rather the insurer of the loan made by an institutional lender. The FHA will pay any loss to the lender following foreclosure. The lender may also assign the loan to the FHA, with its approval. A loan-assignment program is also available from the FHA, which allows loans to be assigned to the U.S. Department of Housing and Urban Development (HUD). HUD will pay the loan, and then homeowners make payments to HUD on terms that meet their needs.

Department of Veterans Affairs

The Department of Veterans Affairs (DVA) guarantees loans for veterans who default on their mortgages. The DVA will pay up to 25 percent of the loan balance, up to certain limits.

Private Mortgage Insurance (PMI)

Private mortgage insurance (PMI) is available from private companies. As previously noted, the insurance premium is paid on a monthly basis. Homebuyers who make a down payment of less than 20 percent are usually required to pay PMI.

PMI indemnifies (compensates for a particular loss suffered) the lender, not the borrower. If the buyer defaults, and the property is sold at a foreclosure sale, the PMI will reimburse the lender for a loss up to 20 percent of the loan amount. The presence of PMI reduces the lender's exposure to loss at foreclosure.

> *Example:* Assume that Julio purchases a $200,000 home with 5 percent cash down and a $190,000 mortgage. The loan-to-value ratio of 95 percent exceeds the 80 percent required for conventional (standard) financing. Suppose the borrower defaults when the loan has been paid down to $188,000; if PMI is in place and a foreclosure sale results in a sales price of $180,000, the lender looks to the mortgage insurer for a payment of $8,000.

Key Terms and Concepts

- Default, page 305
- Secured creditor, page 305
- Workout, page 305
- Pre-workout agreement, page 307
- Deed-in-lieu of foreclosure, page 308
- Short sale, page 309
- Receivership, page 309
- Receiver, page 309
- Servicemembers Civil Relief Act (SCRA), page 310
- Foreclosure, page 310
- Judicial foreclosure, page 311
- Notice of pending action, page 311
- Mortgage Electronic Registration Systems, Inc. (MERS), page 311

- Equity of redemption, page 312
- Statutory redemption period, page 313
- Shock the conscience standard, page 313
- Gross inadequacy standard, page 313
- Certificate of sale, page 314
- Sheriff's deed, page 314
- Foreclosure by power of sale, page 315
- Credit bid, page 315
- Strict foreclosure, page 317
- Absolute priority rule, page 317
- Deficiency judgment, page 317
- Purchase money mortgage, page 318
- Nonrecourse obligations, page 318

Chapter Summary

- If the borrower defaults, the lender may allow a workout or pursue foreclosure. A default occurs when the borrower fails to observe these duties and promises.

- A secured creditor has several alternatives to pursue against a borrower who has defaulted on the terms of the loan. The lender has four basic collection strategies: (1) collection methods, (2) judicial foreclosure, (3) non-judicial foreclosure, and (4) lender takes over the property.

- A workout is a situation in which both the borrower and the lender attempt to compromise their respective positions and rights.

- A workout may involve modifying the terms of the loan, reinstating the loan, making a voluntary conveyance to the lender (that is, a deed-in-lieu of foreclosure), or selling the property to a third party. In addition, the lender may also take over a commercial property through a receivership and operate the property to minimize its losses resulting from the borrower's default.

- A borrower may also have options for common law remedies against the lender, including actions for fraud, negligence, or duress; an action for breach of contract; fraud or negligence claims relating to loan assignments and loan servicing; or a bad-faith action in negotiating loan modification.

- Foreclosure is the legal process of terminating the borrower's claims of ownership in the real property. It allows the lender to sell the real property to satisfy the mortgage debt. Judicial foreclosure begins with the filing of a lawsuit, and the actual foreclosure sale takes place under the supervision of a government official, usually the sheriff.

- The lender in a judicial foreclosure is usually required to use good faith and fair dealing in selling the property at a sale. When the inadequacy of the sale price is at issue, the lender may have to respond in damages to the mortgagor (the borrower).

- With a judicial foreclosure, most states allow a borrower to stop the foreclosure sale by paying the indebtedness before the foreclosure sale. This is satisfying the debt. This process is commonly known as equity of redemption. Once the court has confirmed the sale, some states give the borrower an additional right to redeem the property, called a statutory redemption period.

- Some states allow the mortgage lender to use a deed of trust. The deed of trust allows the lender or a third party to hold the property as a trustee. The property may be sold at a sale much more quickly and economically than is possible through a judicial foreclosure.

- Equity of redemption allows the mortgagor to stop the foreclosure by paying the entire balance before the foreclosure sale. This right must be exercised within a certain period of time to allow the mortgagor to cure the default and reinstate the mortgage.

- Following a foreclosure sale, some states allow the mortgagor the right of statutory redemption. The mortgagor is given the right to redeem the property after the sale by paying the amount for which the property was sold.

- Sale proceeds are disbursed according to the absolute priority rule. With this rule, the first-priority debts (those that have the highest seniority) are paid in full before any second-tier debts (junior liens) are paid.

- With the exception of certain tax liens, the foreclosure proceeding wipes out the equity positions of all interests that are junior to the foreclosing creditor.

- Mortgage guaranty insurance reduces the lender's risk of loss in the event of foreclosure.

Chapter Problems and Assignments

1. What legal remedies are available for the lender when the borrower defaults on the promissory note and mortgage?

2. Why should a borrower with a second mortgage be concerned about entering into a deed-in-lieu of foreclosure with a lender?

3. Barclay owns a property and has been unable to make the monthly payments. The lender has sent a notice to Barclay indicating that it will soon start foreclosure proceedings. Barclay desires to hand the property back to the lender, First Bank. Why would Barclay use this process? What advantages does avoiding foreclosure have for Barclay and for First Bank? Are there any concerns that Barclay should have about utilizing this method?

4. Andrea owns a commercial property. She has a mortgage with First Bank and has been unable to make the monthly payments. First Bank has initiated foreclosure proceedings against Andrea. The state provides Andrea with a one-year statutory redemption period from the foreclosure sale date. What rights does Andrea have during the statutory redemption period? At the foreclosure sale, what does the purchaser receive?

5. Assume you represent a homeowner who purchased a home five years ago with a $250,000 loan from First Bank. Due to a decrease in market conditions, the property has decreased in value to $200,000. The homeowner has lost his job, and First Bank seeks to foreclose on the property. The loan principal with First Bank is $230,000. If the property sells at a foreclosure sale for $200,000, how are the proceeds distributed? Is the homeowner liable for the additional $30,000 to First Bank?

6. Corey purchases a residential property through a foreclosure sale. The state provides a 60-day statutory redemption period. At the foreclosure sale, what does Corey receive? Once the 60 days have elapsed, what type of deed does Corey receive, and what warranties concerning title does he receive?

7. What is the purpose of MERS?

8. Rank the following debts from highest priority (first paid to last paid) when proceeds from a foreclosure sale are dispersed:
   a. Expenses and costs of the foreclosure process
   b. First mortgage obtained on May 30, recorded June 1
   c. Property taxes
   d. A second mortgage, obtained on May 30, recorded May 31

9. Research whether your state allows a lender to pursue a deficiency judgment against a borrower. Does your state provide for an antideficiency judgment statute?

10. Research your state's statutory redemption period. Identify what, if any, what rights the borrower has to redeem a property under a statutory redemption right.

End Notes

1. 15 USC §§1601-1667f.
2. Strict foreclosure can be used in Connecticut and Vermont. In addition, a few other states allow for strict foreclosure to handle special issues.

Part III
Owning, Operating, and Insuring Real Estate

Chapter 12
Ownership of Real Property

As long as our civilization is essentially one of property, of fences, of exclusiveness, it will be mocked by delusions. —Ralph Waldo Emerson

Learning Objectives

1. Define the characteristics of individual ownership of property.
2. Describe the requirements for a tenancy in common.
3. State the elements of a joint tenancy.
4. Discuss tenancy by the entirety.
5. Explain the requirements for community property.
6. Identify differences in holding title in business entities.

Chapter Outline

- Introduction
- Concurrent Ownership
- Case 12.1: *Reicherter v. McCauley*
- Marital Property Concurrent Ownership
- Case 12.2: *RBS Citizens v. Ouhrabka*
- Case 12.3: *Obergefell v. Hodges*
- Rights and Duties of Co-Tenants
- Case 12.4: *Anderson v. Joseph*
- Business Organization Forms of Holding Property
- Real Estate Securities Issues

Opening
scenario

Three sisters — Ashley, Brittany, and Courtney — inherited a commercial building from their parents as "joint tenants with rights of survivorship." Initially, all of the sisters were happy to own the property jointly as a family, and each promised that they would never sell it to anyone outside of the family. Ashley, who was ten years older than her two sisters, later decided to sell her interest in the building to Daniel. The transfer of Ashley's interest to Daniel met all of the conveyancing requirements. Once Brittany and Courtney learned of the sale, they became furious and wanted to know what their legal rights were against Daniel. After you read the chapter, consider what rights, if any, Daniel has in the property. Can Brittany and Courtney rescind (that is, cancel) the transaction completed with Daniel?

Introduction

Real property may be owned individually, jointly (by two or more persons), or by business entities. Concurrent or co-tenant ownership occurs when two or more persons own property together. The major forms of concurrent or co-tenant ownership are tenancy in common, joint tenancy, and tenancy by the entirety. Concurrent ownership of property involves concurrent rights and obligations between and among the co-tenants. Most states apply the concept of tenancy by the entirety in determining the marital property rights of married persons upon their death or divorce. Those states that do not follow tenancy by the entirety typically follow community property laws.

Both individuals and businesses may choose different types of ownership entities based on their tax benefits, liability protections, transferability, and other differences discussed in this chapter. Each type of entity has its advantages and disadvantages. For that reason, over time, new types of business entities can emerge with characteristics that the other business entities do not possess. In this chapter, we will review the laws that apply to the dealings by and between co-tenants; in addition, we will briefly review the legal aspects of holding title to real estate within a business entity

Concurrent Ownership

Concurrent ownership means that two or more persons own the same property at the same time. It may also be considered a form of joint ownership. The laws in which the real property is held determine which form of concurrent ownership is available.

See Figure 12.1 for a chart comparing the characteristics of concurrent ownership. There are four main forms of concurrent ownership of property:

1. Tenancy in common
2. Joint tenancy
3. Tenancy by the entirety
4. Community property

Tenancy in Common

Tenancy in common is a form of co-ownership of real property in which parties may hold equal or unequal shares in the land and have separate but undivided interests in the entire property. An undivided interest allows a tenant in common to share in the whole of the property, not just the portion of interest owned.

Creation of Interest

Under most states' common law, tenancy in common is the default manner of holding title if the intention of the parties is not clear as to what type of co-ownership interest was created. A tenancy in common status is presumed unless contrary intent is expressed. Where a tenancy in common interest is created, the parties equally share the interest in the property unless the ownership percentages are explicitly stated.

> *Example:* Patrick and Donna inherit a house from their mother. The will under which they inherited the property does not identify their respective ownership interests. A tenancy in common interest is created, with Patrick and Donna each owning a 50 percent interest.

Tenancy in common interests can be acquired at different times and can be conveyed *inter vivos* (during the life of the tenant in common), by will, or by intestate succession.

Possession

Each tenant in common is entitled to equal possession of the entire property so long as no other co-tenant objects. The interests owned by the tenants in common may be equal or unequal.

> *Example:* Kevin may own two-thirds of the property while Brian owns one-third, and they may have obtained their interests at different times. Even though Kevin owns two-thirds of the property, he must share the property fifty-fifty with Brian.

Conveyance of Interest

No survivorship rights exist between tenants in common. If one tenant in common dies, the other remaining tenants in common do not automatically inherit the interest of the deceased tenant in common.

Each tenant may sell, or convey by deed or will, her interest in the property. The grantee receives the same interest that the grantor owned, unless the grantor conveyed to the grantee less than her full interest.

Example: Patrick dies, and his will conveys his one-half tenant-in-common interest in Blackacre to Casey, Colleen, and Cameron. Casey, Colleen, and Cameron will each own a one-sixth interest in Blackacre (that is, one-third of the one-half interest that Patrick held). If Casey was the only person Patrick wished to inherit his property, Casey would inherit Patrick's entire one-half interest in Blackacre.

A tenancy in common can be divided into many other types of property interests that we have previously studied, such as a fee simple, a fee simple subject to condition subsequent, or a life estate.

Joint Tenancy

Joint tenancy is a form of concurrent ownership in which two or more persons own equal shares of property, with the right of survivorship between the joint tenants. While each joint tenant owns an equal share, each joint tenant also has an equal right to possession. The biggest advantage to holding property in this manner is that upon the death of the joint tenant, the property is automatically transferred to the surviving joint tenant(s). This automatic transfer to the other surviving joint tenants is known as the **right of survivorship**. Right of survivorship distinguishes joint tenancy from tenancy in common.

Right of survivorship Upon the death of one joint tenant, the surviving joint tenants automatically receive equal shares from the deceased joint tenant.

Because of this advantage, joint tenancies are popular between spouses. The disadvantage of titling property this way lies in the potential that your heirs will not inherit anything if you decease before the other joint tenant(s).

Creation of Interest

Most states require express language of "joint tenants" or "joint tenants with right of survivorship" when creating a joint tenancy. They demand clear expressions of intent to overcome the presumption of tenancy in common. In addition, many states require that four characteristics of unity must be present for a joint tenancy to exist. Where a unity is missing, the interest is held as a tenant in common. The four unities are as follows.

1. *Time.* The interest of each tenant (that is, title to the property) must be acquired at the same time.

    Example: Tom conveys 50 percent of his cabin to his brother John on January 1 as a joint tenant. A few hours later, Tom conveys the remaining 50 percent interest in his cabin to his sister, Megan, as a joint tenant. Because John and Megan's interests were not acquired at the same time, they do not hold title as joint tenants. Instead, they hold title as tenants in common.

2. *Title.* The joint tenants must acquire title by the same deed or will.
3. *Interest.* All joint tenants must have an equal interest in the property. Each joint tenant must have the same share of the undivided whole.

Example: "To Ashley, Tyler, and Daniel, as joint tenants with rights of survivorship" creates a joint tenancy among Ashley, Tyler, and Daniel, with each joint tenant owning one-third of the property. If they did not have equal interests, then the interest created would instead be a tenant-in-common interest.

4. *Possession.* Each tenant must have an equal right to possess the entire property. Where a joint tenant divides the property by time (such as by present and future interests discussed in chapter 5) or geography, this unity is not met.

What to Do When a Unity Is Missing

If any one of these elements is lacking, the estate is not one of joint tenancy but one of tenancy in common. Where a unity is missing, parties can meet the four unities by using a strawman transaction. A **strawman** is a third party to whom the property is transferred temporarily. The strawman then transfers the property back to the original parties, thereby creating the required unity of time and title to the transaction. As long as the other unities are present (interest and possession), a joint tenancy interest is created. Often an escrow company will be used as a strawman.

Strawman
A third party that receives temporary title transfer so that the four unity requirement of joint tenancy can be met.

In the following case, the court held that a joint tenant may unilaterally sever the joint tenancy without providing notice to the other tenant.

CASE 12.1

NOTICE TO OTHER COTENANTS IS NOT REQUIRED TO SEVER THE JOINT TENANCY

REICHERTER v. McCAULEY

283 P.3d 219 (2012)

Kansas Court of Appeals

Richard Reicherter, and his cousin, Douglas Reicherter acquired an 80-acre farm as joint tenants with a right of survivorship. Decades later, while residing in a long-term care facility, Richard executed a quitclaim deed conveying his interest in the farm to himself. This was an attempt to sever the joint tenancy and create a tenancy in common. Richard's attorney then mailed the deed to the recorder's office before Richard died. Douglas was unaware that Richard had recorded a quitclaim deed until after Richard's death.

Upon Richard's death, Barbara McCauley was appointed executrix of Richard's estate. Douglas then filed a quiet title action seeking title to the entire 80-acre farm. Douglas claimed that Richard's unilateral attempt to destroy the joint tenancy was

ineffective since he had no prior notice of Richard's intent to sever the joint tenancy. McCauley counterclaimed seeking half ownership interest of the farm and partition. The district court found in favor of McCauley, finding that the joint tenancy was severed when Richard delivered the quitclaim deed to be filed by his attorney prior to his death. Douglas appealed.

Language of the Court. *A joint tenancy may be terminated (1) by mutual agreement of the parties, (2) by course of conduct indicating tenancy in common, or (3) by operation of law upon destruction of one or more of the required unities (time, title, interest, and possession). We have no doubt that Richard intended to sever the joint tenancy because Richard demonstrated a clear intent to sever the* *joint tenancy by signing the quitclaim deed and giving it to his lawyer.*

We hold that a joint tenant can self-convey and thus destroy a joint tenancy in this case where there are just two joint tenants.

Decision. The court of appeals affirmed the trial court's decision. Richard had severed the joint tenancy, and McCauley was entitled to half ownership interest.

FOCUS ON ETHICS

As Douglas was unaware that Richard was going to sever the joint tenancy, is this outcome fair to Douglas? What if a grantor desired the property to remain in joint tenancy to keep a property within the family?

Conveyance of Interest

When a party holds property as a joint tenant, upon the death of the first joint tenant the surviving joint tenant(s) inherit the property automatically, regardless of what the deceased joint tenant's will provides.

> *Example:* Amir and Natasha share title to Blackacre as joint tenants with rights of survivorship. If, in Amir's will, his 50 percent interest in Blackacre is transferred to his daughter Alexis, upon Amir's death the interest will automatically transfer to Natasha as a joint tenant (not to Alexis). The will provision transferring Amir's 50 percent interest is ignored.

Disclaimer of Interest

It is possible for a surviving joint tenant to reject a transfer of a property interest by right of survivorship. This action is sometimes used to prevent a survivor from accepting some distressed property interest that may cost more money than the property is worth.

Severance of Joint Tenancy

Any joint tenant can destroy his or her right of survivorship by severing the joint tenancy. The severing joint tenant's joint tenancy interest becomes a tenancy in common. The remaining joint tenants can continue to hold title to the property as joint tenants. The advantage of severance is that it promotes the property's free transferability. Each joint tenant has the right to enjoy the benefits of ownership without obtaining any of the co-tenants' consent. Severance can occur as a result of any of these situations:

1. *Conveyance.* Severance can occur when a joint tenant's interest is conveyed to a third person or to another joint tenant. A deed to a third person severs the joint tenancy as to the conveyed share.

   > *Example:* A, B, and C are joint tenants. If A conveys his joint tenant share to D, B and C remain joint tenants between themselves, but D holds her share as a tenant in common with them.

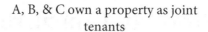

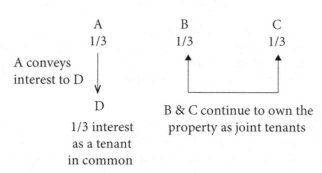

Example: In the above example, when B dies, C owns a two-thirds interest, and D owns a one-third interest as tenants in common.

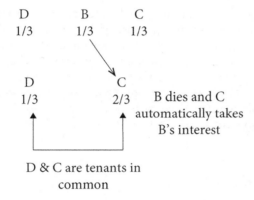

Creditors have concerns regarding property held in joint tenancy. A creditor may act to seize a joint tenant's interest in the property. When that interest is sold or conveyed to the creditor, the joint tenant's interest is severed. Any remaining joint tenants will continue to hold title as joint tenants, with the creditor holding title as a tenant in common. The creditor must act to sever the interest before the joint tenant dies. Once the joint tenant to whom it owes money dies, the surviving joint tenants automatically receive the property, and the creditor will have no interest in the property.

2. *Simultaneous death of joint tenants.* When all joint tenants die simultaneously (for example in a plane crash), each joint tenant is treated as if the interest were a tenancy in common; therefore, each party can transfer their interest in the property by will or intestate succession.

3. *Mortgage.* In many states, if one joint tenant, but not all joint tenants, mortgages the joint tenancy property, the mortgage destroys the unity of interest and severs the joint tenancy upon the effective date of the mortgage.

Marital Property Concurrent Ownership

While spouses in many states can hold property as tenants in common and as joint tenants, some forms of property co-ownership require that the parties be married. Specifically, tenancy by the entirety, community property, and dower and curtesy rights are forms of co-ownership that require the parties to be married.

Tenancy by the Entirety

Tenancy by the entirety is a form of joint tenancy limited to married couples. About half of the states allow this form of spousal ownership. Many of the states that do not recognize tenancy by the entirety recognize community property.

Creation of Interest

The creation of an interest held in tenancy by the entirety is similar to the creation of joint tenancy because it requires the presence of the four unities of joint tenancy (time, title, interest, possession), plus a fifth: unity of person. Unity of person requires that the parties be married at the time they acquire the property. Where unmarried persons attempt to purchase property in tenancy by the entirety, depending on state law, the couple will hold the interest as either joint tenants or tenants in common.

In states that provide for tenancy by the entirety, most states presume that a conveyance to the spouses creates a tenancy by the entirety, unless the deed states otherwise.

Conveyance Rights

In this form of title, unlike joint tenancy, the survivorship right cannot be destroyed by the one spouse's acts. Most states require that both spouses act in order to terminate the interest. A divorce or dissolution of marriage terminates a tenancy by the entirety interest and converts the interests into a tenancy in common with each former spouse owning one-half of the interest.

Creditor's Rights

Many courts hold that the creditors of one spouse may not attach the property because it would adversely affect the interest of the other, nondebtor spouse. The underlying debt must be a joint debt in order to attach the property.

In the following case the court addressed the issue of whether an asset held as tenancy by the entirety could be used to satisfy the debt owed to a creditor of only one of the spouses.

CASE 12.2

NONDEBTOR SPOUSE'S INTEREST IN PROPERTY HELD AS TENANCY BY THE ENTIRETY IS PROTECTED FROM CREDITORS

RBS CITIZENS v. OUHRABKA

2011 Vt. 86 (2011)

Vermont Supreme Court

Jan Ouhrabka was the sole owner of the Providence Chain Company, a Rhode Island jewelry store. In 2010, a Rhode Island superior court placed the business into receivership. At that time, the company owed RBS more than $15,000,000. Ouhrabka executed a personal guarantee in favor of RBS that made him personally liable for the debts of the company. As part of the loan agreement with RBS, Ouhrabka submitted a personal financial statement that listed a personal residence in East Ryegate, Vermont. Vermont is a tenancy by the entirety law state. Following liquidation of the jewelry store assets, RBS sought to satisfy the balance of the debt by attempting to execute a mortgage on the Vermont residence. The trial court held that a creditor such as RBS cannot attach property owned jointly by a debtor and a nondebtor when the debtor and nondebtor hold the property as tenants by the entirety. RBS appealed.

Language of the Court. *RBS contends that the estate of tenancy by entirety is an anachronism whose continuing utility should be reconsidered. RBS contends that because the original purpose of the estate of tenancy by entirety was to protect the survivorship rights of married women at a time when those were the only property rights that could be held by married women, such an estate is an anachronism with no place in our modern jurisprudence.*

The theoretical basis of tenancy by entirety was and is premised on the manner in which the spouses take title — in its entirety — and the manner in which the parties are seized — of the whole. It is

not, as RBS contends, based on the concept of a married woman's inability to freely own property at common law. While the Rights of Married Women Act vested married women with equal rights to manage marital property, it did nothing, explicitly or implicitly, to alter the quality of the marital unity, seizing, or title.

The effect of the Married Women's Property Acts was to abrogate the husband's common-law dominance over the marital estate and to place the wife on a level of equality with him as regards the exercise of ownership over the whole estate. No longer could the husband convey, lease, mortgage, or otherwise encumber the property without her consent. We conclude that the theoretical basis of tenancy by entireties remains intact and that the estate enjoys continued validity in Vermont.

This Court has long held that the estate of the wife and the husband's interest in her tenancy by the entirety, if validly created, is protected from the husband's sole creditors.

Decision. The Supreme Court of Vermont affirmed the trial court, finding RBS could not attach property owned jointly by a debtor and a nondebtor when the property is held as tenants by the entirety

FOCUS ON ETHICS

Is it fair that creditors of one spouse cannot attach property held in tenancy by the entirety? Is it fair that in other states, that same married couple's property could be subject to a creditor's claim?

Community Property

Originating with a system traceable to French and Spanish legal influences in the southern and western parts of the United States, nine states have adopted a community property law system available to married couples. These states are Washington, Idaho, California, Nevada, Arizona, New Mexico, Texas, Louisiana, and Wisconsin. In Alaska, married couples may elect to have their property governed by community property laws.

Community property
Property acquired during marriage that is owned equally by the spouses.

Many variations of the community property system are found among these states. Generally, with **community property**, absent an agreement to the contrary, assets and liabilities acquired during marriage by the labor of either spouse are presumed to be community property. The spouses could change the status of property by entering into a premarital or postnuptial agreement. With community property, both spouses enjoy equal ownership and equal control over the community assets. The basic theory of community property is that both the spouses contribute to the financial success of the marriage and that both should share equally in the results.

> *Example:* Trenton is married and works as a public-school teacher. His salary, though earned only by Trenton, is a community property asset of both spouses.

Once property is characterized as community property, income generated from that property is also deemed community property. Assets purchased with community funds are also considered community property,

In the following case, the U.S. Supreme Court held same-sex marriages to be a fundamental right guaranteed by the U.S. Constitution under the Due Process Clause and Equal Protection Clause. This decision struck down all state-level bans on same sex marriage, thereby requiring all states to not only recognize same-sex marriages, but to afford those couples the same rights as couples of the opposite sex.

CASE 12.3

PERSONAL RIGHTS OF LIBERTY MAY NOT BE UNREASONABLY INTRUDED UPON BY STATE LAWS

OBERGEFELL v. HODGES

135 S. Ct. 2584 (2015)

United States Supreme Court

The plaintiffs are 14 same-sex couples and two men whose same-sex partners are deceased from the states of Michigan, Kentucky, Ohio, and Tennessee ("Obergefell"). Obergefell filed suit in their home states claiming that state officials violated the Fourteenth Amendment when the officials denied Obergefell the right to marry or recognize marriages lawfully performed in another state in which same-sex marriages are allowed. Obergefell prevailed at the trial court level; however, the Sixth Circuit consolidated the cases and reversed. Obergefell appealed to the U.S. Supreme Court.

Language of the Court. *The fundamental liberties protected by the Fourteenth Amendment's Due Process Clause extend to certain personal choices central to individual dignity and autonomy, including intimate choices defining personal identity and beliefs.*

Courts must exercise reasoned judgment in identifying interests of the person so fundamental that the State must accord them its respect.

For that reason, just as a couple vows to support each other, so does society pledge to support the couple, offering symbolic recognition and material benefits to protect and nourish the union. Indeed, while the States are in general free to vary the benefits they confer on all married couples, they have throughout our history made marriage the basis for an expanding list of governmental rights, benefits, and responsibilities. These aspects of marital status include: taxation; inheritance and property rights; rules of intestate succession; spousal privilege in the law of evidence; hospital access; medical decision making authority; adoption rights; the rights and benefits of survivors; birth and death certificates; professional ethics rules; campaign finance restrictions; workers' compensation benefits; health insurance; and child custody, support, and visitation rules.

These considerations lead to the conclusion that the right to marry is a fundamental right inherent in the liberty of the person, and under the Due Process and Equal Protection Clauses of the Fourteenth Amendment couples of the same-sex may not be deprived of that right and that liberty. The Court now holds that same-sex couples may exercise the fundamental right to marry. No longer may this liberty be denied to them and the state laws challenged by Obergefell in these cases are now held invalid to the extent they exclude same-sex couples from civil marriage on the same terms and conditions as opposite-sex couples.

Decision. The Supreme Court held same sex couples had the right to marry and invalidated any contrary state laws.

FOCUS ON ETHICS

Who should decide the issue of the legality of fundamental rights and whether or not something classifies as a fundamental right (courts, state legislatures, or another entity)?

Separate Property

Some property does not become part of the community and remains the **separate property** of a spouse. Generally, the following remains separate property:

Separate property
Property of a spouse that does not become part of the community property.

1. *Property acquired before marriage.* Property that is acquired before marriage remains the spouse's separate property. This includes real property owned before marriage.
2. *Gifts and inheritances.* Property that is acquired by a spouse by either gift or inheritance is treated as separate property.
3. *Property acquired after permanent separation.* Generally, when spouses intend to dissolve the marriage and physically separate, any property acquired after this permanent separation is treated as separate property.
4. *Spouses opt out of community property rights.* Commonly, spouses can opt out of community property rights by entering into prenuptial (before marriage) or postnuptial (after marriage) agreements.
5. *Income generated by separate property.* In most states, income generated from separate property (such as rental property, stock investments) is treated as separate property.

Conveyance of Interest

Because both spouses enjoy equal ownership and equal control over community property assets, both spouses must consent to transfer real property held as community property. Upon the death of one of the spouses, the surviving spouse retains his or her one-half interest in the community assets. The deceased spouse's one-half share can pass according to his or her will.

Creditor's Rights

Subject to a few exceptions, a creditor of one spouse can attach community property assets because both spouses are responsible for debts incurred by the other spouse. It does not matter which spouse created the liability. In addition, the separate property interest of the spouse who has the debt may also be attached.

Community Property with Right of Survivorship

Some community property states allow the creation of a hybrid form of joint tenancy and community property called community property with right of survivorship. Under this form of co-ownership, the rules of community property are followed, but spouses cannot convey their one-half community property interest upon their death; the interest passes automatically to the surviving spouse.

Pre- and Postnuptial Spousal Property Agreements

Prenuptial agreements are agreements made prior to marriage between prospective spouses that limit or waive a spouse's right to marital property. Prenuptial agreements are more common in community property states because of the presumption that assets are part of the community. **Postnuptial agreements** are agreements made after a marriage that limit or waive a spouse's right to marital property.

Many states allow the agreements to be enforced if the parties' assets, earning power, and liabilities were fully disclosed to each other and the terms are fair, reasonable, and not unconscionable.

A majority of states and the District of Columbia have adopted the Uniform Premarital Agreement Act (UPAA), drafted by the National Conference of Commissions on Uniform Laws.[1] The act was designed to create uniform governing laws regarding premarital agreements and to permit engaged couples to arrange for the disposition of their property in accordance with their personal wishes. The act requires that such agreements be made in writing and signed by both parties. The scope of the agreements can be expansive. The agreements must be voluntarily entered into by the parties against whom enforcement is sought.

Ownership of Real Property				
			Marital Property	
	Tenancy in Common (TIC)	Joint Tenancy (JT)	Tenancy by Entirety (TE)	Community Property
Owners / Parties	Two or more persons	Two or more persons (cannot be business entities)	Married persons	Married persons
Must interest be equal	No	Yes	Yes	Yes
Possession	Equal right of possession	Equal right of possession	Equal rights of control	Equal rights of control
Right of survivorship to surviving co-owner(s)	No	Yes	Yes	No
Conveyancing Rights	Each co-owner's interest may be conveyed separately	A co-owner can sever his/her interest and become a TIC with remaining co-owners treated as JTs	Both spouses must agree to convey the property	Both spouses must agree to convey the property
Creditor's rights	Owner's interest may be sold in order to satisfy the creditor; creditor becomes a TIC with remaining owners	If attached before joint tenant dies, owner's interest may be severed to satisfy the creditor; creditor becomes a TIC with remaining owners If attached after joint tenant dies, there is no attachment to the JT interest	Debt must be a joint debt to attach to tenancy by entirety interest	Creditor of one spouse can attach community property interests and separate property of the defaulting spouse
Death	Decedent's interest passes by will or intestate succession	Decedent's interest passes to other surviving JT	Decedent's one-half interest passes to surviving spouse	Decedent's one-half interest transfers by their will or intestate succession; surviving spouse keeps her/his one-half interest

FIGURE 12.1. Ownership of Real Property

■ ■ ■ Unique Prenuptial Agreements Clauses

With the popularity of prenuptial agreements, some interesting and unique clauses have developed. The law is not yet settled on the legal enforceability of some of these unique and bizarre clauses. One such type of clause is lifestyle clauses. These clauses set behavior expectations for the parties during marriage. Below are some provisions couples have adopted in their prenuptial agreements. Which of these appeal to you?

1. *Social media use limitation clauses.* The parties can agree to limit the use of social media as well as whether or not a spouse has permission to post photos of their spouse without permission.
2. *In-law clauses.* These limit how often and how long in-laws are allowed to visit overnight.
3. *Pet clauses.* Prenuptial agreements can cover what happens to pets in the event of a divorce (including visitation rights).
4. *Weight gain clauses.* A spouse who is concerned that their significant other may gain weight after marriage can include a clause penalizing the spouse for gaining above a specified weight or can include a per-pound penalty in the event of divorce.
5. *Right to random drug testing.* These clauses indicate a right to conduct random drug tests of a spouse and penalizing him or her if the drug test results are positive.
6. *TV watching clauses.* For spouses who watch too much television or too many live events (such as college football or professional sporting events), watching time can limited in a prenuptial agreement.
7. *Cheating clauses.* In the event a spouse is unfaithful, the faithful spouse can be awarded additional compensation in the event of divorce.
8. *Religious preferences.* Prenuptial agreements can control the religious upbringing of children. This may be especially important for couples from separate faith traditions.

Common Law Marriage

Common law marriage
A state recognition of marital status for unmarried couples who hold themselves out to the public as if they are married.

Common law marriage is a status given to an unmarried couple who hold themselves out to the public as married and act as if they are married. Cohabitation alone does not create a common law marriage. The couple must hold themselves out to the public as spouses. In states recognizing common law marriages, the states treat the couple with all the rights of married persons. While no court is involved in the creation of a common law marriage, a common law marriage must be dissolved by a court order. Presently, a minority of states and the District of Columbia allow the creation of this form of marital interest.[2]

Dower and Curtesy

Dower rights were created to protect widows from being disinherited by their deceased husbands. **Dower** is the right of a wife to take a life estate in one-third of the real property held by the husband during marriage. Any buyer of the land from the husband's estate would take subject to the wife's life estate. Dower has been abolished in all states except Arkansas, Iowa, Kentucky, Michigan, and Ohio. The effect of dower is that both spouses must execute deeds and contracts in dower states.

Curtesy is the right comparable to dower that is given to a surviving husband. However, the husband has curtesy rights only if issue (children) were born from the marriage, and he receives a life estate in all his wife's lands (not merely one-third). Under modern law, curtesy has been abolished wherever dower has been abolished or modified.

Today, almost all common law property states give the surviving spouse an elective share in the decedent's property owned at death. The share is usually one-half or some other amount, based on factors such as children or the length of the marriage.

Rights and Duties of Co-Tenants

Generally, the rights and duties of the co-tenants are the same regardless of the type of co-tenancy. As previously stated, joint tenants and tenants by the entirety enjoy the right of survivorship, but tenants in common do not. Moreover, state law may require a tenant by the entirety to have spousal consent in order to convey an interest in real property. The rights of co-tenants include the following:

1. *Right to possession*: Each co-tenant is entitled to equal possession. No co-tenant may exclude another co-tenant from any part of the property. If a co-tenant is either forcibly removed from the property or not allowed access to the premises, **ouster** has occurred.

2. *Rents from co-tenant in possession*: In the majority of jurisdictions, a co-tenant not possessing the property is not entitled to collect rent from the co-tenant in possession of the property.

> **Ouster**
> A forceful removal or not allowing a co-tenant access to the premises.

Example: If co-tenant A is in exclusive possession and co-tenant B is voluntarily not in possession (such as might be the case with a personal residence that A and B inherited and in which A resides), A may use and occupy the property without paying rent to B. However, A must pay the ordinary expenses of the premise's upkeep, including mortgage interest, taxes, and ordinary repairs.

3. *Rents from a third party*: Any rents or other income collected by a co-tenant from a third party must be shared with the other co-tenants.

4. *Natural resources*: A co-tenant must pay a proportionate part of the net sums received from the operation of mineral interests (for example, mines and oil wells). In contrast, if the co-tenant operated a farm, the co-tenant who excludes the other co-tenants and farms the land is accountable for the land's fair rental value, not the net sums received from the farming operation.

The duties of a co-tenant include protecting the co-owned property. These duties include the following:

1. *Mortgage costs and taxes*. Each co-tenant must pay a proportionate share of mortgage costs and taxes based on the interest held in the property. In some states, a co-tenant in sole possession has the duty to pay mortgage costs and

taxes up to the amount of the reasonable rental value of the property. Thereafter, any additional amount owed for taxes is shared in proportion to the co-tenants' interests.

2. *Necessary repairs.* Many states provide that if a co-tenant gives notice to the other co-tenants of the need for repairs necessary for the property's preservation, the co-tenant may seek contribution from the nonpaying co-tenants.

Example: After a significant storm, damage to the roof has occurred, allowing water to penetrate the property. Fixing the roof leak is considered a necessary repair to preserve the property; the co-tenant can seek a contribution from the other co-tenants.

3. *Improvements and ordinary repairs.* Improvements and ordinary repairs are not treated in the same way as necessary repairs. There may be no reimbursement for them at all, and the improver bears the risk of not receiving contributions from the other co-tenants.

Example: A co-tenant replaces the light fixtures throughout an expensive home to match the wall furnishings. The co-tenant does not have a right to a contribution from the other co-tenants for this improvement.

Partition

Partition
A legal remedy in which the court can order the division and sale of a property.

Concurrent owners of property may decide to terminate a co-tenancy. Such a termination may occur if the owners cannot agree as to the division of the property or the distribution of the proceeds from the property's sale. In such a case, the co-tenants may ask the court to **partition** (divide or sell) the property. Partition is available to tenants in common and joint tenants but not to tenants by the entirety. It cannot occur among tenants by the entirety because neither spouse can destroy the other spouse's right of survivorship.

In partition, the court either physically divides the property or sells it. If the property can be equally divided, the court may do so and issue a judicial deed providing for separate ownership interests in the previously unified property. If the separate tracts are not equal in value, in order to equalize the difference, the court will order the party with higher-value property to pay a cash sum to the other party.

Example: A tract of land may be partitioned when two heirs cannot agree upon its future development. If one heir receives a greater or more valuable portion than the other heir (which may occur for a variety of reasons, such as road access, natural beauty, or topography), the first heir will pay the other tenant a cash payment to equalize the distributions to both.

If a division of the property is not possible or is not in the parties' best interests, the court will order the sale of the property. Upon partition of the property, each co-tenant is entitled to proportionate shares in the proceeds. The following case addresses the issue of whether a co-tenant has the right to deduct a mortgage following partition when the other co-tenant had no knowledge of and did not consent to the mortgage.

CASE 12.4

RIGHTS OF CO-TENANTS MAY APPLY TO POST PARTITION PROCEEDS

ANDERSON v. JOSEPH

26 A.3d 1050 (2011)

Maryland Court of Special Appeals

Alda A. Anderson owned property located in Hyattsville, Maryland ("Property"), as a tenant in common with Nero Joseph ("Joseph"). Joseph obtained a $49,552.79 loan secured by the Property without Anderson's knowledge or consent. Anderson filed a motion for the court to sell the property and appoint a trustee. Anderson asserted Joseph refused to list the Property for sale and had collected rent and insurance money on the Property without paying any profits he made to her. The court granted the motion and ordered the sale of the Property. The trustee proposed a distribution schedule that deducted Joseph's loan from the proceeds prior to determining the 50 percent share for each of the parties. Anderson contended that this distribution scheme was improper and that the loan should have been deducted only from Mr. Joseph's share of the proceeds.

Joseph testified that he obtained the Bank of America loan to repair a flood in the basement of the Property, as well as to do some kitchen remodeling. He acknowledged that he did not discuss the flood or the loan with Ms. Anderson, explaining, "We weren't talking. She never spoke to me. She never lived in Maryland. She lives in Las Vegas." Joseph stated that he had spoken about the flood with his previous lawyer.

Language of the Court. *There is no dispute that Anderson and Joseph were tenants in common. As tenants in common, Anderson and Joseph each had an equal right to possess, use, and enjoy the property. They each possessed the authority to sell or encumber their own individual interests. The question here is whether Joseph had the authority to encumber Anderson's one-half interest in the Property.*

A tenant in common who takes out a loan on jointly held property can encumber only his or her interest, and another co-tenant's interest in the prop-

erty cannot be used to satisfy the loan. Under these circumstances, the loan encumbered only Joseph's half interest in the Property. Accordingly, it should have been deducted solely from Mr. Joseph's share of the proceeds of the sale.

Generally, one co-tenant who pays the mortgage, taxes, and other carrying charges of jointly owned property is entitled to contribution from the other. With respect to repairs, however, the Court of Appeals has explained: the general rule is that one co-tenant is entitled to contribution from another for necessary repairs and improvements when those repairs were made with the assent of the other, or when the repairs were necessary for the preservation of the building or other erection on the land, and were performed by one co-tenant after making a request of and being refused by the other co-tenant.

Here the evidence shows that Joseph did not give Anderson the opportunity to determine the expediency or necessity of making the repairs prior to the money's expenditure. Moreover, Joseph did not show that the repairs here were necessary for the preservation of the house; he did not even introduce evidence of the specific repairs made.

Decision. The court of appeals reversed, finding Anderson was entitled to the proceeds of the half interest without deduction for the mortgage balance.

FOCUS ON ETHICS

Should Joseph be entitled to a deduction for the mortgage taken out on the property if it was related to necessary repairs, even though he failed to give Anderson notice? Would your answer change if you knew that Anderson would have refused to contribute even if given notice about the necessity of the repairs?

Business Organization Forms of Holding Property

Ownership of real property used for business differs considerably from the characteristics discussed so far in this chapter. The most common business organization forms that hold real property include (1) sole proprietorships, (2) general partnerships, (3) limited partnerships, (4) corporations, (5) limited liability companies, and (6) real estate investment trusts.

Sole Proprietorship

Sole proprietorship
A business organization form whereby title of property is held by an individual owner.

The most common and simplest form of holding title to property is as an individual owner. Generally, when an individual holds title to property for business purposes, the business entity is known as a **sole proprietorship**. With a sole proprietorship, an individual owns and manages the property. He is personally responsible for all costs, risks, and liabilities of owning the property. Sole proprietorships are not separate legal entities because there is no legal distinction between the owner and the business.

Advantages

Sole proprietorships are not as costly to own and operate as the other business entities discussed below. No specific business taxes apply, because the sole proprietorship is not treated as a separate legal entity. The individual owner has complete control and decision-making power over the property's operation. Property may be sold by the owner as desired or can be gifted to or inherited by the owner's heirs.

Disadvantages

Individual ownership of property has some disadvantages. The owner is personally liable for the debts and obligations arising from the ownership of the property. For this reason, the owner should evaluate those risks and obtain proper insurance coverage. Cautious business owners avoid operating a business on real property that is individually owned.

General Partnerships

Partnership
An association of two or more persons who carry on as co-owners of a business for profit.

A **partnership** is an association of two or more persons to carry on as co-owners of a business for profit. A business is any trade, occupation, or profession. Partnerships are governed by the Uniform Partnership Act (UPA), which has been adopted in every state except Louisiana. The UPA currently treats partnerships as stand-alone entities that own property; the partners have ownership rights in the partnership.

Creation

Sharing business profits creates a presumption that a partnership exists. Partnerships can be formed without any formalities and can be created by the agreement and consent of the owners, who are known as "partners." This agreement and consent may be oral; a written agreement is not required to create a partnership.

Characteristics

In a partnership, each partner is entitled to manage the affairs of the partnership and enter into contracts on the partnership's behalf. Partners are personally liable for the debts of the partnership. This liability is unlimited, and partners are jointly and severally liable for partnership debts. With joint and several liability, each partner is liable individually for the entire partnership's debt.

> **Example:** Ryan and Lori are partners in a real estate development partnership. A person is injured through the fault of the partnership, and the partnership is sued. Both Ryan and Lori can be held personally liable for all of the damages sought against the partnership.

Taxation

A partnership is not a separate taxable entity for the purposes of federal income tax. The individual partners pay all profits, losses, and taxes.

Limited Partnerships

A **limited partnership** is a partnership created by filing a certificate of limited partnership with the state. Limited partnerships have general and limited partners. Each limited partnership must have at least one general partner and one limited partner.

Limited partnership
A partnership that has both general and limited partners.

Creation

Unlike general partnerships, which may be orally created, limited partnerships require the filing of a certificate of limited partnership. This document sets forth the rights and duties of the general and limited partners; the terms and conditions regarding the partnership's operation, termination, and dissolution; the partners' voting rights; and the partnership's distributions of profits and losses.

Characteristics

General management of the entity is conducted by the general partners, who have unlimited personal liability for the debts and obligations of the partnership, similar to a general partnership. However, in a limited partnership, a corporation can act as the general partner. This setup provides a form of protection because only the corporation, and not the shareholders of the corporation, will have liability as a general partner.

The limited partners are liable only up to the amount of their capital investment and do not have personal liability for the debts of the partnership unless they enter into personal guarantees to creditors or actively engage in managing the business. Limited partners have no control over partnership management. A person may be both a general and a limited partner at the same time.

Taxation

Limited partnerships are taxed similarly to general partnerships. Limited partnerships are not separate taxable entities for the purposes of federal income tax. The individual partners pay all profits, losses, and taxes.

Corporations

Corporation
A fictitious legal entity created according to statutory requirements.

A **corporation** is a separate legal entity holding rights and duties distinct from those of its owners, who are known as shareholders. Shareholders are not personally liable for the corporation's debts. Absent a personal guarantee of debts, the shareholders' financial exposure is limited to their investment in the corporation (that is, their capital contribution).

Creation

Corporations are created by filing articles of incorporation with the secretary of state. The majority of states also require that the corporation execute bylaws. Bylaws are the rules that govern the corporate structure and provide operating procedures describing how the corporation should conduct its business. The corporation is also required to file annual statements with the secretary of state.

Characteristics

Corporations offer limited liability to all shareholders of the corporation, and corporations can last in perpetuity. State law defines the rights and duties of the shareholders and the directors whom they elect to advance their interests in the corporation's operation.

Taxation

Unlike general partnerships and limited partnerships, corporations are subject to double taxation; that is, the corporate entity is taxed on its earnings, and shareholders are taxed on the distributions made by the corporation.

S corporation
A small form of corporation that elects to be taxed as a partnership.

If shareholders desire to reap the benefits of corporate limited-liability protection along with the pass-through tax treatment that partnerships provide, the shareholders may elect Subchapter S or **S corporation** status. Certain limitations and restrictions apply to forming an S corporations. Because of the depreciation deductions available for real property, many real estate investors create S corporations so that the properties' depreciation can be deducted from their personal income tax returns.

Limited liability company (LLC)
A business entity created under state law in which the owners (members) are not personally liable for the debts and obligations of the entity.

Limited Liability Companies

A **limited liability company** (LLC) is an unincorporated business entity that combines the most favorable attributes of general partnerships, limited partnerships, and corporations.

Creation

State laws govern the creation, operation, and management of LLCs. Generally, the legal requirements include filing articles of organization with the secretary of state. LLCs also execute operating agreements, which are similar to corporation bylaws. The operating agreement is an agreement entered into between and among members that governs the affairs and business of the LLC and the relationship among the members, managers, and the LLC. The operating agreement usually covers the obligations to contribute capital, the allocation of profit and loss, distributions and management, and voting rights.

Characteristics

Like corporate shareholders, the owners of the LLC, known as *members*, are not personally liable for the LLC's debts or obligations, unless these members have executed a personal guarantee. In addition, limited liability applies regardless of the member's participation in the management.

LLCs are managed either through a member-managed structure (in which all members govern and manage the LLC) or through a manager-managed structure (in which the members elect one or more managers to actively manage the LLC on the members' behalf). Like the other entities discussed in this chapter, the LLC is a legal person who can own property, sue and be sued, and enter into and enforce contracts.

Taxation

An LLC is a business entity that can be taxed like a partnership with the Internal Revenue Service allowing the income and losses of the LLC to pass through directly to the individual members of the LLC. Unlike a corporation, no income tax applies at the entity level.

Real Estate Investment Trusts

A **real estate investment trust** (REIT) is a corporate entity or trust that invests in real estate. A REIT operates very much like a mutual fund that invests in stocks, but in this instance, it invests in one or more real estate properties. REITs allow investors to invest in a diversified portfolio of real estate holdings; this arrangement helps reduce the risk and volatility of owning a single piece of real estate.

Real estate investment trust (REIT)
A corporate entity or trust that invests in real property.

REITs are beneficial to investors because they receive a tax treatment designed to reduce or eliminate corporate tax on income and capital gains distributed to shareholders. To qualify for the advantages of not paying taxes, a REIT must, among other requirements:

- Be structured as a corporation, trust, or association
- Be managed by a board of directors or trustees
- Have transferable ownership interests
- Be owned by 100 or more shareholders/persons/beneficiaries
- Distribute at least 90 percent of its taxable income to investors
- Derive 95 percent or more of its income from dividends, interest, and property income

Most of the large REITs are publicly traded securities. Developers often form them to provide capital for a number of projects, with the completed projects acting as the REIT's assets. Frequently, REITs will invest in shopping centers, office buildings, and parks.

	General Partnership	Limited Partnership	Corporation	Limited Liability Company (LLC)
How Created	Two or more partners sharing business profits; no formal requirements	Filing a certificate of limited partnership	File articles of incorporation. Execute bylaws	File articles of organization
Ownership	Two or more partners	One or more general partners and one or more limited partners	Shareholders who may be individuals or other business entities	Members who may be individuals or other business entities
Liability	Unlimited personal liability	General partners have unlimited personal liability; limited partners have liability to investment contribution	Limited to investment contribution	Limited to investment contribution
Taxes	Passed through to individual partners	Passed through to individual partners	Corporation taxed on income; shareholders taxed on distributions	Passed through to individual members

FIGURE 12.2. Common Business Organization Forms of Holding Property

Real Estate Securities Issues

Security
A passive investment not actively managed by the investor.

Persons seeking to attract investors in a real estate transaction must be aware of the requirements imposed by federal and state securities laws. A **security** is an investment, with a reasonable expectation of profits, in a common enterprise which the investor is not managing. Unless an exemption exists, the securities must be registered at the state and federal level.

Ownership in limited partnerships, limited liability companies, and corporations involving real estate investments create the need to comply with securities laws. This occurs because some of the owners may not be actively managing the business. They are subject to the decisions by others that may adversely affect their investment. The ownership of a general partnership interest usually does not create a securities law issue because general partners have the right to manage the business. As active participants in a business, general partners have the opportunity to stay informed about the operations of the business and actively manage the partnership.

Key Terms and Concepts

- Tenancy in common, page 329
- Joint tenancy, page 330
- Right of survivorship, page 330
- Strawman, page 331
- Tenancy by the entirety, page 334
- Community property, page 336
- Separate property, page 337
- Prenuptial agreements, page 338
- Postnuptial agreements, page 338
- Common law marriage, page 340
- Dower, page 340

- Curtesy, page 341
- Ouster, page 341
- Partition, page 342
- Sole proprietorship, page 344
- Partnership, page 344
- Limited partnership, page 345
- Corporation, page 346
- S corporation, page 346
- Limited liability company, page 346
- Real estate investment trust (REIT), page 347
- Security, page 348

Chapter Summary

- A tenant in common can sell or dispose of an undivided interest as if the person were the sole owner of the property.

- Tenancy in common is the default manner of holding title if the intention of the parties is unclear.

- Joint tenancy is a form of concurrent ownership in which two or more persons own equal shares of property, with the right of survivorship between the joint tenants.

- Each joint tenant has an equal right of possession of the whole, regardless of the actual share owned. The right of survivorship allows the survivors to take the property free and clear of the deceased co-tenant's interest.

- Where a unity is missing, parties can meet the four unities by using a strawman transaction.

- Any joint tenant can destroy his right of survivorship by severing the joint tenancy. The joint tenancy interest of the severing joint tenant becomes a tenancy in common.

- Tenancy by the entirety, community property, and dower and curtesy rights are

forms of co-ownership that require the parties to be married.

- The creation of an interest held in tenancy by the entirety is similar to the creation of joint tenancy because it requires the presence of the four unities of joint tenancy (time, title, interest, possession), plus a fifth: unity of person.

- With community property, both spouses enjoy equal ownership and equal control over the community assets.

- Prenuptial agreements are agreements made prior to marriage between prospective spouses that limit or waive a spouse's right to marital property.

- The rights and duties of co-tenants are usually the same regardless of the type of co-tenancy. Each co-tenant is equally entitled to the possession and enjoyment of the whole property.

- Every co-tenant, except tenants by the entirety, has the right to partition the property into separate interests.

- The most common business entities that hold real property include (1) sole proprietorships,

(2) general partnerships, (3) limited partnerships, (4) corporations, (5) limited liability companies, and (6) real estate investment trusts.

■ When an individual holds title to property for business purposes, the business entity is known as a sole proprietorship.

■ Partnerships are a basic form of doing business and holding title to property. A partnership is an association of two or more persons to carry on as co-owners of a business for profit. Partnerships can take two forms: general and limited.

■ In the United States, corporations are the most frequently used form by which to conduct business through a business entity.

■ A limited liability company (LLC) is an unincorporated business entity combining the most favorable attributes of general partnerships, limited partnerships, and corporations.

■ A real estate investment trust (REIT) is a corporate entity investing in real estate with a tax treatment designed to reduce or eliminate corporate tax.

Chapter Problems and Assignments

1. University Hospital sued Smith for unpaid medical services provided to her. University Hospital became aware that Smith owned a home held in joint tenancy. Thereafter, Smith died before University Hospital was able to obtain a judgment against Smith. After Smith's death, can University Hospital place a judgment lien on the survivor's interest in the property?

2. What form of co-ownership interest is conveyed by a deed under the following situations, and what ownership interest is held by each person?
   a. Twenty percent of the property to Lucy, 50 percent of the property to Nix, and 30 percent of the property to Ally.
   b. "To Kevin, Brian, and Megan with right of survivorship."
   c. "To Kevin, Brian, and Megan."
   d. "To Kevin and Devon" (Kevin and Devon are married).
   e. FLG Investments and SLG Investments get together to purchase a property and agree to share profits and losses together.

3. Alan and his wife Liz own real property as tenants by the entirety. Liz has a judgment entered against her personally. What advice would you give Alan regarding his liability

for Liz's judgment? Is the creditor able to sell the property held by Alan and Liz as tenants by the entirety?

4. Three sisters, Mollie, Annie, and Maggie, own a property as joint tenants. Mollie has become very upset with her sisters and wishes to sever her interest in the property. Without Annie or Maggie's consent, Mollie sells her interest to a third person. Was Mollie legally able to sell her interest without the consent of Annie and Maggie? Who holds title to the property and how?

5. Kevin, Brian, and Megan own a property as joint tenants. When Kevin turns 60 years old, he wants to make sure that his daughter and son (Kaitlyn and Ryan) will receive the property. What, if anything, can Kevin do to make sure that Kaitlyn and Ryan will receive a portion of the property he owns as joint tenancy?

6. Four individuals borrowed money to purchase a commercial property as a general partnership. One of the partners is responsible for failing to make a roof repair before the roof collapses. The resulting damages are substantial. Are the non-negligent partners personally liable for the harm caused?

7. Ryan and Jenny purchased a property and held title as community property. While married, Jenny inherited a vineyard in Napa, California. After several years of marriage, Jenny and Ryan decided to divorce. Ryan argues that he is entitled to a fifty percent (50%) interest in the Napa vineyard. Is Ryan entitled to an interest in the vineyard?

8. Vick and his two brothers are joint tenants and full-time residents of Old Ranch. The roof and windows are leaking and need replacing. Vick performs these repairs and asks his two brothers to contribute to the cost. Do the brothers have to contribute?

9. Research the laws of your state to determine if it is governed by the community property law system or tenancy by the entirety.

10. Does your state recognize common law marriages? If so, what are your state's requirements to create a common law marriage?

End Notes

1. Arizona, Arkansas, California, Connecticut, Delaware, District of Columbia, Florida, Hawaii, Idaho, Illinois, Indiana, Iowa, Kansas, Maine, Montana, Nebraska, Nevada, New Jersey, New Mexico, North Carolina, North Dakota, Oregon, Rhode Island, South Dakota, Texas, Utah, and Virginia.

2. Colorado, Iowa, Kansas, Montana, Rhode Island, South Carolina, Texas, and Utah allow for the creation of common law marriages.

Chapter 13
Multiunit Dwellings and Property Management

The fairies, as their custom, clapped their hands with delight over their cleverness, and they were so madly in love with the little house that they could not bear to think they had finished it.
—*J.M. Barrie, Peter Pan in Kensington Gardens (1906)*

Learning Objectives

1. Describe different types of common interest communities.
2. Explain the differences between condominiums and townhouses.
3. Understand how a cooperative is financed and operated.
4. Recognize how timeshares work.
5. Explain how property owners' associations are created.
6. Describe the rights and duties of association boards.
7. State the responsibilities of property managers.

Chapter Outline

- Introduction
- Common Interest Communities
- Types of Common Interest Developments
Case 13.1: *Kephart v. Northbay Property Owners Ass'n.*
- Creating a Homeowners' Association
Case 13.2: *Broadway-Flushing Homeowners' Ass'n Inc. v. Dilluvio*
Case 13.3: *Ebel v. Fairwood Park II Homeowners' Ass'n.*
- Property Management

Opening
scenario

As a real estate developer planning a 500-unit residential subdivision, you must decide how the residents will share the common recreational facilities you will control. The completed project will have private parks and recreational facilities, including clubhouses, basketball courts, and gyms. The extensively landscaped project will make many facilities available to all residents within the subdivision. Each of the units will share party walls, so the proposed layout will consist of 125 structures, each having four attached living units.

After reading this chapter identify what should be included in the covenants, conditions, and restrictions (CCRs) recorded on title to each lot.

Introduction

Historically, homeownership involved a single-family residence on a single lot. Over time, in areas where land was scarce, developers began to offer row housing with party-wall lot lines and high-rise cooperative apartment living. In residential subdivisions, recorded conditions, covenants, and restrictions provided private land-use regulation. In concert with these forms of ownership, a new type of real estate development has become popular: the common interest community.

Explosive growth in common interest communities has occurred in the United States. Real estate developers and buyers of both residential and commercial properties desire to purchase property that is subject to a common property management and use plan.

Local governments embrace the self-managing character of these common interest communities. Issues relating to complaints among neighbors regarding the behavior of a particular property owner no longer engage city councils; instead, homeowners' association boards deal with these issues. Association-governed communities include homeowners' associations, condominiums, townhouses, cooperatives, and other planned communities.

In this chapter, we will review the framework for each type of common interest dwelling unit and discuss the common legal issues that arise with regard to their operation. These matters arise from the laws and procedures that apply to communities controlled by covenants recorded on the title to the properties.

Common interest communities
Communities under the control of a homeowners' association and/or a condominium association.

Common Interest Communities

Common interest communities can operate under a variety of names and with many forms of ownership. A property owner in a common interest community may be under the control of both a homeowners' association (HOA) and a condominium association. The common interest is based on the fact that the property owners are subject to **covenants** that have been recorded on their titles and to a board of directors that can enforce the common restrictions and collect per-unit assessments from the owners. The covenants on title pass with the conveyance of title to the individual units.

Covenant
An unconditional promise to another.

Laws Governing Common Interest Communities

State laws vary greatly with common interest communities. The National Conference of Commissioners on Uniform State Laws has offered model legislation that would apply not only to condominiums but also to other forms of common-ownership communities. These acts have included the following:

- Uniform Condominium Act (1977; amended in 1980)[1]
- Uniform Planned Community Act (1980)[2]
- Model Real Estate Cooperative Act (1981)
- Uniform Common Interest Ownership Act (UCIOA) (1982; amended in 1994)

The model acts become state law only if a state adopts them, and states have taken various routes, with some adopting one of the above acts, and others creating their own statutes governing common interest communities. Differences exist among the states' laws relating to the duties and limitations of boards, board members' fiduciary duties, unit owners' rights to participate in association affairs, voting rights, rights to foreclose for unpaid association dues, and the process of amending association documents.

Types of Common Interest Developments

Common interest developments comprise the following types of multiunit housing: (1) condominiums, (2) townhouses, and (3) cooperatives. Related to the discussion of common interest communities are timeshares and condominium hotel. The creation and characteristics of each type of multiunit housing are discussed in detail below.

Condominiums
A form of housing in a subdivision in which there is individual ownership of the units, but joint ownership of common areas.

Condominiums

Condominiums are a form of multiunit property ownership in which each unit in the condominium complex is individually owned. At the same time, the owner of the unit also holds title, as a tenant in common, to an undivided interest of the common areas. A condominium owner's interest in the unit includes the air space between the unit walls and from the floor to the ceiling of the unit. The exterior of the building (the building's shell), the land, and the amenities provided in the development (pools, parks, landscaping) are part of the **common areas**; the unit holder owns these areas through an undivided tenant-in-common interest.

Common areas
An area of common ownership within a subdivision.

Some common areas are limited common areas. A **limited common area** is a location the use of which is limited to one or more owners. Common examples of limited areas include the owner's balcony on a high rise, or patios and backyards in low-

Limited common areas
Areas where the use is limited to one or more owners within a subdivision.

rise condominiums. An owners' association manages the common areas and assesses each unit a cost to maintain and preserve the common areas.

As to the interior space, the owner has the same set of rights and duties as any other homeowner. For example, the owner must maintain the condition of the unit's interior. While condominiums are often found in residential high-rise buildings, this form of ownership is also used in office buildings, with suites sold to professionals (architects, attorneys, dentists, and doctors) and other users; low-rise buildings and even detached single-family homes sharing a parcel of land (such as the driveway) may also have limited common areas.

Condominium Creation

State statute and contractual laws create condominiums. Every state has a statute regulating condominium ownership. Although state statutes vary, the recordation of a declaration of condominium (also known as a master deed, a condominium subdivision, or a declaration of covenants, conditions, and restrictions [CCRs]) creates a condominium.

The **declaration of condominium** is a contract between and among the unit owners and the association stating the mutual rights and duties of the parties. It establishes individual separate condominium units from one or several parcels of land. The individual unit owners will pay monthly fees to the condominium association for the purposes of maintaining the common areas and securing insurance. Frequently, the declaration of condominium will include covenants restricting the use both of the condominium complex and of the individual units. Many purchasers do not read the declaration of condominium or note the restrictions placed on their unit until they find that they are in violation of a restriction.

> **Example:** Natalie purchased a condominium within a condominium development that consisted of 530 condominium units. When she moved into her condominium, her three cats accompanied her. When the association learned of the cats' presence, it demanded their removal and assessed fines against her for each successive month that she remained in violation of the condominium project's pet restriction. Although Natalie was unaware of the cat restriction, she was still required to remove the cats.

While states differ on what a declaration of condominium must provide, often a declaration of condominium includes the following:

- The name of the condominium
- The legal description of the condominium
- Description of the individual unit boundaries
- Description of the common areas and designation and description of any limited common areas
- Allocation of percentage interests in the common areas to each individual unit
- Creation of a governing body over the condominiums; state law often requires that it be a nonprofit corporation
- Description of any covenants, conditions, or restrictions often related to use, occupancy, or transfer

The declaration of condominium also authorizes the association to adopt **bylaws**, which are the rules governing the condominium association. The law does not require bylaws to be recorded in public records. Each owner of a condominium is provided a copy of the bylaws prior to the purchase of the unit. The bylaws provide the operating procedures of the condominium board, determine the election procedures for the board of directors, and discuss any other relevant matters of the association.

In the following case, a homeowners' association brought suit against a homeowner, claiming that the homeowner's leasing of their property was prohibited.

CASE 13.1

DECLARATION CAN ONLY BE AMENDED BY ASSOCIATION MEMBERS

KEPHART v. NORTHBAY PROPERTY OWNERS ASS'N.
134 So.3d 784 (2013)
Mississippi Court of Appeals

The Kepharts purchased a property within the Northbay Property Owners Association ("NPOA"). Northbay is subject to a "Declaration of Covenants, Conditions, and Restrictions" as well as the Bylaws of NPOA. The Declaration allows homeowners to lease their properties for residential purposes. The Declaration gives the Board power to make rules and regulations, but the power to amend the Declaration was reserved to the homeowners.

Several years before the Kepharts purchased their property, the Board of Directors, acting without the consent of the homeowners, adopted a resolution prohibiting homeowners from renting or leasing their property. Thereafter, the Kepharts purchased their property in Northbay. They then leased the property to Janelle Phillips, despite being notified by Northbay that leasing the property was prohibited. Northbay brought suit against the Kepharts alleging a violation of the Declaration prohibiting renting or leasing the property. The trial court found the resolution prohibiting the Kepharts from leasing the property was valid and ordered the Kepharts to terminate their lease with Phillips. The Kepharts appealed and argued that the removal of the right to lease property was an amendment to the Declaration and the resolution prohibiting leasing the property was void.

Language of the Court. *Because the Bylaws state that changes to the leasing of residences need to be made by amendment, it is clear that these changes could not be made by the Board through passing the Resolution. While the Board has the power to enact rules and regulations, those rules cannot involve rights that "may be exercised only by or are reserved only to the Members." We find that prohibiting the leasing of residences would be considered an amendment and not a rule. Because the right to amend the Declaration is "reserved only to the Members," the Board did not have authority to enact the Resolution; therefore, the Resolution is void.*

Decision. The court of appeals reversed the decision of the trial court, finding the resolution to be void and allowing the Kepharts to continue their lease to Phillips.

FOCUS ON ETHICS

Suppose the bylaws of the association require unanimous consent to amend the recorded declaration. If obtaining unanimous consent is impossible, would it not be fair for the law to permit the board to amend the declaration without unanimous consent?

Assessments

The common areas are maintained through an assessment collected by the individual unit owners. The assessments are often collected monthly and provide for the insurance, maintenance, and repair and replacement of common-area property. The association board creates a yearly budget and establishes an assessment amount on a per unit basis needed for the common areas of the property. Occasionally, an association may incur unplanned expenses, and the association may require a special assessment to pay for the unplanned issues.

> ***Example:*** Within the first three months after the condominium community's completion, a strong wind destroys the recently planted trees throughout the association. Replanting the trees so quickly after the community's completion would not be within the association's maintenance budget and would require a special assessment from all members.

Owners who do not pay their association dues may be responsible for paying late fees and interest and may be subject to an assessment lien placed on the title to their property. While an association can sue an owner for the unpaid assessments, the lien provides a remedy allowing the association to foreclose on the unit owner's property, sell the property, and use the proceeds to pay the association for the dues owing.

Conveyance Rights

A condominium's title may be conveyed just like any other interest, but no actual land interest is transferred with a condominium title. The seller conveys the individual unit, consisting of the air space within the interior, coupled with the fractional interest of ownership in the common area. Condominium owners can transfer and convey their interests subject to any restrictions on transfer provided in the declaration of condominium.

Each condominium owner finances the purchase of his or her individual unit by securing a mortgage. In the event of default under the mortgage, the lender will foreclose on the individual unit. In the event of a foreclosure sale, the lender would sell the title to the individual unit and the interest in the common area. A mortgage secured by one owner does not affect the title held by owners of other units in the community.

Insurance

The condominium owner secures insurance covering the damages to the interior of the unit (for example, fire, smoke damage, theft, and general liability). The condominium association obtains insurance for the building exterior and common areas. The association secures the policy and divides the cost in equal shares as part of the association fees. The association is required to insure all buildings and common areas for both replacement and liability purposes.

Condominium Advantages ■ ■ ■

Owning a condominium offers several advantages. Because a unit owner does not individually own the building's exterior or common areas, the costs for repairing damage to those areas are apportioned to the members of the condominium community.

A condominium owner does not have to maintain the exterior of the building or its landscaping. The owner benefits from the maintenance of the amenities provided within the common areas such as pools, tennis courts, parks, and social facilities.

Prospective purchasers should weigh the inconveniences of condominium living, which can include higher residential density than that found in single-family residences, the amount of the association's dues, and the subjection to rules, regulations, and restrictions on the use of their property.

Townhouses

A townhouse development is different from a condominium development. A **townhouse** can be characterized as a style of housing in which most units are built in a two- or three-story design with common walls between each unit. The townhouse owner owns the entire unit (including the interior and exterior walls, decks, and any side yards) and owns the land upon which the townhouse is built. The inclusion of land in townhouse ownership distinguishes it from condominium ownership.

Townhouse
A form of housing in which the houses have two or more stories and common walls, and the owner owns the land on which the unit is built.

Because land is included in the purchase, townhouses are usually more expensive than condominiums located in the same area. Townhouses may provide more privacy than condominiums because while both may share neighbors on either side, a townhouse does not have a neighbor above or below the unit, as do most condominiums.

Common Areas

As with a condominium, townhouse owners have an interest in the common area of the townhouse community through a homeowners' association. In many states, no specific laws govern townhouse creation, and courts apply the same laws that governs single-family residences.

Townhouse Creation

Townhouses are created in the same manner as condominiums. A declaration of covenants, conditions, and restrictions (CCRs) is recorded, and bylaws are established.

Insurance

When a townhouse owner buys insurance for the unit, the insurance covers the unit and all outdoor areas to which the owner has received title. This would include the interior of the unit, its exterior, and all related patios, garden areas, and balcony areas. Unlike condominium owners, who do not own the land beneath their units individually, townhouse owners need to secure insurance that protects their interests on their property, including both the interior and exterior portions.

Cooperatives

Cooperative
A form of housing ownership in which each owner owns stock with a right to occupy the unit under a proprietary lease.

Owning a cooperative is different than owning a condominium or townhouse. In a **cooperative**, the entire building, all common areas and the land, are owned by a single corporation. Sometimes a limited liability company holds the title. Most often, the cooperative corporation is a nonprofit corporation. Because a corporation usually owns the entire building, individual owners buy shares in that corporation.

Cooperatives were first popular in the early twentieth century. They are primarily found in the Midwest and the eastern United States and are frequently used in New York City. Cooperatives are not as common today as they once were because lenders do not have improved real property as their security for repayment of a loan. Instead, lenders have owners' stock as collateral for the loan.

Proprietary Lease

Proprietary lease
A lease from a cooperative to a tenant providing for the unit's occupancy.

Owners of a cooperative occupy the living units under long-term exclusive leases. These long-term exclusive leases, known as **proprietary leases**, provide the cooperative owners the rights to occupy a particular unit. In contrast to a standard residential lease between a landlord and tenant, the proprietary lease and the bylaws of the cooperative corporation define the cooperative owners' rights and obligations among themselves.

Creation of a Cooperative

Because a corporation usually owns a cooperative, the state's incorporation laws must be followed to create a legal corporation in the state. This requires the filing of articles of incorporation with the secretary of state. The corporation comes into existence once the articles of incorporation are filed.

In addition, the cooperative corporation must execute bylaws for itself. The bylaws are similar to those established through a condominium or homeowners' association. They establish the operating procedures, meetings, voting rights, use restrictions, conveyancing restrictions, and ownership rights of the cooperative shareholder.

Building Operating Costs

In a cooperative, the unit holders do not pay rent. Instead, under the proprietary lease, each owner-lessee must pay a maintenance fee for the proportionate share of the entire cost of owning the building. A cooperative unit owner's failure to keep current in those obligations places a financial burden on all the other owners.

Financing

A single mortgage loan obtained by the cooperative corporation finances the cooperative. The monthly proprietary lease payments cover the unit owner's share of the mortgage, as well as maintenance and management fees. Other cooperative unit holders will make up payment shortfalls of other owners to avoid defaulting under the mortgage of the cooperative corporation.

Conveyance Rights

Cooperative owners are often subject to transfer restrictions in their cooperative stock. A cooperative's board of directors often has the right to approve the sale of individual units and may screen prospective owners before allowing them to purchase their units.

Courts allow the directors to manage the cooperative property and permit the board to deny ownership to anyone for any reason, except when those reasons violate statutory and fair housing laws. This right allows the corporation to screen for the compatibility of building tenants and to pursue eviction remedies for a tenant's failure to abide by reasonable rules of the cooperative.

Timeshares

Related to the common interest community is the timeshare. A **timeshare** is a form of ownership or right to the use of a particular property. Most timeshares that have been created involve recreational or resort property. The concept involves the division of a property's ownership into time periods during a year. The owners are usually known as "members"; all members collectively hold the rights to use the property throughout the year.

Timeshare
A form of ownership characterized by a fractionalized ownership with a specified period of use.

Types of Timeshares

Each owner of a timeshare unit has the right to exclusively occupy and use the property. Most frequently, the right lasts a week or two in duration, and a management company arranges for the reservations and use of the timeshare. Members may have the right to occupy a predetermined unit or have the use of a floating week, whereby the owner can choose a use time throughout the year or during select quarters, months, or weeks established at the time of purchase. Other timeshares allow for the accumulation of points that can be used to purchase time at specific properties and at specific times throughout the year. Each property, unit type (studio, one bedroom), and date of stay will vary in the points required for purchase. Each timeshare company has some latitude as to the type of timeshare offered and the rights each member has when a timeshare is purchased.

Timeshares usually require an annual maintenance fee in addition to the purchase price for property maintenance.

> **Example:** For a $30,000 initial purchase price, Loretta may have the ability to use unit 227 at a Maui timeshare during the 26th week of each calendar year (Sunday to Saturday). In addition to the purchase price, Loretta may be required to pay an annual maintenance fee of $2,100 per year.

Conveyance Rights

The ability to convey the timeshare interest to another person is determined under the terms of the timeshare agreement by which the member acquired the interest. Subject to the terms of such agreements, timeshares can usually be conveyed to another person by deed, will, or intestate succession. Any conveyance is still subject to the terms of the timeshare agreement by which the member acquired her or his interest.

Regulation

Frequently heard criticisms of the timeshare industry include the following: allegations of misrepresentation of gifts and prizes offered to prospective purchasers, the sellers' failure to disclose the material terms of the ownership, and the use of high-pressure sales tactics in timeshare presentations. In response, many states have become concerned over developers' marketing practices and have enacted regulations governing the solicitation and disclosure requirements for to timeshare sales. These regulations may include a right to rescind the purchase contract within a certain number of days after executing it.

Some states regulate timeshares under their real estate commission acts, while others regulate them under securities laws or consumer protection acts. Frequently found in all states' laws are regulations mirroring either the Model Uniform Real Estate Time-Sharing Act[3] or the ALDA/NARELLO Act.

■ ■ ■   Timeshare Advantages and Disadvantages

With timeshares, owners have a fixed vacation cost at a location of their choosing without having to pay for the cost of owning a property year-round. Often, owners can exchange the right to use a unit for the use of a unit at another property location, allowing the owner to enjoy different properties within a portfolio owned by a timeshare company. In addition, many timeshares provide for the interest to be transferred to the owners' children, so that the children can continue to use the property.

Reselling a timeshare is usually not profitable, as timeshares often do not appreciate in value, and the supply of resale timeshares often exceeds the demand for them. It is not uncommon to be able to purchase a timeshare for 50 percent of the purchase price in a secondary market. In addition, owners do not control the property's maintenance fees, which can make owning a timeshare more expensive than originally anticipated.

Condominium Hotels

A trend in multiunit construction is the creation of condominium hotels. A **condominium hotel** involves a project in which condominium owners and hotel guests jointly occupy the property wherein the condominium units can be used for hotel guests.

The condominium owner benefits from the services offered to hotel guests, receives a portion of the income generated from the condominium being offerred to hotel guests, and retains the ownership rights and responsibilities characteristic of a condominium. For a period each year when the condominium owner is not using the unit, he or she may be required to make the unit available to the hotel to rent to hotel guests. Some developers require the owner to use the developer's rental program, and the hotel operator receives a sizeable portion of the revenue collected from the rental of the unit. Condominium hotel owners may feel that they do not have exclusive use of the property, and the owners may take better care of their unit than would a hotel guest.

Creating a Homeowners' Association

Homeowners' associations, also known as property owners' associations, are required in many common interest communities, including condominiums, cooperatives, and townhouses. Homeowners' associations are common in gated communities and **planned communities**, in which a developer designs private streets, recreational facilities, and other amenities among a mix of housing types.

Planned communities
A community developed with a common design for streets, recreational facilities, and other amenities among a mix of housing types.

Homeowners' associations are similar to condominium associations in that homeowners pay regular or special assessment fees to the association. One major difference is that, in the case of the homeowners' association, the association owns the common area, rather than the condominium owners as tenants in common. Aside from this distinction, the law often treats these two associations similarly.

Regulation

State laws regulate the organization of these associations and define their basic structure. Most statutes require a declaration, a set of bylaws, and requirements for voting on certain decisions of the association. Compliance with the requirements of the state common interest statute is required to attain common interest community status.

Recorded Declaration

Like the creation of a condominium association, a homeowners' association is created through a declaration recorded by the developer prior to the sale of the first lot. Each of the homeowners is a member of the association and is subject to the declaration's covenants, conditions, and restrictions (CCRs), even if they never read or reviewed the CCRs before moving into the community.

Owners can vote for members of the homeowners' association's board of directors, which manages the association's common interest areas. The board of directors is composed of homeowners from within the community they manage. Only owners have voting rights; tenants leasing a property are not entitled to vote in board elections.

Association Powers

The power to issue rules regulating common-area use is usually stated in the declaration. The declaration provides the rules, regulations, and limitations regulating ownership throughout the property. Many CCRs are designed to protect neighborhood aesthetics and help support property values by maintaining the appearance and repair of all properties in the community. Some declarations are very detailed and provide specific requirements by which owners are expected to abide (such as limiting the number of domestic animals each homeowner may have in their home).

> *Example:* An architectural guideline may require the selection of certain plant materials to complement the architectural style of the home (for example, Colonial, Italian, French, or Spanish). The guideline may even provide a list of plants that are acceptable based on the style of the home.

The declaration may establish committees, such as architectural and landscaping committees, to review proposed modifications to a property. Owners who fail to abide by the CCRs may be subject to fines, liens by the association, foreclosure of their homes, and other remedies provided for in the declaration.

Resolving Disputes

As common interest communities have increased in popularity, disputes have arisen between the individual unit owners and the governing associations. In resolving these disputes, courts will review the governing documents: the recorded declarations, the articles of incorporation (if the association is incorporated), the bylaws of the association, and the governing board's prior acts. The most common litigation arising in homeowners' associations includes enforcement of CCRs and issues related to appearance and structural modifications made by homeowners in the association.

The association has three common methods to address violations by homeowners: (1) monetary penalties assessed to the homeowner, (2) liens, and (3) foreclosure of the property. Each of these will be limited by the powers provided in the governing documents of the HOA as well as local or state law.

> *Example:* The Northpark Maintenance Association CCRs dictate that each home must at all times be kept in good condition and repair. If Devon allows her home's exterior paint to deteriorate, she is in violation of the CCRs. To compel compliance, the association may levy a fine or special assessment against her.

Standards of Review

Reasonableness review standard
A rule wherein rules based on reasonable decisions and adopted by the board of directors will be upheld.

Courts will review the HOA board's actions using either the **reasonableness review standard** or the business judgment rule. Most states follow the reasonableness review standard. Under this standard, owners are on notice of the restrictions provided in the declaration. Reasonable rules adopted after the purchase will be upheld under the reasoning that the owner impliedly agreed to be bound by new rules agreed upon by a majority of owners. If the new rules meet that standard, they will be upheld.

Business judgment rule
A rule that protects the decisions of a corporation's board of directors if the board has acted on an informed basis, in good faith, and in the honest belief that the action taken was in the best interests of the corporation and its shareholders.

Other states apply the **business judgment rule**. Under this rule, a court will not second-guess the decisions made by the association's board if that decision was made in good faith, was reasonably prudent, and made in the belief that the decision was in the association's interest.

These rules avoid judicial "second-guessing" of board actions. Both municipalities and courts recognize that the individual's choice to purchase a property governed by a common interest declaration should be respected. Deference is given to the decisions of a board of directors that, when acting within its authority, interprets association bylaw provisions.

In the following case, a homeowners' association sued homeowners to enforce a restrictive covenant regarding fences.

CASE 13.2

**HOMEOWNERS' ASSOCIATION CAN ENFORCE
RESTRICTIVE COVENANTS AGAINST HOMEOWNERS**

BROADWAY-FLUSHING HOMEOWNERS' ASS'N INC. v. DILLUVIO

97 A.D.3d 614 (2012)

New York Supreme Court, Appellate Division

The Dilluvios purchased real property subject to CCRs. One such restriction stated, "no fence except hedge or shrubbery will be permitted within 20 feet of the front line or side street line of any lot." After moving in, the Dilluvios constructed a seven-foot high concrete wall to enclose a swimming pool they had installed in the back of their property. The homeowners' association filed a lawsuit against the Dilluvios to enforce the CCRs and secure an order for the Dilluvios to remove the wall. The trial court ruled in favor of the homeowners' association and required the Dilluvios to remove the wall. The Dilluvios appealed, arguing the CCR provision was ambiguous.

Language of the Court. *We reject the Dilluvios contention that the covenant should not be enforced because it is ambiguous. "Restrictive covenants will be enforced when the intention of the parties is clear and the limitation is reasonable and not offensive to public policy." The party claiming that a restriction is unenforceable bears the burden of proving it. Here, the Dilluvios failed to meet their burden of proving that the covenant was unenforceable. The evidence showed that the purpose of the covenant was to benefit and preserve the open yard, as well as the*
"unobstructed, open character of the neighborhood, unimpeded and unburdened" by man-made structures, such as a fence or, in this case, a concrete and stucco wall.

Under the facts of this case, where the homeowner's association provided clear and convincing evidence of the covenant and its scope, where the Dilluvios had knowledge of the covenant but chose to continue with their construction, where the homeowners' association suffered irreparable harm in the form of the obstruction of the open views intended by the covenant, and where the equities are balanced in the homeowners' association favor, the Supreme Court correctly granted a permanent injunction.

Decision. The appellate court found the Dilluvios did not prove the covenant was ambiguous and affirmed the trial court's ruling.

FOCUS ON ETHICS

With the proliferation of homeowners' associations, is it fair that owners' uses can be constrained by the HOA board?

Amending the CCRs

The terms and conditions of the recorded CCRs greatly affect homeowners' ability to amend them. A modification clause may permit changes to allow additions of reasonable new covenants and dictate the percentage of homeowners who must agree to CCR amendments.

In the following case, homeowners sought a court ruling that the homeowners' association lacked the authority to act because it was not properly formed.

CASE 13.3

ASSOCIATION HAS IMPLIED AUTHORITY TO MANDATE ASSESSMENTS

EBEL v. FAIRWOOD PARK II HOMEOWNERS' ASS'N.
150 P.3d 1163 (2007)
Washington Court of Appeals

Evergreen Highlands Association is a homeowners' association consisting of 63 lots, roads, and a 22-acre park. The park contains hiking and equestrian trails, a barn and stables, a ball field, a fishing pond, and tennis courts. The park is almost completely surrounded by private homeowners' lots, with no fences or other boundaries separating the park from the homes.

The recorded covenants did not require lot owners to be members of or pay dues to the association. Over time the voluntary assessments failed to meet the cost of maintaining and improving the park facility. A majority of the homeowners then voted to add a new article to the covenants that required all lot owners to be members of and pay assessments to the association. They further voted to allow the association to impose liens on the properties of those owners who failed to pay their assessments.

Robert West purchased his lot when membership in the association was voluntary. He did not vote for the new article, and he refused to pay his lot assessment of $50 each year. When the association threatened to lien his property, he filed suit, challenging the validity of the amendment. The trial court ruled in favor of the association, but the court of appeals reversed, finding that the original covenants provided that a majority of lot owners could "change or modify any one or more of said restrictions" did not empower the association to add a new covenant. The association appealed.

Language of the Court. *Although many subdivisions have covenants that mandate the payment of assessments for this purpose, others do not. Without the implied authority to levy assessments, these latter communities are placed in the untenable position of being obligated to maintain facilities and infrastructure without any viable economic means by which to do so. In order to avoid the grave public-policy concerns this outcome would create, we today adopt the approach taken by many other states which provides that the power to raise funds reasonably necessary to carry out the functions of a common interest community will be implied if not expressly granted by the declaration.*

We hold that even in the absence of an express covenant mandating the payment of assessments, the association has the implied power to levy assessments against lot owners in order to raise the necessary funds to maintain the common areas of the subdivision.

Decision. The decision of the court of appeals was reversed and the Evergreen Highlands Association could add the covenant to the declaration.

FOCUS ON ETHICS

Was it ethical for the court to imply powers to the association that it did not have under the recorded declaration?

Fiduciary Duty of Boards

Boards may not act impulsively or unreasonably in their decision making. Both the association and the board must act reasonably and in good faith in carrying out their duties. They are representatives of the members and have fiduciary duties. As fiduciaries, they must act with utmost loyalty and good faith solely for the promotion of the members' interests.

Liability

Liability can arise from the ownership of an individual lot, a condominium, or a townhouse, or from common-area activities. A property owner is responsible for all harm to others caused by the owner's intentional or negligent acts.

Personal injuries within a unit are the responsibility of the unit owner. In contrast, if that injury occurred in the common-area clubhouse, the association would be liable. If the homeowners' association is unincorporated, the liability for the common-area injuries becomes the responsibility of the individual members.

Example: A guest slips and injures herself on a wet kitchen floor recently mopped by a townhome owner. The owner is liable for the injury.

Differences Among Homeowners' Associations, Condominiums, and Cooperatives			
	Homeowners' Associations	**Condominiums**	**Cooperatives**
	Individuals own the individual unit and are members of the association.	Individuals own the individual unit.	Individuals hold shares of stock in the cooperative corporation and have proprietary leases allowing them possession of individual units.
Common Areas	Association owns common areas (pools, trails).	Ownership held by unit owners as tenants in common.	Owned by cooperative corporation.
Lender Financing	Individuals may secure personal financing of their units. Association can secure financing on common areas to finance improvements and repairs.	Owners can secure financing of their units. Common areas may be of little worth as collateral; member assessments may act as loan collateral.	Corporation secures blanket mortgage. Individual owners may borrow against their interests in stock in cooperative and proprietary lease.
Management	Members elect board of managers or directors.	Members elect board of managers or directors.	Shareholders elect board of managers or directors.

FIGURE 13.1. Differences Among Homeowners' Associations, Condominiums, and Cooperatives

Property Management

Property management involves the administration, operation, and management of real property. The concept is widely employed in common interest communities, especially larger homeowner communities with hundreds or more homes. Property managers act as an agent for homeowners' association and assist their boards of directors with association administration. Because residents serve voluntarily on these boards, they often lack the background, contacts, experience, and legal knowledge that a property management company can offer.

Services Offered

Property management companies offer various services to help homeowners' associations and condominium associations to manage their properties effectively. Management companies often provide emergency services 24/7 and education to community board members.

In addition, these companies assist boards to establish annual budgets, conduct elections, and retain contractors for necessary repairs. Management companies act as the public face to the community on association's behalf. Depending on the size of the homeowners' association, some property management companies provide on-site community support to property owners. These onsite property managers can assist residents with association-related issues and concerns (such as approved paint colors, architectural modifications, gate access passes, and the like).

Compensation

Property managers receive compensation from the association; those costs are part of the monthly assessments paid by the member-owners. Property managers may be compensated under a fixed-fee arrangement or as a percentage of the effective rental income (net of vacancies). Bonuses may be included in the compensation to incentivize efficient management of the association and decrease operating expenses.

Commercial Property Management

Property management companies do not only work with homeowners' associations, they are also often instrumental in the management of commercial properties. Property managers assist in marketing and leasing commercial property on the owner's behalf. In the case of an apartment project, the on-site manager or rental-office staff will usually show vacant apartments to prospective tenants. If standard-form leases are used, the manager may handle all the activities.

The use of professional property managers can enhance a property's market value. Most investors do not have the time or expertise to manage their income-producing properties. Investors hire property managers to perform two types of functions:

1. *Management of the daily operations.* Every project will have ongoing maintenance, repair, and tenant issues. The presence of property managers who are personally familiar with a project's construction and maintenance history will reduce ongoing maintenance costs. The ability to retain experienced contractors to perform repairs and remodels on the premises allows units to be returned to the rental market more quickly. Property managers must observe the fair housing laws in selecting qualified tenants; they must also be knowledgeable about local landlord-tenant laws.

2. *Financial reporting of operations.* Investors in income producing properties are investing in the cash flow generated from the rental operations. They seek a return on their investments in an asset, which in this case is the real property. The property manager assists by preparing financial statements for the investors. Rental and other income generated from the operations is reported, along with a detailed accounting of all expenses incurred in the property's management.

Licensure

Most states regulate property management by including activities such as leasing, negotiating and making lease offers, and renting in their real estate licensing statutes. Nevertheless, the states lack uniformity as to whether property managers are exempt from real estate licensure. The Institute of Real Estate Management™ is an international association of real estate managers and an affiliate of the National Association of Realtors.™ It is dedicated to serving the needs of managing both the multifamily and commercial real estate sectors. It has taken the following position with regard to the licensing of property managers:

> The Institute of Real Estate Management believes that the management of residential apartments, condominiums, cooperatives and homeowners' associations involves real estate activities and should require a license under existing state license laws. IREM National supports professional community association management but is opposed to a separate state mandated license or certification for community association management and urges all forms of real estate management to be under the jurisdiction of existing state real estate broker and agent licensing laws.
>
> In states where state mandated community association manager certification or licensing already exists, IREM supports placing the ongoing regulation and management of the certification or licensing process under the jurisdiction of the state real estate commission. IREM believes that the state real estate commissions provide the most appropriate means to regulate and monitor the real estate industry and protect the consumer.[4]

The concern about licensing of property managers springs from the importance of the fiduciary duties undertaken by them. Normally, a broker's license is required if the activities include collecting rent, listing properties for rent, or negotiating the terms of leases. A property manager may hold a licensed salesperson's license, but she or he must be working under the supervision of a licensed real estate broker.

Key Terms and Concepts

- Common interest communities, page 354
- Convenant, page 355
- Condominiums, page 355
- Common areas, page 355
- Limited common areas, page 355
- Declaration of condominium, page 356
- Bylaws, page 357
- Townhouse, page 359
- Cooperative, page 360
- Proprietary leases, page 360
- Timeshare, page 361
- Condominium hotel, page 362
- Planned communities, page 363
- Reasonableness review standard, page 364
- Business judgment rule, page 364
- Property management, page 368

Chapter Summary

- Common interest communities can operate under a variety of forms. The common characteristic includes the owners electing a board of managers or directors with the power to make and collect assessments upon and from individual unit owners.

- Condominiums, townhouses, and cooperatives are among the most common forms of common interest communities.

- Condominiums are a form of multiunit property ownership in which each unit in the condominium complex is owned individually, and the owner of the unit concurrently holds title, as a tenant in common, to an undivided interest in the common areas.

- A condominium association governed by a board of owners creates and enforces reasonable rules relating to the use of the units and common areas.

- Condominiums are created by state statute. The state statutes often require a declaration of condominium and the execution of bylaws.

- A townhouse development is different from a condominium development. Townhouse owners own both the interior and exterior walls and the land on which the townhouse is built. Townhouse owners share the common areas through membership in their homeowners' association.

- A cooperative corporation owns the entire building and secures a mortgage on the whole structure. The owners of the cooperative pay the mortgage payments and routine maintenance and operating costs.

- The individuals who own shares in the cooperative occupy the living units under long-term exclusive leases. These long-term exclusive leases, known as proprietary leases, provide the cooperative owners the rights to occupy a particular unit.

- A timeshare is the right to use a particular property during given periods of the year. Developers sell timeshares to those who wish to decrease the costs of their vacation and resort expenses.

- A condominium hotel involves the construction of a building in which a portion of the building is a hotel and the other portion is owned as condominium units that can also be utilized for hotel guests.

- A developer creates a homeowners' association and records a declaration on the title to the property. Before the first unit is sold, the developer records conditions, covenants, and restrictions (CCRs) on the property's title.

■ Courts will either review actions of the homeowners' association board using either the reasonableness review standard or the business judgment rule. Most states follow the reasonableness review standard.

■ Property managers are fiduciary agents of the owners. The scope of property managers' duties can be quite broad. They are responsible for the day-to-day operations of the development and issue periodic financial statements to the owners. States differ as to whether property managers must be licensed under state real estate licensing laws.

Chapter Problems and Assignments

1. What are the common types of common interest communities?

2. How do bylaws differ from a declaration of condominium?

3. Assume that you are a member of the board of directors for your homeowners' association. Because many homeowners park on the street and in designated open spaces, the association has limited parking spaces available for guests. The limited parking is attributable to most homeowners not parking one or both of their vehicles in their garages. What are your options as a member of the board of directors to alleviate this problem?

4. Charlie is attempting to sell his cooperative unit to Sarah, a real estate lawyer. Charlie seeks the approval of the cooperative board to sell his unit to Sarah but is denied because the board states there are too many lawyers in the cooperative and "they have been nothing but trouble." Does the cooperative board have the power to deny ownership to Sarah because she is a real estate lawyer?

5. Kayla resides in a condominium association. The roof to her condominium unit leaks when it rains. She has submitted a repair claim to her association. The association has denied the repair claim, stating that the roof is not part of the common area. Kayla alleges

that the roof is the association's responsibility. Who is correct?

6. The Meadowood Estates homeowners' association has monthly dues of $50. As a result of a recent heavy rainy season, $35,000 of unexpected damage occurred to the common areas. The association does not have the reserve funds to pay for the repairs necessary and decides to implement a one-time $85 special assessment of all owners in the association. Elijah, one of the homeowners, refuses to pay the special assessment. Does the association have the ability to collect a special assessment? If so, what remedies does the association have against Elijah?

7. The Osbornes are holiday display fanatics. They have displays for every major holiday and religious observance throughout the year. Large crowds gather and caravans frequently drive through the neighborhood to view them. Their neighbor, Mr. Curmudgeon, does not like the crowds or the displays. After reading the association declaration and bylaws, he becomes aware that the policies state, "Holiday decorations may be displayed 10 days prior to and 10 days after the date of the actual holiday." It further provides, "Holiday lighting may be operated after November 22 of each year." What rights does Mr. Curmudgeon have to limit the displays and the traffic? Does it matter if the Osbornes had been doing this in the

association for the past five years without any previous complaints?

8. States are divided when it comes to whether a homeowner may sue for personal injuries suffered due to the association's failure to maintain common areas. Research the laws of your state to determine whether a homeowner in such a situation may sue an association.

9. Research the type of review standard your state follows for resolving disputes in a homeowners' association.

10. Research an association that imposes covenants, conditions, and restrictions. Review the restrictions imposed and draft a short memorandum to a prospective purchaser on the homeowner's rights and duties.

End Notes

1. http://www.uniformlaws.org/shared/docs/condominium/uca_80.pdf (last accessed November 2, 2017).
2. http://www.uniformlaws.org/shared/docs/planned%20community/upca80.pdf (last accessed November 2, 2017).
3. Uniform Real Estate Time-Share Act, National Conference of Commissioners.
4. http://www.irem.org/File%20Library/Public%20Policy/IREMStatementOfPolicy.pdf (last accessed November 2, 2017).

Chapter 14
Residential and Commercial Leases

It is not easy to steal where the landlord is a thief. —Irish saying

Learning Objectives

1. Explain the four types of tenancies.
2. Differentiate between the different types of rental rates.
3. Define the duties of landlords and tenants.
4. State the implied covenants contained in residential leases.
5. Recognize the remedies of landlords and tenants.
6. Understand what terms are included in commercial leases.
7. Explain assignments and subleases.

Chapter Outline

- Introduction
- Types of Tenancies
- Rental Rates
- Writing Requirements
- Common Lease Provisions
- Tenant Rights and Landlord Duties

Case 14.1: *Terry v. O'Brien*

- Landlord Rights and Tenant Duties
- Americans with Disabilities Act (ADA)
- Landlord's Tort Liability
- Lease Defaults and Evictions

Case 14.2: *Kayla West v. DJ Mortgage, LLC*

- Selecting Tenants

Case 14.3: *White v. U.S. Department of Housing & Urban Development*

- Assignments and Subleases

Opening
scenario

Franklin entered into a five-year lease with Steven for part of a commercial storefront building in downtown Omaha, Nebraska. The building was under construction when they entered into the lease; however, the lease required the property to be delivered to Franklin in an improved condition at the lease commencement date. The lease also included a rent abatement provision excluding rent for the period during which the building was unavailable to Franklin.

Because the construction of the improvements was delayed, Franklin did not pay rent. Franklin could not open his store. Steven and Franklin disagreed upon the duration of the rent abatement. Steven put a cable lock on the Franklin store door and placed signs reading "Your Rent Is Due — Pay It" in the store windows. Franklin had the lock cut off and moved out of the building within two days after the lockout; Franklin also returned the store's keys to Steven. Steven sued Franklin for unpaid rent. Franklin asserted that it had been constructively evicted. After reviewing this chapter, did the landlord's actions constitute constructive eviction?

Introduction

Lessor
A person who transfers the right to exclusively possess and use property for a duration of time.

Lessee
A person who acquires the right to exclusively possess and use property for a duration of time.

Nonfreehold estate
An estate in which the tenant has a right to possess the real property but does not obtain a real property interest.

Lease
Contract transferring exclusive possession of a property from one party (the landlord) to another (the tenant) for a period of time (the tenancy).

In this chapter, we review both residential and commercial leases and the terminology required to understand lease transactions. While landlords and tenants are sometimes referred to as **lessors** and **lessees** respectively, in this chapter we shall refer to them as landlords and tenants. Before we start our study, we need to recognize where leases fit within the real estate landscape.

Recall from chapter 5 that real property is classified as freehold and nonfreehold estates. A freehold estate includes the fee simple estate and several types of defeasible estates, including the fee simple determinable. In this chapter, we consider the **nonfreehold estate** (or leasehold), in which the person's interest is a personal property interest arising from contract giving the right to possession to the tenant. A leasehold interest lacks the rights of absolute ownership in the real property.

The landlord-tenant relationship is a blend of both contract law and real property law. Some states have statutory authority governing leasing and have adopted the Uniform Residential Landlord and Tenant Act (URLTA) or follow the principles in the Act. A **lease** transfers to the tenant the right to exclusively possess and use the landlord's property for a period of time. The period of a tenant's occupancy or possession is a **tenancy**. When the tenancy expires, the right to possession reverts to the landlord, and the tenant retains no interest in the property.

A **residential lease** covers use of property for a personal purpose, such as residence in an apartment or house. **Commercial leases** cover use of property for business or commercial purposes, such as retail, restaurants, offices, or warehouses.

Leases Distinguished from Other Property Interests

Easement

- A nonpossessory land interest
- Creates only a right to use another's land
- Holder usually pays a lump sum for acquiring it

License

- Nonexclusive access to the premises
- Terminable at any time
- Licensee cannot deny others access to and possession of the premises
- Owner retains control of and access to the premises
- Owner often provides utilities and furnishings and must repair and maintain the premises (hotel guests are licensees)

Freehold Interest (such as fee simple)

- Holder has title (ownership) to the property
- Interest inheritable or transferable during life or after death
- Key characteristic is whether duration is uncertain or unlimited
- A fee simple determinable or a fee subject to a condition subsequent creates interests in the real property beyond mere possession.

Types of Tenancies

There are four types of leasehold estates:

1. Tenancy for years
2. Periodic tenancy
3. Tenancy at will
4. Tenancy at sufferance

Tenancy for Years

One of the most common types of tenancies is a tenancy for years. A **tenancy for years** is a lease for a fixed period of time. While the name of this tenancy sounds as though it necessarily lasts more than a year, a tenancy for years can be for any fixed period, including weeks, months, or years. Some states limit a tenancy for years to 99 years. Leases lasting longer than 99 years may be considered fee simple estates by statute.[1]

Tenancy for years
A lease for a fixed period of time.

> **Example:** A student leasing a dormitory room for an academic year would hold a tenancy for years.

Termination

In this type of tenancy, the landlord and tenant have agreed to a fixed lease duration, and the right to possession expires at the end of the term. Neither party needs to give notice to the other of the lease's expiration. The lease terminates automatically, and the right to possession is transferred back to the landlord. Interestingly, the death of a party does not terminate a tenancy for years. The rights and duties of the deceased are transferred to the decedent's heirs or beneficiaries.

Writing Requirement

The Statute of Frauds requires that a tenancy for years covering a period of time exceeding one year must be in writing. If a lease is not in writing when one is required, a periodic tenancy (discussed below) is created.

> **Example:** Travis enters into an oral lease with Rose from January 1, 2018, through June 15, 2019, with rent payable monthly at the rate of $750 each month. Under the Statute of Frauds, the tenancy for years was required to be in writing to be enforceable. The lease is an implied month-to-month periodic tenancy at $750 each month.

■■■ Duration of Tenancy for Years Leases

So long as state law permits it, tenancies for years may have very long durations. While not an American lease, one such example is the Guinness Brewery lease. The lease was executed on December 31, 1759. It is a 9,000-year tenancy for years at an annual rent of £45.

Periodic Tenancy

A **periodic tenancy** is a tenancy that lasts for a fixed period of time and continues to renew for like periods of time until either the landlord or the tenant gives notice of termination. The tenancy may be year-to-year, month-to-month, week-to-week, or for other periods.

Periodic tenancy
A lease that lasts for a fixed period and continues to renew for like periods until terminated.

> *Example:* The month-to-month lease beginning January 1 for $800 a month is a periodic tenancy.

Creation

Periodic tenancies are created either by express agreement between a landlord and a tenant or through implication. When parties agree to the tenancy period, they create an express periodic tenancy.

> *Example:* Landlord and Tenant agree: "Starting June 1, on a month-to-month basis, Tenant to have the use of my guest house for the sum of $1,500 per month, due on the 10th." The landlord and tenant have created an express periodic tenancy because they agreed on the tenancy period (month-to-month tenancy).

Where a landlord and tenant agree to the terms of the lease, but the lease fails to mention its tenancy period, an implied periodic tenancy is created with the tenancy period being the frequency of the payment intervals.

> *Example:* Landlord and Tenant agree: "Starting June 1, Tenant to rent the apartment for the sum of $1,250 per month, with payment due on the 10th." The landlord and tenant have created an implied month-to-month periodic tenancy because rent is due monthly.

In addition, a tenancy for years that violates the Statute of Frauds creates an implied periodic tenancy. The tenancy period is the frequency at which rent is collected. When the tenancy period has terminated following the expiration of a tenancy for years, and the landlord continues to receive and collect rent, an implied periodic tenancy is created.

> *Example:* Travis enters into an *oral* lease with Rose for two years, with rent payable at the rate of $750 each month. Under the Statute of Frauds, the tenancy for years was required to be in writing to be enforceable. Instead of a tenancy for years, the lease is an implied month-to-month periodic tenancy with rent of $750 due each month.

Some leases may initially start as a tenancy for years and then provide for the lease to automatically convert to a periodic tenancy at the end of the tenancy for years.

> *Example:* Possession of apartment 1418 to tenant for one year; at the end of that period, the lease shall continue on a month-to-month basis, unless the landlord or tenant terminates this lease by notice in writing delivered to the other at least one month prior to the end of the term. In this example, the lease starts as a tenancy for years that at the end of one year would continue as a periodic tenancy until terminated by proper notice.

Continuous Renewal

Periodic tenancies do not have a fixed ending date and continuously renew until either party gives proper and timely notice. The lease renews with the same terms and conditions for another tenancy period (such as another month in a month-to-month tenancy). This is different from a tenancy for years, which ends upon a specific date. The key characteristic of this type of tenancy is that a periodic tenancy has a known beginning date and duration of successive periods. It does not have a fixed ending date and continues until proper and timely notice to terminate is given by either party.

Termination

To terminate a periodic tenancy, one party must give notice of termination to the other party. Except as required by statute, the notice of termination can be given either orally or in writing. This notice must be given to the other party at least as far in advance as the length of the lease period, with the exception that if the tenancy is year to year, only six months' notice is required. However, the parties can agree in the lease to shorten the amount of time required to terminate the tenancy.

> *Example:* To terminate a month-to-month periodic tenancy, one month's notice must be provided.

Tenancy at Will

Tenancy at will
A lease with no stated term and no provision for the collection of rent.

A **tenancy at will** has neither a stated term nor a stated rent amount. It lasts only so long as both the landlord and the tenant agree to it. Either party can terminate it at any time.

> *Example:* After graduating from college, Jerry moves back into his parents' home. Jerry's parents do not charge him rent and provide that he is free to stay as long as he and his parents agree. Jerry has a tenancy at will.

Termination

Either party may terminate a tenancy at will at any time, although some states are now requiring that some advance notice be given to terminate a tenancy at will.

Tenancy at Sufferance

The last type of tenancy is the **tenancy at sufferance**, sometimes referred to as a holdover tenancy. This tenancy is created when a tenant remains in possession of the property after the tenancy period has terminated. The tenant stays in possession without permission and "holds over" after termination of the tenancy. A tenancy at sufferance allows the landlord to collect rental payments against the holdover tenant.

Despite the title given to the occupant, the tenant is not really a tenant at all because the occupant is holding over without the landlord's consent. There is no tenancy to terminate, and notice to terminate is unnecessary. Although the lease has ended, the landlord and tenant may negotiate a new lease to permit the tenant to remain in possession; alternatively, the landlord may collect rent from the tenant, creating an implied periodic tenancy. If one of those events occurs, the tenant's status changes from one of a tenant at sufferance to a tenancy for years or a periodic tenancy, depending on the terms of the lease created.

Example: On January 1, Whitney leases her apartment to Sarah on a month-to-month basis. Assume Sarah gives timely notice to Whitney to terminate the periodic tenancy, with a tenancy end date of December 31 of that same year. If Sarah remains in possession after January 1 of the new year, she is a tenant at sufferance. If Sarah makes a monthly rental payment to Whitney after the beginning of the new year, and Whitney accepts it, this creates a periodic tenancy.

Are Holdover Tenants Trespassers?

Generally, tenants at sufferance are not considered trespassers; however, state laws vary greatly in this regard. A tenant enters into possession with the landlord's consent. By contrast, a trespasser takes possession of land without the permission of the real property's owner. In some states, when a tenant stays in possession after the expiration of the lease, the landlord may treat the tenant as a trespasser; alternatively, the landlord may renew the lease under the same or new terms.

When the holdover tenant is treated as a trespasser, some states allow the landlord the right to use reasonable self-help steps to remove the trespasser from the premises. A self-help eviction may take many forms, including changing the locks, adding a lock without providing keys, turning off utilities, and refusing entry to the leased premises. Caution must be exercised in self-help eviction situations because they can often involve highly charged emotions and legal risks of injury or damage to property. Self-help must be peaceful. Landlords may not use violence or force to retake the premises. If the tenant objects to the landlord's actions, the landlord must leave and resort to judicial processes to evict the tenant.

Type	Definition	Example	Termination
Tenancy for years	Lasts for a fixed period	"Lease of apartment for six months"	Ends at the end of the stated tenancy period (such as at the end of the sixth month)
Periodic tenancy	Tenancy for a fixed period that automatically continues for succeeding periods until either party gives notice of termination	"Lease of apartment on a month-to-month basis"	Ends by notice from one party to the other, given at least as far ahead as the length of the period
Tenancy at will	Tenancy of no fixed duration; lasts as long as the landlord and tenant agree	"Lease of apartment for as long as either party desires"	Ends as soon as one party terminates the tenancy
Tenancy at sufferance	Tenant wrongfully stays in possession after the termination of a tenancy	Tenant's lease expires on May 1, but tenant wrongfully stays in the apartment after the lease has expired	Terminated when the landlord evicts the tenant, the tenant leaves, or a new lease is executed

FIGURE 14.1. Types of Tenancies

Rental Rates

Rent is the amount of money a tenant pays a landlord to use and possess the property. Rental rates usually differ substantially between residential and commercial leases. Residential leases usually have a fixed monthly rental amount. However, commercial leases can vary considerably and often require the tenant to pay a larger share of the property's operating and maintenance costs.

Factors That Influence Rental Rates

Rental rates are generally influenced by the following factors:

- Location of the property
- Rental rate charged for similar properties in the area
- Vacancy rates in the area
- Proposed use of the premises
- Length of the lease term
- Rent control ordinance limitations

Types of Rental Rates

The most common types of rental rate terms include the following:

1. Gross lease
2. Percentage lease
3. Triple net lease (NNN)

Gross Lease

Gross lease
A lease in which the tenant pays a fixed amount.

In a **gross lease**, the tenant pays a fixed monthly amount. The landlord pays for the real estate taxes, insurance, and maintenance of the property. Because rent is fixed each month, the landlord becomes responsible for any increases in utility costs throughout the term of the lease. Gross leases are quite common in residential leases but are not common in commercial leases. A gross lease may be stated as a cost per square foot or given as a fixed sum for the unit or property.

Example: A 650-square-foot space may be priced at $1.85 per square foot per month.

Gross leases may be modified to include costs in addition to the fixed monthly rent. Landlords often require tenants to pay for utility costs. Where the tenant pays a fixed rate each month, as well as a share of other costs of operating the property, the lease is a **modified gross lease**. For example, an office tenant may pay $350 per month plus a percentage of the electricity cost each month.

Percentage lease
A lease in which the tenant pays a fixed base rent amount plus a percentage of sales earned by the business.

Percentage Lease

In a **percentage lease**, the tenant pays a fixed base rent and a percentage of the sales earned from the business. Percentage leases are often used in retail tenancies. The percentage lease may be calculated on gross sales or net sales. If net sales are used, the lease should define how net sales are calculated to avoid any ambiguity in the lease.

While a landlord may require a percentage on all sales, usually the percentage of sales payments begin after the business meets a certain sales threshold. The landlord receives a percentage of the revenue above the sales threshold. As part of the rental amount is based on the business's sales, the landlord requires the tenant to disclose its financial records and to allow the landlord to verify and audit the sales amount. The percentage of sales may be paid monthly, quarterly, or yearly depending on the lease requirements

Triple Net Lease

Under **triple net leases** (NNN leases) the tenant pays the landlord a fixed gross amount each month and also pays for the property's operating costs. Operating costs include the property taxes, property insurance, and property maintenance. The tenant is solely responsible for all the property's operating costs. Because the tenant is covering costs that the landlord would otherwise pay, the base rent under an NNN lease is lower than that under a gross lease.

> **Triple net lease**
> A lease in which the tenant pays the landlord a fixed gross amount each month and also pays for the property's operating costs (property taxes, property insurance, and property maintenance).

Rental Rate Increases

A landlord and a tenant can agree to rental rate increases in a lease. The lease may provide that the rent will increase by a set percentage in the future (for example, "rent shall increase by five percent (5%) on the first of the year") or by an indexed rate. An **indexed rate** is a rate tied to a cost of living index or similar index (such as the consumer price index (CPI)). Tying a rental increase to an indexed rate protects the landlord during periods of high inflation.

Rent Control

Many cities have enacted rent control ordinances. **Rent control** is price regulation imposed on landlords. It consists of setting rental rates and regulating leases to provide affordable housing options to tenants. Cities can control the degree to which and how often rent can be increased and can limit late fees and the total amount chargeable to a tenant. Usually, landlords can raise the rent only when the tenant has decided not to renew the lease and has vacated the premises. In addition, many cities place restrictions on the landlord's ability to evict tenants.

> **Rent control**
> Local ordinances that can regulate and restrict a landlord's ability to increase rent and other fees.

Some rent control ordinances exempt luxury housing units. Other ordinances may exempt substantially rehabilitated housing units that have met required costs of renovation or have been repaired to meet housing code standards.

Legal Challenges to Rent Control Ordinances

Many challenges to rent control ordinances have been raised, but the Supreme Court has ruled that rent control advances a legitimate public purpose and is lawful. Rent control laws will be upheld so long as the landlord receives a reasonable rate of return on the investment.[2] The effect of this decision is that local rent control ordinances may supersede rental agreements on such things as maximum rent increases and grounds for eviction.

Writing Requirements

Creating a lease requires no formal words or special language. Oral leases are permissible so long as they do not violate the Statute of Frauds. Many states permit oral lease agreements with a duration of one year or less. An oral lease for a term exceeding one year is not legally enforceable in most states because the state's Statute of Frauds will require that the lease be in writing.

When a lease is required to be in writing according to the Statute of Frauds, it must do the following:

1. Provide the names and signatures of the parties
2. Adequately describe the leased property
3. Identify the term (duration) of the lease
4. State the amount of rent to be paid

The writing need not take the form of a formal written lease. Leases may be handwritten and may be notated on any type of material (even a napkin). The writing requirement for a lease may be satisfied by a single document or a series of documents (such as emails). One important required element is that the writing must be signed by the party against whom enforcement is sought. For this reason, both parties must have — and request, if necessary — a fully executed copy of the lease.

Example: If a tenant sues a landlord for breach of the lease, the landlord must have signed a writing indicating the lease and its terms. Likewise, if the landlord wants to enforce a breach of the lease against the tenant, the tenant must have signed a writing indicating the lease and its terms.

Common Lease Provisions

Leases may provide a variety of provisions. Some of these provisions include the following: provisions limiting the use of the premises, common area maintenance, security deposits, maintenance and repairs, and the like. Unless identified or distinguished below, the following provisions apply to both residential and commercial leases.

Premises

The lease will describe the premises to be rented by the tenant. The **premises** are the actual space or property to be occupied by the tenant. The tenant will have exclusive use of the premises and a right to use the common areas covered by the lease. The street address and location of the property should be described. If the lease involves large spaces, or if the property is part of a larger project, a survey may be necessary to verify that the description of the premises is consistent with the survey.

Possession

Possession usually begins on the day the lease commences. A lease may provide the tenant the right to take early possession of the property without the obligation to pay rent. This may arise when a tenant desires to complete tenant improvements before the commencement date of the lease. When a property is being constructed, possession may occur months after the execution of the lease to allow for the completion of construction.

Rent

The landlord has the right to collect rent, even if the amount of rent is not stated in the lease. In that situation, courts will infer that the tenant must pay a reasonable amount of rent at the end of the term.

> *Example:* If the landlord states the amount of the security deposit but fails to state an amount of rent in the landlord's preprinted lease agreement form, the courts will imply that the tenant must pay a reasonable amount of rent.

When the lease does not state the day on which rent is due, the rent obligation does not arise until the last day of the rental period. Thus, rent is not due in advance of the rental period unless stated in the lease.

> *Example:* If a month-to-month periodic tenancy had a rental provision of $750 each month and did not provide a date on which rent was payable to the landlord, the rent would be due at the end of the month (that is, at the end of each rental period).

Common Area Maintenance

Many commercial leases require the tenant to pay a prorated share of the common area expenses. These expenses are known as **common area maintenance** (CAM) payments. The charges can include anything that the parties agree to, but they often include such items as the costs of common area utilities, marketing and advertising expenses, elevator expenses, landscaping expenses, building renovation costs, maintenance costs, and so on.

Common area maintenance (CAM)
A pro rata share of costs a tenant is required to pay for common area expenses. Frequently found in commercial leases.

Use

The lease should provide the purpose for which the tenant intends to use the property. Tenants desire freedom of use in their tenancy and often request that their use be broadly defined as "any lawful purpose." Landlords, however, will want to specifically define the uses allowed by the tenant on the premises.

> *Example:* The agreed use of the property shall be for general office space.

Deposits

Landlords often require tenants to make an advance payment to cover certain expenses or costs that may be incurred by the landlord when the tenant vacates. These advance payments are known as **deposits**. States often regulate the collection and use of deposits for residential leases more than they do for commercial leases. Usually there are few, if any, restrictions on a landlord's ability to obtain deposits from commercial tenants, who are thought to be more sophisticated than residential tenants and thus not in need of the statutory protections that residential tenants may require.

Security Deposits

Security deposit
A type of deposit used to protect landlords and that covers expenses for any damage caused to the property or damages suffered because of a tenant's nonperformance of obligations under a lease.

One common type of deposit is the **security deposit**, an advance payment used to protect the landlord from damage the tenant causes to the property or to compensate the landlord for lost rent if the tenant vacates before the term of the lease or fails to pay the amount owed under the lease.

State law may limit the amount of the security deposit and the purposes to which the security deposit may be applied. Many state laws govern the period for refunding unused portions of the deposits, whether the tenant must receive an itemized record demonstrating that use of the security deposit was required, and whether accrued interest must be paid to the tenant on the security deposit.

Prepaid Rent

Another form of deposit sometimes required at the beginning of the lease term is prepaid rent. With prepaid rent, the landlord can require that the tenant pay the first and last months' rent, several months' rent, or a combination of the two. Many states limit the total amount of money a tenant must pay for deposits. This limitation may include amounts sought for prepaid rent.

Lease Guaranty

A landlord may require that a third party guarantee the tenant's performance of the lease. When a rental application indicates that the prospective tenant may have insufficient income or assets to make the monthly payments on a lease, a landlord may require that a third party guarantee the lease payments. When a corporation leases a property, the landlord may require that a shareholder, principal, or officer of a corporation personally guarantee the lease obligations.

Maintenance and Repairs

Unless the lease requires that a tenant correct defects, a tenant has no general duty to correct defective conditions on the premises. On termination of the tenancy, however, the tenant must return the property to the landlord in the same condition it was in when the lease began, except for ordinary wear and tear.

> **Example:** Assume a tenant leased space for four years and was provided new carpeting at the beginning of the lease. At the end of the four years, the law requires the tenant to return the premises in the same condition as when it was leased, except for ordinary wear and tear. If the carpeting was supposed to last for seven years and had been excessively worn in those four years, the tenant will be responsible for the excessive damage to the carpet.

In essence, tenants must protect the premises from damage so that their possession does not substantially harm the property. Tenants may also face eviction if they fail to make required repairs.

In commercial leases, it is common for a landlord to require a tenant, at the tenant's expense, to maintain and repair the premises. Commercial landlords commonly require tenants to maintain and repair the plumbing, HVAC equipment, electrical systems and lighting, interior and exterior walls, ceilings, floors, windows, doors, and roof.

Waste

If the tenant damages the property, he or she is liable to the landlord for **waste**. To recover for waste, the damage must be extraordinary and beyond ordinary wear and tear. The landlord can recover from the tenant the cost to repair waste.

Waste
Destruction, harm, or injury caused to real property by a person in possession of the property.

Notice of Repair

When a tenant discovers a defective condition that it is the landlord's responsibility to repair, the tenant must provide the landlord with notice of the condition. The tenant must allow the landlord a reasonable opportunity to make the needed repairs.

Alterations

Both residential and commercial leases will often prohibit alterations to the premises without the written consent of the landlord. This allows the landlord to secure appropriate insurance, review the qualifications of the contractor, and protect itself from mechanic's liens and other remedies a contractor may seek against a landlord. (Mechanic's liens are discussed in chapter 20.)

Noncompetition Clauses in Commercial Leases

Commercial landlords and tenants may create a lease that includes noncompetition clauses. A noncompetition clause is a covenant prohibiting the landlord from leasing to another tenant in the same or a similar business as the tenant.

> **Example:** A landlord may covenant to a grocery store that the grocery store will be the sole retailer of food, alcohol, and bakery products within a given shopping center.

Landlords may also insert competitive restrictions on tenants by prohibiting or restricting them from doing similar business within a certain radius of the leased premises. If the tenant does operate within that radius, the sales generated within the described radius may be added to the store's sales, with the tenant agreeing to pay a percentage rent on the total. In this way, the landlord's rent is not jeopardized by the tenant's desire to operate from a cheaper or more desirable location.

Tenant Rights and Landlord Duties

Implied Warranty of Habitability

Historically, the common law did not imply that premises would be fit for the purposes intended. Tenants took premises "as is." Today, most states provide that residential (not commercial) leases are subject to an **implied warranty of habitability**. Generally, this duty requires landlords to provide premises that are fit, safe, and suitable for basic human habitation. States do not allow a tenant to waive the implied warranty of habitability in a lease. Generally, the duties imposed upon the landlord require the following:

Implied warranty of habitability
An implied warranty requiring landlords to provide premises that are habitable. Landlords warrant they will make the premises fit for habitation if they are not.

- The landlord must maintain safe and sanitary common areas (elevators, garages, and stairways).

- The landlord must provide basic living conditions in the leased premises, including proper plumbing, running water, and lockable doors and windows.
- The landlord must fix known latent (hidden) defects or other dangers that are not easily discovered by an ordinary inspection.
- The landlord must maintain the premises so as not to violate building or fire code regulations.

Tenants' Remedies for Breach of the Implied Warranty of Habitability

Failure to maintain the premises in a safe and sanitary condition is a material breach of the lease. The tenant may terminate the lease and abandon the premises. Alternatively, the tenant may continue the lease and sue for damages. The measure of damages will usually be a rent reduction for the difference between the fair market rental value of habitable premises and the fair market value of the premises in their current uninhabitable condition. The tenant may also cancel the lease for a condition of continuing uninhabitability.

In some states, a "repair and deduct" remedy is available. If the landlord fails to repair a material condition affecting the habitability of the premises after reasonable notice, the tenant may use a reasonable amount of rent to repair the defective condition.

> *Example:* In California, the tenant may expend up to one month's rent for such repairs and may use this remedy no more than twice in a one-year period.[3]

The following case discusses the notice requirement when determining if there is a breach of the warranty of habitability.

CASE 14.1

PRIOR NOTICE TO LANDLORD REQUIRED FOR BREACH OF WARRANTY OF HABITABILITY

TERRY v. O'BRIEN
134 A.3d 203 (2015)
Vermont Supreme Court

Timothy and Penny Terry ("Terry") rented a property owned by William and Susan O'Brien ("O'Brien"). The parties agreed orally that Terry would pay monthly rent. During the lease, a fire started in the attic of the house, resulting in heavy fire damage to one of the bedrooms, as well as smoke and/or water damage to the other rooms. A fire investigator concluded that the fire began due to overuse of the older electrical system and the improper installation of insulation.

Terry filed a complaint alleging breach of warranty of habitability. At trial, the jury determined the O'Briens had breached the warranty of habitability by renting an unsafe residence. The court determined that the O'Briens were not entitled to any unpaid rent due to their breach of the warranty of habitability.

The O'Briens appealed to the Supreme Court of Vermont. They argued the trial court erred by instructing the jury that prior notice of a latent defect was not required to trigger the warranty.

Language of the Court. *To bring a cause of action for breach of the implied warranty of habitability, the tenant must show that: (1) the landlord had notice of the previously unknown defect and failed, within a reasonable period of time, to repair it; and (2) the defect, affecting habitability, existed during* *the time for which rent was withheld. The trial court's ruling must be reversed because of our vacation of the jury's verdict in favor of tenants with respect to their statutory warranty of habitability claim. Absent their habitability claim, there is no basis for Terry to withhold rent.*

Decision. The Supreme Court of Vermont reversed, finding the O'Briens did not have notice of the defect; and Terry could not sue under the implied warranty of habitability.

FOCUS ON ETHICS

Should tenants be required to pay landlords for uninhabitable spaces, if the tenants are unaware that the premises are not habitable?

Application to Commercial Leases

The implied warranty of habitability does not apply in commercial leases. This trend follows from the reality that residential tenants frequently do not have the skills or resources necessary to identify whether the premises are fit for use.

A few state courts are beginning to recognize an implied covenant of suitability (fitness for the purpose of the intended use) at the time the commercial tenant enters into the lease. This covenant is similar to the implied warranty of habitability found in residential leases. With this warranty, the landlord covenants that the leased premises are free from latent defects in regard to the essential facilities needed by that commercial tenant. Unlike a residential implied warranty of habitability, commercial tenants can waive the implied covenant of suitability.

Covenant of Quiet Enjoyment

The landlord impliedly promises the tenant the right to use and enjoy possession of the premises without the landlord's interference. Even if this covenant is not expressly stated in the lease, it is implied in every lease. The covenant of quiet enjoyment protects the tenant from the following.

1. Landlord interference with the tenant's possession of the property.

Example: If the tenant is not in breach of the terms of the lease and the landlord changes the access codes to the premises or the locks, the landlord has breached the tenant's covenant of quiet enjoyment.

2. Any acts that substantially threaten or actually interfere with the beneficial enjoyment of the premises.

Example: A landlord who does not undertake reasonable measures to remedy substantial annoyances caused by neighboring tenants may have breached the covenant of quiet enjoyment.

Duties of Landlords Under the Uniform Residential Landlord and Tenant Act (URLTA)

Section 2.104(a) of the URLTA provides for the following duties for landlords:

(1) Comply with the requirements of applicable building and housing codes materially affecting health and safety;

(2) Make all repairs and do whatever is necessary to put and keep the premises in a fit and habitable condition;

(3) Keep all common areas of the premises in a clean and safe condition;

(4) Maintain in good and safe working order and condition all electrical, plumbing, sanitary, heating, ventilating, air-conditioning, and other facilities and appliances, including elevators, supplied or required to be supplied by the landlord;

(5) Provide and maintain appropriate receptacles and conveniences for the removal of ashes, garbage, rubbish, and other waste incidental to the occupancy of the dwelling unit and arrange for their removal; and

(6) Supply running water and reasonable amounts of hot water at all times and reasonable heat [between [October 1] and [May 1]], except where the building that includes the dwelling unit is not required by law to be equipped for that purpose, or the dwelling unit is so constructed that heat or hot water is generated by an installation within the exclusive control of the tenant and supplied by a direct public utility connection.[4]

Tenant Remedies

Where the landlord breaches the lease with the tenant, the tenant can often choose among several remedies against the landlord. The tenant can (i) file a lawsuit against the landlord, (ii) withhold rent from the landlord, (iii) repair the issue and deduct the costs of the repair from the rent owed the landlord, (iv) abate the rent, or (v) terminate the lease.

The tenant can file a lawsuit against the landlord to fix the problem on the premises. While a tenant has this option, for many landlord breaches, suing the landlord would be too costly and time consuming. The tenant may also withhold rent from a landlord until the landlord fulfills its obligations under the lease. Once the landlord has done so, the tenant must then pay the landlord the withheld rent.

> *Example:* If the tenant and landlord agreed that the landlord would replace the air conditioner within one month of the tenant taking possession and the landlord fails to replace timely the air conditioner, the tenant may withhold rent payments until the landlord replaces the air conditioner. One the landlord has replaced the air conditioner, the tenant must pay the landlord the rent withheld.

Where the landlord has failed to maintain the tenant's premises as required under a lease, and the tenant has given the landlord notice, the tenant may repair the defect and deduct the cost of repair on the rent payment. The tenant can only deduct the repair costs for damages not caused by the tenant or the tenant's occupants and is usually limited to deducting up to one month's rent toward the repair.

> *Example:* If the garbage disposal in the kitchen sink has stopped working and the maintenance and repair was the responsibility of the landlord, the tenant may be able to hire a plumber, fix the problem, and deduct the costs of the repair on the tenant's rent.

A tenant may also be entitled to abate the rent. When a tenant abates the rent, it pays a reduced amount of rent. The reduced amount of rent is the value of the premises in the condition it is in because of the lack of maintenance and repair.

> *Example:* Assume a tenant rents a 5,000-square-foot commercial warehouse and because of a flood, 1,000 square feet become unusable. The tenant would only be responsible for paying for 80 percent of the rent due to abatement.

A tenant may be **constructively evicted**. In circumstances where the landlord substantially interferes with the tenant's use and enjoyment of the premises, the tenant may terminate the lease, vacate the premises, and be excused from further rent liability.

A tenant claiming constructive eviction must give notice to the landlord and must vacate the premises. If the tenant remains on the premises, no eviction has occurred, and the lease obligations continue. The tenant must abandon the premises within a reasonable time after the interference by the landlord; otherwise, the tenant will have waived the right to object to the interferences.

What constitutes a substantial interference depends on the purposes for which the premises were leased, the foreseeability of the type of interference encountered, the frequency and duration of the interference, and the nature of the harm caused.

> *Example:* If the landlord begins the construction of another apartment building adjacent to a tenant's premises, the constant noise generated by the construction may give rise to a constructive eviction. Courts would more likely find constructive eviction if the tenant was not made fully aware of the anticipated construction prior to entering into the lease.

Constructive eviction
A wrongful eviction in which the tenant may terminate the lease, vacate the premises, and be excused from further rent liability.

Generally, the interference must arise from the wrongful acts of the landlord and not from the actions of a third person, such as another tenant. The landlord's failure to act is essential to this breach of covenant. The landlord is responsible for ensuring that public nuisances (such as drug dealing) do not occur on the premises. Public nuisances can create a constructive eviction situation.

Landlord Rights and Tenant Duties

Landlord's Right to Access the Premises

Tenants have the exclusive right to possess the leased premises during the tenancy. The landlord's right to access the premises is limited. The parties may agree in the lease regarding when access is permissible and what, if any, notice is required to the tenant before the landlord may enter the premises. If states have adopted the URLTA, section

3.103 of the Act in pertinent part provides the landlord the right to access the premises as follows:

(a) A tenant shall not unreasonably withhold consent to the landlord to enter into the dwelling unit in order to inspect the premises, make necessary or agreed repairs, decorations, alterations, or improvements, supply necessary or agreed services, or exhibit the dwelling unit to prospective or actual purchasers, mortgagees, tenants, workmen, or contractors.

(b) A landlord may enter the dwelling unit without consent of the tenant in case of emergency.

(c) Except in case of emergency or unless it is impracticable to do so, the landlord shall give the tenant at least two days' notice of intent to enter and may enter only at reasonable times.

Landlord's Rights to Cure Tenant Defaults

The landlord has the right to cure and perform obligations of the tenant where the tenant fails to perform those obligations. The landlord can also demand that the tenant pay for these costs. Where a tenant fails to perform its obligations, the landlord may seek to perform those obligations to prevent the property from falling into further disrepair or causing further harm to other parts of the property.

> *Example:* If a commercial tenant was responsible for maintaining the premises, and the tenant became aware of a roof leak and did nothing to fix it, the landlord may hire a roofer to fix leaks in the roof and demand the tenant pay for the costs of the repair.

■ ■ ■ Residential Lease

THIS RESIDENTIAL LEASE ("Lease") is made effective as of the _____ day of _____ by and between _____("LESSOR") and _____ ("LESSEE") and "the Parties" collectively.

Recitals

A. LESSOR owns the single family residence located at _____ ("Leased Premises").

B. LESSEE desires to lease the Leased Premises upon the terms and conditions set forth herein.

C. LESSOR enters into this Lease relying upon the truthfulness of the information LESSEE provided in his/her/their application to lease to LESSOR.

NOW THEREFORE, the Parties agree as follows:

1. Recitals. The foregoing recitals are incorporated herein as if set forth in full.

2. Lease. LESSOR, for and in consideration of the rents and covenants herein specified to be paid and performed by LESSEE, LESSOR hereby leases to LESSEE, and LESSEE hereby hires from LESSOR, on the terms and conditions and for the purposes herein set forth, that certain real property commonly known as the "Leased Premises."

3. <u>Term</u>. The term of this Lease shall be a month to month tenancy commencing at 12:01 a.m. on _____. If LESSOR for any reason cannot deliver possession of the Leased Premises to LESSEE at the commencement of the term hereof, LESSOR shall not be liable to LESSEE for any loss or damage resulting therefrom, but there shall be a proportionate reduction of rent. If for any reason the Leased Premises cannot be delivered within ten (10) days of the lease commencement date, then LESSEE may elect to declare this Lease null and void and all money paid to LESSOR shall thereupon be refunded to LESSEE.

4. <u>Rent</u>.

    a.   <u>Amount</u>. LESSEE agrees to pay LESSOR as rent for the Leased Premises for each month during the term of this Lease the sum of _____ Dollars ($_____) ("Rent").

    b.   <u>Payment</u>. All Rent shall be paid monthly, in advance, and delivered on the first day of each calendar month, without deduction or offset, at the address noted below or at such other place(s) as LESSOR may designate in writing. LESSEE acknowledges that LESSOR need not send notices or invoices as a condition to LESSEE's payment of Rent due under this Lease. Receipt of the sum of _____ Dollars ($_____) is hereby acknowledged which shall be Rent for the period of _____, through _____.

    c.   <u>Service Charges</u>. LESSOR shall be entitled to collect a late charge of _____ Dollars ($_____) on any Rent received after the due date. LESSOR shall be entitled to assess and collect a Twenty-Five Dollar ($25.00) charge for administrative costs whenever a check for Rent is returned from the bank to LESSOR unpaid for any reason. Such late charge shall be considered an additional item of rent under the terms of this Lease.

    d.   <u>Interest</u>. LESSOR shall be entitled to collect interest on all unpaid rent at the maximum legal rate of interest for the period when LESSEE's rent is due and unpaid.

5. <u>Security Deposit</u>. LESSEE deposits with LESSOR the sum of _____ Dollars ($_____), receipt of which is hereby acknowledged, as a Security Deposit for the performance by LESSEE of the provisions of this Lease. LESSOR may use therefrom such amounts as are necessary to remedy LESSEE's defaults in the payment of Rent, to repair damage to the Leased Premises caused by LESSEE or LESSEE's guests and invitees, or others coming into the Leased Premises with or without LESSEE's consent, excluding ordinary wear and tear, to replace any key(s) not returned to LESSOR by LESSEE, or to cause such cleaning work to be accomplished as LESSOR deems necessary and appropriate to the Leased Premises upon the termination of the tenancy. If used toward Rent or damages, LESSEE shall reinstate the Security Deposit so as to maintain the Security Deposit in the sum initially deposited with LESSOR, upon receipt of five (5) days' written notice.

6. <u>End of Term Obligations</u>. Upon surrender of the Leased Premises and all fixtures, equipment and keys in good working order, repair and clean condition, provided LESSEE is not then in default under this Lease and has paid all sums due pursuant thereto, LESSOR shall return the balance of the Security Deposit, if any, together with an itemized written accounting to LESSEE at LESSEE's last known address. LESSOR

shall be under no obligation to pay interest on or maintain the Security Deposit separate and apart from LESSOR's general funds.

    7. <u>Use and Occupancy</u>.

    a.   <u>Use and Occupancy</u>. The Leased Premises shall be occupied by no more than four adults and shall be utilized solely and exclusively for residential purposes and for no other purpose without LESSOR's prior written consent. No more than two automobiles may be parked in the driveway at any one time. LESSEE shall not park, store or allow the continued placement of any boat, recreational vehicle, automobile (whether operable or otherwise) upon the premises without LESSOR's prior written consent.

    b.   <u>Pets</u>. LESSEE will not keep, or permit to be kept, in the Leased Premises any dog, cat, parrot, or other kind of bird, animal, or reptile of any kind, or an aquarium.

    c.   <u>Uses Not Permitted</u>. LESSEE agrees: (i) not to use, or permit the use of, the Leased Premises or any part thereof for any purpose or use in violation of any law, ordinance, or regulation of any governmental authority or in any manner that will constitute waste or nuisance or which may disturb the quiet enjoyment of any other resident or occupant of the building in which the Leased Premises is located, or of any adjoining or neighboring property; (ii) not to do, suffer, or permit any act to be done which will increase the existing rate of insurance upon the building in which the Leased Premises is located, or any part thereof, or violate any provisions of or cause the cancellation, suspension, or other inoperativeness of any insurance policy covering the building or any part thereof; (iii) not to keep, or permit to be kept, items and articles prohibited by the standard form of fire insurance policy; and (iv) not to use, or permit the Leased Premises or any part thereof to be used, in any way that will injure, impair, or affect the structural strength of the Leased Premises by virtue of the weight or vibration of machinery, or otherwise. The use or location of water beds or other liquid-filled furniture, air conditioning or other heating units, belonging to the LESSEE and located within the Leased Premises, are expressly prohibited unless their use is authorized in writing by LESSOR before installation thereof.

    8. <u>Repairs and Alterations</u>. LESSEE shall not make or permit to be made any alterations, decorations, improvements, or additions to the Leased Premises, or any part thereof, without the prior written consent of LESSOR, except such repairs, if any, as LESSEE is reuqired to make by the provisions of this Lease. Decoration is deemed to include, without limitation, painting, wallpapering, hanging of murals, or posters. LESSEE agrees not to change or add any lock to the Leased Premises without the prior written consent of LESSOR. Any additions or alterations to the Leased Premises except movable furniture, shall become at once a part of the realty and belong to the LESSOR, unless prior to termination of occupancy, LESSOR gives LESSEE written notice to remove some or all of such additions or alterations, in which case LESSEE shall cause the items so designated to be removed and the Leased Premises to be restored to their original condition, all at the expense of LESSEE.

    9. <u>Maintenance</u>. LESSEE shall maintain all lawns, landscaping, pool and at LESSEE's sole expense. LESSOR shall maintain the exterior of the Leased Premises, including the roof, doors, and windows. LESSOR shall maintain a service contract for the maintenance and repair of the heating, ventilation and air conditioning sytems.

10. <u>Utilities</u>. LESSEE shall during the term hereof pay all charges for telephone, gas, electricity, cable and or satellite reception and water used in or on the Leased Premises, and for the removal of rubbish therefrom. Placement of all satellite dishes are subject to the LESSOR's prior approval.

11. <u>Conditions, Covenants, and Restrictions</u>. LESSEE shall abide by, and not act in violation of, any Conditions, Covenants, and Restrictions which may have been adopted by any representative homeowner's association, or governmental or quasigovernmental body having jurisdiction over the Leased Premises, and which Conditions, Covenants, and Restrictions have application to the owner or resident of the Leased Premises. LESSOR shall present a copy of any such Conditions, Covenants, and Restrictions to LESSEE within five (5) days after the commencement of the term of this Lease.

12. <u>Surrender at Termination</u>.

    a.   <u>Month-to-Month Lease</u>. If this Lease has a month-to-month term, then it may be terminated at any time by either party hereto by giving to the other party not less than thirty (30) days' notice in writing prior to the date upon which the lease is tp be terminated.

    b.   <u>Lease Agreement</u>. If the term of this Lease is other than month-to-month, LESSEE shall give LESSOR at least thirty (30) days' written notice of LESSEE's intention to vacate (the Leased Premises upon the expiration of the term of this Lease, or at the option of LESSOR, this Lease shall continue on a month-to-month basis under the terms and conditions stated herein, and LESSOR shall continue to hold the deposits set forth herein.

13. <u>Delivery</u>. Upon termination of this Lease, the Leased Premises shall be delivered to LESSOR in as good condition as that in which they were received by LESSEE from LESSOR, reasonable use and wear and damage by act of God, fire, earthquake, war, riot, insurrection or sudden violent action of the elements beyond the control of LESSEE excepted. LESSEE shall not vacate or abandon the Leased Premises at any time, and if LESSEE shall abandon, vacate, or surrender the Leased Premises or be dispossessed by process of law or otherwise, any personal property belonging to LESSEE and left on the Leased Premises shall, at the option of LESSOR, be deemed abandoned.

14. <u>Abandonment</u>. When LESSEE is in default under the terms of this Lease, LESSEE's failure to actually and continually occupy the Leased Premises for a period of seven (7) consecutive days without the LESSOR's consent in writing, may, at LESSOR's option, be deemed an abandonment of the Leased Premises. Upon abandonment LESSOR may dispose of all personal property left on the Leased Premises in any manner LESSOR shall deem proper, and LESSOR is hereby relieved of any liability therefor.

15. <u>Holding Over</u>. If LESSEE remains in possession of all or any part of the Leased Premises after the expiration of the term hereof, with or without the express or implied consent of LESSOR, such occupancy shall be from month-to-month only, and not a renewal hereof or an extension for any further term. LESSEE shall pay Rent during the hold over period at the rate of _____ Dollars ($_____) per month. All other monetary sums due hereunder shall be payable in the amount and at the time specified in this Lease. Month-to-month occupancy shall be subject to every other term, covenant and agreement contained herein.

16. <u>Non-Liability</u>. LESSOR shall not be liable to LESSEE or to any other person for or on account of any injury or damage of any kind whatsoever to persons or property occasioned in or about the Leased Premises or anywhere else, or resulting from any patent or latent defect, structural or otherwise, in the construction, condition or present

or future lack of repair of the Leased Premises, including the wiring and equipment thereof, or of the building or buildings where the Leased Premises are situated, or the sidewalk adjacent thereto.

17. <u>Indemnification</u>. LESSEE indemnifies LESSOR against and agrees to hold LESSOR harmless from any loss, damage, claim of damage, liability, or expense arising out of or resulting from any of the matters or events hereinabove specified and from any loss, damage, claim of damage, liability or expense arising out of or resulting from any damage or injury to any person or the property of any person arising from the use of the Leased Premises by LESSEE or by any other person by license or invitation of LESSEE, or from the failure of LESSEE in any respect to comply with any of the requirements or provision of this Lease, and from and against any expenses, including costs of litigation and reasonable attorneys fees, incurred in investigating, resisting, or compromising any claim asserted with respect to any of the foregoing.

18. <u>Entry By Lessor</u>. LESSOR reserves the right and LESSEE shall permit LESSOR, and the authorized representative of LESSOR, to enter into and upon the Leased Premises at all reasonable times for the purpose of maintaining the Leased Premises or the building of which the Leased Premises may be part, or for the purposes of exhibiting the Leased Premises to prospective residents or purchasers. Nothing herein contained shall imply any duty upon LESSOR to do any work which, under any provisions of this Lease, LESSEE may be required to perform and the performance thereof by LESSOR shall not consitute a waiver of LESSEE's default in failing to perform the same.

19. <u>Assignment And Subletting</u>. LESSEE shall not assign this Lease or any interest therein, and shall not sublet the Leased Premises or any part thereof or any right or privilege appurtenant thereto without the prior written consent of LESSOR. A consent to one assignment or subletting shall not be deemed to be a consent to any subsequent assignment or subletting. Any assignment of this Lease or of any right or interest therein, whether voluntary or involuntary, by operation of law, or otherwise, without the prior written consent of LESSOR; shall be null and void and shall, at the option of LESSOR, terminate this Lease immediately, together with all of LESSEE's rights hereunder.

20. <u>Impairment Of Use Of Premises</u>. In the event of destruction of the Leased Premises, or the building of which the Leased Premises are a part, or damage thereto by fire or any other casualty, LESSOR may, at his option, elect to terminate this Lease as of the date of such happening. In no case shall LESSEE be entitled to compensation or damages on account of any annoyance or inconvenience arising out of any destruction or damage or the repair thereof.

LESSOR shall not be liable for any damage occasioned by water being upon or coming through a opening of any nature in the building of which the Leased Premises are a part. In the event of any penetration of water, LESSEE shall promptly notify LESSOR. LESSEE shall use reasonable care to cause all windows and other openings in the Leased Premises to be closed in the event of rain. LESSOR shall not be liable, in damages or otherwise, for any failure or interruption of any utility service furnished to the Leased Premises, and no such interruption shall entitle LESSEE to cancel this Lease or to withhold or deduct Rent or other sums due hereunder.

21. <u>Insurance</u>.

    a.   <u>Lessor's insurance</u>. LESSOR agrees to and shall, at LESSOR's sole cost and expense, within ten (10) days from the date hereof, secure from a responsible company or companies doing insurance business in the State of _____, and maintain during the entire term of this Lease, the following insurance coverages, insuring its interests alone:

(a) Fire and extended coverage insurance in an amount not less than one hundred percent (100%) of the value of the Leased Premises, provided that insurance in that percentage can be obtained, and, if not, then to the highest percentage that can be obtained.

(b) Comprehensive public liability insurance in the minimum amount of _____ Dollars ($_____) for loss from a bodily injury to or death of a person, and _____ Dollars ($_____) for loss resulting from damage to or destruction of property.

b. <u>Lessee's insurance</u>. LESSEE will be solely responsible, at LESSEE's sole cost and expense, for obtaining and maintaining insurance coverage protecting against the loss, theft, destruction or damage to the personal property of LESSEE which is located on the Leased Premises. LESSOR shall expressly not be responsible or liable for any damage or loss suffered by LESSEE as a result of LESSEE's failure to obtain such insurance coverage, or for the damage, loss, destruction or theft of LESSEE's property which is not compensated by such insurance coverage. In the event of a covered loss, LESSEE's insurance shall be primary. LESSEE shall name LESSOR as an additional insured and such insurance shall waive the right of subrogation against LESSOR's insurance carriers.

22. <u>Remedies</u>. In the event of non-payment of Rent or other charges hereunder or in the event of the breach of any other provisions of this Lease by LESSEE, LESSOR, in addition to other rights and remedies LESSOR may have, shall have the immediate right, with or without terminating this Lease, to re-enter the Leased 'remises and to remove all persons and property from the Leased Premises. Such right shall include, but not be limited to, the right to store the property in a public warehouse or elsewhere at the cost and for the account of LESSEE. If LESSOR's right of reentry is exercised following abandonment of the Leased Premises by LESSEE, then LESSOR may consider any personal property left on the Leased Premises by LESSEE to also have been abandoned. If LESSEE should breach this Lease and abandon the Leased Premises, this Lease shall continue in effect so long as LESSOR does not terminate LESSEE's right to possession, and LESSOR may enforce all LESSOR's rights and remedies under this Lease including LESSOR's right to recover the Rent as it becomes due under this Lease.

23. <u>Waiver</u>. No covenant, term, or condition or the breach thereof shall be deemed waived, except by written consent of the party against whom the waiver is claimed, and any waiver of the breach of any covenant, term, or condition shall not be deemed to be a waiver of any other covenant, term, or condition. Acceptance by LESSOR of any performance by LESSEE after the time performance is due shall not constitute a waiver by LESSOR of the breach or default of any covenant, term, or condition unless otherwise expressly agreed to by LESSOR in writing.

24. <u>Joint Rental Responsibility</u>. The term "LESSEE" as used herein shall be construed to mean "LESSEES" whenever used in this Lease, and all such parties shall be jointly and severally liable for all rental payments set out in this Leasae and for all other sums due pursuant to this Lease, it being the understanding that each LESSEE shall be

individually liable for any and all payments made. Each LESSEE's community property (or property held in tenancy in the entirety, as the case may be) and separate property shall be liable for any sums due under this Lease.

25. <u>Acceptance of Premises</u>. LESSEE acknowledges that no warranties, express or implied, and no statements or representations not herein expressed, as to the past, present, or future condition or repair of the Leased Premises, or of any building of which the Leased Premises is a part, have been made by or on behalf of LESSOR. By taking possession hereunder, LESSEE acknowledges that the Leased Premises is ready for occupancy and in good and sanitary order, condition, and repair, and hereby waives any claim or right on account of the condition or repair of the Leased Premises. LESSEE shall pay LESSOR, on demand, for all loss, breakage, damage, and plumbing stoppages occuring during LESSEE's tenancy or occupancy of the Leased Premises.

26. <u>Notices</u>. Notice to LESSEE may be served at the Leased Premises. Notice to LESSOR may be served at _____. Notices shall be deemed given on the date postmarked by the United States Post Office, or upon personal delivery by either party hereto.

27. <u>Attorneys' Fees</u>. If any legal action or proceeding is brought by either party to enforce any part of this Lease, the prevailing party shall recover, in addition to all other relief, reasonable attorneys' fees and costs.

28. <u>Eminent Domain</u>.

   a. <u>Taking</u>. If the Leased Premises are taken under the power of eminent domain, or sold to any authority having the power of eminent domain either under threat of condemnation or while condemnation proceedings are pending, this Lease shall automatically terminate as of the date of the taking.

   b. <u>Awards</u>. Any award for any taking of all or any part of the Leased Premises shall be the property of LESSOR.

   c. <u>"Taking" Defined</u>. The "date of the taking" as used in this Paragraph 28 relative to an eminent domain proceeding shall mean the earlier of (i) final judgment (not subject to appeal or other relief) or (ii) the taking of possession of the Leased Premises.

29. <u>Quiet Enjoyment</u>. LESSOR covenants and agrees that LESSEE, upon paying the rent and all other charges herein provided for and observng and keeping all covenants, agreements, and conditions of this Lease on its part to be observed and kept, shall quietly have and enjoy the Leased Premises during the term of this Lease without hindrance or molestation by anyone claiming by or through LESSOR, subject, however, to the exceptions, reservations and conditions of this Lease.

30. <u>Partial Invalidity</u>. If any term or provison of this Lease or the application thereof to any person or circumstance shall, to any extent, be invalid or unenforceable, the remainder of this Lease shall be valid and enforced to the fullest extent permitted by law.

31. <u>Governing Law</u>. This Lease shall be construed and enforced in accordance with the laws of the State of _____.

32. <u>Entire Agreement; Attachments</u>. This Lease, along with the attachments indicated below and fully executed by LESSEE and LESSOR, constitutes the entire Lease between the parties. The Lease and the attachments thereto may be altered or amended only by an instrument in writing signed by both parties.

LESSOR

By: _____

Print Name and Title: _____

Address for payment of Rent: _____

LESSEE(s)

By: _____

Print Name: _____

By: _____

Print
Name: _____

Americans with Disabilities Act (ADA)

The Americans with Disabilities Act of 1990 (ADA), as amended by the Americans with Disabilities Act Amendments Act (ADAAA) of 2008, prohibits discrimination against disabled individuals. The Act is very important to landlords and tenants in the commercial setting, as it can become quite expensive for a party to comply with ADA provisions.

When Does the ADA Apply?

The ADA prohibits discrimination in places of public accommodation and commercial facilities. A **place of public accommodation** is a facility whose operation affects commerce; this includes places of lodging (hotels, motels, etc.), restaurants, theaters, shopping centers, grocery stores, office buildings, and professional offices.

> **Place of public accommodation**
> Businesses, buildings, or facilities open to or offering services to the general public.

What Does the ADA Require?

Where premises are covered under the ADA, the landlord or tenant responsible for them must make reasonable modifications for or accommodations to individuals with disabilities. This often requires new construction to be designed, constructed, and built in compliance with the Act's provisions. Moreover, improvements and alterations to an existing building must be made in compliance with the Act's provisions to the maximum extent feasible, unless the modification would create an undue burden (significant difficulty or expense). The nature of "an undue burden" is determined by considering the cost of the modification, the financial resources of the entity required to make the change, and the type of business operations conducted at the premises.

The Act requires the removal of barriers for persons with disabilities. These restraints can include architectural, structural, and communicational issues. Common examples of ways in which barriers must be removed include the following:

- Installing ramps
- Making curb cuts in sidewalks and entrances
- Widening doors
- Installing accessible door hardware
- Installing grab bars in toilet stalls
- Rearranging toilet partitions to increase maneuvering space
- Installing a tactile Braille restroom sign

Tenant Issues

Because of the substantial costs involved in complying with ADA provisions, commercial landlords often shift the burden to tenants. Tenants should make sure, in their due diligence prior to executing a lease, that they review the current premises for compliance with ADA provisions. If the premises are not in compliance, tenants may seek an offset in rent to fund the construction necessary to comply with ADA provisions or may require the landlord to make the necessary modifications.

Landlord's Tort Liability

A landlord is responsible to the tenant for the landlord's negligent acts and omissions toward the tenant. **Negligence** is conduct falling below the standard of care that a reasonable person would perform under similar circumstances. The landlord who fails to make the premises safe may be liable for the tort of negligence.

The damages that can be assessed from the landlord may exceed the amount of rent because damages recovered are intended to compensate the tenant for damages suffered. Landlords can obtain insurance to cover the risk of injury arising from the condition of the property. Those who can present claims for injuries or damages arising from the tenancy include tenants, their guests, and third parties.

The most common risks encountered by landlords include the following:

- Failing to disclose a dangerous condition about which the landlord knows or should have known and that the tenant will not discover.

    If disclosure is made to the tenant, the landlord's liability is either eliminated or reduced. The landlord will be responsible for addressing the risk posed by the defective condition, but any harm the tenant could have avoided by taking precautions is attributable to the tenant and not the landlord.
- Failing to exercise reasonable care over the maintenance of the common areas that remain under the landlord's control (such as stairwells and parking structures).
- Damages arising from negligent repairs. When the landlord undertakes to perform a repair, he must exercise reasonable care in performing the repair. Negligently performed repairs create a risk of harm to others, and the landlord is liable.

Landlord's Liability to Third Parties for Tenant's Activities

Generally, a landlord is not liable for a tenant's conduct. However, where a landlord has actual knowledge of the potential for injury and the potential for injury is foreseeable, the landlord may be liable to a third party for the injury.

> *Example:* The landlord is aware that a tenant possesses a pit bull. He has seen the pit bull act aggressively toward children at various times but has not said anything to the tenants or taken any other action regarding the dog. If the pit bull attacks a child and the child is injured, the landlord may face liability for failing to take reasonable steps to prevent the foreseeable injury.

Landlord's Liability for Criminal Acts by Third Parties

The landlord may also be held liable to a tenant injured by the criminal acts of third parties. If the crime was due to a landlord's negligence and the crime was reasonably foreseeable as a result of that negligence, the landlord may be liable to the tenant. Where the crime was not reasonably foreseeable or the landlord was not negligent, the landlord is usually relieved of liability for the criminal acts of third parties.

> *Example:* A negligent maintenance and repair of common area facilities exposes the landlord to damages by tenants and third parties. For example, if burglaries have taken place because of the landlord's failure to provide lockable entry doors to the property, the landlord will be liable for the stolen property.

Exculpatory Clause

Sometimes, landlords will attempt to insert into a lease a provision releasing them from some or all liability arising from the landlord's negligent acts that cause injury to tenants or tenants' guests. This provision is called an **exculpatory clause**. Many states hold that landlords cannot release themselves from liability for their own intentional or gross negligent acts.

Exculpatory clause
A contract provision that relieves a party (or both parties) from liability for ordinary negligent acts.

Lease Defaults and Evictions

When the tenant defaults under the terms of the lease, the landlord may evict the tenant through an **unlawful detainer** proceeding after giving notice and an opportunity for the tenant to cure the default. An unlawful detainer results in the termination of the lease. Common defaults under leases include the failure to pay or failure to timely pay rent, or the failure to abide by a covenant, term, or condition of the lease. In some jurisdictions, the judicial process for eviction is known as an **action for ejectment** (or summary ejectment, in other jurisdictions). At the conclusion of the unlawful detainer proceeding, the landlord is awarded damages for unpaid rent and possession of the premises is restored to the landlord.

When a tenant is in breach of the terms of the lease, the landlord must notify the tenant of the default and the reasons for the default (such as a demand for unpaid rent) and then give the tenant a reasonable time to cure the defaults. State laws control the notice requirements.

Unlawful detainer
A legal proceeding a landlord must use to evict a tenant.

Mitigation of Damages

Mitigation of damages
A legal doctrine requiring the nonbreaching and injured party to take reasonable steps to avoid or reduce damages.

When a tenant vacates the premises and refuses to pay further rent prior to the expiration of the lease, the landlord is required to **mitigate damages**. This doctrine requires a person who has suffered damages to take reasonable action to avoid additional injury or loss. The burden is upon the former tenant to show that the landlord did not mitigate.

> *Example:* If the tenant were to abandon the premises prior to the end of the term, the landlord would be required to seek a new tenant to mitigate the damages caused by the prior tenant.

In some states the landlord is not required to mitigate damages. These jurisdictions allow the landlord to treat the tenant's actions as a surrender of the premises. The landlord may reenter and take possession, and the tenant's rent obligation ceases.

> *Example:* When Kotis Properties sued its former tenant for breach of its lease, the defendants argued that Kotis had failed to mitigate its damages. The North Carolina Court of Appeals enforced the lease provisions that exempted the landlord from mitigating its damages. It awarded damages and attorney's fees to Kotis.[5]

Retaliatory Eviction

Retaliatory eviction
A wrongful eviction that occurs when the landlord retaliates against a tenant's good faith complaint.

Retaliatory eviction occurs when the landlord retaliates against a tenant who is exercising some right under the lease or by statute by evicting the tenant or refusing to renew the lease at the end of the lease term. Retaliatory evictions may arise after a tenant reports that the landlord has breached a covenant under the lease, violated the housing code, committed a tort, and so on. Most retaliatory evictions involve tenants' complaints about a housing code violation. A tenant in default or breach of the lease cannot assert a retaliatory eviction defense.

In the following case, a district court considered the relationship between the landlord's treatment of the tenant and the reasonableness of the tenant's withholding of rent.

CASE 14.2

RETALIATORY CONDUCT CAN DEFEAT A LANDLORD'S EVICTION PROCEEDING

KAYLA WEST v. DJ MORTGAGE, LLC
164 F.Supp.3d. 1393 (2016)
United States District Court for the Northern District of Georgia

Kayla West ("West"), a single mother of four children, emailed the landlord, DJ Mortgage, regarding its Craigslist advertisement for one of its rental units. Its property manager, Gene Andrews ("Andrews") responded on behalf of DJ Mortgage and agreed to rent the home to West. A few days later the two agreed to meet for West to sign the rental lease and obtain the key to the property from Andrews. During this meeting Andrews lifted West's skirt and inappropriately touched her. West slapped his hand away and left. However, West still rented the home from DJ Mortgage as she had already paid her rental deposit and was in need of a place for her and her four children to live.

After West moved into the home, any time she approached Andrews regarding repairs or an issue with the home, Andrews would ask her on a date or for nude pictures. Andrews grew tired of West's rejections and began ignoring her requests for repairs. West then wrote a letter to DJ Mortgage explaining the situation. DJ Mortgage did not respond for several weeks and continued to ignore West's requests for repairs. West then decided to withhold rent until improvements were made. This led DJ Mortgage to initiate an eviction proceeding against West, ultimately resulting in West's eviction.

West then filed a complaint alleging sexual discrimination and unlawful interference in violation of the Fair Housing Act. The court found in favor of the West despite DJ Mortgage's successful eviction proceeding.

Language of the Court. *DJ Mortgage's primary contention is that the conduct alleged is not sufficiently severe or pervasive to state a hostile housing environment claim. Simple teasing, offhand comments, and isolated incidents that are viewed only as annoying or offensive are not sufficiently severe or pervasive to support a FHA hostile housing environment claim. Even one act of harassment, if it is severe enough, may support a claim for sexual harassment. For example, direct contact of an intimate body part will support such a claim.*

These facts plausibly suggest that DJ Mortgage considered West a problem tenant because of her complaints about sexual harassment, failed to make crucial repairs to her home, and evicted her under the pretext of her withholding rent (which, to complete the circle, only started because of Andrews' sex-for-repairs harassment in the first place). This sort of retaliatory conduct is indicative of both interference and intent.

Discriminatory intent does not always wear a top hat, twirl its mustache and cane, and laugh maniacally like an out-in-the open super villain. West's claim appears more subtle. In essence, she alleges that the DJ Mortgage silently refused, during winter, to repair her furnace after she had accused its employee property manager of sexual harassment, compelling her to temporarily move to a hotel and withhold rent in response, and then evicting her.

Decision. The court found West's complaint was sufficient for her claim of sexual discrimination and violation of the Fair Housing Act.

FOCUS ON ETHICS

Why should the employer be held liable for the egregious behavior of its employee?

Selecting Tenants

Under common law, landlords were free to choose their tenants on any basis. Federal, state, and local laws have since inhibited the landlord's unrestricted choice of tenants. These laws now prohibit discrimination in the sale or rental of property.

Federal Laws

Two main federal laws operate regarding the selection of tenants. The Civil Rights Act of 1866 "prohibits all racial discrimination, private and public, in the sale and rental of property."[6] The second law is the Fair Housing Act (discussed in chapter 7). The Fair Housing Act provides everyone an equal opportunity to buy, rent, sell, and live in residential properties. The Act prohibits discrimination on the basis of race, color, religion, sex, handicap, familial status, or national origin.

In the following case, a prospective tenant petitioned for review of a Department of Housing and Development decision that found the landlord did not discriminate against the prospective tenant based on familial status.

CASE 14.3

DISCRIMINATION BASED ON FAMILIAL STATUS VIOLATED THE FAIR HOUSING ACT

WHITE v. U.S. DEPARTMENT OF HOUSING & URBAN DEVELOPMENT
475 F.3d 898 (2007)
United States Courts of Appeals for the Seventh Circuit

White was living with her grandfather and was looking for an apartment for herself and her two children. She saw a newspaper advertisement for a two-bedroom apartment for rent in Harvey, Illinois. White called and spoke to an elderly woman with broken English who stated she would not rent to White because White had children and was not married. White hung up before she obtained the woman's name.

Several weeks later, White saw another advertisement for the same apartment with the same number listed. She called again to ask about the apartment, and she alleges she spoke to the same elderly woman with broken English. This time White stated she was married rather than single, and she asked for the woman's name, which was Gertie Wooden. She claims that Gertie Wooden was the name that showed up on her caller ID after every phone call.

After the second telephone conversation White filed a complaint with the Dept. of Housing and Urban Development (HUD) alleging she was denied the opportunity to rent an apartment due to her marital and parental status. HUD concluded that White failed to show by a preponderance of evidence that Wooten violated the Fair Housing Act (FHA) because White failed to prove it was Wooten she spoke with during her first call. In its decision, HUD continued to reason that even if White could prove she had spoken with Wooten there was no proof the call violated the FHA because an ordinary listener would not believe the speaker discriminated against White based on her familial status, but would assume the denial to rent the apartment simply related to financial matters. White petitioned for review by the federal court of appeals.

Language of the Court. *It is illegal to "make, print, or publish, or cause to be made, printed, or published any notice, statement, or advertisement, with respect to the sale or rental of a dwelling that indicates any preference, limitation, or discrimination based on familial status or an intention to make any such preference, limitation, or discrimination." As a result, White needed to present evidence that: (1) Wooten made a statement; (2) the statement was made with respect to the sale or rental of a dwelling; and (3) the statement indicated a preference, limitation, or discrimination against her on the basis of her status as a parent living with minor children. The parties do not dispute that the statements were made in connection with the sale or rental of a dwelling.*

In the first telephone call, Wooten stated repeatedly that she would not rent to White because she had children but not a husband. Wooten's statements suggest that she would have been willing to rent to a single woman; because White stated she had children, however, Wooten told White she would not rent to her. We conclude that White has demonstrated that Wooten's statements indicate disfavor for her familial status because her statements would allow an "ordinary listener" to infer she had a preference against White due to her familial status.

Decision. The court of appeals reversed the HUD's ruling and found that the landlord discriminated against White on the basis of her familial status.

FOCUS ON ETHICS

What can landlords lawfully do to screen prospective tenants?

State Laws

Many states have enacted statutes prohibiting discrimination on grounds broader than those stated in the federal act.

> *Example:* Illinois's Human Rights Act prohibits discrimination based on race, color, religion, national origin, ancestry, age, sex, sexual orientation, marital status, familial status, or disability.[7]

Assignments and Subleases

Unless prohibited by a state statute or the lease, a tenant may assign the lease or sublet the rented premises without the landlord's consent. An assignment or sublease transfers some or all of the tenant's rights to the assignee.

Assignments

An **assignment** arises when a tenant, the **assignor**, transfers all of the tenant's unexpired lease to a third party, the **assignee**. The entire interest and the entire remaining duration of the lease must be transferred for an assignment. Leases usually prohibit assignments without the landlord's written consent. In such cases, if the tenant assigns her interest without the landlord's consent, the landlord may void the assignment and sue for damages. If the landlord knowingly accepts rent from the assignee, then the landlord has impliedly consented to the assignment, and any right to enforce the anti-assignment covenant is waived.

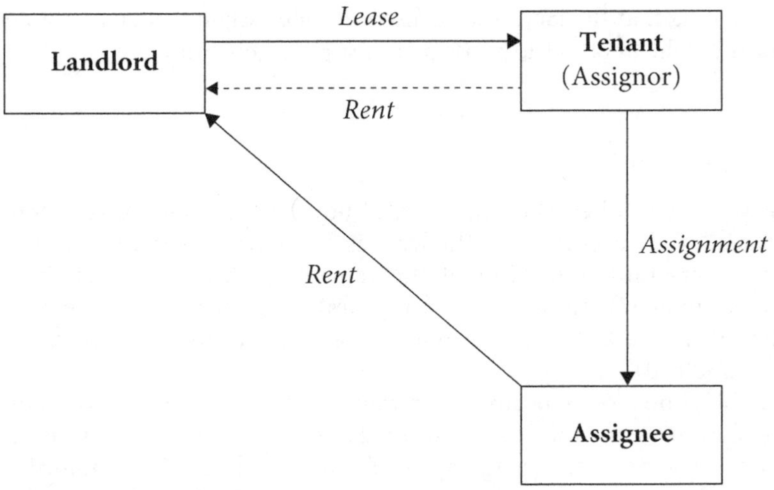

Assignment
A transfer of a tenant's unexpired lease to a third party.

Assignor
A tenant that transfers all his or her interests under a lease to a third party.

Assignee
A new tenant who received an assignment by an assignor.

FIGURE 14.2. Assignment of a Lease

Rights and Duties

With an assignment, the assignee takes the position that the tenant (assignor) had with the landlord. The assignee receives and owes no greater or lesser rights and duties than the tenant (assignor) had regarding the landlord; that is, the assignee takes over the rights and duties of the assignor, and the landlord can enforce those duties against the assignee. The tenant's obligations do not end with the assignment, however. The tenant continues to remain liable to the landlord if the assignee defaults in any of the duties owed under the lease. This allows the landlord to sue either the assignor or the assignee for any breach of a duty owed to the landlord. The landlord can release the assignor from liability and accept the assignee as having sole liability under the lease. This substitution is called a novation.

> **Example:** A tenant and landlord enter into a 12-month lease. After two months, the tenant's employer transfers him to another state. With the landlord's permission, the tenant assigns the lease's remaining ten months to a third party, the assignee. The assignee now has the rights and duties of the tenant and owes the landlord rent; the assignee also has the benefits of the rights owed by the landlord to the tenant. If the tenant breaches a covenant in the lease, the landlord can sue to collect from either the tenant or the assignee.

Rule in Dumpor's Case

Once a landlord consents to one assignment, does she or he waive objection to subsequent transfers? The **Rule in Dumpor's Case**[8] answers this question. The English court found that the landlord's consent to one assignment destroyed the anti-assignment clause of the lease. If the landlord consented to one assignment, all other assignments were valid.

Many states have eliminated this rule or restricted its application to assignments only and not subleases. To avoid the application of this rule, landlords insert a lease provision stating that the landlord's consent to one assignment shall not constitute a waiver of the right to object to subsequent lease assignments.

Subleases

Sublease
A transfer of a portion of the lease from a tenant to a third party (a subtenant).

A **sublease** occurs when the tenant does not transfer the entire interest in the lease. Instead, only a portion of the lease is transferred. Subleases arise when the tenant transfers only a portion of the remaining term (such as three months of the remaining six-month term for years) or a portion of the property (as when the tenant leases to another one of the two bedrooms the tenant has leased from the landlord).

Subleasing most often occurs when rental properties are in scarce supply or the tenant wishes to vacate for only a short period of time. As with assignments, most leases contain a prohibition against subleasing without the landlord's consent. A violation of that covenant will entitle the lessor to void the sublease and/or recover damages.

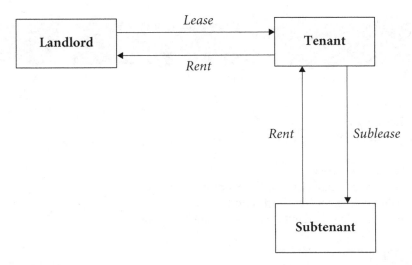

FIGURE 14.3. Sublease

Rights and Duties

With a sublease, two leases exist. The landlord has rights only against the tenant, because the landlord has a contract with the tenant but not with the subtenant. The tenant remains liable to the landlord under the terms of its lease. The subtenant is not liable to the landlord.

The lease between the tenant and the subtenant governs the rights with the subtenant. The subtenant is liable to the tenant, and the tenant owes rights and duties to both the landlord and the subtenant.

Potential Issues

It is important that the lease between the tenant and the subtenant mirror the lease terms contained in the lease between the landlord and the tenant or incorporate the terms and conditions of the lease between the landlord and tenant into the lease between the tenant and subtenant. Otherwise, situations may arise in which the subtenant is in breach of a covenant the landlord has with the tenant, but the subtenant is not in breach of a covenant in the lease with the tenant.

> *Example:* The lease between the landlord and the tenant contains a no-dog policy. Unfortunately, the lease between the tenant and the subtenant does not contain such a policy. If the subtenant possesses a dog, the tenant would be in violation of the covenant with the landlord against dogs, yet the subtenant would not be in breach of a covenant with the tenant. The tenant and subtenant could be evicted, with the subtenant suing the tenant for damages. The tenant could have avoided this problem by incorporating the lease terms into the sublease.

Prohibition Against Assignments and Subleases

Landlords can prohibit an assignment or a sublease in the lease. However, courts narrowly construe this prohibition. A prohibition against an assignment does not prevent the tenant from subleasing. Similarly, a sublease prohibition does not prevent the tenant from assigning the lease.

Checklist for Preparation of a Lease

1. Type of Lease
   - ☐ Residential
   - ☐ Commercial

2. Parties to the Lease
   - ☐ Names and capacities of the landlord and tenant
   - ☐ Addresses of the landlord and tenant
   - ☐ Brokers identified;entitled to real estate commissions

3. Description of the Premises
   - ☐ Legal description of the premises provided
   - ☐ Does tenant have option for additional space or expansion
   - ☐ Does landlord have right to relocate the tenant within the property

4. Common Areas
   - ☐ Rights to the common areas
   - ☐ Common area expenses and maintenance costs

5. Rent
   - ☐ Gross lease
   - ☐ Modified gross lease
   - ☐ Percentage lease
     - ☐ When paid
     - ☐ Gross or net sales
     - ☐ How calculated
     - ☐ Sales threshold
     - ☐ Disclosure of financial records
     - ☐ Audit and inspection rights
   - ☐ Triple net lease
   - ☐ Security deposit
   - ☐ Prepaid rent
   - ☐ Miscellaneous
     - ☐ Rent control
     - ☐ Rental increases
     - ☐ When is rent due

6. Term of the Lease
   - ☐ Tenancy for years
   - ☐ Periodic tenancy
   - ☐ Tenancy at will
   - ☐ Option(s) to renew

7. Use
   - ☐ Specific use
   - ☐ General purpose

8. Guaranty
   - ☐ Personal guaranty

9. Maintenance, Repairs, and Alterations
   - ☐ Landlord obligations
   - ☐ Tenant obligations
   - ☐ Notice of repair requirements
   - ☐ Alteration rights

10. Insurance
   - ☐ Insurance required
      - ☐ Commercial general liability (CGL)
      - ☐ Business interruption insurance
      - ☐ Other

11. Miscellaneous
   - ☐ Covenant of quiet enjoyment
   - ☐ Noncompetition
   - ☐ Americans with Disabilities Act
      - ☐ Due diligence performed
      - ☐ Responsibility for compliance
   - ☐ Exculpatory clause

12. Assignment and Subleasing
   - ☐ Assignment rights
   - ☐ Sublease rights

Key Terms and Concepts

- Lessors, page 374
- Lessees, page 374
- Nonfreehold estate, page 374
- Lease, page 374
- Tenancy, page 374
- Residential lease, page 374
- Commercial lease, page 374
- Tenancy for years, page 375
- Periodic tenancy, page 377
- Tenancy at will, page 378
- Tenancy at sufferance, page 378
- Gross lease, page 380
- Modified gross lease, page 380
- Percentage lease, page 380
- Triple net lease, page 381
- Indexed rate, page 381
- Rent control, page 381
- Premises, page 382

Chapter Summary

- There are four types of leases: (1) tenancy for years, (2) periodic tenancy, (3) tenancy at will, and (4) tenancy at sufferance.

- A tenancy for years is a tenancy for a fixed period of time.

- In a periodic tenancy, the tenancy continues for a stated period and automatically renews for successive periods unless either party gives proper and timely notice of termination.

- In a tenancy at will, the tenancy is of no fixed duration. Either party can terminate it at any time.

- A tenancy at sufferance occurs when a tenant remains in possession of the leased property after the lease period has terminated.

- There are three common types of rental rates: (1) gross lease, (2) percentage lease, and (3) triple net lease (NNN).

- Gross lease is a fixed sum that the tenant pays the landlord.

- A percentage lease is used in retail leasing; the tenant pays a percentage of its gross sales to the landlord.

- A triple net lease is one in which the tenant pays a base rent plus a proportionate share of property taxes, insurance, and property maintenance.

- Many cities may impose rent control ordinances on landlords to regulate rental rates.

- Landlords may require tenants to make advance payments, known as deposits, to cover certain expenses or costs that may be incurred by the landlord when the tenant vacates.

- Tenants have several remedies: they can (1) file a lawsuit against the landlord, (2) withhold rent from the landlord, (3) repair the issue and deduct the costs of the repair from the rent owed the landlord, (4) abate the rent, or (5) terminate the lease.

- If the premises become damaged during the tenancy, the landlord must be timely notified and given a reasonable amount of time to make the repair.

- Landlords have a limited right to access during this time.

- The Americans with Disabilities Act prohibits discrimination against disabled individuals in places of public accommodation or commercial facilities. The Act requires reasonable modifications unless they are unduly burdensome.

- Landlords may face liability for their negligent acts and omissions to the tenant where a landlord fails to make the premises safe.

- When a tenant assigns the lease, he or she remains fully liable to the landlord for obligations remaining under the lease.

- A sublease transfers less than all the lease interest, usually as to term and sometimes as to physical leased area, and creates a separate landlord-tenant relationship.

Chapter Problems and Assignments

1. How is a tenancy terminated in each of the following types of leases?
   a. Tenancy for years
   b. Periodic tenancy
   c. Tenancy at will
   d. Tenancy at sufferance

2. What is the difference between a gross lease and a modified gross lease?

3. You are a business tenant. Unfortunately, business has been slow, and you are forced to close your business. You have four years remaining on your lease. The landlord refuses to terminate your company's obligations under the terms of the lease. You find a replacement tenant for the landlord, and the landlord agrees to an assignment of the lease from your company to the new tenant. After the assignment, what is your company's remaining liability, if any, to the landlord?

4. Brian applies to become a tenant in an apartment complex designed for families with children. While he is filling out the application, the project manager asks him if he has any children or is married. Although he is dating, he is not married and does not have any children. After completing the application, he is told that his application is denied because he isn't the type of person the apartment community desires. Does Brian have a claim against the apartment community over how they select tenants?

5. Janet had a lease with her landlord from January 1 through December 31 of the current year. The lease contained a provision that after December 31, if the tenant stayed in possession and the landlord accepted rent, a month-to-month tenancy would be created. Janet stayed in the premises for an additional three months after December 31, and thereafter the landlord gave notice to terminate the lease. The termination of the lease was effective on April 30.

Janet was unable to find another apartment timely and continued to stay in the apartment until May 4, when she was able to obtain another lease and move out of the apartment. How would you characterize the types of tenancies Janet had during her entire stay in the apartment?

6. Felix has been leasing his apartment on a month-to-month basis for the past three years. He has an oral lease with his landlord. Recently, he has had a few disagreements with the landlord, who has stated that Felix is lucky because the lease Felix has with the landlord needs to be in writing to be enforceable, and the landlord has just been accommodating Felix by allowing him to stay. Is the landlord correct? Must the lease be in writing to be enforceable?

7. You represent a commercial landlord. She has always used modified gross leases in the past, believing there is no real difference between a modified gross lease and a triple net lease. Why is a triple net lease more advantageous to a landlord?

8. Julie moved into Manor Estates in September, at which time she was told her apartment had central heat and air. It is now December, and the temperatures have dropped to almost freezing levels. Julie quickly realizes that the heat in her apartment does not work. Julie has contacted her landlord several times to discuss this issue, and each time he simply ignores her request for repairs. What remedies does Julie have against her landlord?

9. Jermaine rents an apartment from Luci. Before he signs the lease and moves in, the building manager, Nancy, tells him the pipes throughout the building are being repaired and replaced, so there may be intermittent hours during which he will not have running

water. The repairs are not anticipated to last more than two weeks. One day, Jermaine tries to take a shower and is unable to do so because he has no water. Can Jermaine terminate the lease and allege constructive eviction? Can Jermaine allege a breach of the implied warranty of habitability?

10. Landlord Larry rented out a second-floor apartment, which included a balcony, to Tenant Tom. A section of the railing on one side of the balcony became loose. Tom notified Larry of the loose railing, and Larry repaired the loose railing on one side of the balcony. Larry did not inspect or repair any other sides of the balcony. Two weeks later, Alex, Tom's best friend came for a visit; when he leaned against the balcony railing, it collapsed. Alex fell and was seriously injured when the railing gave way. As a guest, rather than a tenant, should Alex be entitled to recover damages against Larry for failing to reasonably inspect and repair the balcony?

11. A shopping center was operated by Fields Commercial Enterprises. Each of the tenants rented the premises under leases that included common area maintenance (CAM) expenses. The CAM provision in the lease stated, "Tenants shall be responsible for all costs incurred by lessor relating to the ownership and operation of the project." After several years, several tenants sued Fields Commercial Enterprise, asserting that the CAM charges were excessive. Among the required CAM expenses were the costs to renovate the property when the landlord replaced concrete with brick and stone to beautify the property. Are the tenants responsible for these expenses?

12. Research whether your state requires any advance notice to terminate a tenancy at will.

13. Research to determine if your city has a rent control ordinance. Prepare a memorandum summarizing the rent control ordinance, and be sure to attach the rent control ordinance to your memorandum. Do you believe the rent control ordinance is fair to both landlords and tenants?

14. One frequent argument against rent control ordinances is that they lead to the deterioration of existing housing because the restrictions, by reducing the landlords' revenues, lead landlords to substantially reduce maintenance and repairs. Is the practice of rent control worthwhile? How should cities balance the equities between tenants and landlords?

15. Research if your state has a law regarding housing discrimination. Be ready to discuss its provisions during class.

End Notes

1. California and Massachusetts are two states that limit tenancy for years to 99 years or less.
2. 485 U.S. 1, 14 (1988).
3. Cal. Civil Code §1942.
4. National Conference of State Legislatures, *State Adoptions of URLTA Landlord Duties*. http://www.ncsl.org/issues-research/env-res/state-adoptions-of-urlta-landlord-duties.aspx# (last accessed November 2, 2017).
5. *Kotis Properties v. Casey's*, 183 N.C. App. 617 (2007).
6. 42 U.S.C Section 1981.
7. 775 Ill. Comp. Stat. 5/3-103.
8. 76 Eng. Rep 1110 (K.B. 1603).

Chapter 15
Insuring Real Property

I called an insurance company to get a quote. They gave me one of Oscar Wilde's best.
  —*Jarod Kintz, humorist*

Learning Objectives

1. Understand the terminology used in insurance contracts.
2. Explain an insurable interest.
3. Define who can be considered an insured.
4. Describe the differences between an insurance agent and a broker.
5. Explain the process of forming an insurance contract and the key provisions of such a contract.
6. Define the common types of real property insurance.
7. Understand the different methods an insurer can use to calculate the amount to be paid under a property loss claim.
8. Describe the duties of the insured and the insurer following an insured loss.
9. Discuss the emerging issues affecting property insurance coverage.

Chapter Outline

- Introduction
- Why Is Insurance So Complex?
- Insurable Interest
Case 15.1: *Arthur Andersen LLP v. Federal Ins. Co.*
- Who Is the Insured?
- Insurance Agents and Brokers
Case 15.2: *United Fire & Cas. Ins. Co. v. Garvey*
- The Insurance Contract
- Common Types of Property Insurance
- What Will the Insurance Carrier Pay?
- Duties of the Insured
- Duties of the Insurer
Case 15.3: *Maloney Cinque, LLC. v. Pacific Ins. Co.*

Opening scenario

Michelle, mother of 6-year-old Ryder, invites children over to her house for a birthday party for Ryder. During the party, the children are playing upstairs when one of them leans on a loose banister and falls to the floor below, severely injuring himself. The distraught parents are unable to pay for the medical bills, and they file a lawsuit against Michelle for pain and suffering and medical costs. As you review this chapter, consider what forms of property insurance would provide Michelle coverage for this unfortunate and unforeseen accident. What insurance limits would you recommend that a homeowner carry?

Introduction

Life is unpredictable and can subject any of us to financial losses. Sometimes our real property is damaged by a calamity such as a fire, hurricane, earthquake, flood, windstorm, or building design defect. These are frequent hazards, but insurance proceeds can mitigate some of their financial effects.

Owners of real property need property and liability insurance to protect their substantial investments. Insurance plays a significant role in stabilizing the economy and preventing widespread panic and financial ruin when large-scale catastrophes occur. Because it is so important to society, insurance is heavily regulated by state insurance commissioners. In this chapter, we review the requirements for an insurance contract, common real property insurance coverages, and the good faith duties of the parties to the insurance policy.

Insurance Terminology

Insurance is a contract transferring the risk of loss from one party to another in exchange for a premium payment. The party obtaining and paying for the insurance is called an **insured**. Insurance allows insureds to recover from financial losses they would otherwise suffer. The insurance company receiving payment is known as the **insurer**. The insurer assumes the risk it might have to pay the insured for a covered loss if one occurs. The payment made by the insured to the insurer is known as the **premium**. Premiums are collected from a large pool of insureds, allowing the risk of loss to be spread among many insureds. The assumption underlying the insurance concept is that not all insureds will suffer a loss at the same time. In the event of a loss covered by the insurance policy, the insurer pays the insurance proceeds to the insured.

Premiums are based upon determinations made by actuaries, who apply mathematical, economic, and statistical models to price policies so that if insured losses occur, the insurer (the insurance company) will have the financial resources to pay the claims.

Insurance
A contract that shifts the risk of loss for individuals and businesses to another in exchange for a premium payment.

Insured
The person who obtains insurance.

Insurer
The insurance company which receives payment from an insured.

Premium
The cost of insurance paid by an insured.

An insured selects the amount of insurance, called the **policy limits**, that are payable under the policy. By paying the premium to the insurer, the insured seeks to avoid a larger loss. An insurer is only required to pay a loss covered by the policy up to the amount of the policy limits. Losses in excess of the policy limits are the responsibility of the insured.

The insurance contract is known as the insurance policy and must follow all the requirements necessary to form a valid legal contract. The premiums received are invested by the insurer in the stock market, real estate holdings, and other investments to realize investment returns to pay for future claims.

Why Is Insurance So Complex?

Developing, constructing, financing, managing, and litigating real property presents a unique set of problems. The questions "What kind of insurance do I need?" and "How much insurance do I buy?" are potentially problematic. It is best to proceed cautiously with regard to insurance coverage. To answer these questions, the insurance applicant should consult experienced insurance professionals for assistance in evaluating insurance coverage.

Complex Jargon

The insurance industry loves jargon and indecipherable policy language, which can baffle even the most talented linguist. Understanding insurance coverage terminology is not always easy because insurance carriers do not use common language in the policies. As in every other business, insurance carriers try to distinguish themselves from their competitors. Increasing coverages or reducing premiums along with coverages is common.

The complexity of insurance law is not lost upon the courts. The courts have developed insurance contract interpretation rules that favor the insured.

Regulation and Conflicting State Laws

The insurance market is heavily regulated and is the subject of legislation and enforcement at the state level. The **McCarran Ferguson Act of 1945**[1] is a federal law that delegated regulation of the insurance industry to the states. Many policies are prepared on forms developed by the Insurance Services Office (ISO), a nonprofit association. These policy forms, after approval by the insurance carriers, are then submitted to state agencies for review. Each state has the ability to make the insurance carriers include or exclude certain types of coverage. While many states use standard ISO forms, just as many modify the forms on a state-by-state basis.

Manuscript Policies

Carriers may also develop their own forms or issue a manuscript policy, which is a policy negotiated between the insurance carrier and the policyholder. Large real estate developers and owners will often persuade their insurance carriers to modify standard policy forms due to the large premiums to be paid to the carriers.

■ ■ ■ Property Insurance Terms

Below is an overview of common terminology used in insurance policies.

Certificate of insurance	A written verification that an insurance policy has been issued. It is an informational document and not a substitute for an actual policy of insurance.
Deductible	The amount the insured pays before the insurance policy benefits become payable.
Endorsements	Also known as a rider. This is a modification of or change to the policy. It can add or reduce coverage or add additional insureds.
Exclusions	Risks of loss not covered by the insurance policy. Common exclusions relate to earth movement, mold, and pollution claims.
Indemnity	The agreement to compensate and make whole achieved by payment, repair, or replacement.
Insurable interest	An interest in property sufficient to result in a financial or other kind of loss when that property is lost or damaged.
Insured	Owner of the insurance policy who is entitled to policy coverage benefits in the event of a covered loss.
Insurer	The insurance company that receives payment and provides coverage to the insured.
Limits of liability	A limit on the amount the insurer will pay. A per-occurrence or per-claim limit limits the amount the insurer will pay arising out of a single claim. An aggregate limit is the most the insurer will pay under the policy, regardless of the number of claims made during the policy period.
Self-Insured Retention	Also known as a retained limit, this is the amount paid by the insured before the insurance policy will respond to (that is, indemnify) a loss.
Underwriting	The process by which insurers analyze an insured's risks and set the amount of premium to charge him.

Insurable Interest

To obtain insurance on real property and recover in the event of a covered loss, a person must have an insurable interest in the property. An **insurable interest** exists when an insured would sustain a financial loss if the property were lost or damaged. The insurance company will pay only those who have an insurable interest in the property. Otherwise, without an insurable interest, an insurance policy would merely be gambling on the occurrence of an event. Gambling contracts are unenforceable.

Insurable interest
A requirement that a person have a property or personal interest in the insured goods, property, or person.

Persons with an Insurable Interest

States generally agree that the following persons have insurable interests in real property:

1. Buyers and sellers (owners) of real estate
2. Owners of nonpossessory real property interests (easements) and holders of future estates (less than fee interests)
3. Persons holding a security interest (mortgage or deed of trust)
    Mortgage lenders require borrowers to insure the property as a condition of making the loan. The insured's failure to maintain the required insurance will trigger a default under the mortgage deed of trust.
4. Tenants who have agreed to insure the premises under the terms of the lease
5. Owners of a common interest in real property (such as a condominium owner and his or her homeowners' association, both of whom have an interest in the common area)

Extent of an Insurable Interest

The insurable interest in real property is limited to the extent of the person's interest in the insured property.

> *Example:* Aiden and Mia own a commercial building as tenants in common. Aiden has a two-thirds interest, and Mia has a one-third interest in the building. If the building is damaged by fire, Aiden and Mia can each recover only up to the amount of their insurable interest (two-thirds and one-third, respectively) in the policy proceeds.

When Must a Person Have an Insurable Interest?

An insurable interest must exist for property insurance *at the time of the loss*. If the insured does not have an insurable interest in the property, the insured may not enforce a claim under the policy.

> *Example:* Jamie sells his real property to a third person. After his property has been sold, Jamie no longer has an insurable interest in the property.

In the following case, the international accounting firm Arthur Andersen LLP sued its insurance carrier for business losses caused as a result of property damage to the World Trade Center and the Pentagon on September 11, 2001. In its decision, the court considered whether Arthur Andersen had an insurable interest in damaged insured property covered by the policy.

CASE 15.1

AN INSURABLE INTEREST INVOLVES A DIRECT MONETARY BENEFIT OR LOSS FROM DAMAGE TO COVERED PROPERTY

ARTHUR ANDERSEN LLP v. FEDERAL INS. CO.

3 A.3d 1279 (2010)

New Jersey Superior Court Appellate Division

Arthur Andersen filed a claim for business losses for $204 million in lost earnings in the three- and-one-half months following the 9/11 terrorist attacks. Andersen's business interruption clause in its insurance policy covered losses "caused by property damage that prevented the flow of goods or services to or from the insured and necessarily interrupted the insured's business." Andersen did not own or lease any property at the WTC or the Pentagon and could not identify any supplier or client whose property was damaged to support its claim. Nonetheless, Andersen filed a claim under its all-risk commercial property insurance policy for business losses that it claimed it had suffered due to the property damage to the WTC and the Pentagon, based on a comparison between expected revenue trends and actual revenue earned. Andersen sued its insurer under the policy, but the trial court granted summary judgment in favor of the insurer. Andersen appealed.

Language of the Court. *No evidence has been presented that Andersen insured or was responsible for insurance for either site or the airplane. Andersen did not own or lease any of this property. One must have an insurable interest in property to sustain recovery under a policy that insures risks for property damage.*

Andersen's theory would permit an insured to allege an insurable interest in a class of property so broad as to be impossible to define and certainly not susceptible to a predictable level of risk. Just as an insurable interest cannot be viewed so narrowly as to create a windfall for the insurer, allowing it to retain the premiums without providing anything in return, the interest cannot be read as broadly as Andersen argues, allowing the insured to reap a windfall recovery for a loss so clearly unanticipated in the calculation of the premium. Such an application would undermine the very purpose of an "insurable interest" requirement, reducing an insurance contract to a "pure gamble," and we reject it as a matter of law.

Decision. The court affirmed judgment in favor of the insurer, finding Andersen had no insurable interest.

FOCUS ON ETHICS

Was it ethical for the CPA firm to make a claim for property damage in this case?

Who Is the Insured?

Most policies contain a specific definition of who qualifies as an insured under the policy. These parties may include the "named insured" and "additional insureds." The **named insured** is the policy owner and is usually the party purchasing the insurance. This person has the power to cancel, modify, or renew the policy.

An **additional insured** is a party unrelated to the named insured who receives the benefits of the insurance policy without having to pay the premium. Often landlords, mortgage lenders, construction project owners, and general contractors require that they be named as additional insureds to provide insurance coverage for their benefit. In this situation, the insurance company owes the additional insureds the same duties to defend and indemnify that the insurer owes the named insured. While it may seem unfair, it does allow the additional insureds to reduce their premium costs, and it provides policy coverages consistent with those whom the additional insureds deal with on a continuing basis.

Named insured
In the event of a covered loss, the person or business receiving payment from the insurance company.

Additional insured
A party unrelated to the named insured who receives the benefits of the insurance policy without having to pay the premium that the named insured pays.

Insurance Agents and Brokers

The insurance marketplace and prior claims history will dictate the availability of particular coverages and the pricing of those policies. Because insurance coverages and products are constantly changing, it is prudent for a property owner to stay informed about what is available in the marketplace.

Insurance Agents and Brokers

In most cases, a person does not purchase insurance directly from an insurer. Insurance is sold primarily through agents and brokers. Agents sell insurance for only one insurance carrier. Although **insurance agents** advise consumers on the insurance policies that best suit their needs, the insurance agent is an agent of the insurance company, not of the applicant.

An **insurance broker** can place insurance with a number of different insurance carriers. In most states, the broker is the agent of the insured with regard to matters connected with the application for insurance.[2] Agents and brokers owe fiduciary duties of good faith and reasonable care in handling insurance related matters. Mistakes do occur during the application and claim management process, and the distinction between an agent and a broker can have significant consequences for the insured.

Fiduciary Duties

Insurance Agents

The agent owes a fiduciary duty to act in the best interest of the insurance company. Because the insurance agent works for the insurance company, the insurance company is liable for acts he commits. If an agent acts negligently toward a person in the process of securing the insurance policy, those acts are attributable to the insurance company.

Example: If Property Insurance Company sells policies only through employed agents, and one of them negligently fails to list a co-insured on the application (such as a co-tenant), the insurer would be liable to the nonnamed person if she or he was harmed because of an insured loss.

Insurance Brokers

Insurance brokers owe a fiduciary duty to act in the best interests of the insured regarding matters related to the application for insurance. Because of this fiduciary relationship, misrepresentations made by the broker are deemed to be misrepresentations of the applicant.

Example: When the insured advises its broker of certain information and the broker provides contrary information to the insurer, the insurance company can later cancel the policy because of the broker's misrepresentations.

In the following case, the insurer brought action against the insured seeking a declaration that it did not have a duty to indemnify under the property insurance policy.

CASE 15.2

AN AGENCY RELATIONSHIP MAY REFLECT THE OWNER'S PROPERTY INTEREST

UNITED FIRE & CAS. INS. CO. v. GARVEY

419 F.3d 743 (2005)

United States Court of Appeals for the Eighth Circuit

The Garveys purchased a residential property and instructed their son Paul to obtain insurance coverage for the property. Paul called the family's insurance agent, Dan Hebbeln to obtain insurance on the property. Hebbeln completed the application, which was reviewed and signed by Paul. The policy with United Fire & Cas. Ins. Co. ("United Fire") listed Paul as the insured. Thereafter the property was destroyed by a fire. Paul reported the loss to Hebbeln, who notified United Fire. United Fire denied the claim, asserting that Paul, who was the named insured, had no insurable interest in the property. The trial court found United Fire had no duty to indemnify as Paul had no insurable interest. Paul appealed. On appeal the court determined Paul had no insurable interest in the property, but it required the lower court to determine if Paul was acting as an agent for his parents when he obtained the policy. The court determined Paul never disclosed he was acting for his parents when obtaining insurance, and thus the court held for United Fire. Paul Garvey appealed.

Language of the Court. *Under Missouri law, an insurance broker is one who, on behalf of the insured, shops around for insurance among multiple insurance companies. In such instances, the broker is acting as the agent of the insured. Conversely, "[a] person delegated to solicit insurance for a particular company, and to refrain from soliciting insurance for any other company, is an agent [of the insurer], and not a broker." Absent special conditions or circumstances suggesting otherwise, the presumption is a broker is the agent of the insured, and any mistakes made by the broker are attributable to the insured.*

As Hebbeln testified, the agreement imposed an affirmative duty on him to solicit the coverage on behalf of United Fire if it was available. Based on this evidence, a jury could reasonably conclude Hebbeln was precluded from shopping the coverage to other insurers, and was not acting as a broker.

Paul does not claim an insurable interest in the property. Rather, the evidence viewed in the light most favorable to the verdict, shows he was acting as agent for his parents when he obtained the insurance. By virtue of this agency relationship, the Garveys interests in the property are reflected in the policy.

Decision. The court of appeals reversed, holding that the Garveys had an insurable interest and United Fire had a duty to indemnify them for the fire loss.

FOCUS ON ETHICS

Do you believe the outcome would be different if Paul wasn't the Garveys son? How can an insurance company protect itself from third persons claiming to have a principal/agent relationship to circumvent the insurable interest requirement?

The Insurance Contract

An insurance policy is a contract, and the basic contract law principles discussed earlier in the text apply to it. As noted, because of the state regulation of insurance, each state may have unique requirements or may vary the general provisions discussed below.

Application

The process of entering into an insurance contract begins with the application. The completed application of the insured becomes part of the policy. Subject to certain exceptions, the applicant is liable for his misrepresentations in the application.

> *Example:* If the property owner was aware that leaking plumbing existed at the time of applying for property insurance, the insurer could seek to deny a later claim for water damage to the building, especially if the insurer would not have extended insurance to the insured had it known all the material facts regarding the property.

Effective Date

The effective date of a policy is the date on which coverage begins. The insurer may wish to conduct a visual inspection of the property before it issues a policy, and the effective date may occur well after the application is submitted. The general rule is that the insurer has no liability to the insured until the policy is issued. Because it sometimes takes time to issue the policy, a binder may be provided by an insurance agent (usually not by a broker) to obtain coverage from the date of the application. A **binder** is a form of temporary insurance contract that provides coverage subject to the same terms and conditions as the insurance policy the carrier will eventually issue.

Binder
Temporary insurance lasting until a policy is issued.

Insurance Contract

The insurance contract, also known as an insurance policy, sets forth the covered losses and exclusions from coverage under the policy. Most insurance carriers provide insurance coverage using standardized insurance contract forms. States may require the use of standardized forms and can mandate that certain covered losses be included and can limit the extent to which an insurer may attempt to limit coverage.

■■■ Important Policy Clauses

Choice of law	Policies can identify the state law to be applied in interpreting the policy. As insurance is regulated by the states, the insurer will attempt to select the law of a state that is most favorable to its interests.
Co-insurance	Co-insurance clauses encourage applicants to insure their properties for amounts close to their full value by penalizing insureds in the event of a loss if they fail to purchase insurance at least equal to a specified percentage of property value (usually 80 percent).
	If the face value of the policy is less than the required percentage, the insurer pays only a proportionate amount of the loss. The balance is paid by the insured.
	Example: Acme Manufacturing owns a plant valued at $2 million and has a $1.5 million fire insurance policy. If the insurance policy required that 80 percent of the property value be covered by insurance, and Acme suffered $1 million in property damage, Acme's insurance recovery would be $937,500.
	$$\frac{\text{Amount of insurance}}{(\text{Stated \%}) \times (\text{Value at time of loss})} \times \text{Loss} = \text{Recovery Amount}$$ $$\frac{\$1,500,000}{(80 \text{ \%}) \times (2,000,000)} \times \$1,000,000 = \$937,500$$
Deductible clause	The policy will often state the amount the insured is required to pay before the insurance policy benefits become payable.
	Example: If a building owner has a $1 million fire-insurance policy with a $10,000 deductible, and the structure suffers severe damage caused by a fire, the insured must pay the first $10,000 in damages.
Subrogation	Subrogation is the insurer's right to pursue a third party that caused the insured loss. Once an insurer pays the insured's liability, the insurer takes over the legal rights the insured may have had against third parties who caused the damages. The insured cannot pursue a claim for damages against the wrongdoer.
	Subrogation prevents the insured from double recovering. Without subrogation, the insured could recover from the insurer and then sue and recover against the third party who caused the damage, thereby receiving a windfall. With subrogation, the insurer has the right to recover against the third party.
	Example: If a contractor's liability insurance pays for property damage caused to a project owner, the insurer obtains the right to recover this sum from other responsible parties, such as negligent subcontractors who caused the harm.
Statute of limitations	The statute of limitations, as applied to insurance contracts, requires that an insured seek to enforce an insurance claim within a certain period of time after the covered loss occurs.

Covered Losses

The insurance contract identifies what losses are covered under the policy. A **covered loss**, also known as an insured loss, is the unforeseen, unanticipated destruction, diminution, or loss of something of value triggering the duty of the insurance carrier to investigate and potentially pay an insurance claim.

A covered loss is caused by a peril. Examples of perils to real property include fire, explosion, soil movement or failure, lightning, hail, water damage from floods, faulty plumbing, smoke damage, earthquakes, and windstorms. A single peril may cause more than one type of real property loss.

> **Example:** A broken water pipe may damage flooring and create conditions favorable to the growth of mold. The sudden occurrence of the broken pipe will be a covered peril, and the resulting mold may or may not be a covered peril under the policy.

Insureds should carefully review their policies to confirm that they have the property coverage needed. If a covered loss is not stated or reasonably inferable from the policy terminology, then a loss may be uninsured.

Covered loss
An event or occurrence that triggers the duty of the insurance carrier to investigate and potentially pay an insurance claim.

Separate Forms of Property Insurance

Four forms of insurance policy protections exist: basic (or named risk), broad, special (or all risk), and earthquake.

1. *Basic.* Under this coverage, the insurer indemnifies the insured only from losses specifically listed in the policy, such as fire, flood, or design liability. Anything not specifically named in the policy is not covered. Many mortgage lenders require that, as a condition to obtaining and not defaulting on the loan, borrowers secure basic insurance.
2. *Broad.* A broad policy includes all the items covered under a basic policy, as well as glass breakage; damage caused by falling objects; damage from the weight of snow, ice, or sleet; water damage; and additional collapse coverage.
3. *Special.* Under this coverage, the insurer indemnifies the insured from losses from any perils except those specifically excluded. The insurer bears the burden of proving that the loss was caused by an excluded peril. Virtually any physical loss to the insured property is potentially covered by an all risk property policy.
4. *Earthquake.* Special or all risk insurance does not provide coverage for earthquake damage. Most lenders do not require earthquake coverage, even if the property is located in an earthquake prone area.

Exclusions

Under the law of most states, an insurer is free to select the type of risk it will assume and is liable only for the loss it defines within the terms of the policy. An insurer has the right to limit the coverage it issues, so long as the exclusion (limitation of coverage) is plainly stated. The insurer bears the burden of drafting clear exclusionary language comprehensible to the average person.

When an insured has a noncovered loss, it is likely because an exclusion was stated in the policy. Some of the most common exclusions found in policies include the following:

- *Earth movement.* Policies typically define earth movement as including earthquakes; landslides; mudslides or mudflows; land subsidence; sinkholes; and the sinking, rising, or shifting of earth.
- *Deterioration, latent defect* (a hidden defect not discoverable through reasonable inspection), *or wear and tear.* These exclusions are intended to remove coverage for any covered event that is not sudden or accidental (such as lack of maintenance claims).
- *Water damage, whether caused by floods, subsurface water, waves, sewer backups, sprays, or otherwise.* Mold is commonly excluded, or coverage is limited to a small sum.
- *Pollution, war, terrorism, and intentional acts.*
- *Vacant buildings.* Often excluded because of the higher risk of vandalism.

Interpretation of Ambiguities

If an exclusion appears ambiguous, courts favor an interpretation most favorable to the insured, because the insurer drafted the exclusion causing the ambiguity. If the ambiguity is found in a special form insurance policy, the insurer has the burden of showing that the loss is within an exclusion.

Prohibited Conduct by Insured

State laws prohibit insurance carriers from providing coverage for intentional wrongdoing by the insured. An insurance company is liable to defend and indemnify its insured from the insured's acts of negligence but not from the insured's willful and intentional acts. Thus, if a building owner negligently maintained the electrical system in a building, the structural damage resulting from a fire would be covered. The building owner's intentional damage causing acts (such as arson) would not be covered by insurance.

Common Types of Property Insurance

An insurance policy does not cover every conceivable type of risk. Instead, insurance policies are purchased according to the nature of the risk involved. Below are several common types of insurance relevant to real property.

Business Insurance

Commercial General Liability Insurance

Commercial general liability policy
Policy covering bodily injury, property damage, and personal injury liability arising from the operations of a business.

A **commercial general liability policy** is one of the most common liability protection insurance policies issued to business organizations. This insurance covers bodily injury, property damage, and personal injury liability arising from the operations of the business. While coverage excludes intentional conduct, liability arising out of gross negligence or recklessness is a covered peril for the insured.

Seller's Warranties Policies

A **representations and warranties insurance policy** provides insurance to guarantee the representations made by sellers in real estate transaction contracts. It extends to any resulting financial loss if representations and warranties in the property purchase agreement are untrue. The policy can be obtained in conjunction with a general liability policy.

Representations and warranties insurance policy
A policy used in real estate transactions to guarantee the representations made by sellers in real estate transactions.

Errors and Omissions Policies

Real estate brokers can be sued for negligence in a real estate transaction. To protect themselves, they can procure an **errors and omissions policy**. Liability coverage extends to claims arising out of any act or omission or "personal injury" caused by a failure to render "professional services."

Errors and omissions policy
Policy procured by real estate brokers to insure against negligence in real estate transactions.

Insurance Related to Personal and Real Property

Fire Insurance Policy

A **fire insurance policy** protects real and personal property against damages resulting from a fire and certain other perils (often lightning, smoke, and water damage). Liability insurance protection is not covered in standard fire insurance policies. It is one of the lowest levels of insurance protection a homeowner can secure.

Fire insurance policy
Insurance that protects real and personal property against damages resulting from a fire and certain other perils.

Homeowner's Insurance

A **homeowner's insurance policy** is considered a comprehensive insurance policy providing coverage for damage to the home and the homeowner's personal property, protections against personal liability, some legal claims by third parties (including damages caused by household members and family pets), and a limited amount of medical expenses incurred by guests injured on the property. It does not cover business or professional activities (such as activities related to a home office or home day-care services).

Homeowner's insurance policy
Comprehensive policy covering damage to the home and the homeowner's personal property, protections against personal liability, some legal claims, and limited medical expenses for injured guests.

Covered perils usually include those contained in a fire policy, as well as coverage for winds or hail, explosions, riots, civil commotions, aircraft incidents, vehicles causing damage, smoke, volcanic eruption, vandalism, theft, and falling objects. In contrast to fire insurance policies, homeowner's insurance policies cover personal liability. This coverage provides protection against claims by third parties injured on the insured's property (such as a slip and fall) and third parties injured by the insured away from the home (for example, by a defamatory statement).

Homeowner's insurance policies typically exclude losses caused by lack of property maintenance and repair. Common exclusions include, but are not limited to:

- Structural defects whether known or unknown
- Known or hidden defects in the plumbing, heating, and electrical systems

- Known or unknown soil conditions or draining problems
- Concealment or misrepresentation of any known defects in the residential property (including soil movement and defective appliances)

Condominium Policies

The condominium policy insures the personal property inside the condominium unit. Condominiums present unique problems because of the potential for shared insurance responsibility with homeowners' associations over common walls and common areas, as well as shared responsibilities for maintenance and repair. The conditions, covenants, and restrictions (CCRs) on a condominium development may divide the responsibility for maintaining insurance between the homeowners' association and the individual unit owners. Often, the condominium will insure the building walls, roof, and floors, while the condominium owner is responsible for insuring the personal property inside the unit.

Renter's Insurance

Tenants leasing a premises can purchase renter's insurance to protect from any loss or damage to their personal property. A homeowner's insurance policy does not cover the personal property of tenants residing on the premises in the event of a peril to the property. Renter's insurance is very affordable and significantly cheaper than a homeowner's insurance policy. Landlords should require tenants to secure renter's insurance and name the landlord as an additional insured under the policy to ensure that the tenants have insurance to protect their personal property. Without such insurance, a tenant could sue a landlord for any damage caused to the tenant's personal property.

Flood

Flood insurance provides insurance for property damage caused by a flood. In response to the rising cost of taxpayer-funded relief for flood victims, the federal government administers the National Flood Insurance Program (NFIA).[3] The NFIA makes flood insurance available to properties at a reasonable cost. Policies are issued by private insurers participating in the program. The Federal Emergency Management Agency (FEMA) establishes standard flood insurance policies.

Earthquake Insurance

Earthquake insurance
Provides insurance to protect against property damage caused by an earthquake.

Earthquake insurance protects against property damage caused by an earthquake and earth movements. Recall that standard CGL policies exclude earth movements and earthquakes from coverage. Earthquakes have caused billions of dollars in damage to residential property. As a result, many insurers have severely restricted or refused to write new policies.

Title Insurance

Title insurance protects owners of real property against any defects in title, liens, or other encumbrances not disclosed in a title insurance policy at the close of a real estate transaction. Owners seek title insurance to ensure that clear and accurate title to the property is transferred. A title insurance policy reimburses costs incurred to defend a title case and pays for the costs involved in clearing the title, up to the policy limit. A more detailed discussion on title insurance appears in chapter 10.

> *Example:* If a buyer purchased a piece of real property and secured title insurance to it, and the title to the property did not disclose unpaid taxes on the property, title insurance would pay for any costs associated with paying the unpaid taxes on the property.

Builder's Risk Insurance

Builder's risk policies indemnify for loss of, or damage to, a building under construction. They are normally written for a specific dollar amount and apply only during construction. Most often, a contractor will be required to obtain insurance to indemnify the owner and any construction lender from damages arising from the contractor's work on the project.

Builder's risk insurance
Provides insurance for a loss or damage to a building under construction.

> *Example:* While building a home, a welder accidentally ignited a fire that consumed the almost completed home. Builder's risk insurance funds the rebuilding of the residence.

Terrorism Insurance

Property owners may purchase **terrorism insurance**, which protects against damages caused by terrorist activities. Prior to September 11, 2001, insurers often provided terrorism coverage free of charge in all risk insurance policies. Most terrorism insurance policies cover damaged or destroyed property (such as buildings, equipment, furnishings, and inventory). Exclusions from coverage typically include nuclear, biological, chemical, and radiological attacks.

Umbrella Policy

An **umbrella policy** is a liability insurance policy that offers limits of liability protection in addition to the primary policy. Often, commercial general liability policies and homeowner's policies limit coverage to a certain sum. Property owners seeking additional insurance protection can secure an umbrella policy to increase their liability coverage beyond the coverage from the commercial general liability policies and homeowner's policies. In addition, umbrella policies are broader and can cover risks excluded from underlying policies.

Umbrella policy
Liability insurance coverage that covers damages in excess of the basic liability policy covering real or personal property. Umbrella insurance pays only where the underlying policy limits have been exhausted.

> *Example:* A homeowner's insurance policy may exclude recovery for the insured's liability under defamation. An umbrella policy will often include coverage for defamation; therefore, the insured would be covered for defamation under its umbrella policy.

Umbrella policies are so called because they provide additional coverage to all policies underneath them (such as a homeowner's and auto insurance policies). Umbrella insurance often is less costly to purchase than commercial general liability policies and homeowner's policies, making it an affordable method of increasing insurance limits. It often provides broader coverage than primary coverage.

> *Example:* If a homeowner had a homeowner's policy with a limit of $500,000 and then purchased an umbrella policy for $1 million of coverage, the homeowner would have insurance coverage up to $1.5 million.

What Will the Insurance Carrier Pay?

Insurance carriers use several methods to calculate the amount they will pay the insureds in the event of a covered peril. The insurance contract between the insurer and the insured will establishes the method to be used. Typically, the insurer pays either the actual cash value or the replacement cost value. An insured, by paying a higher premium, can obtain a replacement cost value or guaranteed replacement cost coverage policies, as discussed below.

Actual Cash Value

The actual cash value is the insurer's standard method of reimbursement and is the most favorable reimbursement method for the insurer. The actual cash value of a piece of property is determined by subtracting the item's depreciation from its replacement cost.

Depreciation
The gradual loss in value of property due to its deterioration and obsolescence.

Depreciation is calculated by establishing the useful life of an item and determining what percentage of that life remains. This method of calculating depreciation measures the replacement life percentage against the current replacement cost, not the original purchase price or cost. Actual cash value is equivalent to the value one should receive in the marketplace for the covered property.

> *Example:* If a garage was damaged by lightning, the carrier would consult industry guidelines on useful life and replacement cost. If a homeowner's garage had a 40-year useful life, had been in place for 20 years, and would cost $15,000 to replace today, then the insured would be paid a maximum of $7,500.

Replacement Cost

Under a replacement cost value policy, the insurer will pay the amount required to replace the damaged property, in today's marketplace, with comparable material and quality, up to the amount of the policy. If the cost to replace a covered loss on the property exceeds the policy limit, the insurer is only obligated to pay the policy limit (that is, the owner may not be able to actually replace the property through insurance proceeds alone). Unlike actual cash value, depreciation is not deducted from the value of the damaged property. Insureds prefer replacement cost value to actual cash value.

> *Example:* In the above example, the insured would be paid a maximum of $15,000, which is the cost to replace the damaged garage in today's marketplace.

Extended Replacement Cost

Extended replacement cost coverage will pay for the replacement costs up to a specified percentage above the policy limit. Insurance carriers typically agree to pay 20 or 30 percent above the policy limit under extended replacement cost policies.

> *Example:* If a home destroyed by a fire had extended replacement cost value coverage of $100,000, the insurer would typically agree to pay benefits in the sum of either $120,000 or $130,000. If the cost to replace the home exceeded these amounts, it would be the insured's responsibility to pay for the difference.

Guaranteed Replacement Cost

Guaranteed replacement cost coverage is the best policy for an insured. It provides that the insurer will pay the full cost of repairing or replacing the damaged or destroyed structure, regardless of policy limits. The insurer bears the risk of securing insurance at an amount close to the actual replacement cost of the structure.

> *Example:* In the above example, if the cost to replace the home were $175,000 and the guaranteed replacement cost policy was issued for $100,000, the insurer would pay the $175,000 to pay for the cost of replacing the structure.

Building Code Upgrades

An insured may also obtain an endorsement to provide additional reimbursement costs required to bring the structure up to current building codes or ordinance requirements. Under the above policies, the insurer must replace the structure only with comparable material and quality. If building codes or ordinance requirements have changed, the insured is typically required to pay those additional costs, unless a building code upgrade endorsement is purchased.

Underinsurance: How Much Insurance Is Enough?

It is estimated that two out of every three homes in America are underinsured. **Underinsurance** occurs when the insurance policy is insufficient to cover the costs of rebuilding a property after a peril. To keep policy premiums at a minimum, many insureds buy only the minimum mandated coverage required by statute or their mortgage lender. In addition, insureds fail to update their insurance policy limits over time or fail to increase coverage when additions and improvements are made to the property.

As construction costs rise, the cost to rebuild the property may significantly exceed the policy limit, leaving the insured to fund the balance of the costs. An insured is still responsible for paying its mortgage after a peril, even if the insurance proceeds are not sufficient to rebuild the property. In those situations, many property owners are forced to file bankruptcy; therefore, it is prudent for an insured to check annually the amount and type of insurance on the property.

Duties of the Insured

Both the insurer and the insured owe certain duties in an insurance contract. Both parties must perform the obligations imposed under the insurance contract. In addition, each party owes certain duties to the other party. An insured owes to the insurer the duties to notify and cooperate and to mitigate.

Duty to Notify

Insurance policies require that the insured provide notice of a claim for a covered loss as soon as practicable. In most cases, this means that notice must be given to the insurer within a reasonable time after a loss. Failure to give notice within a reasonable time after the loss may result in a denial of coverage.

Duty to Cooperate

An insured also has the duty to cooperate in the investigation, settlement, or defense of the claim or lawsuit. Many property policies impose a duty on the insured to submit to an examination under oath to obtain information relevant to the claim's investigation.

Voluntary payments clause
If an insured fixes a problem or damage and then notifies the insurer and seeks coverage, the insurer can deny coverage.

Under the **voluntary payments** clause, an insured cannot fix a problem or damage attributable to the insured and then notify the insurer of the claim or lawsuit. Generally, this means when an insured settles a claim without informing or obtaining the consent of the insurance company, the expense of settling the claim falls entirely on the insured. Repairing damage before giving notice to the insurance carrier may result in the denial of coverage.

Duty to Mitigate

The insured also has a duty to mitigate. The duty to mitigate requires the insured to take steps to avoid incurring expenses or other unnecessary costs. Failure to mitigate may result in coverage reduction and, in some instances, a denial of coverage.

> *Example:* If an insured's home suffers water damage due to a broken water pipe, the insured has a duty to mitigate by turning off the water supply to a home.

Duties of the Insurer

As discussed, the insurer and the insured owe duties to each other. The insurer owes the duty of good faith and fair dealing, the duty to indemnify, potentially the duty to defend, and the duty to settle claims.

Duty of Good Faith and Fair Dealing

Duty of good faith and fair dealing
An implied promise that neither party will do anything to injure the other party's right to receive the rights of the agreement.

Courts and legislatures have imposed on insurance companies the **duty of good faith and fair dealing** with their insureds. The duty of good faith and fair dealing is an implied promise (covenant) in every contract that neither party will do anything to injure the other party's right to receive the rights of the agreement. All states recognize this covenant in insurance policies and the insured may sue the insurer for damages in the event of a breach.

Insurer's Response to a Claim

Insurers can respond to a notice of claim in several ways. They may unconditionally accept the demand, require additional information, deny coverage, or agree to provide a defense to the insured under a reservation of rights as to indemnity coverage. With a **reservation of rights**, the insurer agrees to defend the insured by hiring a lawyer and paying defense costs, but it reserves the right to withdraw that defense and decline coverage if all or some of the claim involves damages or injuries falling outside of the policy coverage. State laws require a carrier to issue timely, clear, and specific reservation of rights letters.

Reservation of rights
An insurance carrier's notification to an insured that coverage for a claim may not exist under the policy.

Insurer's Right to Investigate

Some jurisdictions hold that an insurer has the right to investigate the insured's claim. Where the duty to investigate is imposed on the insurer, most courts hold that the insurer must consider all reasonably ascertainable facts before denying coverage.

Insurer's Duty to Indemnify

The **duty to indemnify** means the insurer has a duty to pay covered claims up to the limits of the policy. If the claim or damage is not covered under the policy or is excluded from it, the insurer can decline to indemnify the insured. Moreover, the insured's recovery is limited to reimbursement for losses actually suffered.

Duty to indemnify
A contractual duty to pay for any loss or damage suffered by another.

In the following case, insureds filed suit against an insurer for breach of contract when the insurer failed to timely pay the damages associated with a claim.

CASE 15.3

INSURER'S FAILURE TO TIMELY PAY A CLAIM MAY RESULT IN A BREACH OF CONTRACT

MALONEY CINQUE, LLC. v. PACIFIC INS. CO.

89 So.3d 12 (2012)

Louisiana Court of Appeal

Maloney Cinque, LLC ("Maloney") owned several truck stops in the New Orleans area. Two of their properties, Big Easy and Mardi Gras, were damaged as a result of Hurricane Katrina. Damage to the properties were caused by wind and flood. Maloney brought suit against Pacific Ins. Co. ("Pacific"), arguing that although the amounts due were paid under the policy, the amounts were not paid timely as required by law. Louisiana state law requires all insureds to pay the amount of any claim due within thirty days after receipt of satisfactory proof of loss. The parties disagree when the satisfactory proof of loss occurred. Maloney argues that satisfactory proof of loss was provided to Pacific on December 13 and 18, 2005, for both locations. Pacific contends that it did not have satisfactory proof of loss until

April 17, 2006, and that its payments on May 9 and 10, 2006, were timely. The disagreement arises from the parties' dispute as to the amount of loss that existed. The trial court found that satisfactory proof of loss occurred on December 13 and 16, 2006, and thus Pacific's payments were untimely. The trial court subjected these late payments to penalty and awarded Maloney $2,386,354.50. Pacific appealed.

Language of the Court. *Where a reasonable disagreement between the insured and the insurer as to the amount of a loss exists, the insurer's refusal to pay is not arbitrary, capricious, or without probable cause, and failure to pay within the statutory delay does not subject the insurer to penalties.*

However, if part of a claim for property damage is not disputed, the failure of the insurer to pay the undisputed portion of the claim within the statutory delay will subject the insurer to penalties on the entire claim.

We cannot agree with Maloney on the date that a satisfactory proof of loss was received by Pacific. We find that the 30-day period began to run no later than March 1, 2006. Pacific had, or should have had, all the information it needed to determine the plaintiffs' loss at that time. As determined by the trial court, the final payments of $190,348 for the Mardi Gras and $415,974 for the Big Easy made by Pacific on May 9–10, 2006 were untimely.

However, Pacific failed to pay the claim in a timely manner; it failed to timely pay even the undisputed amount of the claim. This failure exposes Pacific to statutory penalties in an amount that far exceeds the penalties awarded.

Decision. The court of appeal affirmed the trial court's finding that payment on the claim was untimely and increased the penalty amounts to meet the statutory requirements.

FOCUS ON ETHICS

Was Pacific acting ethically in not timely paying Maloney's claim?

The Insurer's Duty to Defend

Duty to defend
A contractual duty obligating the insurer to provide the insured with a defense of claims typically by hiring legal counsel.

Under the **duty to defend**, an insurer has a duty to provide defense to its insured (such as paying an attorney to defend) when a complaint alleges facts that could, if proved, impose liability on the insured within the policy's coverage. It is estimated that over 40 percent of premiums paid are allocable to paying for the costs of litigation relating to claims and coverage disputes.

The Insurer's Duty to Settle Claims

The duty to settle claims requires that, when coverage for the claim exists, the insurance company must attempt to settle the case within the policy limits. An insurer can settle solely the claims covered under the policy and withdraw its defense as to the claims for which the policy provides no protection to the insured.

■ ■ ■   Policy Cancellation and Nonrenewal

The insurer is contractually bound to cover the risk for the period provided for in the policy. An insurer has no right to cancel a policy midterm unless certain conditions arise such as nonpayment of premiums, fraud, or misrepresentation by the insured. An insurer's bad faith cancellation of a policy can subject it to damages. However, the insured may cancel the insurance contract during the policy term.

Subject to state restrictions, the insurer has no obligation to continue the policy with the insured beyond the policy period. The insurer may refuse to renew policies for any reason whatsoever or for no reason at all. Quite often insurers will not renew a policy when the insured has presented a claim in a substantial sum.

Acting in Bad Faith

An insurer acts in **bad faith** when it unjustifiably refuses to defend its insured or mishandles the claim's adjustment. When that happens, the insurer is liable to the insured for a judgment or settlement beyond the policy limits and for the cost of the insured's reasonable attorney fees in defending the case, plus any damages suffered due to the breach. Such damages could include the loss of prospective business, the cost of funds needed to pay for its defense, and mental distress to the insured. Some states permit the award of punitive damages against insurers who breach this duty.

Bad faith
Where the insurance company acts in a blatant and unfair manner against the insured with conduct exceeding mere negligence.

Key Terms and Concepts

- Insurance, page 412
- Insured, page 412
- Insurer, page 412
- Premium, page 412
- Policy limits, page 413
- McCarran Ferguson Act of 1945, page 413
- Insurable interest, page 415
- Named insured, page 417
- Additional insured, page 417
- Insurance agents, page 417
- Insurance broker, page 417
- Binder, page 419
- Covered loss, page 421
- Commercial general liability policy, page 422
- Representations and warranties insurance policy, page 423
- Errors and omissions policy, page 423

- Fire insurance policy, page 423
- Homeowner's insurance policy, page 423
- Earthquake insurance, page 424
- Builder's risk insurance, page 425
- Terrorism insurance, page 425
- Umbrella policy, page 425
- Depreciation, page 426
- Extended replacement cost coverage, page 426
- Guaranteed replacement cost coverage, page 427
- Underinsurance, page 427
- Voluntary payments, page 428
- Duty of good faith and fair dealing, page 428
- Reservation of rights, page 429
- Duty to indemnify, page 429
- Duty to defend, page 430
- Bad faith, page 431

Chapter Summary

- Insurance is a contract transferring risk of loss from one party to another in exchange for a payment. The insured pays premiums to the insurer; these premiums are set by the insurer after underwriting the risk of probable loss arising from the coverage.

- The policy limit is the maximum amount payable by the insurer under the policy. The actual loss suffered is the amount of indemnity that the insurer pays.

- The McCarran Ferguson Act gives states the power to regulate insurance. The complexity of insurance coverage is attributable, in part, to allowing differing state laws to develop regarding the rights and duties of parties to an insurance contract.

- A deductible is the amount of the claim that the insured must pay before the insurer pays benefits under the policy.

- An occurrence policy covers property losses when they occur, whether or not they occurred during a period outside of the policy term.

- To enjoy a policy's benefits, the insured must have an insurable interest in the insured property. This interest exists if the insured would sustain a financial loss if the property were lost or damaged.

- An insurable interest in the property must exist at the time of the loss.

- A named insured is the policy owner and usually the party purchasing the insurance. An additional insured is a person unrelated to the insured who receives the benefits of the insurance policy without having to pay the premiums.

- An insurance agent is an authorized agent of the insurer and can bind the insurer. An insurance broker is an agent of the insured.

- The effective date of a policy is the date on which coverage begins. A binder provides temporary insurance until the carrier issues the insurance policy.

- The insuring agreement sets forth the covered losses and exclusions from coverage under the policy.

- Co-insurance clauses require the insured to insure the property up to a stated percentage of the property value.

- Subrogation is the right of an insurer to pursue a third party that caused the insured loss.

- A covered loss is one that is unforeseen or that involves unanticipated destruction, diminution, or loss of something of value. State laws prohibit coverage for intentional wrongdoing by the insured.

- An exclusion is a coverage limitation that an insurer may use to exclude coverage within a policy.

- A commercial general liability policy is one of the most common liability protection insurance policies issued to business organizations.

- A homeowner's insurance policy usually provides coverage for damage to the dwelling and the owner's personal property. It also has liability coverage for the insured's home activities.

- Tenants may purchase renter's insurance to protect from any loss of or damages to their personal property during their tenancy.

- Builder's risk insurance indemnifies for loss of or damage to a building under construction. The owner and/or general contractor can receive policy proceeds to rebuild a structure damaged or lost because of a covered loss.

- Insurance carriers can use several methods to calculate the amount they will pay the insureds in the event of a covered peril. The most common are actual cash value, replacement cost, extended replacement cost, or guaranteed replacement cost.

- Actual cash value is the replacement cost less depreciation. Replacement cost value is the amount required to replace the damaged property in the current market without deducting depreciation.

- With extended replacement cost policy, the carrier will pay a specified percentage above the policy limit to replace property.

- Guaranteed replacement cost coverage pays the full cost to repair or replace the damaged or destroyed structure, regardless of policy limits.

- An insured has duties to the insurer to notify and cooperate and to mitigate.

- The insurer owes the insured the duty of good faith and fair dealing, the duty to indemnify, potentially the duty to defend, and the duty to settle claims.

- The duty of good faith and fair dealing is an implied promise (covenant) in every contract that neither party will do anything to injure the other party's right to receive the rights of the agreement.

- The insurer must timely investigate the claim, defend the insured, and indemnify the insured from covered losses.

- The duty to indemnify means the insurer has a duty to pay covered claims up to the limits of the policy.

Chapter Problems and Assignments

1. Explain why the distinction between an agent and a broker is important for the insured in instances where the agent or broker makes a mistake.

2. Matthew's home is damaged when a water pipe breaks and causes damage to a room in his house. He submits a claim to his insurer, who pays Matthew $7,500, representing replacement cost less depreciation. What method was used by the insurer to calculate the amount to be paid?

3. A concert promoter wants to rent out the Fields Auditorium for a concert performance. Fields Auditorium is concerned about liability resulting from the concert and does not want its insurance carrier to have to pay any claims resulting from the concert. What can Fields Auditorium do to protect its insurance carrier if it rents the facility to the concert promoter?

4. Adoree has submitted an insurance application but is concerned that liability may arise between the time he submitted the application and the time the policy becomes effective. What can Adoree do to alleviate this concern?

5. Jaclyn and Denae embark on a six-month-long world cruise. One month into the trip, their house is damaged by a fire, but Jaclyn and Denae are unaware of the damage. When they return from their cruise, they immediately notify their insurance carrier. Their carrier denies coverage due to their failure to notify the insurer within 30 days of the peril as stated in the policy. Can the insurer deny coverage in this situation?

6. Mitchell operates a consulting business out of his home. Mitchell's house suffers extensive damage from a fire, and his home office and business supplies are destroyed. Mitchell maintained homeowner's insurance, but not commercial general liability insurance. Mitchell submits a claim to his insurer. Will the insurer indemnify Mitchell for the loss?

7. Bryce owns a commercial property that was vandalized. His insurance carrier, Large Insurance, paid Bryce under the terms of his policy. Does Large Insurance have any rights against the person who vandalized the property? If so, what are they?

8. David knows that his friend has installed several electrical panels that are not in conformance with the current electrical code. David believes that this poses a risk of fire. Instead of alerting his friend, David seeks to obtain insurance on his friend's property. Can David obtain insurance on his friend's property?

9. Elena's one-bedroom apartment was destroyed by an accidental fire. She did not maintain renter's insurance. Her personal property worth $10,000 was destroyed. Is her landlord responsible for the damage to her personal property?

10. Research whether your state has a privately financed, publicly managed entity to insure natural disasters such as flood, tornado or earthquakes.

End Notes

1. 15 U.S.C. §§1011-1015.
2. Oregon law provides that a person who solicits and procures the application is deemed to be the agent of the insurer. *See Seidel v. Time Ins. Co.*, 970 P.2d 255, 258 (1998).
3. 42 U.S.C. §4001-4129.

Chapter 16
Transfers by Operation of Law and Gift

Laws should be like clothes. They should be made to fit the people they are meant to serve.
—Clarence Darrow, American lawyer (1857–1938)

Learning Objectives

1. Define the elements of adverse possession.
2. Distinguish adverse possession from prescriptive easements.
3. Define eminent domain.
4. Detail when a government regulation can constitute a taking.
5. Explain the importance of a donor's intent in making a gift.
6. Describe the elements of a valid gift.

Chapter Outline

- Introduction
- Adverse Possession
Case 16.1: *Galli v. Galli*
- Eminent Domain and Regulatory Takings
Case 16.2: *Kelo v. City of New London, Connecticut*
- Transfers by Gift
Case 16.3: *Bader v. Digney*

Opening

scenario

The Dakotas live next door to the Brinks. The Brinks have a beautiful rose garden at the fence line between the properties. For the past 25 years, both parties believed the fence line to be the dividing line between the properties, but it turns out that the Brinks' rose garden has encroached on the Dakotas' property by one foot. The Dakotas now want the rose garden moved back a foot and the fence moved, and the Brinks contend that they now own the extra one foot. As you read this chapter, determine how a court should rule if a lawsuit is filed to determine the parties' rights as to the disputed land.

Introduction

Possession of property is a powerful right. Ordinarily, the fee simple owner of property retains the ability to convey the property in the manner he or she desires and may voluntarily transfer the property without compensation as a gift. However, the law may provide for third parties, private persons, and the government to take private property. In some situations, the government is required to pay just compensation; in other situations, no payment to the legal owner of the property is required. These concepts are discussed in this chapter.

Adverse Possession

Adverse possession
A method of acquiring title by wrongfully possessing the real property of another, subject to state law requirements.

Under the doctrine of **adverse possession**, a person who does not have title to property but possesses it for a statutory period of time and meets other requirements can cause a court to convey title to the adverse possessor. This doctrine rewards a trespasser with title to the property. Moreover, the adverse possessor is not liable to the original owner for the loss of title to the property. This odd concept encourages the full and beneficial use of land and can be used to help resolve disputed boundary lines between properties.

Every state has its own laws defining the requirements for acquiring title by adverse possession. Adverse possession is recognized by statute or by complying with common law requirements. One common element is that adverse possession can only occur on privately owned property; it does not apply to publicly owned property, such as federally or state governed land. In some states, the adverse possessor must pay taxes. Generally, the requirements that enable adverse possession are as follows:

1. Adverse to that of the landowner
2. Actual possession
3. Exclusive possession

4. Open, visible, and notorious

5. Continuous for the statutory period

Each of these elements must exist for an adverse possessor to acquire title by adverse possession. Whether each of them exists is a question of fact and a burden that the adverse possessor must prove.

Adverse

The first element is met when the adverse possessor takes possession without the owner's permission and in a manner inconsistent with the true owner's legal title to the property. The adversity of the claim is measured by what a third party would think about the possession. Would third parties believe that the property's owner permitted possession? This element does not require that the adverse possessor have any negative feelings, ill will, or hatred toward the owner, simply that the use must not be permissive.

> *Example:* A trespasser is an adverse user. A permissive user never becomes adverse because, no matter how long the use continues, it began and continued without the user making any adverse claim against the landowner.

Boundary Line Disputes

Most states hold that a person using a neighbor's property due to a mistaken belief about the location of the boundary line between the properties — that is, the user believes the property belonged to him or her rather than to the neighbor — is enough to establish the adverse element under the doctrine of adverse possession.

> *Example:* A woman plants rosebushes on what she believes to be her property. In fact, they are planted two feet into her neighbor's property. Most states hold that the woman has met the adverse element for adverse possession.

Application to Landlords and Tenants

In a landlord-tenant situation, the landlord grants permissive possession to the tenant. Because of the permission, the tenant does not become an adverse possessor. Many courts hold that, where a tenant remains on the premises following the tenancy (when a tenancy at sufferance occurs), the tenancy at sufferance begins to accrue adverse possession rights. Other states require the tenant at sufferance to vacate the property and reenter it to establish the adverse element necessary for adverse possession.

> *Example:* A tenant with a 99-year lease on real property makes substantial improvements to the land. The business operated on the property has changed ownership several times. The tenant does not hold title by adverse possession because the possession granted was permissive.

Application to Co-Tenants

The adverse element may also be met between co-tenants. Recall from chapter 12 that co-tenants share equal use and equal possession of the property. Where a co-tenant refuses to allow equal possession to the other co-tenant and ousts him or her, the adverse element can be established.

Example: Melanie is a tenant in common with Cynthia. Melanie has a 90 percent interest in the property, and Cynthia has the remaining 10 percent interest. If Melanie ousts Cynthia by refusing to allow her any use of the property, Melanie can establish the adverse element for adverse possession.

Actual Possession

Actual possession requires that the adverse possessor use the property in a manner consistent with its nature and use. The property's nature and use will be determined by the property's location and the uses to which that type of property is expected to be put in the community.

Example: If the property is residential, then the adverse possessor must utilize the property as a residential property. The adverse possessor must reside on the property and use the property as would a residential owner.

The adverse possessor can only acquire by adverse possession interest in land that the adverse possessor actually occupies. However, when the possessor claims the property under color of title (discussed below) to the entire parcel, the possessor's act of maintaining continuous and actual possession of a small part of the parcel is sufficient to preserve his title of the entire parcel.

Example: If an adverse possessor desires to obtain title to farmland from an owner who owns ten acres, and the adverse possessor actually possesses one-quarter of an acre, the adverse possessor would be able to obtain title to just that one-quarter of an acre, not the entire ten acres.

Color of Title

Color of title
A defective legal instrument that the holder believes is effective to transfer title but cannot operate as a legal conveyance of title.

Some jurisdictions also require the adverse possessor to occupy the land under color of title. **Color of title** is a legal instrument (often a deed, judgment, or court decree) that the holder believes is effective to transfer title, but the legal instrument is in some way defective and cannot operate as a legal conveyance of title. Often states will shorten the stated statutory period of possession necessary to transform ownership under a claim for adverse possession when there is color of title.

Example: Color of title might occur under a deed claiming to transfer ownership of property that included more land than the grantor actually owned at the time of the conveyance.

Other grounds for color of title include the lack of a signature on a deed, the land's procurement through a faulty foreclosure sale procedure, or transference by a party lacking the mental or legal capacity to convey the property.

Exclusive Possession

While some states include actual possession and exclusive possession as one element, exclusive possession requires that the adverse use be exclusive. *Exclusive* in this context typically means that the adverse possessor cannot share possession with the legal titleholder of the property or with the general public. Most states allow two or more adverse possessors to obtain title to property jointly through adverse possession at the same time. However, most states do not allow two adverse possessors not acting in concert to obtain title to the land because each adverse possessor must have exclusive possession.

> *Example:* An adverse possessor who desires to obtain title to an abandoned residential property would not have exclusive possession if the adverse possessor allowed other individuals to reside in different rooms on the property.

Open, Visible, and Notorious Use of the Property

This element requires that the adverse possessor's acts be visible and obvious enough to put a reasonable owner on notice that someone is attempting to claim the property. Under this requirement, an observant landowner should or would know of the possessor's possession. The use may not be carried on in secret or concealed from observation. It is not necessary that the landowner be aware that the adverse possessor has taken possession of the property.

> *Example:* Enclosing property with a fence or building a dwelling on property is open and notorious.

This element is a subjective standard, and more than minimal activity might be required to place a reasonable owner on actual notice in a rural area than might be required in an urban one. The urban area might be frequently traveled, and changes in occupation thus might be noticed more quickly than if the possession occurred in a rural area.

Continuous for the Statutory Period

The adverse possessor must also continuously occupy the property without significant interruption during the statutory period. Each state provides a length of time for which the claimant must use the property before satisfying the statute of limitations for adverse possession. The statutory period varies from three years to 40 years, with many states having a 20-year statutory period.

During the statutory period, the possession must not be interrupted by either physical ouster or court-ordered eviction. This requirement does not mean that the adverse possessor must be on the property 24 hours a day for the statutory period. The adverse possessor can leave the land (for example, for work and vacations). The continuous use is established by taking into account the nature and use of the property.

> *Example:* Maggie is occupying an abandoned residential property under a claim of adverse possession. She has started to improve the property and leaves for work each day and returns home. She typically takes a two-week vacation each year. Even though Maggie leaves daily during the workweek and takes vacations, she has still met the continuous element for adverse possession.

Tacking of Time

Periods of possession by successive adverse possessors can be added together to attain the statutory period for adverse possession. This process is known as **tacking** and is allowed where privity exists. **Privity** occurs when possession of the subject land is passed from one person to another by deed, will, the laws of intestacy (distributing the property of those dying without a will), or contract.

> **Example:** In a state that had a 20-year statutory time period for adverse possession, if Juan adversely possessed Gabriella's property for 19 years and then died, but Juan's son continues to possess the property following Juan's death, the son's possession may be added to the time Juan possessed the property to reach the applicable 20-year statutory period.

Where an adverse possessor ousts another party (such as by forcibly removing another adverse possessor), no tacking of time occurs. If an adverse possessor abandons the property and another adverse possessor begins possessing the property, no privity between them exists. The statutory period for adverse possession begins anew for the second adverse possessor

> **Example:** Nolan has been an adverse possessor for nine years in a state that has a ten-year statutory period. Gabriella desires to have the property and forcibly ousts Nolan from the property. Gabriella is not able to tack Nolan's nine years of adverse possession because she ousted him from the property.

Stopping Adverse Possession

Before an adverse possessor has accrued the statutory time required to obtain title through adverse possession, the legal owner of the property can take several steps to halt the adverse possession claim.

1. *File a lawsuit against the adverse possessor for trespass or a quiet title action.* The trespass action will provide for the removal of the trespassing adverse possessor. The quiet title action, as discussed previously, will determine the rights between the parties to the property. Once either lawsuit is filed, the continuous period of possession is interrupted; an adverse possessor would need to start anew the statutory time required for possession.
2. *Grant permission.* If the landowner grants permission to the adverse possessor to use or possess the property, the adverse element is destroyed. The legal owner could deny permission later, which would start the statutory period. The landowner would have also the rights to remove the trespasser through a trespass action.

In the following case, an owner with 75 percent interest in a property claimed to have acquired the remaining 25 percent from the other owner by means of adverse possession. The majority owner brought action to quiet title to the property.

Tacking
Rule allowing an adverse possessor who has not been in possession for the statutory period to add the periods of adverse use by prior adverse possessors.

Privity
The state of two parties being in contract with each other, which can be met by a contract, deed, will, or the laws of intestacy.

> ### CASE 16.1
>
> ## ADVERSE POSSESSION MAY OCCUR AS TO A PARTIAL OWNERSHIP INTEREST

GALLI v. GALLI

117 A.D.3d 679 (2014)

New York Supreme Court, Appellate Division

Robert Galli ("Robert") sought to quiet title to property that has been owned by members of the Galli family since 1946. Since 1972, Robert and his parents have owned a 75 percent interest in the property and lived there. The defendant, Mary Jean Galli ("Mary Jean"), was married to Robert's uncle, Henry, and the two owned the remaining 25 percent of the property. Neither Mary Jean nor Henry made any contribution to the maintenance of the property or lived there. Henry died in 2000 and left Mary Jean the 25 percent interest. After the death of his parents, Robert became the sole owner of the 75 percent interest in the property. In 2010, Robert brought action to determine that he was the owner of what had been Henry's 25 percent interest by means of adverse possession. In his lawsuit, Robert stated that since 1972 he and his parents had continuously possessed, controlled, managed, and maintained the property exclusively, openly and notoriously and under a claim of right hostile to any ownership interest that any other individual might claim to have once had. Robert further argued that neither Henry nor Mary Jean had made any claims to the property since 1960, and they "did not believe they were owners of the property having exercised no control, possession or claim to the property since 1960." Lastly, Robert argued that the property has been in the exclusive possession of himself and his mother for more than twenty years prior to the commencement of the instant action. The trial court determined that Robert possessed 100 percent interest in the

property and that Mary Jean had no interest in the property. Mary Jean appealed.

Language of the Court. *To establish a claim of adverse possession, the following five elements must be proved: Possession must be (1) hostile; (2) actual; (3) open and notorious; (4) exclusive; and (5) continuous for the required period.*

Here, Robert established by clear and convincing evidence that his possession of the subject premises had been actual, open and notorious, exclusive, and continuous for the required 20-year period, giving rise to an inference of hostile possession. Thus, Robert established that he had acquired, by adverse possession, the 25 percent interest in the property previously owned by Henry, which Mary Jean argues had actually passed to her through intestate succession. In opposition to Robert, Henry failed to raise a triable issue of fact. Accordingly, the trial court properly held for Robert.

Decision. The appellate court affirmed the trial court's ruling, finding Robert acquired full interest in the property through adverse possession.

FOCUS ON ETHICS

Does it seem fair that family members, residing in a property, can take property by adverse possession from non-residing family members? Why did the court not infer implied permission between the family members in this case?

Other Potential Requirements

Because adverse possession is state specific, each state can create its own requirements for adverse possession. The following two requirements are among the most common additional requirements across the states:

1. Payment of taxes
2. Perfecting title by adverse possession

Payment of Taxes

In some states, the adverse possessor must pay taxes (such as property taxes) upon the land subject to the adverse possession. In these states, if all other requirements are met except the tax payment, the court will usually grant the trespasser a prescriptive easement rather than ownership through adverse possession.

■ ■ ■   Adverse Possession and Prescriptive Easements Compared

The nature of the right acquired is the principal difference between title acquired by adverse possession and an easement by prescription. Adverse possession grants more than a right to use; it grants ownership of the property. A prescriptive easement grants a specific use over another's property. Quite often, boundary line disputes generate claims regarding these two types of rights.

> *Example:* Susan constructs a driveway on what she believes is the edge of her property, but the land actually extends onto her neighbor's property. She might claim either a prescriptive easement or adverse possession. The result will be determined through her actions on the strip of land upon which the driveway is built.
>
> If her use was merely to access her own property, the right she acquires might well be a prescriptive easement. If she removed the driveway and landscaped the area, her actions might be interpreted as supporting adverse possession. The facts of each case will determine the extent of these rights regarding the property of an adjoining landowner.

Payment of property taxes is never necessary for a successful prescriptive easement claim. In the states where tax payment is required for a trespasser to obtain ownership, courts will grant the trespasser a prescriptive easement, but not ownership by adverse possession, when all requirements for adverse possession have been met except the payment of taxes.

Focus on Ethics

The doctrine of adverse possession transforms a wrong (trespassing on another's property) into a right (title to the property). The rule grants title to someone who did not respect the property rights of another. This rule appears to punish those who are negligent in their supervision of their real property. On the other hand, it may be argued that it grants title to the person who values the property the most.

What ethical conflicts are posed by this rule promoting title theft? Why should long-standing possession transfer title? Do we continue to recognize this rule because in our society we value highly the possession of property?

Eminent Domain and Regulatory Takings

All governments in the United States have the power to take private property for public uses. That power is known as **eminent domain**. The government may take property from private owners as long as the owner receives just compensation. Eminent domain and condemnation are terms used interchangeably, but eminent domain refers to the right of the government to take property, while **condemnation** is the legal proceeding by which the government exercises its eminent domain powers. The source of the government's eminent domain power springs from the Takings Clause of the U.S. Constitution.

Eminent domain
The government's power to seize private property for public use.

Takings Clause (Eminent Domain Clause)

" . . . nor shall private property be taken for public use, without just compensation." — U.S. Constitution, Amendment V

The Takings Clause applies to both the taking of title and depriving the owner of the possession of property.

The purpose of eminent domain is to prevent the government from forcibly taking property without paying just compensation to the private owner. Eminent domain also serves a public purpose by promoting the public interest. These interests can be advanced by the use of eminent domain to secure and expand transportation corridors, facilities, and other rights and services that are better protected by government than by private ownership.

Three important questions relate to the Takings Clause:

1. Is there a taking of private property?
2. Is the taking for a public use or public purpose?
3. Has just compensation been paid to the private property owner?

Taking of Private Property

Eminent domain requires that the government take private property. A taking of private property occurs where (1) the landowner is deprived of any use of the property, (2) there is a permanent physical invasion on the property, or (3) a regulatory taking occurs that denies the landowner all economic uses of the property.

Landowner Deprived of Any Use of the Property

If a landowner is deprived of any portion of its private property, a taking has occurred.

> **Example:** The state requires that only one inch of your property be taken to allow for the highway's expansion. While you are deprived of only one inch of your property, you have still been deprived of one inch of property, and a taking has occurred.

Permanent Physical Invasion

A taking has occurred when the government permanently takes possession of or physically occupies all or a part of a property. A taking has occurred when a government regulation authorizes a third party to physically invade private property.

> **Example:** The installation of cable wires and a steel cable box on private property, authorized by a New York law, was considered a permanent physical invasion and a taking.[1]

Regulatory Takings

Regulatory takings
A government regulation that deprives the owner of all economically beneficial use of the property.

With **regulatory takings**, the government may issue regulations so severe in their effect on a landowner that those regulations are equivalent to the governmental taking of the property. A regulation that deprives the owner of all economically beneficial uses of the property constitutes a regulatory taking. If the regulation only decreases the property's value, a taking has not occurred.

> **Example:** A developer acquired beachfront lots for approximately $1 million. Before he started construction on them, a new state law barred construction on them for public safety reasons. The lots were rendered valueless. The Supreme Court held that a regulatory taking had occurred that deprived the landowner of all economically viable uses of the property.[2]

Taking for Public Use or Public Purpose

Public use
In the context of eminent domain, any conceivable benefit to the public welfare can be deemed a public use.

Property cannot be taken by eminent domain unless it is for a **public use**. The Supreme Court's current position is that public use is met if the taking is rationally related to a conceivable public purpose. As part of the explication of its position, the Supreme Court defined public use quite broadly. The expansiveness of the public use definition will accommodate virtually any need that addresses the advancement of the public welfare (such as increasing sales taxes). This purpose may be achieved even if it involves taking private property from one owner for the purpose of conveying it to another private owner, as long as the public may benefit.

In the following case, the Supreme Court held that a city's taking of private property to sell to a private developer was a taking for a "public use."

PUBLIC USE IS SATISFIED IF THE TAKING BEARS A RATIONAL RELATIONSHIP TO A LEGITIMATE PUBLIC PURPOSE

KELO v. CITY OF NEW LONDON, CONNECTICUT

545 U.S. 469 (2005)

United States Supreme Court

The city of New London sits at the junction of the Thames River and the Long Island Sound in Southeastern Connecticut. After decades of economic decline, a state agency in 1990 designated the city as a distressed municipality. In 2000, the city approved a development plan that would create in excess of 1,000 jobs, increase tax and other revenues, and revitalize an economically distressed city, including its downtown and waterfront areas. The development plan included a small urban village in the center that would include restaurants and shopping, marinas, a pedestrian river walk, and a new $300 million Pfizer pharmaceutical company facility containing at least 90,000 square feet of research and development office space.

The city authorized the New London Development Corporation ("NLDC"), a private nonprofit entity, to develop the property. While the NLDC purchased property from willing sellers, the city council also authorized the NLDC to acquire property by exercising eminent domain in the city's name.

Kelo's property was acquired through eminent domain powers. Kelo lived in an area that was not blighted or otherwise in poor condition. Instead, it was condemned only because Kelo happened to be located in the development area. Kelo brought suit claiming that the taking of the property violated the public use restriction in the Fifth Amendment. The state's superior court held that the taking violated the public use restriction in the Fifth Amendment. The appellate court reversed authorizing the takings under the Fifth Amendment. Both sides appealed to the U.S. Supreme Court.

Language of the Court. *This is not a case in which the City is planning to open the condemned land — at least not in its entirety — to use by the general public. Nor will the private lessees of the land in any sense be*

required to operate like common carriers, making their services available to all comers. This Court long ago rejected any literal requirement that condemned property be put into use for the general public.

The disposition of this case turns on the question whether the City's development plan serves a public purpose. Without exception, our cases have defined that concept broadly, reflecting our longstanding policy of deference to legislative judgments in this field.

The City has carefully formulated an economic development plan that it believes will provide appreciable benefits to the community, including — but by no means limited to — new jobs and increased tax revenue. The City is endeavoring to coordinate a variety of commercial, residential, and recreational uses of land, with the hope that they will form a whole greater than the sum of its parts. To effectuate this plan, the City has invoked a state statute that specifically authorizes the use of eminent domain to promote economic development. Given the comprehensive character of the plan, the thorough deliberation that preceded its adoption, and the limited scope of our review, it is appropriate for us to resolve the challenges of the individual owners, not on a piecemeal basis, but rather in light of the entire plan.

Decision. The city's proposed use of Kelo's property serves a public purpose. The takings challenged here satisfy the public use requirement of the Fifth Amendment. Public use in this case was broadly interpreted to mean "public purpose."

FOCUS ON ETHICS

Should cities be allowed to redevelop non-blighted areas if the purpose is purely to increase tax revenues? Do you agree with the Supreme Court's decision in *Kelo*?

While the *Kelo* decision had many supporters, *Kelo* was unpopular in many states. In response, many states passed laws limiting the power of local governments to use eminent domain for economic development purposes.

Just Compensation to the Property Owner

Just compensation is the payment of a property's fair market value at the time of the taking. If a partial taking of a property occurs, the government must pay the fair market value for the portion of the property taken. In addition, the government is responsible for paying any damages that might result from the severance and cause a reduction in the value of the land remaining in the owner's hands.

> *Example:* If the government took 30 acres of a 100-acre tract, it must pay just compensation not only on the 30 acres but also for any diminution in value to the remaining 70 acres. If the remaining land increases in value, then the increased value is offset against any of the owner's losses. This might occur, for example, if the 30 acres were taken to construct a major road, which then improved access to the remaining 70 acres and increased the remainder's value. However, some states have adopted a variety of approaches to partial takings. Some allow payment of the full value of the 30 acres without offset, while others take the offset into account.

Transfers by Gift

Gift
A voluntary transfer of property without payment or the expectation of repayment.

A **gift** is a voluntary transfer of property. When one person (the "**donor**") transfers title to real property to another (the "**donee**") without any consideration, it is a gift. Generally, persons are free to give their property to whomever they wish. The key characteristic of a gift is that it is done without payment or the expectation of repayment. With real property gifts, the execution, delivery, and acceptance of a deed make the gift irrevocable. Prior to such time, the gift is revocable. Where the gift is revoked and the donee detrimentally relied on believing a gift would be made, the donee is entitled to recover the costs related to the detrimental reliance.

Donor
Person who gives a gift to another.

Donee
Person who receives a gift from a donor.

> *Example:* Nelly informs John that she will gift him her house. In reliance, John insures and paints the house. If Nelly revokes the promise, John may recover from Nelly the costs of the property insurance and the cost to have the house painted.

Gifts are classified by whether they are made during the donor's life (***inter vivos***) or in contemplation of the donor's death (**gifts *causa mortis***). Transfers made after death by will, trust, or intestate succession are not considered gifts and are discussed in chapter 17.

Inter Vivos Gift Requirements

***Inter vivos* gift**
A gift made during the donor's lifetime.

Three legal requirements exist to make a valid *inter vivos* gift:

1. Donor's intention to make a gift

2. Delivery of the gift to the donee
3. Acceptance of the gift by the donee

Donative Intent

The donor's intent is essential. The actions or intentions of the donor must be clear, unmistakable, and unequivocal to evidence the voluntary making of a gift. In making the gift, the donor must relinquish control of and all rights to the property gifted. Determining the donor's intent is frequently litigated in circumstances involving post-death disputes relating to gifts made prior to death and to gifts made during marriage to persons other than the decedent's spouse. The evidence of donative intent may be expressed in words or actions or inferred from the surrounding circumstances, including the relationship of the parties.

Delivery

Delivery is accomplished by the unconditional transfer of property to the donee. The intention to make a gift does not constitute delivery because it is an expression of a promise to make a gift in the future. Until delivery occurs, the promise to make a gift can be revoked.

With delivery, the owner must surrender possession of and control over the gift. Delivery may occur through either actual delivery or constructive delivery. With actual delivery, the donor physically delivers the gift (for example, by physically handing over a deed) to the donee. **Constructive delivery** occurs when the donor delivers to the donee the exclusive means of obtaining possession or control of the property and relinquishes control over the property.

> **Constructive delivery**
> A method that can be used in making gifts where the donor makes a symbolic delivery of the property to the donee.

> **Example:** John had his attorney prepare deeds to transfer property John owned to his niece. He placed the executed deeds in a safe-deposit box and gave his niece the only key. John has constructively delivered the deeds to his niece as he has relinquished control over the property and has given the donee the exclusive means of obtaining possession.

Acceptance

Acceptance of the gift is presumed unless the donee makes the rejection clear by refusing to take physical possession of or assert control over the property. When the donee exercises control over the object of the gift, acceptance by the donee is presumed. A donee is not under any legal obligation to accept a gift; however, once the gift has been accepted, it becomes an irrevocable transfer of ownership from the donor to the donee.

In the following case, an administrator for a decedent's estate sued to set aside a gift of real property.

BADER v. DIGNEY

55 A.D.3d 1290 (2008)
New York Supreme Court, Appellate Division

Prior to her death, Beryl Digney executed a deed granting title to her home to her son, Kevin. She handed (delivered) the deed to him in the presence of his attorney. She chose not to record the deed because she feared his sisters would be upset by her gift to him.

Beryl and Kevin continued to live in the home until her death, and during her lifetime she paid the real property taxes. Bader, the public administrator of the her estate following her death, sought to have the deed of real property to Kevin Digney set aside. At trial, the court held Beryl had made an inter vivos gift to her son, Kevin.

Language of the Court. *An inter vivos gift is valid only if the donee establishes the following three elements by clear and convincing evidence: (1) intent on the part of the donor to make a present transfer of the property; (2) actual or constructive delivery of the gift to the donee; and (3) acceptance of the gift by the donee.*

The intent element requires an irrevocable present transfer of ownership, or title, although the donor may retain possession of the property for the remainder of his or her life. The delivery element requires a delivery sufficient to divest the donor of dominion and control over the property. The acceptance element is presumed when the gift is of value to the donee.

Here, Digney established that decedent intended to make a present transfer of her property to him but that she did not want the deed recorded "until things settle down," because she was concerned that her daughters would "cause trouble" if they found out that she had given the property to Digney. Digney further established that he, decedent, and decedent's attorney were present when decedent executed the deed and related documents, that the deed was handed to Digney at decedent's direction, and that Digney accepted it.

The fact that decedent continued to pay taxes on the property until her death is not inconsistent with her continued possession of the property and intention to make a present transfer of the title and ownership to Digney. The evidence establishes that decedent continued to pay the taxes on the property because she was residing in the house on the property.

Decision. The appellate court affirmed, finding the deed to be an *inter vivos* gift made to Digney by the decedent.

FOCUS ON ETHICS

Should a deed of real property have to be recorded for it to be considered delivered?

Causa Mortis Gifts

Causa mortis **gifts**
A gift made in contemplation of an impending death.

Causa mortis **gifts** (sometimes referred to as deathbed gifts) occur when a donor makes a gift in contemplation of her impending death. The requirements of a valid gift *causa mortis* are as follows:

1. The donor intended to make a gift effective at death.
2. The donor made the gift in anticipation of an impending death from an illness, disease, or peril.
3. The donor died as a result of the illness, disease, or peril.
4. Delivery of the gift occurred.

If the donor dies as a result of the illness, disease, or peril, the gift becomes irrevocable. If the donor survives, the gift is automatically revoked.

Example: John is scheduled for major surgery. John tells his brother, Joseph, that he wishes Joseph to have John's art collection in the event John dies as a result of the surgery. Joseph agrees to the gift. John survives the surgery, and the gift to his brother is automatically revoked.

Setting Aside Gifts

A gift must reflect the donor's free will. Many of the same defenses to the enforcement of contracts discussed in chapter 8 can be used to set aside a gift. Specifically, when a gift results from fraud, duress, material mistake, or undue influence, it may be set aside.

Example: If a donor makes a gift to a short-term caretaker and ignores a spouse of many decades, the gift can be set aside as made under undue influence if the donor was vulnerable to a manipulation of her free will and judgment.

Key Terms and Concepts

- Adverse possession, page 436
- Color of title, page 438
- Tacking, page 440
- Privity, page 440
- Eminent domain, page 443
- Condemnation, page 443
- Takings Clause, page 443
- Regulatory takings, page 444

- Public use, page 444
- Gift, page 446
- Donor, page 446
- Donee, page 446
- *Inter vivos* gifts, page 446
- Constructive delivery, page 447
- *Causa mortis* gifts, page 448

Chapter Summary

- Under certain circumstances, a trespasser can enter land, occupy it, and gain legal title to it through adverse possession.

- The adverse possessor receives title to the real property in fee simple, just as if title were conveyed in fee simple by deed.

- Adverse possession requires adverse use to that of the landowner; actual possession; exclusive possession; open, visible, and notorious possession; and continuous possession for the statutory period.

- Adverse possessions in some jurisdictions also require the adverse possessor to occupy the land under color of title.

- Color of title is a legal instrument (often a deed, judgment, or court decree) that the holder believes is effective to transfer title, but the legal instrument is in some way defective and cannot operate as a legal conveyance of title.

- Tacking allows periods of possession by successive adverse possessors to be added together to attain the statutory period for adverse possession as long as privity exists between the parties.

- A landowner may stop adverse possession by filing a lawsuit against the adverse possessor for trespass or a quiet title action against the trespasser.

- Eminent domain allows the government to take private property for public use.

- If the government takes private property under its eminent domain power for a public purpose, the government must pay just compensation.

- Just compensation is the fair market value of the property.

- A permanent physical occupation authorized by the government is a taking that must be compensated.

- Where a regulation deprives the owner of all economically beneficial uses of the property, there is a regulatory taking.

- Property cannot be taken by eminent domain unless it is for a public use. The Supreme Court's current position is that public use is met if the taking is rationally related to a conceivable public purpose.

- A gift is a voluntary transfer of property.

- Gifts are classified by whether they are made during the donor's life (*inter vivos*) or made in contemplation of the donor's death (gifts *causa mortis*).

- *Inter vivos* gifts require that the donor intends to make a gift, that the gift be delivered to the donee, and that the donee accept the gift.

- Constructive delivery occurs when the donor delivers to the donee the exclusive means of obtaining possession or control of the property and relinquishes control over the property.

- A *causa mortis* gift requires that the donor to intend to make a gift effective at death; the donor makes the gift in anticipation of an impending death from an illness, disease, or peril; the donor delivers the gift to the donee; and the donor dies as a result of the illness, disease, or peril.

Chapter Problems and Assignments

1. Detail the elements necessary to take a property by adverse possession.

2. When does a taking of private property occur?

3. Ryan and Elliot are brothers who own a beachfront property as tenants in common. Ryan owns 75 percent, and Elliot owns 25 percent. Several years into their ownership of the property, Ryan decides he is tired of giving Elliot equal possession when he owns less, so he prohibits Elliot from using the beachfront property. Ryan wants to buy Elliot's interest, but Elliot refuses to sell. Will Ryan be able to take the property by adverse possession?

4. Omar inherits a vacation home distant from his residence. He takes no action to inspect the property at any time. Without his knowledge, the Forche family has started using the property as their own home. The neighbors believe that the Forches purchased the property.

Assuming the Forches meet the state's statutory period of time for occupation, can they take title to the property by adverse possession?

5. Kyle has a rare coin that he wants to ensure his brother receives upon Kyle's death. With his brother and sister present, he tells them his brother is to receive the rare coin upon Kyle's death. He places the coin in his desk drawer so that it could be accessible upon his passing. When Kyle dies, his sister asserts there was no delivery of the coin and no gift. Is she entitled to a share of its value?

6. Lance owns a commercial property in the city of Yorba. Lance has plans to develop his property and build a five-story apartment complex. The city of Yorba enacts an ordinance prohibiting construction of buildings over three stories in the city. Lance's property is now worth many millions of dollars less than the purchase price. Is he entitled to sue for a taking?

7. The Jamesons own a house in a blighted area. The city has plans to develop the blighted area and wants to use eminent domain to take the property. It will then transfer the property to private commercial developers who will construct a commercial and residential district, thereby increasing the city's sales tax and property tax revenues. The Jamesons object that the transaction is not for a public purpose. Who is correct?

8. The Muchados have a family farm with ten acres of land that has been in their family for generations. Due to suburban growth, their farmland is now being encroached on by neighboring communities. The county seeks to take a portion of the Muchados' farmland under eminent domain and use the land for a public school. The Muchados have been offered $250,000 for a portion of the land for use as a school site. That is a fair price. The Muchados don't want to sell for any price because of the sentimental value of the property of this multigenerational asset. Can they be forced to sell? Will the price include payment for the emotional loss suffered by the family members?

9. Research your state's law on adverse possession. Do the requirements vary from those in the text?

10. Following the *Kelo* decision, has your state sought to narrow the definition of "public use" to restrain the taking of private property. Research the question.

End Notes

1. 458 U.S. 419 (1982).

2. 505 U.S. 1003 (1992).

Chapter 17
Transfers After Death: Wills, Intestacy, and Probate

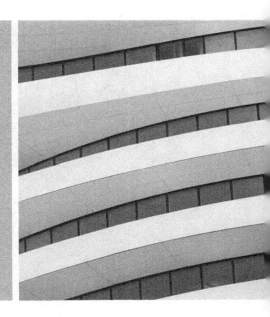

"The key here, I think, is not to think of death as an end. But think of it more as a very effective way of cutting down on your expenses."
    —Boris, Love and Death (1975)

Learning Objectives

1. Understand the requirements for making a will.
2. Explain how property is transferred under the laws of intestate succession.
3. Describe the process of probate.
4. Distinguish between an *inter vivos* trust and a testamentary trust.
5. Identify the benefits of using a trust.

Chapter Outline

- Introduction
- Wills
- Case 17.1: *Ferguson v. Critopoulos*
- Intestate Succession
- Probate
- Trusts

Opening scenario

Arman passed away without a will. His wife, two children, brother, and sister all claimed an interest in his estate. As you read this chapter, consider how Arman's estate will be distributed.

Introduction

We all will die, and how our property is distributed can be of great importance to us. Property may be distributed voluntarily after a person's death through a deceased person's will or trust. It may also be distributed through the laws of intestacy. Depending on how property is transferred, probate court may be required. This chapter discusses these concepts.

■ ■ ■ Key Terms and Concepts

This area of law has many key terms. Several are important to know as we begin our study of this area of the law:

- A **testator** (male) **or testatrix** (female) is a person who makes a will.
- A **decedent** is the person who dies.
  - ☐ If the decedent dies **testate**, it means the person had a valid will at the time of death.
  - ☐ If a decedent dies without a valid will, the person dies **intestate**.
- **Issue** is the descendants (such as children, grandchildren, great-grandchildren and so on) of the decedent.
- A **devise** is a gift of real property under a will.
- A **bequest** is a gift of personal property.
- A **beneficiary** is the person who receives the testator's property from a will.

Will
A legal instrument declaring how a person wants their property distributed upon death.

Wills

A **will** is the legal instrument by which a person dictates how his or her property will be disposed of at death. A will allows a decedent to be specific or general with gifts.

For example, each individual piece of china could be given to different individuals, or a will could provide that all personal and real property be given to a specified person. Further, decedents can name who they wish to have handle their estates upon their passing and distribute their property.

Unlike a deed, a will may be changed and amended at any time prior to the death of the decedent. Upon death, however, the property is transferred, and no changes may be made to the will. In addition, the will cannot change the characteristics of how property is held by co-owners. In chapter 12, we discussed joint tenancy, community property, and other co-ownership scenarios. A will cannot change these characteristics.

> *Example:* Nelly dies with property held in joint tenancy with her brother. If Nelly stated in her will that she wanted that property to be distributed to her sister Sarah, that provision of the will would be void. Her property would pass automatically upon Nelly's death to her brother because of laws of joint tenancy (see chapter 12).

Requirements for Creation

Although wills can be simple documents, certain requirements must be met if a will is to be enforced. Most states require four elements to make a will enforceable: (1) a writing, (2) capacity, (3) the testator's signature, and (4) witnesses.

Writing Requirement

A will must be in writing to be enforceable. A few states do provide for oral wills (known as nuncupative wills). Because the circumstances of making such a will could be subject to fraud and perjury of witnesses, if a state permits the use of an oral will, it usually limits its use to the distribution of personal property and only if made in the circumstances of imminent death.

The type of document used as a will may be informal. However, for a document to be treated as a will it must contain a clearly expressed intention to dispose of property after death as well as compliance with other requirements discussed below.

> *Example:* Letters have been admitted to probate as a decedent's last will and testament.

Wills may be handwritten. Handwritten wills are known as **holographic wills**. They have slightly different requirements for validity. Generally, the material portions of the will (such as the gifts and beneficiary names) must be in the testator's own handwriting. The will must also be signed by the testator. Usually no witnesses are required for holographic wills, but a few states require that holographic wills be witnessed to be valid. Because holographic wills can provoke litigation among the heirs if all the formalities required for a will were not followed and the will was not dated.

Holographic wills
A will that is entirely handwritten and signed by the testator.

> *Example:* The death of the painter Thomas Kinkade resulted in a will contest between Kinkade's wife of 30 years and his girlfriend of 18 months. The painter left two holographic wills favoring his girlfriend. His widow sued to have them set aside and a previous estate plan enforced. The matter was resolved through a confidential settlement between the parties.

■ ■ ■   Electronic Wills

Wills written and stored in an electronic record are not allowed in most states. Nevada was the first state to enact a statute providing for enforcement of electronic wills. Other states have proposed legislation to enact their own electronic wills acts. Where proposed and enacted, the testator's electronic signature must be authenticated by at least one "authentication characteristic." The authentication characteristic examples include a fingerprint, a retinal scan, voice recognition, facial recognition, a digitized signature, or other authentication using a unique characteristic of the person. The will must still meet the remaining requirements, namely testator capacity and witness.

Capacity

The testator must have the capacity to execute (sign) a will at the time of the will's execution. Capacity requires that the testator possess both age capacity and mental capacity at the time of the will's execution.

Every state requires a testator to be of a certain age to execute a will. In most states, the testator must be at least 18 years of age. In addition to the age requirement, the testator must also have the mental capacity to execute a will. The testator must be able to understand the nature and extent of the property, name the persons to whom they wish to distribute the property, and have a general understanding of the purpose of a will. When an individual lacks the sound mind required to make a will, the resulting instrument is void.

Testator's Signature

Acknowledge
The process of verifying the identity of the testator and witnesses of the executed the will before a notary public.

Notary public
A commissioned representative of a state who is charged with verifying the identity of the signor of documents.

The testator must either sign the will or direct someone else to sign the will on the testator's behalf. Where the testator is unable to sign the will (such as by disease or physical impairments), the testator may direct another person to execute the will in his or her presence. A will signed by a third party on behalf of the testator requires that the will be acknowledged to be valid. A will is **acknowledged** when the testator and witnesses confirm the authenticity of their signatures before a notary public.

Frequently, even when the testator signs the will, the will is acknowledged by a **notary public**. In many states an acknowledged will before a notary public carries a presumption that the will was validly executed. Known as "self-proving" wills, these acknowledged wills save time in probate court of otherwise having the witnesses to the will testify to the will's validity.

Witnesses

Most states require that wills be witnessed, usually by either two or three mentally competent witnesses. States may also require that the witnesses be disinterested (without a beneficial interest in the will). The witnesses sign as witnesses to the will's execution in the presence of the testator and each other.

Contents of a Will

While certain requirements are necessary to create a legal will, no specific requirements cover the contents to be included in a will. Lawyers have developed standard procedures for the preparation and execution of wills. Wills usually contain the following provisions:

1. *Publication clause.* The publication clause identifies the testator and states that the testator has capacity (for example, "being of sound mind") and that the document represents their intention to make a will.
2. *Revocation clause.* In this clause, the testator usually revokes all previous wills and codicils. However, instead of revoking previous will and codicils, the testator may amend certain provisions of a previously executed will.
3. *Funeral and debt clauses.* The testator can dictate and provide any funeral or burial instructions they desire and specify the property to be used to pay the decedent's debts and inheritance taxes.
4. *Gift clauses.* The testator can dispose of real and personal property through either specific dispositions (such as my diamond ring to my daughter, Eva) or general dispositions (all of my personal property to my daughter, Eva).
5. *Residuary clause.* Usually a residuary clause is inserted that governs how property that remains in the estate after satisfaction of all gifts should be distributed.
6. *Appointment of representative.* The testator may appoint a representative of the estate, also referred to as an executor/executrix, and specify their powers.
7. *Appointment of guardian.* In the event a testator has minor children, the will typically appoints a guardian for the children.
8. *Penalty clause.* The testator may penalize or minimize the distribution to a person who contests the will.
9. *Distribution clause.* A testator may intentionally declare that a person (such as a child) will receive nothing from the estate.
10. *Execution clause.* The will must be signed and witnessed, and sometimes the signatures must benotarized.

Joint and Mutual Wills

Joint wills and mutual wills are contracts in which the parties agree as to how the property should be distributed upon their deaths. A **joint will** is created when two or more testators, often spouses, execute the same instrument as their will. Not all states recognize the validity of a joint will.

Mutual wills, also called reciprocal wills, occur when two or more testators execute separate wills and make reciprocal gifts of their property to each other on the condition that the surviving person, on their death, leaves the remaining property as agreed upon by the testators. All states recognize the validity of mutual wills. Because they are

Joint will
A will created by two or more testators.

Mutual wills
Where two or more testators execute separate wills and leave their property to the other testators on the condition that the surviving persons, on their deaths, leave the remaining property as agreed upon by the testators.

enforceable contracts, they cannot be unilaterally revoked after the death of any of the testators.

Changing a Will: Codicils

Codicil
A revision to a will that can amend, modify, or revoke a prior will.

A **codicil** is a revision to a will that can modify, amend, or revoke a prior will. A codicil must be executed in the same manner as the original will to be valid. If the codicil amends a prior will, it must reference the will it is amending. If the codicil does not specifically state that it is revoking a prior will, the will and codicil must be read together to determine the testator's wishes. Codicils may change the testator's estate plan in a variety of ways.

> *Example:* A codicil may add or delete beneficiaries, change the assets to be distributed, or place conditions upon the receipt of gifts made in the will (for example, the codicil may require that a donee have attained a college degree in order to receive her gift).

Revoking a Will

A will can be revoked by the acts of the testator. A subsequent will or codicil can revoke a will, the testator may physically destroy the will, or the will may be revoked by operation of law.

To revoke a will by physical destruction, the testator must intend to destroy the will and then actually do so. Many states do not require the will to be completely destroyed to be revoked. States may provide for physical destruction when a testator intends to destroy a will by tearing material portions of the will, burning the will, writing cancelled or void across the will, or completely obliterating it (for example, by shredding it).

> *Example:* A testator who intends to revoke his will may do so by taking the will and placing it through a document shredder.

Many states revoke or partially revoke a will by operation of law when the testator's family situation changes between the will's execution and the testator's death.

> *Example:* A divorce often revokes a will, at least as to property left to the former spouse.

Disinheritance Limitations

Occasionally, a spouse may be omitted from a will. This may arise when, after marriage, a will was not amended to include the spouse. States vary on the treatment of an omitted spouse. Some states provide for dower or curtesy rights (see chapter 12 for a discussion of dower and curtesy rights); others follow community property laws, if applicable; and still others provide for a statutory share of the testator's estate as determined under state laws. Note too that a spouse may have signed a waiver, such as a prenuptial or postnuptial agreement, eliminating or reducing their share of the estate.

Children may also be omitted from a will. Children born or adopted after the execution of a will are known as **pretermitted children**. State laws often provide that these pretermitted heirs will receive at least what they would have received under intestate succession (discussed below). An exception occurs where the omission from the will was intentional and that intention is apparent upon reading the will. In that case, the children will not inherit under the will or intestate succession.

Pretermitted children
A child who is born or adopted after the execution of a will.

> *Example:* Testator executes a will with no children and provides the following clause in his will, "I presently have no children, but if I ever do, they are to take nothing from my will." In this example, if the testator then had children after execution of the will, the omission from the will would be considered intentional and the children will not inherit under the will.

Generally, if an omitted child is born or adopted before the execution of the will, the child will not inherit anything unless the omission was accidental.

> *Example:* Testator executes a will with two known children and leaves his estate to those two known children. If it is discovered that the testator had conceived another child and was unaware of that child, the child will be entitled to a share of the estate.

In the following contested will case, the stepson of the decedent petitioned to have the court declare him a residual beneficiary. The decedent's wife filed her own petition for an omitted-spouse share of the decedent's estate.

CASE 17.1

AN OMITTED SPOUSE WHO WAS PROVIDED FOR OUTSIDE OF THE WILL MAY NOT BE ENTITLED TO COLLECT INHERITANCE

FERGUSON v. CRITOPOULOS

163 So.3d 330 (2014)

Alabama Supreme Court

Dimitrios Critopoulos had been married to Dorothy Marie Hayes Critopoulos for 35 years when she preceded him in death. Dorothy had three children from a prior marriage, one of whom was the plaintiff, Tiger Ferguson ("Ferguson"). Dimitrios never adopted Dorothy's three children; however, he and the children enjoyed a parent-child relationship. The three children were named residual beneficiaries under his will. Prior to his death, he married Katina Critopoulos ("Katina"). At the time of his death, he had a valid will; however, the will was executed prior to his marriage with Katina and made no provision for her.

Ferguson filed a petition to probate Dimitrios's will. Katina filed a petition for an omitted-spouse share of the decedent's estate. Ferguson filed a response to Katina's petition, claiming the decedent had provided for Katina outside of the will, including checking accounts, life insurance, and retirement benefits, and thus she was not entitled to an omitted-spouse share. The probate court held for Katina. Ferguson appealed.

Language of the Court. *The purpose of the probate statute is to avoid an unintentional disinheritance of the spouse of a testator who had executed a will prior* *to the parties' marriage. It serves to give effect to the probable intent of the testator and protects the surviving spouse. There are two exceptions to allowing an omitted spouse an intestate share: (1) if it appears from the will that the omission of the surviving spouse was intentional or (2) if the testator provided for the surviving spouse with transfers outside the will with the intent that those transfers were in lieu of a provision in the will. If either exception exists, the surviving spouse is not entitled to a share as an omitted spouse.*

Nothing in the decedent's will indicates that the omission of Katina from the will was intentional; therefore, the first exception to the omitted-spouse share is not applicable.

As to the second exception, the decedent, during his brief marriage to Katina, changed beneficiaries on his retirement accounts and insurance policies. He was considering changing his will, but did not do so. In short, he considered his old will in relation to his new marriage. He also substantially provided for Katina; Katina

acknowledges that, if she received the intestate share, she would be receiving more than the decedent intended her to have.

In the present case, the amount of the transfers made during the marriage, along with the testimony that the decedent considered the terms of his will, the fact that Katina was not included in the will, the fact that the decedent did not change his will, and the fact that the will ultimately benefited Dorothy's children provide reasonable proof to satisfy Tiger's burden of proving an exception to the omitted-spouse share under the facts of this case.

Decision. The Supreme Court of Alabama reversed, finding Katina was not entitled to an omitted-spouse share.

FOCUS ON ETHICS

Is it fair for a court to determine the decedent's intent to omit a spouse through the actions of providing for a spouse consistent with actions most spouses would undertake?

Challenging the Validity of a Will

A will may be challenged only by those persons who have an interest or allege an interest in the estate of the decedent. An omitted heir, an heir, or anyone named as a beneficiary in a will can challenge that will's validity.

The same defenses that can be used to set aside a gift are grounds for challenging a will's validity: Fraud, duress, mistake, and undue influence are grounds for contesting a will. Fraud can occur in many ways, including inducing the testator to make or change a will, committing fraud during the will's execution, and committing fraud by preventing the testator from changing or revoking a will.

Intestate Succession

Intestate succession
The process of distributing property in the absence of a valid will.

Descent and distribution statute
A state statute governing how property is distributed under intestate succession.

The laws of intestate succession govern the disposition of property where (1) there is no will, (2) the will is invalid, or (3) property was not included in the will. Several surveys over the years have estimated that more than half of Americans die intestate. When intestacy occurs, state law controls how the decedent's property is to be distributed in a process known as **intestate succession**.

Each state has adopted a **descent and distribution statute** describing who receives the decedent's property in cases of intestacy. Property that transfers by operation of law, such as property held as joint tenancy and life estate, are not included in intestate succession because they transfer automatically upon the death of the decedent. In addition, in states that provide for community property, the surviving spouse is entitled to his or her one-half share of community-property assets.

Distribution of Property with a Surviving Spouse

Under state law, title to the decedent's property passes immediately upon his death to the closest living heirs, subject to the payment of any nonexempt debts. Usually most descent and distribution statutes provide for the surviving spouse to inherit the whole estate or a portion of it. Often these statutes provide for the surviving spouse to inherit a different percentage of the estate depending on the number of children or grandchildren surviving the decedent.

> *Example:* A state may provide that the surviving spouse is entitled to a one-half share of the estate and must share the remaining half of the estate with a surviving child. If two or more children survive, the surviving spouse may receive one-third of the estate, while the surviving children receive two-thirds.

Distribution of Property Without a Surviving Spouse

While the descent and distribution statute controls the distribution of property, generally, in the absence of a surviving spouse, property flows first to any living **lineal descendants** (children or issue of the children). If there are no surviving lineal descendants, the property goes to the parents of the decedent. If the parents have predeceased the decedent, then the property flows to the decedent's brothers and sisters. Many states then provide that grandparents of the decedent will inherit if none of the above exists. In such cases, one-half of the estate will go to the paternal grandparents and the other half to the maternal grandparents. The descent and distribution statute will provide for further heirs to inherit.

At some point, if no heirs exist to receive the decedent's assets, the decedent's property **escheats**. When property escheats, the probate court will order that the property be distributed to the state. The state's descent and distribution statute dictates when property will escheat to the state.

> *Example:* The property of a single adult who dies without children or siblings and has no surviving parents or relatives may escheat.

How Property Is Distributed

Usually, a will states how the decedent's estate will be distributed to her or his descendants. However, where intestate succession is required, states have for the most part adopted one of two theories of property distribution. The two most common property-distribution methods are *per stirpes* and *per capita* distribution.

State laws vary in defining these two methods of distributions to grandchildren. In part, some variation exists among states because they adopted different versions of the **Uniform Probate Code** (UPC) or made modifications to the UPC. The UPC is a

Lineal descendants
A relative in the direct line of descent of the decedent including children, grandchildren and so on.

Escheat
A process whereby, if there are no living heirs under a state's intestacy laws, the court orders that the property be distributed to the state.

Uniform Probate Code
A uniform law governing inheritance and probate matters adopted in approximately one-third of the states.

uniform act governing inheritance and probate matters. It has been adopted in about one-third of the states.

Per Stirpes *Distribution*

Per stirpes distribution
Form of distributing the decedent's estate in which surviving lineal descendants inherit through representation of their parents' inheritance share.

Under *per stirpes* distribution, surviving lineal descendants inherit through representation of their parents' inheritance share. The first question is to determine whether the decedent's children are living. If they are deceased, do they have living issue? Under a per stirpes distribution, all living lineal descendants (children, grandchildren, and so on) take the representative share that their deceased parent would have been entitled to inherit. That means the living lineal descendants split among themselves what their deceased parent would have received. If their parent is alive, they receive nothing.

> *Example:* A, whose husband has predeceased her, had three adult children, B, C, and D. B had two children, E and F. C had one child, G. D had no children. Both B and C predecease A, but D is still alive at the time of her mother's death. When A dies, the estate is distributed per stirpes. In such case, D receives a one-third share of the estate, E and F each receive one-sixth of the estate, and G receives one-third of the estate.

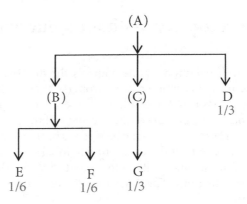

FIGURE 17.1. *Per Stirpes* **Example**

Per Capita *Distribution*

Per capita distribution
Form of distributing the decedent's estate in which the living lineal descendants equally share the property of the estate.

Under a *per capita* distribution, the living lineal descendants equally share the property of the estate. The heir's degree of relationship to the decedent does not matter. That means children, grandchildren, and so on, of the decedent receive equal shares. A common exception adopted in many states, and the approach the UPC takes, is that the distribution stops at the first living lineal descendant.

> *Example:* In the example used above for per stirpes distribution, if A's estate were instead distributed on a *per capita* basis, then each person would receive an equal share. In that case, E, F, G, and D would each receive a one-fourth share of the estate.

> *Example:* In the above example, if D had a living lineal descendant, the distribution under a *per capita* basis would not change. This is because many states and the UPC approach do not distribute down beyond the first living lineal descendant under a *per capita* basis.

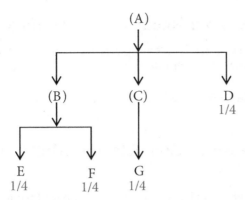

FIGURE 17.2. *Per Capita* **Example**

Intestate Succession: Children

With intestate succession, questions may arise as to whether all types of children are entitled to inherit from a decedent or if any restrictions from inheritance exist. Some of the more common questions include the rights of (1) nonmarital children, (2) adopted children, and (3) posthumous children. The UPC provides uniform laws that assist in our analysis.

Nonmarital Children

The decedent's marital status does not preclude distribution to children from their biological mother. An illegitimate child — that is, a child born outside of marriage — is eligible to take from the mother's estate. The child can also take from the biological father's estate if paternity has been established by a court proceeding or paternity is admitted by the father; otherwise, the child does not inherit from the father.

Adopted Children

Children who are legally adopted inherit just as if they were biological children of the adopting parents. Once adopted, the children do not inherit from their biological parents through intestate succession. To allow otherwise would provide a windfall to the adopted child. They may still inherit through a will provision of their biological parents.

Posthumous Child

A **posthumous child** is a child born after the decedent's death. Generally, a posthumous child is treated as an heir and entitled to inherit. Some states limit the rights of posthumous children by requiring that the child be born within ten months of the decedent's death. This allows a child conceived on the day of the decedent's death to be an heir to the decedent.

    Other states allow children to be born years after the decedent's death and still be treated as an heir. Such circumstances may arise from instances of post mortem in vitro fertilization of a widow.

Posthumous child
A child born after the decedent's death.

Intestate Succession: Relatives by Marriage

In most states, relatives of the decedent by marriage, other than a surviving spouse, do not receive any property through intestate succession.

> *Example:* Stepchildren (unless adopted by the decedent) do not inherit property through intestacy.

Intestate Succession: Convicts and Murdering Heirs

The UPC provides that a convict is still entitled to inherit through intestate succession. If the heir is convicted of murdering the decedent, however, the murderer does not inherit and is treated as if she or he had predeceased the decedent. The murder's issue can still inherit, but some states do not provide for an inheritance to the issue of a murderer of the decedent. Note that a murderer can still inherit from parents and siblings, as long as the murderer did not murder the person from whom she is inheriting.

Simultaneous Deaths

While rare, sometimes both spouses die at the same time, such as can happen in accidents and natural disasters. In these cases, it is often unknown which spouse died first, and thus the laws of intestate succession cannot be applied. The UPC provides that heirs must survive for 120 hours (approximately five days) before they are entitled to inherit. Other states have created similar survival periods before an heir can inherit under intestate succession and not be treated as having a simultaneous death. Simultaneous death provisions can have significant impacts on the distribution of an estate.

> *Example:* Henry and Ziva are involved in a car accident in a state that has a 120-hour survival provision. Ziva passes away immediately, but Henry survives for three additional hours. If Henry and Ziva have two children together, and Ziva had one child from a previous marriage, the application of the simultaneous death provisions changes the inheritance considerably. Without such a provision, Henry's two children would receive the entire estate, while Ziva's child from the previous marriage would receive nothing. If the roles were reversed and Ziva survived Henry for three hours, the couple's two children and Ziva's child from the previous marriage would each inherit one-third of the estate.

To address these concerns, some states have adopted the Uniform Simultaneous Death Act, which provides that in such situations each spouse is treated as if they predeceased the other. In such situations, each spouse's assets are then distributed as if they had died without a surviving spouse.

> *Example:* A married couple is killed in a boating accident. Spouse A's assets are treated as if Spouse B had predeceased Spouse A through intestate succession. Spouse B's assets are treated as if Spouse A had predeceased Spouse B through intestate succession.

Related Transfers Following Death ■ ■ ■

Some transfers occur outside of the laws of intestate succession. These nonprobate transfers are operative upon death but follow rules other than intestate-succession rules. They include the following:

- A life estate held in real property
- Real property assets held in joint tenancy
- Real property assets held in trust or partnership arrangements that provide for transfers upon death
- Marital real property that transfers upon the death of a spouse
- Real property assets subject to a buy-sell agreement
- Transfers stated in prenuptial and postnuptial agreements

While not directly related to real property, other important asset transfers that occur following death include bank accounts, life-insurance policies, annuities, and pension and retirement plan transfers to designated beneficiaries.

Probate

The process of administering the decedent's estate is known as **probate**. Probate is used when a person dies testate or with a will. Nonprobate transfers, discussed above, and transfers when a person utilized a trust (discussed below), do not have to go through probate.

The probate court, a special state court, supervises the administration of the estate and approves the distribution of the state's assets. In probate, the will is authenticated as the last, final, and true will of the testator; the court then determines heirs for intestate succession, collects the decedent's property, pays the estate's debts, and distributes the estate's remaining assets.

Probate can last from several months to several years depending on the size of the estate, its complexity, and challenges by heirs in probate court. Additionally, the probate court and attorneys are paid based on the size of the estate. Due to these issues, probate court is time consuming and costlier than if a person was able to use nonprobate transfers or a trust.

Probate
The process of collecting a decedent's property, paying the decedent's debts and taxes, and distributing the remainder of the estate.

Petition for Probate

Probate court opens with the filing of an application or petition for probate. Any person who has an interest in the estate (such as an heir) can open probate. Usually, probate is opened in the court nearest to where the decedent resided prior to death.

Appointment of Probate Representative

A representative of the estate is appointed to administer the estate. The representative is known as an administrator (male) or administratrix (female) if the decedent died intestate. If the decedent died testate, the representative appointed in the will is known as an executor (male) or executrix (female). The UPC uses the gender-neutral term personal representative to denote the person who administers the estate.

An attorney is often appointed to help with the administration of the estate, the preparation of all estate tax filings (a federal estate tax return and, in some jurisdictions, state inheritance filings and taxes must be considered), and the identification of all heirs who are to receive the property.

Collection and Distribution of Estate Assets

During the probate process, the executor or administrator collects all of the decedent's assets. Usually, a written inventory of these assets is filed with the court within a specific time from the opening of probate. The inventory is sent to all estate heirs and beneficiaries. During this time, an appraisal is completed for noncash assets. In addition to collecting the assets, the decedent's debts are paid.

Most states require that a notice to creditors be published or served so that they may timely submit a claim for payment by the estate. Creditors then have a fixed period within which to submit their claims or be barred from recovering from the estate. The heirs are not personally liable for the payment of those debts.

If the decedent died testate, the will can only dispose of property owned by the decedent at the time of death. **Ademption** arises when a specific item of property, a **specific gift**, to an heir fails because the testator does not own the property at death. If the testator dies without owning the specific gift, the beneficiary receives nothing.

> ***Example:*** Shawn's will provides that his classic 1967 Ford Mustang Shelby GT500 fastback will go to his niece, Ariana. If Shawn sold the classic car before his death, the property has adeemed, and his niece receives nothing from this specific gift.

If a testator's estate does not have enough assets to pay all the gifts, abatement results. **Abatement** is the process by which gifts are decreased. Abatement may also arise when it is necessary to pay for a share owed to an omitted child, omitted spouse, or omitted domestic partner. In abatement, no distinction is usually made among the types of gifts provided for to heirs.

Ademption
When an heir receives nothing because the testator leaves a specific device of property and that property is no longer in the estate.

Specific gift
A gift of a specific item of property in a will.

Abatement
The proportional reduction in the distribution of an estate when the funds or assets are insufficient to pay all beneficiaries in full.

Buying Property from a Probate Estate

When a person wishes to purchase property from a probate estate, the sale must be approved by the probate court. The executor must establish the fair market value by means of an appraisal, the sale must have been exposed to the market by public advertising and through the receipt of one or more bids, and the executor must receive permission from the court to sell the property. Real estate brokers may receive a reduced commission when handling sales in probate court. The probate court must approve all commissions and expenses of sale prior to the sale. The executor's deed to the purchaser is usually in the form of a special warranty deed offering little to no protection.

Closing of the Estate

Once all the foregoing activities have occurred, the estate may be closed in probate court. The closing may require a hearing or the submission of a final accounting and inventory of the assets. The estate is then deemed closed and can only be reopened by order of the court.

Trusts

A **trust** is a legal relationship in which property is transferred (by the settlor or trustor) and held and managed (by the trustee) for the beneficiaries named in the trust. The grantor has control over the property in the trust during the grantor's lifetime and can amend, alter, or terminate a trust during the grantor's lifetime. The grantor may serve as a trustee and the trustee may be either a person or a company (such as a bank acting as a trustee). During the grantor's lifetime, the income produced from the trust assets are often distributed to the grantor as a beneficiary. A trust is essentially an empty shell into which assets may be transferred for the benefit of the beneficiary identified in the trust.

Trust
A legal arrangement in which one person transfers property to another to be held and used for the benefit of a third person.

> *Example:* Keith Yang creates a trust and executes a deed transferring his residential home to the trust. He wishes to act as the trustee of the trust and receive the income from the trust during his lifetime. Upon his death, his children, Carson and Lenara, will have ownership of the trust property as the residential home will pass to them without having to go through probate. This is illustrated in Figure 17.3 below.

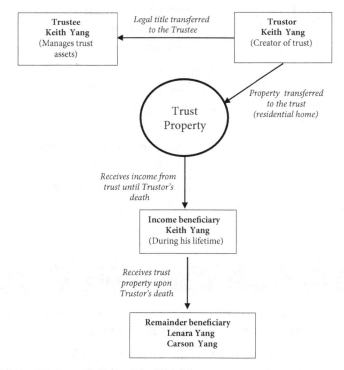

FIGURE 17.3. Revocable Trust Example

Types of Trusts

Inter vivos **trust**
A trust created during a trustor's life.

Testamentary trust
A trust created by a will that comes into existence upon the death of the trustor.

While many types of trusts exist, trusts can be characterized as either *inter vivos* or testamentary. An ***inter vivos* trust** is a trust created during a trustor's life. A **testamentary trust** is a trust that takes effect upon the settlor's death. This type of trust must comply with the state laws on creating wills.

Trusts are also classified as being either revocable or irrevocable. The most common type is a revocable trust. A **revocable trust** can be changed or revoked at any time by the trustor prior to the trustor's death. Revocable trusts are also known as revocable living trusts. **Irrevocable trusts** cannot be changed or revoked during the trustor's life. The type of trust chosen can affect creditor rights to the trust assets and reduce estate taxes upon death.

Key Terms and Concepts

- Testator/testatrix, page 454
- Decedent, page 454
- Testate, page 454
- Intestate, page 454
- Issue, page 454
- Devise, page 454
- Bequest, page 454
- Beneficiary, page 454
- Will, page 454
- Holographic wills, page 455
- Acknowledged, page 456
- Notary public, page 456
- Joint will, page 457
- Mutual wills/reciprocal wills, page 457
- Codicil, page 458
- Pretermitted children, page 459
- Intestate succession, page 460

- Descent and Distribution statute, page 460
- Lineal descendants, page 461
- Escheat, page 461
- Uniform Probate Code (UPC), page 461
- *Per stirpes* distribution, page 462
- *Per capita* distribution, page 462
- Posthumous child, page 463
- Probate, page 465
- Ademption, page 466
- Specific gift, page 466
- Abatement, page 466
- Trust, page 467
- *Inter vivos* trust, page 468
- Testamentary trust, page 468
- Revocable trust/living trust, page 468
- Irrevocable trust, page 468

Chapter Summary

- A will is the legal instrument by which a person dictates how his property will be disposed of at death

- A person who makes a will is a testator or testatrix. The person's estate, following that person's

death, will be administered by an executor or executrix appointed by the court.

- If a person dies without a will, he or she dies intestate. The laws of intestacy govern the conveyance of the decedent's property.

- Most states require four elements to make a will enforceable: (1) a writing, (2) capacity, (3) the testator's signature, and (4) witnesses.

- Handwritten wills are known as holographic wills.

- A joint will is created when two or more testators, often spouses, execute the same instrument as their will.

- Mutual wills occur when two or more testators execute separate wills and make reciprocal gifts of their property to each other on the condition that the surviving person, on his or her death, leaves the remaining property as agreed upon by the testators.

- A codicil is an amendment to a will that can modify, amend, or revoke a prior will. It must be executed in the same manner as the original will to be valid.

- A will can be revoked by the acts of the testator. A subsequent will or codicil can revoke a will, the testator may physical destroy the will, or the will may be revoked by operation of law.

- States may provide for physical destruction when a testator intends to destroy a will by tearing material portions of the will, burning the will, writing cancelled or void across the will, or completely obliterating it.

- Children may be omitted from a will. State laws often provide that these pretermitted heirs will receive at least what they would have received under intestate succession.

- A will may be challenged only by those persons who have an interest or allege an interest in the estate of the decedent. An omitted heir, an heir, or anyone named as a beneficiary in a will can challenge that will's validity.

- The laws of intestate succession govern the disposition of property where (1) there is no will, (2) the will is invalid, or (3) property was not included in the will.

- Each state has adopted a descent and distribution statute describing who receives the decedent's property. Most descent and distribution statutes usually provide for the surviving spouse to inherit the whole estate or a portion of the estate.

- In the absence of a surviving spouse, property flows first to any living lineal descendants.

- The laws of intestacy distribution of property vary from state to state. *Per stirpes* distribution means that surviving lineal descendants inherit by representation of their parent's inheritance share.

- *Per capita* distribution provides that all living lineal descendants share equally in the property of the estate.

- Parental marital status is irrelevant to a child's ability to inherit property. Adopted children are treated as if they were biological children; however, once adopted, they cannot inherit from their biological parents through intestate succession.

- Probate is the process of administering the decedent's estate.

- A trust is a legal relationship in which property is transferred by a trustor or settler and held and managed by a trustee for the beneficiaries of the trust.

- An *inter vivos* trust is created during the trustor's life, while a testamentary trust takes effect upon the settlor's death.

Chapter Problems and Assignments

1. Identify the requirements necessary to create a valid will.

2. Describe the differences between a will and a trust.

3. Thomas holds property in joint tenancy with his brother Derrick. Thomas's will states that the property Thomas holds in joint tenancy is to transfer to his other brother Ben. Upon Thomas's death what happens to the property held in joint tenancy?

4. Maurice and Nancy are husband and wife. They have their lawyer draft separate wills in which each party agrees to leave the property to the surviving party and that upon the death of the last surviving person, the property will go to their only daughter, Gabby. What type of will was used by Maurice and Nancy?

5. Brad has a validly executed will, but he wants to physically revoke his will so he sets the will on fire. After he has burned half of the will, he blows the fire out and throws the will in the trash can. Was the will revoked?

6. Eric had a validly executed will. Upon his death, his will left his property to his two sons, Aiden and Greyson. Unbeknownst to Eric, he had conceived a third child, Carly. Upon Eric's death, Carly comes forward and seeks to obtain a share of the will. Will Carly be entitled to a portion of Eric's estate?

7. Rosita died intestate. She was survived by her husband, George, and their two children, Michael and Christian. She had a net worth of $100,000 upon her death. How should Rosita's estate be distributed?

8. Addison died testate. She was predeceased by her husband, Neil. The couple had three children, Brent, Christina, and Dominic. Both Dominic and Christina had predeceased Addison. Christina had two children, Eliza and Fred. Dominic had one child, Garrett. When Addison dies, how is the property distributed under the *per stirpes* method of distribution? How would the estate be distributed under the *per capital* method of distribution?

9. Conduct Internet research to locate an example of a celebrity's will. Determine if the requirements for a valid will are present.

10. Research your state law to determine what method your state uses to distribute property under intestate succession. Does your state follow one of the methods discussed in the book, or does it apply another method?

Part IV
Special Topics

Chapter 18
Zoning and Land Use Issues

Architecture is the very mirror of life. You only have to cast your eyes on buildings to feel the presence of the past, the spirit of a place; they are the reflection of society.
— *Ieoh Ming Pei, Architect, with E. J. Biasini, in* Les Grands desseins du Louvre *(1989)*

Learning Objectives

1. Define the differences between public and private land use restrictions.
2. Identify the various types of zoning ordinances.
3. Discuss how zoning can be unconstitutional.
4. Describe when nonconforming use permits and variances may be authorized.
5. Explain common types of private land use restrictions.

Chapter Outline

- Introduction
- Public Control of Land: Zoning
- Case 18.1: *Village of Euclid v. Ambler Realty Co.*
- Case 18.2: *Village of Belle Terre v. Boraas*
- Case 18.3: *Moore v. East Cleveland*
- Private Restrictions on Land Use

Opening
scenario

As a real estate developer, you desire to build several mixed-use projects and several hundred residential units in New City. You approach the zoning board and planning commissions for New City with your proposals. They make it clear that the community wants to retain its small-town characteristics. They propose burdensome and prohibitively expensive conditions upon your projects if you proceed with development. What rights and remedies do you have?

Introduction

In this chapter, we address two significant land use issues affecting real property: zoning and private restrictions imposed by land developers and owners. Land use regulation is the regulation of the use of real property whether by the public or the private sector. This chapter studies the balancing of personal rights and duties with those of the community.

Public Control of Land: Zoning

How best to use land is everyone's concern. As individuals, we want a pleasant, secure environment in which to live, shop, and work. Families desire good schools with safe recreational opportunities nearby. Businesses wish to operate without undue regulations restraining their ability to produce products and services and the freedom to operate their businesses, despite the noise, pollution, and traffic these businesses might generate. Contentious city council and planning commission meetings frequently pit business owners seeking relief from land use regulations against homeowners. Balancing these interests is never easy.

Zoning
Local regulations that control the use of various areas of land.

Most land use regulation is by local governments. It begins with the concept of **zoning**, which divides areas of land into sections called zones and regulates the activities that can occur within them. Each zone permits landowners to use the land in a manner consistent with the overall zoning plan.

> *Example:* One zoning area may permit commercial development, high-density housing, and single-family homes.

The public policy underlying zoning is that it promotes the efficient use of land, permits commercial activity while preserving recreational and historical areas, and enhances a community's health, safety, and welfare.

Zoning Authority

Zoning may regulate land use. Government's source of authority to regulate land is implied in the U.S. Constitution. The police power of government is the authority to control the activities and rights of persons subject to its jurisdiction. Zoning has been held to be a valid exercise of a state's police power.[1]

Zoning is permissible if the zoning law (1) promotes the health, safety, and general welfare of the people and (2) is not arbitrary, unreasonable, or discriminatory. In making zoning-related decisions, courts analyze whether the law or regulation serves a public interest, whether the regulation is a reasonable means by which to attain that purpose, and how public needs and private interests are balanced as a result of the law or regulation.

In the following precedent-setting case, the Supreme Court considered the constitutional challenges to an Ohio city's zoning ordinance posed by Ambler Realty. Ambler argued a zoning change impaired its rights to develop its project. The court's holding has shaped the landscape of land use law ever since.

CASE 18.1

ZONING UPHELD AS A CONSTITUTIONAL EXERCISE OF POLICE POWER

VILLAGE OF EUCLID v. AMBLER REALTY CO.
272 U.S. 365 (1926)
United States Supreme Court

Ambler Realty owned 68 acres of land in the Village of Euclid, a suburb of Cleveland, Ohio. To prevent the industrial sections of Cleveland from growing into the village, the village developed a zoning ordinance based upon six uses of land, three classes of height, and four classes of lot size. The Ambler property was affected by several of these zoning classifications. Ambler sued the village, arguing that the zoning ordinance amounted to an unconstitutional taking of property by reducing the value of the company's property. Ambler argued that the newly zoned area of Ambler's property was worth $10,000 per acre if put to industrial use, but only $2,500 per acre if put to residential use. The district court held in favor of Ambler, and the Supreme Court granted certiorari.

Language of the Court. *Building zoning laws are of modern origin. Until recent years, urban life was comparatively simple; but with the great increase and concentration of population, problems have developed, and constantly are developing, which require, and will continue to require, additional restrictions in respect to the use and occupation of private lands in urban communities.*

The ordinance now under review, and all similar laws and regulations, must find their justification in some aspect of the police power asserted for the public welfare. The line which in this field separates the legitimate from the illegitimate assumption of power is not capable of precise delimitation. It varies with circumstances and conditions. A regulatory zoning ordinance, which would be clearly valid as applied to the great cities, might be clearly invalid as applied to rural communities.

The matter of zoning has received much attention at the hands of commissions and experts, and the results of their investigations have been set forth in comprehensive reports. These reports concur in the view that the segregation of residential, business, and industrial buildings will make it easier to provide fire apparatus suitable for the character and intensity of the development in each section; that it will increase the safety and security of home life; greatly tend to prevent street accidents, especially to children, by reducing the traffic and resulting confusion in residential sections; decrease noise and other conditions which produce or intensify nervous disorders; and preserve a more favorable environment in which to rear children.

Under these circumstances, apartment houses, which in a different environment would be not only entirely unobjectionable but highly desirable, come very near to being nuisances.

Decision. The Supreme Court reversed and upheld the zoning ordinance.

FOCUS ON ETHICS

How does the *Euclid* decision impact a planning commission's decision to approve the construction of university student housing within a residential neighborhood? Would it make a difference if the university was located within a densely populated area as opposed to a sparsely populated area?

Delegation of Authority to Local Governments

Enabling statute
A state law by which the authority to control land use is delegated to local governments.

An **enabling statute** is a state law by which the authority to control land use is delegated to local governments (such as counties, cities, or towns). Several states, including Oregon, have enacted a statewide planning policy to which local agencies must abide. These states establish the goals and guidelines directing the choices made by local governments in their planning processes. Local governments must conform to their statewide directives.

Master Plan

On a local level, zoning begins with the adoption of a master plan (also known as a comprehensive plan or general plan) for the area to be zoned. All land use decisions, such as zoning ordinances and agreements with developers, must be consistent with the master plan.

The master plan can protect existing land uses and ensure that proposed and future land uses will be compatible with each other and with the land. Additionally, zoning ensures that future developments will be served by public utilities and improvements necessary to the use of the affected parcels. Many local governments post zoning plans on their public websites.

Each master plan includes text and diagrams outlining the existing and proposed development of the area. These uses commonly involve the following elements:

- Preserving the quality of its air, light, and water
- Regulation of the uses within the community
- Height restrictions of buildings
- Density of residential and commercial users
- Transportation
- Growth controls
- Conservation and open space
- Structural safety and other similar public interests

Zoning Categories

A local government may create many different categories of zones for regulation, and each zone may be divided into subcategories. Local governments do not always use the same zoning classifications. One city may use a zoning code designation for one type of use (such as single-family dwellings), and another may use the same code for high-density, high-rise apartments. Examples of zones under a typical zoning ordinance might include the following:

1. Residential
   1.1 Low density
   1.2 Medium density
   1.3 High density
2. Commercial
   2.1 Low density
   2.2 Medium density
   2.3 High density
3. Agricultural
4. Recreational/Preservation
5. Institutional/Educational
6. Industrial

Zoning Ordinances

A local government may use several different types of zoning ordinances. The most common zoning ordinances include: (1) exclusive use and cumulative use restrictions, (2) intensity zoning, (3) incentive zoning, (4) aesthetic zoning, (5) spot zoning, (6) exclusionary zoning, and (7) inclusionary zoning.

Exclusive Use and Cumulative Zoning

Exclusive use zoning was one of the earliest types of zoning adopted by local governments. **Exclusive use zoning** (also known as noncumulative zoning) creates zones in which property may be used only as designated for that specific zone. Many zoning ordinances are exclusive use zoning.

Exclusive use zoning
Regulation that limits property uses to those specified in the zoning ordinance.

> *Example:* A location zoned as residential would not permit a commercial development. Under exclusive use zoning, the only type of development allowed would be residential.

In contrast, **cumulative zoning** permits higher priority uses that are not designated for that zone as long as those uses are reasonable under the circumstances. The higher priority uses will be determined by the local zoning ordinance; therefore, the higher priority use can vary by local government.

Cumulative zoning
Regulation that allows more restrictive uses that are not designated for that zone.

> *Example:* In cumulative zoning, a high-density commercially zoned area would permit a low-density commercial development in the area.

Intensity Zoning

Intensity zoning
Regulation controlling the density and intensity of structures on land.

Intensity zoning protects against undue congestion in a location by regulating the density and intensity of structures on land. Intensity zoning may include zoning requirements for the following:

1. Minimum setbacks for buildings (distance from the structure to the street)

   Example: The local zoning ordinance may require that a single-family dwelling have at least a 20-foot setback from the street, be at least 10 feet from the adjacent lots, and sit no closer than 15 feet from the rear property line.

2. Minimum usable open space
3. Building heights and placement locations
4. Minimum lot sizes
5. Maximum number of structures per acre (density)

Incentive Zoning

Incentive zoning
Regulations using a rewards-based system to encourage urban development goals.

Often adopted in densely populated cities (such as Chicago and New York City), **incentive zoning** is a rewards-based system to encourage urban development goals. Incentive zoning may be used to allow a developer to vary from typical zoning requirements (such as density) in exchange for providing public amenities on the site (such as open spaces, public plazas, or affordable housing).

Aesthetic Zoning

Aesthetic zoning
Regulations used to control aspects of a community's beauty.

Aesthetic zoning is used to control aspects of community beauty. Often aesthetic zoning requires conformity with the local area's architectural and landscaping requirements. The U.S. Supreme Court has stated, "It is within the power of the legislature to determine that the community should be beautiful as well as healthy, spacious as well as clean."[2]

   Example: A historical section of a city may limit the architectural style of its homes to Craftsman style to maintain consistency with the section's existing architecture and charm.

In some states, zoning for *purely aesthetic reasons* is illegal. In those states, local governments may combine aesthetic zoning goals with the public health, safety, or moral interests of society.

Spot Zoning

Spot zoning
Regulation permitting a use different from those allowed in that zoned area.

Spot zoning allows a specific property within a zoned area to be rezoned to permit a use different from the zoning requirements for that zoned area. In some states, such as New York, spot zoning is illegal.

   Example: A property owner desires to rezone his residential property for commercial use because the property would then be more valuable.

Exclusionary Zoning

Some communities desire to preserve the historical character of the area and limit future growth. In response to these goals, cities adopt **exclusionary zoning** ordinances to limit and regulate future growth. The courts have upheld these ordinances if they are reasonable in scope and purpose. Where growth is limited to allow city services to grow to meet the needs of an increased population, they are upheld. Where growth is altogether prohibited, such zoning is typically held to be unconstitutional.

> **Example:** In order to limit the city's growth, a city adopts a slow-growth zoning ordinance to cap the number of homes built yearly. The purpose was to ensure that the resulting demands on the municipal infrastructure could be met and the historical character of the city could be preserved. This slow-growth zoning ordinance would be deemed constitutional.

Exclusionary zoning Regulation limiting and regulating future growth in order to preserve the historical character of the area.

Inclusionary Zoning

Inclusionary zoning is the use of zoning to require portions of new construction to be reserved for persons with low and/or moderate incomes. Local government inclusionary zoning plans may be mandatory or voluntary and can have different set-aside requirements, and affordability levels. Where voluntary, inclusionary zoning is often used with incentive zoning to entice developers to add low- and moderate-income housing units. The purpose of inclusionary zoning is to create mixed-use housing allowing people from diverse socioeconomic backgrounds to live in the same developments and have access to the same community services, schools, and amenities.

Inclusionary zoning Regulations requiring portions of new developments to be reserved for low- to moderate-income housing.

Constitutional Challenges to Zoning

Zoning is subject to the Constitution's limitations on intrusion into individual liberties. The basis for all land use regulation is the police power of a local government to protect the public health, safety, and welfare of its residents. A land use ordinance is within the realm of police power if it is reasonably related to the public welfare. As discussed in this chapter, zoning often elicits challenges on constitutional grounds. Common challenges to zoning ordinances include the following:

- *Substantive Due Process and Equal Protection claims.* These claims are based on the Fourteenth Amendment's Due Process Clause, which states, "Nor shall any state deprive any person of life, liberty, or property without due process of law." Courts have interpreted this provision to mean that zoning regulations must advance legitimate governmental interests serving the public health, safety, or general welfare. When zoning regulations do not meet that standard, they may be held unconstitutional.
- *Eminent domain.* The Takings Clause of the Fifth Amendment will invalidate a zoning ordinance if the government's regulations are so severe as to be tantamount to a taking for which just compensation must be paid. Recall from the discussion in chapter 16 the two related concepts of eminent domain (government's direct taking of property) and inverse condemnation (government's indirect taking where the governmental regulation "goes too far" and results in a taking without compensation).

- *Freedom of speech.* Courts have examined whether zoning ordinances interfere with protected expressions of free speech under the First Amendment.

Example: The Supreme Court has upheld a Los Angeles ordinance barring the posting of political signs on streetlight posts. The regulation was adopted to minimize litter and promote aesthetic goals.[3]

■ ■ ■   Zoning Compared to Eminent Domain

Zoning is the *regulation, not the taking,* of property. Zoning does not require reimbursement to the property owner; however, a taking under eminent domain requires that just compensation be paid to the property owner.

As our previous study of eminent domain reflects, it is difficult to distinguish between a "mere" regulation and one that effectively robs an owner of the use of the property so that a "taking" occurs. Although no clear distinctions exist between the two concepts of zoning and eminent domain, they are viewed as deriving from two separate governmental powers: zoning power derives from the government's police power, and eminent domain power derives from the Takings Clause of the Fifth Amendment.

Nonconforming Uses and Structures

Nonconforming use
A preexisting use allowed to continue even though it is incompatible with current allowable uses in that zoned area.

Sometimes zoning ordinances change. When they do, a use that was permissible may become disallowed. A **nonconforming use** structure is one that can remain because it existed when the original ordinance was enacted. The use may continue as long as it was in existence at the time the zoning ordinance was enacted.

Example: A landowner may use part of his residential property as a vehicle repair business. If a new ordinance prohibits that use, the property owner's use is "grandfathered in" as a nonconforming use. The owner can continue to use his property as he has done in the past.

When Nonconforming Uses Must Follow Current Zoning

While nonconforming uses are tolerated, they remain inconsistent with the surrounding zoning. Local governments will want to eliminate the inconsistency, not perpetuate it. For that reason, courts have held that a nonconforming use may be lost in the following situations:

1. The nonconforming use is expanded or altered from the time the zoning law was changed.
2. The nonconforming use is abandoned.
3. The nonconforming building is destroyed by fire or natural events. Even if the building is rebuilt to the same specifications as before, the nonconforming use may not be continued.
4. The nonconforming use creates a nuisance.

Example: A pit mining operation near a residential development (a nonconforming use) might be required to comply with current zoning ordinances if a private nuisance lawsuit against its continued operation succeeds.

Amortization of Nonconforming Uses

Some local zoning ordinances provide amortization (sunsetting) provisions covering the nonconforming use, often for a period of five or ten years. In such situations, the nonconforming use will be permitted only for the period of time stated in the amortization provision. After that, the use will no longer be permitted. Amortization provisions provide the property owner time to convert the property to a conforming use.

Example: Since 1980, Bonnell had been operating an adult bookstore in Oklahoma City. In 1981, the city council adopted amendments to its zoning code that for the first time defined and regulated the location of "adult entertainment uses." Those businesses (including Bonnell's) located outside these zones were deemed a nonconforming use. The city granted these businesses five years to come into compliance with the ordinance. The city denied Bonnell's request for a variance. The court of appeals held that the amortization clause was valid.[4]

Exceptions from Zoning Ordinances

Variance

An exception to a zoning ordinance is known as a **variance.** Variances permit land owners and their successors to use property in a manner inconsistent with the current ordinance. Variances are granted by planning commissions or boards of adjustment only in exceptional cases. For a variance to be approved, two things must be shown:

Variance
An exception to the allowable uses within a zoned area.

1. The owner would suffer an undue hardship if the ordinance was enforced.
2. If granted, the use and character of neighborhood or surrounding land would not be excessively disrupted.

Example: A variance would not be granted to allow a homeowner to open an auto repair business in a quiet neighborhood.

There is no basis on which to grant a variance if the project site is otherwise indistinguishable from the surrounding lots.

Example: Where all lots have a 50-foot setback, no basis exists for allowing one lot to have a reduced setback.

The most commonly requested variance is an **area variance.** Area variances are requested if the property owner wishes to deviate from required setbacks, structure heights, minimum lot sizes, or parking requirements.

Area variance
Variances allowing a deviation from required setbacks, structure heights, minimum lot sizes, or parking requirements.

Example: A property owner has a triangularly shaped property at the end of a cul-de-sac. As configured, the property owner could not build a structure with the required zoning ordinance setbacks. The property owner may seek to deviate from the setback requirements to build an adequate structure through an area variance.

Conditional Use Permits

Instead of requiring property owners to obtain variances, the zoning ordinance may allow different uses without requiring them. A **conditional use permit** allows a municipality to provide for uses inconsistent with the property's existing zoning but essential or desirable to a specific area. The uses permitted will be set forth in the local government's zoning ordinance.

> *Example:* An area may be zoned for single-family residences. A church may seek a conditional use permit to allow for placement of temporary amusement attractions for the church's annual harvest celebration.

The conditional use permit will have specific conditions that must be met to allow for exception. In addition, the permit holder cannot make more intensive use of the property than that authorized by the conditional use permit. Like variances, conditional use permits "run with the land" and allow successor owners of the land to use the property as provided in the conditional use permit.

Changing Zoning Ordinances

Landowner who cannot obtain a variance may wish to petition the local government for a zoning change. This is a difficult process, and communities with comprehensive master plans are unlikely to consider such petitions. Amending a municipality's comprehensive master plan often requires obtaining a supermajority of votes of the city council.

■ ■ ■ Building Codes

Building code ordinances differ from zoning ordinances. While a zoning ordinance addresses uses of property, building codes address the allowable minimum standards for the construction of real property improvements. Building codes are also adopted pursuant to the police power of government. Building codes are responsive to the needs of the area.

> *Example:* As a result of the latest requirements for residential housing, new homes in the southeastern United States are better able to withstand hurricanes than are older homes in the area.

Building code changes can be sweeping, or they may address seemingly insignificant components such as the type, size, and spacing of nails used to attach roofing plywood to rafters, but such small details can save homes. Improving building codes can reduce the cost and damages resulting from natural disasters. Retrofitting buildings to conform to current building codes is now required throughout the United States by municipalities, buyers, mortgage lenders, and property insurers for property improvements, repairs, and remodels.

Zoning's Intrusion into Personal Choice

Zoning is not without controversy. It intrudes upon the basic freedoms of personal expression and association that Americans embrace. Zoning regulates conduct, but the courts are still defining zoning's boundaries within the guarantees provided for in our Constitution. It has been left to the courts to determine the balance between the rights of the community and of the individual.

In the following two cases, the court examined whether zoning laws can be used to regulate the number of persons living in a household. In the first of the two cases, the Supreme Court considered a Belle Terre, New York, ordinance that prohibited people unrelated by blood, adoption, or marriage, but not counting household servants, from living together in a single dwelling unit.

CASE 18.2

REGULATING THE HOUSEHOLDS OF UNRELATED PERSONS IS A LEGITIMATE GOVERNMENTAL INTEREST

VILLAGE OF BELLE TERRE v. BORAAS

416 U.S. 1 (1974)

United States Supreme Court

The Village of Belle Terre, New York, is located on the north shore of Long Island. It is a small community of fewer than a thousand people and is conservative in character. The village enacted an ordinance restricting land use to one-family dwellings. The ordinance defined "family" to mean one or more persons related by blood, adoption, or marriage, or not more than two unrelated persons, living and cooking together as a single household. It excluded lodging, boarding houses, fraternities, and multiple dwellings. The Dickmans were owners of a house in the village; they leased it in December 1971 for a term of 18 months. Later, Bruce Boraas become a co-lessee. Then Anne Parish moved into the house, along with three others. These six people were students from the nearby State University of New York at Stony Brook. None of them were related to the others by blood, adoption, or marriage.

The village served the Dickmans with an "Order to Remedy Violations" of the ordinance. The owners, as well as the tenants, sued for an injunction and a judgment declaring the ordinance unconstitutional. The federal district court upheld the ordinance, but the Court of Appeals reversed. The Supreme Court granted certiorari.

Language of the Court. *This case brings to this Court a different phase of local zoning regulations from those we have previously reviewed. The present ordinance is challenged on several grounds: that it interferes with a person's right to travel; that it interferes with the right to migrate to and settle within a state; that it bars people who are uncongenial to the present residents; that it expresses the social preferences of the residents for groups that will be congenial to them; that social homogeneity is not a legitimate interest of government; that the restriction of those whom the neighbors do not like trenches on the newcomers' rights of privacy; that it is of no rightful concern to villagers whether the residents are married or unmarried; and that the ordinance is antithetical to the nation's experience, ideology, and self-perception as an open, egalitarian, and integrated society.*

We find none of these reasons in the record before us. It is not aimed at transients. It involves no procedural disparity inflicted on some but not on others, such as was presented. It involves no fundamental right guaranteed by the Constitution, such as voting, the right of association, the right of access to the courts, or any rights of privacy. We deal with economic and social legislation where legislatures have historically drawn lines which we respect against the charge of violation of the Equal Protection Clause if the law be reasonable, not arbitrary, and bearing a rational relationship to a permissible state objective.

We have refused to limit the concept of public welfare that may be enhanced by zoning regulations. A quiet place where yards are wide, people few, and motor vehicles restricted are legitimate guidelines in a land use project addressed to family needs. This goal is a permissible one, and police power is not confined to the elimination of filth, stench, and unhealthy places.

It is ample to lay out zones where family values, youth values, and the blessings of quiet seclusion and clean air make the area a sanctuary for people.

Decision. The Supreme Court affirmed the judgment finding the zoning ordinance constitutional.

FOCUS ON ETHICS

Is it right for a community to restrict personal life choices? Would the court rule the same way today?

Three years later, the Supreme Court considered the city of East Cleveland's housing ordinance, which limited occupancy of a dwelling unit to the members of a single family. However, in this case the Court concluded that the ordinance limited personal liberties and declared the ordinance as unconstitutional.

CASE 18.3

ZONING MUST NOT UNREASONABLY INTRUDE UPON PRIVACY RIGHTS

MOORE v. EAST CLEVELAND
431 U.S. 494 (1977)
United States Supreme Court

Mrs. Inez Moore lived in her East Cleveland home together with her son, Dale Moore, Sr., and her two grandsons, Dale, Jr., and John Moore, Jr. The two boys were first cousins rather than brothers; John had come to live with his grandmother and with the elder and younger Dale Moore after the death of Dale Jr.'s mother. In early 1973, Mrs. Moore received a notice of violation from the city, stating that John was an "illegal occupant" and directing her to comply with the ordinance. When she failed to remove him from her home, the city filed a criminal charge. Mrs. Moore moved to dismiss, claiming that the ordinance was constitutionally invalid on its face. Her motion was overruled, and upon conviction she was sentenced to five days in jail and a $25 fine. The Ohio Court of Appeals affirmed the conviction after giving full consideration to her constitutional claims, and the Ohio Supreme Court denied review. The Supreme Court granted certiorari.

Language of the Court. *East Cleveland's housing ordinance, like many throughout the country, limits occupancy of a dwelling unit to members of a single family. But the ordinance contains an unusual and complicated definitional section that recognizes as a "family" only a few categories of related individuals. Because her family, living together in her home, fits none of those categories, the appellant stands convicted of a criminal offense. The question in this case is whether the ordinance violates the Due Process Clause of the Fourteenth Amendment.*

The city argues that our decision in Village of Belle Terre *requires us to sustain the ordinance attacked here. Belle Terre, like East Cleveland, imposed limits on the types of groups that could occupy a single dwelling unit. Applying the constitutional standard announced in this Court's leading land use case,* Euclid v. Ambler Realty Co., *we sustained the Belle Terre ordinance on the grounds that it bore a rational relationship to permissible state objectives. But one overriding factor sets this case apart from* Belle Terre. *The ordinance there affected only unrelated individuals. It expressly allowed all who were related by "blood, adoption, or marriage" to live together, and in sustaining the ordinance we were careful to note that it promoted "family needs" and "family values." East Cleveland, in contrast, has chosen to regulate the occupancy of its housing by slicing deeply into the family itself. On its face, it selects certain categories of relatives who may live together and declares that others may not. In particular, it makes a crime of a grandmother's choice to live with her grandson in circumstances like those presented here.*

When a city undertakes such intrusive regulation of the family, neither Belle Terre *nor* Euclid *governs; the usual judicial deference to the legislature is inappropriate. This Court has long recognized that freedom of personal choice in matters of marriage and family life is one of the liberties protected by the Due Process Clause of the Fourteenth Amendment.*

When thus examined, this ordinance cannot survive. The city seeks to justify it as a means of preventing overcrowding, minimizing traffic and parking congestion, and avoiding an undue financial burden on East Cleveland's school system. Although these are legitimate goals, the ordinance before us serves them marginally, at best. The ordinance would permit a grandmother to live with a single dependent son and children, even if his school age children number a dozen, yet it forces Mrs. Moore to find another dwelling for her grandson John, simply because of the presence of his uncle and cousin in the same household. We need not belabor the point. The ordinance has but a tenuous relation to the alleviation of the conditions mentioned by the city.

Decision. The Supreme Court held the ordinance unconstitutional.

FOCUS ON ETHICS

Had the Court recognized that societal values had changed from the time of its *Village of Belle Terre* decision? What effect did the fact that a grandmother was cited have upon the Court's thinking?

Religious Land Use and Institutionalized Persons Act

Disputes may arise over the use of property for religious purposes. Zoning laws may restrict the location and thereby the religious practices of many churches and religious facilities. Local governments may be confronted with a dispute over the exercise of religious views against local zoning ordinances, increased traffic and congestion near the religious institutions, or the desire of the municipality to maximize the number of tax assessable properties in the community. Tax-exempt religious institutions are not subject to property taxes.

In response, Congress enacted the federal Religious Land Use and Institutionalized Persons Act (RLUIPA). In part, it gives churches and other religious facilities a way to avoid burdensome zoning restrictions on their property use. If a local government imposes or implements a land use regulation that creates a substantial burden on the religious exercise of a person, including a religious assembly or institution, the local government must demonstrate a strict judicial scrutiny standard. Strict scrutiny requires that the government action furthers a compelling governmental interest and is the least restrictive means of furthering that interest.

RLUIPA does not guarantee religious communities the right to intrude upon existing zoning ordinances, and it places the burden of proof on the local government to show that its restrictions accord with RLUIPA requirements.

Private Restrictions on Land Use

Restrictive covenant
An unconditional promise. When recorded on title, it is binding upon successor owners.

Land use restrictions are not limited to zoning laws: Private parties can achieve similar results through deed restrictions (covenants). For example, a homebuilder might sell homes and require that the lots be used only for private residences. An agreement restricting the future uses of property is known as a **restrictive covenant**. The scope of such private land restrictions is almost limitless, subject only to compliance with fair housing laws. Fair housing laws prevent the enforcement of deed restrictions that discriminate against protected groups (such as racial covenants) or that have the effect of discriminating against protected groups (such as requiring that properties be occupied only by single families, which has the effect of prohibiting group homes for the developmentally disabled).

Covenants

A covenant is a written contractual promise relating to land. Covenants are recorded by a landowner on the title to her or his property, and they can last in perpetuity. They are often more restrictive than zoning ordinances. The covenants are binding upon succeeding owners of the property. Covenants are usually made with the intention of preserving a neighborhood's aesthetic character and, indirectly, of preserving or increasing the affected properties' market value.

> *Example:* A property owner may covenant not to park vehicles on the street in front of his home.

Covenants, Conditions, and Restrictions (CCRs)

**Covenants,
conditions, and
restrictions (CCRs)**
A document that regulates the uses and activities permitted on a developer's lots, recorded by the developer prior to the first sale in a development.

Covenants, conditions, and restrictions (CCRs) are often found in multiunit dwellings, a subject discussed in chapter 13. Most commonly, these private limitations on land are created as part of a real estate development's general plan. The developer may record a Declaration of Covenants, Conditions, and Restrictions. Once CCRs are recorded, each deed contains language stating that the CCRs are incorporated by reference. This incorporation reference has the same legal effect as if each deed stated all the CCR terms and conditions. Examples of CCRs can include the following:

> *Example:* No fence, wall, hedge, or other dividing device may be erected, painted, altered, or maintained on any lot or common area that borders or is visible from any public or private street, unless such fence or wall is first approved in writing by the Architectural Committee.

> *Example:* Garage doors shall be kept closed at all times, except as reasonably required for ingress and egress.

Example: No animals, fowl, reptiles, poultry, fish, or insects of any kind ("animals") may be raised, bred, or kept on any lot, condominium, or common area within the properties, except that a reasonable number of birds, fish, dogs, cats, or other customary household pets may be kept on a lot or condominium. An unreasonable quantity ordinarily means more than two household pets per residence.

Each lot owner may enforce the restrictions against any other lot owner. Typically, a homeowners' association in which all owners are members files a lawsuit seeking an injunction to prevent further violations of the CCRs. A lawsuit could also be filed for damages resulting from the loss of value to the property.

Example: A property owner who removes the grass in his front yard and installs a stone ground cover to reduce maintenance and watering costs in violation of CCR requirements may be required by the homeowners' association to remove the stone ground cover and install an alternative approved ground cover.

Defenses to Enforcement

Defenses to the enforcement of land restrictions can include the following:

1. *Changed conditions.* Where the condition or restriction on the burdened land has changed and become obsolete so that enforcement would be unfair, the covenant may not be enforced.

Example: A subdivision of industrial properties had a covenant restricting the sale and consumption of alcohol. Over time, the area has gentrified, and the industrial properties have been converted to commercial and residential properties. Business owners of the commercial properties seek to add restaurants and bars, requiring the sale and consumption of alcohol. The business owners may claim that due to changed conditions, the covenant has become unenforceable.

2. *Abandonment.* If the holder of the covenant demonstrates the intent to relinquish the rights of the covenant, it may be deemed abandoned.

Example: The CCRs of a homeowners' association contain a covenant requiring that all homeowners must park their vehicles inside their garages. Over time, most people in the neighborhood have begun to park their cars in their driveways and on the streets. A homeowner requests that the covenant be enforced, and the homeowners' association elects not to enforce the covenant. The covenant may be abandoned by the inaction of the homeowners' association.

3. *Violation of public policy.* If a covenant is in violation of public policies, the covenant will not be enforced.

Example: If a covenant promotes unlawful discrimination, such as that based on race, religion, national origin, age, or disability, the covenant may not be enforced.

4. *Laches.* Laches occurs when a party waits too long to seek enforcement of their rights. When someone unreasonably delays in seeking enforcement of the CCRs and the delay prejudices the affected party, the covenant may not be enforced.

Example: A neighbor waited until construction of a home in violation of the subdivision setback rules was completed before seeking an injunction.

5. *Expiration of CCRs.* Some CCRs automatically expire unless the owners agree to extend them.

Restrictive Covenants Can Apply to Leasehold Interests

Example: SES owned the Sagamore Shopping Center in Lafayette, Indiana. Kroger, a grocery store chain, leased one of the stores in the shopping center from SES for 20 years with options. The lease contained a covenant that the landlord would not lease to another food or grocery store operating within two miles of the center. After the loss of an anchor tenant and an extensive marketing campaign, the only tenant the landlord could attract was Schnucks, another grocery store chain. Schnucks sought to have the restrictive covenant declared unenforceable as a violation of public policy. The Indiana Court of Appeals enforced the covenant against the landlord. It noted that even the property's loss of value arising from the lack of tenants was not a sufficient reason to set aside the restrictive covenant.[5]

Key Terms and Concepts

- Zoning, page 474
- Enabling statute, page 476
- Exclusive use zoning, page 477
- Cumulative zoning, page 477
- Intensity zoning, page 478
- Incentive zoning, page 478
- Aesthetic zoning, page 478
- Spot zoning, page 478
- Exclusionary zoning, page 479

- Inclusionary zoning, page 479
- Nonconforming use, page 480
- Variances, page 481
- Area variance, page 481
- Conditional use permit, page 482
- Restrictive covenant, page 486
- Covenants, conditions and restrictions (CCRs), page 486

Chapter Summary

- Zoning involves sectioning land into zones; only certain uses of the land may occur in the created zones.

- The local government's authority to create zones comes from the state's police powers.

- Zoning begins with a state enabling statute empowering local jurisdictions to develop comprehensive plans by which they zone and regulate the current and future uses of land.

- Zoning is permissible if the zoning law (1) promotes the health, safety, and general welfare of the people and (2) is not arbitrary, unreasonable, or discriminatory.

- Zoning ordinances may include (1) exclusive use and cumulative use restrictions, (2) intensity zoning, (3) incentive zoning, (4) aesthetic zoning, (5) spot zoning, (6) exclusionary zoning, and (7) inclusionary zoning.

- Nonconforming use is a structure or activity allowed to continue on a property because it existed before the zoning ordinance was enacted.

- When property owners wish to deviate from an existing zoning ordinance, they must obtain a variance that allows them (and successor owners

of the land) to use the land in a manner inconsistent with the current zoning ordinance.

- A grandfather clause allows a nonconforming use to remain, as long as it was in use when a new zoning ordinance was enacted.

- A variance is an exception to an existing zoning ordinance. The most common type of variances is an area variance.

- A conditional use permit allows a municipality to provide for uses inconsistent with the existing ordinance but essential or desirable to a particular area.

- An agreement restricting the future uses of property is known as a restrictive covenant. The scope of such private land restrictions is almost limitless, subject only to compliance with fair housing laws.

- A covenant is a written contractual promise relating to land. Covenants that affect title run with the land and are binding upon succeeding owners of the property.

- A defense to the enforcement of land restrictions may include (1) changed conditions, (2) abandonment, (3) violation of public policy, (4) laches, and (5) expiration of CCRs.

Chapter Problems and Assignments

1. Define when zoning is permissible.

2. Explain the differences between a variance and a conditional use permit.

3. A city zoning ordinance provides the following zoning classifications, in order: (i) residential use, (ii) low-density commercial use, (iii) medium-density commercial use, (iv) agricultural use, and (v) industrial use. A developer purchases a property zoned for agricultural use but desires to build low-density commercial realty. Between

exclusive use zoning and cumulative zoning, which approach would allow the developer to build for the desired purpose?

4. An urban city has a zoning ordinance limiting the height of structures to ten stories and requiring at least a 12-foot-wide sidewalk. The city has recently passed a zoning ordinance allowing a developer who provides a 15-foot-wide sidewalk and installs trees on the sidewalk can build up to 12 stories. What type of zoning ordinance has the city recently enacted?

5. Jaclyn owns a residential property in an area in which the city has recently changed the zoning to low-density commercial. Jaclyn desires to continue using the property as her home; however, an electrical fire occurred on her property through no fault of her own. Her property was destroyed by the fire, and she wishes to rebuild her home to the same specifications as the home that was destroyed. The city is not allowing her to rebuild the home and requires that the property now be used for low-density commercial purposes. Who is correct?

6. Mega Church desires to hold an annual Thanksgiving dinner for the homeless at the church. Local zoning laws prohibit the event the church desires to hold. Would it be best for Mega Church to seek a variance, spot zoning, or a conditional use permit to allow it to hold the Thanksgiving day event?

7. Quinn operates an industrial building in an area that the city has recently zoned residential. The city has provided five years for Quinn to conform the use of her property to residential premises. Quinn does not want to construct a residential building and instead wants to construct a commercial property. Will Quinn be able to construct her commercial property?

8. The Northco homeowners' association has enacted a restrictive covenant that limits to two the number of dogs and cats a homeowner can maintain on the property. Elizabeth is a dog lover and moved into Northco with four dogs. Does Northco have any remedies against Elizabeth? If so, what rights and remedies does the city of Northco have?

9. Review your local government zoning ordinance. List the different zoning categories in which the zoning ordinance regulates.

10. Research whether your local zoning ordinance allows purely aesthetic zoning.

End Notes

1. *Village of Euclid, Ohio v. Ambler Realty Co.*, 272 U.S. 365 (1926).
2. *Berman v. Parker*, 348 U.S. 26 (1954).
3. *City Council of Los Angeles v. Taxpayers for Vincent*, 466 U.S. 789 (1984).
4. *Bonnell, Inc. v. Board of Adjustment*, 791 P.2d 107 (1990).
5. *Tippecanoe Associates II, LLC v. Kimco Lafayette 671, Inc.*, 811 N.E.2d 438 (Ind. 2004).

Chapter 19
Real Estate Taxation

The hardest thing in the world to understand is the income tax.
   —*Attributed to Albert Einstein by Leo Mattersdorf during a private conversation*

Learning Objectives

1. Distinguish tax deductions from tax credits.
2. Describe the limitations on deducting mortgage interest.
3. Explain how taxable gain on the sale of residential and commercial properties is calculated.
4. Determine what property is exempt from real property taxes.
5. Define the concept and requirements of IRC §1031 exchanges.

Chapter Outline

■ Introduction
■ Income Tax and Real Property Transactions
■ Sale of Residential Real Property
■ Sale of Commercial Real Property
■ Real Estate Property Taxes
Case 19.1: *Wells Fargo Bank, Minnesota, N.A. v. Commonwealth of Kentucky*

Opening
scenario

Liam owns and operates a four-unit apartment complex in Palm Beach, Florida. Palm Beach is an affluent area, and his four-unit apartment complex is now worth $1.1 million. He purchased the property decades ago for $250,000 and now desires to sell the apartment complex and purchase a larger apartment complex in a lower cost state. He is considering purchasing a 12-unit complex in Dallas, Texas, with his sales proceeds. He is concerned about paying the taxes on the gain he will realize upon sale of his four-unit apartment. What advice would you give Liam to accomplish his objective and minimize his tax liability?

Introduction

In this chapter, we begin with a brief review of the effect that real property ownership has on income and property taxes. Real property taxation involves personal-, business-, and investment-income taxation, as well as *ad valorem* (value-based) taxes assessed against the owners of real property. We discuss the power of government to tax real property owners, and we review the effect that real property ownership has on income and property taxes.

Income Tax and Real Property Transactions

No one enjoys paying taxes, especially in amounts higher than are actually required. Owners selling real property may encounter a taxable event. It is important to become familiar with the tax consequences resulting from selling residential and commercial real property and to understand how ownership of real property can reduce a home-owner's income taxes. Income tax and the deferral of the income tax resulting from the sale of real property often drive real property transactions.

Tax Deductions Versus Tax Credits

To understand the tax consequences from a real property transaction, it is important to understand a couple of introductory concepts related to taxes. First, is the effect of a tax deduction versus that of a tax credit. In addition, one must understand common real property deductions and credits.

Tax Deductions

A **tax deduction** reduces taxable income. A reduction in taxable income lowers the amount of income taxes paid. Deductions are beneficial because by reducing the income from which taxes are paid, they increase the taxpayer's net income.

The most significant deductions a homeowner can enjoy are those obtained through mortgage interest and property taxes. Congress often encourages taxpayers' preferred behaviors by providing tax deductions.

> **Example:** As a means of increasing home ownership, the Internal Revenue Code (IRC) recognizes certain expenditures in acquiring and financing a property, such as mortgage interest, to be tax deductions.

No matter how many deductions a taxpayer may have, the total sum of all deductions cannot reduce a person's taxable income below zero. Hundreds of possible tax deductions exist. Many of the most common deductions relating to the ownership of real property are discussed in this chapter.

Tax deduction
A reduction to taxable income.

Tax Credits

Unlike tax deductions, which reduce taxable income, **tax credits** lower the amount of taxes to be paid, dollar for dollar. Both the federal government and the state may provide tax credits to incentivize certain consumer behaviors.

> **Example:** A state may provide homeowners tax credits for installing energy efficient appliances or solar panels to conserve the state's energy resources.

Tax credit
A reduction in the amount of taxes a taxpayer is obligated to pay.

Assume a taxpayer had a taxable income of $55,000 and a tax rate of 20 percent.

Tax Deduction

If the taxpayer was entitled to a tax deduction of $5,000, the taxpayer would be obligated to pay $10,000 in income taxes for the year.

$55,000	Taxable income
($5,000)	Tax deduction
$50,000	Adjusted taxable income
x 20%	Tax rate
$10,000	Income tax owed

Tax Credit

If instead of a deduction, the taxpayer was entitled to a tax credit of $5,000, the taxpayer would be obligated to pay $6,000 in income taxes.

$55,000	Taxable income
x 20%	Tax rate
$11,000	Income tax before credits
($5,000)	Tax credit
$6,000	Income tax owed

This simple example presents the differences between a tax deduction and a tax credit.

FIGURE 19.1. Comparison of a Tax Deduction to a Tax Credit

Mortgage Interest Deduction

Amortized
The process of paying regular installments of a debt over a period of time.

Generally, the largest deduction individuals can take on their personal tax returns is for mortgage interest. Only the interest on a mortgage is deductible; the total payment (principal and interest) is not. The largest mortgage interest deductions usually occur when a home has just been purchased or refinanced. Due to a loan **amortization** schedule, in the early years of a mortgage, more of a homeowner's loan payment will be attributable to interest than to the payment of principal. Because of this phenomenon, more of the monthly payment is deductible in the early years of a loan compared to when a loan reaches its maturity date (final payment).

The IRC provides the amount of mortgage interest that may be deducted. Homeowners may deduct as mortgage interest from their personal tax returns up to the property's fair market value, with some limitations concerning total debt, number of properties, and home equity debt.[1]

Number of Residential Properties and Debt Limitation

A taxpayer may deduct the mortgage interest from home mortgage debt totaling $1 million or less ($500,000 if married filing separately). A home includes a house, condominium, cooperative, mobile home, house trailer, boat, or similar property having sleeping, cooking, and toilet facilities. The mortgage debt total includes a principal residence as well as a second residence (such as a weekend or vacation home) owned by the taxpayer.

> *Example:* Anisha owns two residential properties. She has a mortgage of $700,000 on her principal residence and a mortgage of $300,000 on her vacation home. She is entitled to deduct the mortgage interest from both properties on her personal tax return.

Interest on mortgage debt above $1 million is not deductible.

Example: In the above example, if Anisha's mortgage on her principal residence totaled $800,000 and the mortgage on her vacation home totaled $300,000 (for a total mortgage debt of $1,100,000), Anisha would only be entitled to deduct the mortgage interest up to the $1,000,000 in debt on her personal tax return. The mortgage interest on the remaining $100,000 is not deductible on her tax returns.

If the taxpayer has three residential mortgages totaling $1 million in debt or less, only two residences will qualify under the IRC guidelines for mortgage interest deductions.

Example: Anisha owns three residential properties. She has a mortgage of $600,000 on her principal residence, a mortgage of $200,000 on her vacation home, and a mortgage of $100,000 on her third property. She is only entitled to deduct the mortgage interest from two of these properties on her personal tax return.

A person can continue to use the $1 million mortgage interest deduction in perpetuity. If the taxpayer refinances a property or purchases a new property, the taxpayer may continue to use the $1 million mortgage interest deduction.

Example: Joel owns a residential property with a mortgage of $700,000. After 20 years, Joel has paid off the mortgage. He had deducted all the mortgage interest from his personal tax returns. If Joel now purchases a second home with a mortgage of $500,000, he will be entitled to deduct all the mortgage interest from his second home as well.

Home Equity Interest

A taxpayer may deduct the interest from a home equity debt of $100,000 or less ($50,000 for married taxpayers filing separate returns) so long as the home equity loan was not used in the purchase of the first or a second home. Home equity debt is debt secured by a mortgage on the residence for which the loan proceeds were used for purposes other than acquiring the property.

Example: Kari obtains a home equity line of credit in the amount of $25,000, which she uses to purchase a new automobile. The interest from the home equity line of credit can be deducted from Kari's tax return.

The interest on home equity debt above $100,000 is not deductible.

Example: Jennifer has a $300,000 home equity line of credit on her home, which she uses to finance her lifestyle. The interest she pays on borrowings up to $100,000 is deductible, while the interest paid for borrowings above that amount is not deductible.

Business Properties

Generally, for business and investment properties, all interest is tax deductible with no limit.

Deduction for Points

Points are prepaid interest or extra profit lenders charge borrowers for securing a loan. Points are sometimes also referred to as loan origination fees, loan discounts, and

Points
A percentage of a loan given to the lender as additional consideration for making the loan. One point equals one percent of a loan.

discount points. One point equals 1 percent of the loan amount. Points are often used by lenders to allow a borrower to reduce the interest rate on the mortgage loan by purchasing a point.

> *Example:* A lender may provide for a 30-year fixed interest rate of 4.875 percent with zero points or an interest rate of 4.625 percent with one point.

With some exceptions, the amount of money paid for a point(s) used as prepaid interest is fully deductible on income tax returns. Points paid for services provided by the lender, such as those for appraisal fees and preparing legal documents, are not deductible.

Using a Residence for Business Purposes

The costs of operating a residence used solely for residential purposes are not deductible. When a taxpayer uses a portion of a personal residence to operate a business, trade, or income- producing activity, they may be allowed to deduct some of the expenses related to the business if specific requirements are met.

A few of the more common methods qualifying a taxpayer to deduct a portion of household expenses as business expenses arise when a taxpayer *exclusively and regularly* uses part of the residence in one of the following ways:

1. *As the principal place of business for the taxpayer's trade or business.* If the part of the home is used for both business and personal purposes, it does not meet the requirements of exclusive use. Further, while the taxpayer may have more than one business location, to qualify for the deduction, the home must be the principal place of business for that business.

> *Example:* An accountant who works for a firm with an office downtown would not be able to deduct use of a home office on weekends because his principal place of business is the office provided by the firm.

2. *As a place where the taxpayer met or dealt with patients, clients, or customers in the normal course of the taxpayer's business.* Under this test, the taxpayer can carry on business at another location, but must physically meet with patients, clients, or customers and the use of the home must be substantial and integral to the conduct of the business.

> *Example:* If a physician occasionally met with patients in a downstairs room of her house, she would not qualify to deduct the expenses because it fails to be substantial and integral to the conduct of the business.

3. *If the taxpayer uses a separate structure free-standing structure to the home in connection with the taxpayer's trade or business.* The taxpayer must exclusively and regularly use the separate free-standing structure for the business. The structure does not have to be the taxpayer's principal place of business, nor a place where the taxpayer meets patients, clients, or customers.

> *Example:* A carpenter who has a workshop for her finish carpentry business in a separate free-standing structure would be entitled to deduct the business expenses related to that structure.

Generally, because of the exclusivity requirement, the taxpayer may not deduct for space that is used for both business and personal purposes.

Example: The authors of this textbook prepared it while working in areas of their homes that were not exclusively used for business purposes. Their use is not exclusive, and the deduction does not apply.

Sale of Residential Real Property

The sale of a residential real property may create taxable income. However, if certain rules are followed, the tax law allows the tax to be avoided. In addition, certain exceptions to the general rules apply (such as the Servicemembers Civil Relief Act discussed in chapter 11).

Capital Gains or Losses

Ordinarily taxpayers must calculate the capital gain or loss from sales of property to determine whether taxable income must be recognized. Taxpayers may have to pay income tax on the capital gain realized. To understand taxable gains and losses, a few definitions are helpful.

- The **basis** of the property is usually the cost of buying or building the home. The basis can also be the fair market value of the property if one received it through an inheritance, or it can be the basis of the previous owner when the property is received by gift. Adjustments are made over time, including the cost of improvements made to the property.
- **Gain** is the amount of money realized from the sale of the property in excess of the property's adjusted basis.
- **Loss** is the amount of money realized from the sale of the property below the property's adjusted basis.
- **Depreciation** is the decrease in the value of assets over time as a result of wear and tear and obsolescence of the property. Depreciation deductions are available only for commercial and investment properties (not residential properties). It does not apply to land because land does not wear out. The land value and the building value must be separated to arrive at a basis for determining the basis of a property.
- The **selling price** is the total consideration received for the sale of the home.
- **Selling expenses** include the brokers' commissions, advertising fees, legal fees, and loan charges paid by the seller, such as points.

Calculating the Basis

Basis
An amount representing the taxpayer's cost in acquiring an asset with adjustments to allow for changes in the condition of the asset.

The **basis** is adjusted (increased and decreased) to allow for changes in the condition of the house. The most common adjustment is an increase in the basis for the cost of additions and improvements to the real property that have a useful life of more than one year. Ordinary repair and maintenance costs that do not add to the value of a home or prolong its life may not be added to the basis.

> **Example:** The basis in a property increases if the owner adds a room, remodels a bathroom or kitchen, or adds a swimming pool.

Calculation of Realized Gain or Loss

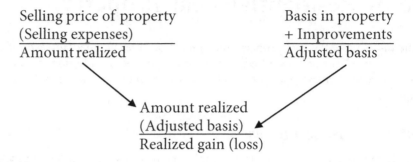

> **Example:** Assume a taxpayer purchased a residential property for $350,000 and spent $50,000 remodeling the kitchen. The taxpayer sold the property for $600,000 and incurred $20,000 in selling costs. The realized gain to the seller is $180,000.

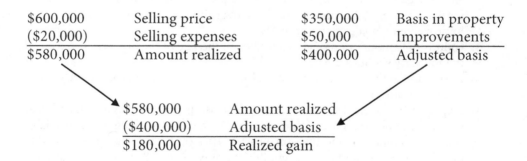

Income Tax on Realized Gain

The amount of income tax owed from the realized gain is taxed at a capital gains tax rate. Established by Congress, the capital gains rate for real property can change.

Principal Residence Exemption

Taxpayers may qualify to exclude part of the gain on the sale of a home if they owned and used the home as a principal residence for two out of the previous five years prior to its sale. The occupancy need not be continuous as long as it totals two years.

Taxpayers who meet these criteria can exclude a portion of the gain from their taxable income. The exclusion from gain from the sale or exchange of a personal residence is $250,000 for single persons and up to $500,000 for married couples. Any gain in excess of these limits is subject to capital gains tax.

> *Example:* Robert and Jane, a married couple, sell their primary residence for a realized gain of $350,000. Because the realized gain was less than $500,000, they will not pay capital gains tax on the sale of their home.

In the event of a taxable loss, instead of a taxable gain, from the sale of the property, the owner is not entitled to any deductions on income taxes.

Sale of Commercial Real Property

The sale of a commercial real property may also create taxable income. However, if certain rules are followed, the tax law allows the tax to be deferred. Under Internal Revenue Code §1031, discussed below, unlike residential real estate, on which taxable gains may be avoided, gains on commercial real property can only be deferred. In addition, when calculating the adjusted basis for commercial property to determine realized gain or loss, depreciation must be deducted from the basis.

Depreciation Deductions

Commercial real property and investments, such as apartment buildings and shopping centers, do not last forever. The Internal Revenue Service (IRS) requires an owner to deduct part of the building cost and the value of improvements (not the value of land) in the form of an annual depreciation deduction. **Depreciation** is the value of the estimated wear and tear and obsolescence of the property as it ages.

Depreciation
The decrease in value of assets over time due to wear and tear and obsolescence of the property.

Depreciation provides a yearly tax deduction, which lowers the yearly income tax of the taxpayer. However, depreciation reduces the taxpayer's basis in the property, thereby increasing the taxable gain a property owner may realize in the future.

Calculation of Realized Gain or Loss

The calculation of the realized gain or loss for commercial real property is similar to the calculation used for residential real property, except for the deduction of depreciation as shown below.

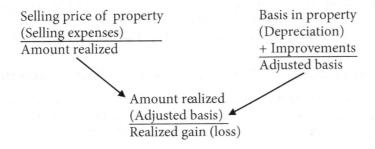

Example: Assume a taxpayer purchased an investment property for $400,000 and spent $125,000 remodeling it. The property had depreciation of $50,000. The seller sold the property for $700,000 and incurred $25,000 in selling costs. The realized gain to the seller is $200,000.

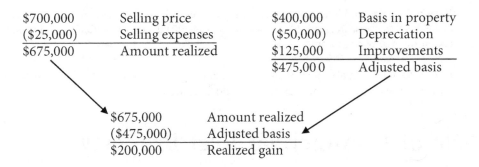

$700,000	Selling price		$400,000	Basis in property
($25,000)	Selling expenses		($50,000)	Depreciation
$675,000	Amount realized		$125,000	Improvements
			$475,000	Adjusted basis

$675,000	Amount realized
($475,000)	Adjusted basis
$200,000	Realized gain

Like-Kind Property Exchanges: IRC Section 1031

IRC §1031 (tax-free exchange)
A deferral of the recognition of gain or loss when property held for business or commercial purposes is exchanged for like-kind property.

Commercial and investment properties do not enjoy the capital gains exemption provided for residential properties; however, capital gains exemptions are allowed for these properties under IRC §1031 rules for exchanges. Exchanges under IRC §1031 allow property owners to defer (postpone) taxes due on sales of qualifying properties. If the parties exchange similar properties, the taxpayer has not realized a profit on the transaction, and the law views the parties as continuing their investment in a property. Because the party is continuing an investment, the IRS does not impose a capital gains tax at that time.

In an exchange under **IRC §1031**, also known as a tax-free exchange, a taxpayer does not realize any gain or loss on the transfer of like-kind property. Most tax-free exchanges of property require some payment of cash or other consideration to equalize the value of the properties, however, which is known as **boot.** The boot amount is taxed at the capital gains tax rates.

Boot
The receipt of cash or other consideration given to equalize the value between two properties being exchanged.

Example: Sam owns a small office building and sells the building for $1.5 million. If Sam identifies a replacement property in Sun Valley, Idaho, for $1.25 million and receives $250,000 in cash in the transaction, Sam has received $250,000 in boot, which is taxable as a capital gain.

With a §1031 exchange, the basis of the original property carries over to the replacement property (the one received in the exchange). In this sense, the capital gain is deferred until the property is sold in the future. At that time, the realized gain or loss will be recognized as taxable income or loss.

Requirements for a Real Property Like-Kind Exchange

Three conditions are required to accomplish a §1031 exchange: (1) the property involved must be a like-kind exchange, (2) a qualified intermediary must be used, and (3) the exchange must occur within the appropriate time.

The Property Involved Must Be a Like-Kind Exchange

The term "like-kind property" is liberally interpreted. It requires that both the real property exchanged (the property given up) and the real property received be business, trade, or investment property. Property held for personal use does not qualify under a §1031 exchange. Property, however dissimilar, is of like kind as to exchanges. If both properties qualify, then nearly any type of real property can be exchanged.

> *Example:* A property owner seeks to exchange a piece of rural unimproved real property with a piece of developed commercial property in an urban environment. This property exchange qualifies for a like-kind exchange.

The Taxpayer Must Exchange Property Through a Qualified Intermediary

A **qualified intermediary** accepts the funds, prepares escrow for the sale, and handles the legal contracts. The involved parties often retain a commercial company specializing in handling §1031 exchanges.

Qualified intermediary
An entity that accepts the funds, prepares escrow for the sale, and handles the legal contracts.

> *Example:* First American Financial Corporation has a separate entity, "First American Exchange Company, LLC" that can assist as a qualified intermediary in commercial transactions.

The Like-Kind Exchange Must Occur Within the Appropriate Time Period

Once the property given up in the exchange has been transferred, the taxpayer has 45 days from the time title is transferred on the property given up in the exchange to identify the replacement property to be exchanged. The taxpayer must close on the replacement property within 180 days from the time title is transferred on the property that was given up in the exchange.

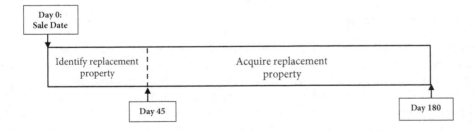

The requirements for a tax-free exchange must be strictly followed; otherwise, the taxpayer must recognize the entire amount of gain or loss on the sale or exchange of property.

Real Estate Property Taxes

Ad valorem taxes
Taxes levied according to the value of property.

Property taxes are an annual tax on the value of real property. These taxes are **ad valorem taxes** because they are taxes levied according to the value of property as determined by an assessment or appraisal. When property values increase, property taxes increase. The receipt of real property taxes is, for most local governments, their largest source of revenue. In the local community, property taxes play a prominent role in financing both public services and infrastructure. Taxes paid on real property are usually deductible on both personal and business tax returns.

Property Exempt from Property Taxes

Certain property is wholly or partially exempt from real property taxation.

1. *Government-owned property.* All property that is owned by the federal, state, or local governments is exempt from property taxation. This exemption has considerably more impact on state government budgets in the western United States than in the eastern or southern states because the federal government owns more land in the West than elsewhere in the country.
2. *Tax-exempt organizations.* Although states may vary in how they define tax-exempt organizations, usually properties owned by nonprofits and tax-exempt organizations do not pay property taxes. Tax-exempt organizations include houses of worship and related facilities, nonprofit hospitals, universities and colleges, charities, and other similar organizations.
3. *Homeowner's deduction (also known as a homestead exemption).* Properties held for household residential use are entitled to limited exemption from taxes in many states. Some states may require the taxpayer to file a homestead exemption to receive the benefit, while other states allow an automatic exemption with no need to file an application.

Example: Hawaii exempts from property taxes the first $48,000 of assessed value and Florida up to the first $50,000, both with certain restrictions.

Tax Assessment

Tax assessor
A public official who appraises all taxable properties within a jurisdiction.

A property tax assessment is made on the property to estimate its value for tax purposes. A **tax assessor** or county property appraiser makes the tax assessment for all taxable properties within a jurisdiction. The frequency of assessment varies among governments. Some assessments are made every two, three, or four years, while others are made annually on the property's value. Usually, the property tax is computed by taking the assessed value multiplied by a tax rate, which can vary by local government and from state to state. In some local governments, the tax rate can be as low as one-quarter of a percent of the assessed value, while in others it may be as high as a few percentage points of the assessed value.

Example: A property assessed at $150,000 in Portland, Oregon, with a property tax rate of 1.141 percent would have an annual property tax of $1,711.

Tax Assessment Valuation Methods

Three common methods exist for valuing real property: (1) the market approach, also known as the sales comparison approach; (2) the income approach; and (3) the cost approach. These methods were discussed in chapter 9 covering the valuation and financing of real estate.

Nonpayment and Tax Lien Sales

Once the local property-tax assessor establishes the property tax, the property tax becomes a lien upon the real property as of a certain date. State laws vary as to whether the real property tax liability is a personal tax obligation or one assessed against the property rather than the owner.

Priority of Property Tax Liens

A **property tax lien** is a lien imposed by law upon a debtor's property to secure the payment of property taxes. A tax lien may be imposed for delinquent taxes owed on real or personal property or the failure to pay income or other taxes.

Property tax lien
A lien imposed upon real property to secure the payment of property taxes.

Generally, state laws provide that property-tax liens are superior to private liens (mortgages and deeds of trust), regardless of the date of the private lien's creation. As a result, most mortgages and deeds of trust provide in the contract that the lender or beneficiary may foreclose immediately to protect its interests if the borrower becomes delinquent in the payment of real property taxes.

In the following case, two lending institutions argued their recorded mortgages were superior to general tax liens recorded on title to the properties because they were recorded first in time.

CASE 19.1

A STATUTE MAY GIVE PRIORITY TO PROPERTY TAX LIENS OVER ALL OTHER LIENS

WELLS FARGO BANK, MINNESOTA, N.A. v. COMMONWEALTH OF KENTUCKY

345 S.W.3d 800 (2011)

Kentucky Supreme Court

This case arises out of the refinancing of a mortgage wherein the property owners failed to satisfy the debt obligations owing to Wells Fargo, and Wells Fargo thereafter foreclosed on the property. Wells Fargo argued that its mortgage was superior to general tax liens that were recorded on the title to the property by the Commonwealth of Kentucky's Department of Revenue ("Commonwealth"). The trial court found in favor of Wells Fargo. The Com-

monwealth appealed and the court of appeals reversed holding in favor of the Commonwealth. Wells Fargo appealed to the state supreme court.

Language of the Court. *This Court has long held that that the first creditor to file its lien enjoys the first right to the debtor's property. This general rule of lien preference has become known as "first in time, first in right." It is without question, however, that* the Kentucky General Assembly is empowered to create statutory liens and establish their priorities; but, absent a statute giving precedence to a statutory lien, its rank is determined under the principle of first in time, first in right.

Kentucky statutes specifically establish a priority for the tax liens created therein. With this underlying policy in mind, the legislature created the machinery for collection of its taxes and provided those tax liens priority over subsequent holders of security interests.

Accordingly, we hold that the plain language of the Kentucky statutes establishes that a tax lien created and filed in accordance with those sections enjoys a priority over all subsequent purchasers, judgment lien creditors, security interest holders, and mechanic's lien creditors.

Decision. The Supreme Court of Kentucky affirmed the court of appeals ruling that the mortgages were not superior to a general tax lien.

FOCUS ON ETHICS

Is it fair that the government is given a superior position to that of a prior lender that may be more seriously damaged in the event of a loan default and resulting foreclosure?

Tax Lien Sale

Tax lien sale
A public sale of real property due to a failure to timely pay property taxes.

If the taxpayer is not timely in paying the property taxes when due, the taxing authority may force a sale of the property, known as a **tax lien sale**. State law establishes the procedures for a tax-lien sale. These statutes often provide that notice must be given to the taxpayer of the delinquency and that a list of delinquent properties must be published in a newspaper of general circulation.

Redemption Rights

The taxpayer has the right to reclaim the property before its public sale by paying the unpaid taxes, plus interest and penalties. The taxpayer also has the right to redeem the property by paying all delinquent taxes and penalties within a certain period following the tax-lien sale. After the period of redemption has expired, the property owner will have no rights in the property.

■ ■ ■   California's Proposition 13

The voters of California adopted a controversial amendment to the California Constitution under Proposition 13. It decreased real property taxes and placed substantial limitations on the ability to increase real property taxes at the state and local levels. The law requires an almost impossible-to-reach two-thirds majority in both legislative houses for future increases in any state tax rate, including income tax rates.

Under Proposition 13, property taxes for both residential and commercial properties are limited to 1 percent of the real property's assessed value. The property's assessed value is determined at the time of sale. Thereafter, the assessed value may increase by a maximum of 2 percent per year unless the property is transferred, sold, or significantly repaired. The result is that adjacent neighbors who acquired their homes at different times can pay radically different amounts of real property taxes.

Certain changes in ownership do not trigger a property-tax reassessment. These include a transfer between spouses, transfers to children, a change in title between co-tenants and joint tenants, and transfers to estate planning trusts. Because residential property is sold more often than commercial properties, the law actually benefits the owners of commercial and industrial buildings because such property is not as frequently subject to reassessment upon sale.

In the wake of this law, state and local government budgets have been starved for revenue. In response, municipalities secured voter approval for special assessments known as Mello-Roos assessments. These assessments levy new taxes and fees that formerly were paid by local property taxes. As a result, moving into a new community can entail paying almost double the real property assessment for the costs of streets, water service and sewers, landscaping and lighting, schools, parks, and police and fire departments. Sales taxes have also increased throughout the state following the enactment of Proposition 13.

Key Terms and Concepts

- Tax deduction, page 493
- Tax credit, page 493
- Amortized, page 494
- Points, page 495
- Basis, page 497
- Gain, page 497
- Loss, page 497
- Depreciation, page 497
- Selling price, page 497

- Selling expenses, page 497
- IRC §1031 (tax-free exchange), page 500
- Boot, page 500
- Qualified intermediary, page 501
- *Ad valorem* taxes, page 502
- Tax assessor, page 502
- Property tax lien, page 503
- Tax lien sale, page 504

Chapter Summary

- A tax deduction reduces taxable income, while a tax credit reduces the amount of tax paid.

- Mortgage interest is deductible up to certain limits with regard to residential property; it is fully deductible without limitation for commercial and investment properties.

- A taxpayer may deduct the interest from a home equity debt of $100,000 or less as long as the home equity loan was not used in the purchase of the first or second home.

- Points are prepaid interest or extra profit charged by a lender in securing a loan. They are deductible on income taxes.

- When taxpayers use a portion of a personal residence to operate a business, trade, or income producing activity, they may deduct some of the costs of operating the residence as a business expense.

- Gain may be excluded from the sale of a principal residence up to set limits for single filers and married couples filing jointly.

- Taxpayers may qualify to exclude part of the gain on the sale of a home if they owned and used the home as a principal residence for two out of the previous five years prior to its sale.

- Gain or loss resulting from a commercial sale can only be deferred.

- Depreciation deductions are available for commercial and investment properties. They must be taken each year and calculated in accordance with formulas provided by the IRS.

- An exchange under IRC §1031 allows a property owner to defer (postpone) taxes due on the sale of qualifying properties.

- Through an IRC §1031 exchange, if the taxpayer receives boot (cash or some type of nonqualifying property), the boot is taxable.

- Three conditions are required to accomplish a §1031 exchange: (1) the property involved must be a like-kind exchange, (2) a qualified intermediary must be used, and (3) the exchange must occur within the appropriate time.

- Real property taxes are assessed on the value of the real property. Certain types of property — those owned by the government and tax-exempt organizations — are exempt from real property taxation.

- If the taxpayer is not timely in paying the property taxes when due, the taxing authority may force a sale of the property, known as a tax lien sale.

- The taxpayer has the right to reclaim the property before its public sale by paying the unpaid taxes, plus interest and penalties. The taxpayer also has the right to redeem the property by paying all delinquent taxes and penalties within a certain period following the tax-lien sale.

Chapter Problems and Assignments

1. Explain the difference between a tax deduction and a tax credit.

2. What real property types of uses exempt the property from the assessment of taxes?

3. For a taxpayer with a taxable income of $100,000 and a tax rate of 20 percent, calculate the income tax owed if he or she received a $10,000 tax deduction. If the taxpayer received not a tax deduction, but a tax credit of $10,000, how much would the taxpayer owe?

4. Jessica, a single woman, owns a residential property that she purchased for $75,000. She sells the property years later for $375,000. She incurred $25,000 in selling expenses to sell the property. Calculate the amount realized in the property. Will Jessica have to pay any income tax on the amount realized? If so, what is the amount realized that will be subject to income tax?

5. Joel and Kirsten are married, file their tax returns jointly, and own three residential properties. One home has a mortgage of $500,000. Their vacation home has a mortgage of $350,000, and they just purchased a smaller home with a mortgage of $150,000. Can Joel and Kirsten deduct any of the mortgage payment amounts on their personal tax return? If so, what can they deduct?

6. Zachary purchased a warehouse and operated his business for several years. He then decides he wants to sell the warehouse and operate his business elsewhere. He sells the warehouse and within 30 days identifies a 20-unit apartment complex as a replacement property for the warehouse. He then closes on the transaction 45 days thereafter. He used an escrow company as a qualified intermediary to facilitate the exchange of the properties. Does this transaction meet the requirements for a §1031 exchange?

7. Garrett obtains a home equity line of credit to purchase a new luxury vehicle. The vehicle costs $50,000. Garrett wants to deduct the home equity line of credit payments on his personal tax return. What, if anything, is Garrett entitled to deduct?

8. Mack opens an accounting practice, and to keep overhead low, he operates the business from a spare room in his house. He occasionally meets clients in this space, and he conducts all of his business in this portion of his house. Is Mack entitled to deduct any expenses on his personal tax return for using the spare office for business purposes?

9. Research whether your state provides any specific tax credits related to real property improvements. List the tax credits provided.

10. Research your state law to determine if real property tax liens are superior to private liens regardless of the date of creation of the private lien.

End Notes

1. At the time of publication, Congress began considering changes to the Internal Revenue Code. The rules and statements that are presented regarding mortgage interest deduction were those in effect prior to any legislative changes.

Chapter 20
Construction Law, Liens, and Remedies

The first principle of architectural beauty is that the essential lines of a construction be determined by a perfect appropriateness to its use.
—Gustave Eiffel (1832–1923)

Learning Objectives

1. Identify the parties involved in a construction project.
2. Distinguish the common types of construction contracts.
3. Understand construction defects.
4. Explain how mechanic's liens work.
5. Describe stop notices and bond claims.

Chapter Outline

Opening scenario

A subcontractor employed by a prime contractor installs electrical work in a commercial property. After completing construction, the contractor cannot obtain payment from the prime contractor who becomes unresponsive and does not return phone calls or emails. The quality of the contractor's work is not in dispute, and the owner has already paid the prime contractor in full for the construction. As you read this chapter, determine what rights the electrical subcontractor has to seek payment against either or both of the prime contractor and the owner.

Introduction

Construction has been a hallmark of civilization for millennia. Safe construction and responsibility for harm caused by unsafe construction can be found in Hammurabi's Code.[1] In the code, the law dictated that builders be punished for injuries to others caused by the collapse of their buildings. In the modern era, the construction process embraces public safety, environmental considerations, and aesthetics.

A significant part of real estate law involves improving raw land or remodeling existing structures. This chapter discusses the many facets of construction law, introduces the construction team and their responsibilities, and identifies the typical construction clauses found in construction project contracts. Construction defects and remedies are reviewed. The chapter concludes with a discussion of mechanic's liens and related construction remedies, including stop notices and payment bonds.

The Construction Process

Prime contractor
A contractor hired directly by an owner of real property to construct an improvement to the land.

Bid
A contractor's estimated cost to construct a project.

Prime contract
A contract created between the owner and the prime contractor chosen to complete the project.

A construction project starts with an owner acquiring an interest in land either in fee or as a leasehold interest. The owner adopts a project design created by architects and engineers and then secures financing for construction.

The owner hires a **prime contractor**, also known as a general contractor or builder. The prime contractor may be selected through either a bidding process or a pricing negotiation with the owner. In a bidding process, prospective prime contractors prepare an estimated cost, known as a **bid**, to construct the project. The contractor with the lowest priced bid is often awarded the project. In negotiated pricing, the owner selects prime contractors and requests them to provide bids. The owner may then negotiate directly with each prime contractor to secure the most cost-effective contract possible.

Once a prime contractor has been selected, the owner and prime contractor create a contract between the parties, known as a **prime contract**. A construction schedule (a timeline for completion of the project by construction activity) is prepared, subcontractor and material supplier bids are received and accepted, and the construction work then proceeds.

The Parties to a Construction Contract

A construction project involves several parties: the project owner, the design professionals, the lender, insurance companies, and the construction team.

The Owner

The owner of a property targeted for a construction project may be either public or private. The owner's classification will control the requirements and legal remedies available to if the contractor defaults in performance.

Public Owners

Public land is owned for the beneficial use of the public. Public owners include federal and state governments, local municipalities, school districts, and special government districts, such as water and sanitation districts.

Private Owners

Private owners include any owner whose land is not owned for the beneficial use of the public. In the private sector, owners may adopt creative design and construction methods. They are not subject to the numerous, often complex regulations and limitations to which public owners must adhere. Private owners potentially pose more risk to contractors, because unlike public works projects, private works projects present the risk of not getting paid. Private projects are financed through owner funds and/or construction loans.

The Design Professionals

Owners will employ design professionals to assist in the preconstruction activities. In addition to architects, design services required include those of engineers and consultants who provide soil, structural, mechanical, and electrical engineering reports and recommendations for the completed structure. Either the architect or the owner contracts with these other professionals before retaining a contracting team.

The Construction Lender

A lender provides a construction loan to fund the purchase of the land and/or construct the planned improvements. Following the project's completion, permanent financing (also called takeout financing) is secured to pay the balance in full of the construction loan.

> **Example:** First Student Bank is a construction lender providing construction loans to homeowners for the construction of backyard renovations.

Insurance Companies

Insurance companies also play a key role in the construction process. Design errors, defective construction, and the risk of worker injuries are inherent in construction. Insurance carriers provide the means for insuring these risks.

The Contracting Team

The term "contractor" is synonymous with "builder." The contracting team includes prime contractors, subcontractors, and construction managers.

Prime Contractors

The builder who has a contract directly with the owner is the prime contractor. As discussed above, the prime contractor is also known as the general contractor. The prime contractor enters into contracts with subcontractors, who usually construct the project. The prime contractor is usually responsible for the daily oversight of the construction site.

> *Example:* Bechtel®, Fluor®, Turner Construction Company®, Kiewit Corporation®, PCL Construction Enterprises Inc.®, and The Walsh Group® are all examples of large prime contractors who perform construction activities throughout the United States.

Subcontractors

Subcontractor
A contractor hired by a prime contractor to perform specific construction-related tasks on a construction project.

Because construction requires technically complex work and a wide range of skills, the prime contractor hires **subcontractors** to perform specific tasks on the construction project. Although the prime contractor may perform some of the work with its own employees (known as self-performed work), such work is usually limited to a particular trade with which the prime contractor is generally familiar, such as concrete or rough carpentry.

> *Example:* A prime contractor may hire a subcontractor to install the drywall; other subcontractors to install the windows, millwork, and mechanical, electrical, and plumbing systems; still others may complete the rest of the scope of construction.

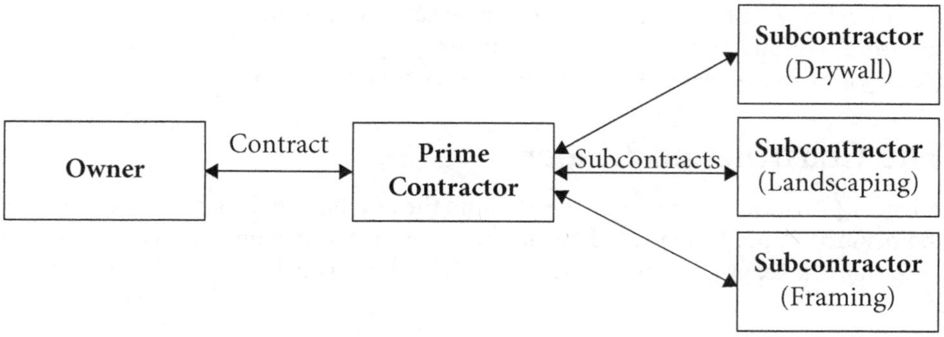

FIGURE 20.1. Typical Owner, Prime Contractor, and Subcontractor Contractual Relationships

Construction Managers

A prime contractor may also act as the owner's construction manager. This arrangement means that subcontractors enter into contracts directly with the owner. The construction manager acts as the owner's agent in managing the project.

In this relationship, the construction manager is not liable to unpaid subcontractors for breaches of contract. The use of a construction manager instead of a traditional prime contractor does not impact the mechanic's lien rights (discussed below).

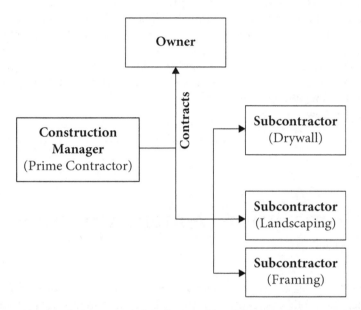

FIGURE 20.2. Typical Contractual Relationships Using a Construction Manager

Licensing of Contractors

Many states require that contractors be licensed by the state to perform certain construction activities. The purpose of these laws is to protect the public from dishonest, fraudulent, and unqualified contactors. In these states, the regulatory boards may discipline contractors and bring court actions to prevent unqualified persons from continuing to act as contractors.

Many states require that the contractor be licensed at all times during the construction project to recover payment for services rendered and materials provided to the work site. Usually, an unlicensed contractor cannot record a mechanic's lien (discussed below). The penalties for a contractor without a license are intended to protect the public from unqualified, unscrupulous handymen who seek to prey upon the unsuspecting.

Example: A handyman who is not licensed in a state requiring a contractor's license renovates a bathroom. State law may prohibit the handyman from recovering compensation for the work performed.

■■■ Ethics: Using an Unlicensed Contractor

As discussed in this chapter, a state may prohibit an unlicensed contractor from collecting compensation for work performed. What if a homeowner is aware that the contractor is not licensed and purposefully hires the contractor to perform work at her house? The contractor has expended money for supplies and goods that were utilized in the project, and the homeowner may be able to obtain the goods and value of the services performed without paying the contractor anything. Is this ethical conduct? Why does the law allow this behavior? Do you believe the law should be changed? If so, how?

The Home Improvement Contract Checklist

As with all other professions, although 99 of every 100 licensed contractors are honest and capable, the public's perception of the industry is damaged by the one dishonest contractor who makes headlines for taking advantage of unsuspecting homeowners. As a consequence of this perception, many states have enacted laws requiring the inclusion of specific language for residential improvement contracts.

Example: New York requires specific disclosures be made to homeowners in a written home improvement contract.

The following factors constitute only general guidance regarding what should be included in a home improvement contract. Local considerations will prevail, because soil (sinkholes, expansive soils, and unstable hillsides), weather (snow, freezing, humidity, floods, and tornadoes), environmental (water, effluents, and storm drains), and zoning requirements vary throughout the United States. This list can only identify generally the concerns that homeowners should address in retaining a contractor for residential work:

■ *Description of the work.* The homeowner should obtain a complete description of the work to be performed, including the materials to be incorporated into the work.

- *Schedule.* Parties should agree upon the dates work is to be scheduled and substantially completed.
- *Payment and payment schedule.* The contract should specify the total amount to be paid and the means by which the homeowner and the contractor can adjust the sum by written change orders. In addition, the contract should specify the payment schedule.
- *Contractor's license.* If required by state law, the contract should indicate the contractor's licensure status.
- *Cancellation rights.* The homeowner's rights to cancel the contract, if any, should be provided. Often homeowners are provided with the right to cancel the contract within three days of its execution.
- *State specific disclosures.* States may require disclosures relating to warranties; the homeowner's right to require the contractor to post a payment and performance bond; the homeowner's right to compel the contractor to obtain building permits for the work, perform in accordance with applicable building codes, and carry workers' compensation insurance; and the homeowner's right to seek arbitration of disputes between the owner and the contractor.

Types of Construction Agreements

Owners and prime contractors often agree on one of several forms of contracts for the construction of commercial buildings. The most common types of construction contracts for commercial buildings are (1) fixed price, (2) cost plus, or (3) guaranteed maximum price.

Fixed Price

In a **fixed price contract** (also known as a lump sum contract), the contractor agrees with the owner to build the structure for a fixed fee, which will include all of the contractor's overhead and profit. If the contractor can build the project less expensively while honoring the contractual requirements, the contractor will increase his or her profit margin. However, the contractor bears the risk that building costs exceed the fixed price stated in the contract.

> **Fixed price contract**
> A contract where the contractor agrees with the owner to build the structure for a fixed fee, and the contractor can increase its profit margin by building the project less expensively.

> *Example:* Owner and contractor enter into a fixed price contract for the total sum of $1 million. If the total cost of construction was $900,000, the $100,000 saved would be allocated to the contractor, increasing the company's profit margin.

Cost Plus

In a **cost plus contract**, the contractor is compensated for all building costs, plus an amount for overhead costs and profit. The total amount paid for overhead and profit is often between 10 and 15 percent but can range below or above those percentages.

> **Cost plus contract**
> A contract where the contractor is paid its costs plus an amount for overhead costs and profit.

Example: Owner and contractor enter into cost plus contract. The parties agree that the contractor shall be paid cost plus 15 percent. If the cost of construction is $1 million, the contractor will be paid the total sum of $1,150,000.

Guaranteed Maximum Price

Guaranteed maximum price contract
A contract where the contractor agrees with the owner to build the structure for a guaranteed price where the contractor bears the risk in the event the project costs more than anticipated to construct.

In a **guaranteed maximum price contract**, the owner reimburses the contractor for costs, overhead, and profit, but the owner stops making those payments once it has paid the guaranteed maximum contract price. The contract is administered just as with a cost plus contract, but it offers the owner a cost ceiling.

A variation on the guaranteed maximum price contract allows a shared savings provision by which the contractor and the owner share any savings in the project's cost. This setup motivates both parties to bring the project in under budget.

Example: Owner and contractor enter into a guaranteed maximum price contract for the total sum of $1 million. The contract provides that the contractor and owner will share in any savings on the project, with 80 percent of the savings going to the owner and 20 percent going to the contractor. If the total cost of construction is $900,000, $100,000 would be divided, with $80,000 allocated to the owner and $20,000 to the contractor.

■ ■ ■ ■ Construction Terms

- **Bid**: A contractor's or subcontractor's offer to render work, labor, or materials to a project owner.
- **Change order**: An amendment to a construction contract. The request for a change order may involve an adjustment to the contract price or a request for a time extension to complete the work.
- **Delay damages**: Delays can cause the owner to suffer losses on the project (such as lost rent or increased loan interest). Contractors may suffer additional supervision costs and overhead expenses or increased material cost pricing. Those responsible for unjustifiable delays may be held liable for damages.

  Not all delays are the caused by the owner or the contractors. Some delays are beyond the control of all parties. Most commonly, such delays arise from acts of God: events caused by nature, such as hurricanes, floods, tornadoes, and earthquakes.
- **Liquidated damages**: Damages assessed for each day during which the project remains unfinished after the agreed upon completion date. The owner seeks to collect liquidated damages from the contracting team to compensate for the finished project's loss of use.
- **No-damage-for-delay clause:** A provision eliminating the contractor's recovery of delay damages in the event of delays in completing the project. This clause limits a contractor's recovery to a time extension (limiting any liquidated damages claim the owner may have against a contractor).

- **Retention**: The amount deducted each month from the contractor's and sub-contractor's billings (usually in the amount of 5 to 10 percent). The owner reserves the amount until the work is completed. The sums are held to ensure that the entire project is completed and that the contracting team remedies minor imperfections in the work.

Green Building Codes ■ ■ ■

Governmental and societal recognition and awareness of environmental issues, together with the development of environmentally friendly building components, have led to an increasing movement toward "green" building construction. The effort focuses on building construction and operational use of energy, water, and waste disposal.

In recent years, states and local governments have been awarding tax credits and preferential building permit processing for green projects. Following these codes is voluntary. Some programs, such as those presented by the U.S. Green Building Council,[2] have evolved to include certification for adhering to specific building standards. Owners can apply for certification (for example, the Empire State Building has been designated as LEED Gold).

Construction Defects

No completed construction project is perfect, and minor defects can be expected after completion. The contracting team will repair or replace these imperfections as needed. It is the magnitude and impact of these deviations that may create liability. While no universal definition exists for a **construction defect**, the concept generally includes an imperfection or shortcoming in a construction component. Construction defects may originate from defects in design, workmanship, and materials or from soil failures (such as failing to properly compact soil, install adequate drains, or achieve the correct finish grade).

Construction defect
An imperfection or shortcoming on a construction project often originating from defects in design, workmanship, and materials or from soil failures.

Filing a Construction Defect Lawsuit

If a property owner believes a construction defect exists, the owner will often hire forensic experts to determine what caused the defective condition (such as defective design, workmanship, or materials, or some external factor, such as expansive soils). If the expert finds that a defect exists, the contractor will be put on notice of the defect and can agree to fix the problem or dispute it. If the contractor disputes the property owner's position, the property owner will invariably file a lawsuit seeking compensation for the repairs necessary to fix the defective condition.

Construction defect lawsuits often bring a wide range of parties into the case. Often, any contractor who performed work on the project is sued as a defendant in the case. The parties to the lawsuit may dispute the existence or extent of and the responsibility for any claimed defects. Moreover, each of the parties may seek to shift the blame for any alleged defect to others and seek the right to investigate the claim and to attempt to cure any identified defects. Because of the number of parties and the difficulty in determining exactly who or what caused the construction defect, litigation becomes complex and taxes the resources of both the courts and the parties to the case.

> *Example:* The Northwood Homeowners' Association has sued a home builder for the numerous cracks and elevation changes in the sidewalks and curbs. The association sued the prime contractor on the project, who in turn filed a cross complaint naming every subcontractor who worked on the project seeking indemnification from them. A contractor who installed decorative exterior iron accents to the homes could be named in the lawsuit. While this contractor may have not been negligent, it (or its insurance carrier) will incur substantial costs and fees before being dismissed from the lawsuit.

Homeowners' association lawsuits over residential construction defects are so prevalent that some insurance companies have ceased insuring condominium construction. The rights of a homeowners' association to file a construction defect lawsuit are often limited to common area property. The issue of whether a homeowners' association would be precluded from asserting claims on behalf of unit owners where the claimed defects are within the common areas was the subject of the following case.

CASE 20.1

ASSOCIATIONS MAY ASSERT COMMON AREA CLAIMS ON BEHALF OF UNIT OWNERS

MARONDA HOMES, INC. OF FLORIDA v.
LAKEVIEW RESERVE HOMEOWNERS ASSN., INC.
127 So. 3d 1258 (2013)
Florida Supreme Court

Lakeview Reserve is a subdivision of homes in Orange County, Florida, that Maronda Homes developed and for which it served as the homeowners' association. As part of the development, Maronda Homes and T.D. Thomson performed all infrastructure and site work, including construction of a storm water drainage system and private roadways. The Declaration of Covenants, Conditions, and Restrictions required that all residents in the subdivision join the homeowners' association ("Lakeview Reserve") and that the association be responsible for the repairs and replacement of common property.

After Lakeview Reserve assumed management control of the subdivision, residents reported water and drainage problems caused by the infrastructure of the subdivision. Residents reported several infrastructure problems, including that the storm water failed to drain properly, which then flooded driveways and completely impeded normal use. Residents also reported the collapse of storm drain run offs. To correct the residential subdivision's infrastructure defects, which directly impacted the homes and access to the homes, Lakeview Reserve filed an action against Maronda Homes, alleging that Maronda Homes defectively designed and constructed the subdivision's infrastructure. The trial court held for Maronda Homes but was then reversed upon an appeal by the homeowners' association. Maronda Homes then appealed to the state supreme court.

Language of the Court. *The law applicable in this case was analyzed and outlined by this Court forty years ago in Gable. The law has clearly recognized that the developer, builder, and seller of new residential real estate is in the best position to have knowledge of, discover, and prevent defects in connection with the design, development, and construction of residential real estate. This is particularly applicable where the residential real estate is within a mass development of many homes.*

The development of large areas of real estate having multiple homes contemplates the design and installation of everything from the complete grading to infrastructure, drainage, and other essential items that enable access to and from each lot and are part of the services necessary for the buildings constructed to be used as residential premises. Building and zoning requirements have been adopted to cover all aspects of the design, development, and construction of structures to be used for residential purposes. The failure to satisfy these requirements would prevent the safe and sanitary use of structures for residential purposes if not corrected, and this burden should not be transferred to innocent purchasers.

A homeowners' association has the legal right to institute an action on behalf of its members for matters that concern the members' common interest.

Decision. The court affirmed the decision of the appellate court. The association could sue the developer for defective construction in the common areas. These claims included those arising from implied warranties of fitness and merchantability because they relate to the residences.

FOCUS ON ETHICS

Why does the law permit a homeowners' association to file a lawsuit in lieu of requiring the individual homeowners to do so?

Owner's Implied Warranty

Sometimes the owner provides an implied warranty of the correctness of plans and specifications to contractors. Even if this warranty is not expressly stated in the contract, it is implied in every construction contract. This warranty is known as the *Spearin* **doctrine**, after the Supreme Court case of that name. When the owner supplies the drawings and specifications on a project, she or he warrants that the design will work for the structure's intended purpose. Where the contractor is required to build the improvement in accordance with owner-supplied plans and specifications, the contractor will not be responsible for defects in those plans and specifications.

Spearin **doctrine**
A warranty provided by the owner promising the correctness of plans and specifications and holding that the contractor will not be responsible for defects in the plans and specifications.

> *Example:* The Supreme Court ruled that a contractor could rely upon the information supplied to it by the owner, which was the federal government, to construct a dry dock in the Navy Yard. The work involved the relocation of a six-foot existing sewer line. The sewer flooded as a result of the presence of a dam that was undisclosed in the contract

documents. The federal government demanded that the contractor reconstruct the damaged sewer line at its own cost. The Supreme Court held that the contractor, in submitting its bid to perform the work, was entitled to rely upon the contract documents, which did not disclose the existence of the conditions causing the damage to the sewer. A contractor may rely upon the drawings and specifications supplied by the owner. A contractor is not liable for defects in construction arising from defects in the owner-supplied documents.[3]

The *Spearin* warranty can be disclaimed in the prime contract (that is, requiring the subcontractor to accept liability for defective plans and specifications). Unless this implied warranty is specifically disclaimed in the contract documents, however, contractors can use it as a defense from owner and lender claims. They can also use it as a basis for a damages claim against the owner if the contractor incurs losses or delays because of deficiencies in the owner-supplied design documents.

No-Damage-for-Delay

No-damages-for-delay
A contract provision preventing a contractor from recovering damages for extra time spent on the project.

Some jurisdictions recognize a limitation to the *Spearin* doctrine known as the **no-damages-for-delay** rule. This rule permits the contractor to recover only an extension of time to complete the project, not damages, in the event the owner has breached its implied warranty to the contractor.

> *Example:* A no-damage-for-delay clause might read as follows: "Contractor shall not receive additional compensation for delays due to any cause, including delays caused by the owner's acts and omissions, and contractor's sole remedy for delay shall be limited to an extension of the contract time."

A substantial number of exceptions to the enforcement of this clause exist and are recognized throughout the United States. No state will enforce the clause based upon delay due to a party's fraud or misrepresentation. A no-damages-for-delay clause was the subject of the following decision of the Supreme Court of Texas involving the construction of a wharf for the city of Houston.

CASE 20.2

A NO-DAMAGE-FOR-DELAY PROVISION IS AGAINST PUBLIC POLICY WHEN IT ALLOWS A PARTY TO INTENTIONALLY DELAY

ZACHRY CONSTRUCTION CORP. v. PORT OF HOUSTON AUTHORITY OF HARRIS COUNTY

449 S.W.3d 98 (2014)

Texas Supreme Court

Zachry Construction Corporation ("Zachry") contracted to build a wharf for the Port of Houston Authority ("the Port") to be used for the loading and unloading of shipping containers. The contract made Zachry an independent contractor in sole charge of choosing the way the work would be con-

ducted. The provision benefitted the Port, insulating it from the liability to which it would be exposed were it exercising control over Zachry's work. Still, the Port was fully engaged in reviewing Zachry's plans and overseeing construction. The contract provided that Zachry's sole remedy for delays encountered would be an extension of time to complete the work. The scope of the project changed over time; however, the Port rejected Zachry's designs for performing this additional work — decision-making Zachry argued the Port had waived in the contract. The Port's actions delayed completion of the project. They resulted in a large damage claim by Zachry for additional costs incurred because of the Port's arbitrary conduct and active interference. At trial, issues of Zachry's waiver of monetary damages and the defense of governmental immunity from those delay damages were considered. Dissatisfied with the amount awarded to it, Zachry appealed on the basis that the jury found that the delay damages resulted from the Port's deliberate, wrongful conduct.

The Texas Court of Appeals found that the no-damage-delay provision barred Zachry's recovery. Zachry appealed to the Supreme Court of Texas.

Language of the Court. *The common law permits a contractor to recover damages for construction delays caused by the owner, but the parties are free to contract differently. A contractor may agree to excuse the owner from liability for delay damages, even when the owner is at fault. The contractor thereby assumes the risk of delay from, say, an owner's change of plans, even if the owner is negligent. But can a no-damages-for-delay provision shield the owner from liability for deliberately and wrongfully*

interfering with the contractor's work? Before this case, a majority of American jurisdictions — including Texas courts of appeals, courts in all but one jurisdiction to consider the issue, and five state legislatures — had answered no. We agree with this overwhelming view.

We have indicated that pre-injury waivers of future liability for gross negligence are void as against public policy. Generally, a contractual provision "exempting a party from tort liability for harm caused intentionally or recklessly is unenforceable on grounds of public policy." We think the same may be said of contract liability. To conclude otherwise would incentivize wrongful conduct and damage contractual relations. The Port argues that withholding enforcement of a no-damages-for-delay provision is in derogation of freedom of contract. But that freedom has limits. Enforcing such a provision to allow one party to intentionally injure another with impunity violates the law for the reasons we have explained.

Decision. The Supreme Court of Texas reversed the court of appeal, holding Zachry was entitled to delay damages.

FOCUS ON ETHICS

Suppose the Port recognized it could not interfere with Zachry's design. Would it have been ethical for it to allow Zachry to proceed with a design the Port thought was defective?

Minimizing Construction Defects

Design details are increasingly being delegated to the construction team. To offset construction defect liability, construction teams have developed strategies to minimize the potential for design and construction defects.

Mock-ups

The use and testing of mock-ups (physical models of the completed work) before constructing the work allow the owner, design team, subcontractors, and suppliers to review the sufficiency of the proposed work. Mock-ups allow potential defects to be identified, including areas where water may intrude into the building, leading to mold infestation and damaged finishes.

Building Information Modeling (BIM)

In addition to mock-ups, building information modeling (BIM) software systems have been developed. Traditionally, building design relied on two-dimensional drawings showing plans, elevations (sides of buildings), and details. Unfortunately, conflicts between building components were often missed (such as ceilings not fitting into the space below steel beams or multiple interfering utility connections put in the same location). Using sophisticated computer programming, the software adds time and cost dimensions for the completed structure to the three traditional spatial relationships of width, height, and depth. In addition, BIM addresses more than geometry and can include lighting, quantities, and the properties of materials to ensure that the completed project meets project requirements.

Sophisticated owners such as the federal government, health care facilities, and commercial developers are routinely employing BIM.

> *Example:* BIM has been used to help develop high-profile projects, including the Mercedes-Benz Stadium in Atlanta, Georgia, and the 12-acre Pandora: The World of Avatar at Disney's Animal Kingdom in Florida.

Liens

Lien
A recorded legal instrument by which property acts as security for the repayment of a debt.

A **lien** is an encumbrance on property used to secure the repayment of a debt. A lien may be recorded or filed on the title to either real or personal property. A lien is a security interest granted to a creditor. It can result in the sale of the property to compensate the creditor or taxing authority (such as the county tax assessor) if the property owner defaults over an obligation.

> *Example:* A mechanic's lien is a lien that encumbers real property.

Specific and General Liens

Liens may be classified by how and to what property they attach. They are classified as either specific or general liens.

Specific Liens

Specific lien
A lien that attaches to a particular parcel of land only.

Specific liens arise out of events or actions related to the ownership, development, or improvement of a property. Specific liens attach to a particular parcel of land only. Mechanic's liens, discussed below, are examples of liens specific to a particular parcel of land.

Example: Brooke hires a contractor to perform work on her property. She does not pay the contractor for work performed, and the contractor records a mechanic's lien on the title to her property. The mechanic's lien is an example of a specific lien.

General Liens

General liens arise out of actions on the part of the property owner unrelated to the property's ownership, and they apply against all real or personal property within a jurisdiction (such as a county). A federal tax lien is an example of a general lien.

The Importance of Specific or General Lien Classification

When a principal residence is designated as a homestead (discussed in chapter 19), the homestead exemption law enacted in many states automatically protects the owner's equity in the residence from general liens, up to a specified limit. These laws protect the homeowner from the forced sale of a home to pay off indebtedness to creditors.

Mechanic's Liens

Certain persons hired to perform work or furnish materials or equipment to improve a third-party owner's real property are entitled to a type of lien known as a mechanic's lien. A **mechanic's lien** is a specific lien that arises from the construction or other improvement of real estate. Every state has its own laws on the requirements, process, and effect of a mechanic's lien.

Mechanic's lien
A specific lien recorded by a contractor, subcontractor, or material supplier for unpaid sums owed under a construction-related contract.

State constitutions, statutes, and case law establish who is entitled to a mechanic's lien. Typically, however, the following are entitled by law to a mechanic's lien: contractors, subcontractors, sub-subcontractors (a subcontractor to a subcontractor), material suppliers (those who supply materials to a project), equipment rental companies, surveyors, and designers (including architects and engineers). These parties, if they do not receive payment for their work on a project, may record a lien (an encumbrance) on the title to the real property upon which the work was performed.

Permanent Improvements

The rights to record a mechanic's lien occur when construction or a permanent improvement occurs. This requires that the items of work or materials remain part of the owner's realty. Nonpermanent improvements include routine gardening services (such as lawn mowing).

> *Example:* Construction of a room addition to a home is a permanent improvement to real property and would justify a mechanic's lien if the contractors were not paid.

Property Subject to a Mechanic's Lien

Only privately owned property is subject to a mechanic's lien. To protect the public's interest, no federal, state, or local government property is subject to mechanic's liens.

> *Example:* National parks, state capitals, and local parks are not subject to mechanic's liens.

In addition, where a contractor performs work for Indian tribes or performs work on Indian reservations, the contracting entity cannot record a mechanic's lien on the property. This is because U.S. law grants sovereign immunity to these entities.

Who Is Affected by Mechanic's Liens?

The property owner (or an agent for the owner) has the power to enter into contracts for the improvement of the owner's land. Only where the property owner (or agent of the owner) has consented to improvement work on the property will the owner's interest be affected by a mechanic's lien. This interest may be affected when any of the persons entitled to a mechanic's lien are unpaid. The lien attaches to whatever ownership interest the owner holds.

> *Example:* An owner who holds a 30 percent tenancy in common interest hires a contractor to perform work on a property. Assuming the other 70 percent of the tenants in common do not consent to the work of improvement, a mechanic's lien will attach to only the 30 percent ownership interest the tenant in common owns.

> *Example:* An owner who holds a joint tenancy interest hires a contractor to perform work on a property. Assuming the other joint tenant did not consent to the improvement, a mechanic's lien will attach only to the interest of the joint tenant who contracted for the work of improvement.

Tenant's Leasehold Improvement

Often, an owner's interest will not be affected when a tenant improves the leasehold interest and the tenant fails to pay a contractor or a person entitled to record a mechanic's lien. Some states allow the owner's interest to be subject to a mechanic's lien for work a tenant orders. These states typically permit the owner to protect his interest from a mechanic's lien by posting a notice of non-responsibility (Exhibit 20.1). Many states require that the notice be posted in a conspicuous location on the land within a given period ranging from three to ten days after the owner learns about the work of improvement being done by a tenant.

> *Example:* A tenant hires a contractor to renovate the tenant's leasehold space. If the owner posts a notice of non-responsibility, the mechanic's lien attaches only to the leasehold interest and not to the owner's interest in the property.

NOTICE OF NON-RESPONSIBILITY

Notice is hereby given that:

    1. _____ (owner) is the owner who has an interest in the property hereinafter described.

    2. Owner's address: _____

    3. Property street address: _____

    4. Legal Description in provided in Exhibit "A." A.P.N.: _____

    5. Name of tenant: _____

    6. On _____ (date), the undersigned first obtained actual knowledge of the work of improvement on the above described property, said date being 10 days or less than the date of this Notice.

    7. The undersigned, as owner or agent for the owner, advises it will not be responsible for any such work of improvements or claims hereto, nor for any labor, services, equipment, or material furnished or to be furnished to said property.

VERIFICATION

The undersigned being duly sworn, says that he/she/it is the owner or authorized agent of the owner of the property; that the foregoing Notice has been read and the contents known; that the facts stated are true; and that this Notice is executed in an authorized capacity.

Date: _____   By: _____

                                 Its: _____

Exhibit 20.1. Notice of Non-Responsibility

Mechanic's Lien Requirements

State laws vary greatly as to what is required to allow a claimant to record a lien on the title to the project property. Generally, a successful mechanic's lien claimant will:

- Have a contract directly with the owner or someone authorized or permitted by the owner to enter into the construction contract
- Successfully perform the work
- Fulfill the procedural requirements of notice and lien recording
- Timely file a lawsuit to foreclose the lien

Notice to Owner

Many states require that mechanic's lien claimants serve a written **notice to owner** (known in some states as a preliminary notice) within a certain time after the claimant's work has begun on the project. Providing a notice to owner alerts the owner that persons performing work on the project expect to be paid.

Notice to owner
A notice given to property owners alerting them that persons performing work on a project expect to be paid.

Often, the notice to owner is served upon the owner, the prime contractor, and occasionally the construction lender. The information required in the notice to owner is determined by each state, but frequently required are the name of the claimant; the work or materials supplied to the project; and the value of the labor, services, equipment, or material the claimant has bestowed or will bestow on the project.

Failure to give notice to owner within the required time may either defeat the notice to owner or limit the amount of the lien to the value given by the claimant after the date of the notice to owner. In most states, not sending a notice to owner, or the presence of a defective notice to owner, voids a recorded mechanic's lien. An example of a preliminary notice is provided in Exhibit 20.2.

PRELIMINARY NOTICE OF INTENTION TO FILE A CLAIM
(49 Pa. Cons. Stat. § 1501(a))

TO: OWNER: _____
  (Name/Address)

  _____

FROM: SUBCONTRACTOR: _____
  (Name/Address)

  _____

PLEASE TAKE NOTICE that Subcontractor has or will provide certain alterations or repairs to your real property for which amounts are due or to become due to Subcontractor. In the event Subcontractor is not paid for said alterations or repairs, this Notice serves as a statement of intention to file a claim therefor:

  1. The name of the contractor is: _____.

  2. A general description of the property against which the claim is to be filed:
  _____

  3. The amount due or to become due to Subcontractor is: $_____.

Dated: _____   _____
                                                (Subcontractor)

                                      By: _____
                                                (Signature)

                                      _____
                                                (Print or Type Name/Title)

Exhibit 20.2. Example of Preliminary Notice

Example: A subcontractor who worked on a project for a prime contractor and failed to timely serve a preliminary notice would be barred from seeking a mechanic's lien if the state required preliminary notice to be given. The subcontractor could still recover payment under a breach of contract remedy but not under a mechanic's lien remedy.

Some categories of mechanic's lien claimants are excused by statute or case law from the preliminary-notice requirement. Laborers working for a daily wage, for example, are excluded in recognition of their weaker bargaining position and sophistication relative to the property owner. In addition, many states provide that the prime contractor need not serve a notice to owner because owners enter into contracts with prime contractors and thus are aware of their identity already.

Recording the Mechanic's Lien

Mechanic's liens must be recorded in the appropriate local recording office within a permitted period of time following the completion of the project. This requirement compels buyers, lenders, and their title companies to make certain that unrecorded liens do not interfere with their title.

What constitutes completion of the project varies among the states. It can mean the cessation of all construction activity, the occupation of the property by the owner, or the certification of completion by the project architect. In some jurisdictions, the owner may record a **notice of completion** to shorten the time within which the lien claimant must record a lien. An example of a mechanic's lien is provided in Exhibit 20.3.

Notice of completion
A notice that construction activities have completed. This starts the time to record mechanic's liens.

NOTICE UNDER MECHANIC'S LIEN LAW
(NEW YORK)

To the Clerk of the County of [Enter County] and all others whom it may concern:

Please Take Notice, that [Enter Lienor] as lienor(s) have (has) and claim(s) a lien on the real property hereinafter described as follows:

1. The names and residences of the lienor(s) is (are): [Enter Names and Addresses], being (a) [Enter Foreign/Domestic Corporation, Partnership, etc.] whose business address(es) is (are) at: [Enter Address] whose principal place (s) of business is (are) at: [Enter Address]
   The name, address, and telephone number of lienor's attorney, if any: [Enter Name, Address of Attorney and Telephone Number]
2. The owner of the real property is: [Enter Owner] and the interest of the owner as far as known to the lienor(s) is (are): [Fee Simple, etc.]
3. The name of the person by whom the lienor(s) was (were) employed is: [Enter Name] The name of the person to whom the lienor(s) furnished or is (are) to furnish materials or for whom the lienor(s) performed or is (are) to perform professional services is (are): [Enter Name]. The name of the person with whom the contract was made is [Enter Name]
4. The labor performed consisted of the following: [Describe Labor Performed]
   The material furnished consisted of the following: [Describe Material Furnished]
   The materials actually manufactured for but not delivered to the real property are: [Describe Material – if None Enter "None"]
   The agreed price and value of the labor performed and the materials furnished is: $_____
   The agreed price and value of the materials actually manufactured for but not delivered to the real property is: $[Enter Amount – if None Enter 0]
   Total agreed price and value: $[Enter Amount]
5. The amount unpaid to the lienor(s) for said labor performed and materials furnished is: $[Enter Amount]. The amount unpaid to lienor(s) for materials actually manufactured for but not delivered to the real property is: $[Enter Amount – if None Enter 0]   Total amount unpaid: $[Enter Amount]
   The total amount claimed for which this lien is filed is: $[Enter Amount]
6. The time when the first item of work was performed was [Enter Date]. The time when the first item of material was furnished was: [Enter Date].
   The time when the last item of work was performed was: [Enter Date].
   The time when the last item of material was furnished was: [Enter Date].
7. The property subject to the lien is situated in the County of [Enter County], State of [Enter State], City of [Enter City] and known as [Enter Address of Property], Block [Enter Block Number], Lot [Enter Lot Number] (See Exhibit 1 annexed for full legal description of property.)

That said labor and materials were performed and furnished for and used in the improvement of the real property herein before described. That 8 months (4 months if a single family dwelling) have not elapsed dating from the last item of work performed, or from the last items of materials furnished or since the completion of the contract, or since the final performance of the work, or since the final furnishing of the materials for which this lien is claimed.

Date: _____
   [Enter Date]

_____
[Enter Corporate/Business Name]

By: _____
[Enter Name and Title]

ACKNOWLEDGEMENT ON NEXT PAGE

Exhibit 20.3. Example of a Mechanic's Lien

Once a lien attaches to the property, it attaches to the entire real property and not just to that portion upon which the claimant provided work, labor, or materials. The mechanic's lien applies to both the land and the improvement.

Example: If a landscaper successfully records a mechanic's lien, the lien attaches to the entire parcel and not simply to the landscaped areas.

Priority of Mechanic's Liens

The recording statutes of each state determine the priority of a mechanic's lien. In most states, mechanic's liens attach to the property as of the date the work first began on the project and not the date on which the mechanic's lien was recorded. If any work started prior to the recording of any other liens (such as a construction loan), all mechanic's liens may take priority over (will be superior to) the liens recorded on the property after the project work commenced. This is referred to as the doctrine of relation back. Under this doctrine, all mechanic's liens will relate back to the period when work started, even though the work or material provided by each individual mechanic's lien claimant was rendered subsequent to other mechanic's lien claimants and were recorded subsequent to other liens (such as a mortgage or trust deed securing the construction loan or other liens). One exception to this rule is that real property tax liens take priority over all other liens on title, regardless of when the liens were recorded.

In the following case, the court considered if a purchase money deed of trust was in superior position to a mechanic's lien on the title to the property.

CASE 20.3

MECHANICS LIENS HAVE PRIORITY OVER A DEEDS OF TRUST RECORDED AFTER CONSTRUCTION ACTIVITY STARTS

BOB DeGEORGE ASSOCIATES v. HAWTHORN BANK
377 S.W. 3d 592 (2012)
Missouri Supreme Court

Blue Springs Xtreme Powersports ("Xtreme") purchased property and obtained a loan from Hawthorn Bank for $2,512,000. The loan was secured by a purchase money deed of trust. Neither the warranty deed to Xtreme nor Hawthorn's purchase money deed of trust were recorded. Before purchasing the property, Xtreme entered into a contract with Bob DeGeorge Associates ("DeGeorge"), a prime contractor, to remodel the building on the property. DeGeorge and a subcontractor began to work on the property two days after Xtreme purchased the property. DeGeorge and the subcontractor completed their work on the project pursuant to the contract; however, Xtreme never paid DeGeorge $147,833.70. Due to the lack of payment, DeGeorge was unable to pay the subcontractor.

DeGeorge recorded a mechanic's lien against the property for the amount due. The next day, the warranty deed to Xtreme and Hawthorn's purchase money deed of trust were recorded. The subcontractor also recorded a mechanic's lien. DeGeorge and the subcontractor filed lawsuits against Xtreme to foreclose on their mechanic's liens. They also sued Hawthorn Bank to establish the priority of their mechanic's lien over Hawthorn's purchase money deed of trust on the property. The trial court held the mechanic's liens to be superior in priority to the purchase money deed of trust. Hawthorn appealed and the case was transferred to the Supreme Court of Missouri.

Language of the Court. *As a written instrument affecting real estate, a purchase money deed of trust falls* *under the requirements of Missouri's recording statutes. In contrast, mechanic's liens are not governed by Missouri's recording statutes because they arise by operation of statute. Mechanic's liens arise for the purpose of giving "security to mechanics and material for labor and materials furnished in improving the owner's property."*

Unlike recording an instrument under the recording statutes, filing a mechanic's lien is irrelevant for the purpose of determining first-in-time priority between competing encumbrances on real property. Two statutory provisions govern the priority of a mechanic's lien against other encumbrances on real property. For encumbrances on the land, the "first spade rule" gives the mechanic's lien relation back priority to the date when work commenced. So long as a mechanic's lien arises on the land and is filed properly, it will have priority over any third-party encumbrance attaching after the date work began.

In applying the recording statutes and the first spade rule to this case, DeGeorge's and the subcontractor's mechanic's liens are superior to Hawthorn Bank's purchase-money deed of trust. Although Hawthorn Bank obtained its purchase-money deed of trust before construction, it failed to record its deed of trust until after the commencement of construction activities.

Decision. The Missouri Supreme Court affirmed the trial court's decision, finding the contractors' mechanics liens were superior in position to that of Hawthorn's purchase-money deed of trust.

FOCUS ON ETHICS

Why should contractors have priority over a mortgage lender who fails to timely record a deed of trust or mortgage?

Timely Foreclosing on the Mechanic's Lien

After the recording of the lien, the mechanic's lien claimant must enforce the claimant's mechanic's lien rights. Usually this requirement is met by the claimant filing a lawsuit seeking to foreclose on the mechanic's lien. States vary as to the time within which the mechanic's lien lawsuit must be filed after a mechanic's lien is recorded. The lawsuit seeks a judgment for the balance of the debt owed to the claimant and a judicial order for the sale of the property.

Foreclosure Sale Proceeds

In most states, when equity in the property upon foreclosure is insufficient to pay all of the mechanic's lien claimants in full, the mechanic's lien claimants share pro rata in the proceeds resulting from the foreclosure sale of the property. Under the pro rata distribution, payments are made in proportion to the claimant's claim to the amount to be distributed.

> *Example:* If a property is sold for $1 million because of a mechanic's lien foreclosure and the mechanic's lien claimants present claims of $2 million, $450,000, and $50,000, the claimants' total claims equal $2.5 million.
>
> The proportionate share of each mechanic's lien claim is:
>
> $2,000,000 /$2,500,000 = 80%
> $450,000 /$2,500,000 = 18%
> $50,000 /$2,500,000 = 2%
>
> Each mechanic's lien claimant receives:
>
> $2,000,000:   80% x $1,000,000 = $800,000
> $450,000:   18% x $1,000,000 = $180,000
> $50,000:   2% x $1,000,000 = $20,000

In this case, each mechanic's lien claimant receives 40 percent of his claim.

■ ■ ■ *Lis Pendens*

Lis pendens means "pending action." A *lis pendens* is recorded in the same location as the mechanic's liens are recorded. When it is recorded on the title to property, a *lis pendens* provides constructive notice to prospective buyers and lenders that another person has a claim that could result in a court order requiring the sale of the property to satisfy that person's claim.

The recording of a *lis pendens* is not a condition for filing a lawsuit, but it will make the title to the property unmarketable (that is, it creates an encumbrance, or **cloud on title**) until the litigation is dismissed or the notice of *lis pendens* is withdrawn.

Release of Mechanic's Liens

A mechanic's lien is effective until it is satisfied, released, or terminated. A mechanic's lien may be discharged by the claimant's failure to commence a lien foreclosure lawsuit within the statutory period to foreclose. The lien may also be discharged by the claimant's written release (see Exhibit 20.4). A claimant may give the release when the owner or contractor has paid the claimant for his or her work. In some jurisdictions, a bond (often called a mechanic's lien release bond) may be issued to release the mechanic's lien from the title.

Release of Lien Form

DISCHARGE OR RELEASE OF NOTICE OF LIEN

NOTICE IS HEREBY GIVEN THAT:

The undersigned did, on the _____ day of the month of _____ of the year _____, record in Book _____, as Document No. _____, in the office of the county recorder of _____ County, [State], its Notice of Lien, or has otherwise given notice of his intention to hold a lien upon the following described property or improvements, owned by _____ located in the County of _____, State of [State], to wit:

(Legal Description or Address of the Property or Improvements)
NOW, THEREFORE, for valuable consideration the undersigned does release, satisfy and discharge his notice of lien on the property or improvements described above by reason of this Notice of Lien.

_____
(Signature of Lien Claimant)

Exhibit 20.4. Release of Mechanic's Lien

Concept Summary

Mechanic's Lien Enforcement

While state laws differ, commonly they require the following:

1. Prior to or subsequent to starting work, a notice to owner is given to the owner, contractor, and lender.
2. A mechanic's lien is recorded on the title to the project property. This lien must be recorded within a certain period following the completion

of the project. In some jurisdictions, the owner may shorten the recording time if the owner records a notice of completion.

3. Once a valid mechanic's lien is recorded, the lien claimant must file a lien foreclosure lawsuit within a statutory period of time.
4. A *lis pendens* is recorded on the title to give notice of the claimant's interest to third parties.

Public Policy Behind Mechanic's Liens

Strong public policy grounds exist for granting claimants a mechanic's lien against the owner's real property. The owner has benefited from the labor and materials supplied by the claimant, which have enhanced the property's value. The real property acts as security for payment. When a seller of personal property sells goods to a buyer, the seller may have a valid security agreement and can repossess the goods. This remedy is not available to material suppliers, whose materials have been incorporated into the work of improvement. Likewise, a worker cannot recover the time and effort expended on a project. Yet, the owner would benefit from the incorporation of these items into the project.

Suits by contractors or subcontractors over unpaid labor and materials are time consuming and expensive; the mechanic's lien affords them an opportunity for expedited payment of money due. When property is transferred, title to the property is affected by existing liens. To give clear title to buyers, liens must either be satisfied by payment or the liability assumed by the grantee.

Stop Notices

A stop notice (see Exhibit 20.5) is a statutory remedy allowing an unpaid subcontractor or material supplier to reach the unexpended construction funds held by the owner. Stop notices may be used on public works projects; in a few states, they may also be used on private projects.

Since mechanic's liens cannot attach to public property, one of the remedies available to an unpaid contractor is to serve a stop notice on the owner. Upon receipt, the public works owner must segregate funds from the amounts to be paid the prime contractor. The stop notice claimant may then proceed against the funds withheld by filing a timely lawsuit for enforcement of the stop notice.

Stop notice
A statutory remedy allowing an unpaid subcontractor or material supplier to reach the unexpended construction funds held by the owner.

STOP NOTICE
(Miss. Code Ann. §85-7-181)

TO:
OWNER: _____
        (Name/Address)

FROM:
CLAIMANT: _____
        (Name/Address)

    PLEASE TAKE NOTICE that Claimant hereby asserts a claim on unpaid funds from owner to the contractor:

    1. Claimant has provided the following labor or materials: _____, for which he has not been paid, and for which he is owed $_____.

    2. Accordingly, pursuant to Miss. Code Ann. §85-7-181, you shall, upon receipt of this Notice, withhold from the contractor sufficient monies due to the contractor to answer this claim.

Dated: _____

_____
(Claimant)

By: _____
    (Signature)

_____
(Print or Type Name/Title)

Exhibit 20.5. Stop Notice (Mississippi)

Payment and Performance Bonds

Unlike insurance, with a payment or performance bond, a surety provides a source of payment should one of the construction contractors, owners, or lenders fail to pay what is due. The types of bonds relevant to construction include payment and performance bonds.

Payment Bonds

Payment bond
A bond guaranteeing that all claims for labor, material, equipment, and services provided to the project will be paid.

Payment bonds guarantee that all claims for labor, material, equipment, and services provided to the project will be paid (see Exhibit 20.6). When the owner purchases a payment bond, a prime contractor or a subcontractor can recover on the payment bond.

When the federal government is the owner of the property, the payment bond is known as a Miller Act bond and has requirements that must be followed.

Usually, all public works projects — construction projects with a public owner — require a payment bond that provides a source of payment to the contractors and material suppliers in the event of nonpayment. Payment bonds are available on private works projects — construction projects with a private owner — but owners may be reluctant to require payment bonds because they can add considerable cost to the project.

NOTICE OF CLAIM ON PAYMENT BOND

(N.C. Gen. Stat. §44A-27)

North Carolina _____ County

TO: CONTRACTOR _____
                (Name/Address)

FROM: CLAIMANT: _____
             (Name/Address)

PLEASE TAKE NOTICE that Claimant is looking to you and your surety for payment:

1. Claimant has provided the following labor or materials: _____ in connection with the public work of improvement located at: _____ for which Claimant has not been paid in full.

2. Claimant is owed: $ _____.

3. The name of the person for whom the work was performed or to whom the material was furnished is: _____.

Dated: _____   _____
                                          (Claimant)

                                  By: _____
                                        (Signature)

                                  _____
                                    (Print or Type Name/Title)

Exhibit 20.6. Payment Bond (North Carolina)

Performance Bond

A **performance bond** protects the owner. With a performance bond, a surety guarantees payment for the completing the project should the prime contractor fail to do so. Performance bonds are available for either public or private works projects.

Key Terms and Concepts

- Prime contractor, page 510
- Bid, page 510
- Prime contract, page 510
- Subcontractor, page 512
- Fixed price contract, page 515
- Cost plus contract, page 515
- Guaranteed maximum price contract, page 516
- Bid, page 516
- Change order, page 516
- Delay damages, page 516
- Liquidated damages, page 516
- No-damage-for-delay clause, page 516
- Retention, page 517

- Construction defect, page 517
- *Spearin* doctrine, page 519
- Lien, page 522
- Specific lien, page 522
- Mechanic's lien, page 523
- Notice to owner, page 525
- Notice of completion, page 527
- *Lis pendens*, page 530
- Cloud on title, page 530
- Stop notice, page 531
- Payment bond, page 532
- Performance bond, page 534

Chapter Summary

- A construction project is created through a complicated series of relationships. It requires coordination among the parties in a construction contract: owner, design professionals, construction lender, and contracting team.

- Most states regulate and license contractors. This regulatory scheme is intended to protect consumers.

- Construction contracts can take many forms, the most common of which are the fixed price, cost plus, and maximum guaranteed price forms.

- Construction defects are imperfections or shortcomings in a component of construction.

Contractors have developed strategies for minimizing construction defects by creating mock-ups and utilizing building information modeling (BIM).

- In providing plans and specifications to the contractor, the owner impliedly warrants (*Spearin* doctrine) that the finished structure can be built according to those plans and specifications. If the contractor follows them and the structure is defective, the contractor may defend against a claim that it defectively constructed the structure.

- A lien is an encumbrance on a debtor's property that secures the repayment of debt.

- A mechanic's lien is a specific lien arising from the construction or other improvement of real estate. The right to record mechanic's liens relate to construction or permanent improvements. Only privately owned property is subject to a mechanic's lien.

- Only where the property owner (or agent of the owner) has consented to improvement work on the property will the owner's interest be affected by a mechanic's lien.

- Some states allow the owner's interest to be subject to a mechanic's lien for work ordered by a tenant. These states typically permit the owner to protect his interest against a mechanic's liens by posting a notice of non-responsibility.

- Prior to recording a mechanic's lien, state laws often require that the lien claimant give the owner, lender, and/or prime contractor a written notice to owner.

- After the lien claimant records a lien, the claimant must enforce the mechanic's lien. This element is usually met by the timely filing of a lawsuit to foreclose the lien.

- While state laws vary, the recording priority of a mechanic's lien relates back to when work commenced on the project, not to the actual date on which the mechanic's lien was recorded.

- Recording a *lis pendens* gives constructive notice of the lien claimant's interest in the property. The *lis pendens* acts as a cloud on title and will make title unmarketable.

- A stop notice is a statutory remedy allowing an unpaid subcontractor or material supplier to reach the unexpended construction funds held by the owner. Stop notices may be used on public works projects; in a few states, they may also be used on private projects.

- Payment bonds guarantee that all claims for labor, material, equipment, and services provided to the project will be paid.

- A performance bond protects the owner and guarantees that the contractor and its subcontractors will complete construction of the project.

Chapter Problems and Assignments

1. How does a subcontractor differ from a prime contractor?

2. Distinguish between a fixed price contract and a guaranteed maximum price contract.

3. What is a mechanic's lien, and what are the typical requirements for a mechanic's lien enforcement action?

4. Alicia hires Sam, a local handyman, to install a whole house fan that Alicia has purchased for her home. The installation requires Sam to cut holes in the ceiling of several rooms, connect electrical wiring to those locations, and patch and paint the ceiling drywall. While Sam is not a licensed electrician, he has the skill set necessary to install the whole house fan and connect the electrical wires. Sam completes the work, patches the holes in the ceiling, and paints the repaired parts of the ceiling. Alicia refuses to pay Sam for the installation because he was not properly licensed as a contractor to perform all these items of work. Can Sam sue Alicia for the cost of installing the whole house fan if he acted as an unlicensed contractor?

5. Cool Conditioning, an air-conditioning contractor, installed an air-conditioning system in an apartment building in Las Vegas, Nevada. Cool Conditioning reasonably relied upon the detailed plans and specifications provided by the owner. Cool Conditioning was not involved in the design of the air-conditioning system. When the apartment complex was completed, the system failed to cool the units by the

required 30 degrees stated in the contract because of defective plans and specifications supplied by the owner. What provision will the subcontractor rely upon to avoid liability?

6. Bad Sports Sporting Goods entered into a lease with Acme, Inc., for a leasehold tenancy at a mall. The tenant improvements were not made under the authority or direction of Acme, Inc. Irvine Acme, Inc. posted a notice of non-responsibility on the premises. Bad Sports Sporting Goods retained a general contractor. After the tenant improvements were completed, the general contractor refused to pay one of its subcontractors. The subcontractor recorded a mechanic's lien on the property. To what interest does the mechanic's lien attach on the property?

7. Courtney wants to build a commercial property and lease it to tenants. She is concerned about the cost of construction. She desires to contract in such a way that her liability for the total amount of the construction will be capped. In addition, she wishes to incentivize the contractor by allowing it to keep any cost savings if the contractor completes the project for less than the stipulated contract price. What type of construction agreement does Courtney intend to create?

8. Logan retains Shady Construction Enterprises to build his home on his real property. He has chosen Shady Construction Enterprises because it was the lowest bidder on the project. In fact, Shady was 30 percent lower than the next lowest bidder. Logan has misgivings that Shady Construction Enterprises may fail to complete the project. What type of bond can Logan obtain to protect himself in this situation?

9. Research your state's laws regarding the licensing of contractors. Does your state require that contractors be licensed to perform construction activities? What are the penalties in your state if a contractor is not licensed but performs unlicensed construction work?

10. Research your state's mechanic's lien law, and draft a memorandum that discusses the following: (1) who is entitled to claim a mechanic's lien, (2) what notice is required to be given to anyone before recording a mechanic's lien, (3) when a mechanic's lien can be recorded, (4) what property is subject to a mechanic's lien, (5) whether the owner is liable when a tenant contracts for improvements on a leased property, and (6) when a mechanic's lien foreclosure lawsuit must be filed.

End Notes

1. Code of Hammurabi, approx. 1750 B.C.
2. U.S. Green Building Council, http://www.usgbc.org/ (last accessed November 3, 2017).
3. *United States v. Spearin*, 248 U.S. 132 (1918).

Chapter 21
Bankruptcy and Restructuring Transactions

Debt, grinding debt, whose iron face the widow, the orphan, and the sons of genius fear and hate; —debt, which consumes so much time, which so cripples and disheartens a great spirit with cares that seem so base, is a preceptor whose lessons cannot be foregone, and is needed most by those who suffer from it most.
—Ralph Waldo Emerson, Nature, American Essayist, Poet, 1803–1882

Learning Objectives

1. Explain the differences between a Chapter 7, Chapter 11, and Chapter 13 bankruptcy.
2. Identify the parties to a bankruptcy proceeding.
3. Discuss the order of events in a bankruptcy case.
4. Describe the importance of a proof of claim.
5. Understand what occurs in a single asset real estate bankruptcy.
6. Explain the rights of landlords and tenants in the bankruptcy context.

Chapter Outline

- Introduction
- Overview of Bankruptcy Law
- Types of Bankruptcy Cases
- Parties to a Bankruptcy Case
- Bankruptcy Procedures
- Case 21.1: *In re Schleier*
- Case 21.2: *In re Franklin*
- Real Property Bankruptcy Issues
- Case 21.3: *In re Alexandra Trust*
- Avoiding Transfers
- Residential and Commercial Leases

Opening scenario

A development company secured a construction loan to develop a small retail center. Failing to attract prospective commercial tenants, the developer was unable to find replacement permanent financing for the project. When reading this chapter, consider what the developer could expect if it filed for bankruptcy protection.

Introduction

The relationship between bankruptcy and real estate is expansive. In this chapter, our study will survey the most common topics of interest to the real estate professional. We discuss the complexities of real property subject to a bankruptcy proceeding, beginning with an overview of bankruptcy law, including the types of proceedings and the effects of the automatic stay. We then cover the most common issues that arise for a secured real property lender, a commercial landlord confronted with a bankrupt tenant, claims in bankruptcy, and the effect of a bankruptcy discharge.

Overview of Bankruptcy Law

Each of the federal district courts across the United States includes a bankruptcy court. The presiding decision maker in each bankruptcy case is the U.S. bankruptcy judge. The bankruptcy judge may decide any matter connected with a bankruptcy case, including whether real estate assets should be sold to pay creditors or may be retained by the debtor. A **creditor** is a person who is owed money. The **debtor** is the person who owes the money to the creditor. Unlike federal court judges, who have lifetime appointments, bankruptcy judges serve terms of 14 years. These judges are appointed by the U.S. Court of Appeals for the circuit in which the federal district court is located.

Creditor
The lender in a credit transaction.

Debtor
The borrower in a credit transaction.

Purpose of Bankruptcy

The bankruptcy court provides a forum in which the debtor's assets are equitably distributed to creditors. Additionally, the debtor is given a fresh start by reducing or eliminating the pre-bankruptcy debt.

Matters Relevant to Bankruptcy

Core proceedings
A legal proceeding over which the bankruptcy court has jurisdiction; it is essential to the disposition of the bankruptcy estate.

Bankruptcy courts focus on a debtor's financial affairs. **Core proceedings** involve issues directly affecting the debtor's reorganization or discharge. These proceedings will consider creditors' claims and the relative priority of those claims between and among one another; proceedings conclude with a plan of reorganization and a grant of discharge. Given the potentially broad definition of what could constitute a core proceeding, courts have adopted the general principal that a core proceeding must invoke a sub-stantive right created by bankruptcy law or a right that would not exist outside of bankruptcy. In core proceedings, bankruptcy judges may "hear and determine" the matter and enter a final judgment.

Sometimes issues in a bankruptcy case are related to the bankruptcy but are not technically bankruptcy matters. These issues are addressed in **noncore proceedings** and are resolved in either state or federal court proceedings addressing issues affecting the creditor or debtor but not related to the bankruptcy.

Noncore proceedings
A legal proceeding that is not essential to the disposition of the bankruptcy estate.

> *Example:* A real estate developer may seek to stay the foreclosure of its development by its lender. The rehabilitation of that developer in bankruptcy will be directly related to whether that foreclosure should occur. This is a core proceeding.

> *Example:* The same developer may have been sued for a personal injury that occurred at the development's model homes. The personal injury lawsuit, pending in state court, is not essential to determining the developer's ability to obtain a discharge in bankruptcy. This is a noncore proceeding.

Types of Bankruptcy Cases

Six types of bankruptcy cases are provided for under the Bankruptcy Code. In our study, we will focus on the three types that primarily relate to real estate interests: Chapter 7, Chapter 11, and Chapter 13. The cases are traditionally named according to the relevant chapter.

Chapter 7

A **Chapter 7** bankruptcy petition, also known as liquidation, provides the debtor with a fresh start in exchange for distributing all the debtor's nonexempt assets to the bank-ruptcy trustee for liquidation. The bankruptcy code allows debtors to keep certain exempt property. The Chapter 7 trustee converts the nonexempt assets into cash, which is then distributed to the creditors. The debtor is discharged from most of the remaining debts. Proceedings under Chapter 7 apply to all debtors, including individ-uals, partnerships, and corporations. Because little or no nonexempt property is usually available in most Chapter 7 cases, an actual liquidation of the debtor's assets may not occur. These types of cases are called no-asset cases. In most Chapter 7 cases, if the individual receives a discharge, she is released from personal liability for certain dis-chargeable assets.

If one spouse files a bankruptcy petition, all community property or marital prop-erty of both spouses is included in the estate of the filing spouse.[1]

Chapter 7
A bankruptcy petition providing the debtor with a fresh start. The debtor's nonexempt assets are sold, and the proceeds are distributed to creditors.

Chapter 11

A **Chapter 11** bankruptcy petition is known as a reorganization or restructuring. A Chapter 11 petition allows a distressed business, such as a partnership or corporation,

Chapter 11
A bankruptcy petition allowing a debtor to restructure the debtor's finances under supervision of the bankruptcy court.

involved in operating real estate to restructure its finances. The restructuring allows the business to continue and the creditors to be paid, though usually not in full.

Reorganization is primarily a negotiation process that allows the debtor and its creditors to develop a plan for the adjustment and discharge of the debts owed by the debtor. In reorganization, the debtor receives a fresh start in exchange for the debtor's paying creditors over time, in an amount greater than the creditors would have received in a Chapter 7 liquidation.

Unlike Chapter 7 petitions, insolvency is *not* a condition for filing a voluntary petition for Chapter 11. Under a Chapter 11 proceeding, the debtor has the exclusive right to file a plan of reorganization during the first 120 days after the order of relief, unless a trustee has been appointed, in which case the debtor may file a plan at any time.

Chapter 13

Chapter 13
A bankruptcy petition permitting the bankruptcy court to supervise the debtor's plan for repayment of unpaid debts over a period.

A **Chapter 13** bankruptcy petition provides for an adjustment of an individual's debts. Businesses cannot file a Chapter 13 petition. It is designed for an individual who has a regular source of income. Chapter 13 is often preferable to a Chapter 7 proceeding for an individual because it enables the debtor to keep valuable assets such as his home; it also allows the debtor to propose a plan for repaying the debt over a period of three to five years.

Parties to a Bankruptcy Case

The parties in the bankruptcy proceeding may include the debtor, a bankruptcy trustee (in Chapter 7 and Chapter 13 cases), a creditor's committee (in most Chapter 11 cases), a U.S. attorney (for the prosecution of bankruptcy crimes), creditors and equity holders, officers and directors of bankrupt corporations and general partners of bankrupt partnerships, and members of the limited liability companies that have filed for bankruptcy protection.

Bankruptcy Trustee

Bankruptcy trustee
A legal representative of the bankruptcy estate before the bankruptcy court.

A **bankruptcy trustee**, who is often an attorney, certified public accountant, or business manager, becomes the legal representative of the bankruptcy estate. The bankruptcy trustee is *not* the same person as the U.S. trustee. Broad powers are granted to the bankruptcy trustee, such as the following: collecting the debtor's property, performing investigations relating to the debtor's affairs, setting aside fraudulent conveyances and other preferential transfers, operating the debtor's business, hiring professionals such as accountants, filing reports, and closing the estate.

The trustee performs these services and is compensated for the fair value of the services rendered. The trustee must be qualified and receive court approval of her appointment.

U.S. Trustee

The **U.S. trustee** is a government employee appointed by the Justice Department to perform administrative tasks for the benefit of the bankruptcy courts. The U.S. trustee supervises the bankruptcy case and monitors the creditor's committees, disclosure statements, and other required bankruptcy duties. A trustee is required in Chapter 7 and Chapter 13 cases but not in a Chapter 11 case. However, the court may, for cause, order the appointment of a trustee, who may then be elected by the creditors.

U.S. trustee
A federal government official who handles and supervises administrative tasks within a bankruptcy case.

Debtor in Possession

Normally, there is no trustee in a Chapter 11 case; instead, the debtor continues in possession of its property as a **debtor in possession**. As a debtor in possession, the debtor enjoys the same rights and powers — as well as the obligations — of a trustee in bankruptcy.

Debtor in possession
The debtor in a Chapter 11 case that retains possession of its property and enjoys the same rights and powers — as well as the obligations — of a trustee in bankruptcy.

Creditor

The Bankruptcy Code defines a **creditor** as "an entity that has a claim against the debtor that arose at the time of or before the order for relief concerning the debtor." Creditors in a real property bankruptcy often include local, state, and federal taxing authorities; lenders; landlords; secured creditors; holders of executory contracts and unexpired leases; trade creditors; and the like.

Creditor
An entity that is owed money from a debtor.

Creditor's Committee

A creditor's committee of unsecured creditors is appointed by the U.S. trustee in Chapter 11 cases. Creditor's committees are appointed in most, if not all, Chapter 11 cases. The members of the creditor's committee are unpaid for their service. The committee represents the interests of the unsecured creditors in the proceeding. Members of the creditor's committee are usually the first to know of events affecting the bankruptcy, which can provide them with invaluable knowledge.

Key Terms Used in Bankruptcy ■ ■ ■

Adversary proceeding	A lawsuit arising in or related to a bankruptcy case that is commenced by filing a complaint.
Assume	An agreement to continue performing duties under a contract or lease.
Automatic stay	An injunction that automatically stops lawsuits, foreclosures, and all collection activity against the debtor the moment a bankruptcy petition is filed.

Bankruptcy estate	All legal or equitable interest of the debtor in property at the time of bankruptcy filing.
Claim	A debtor's assertion of a right to payment from the debtor or its property.
Discharge	A release of a debtor from personal liability for certain debts. A discharge prevents creditors owed those debts from taking any action against the debtor to collect them.
Equity	The value of a debtor's interest in property after liens and other creditor interests are considered. For example: If a house is valued at $100,000 and is subject to a $75,000 mortgage, there is $25,000 of equity.
Executory contract or lease	Those agreements that have duties remaining to be performed. If the agreement is an executory contract, a debtor may assume or reject the contract or lease.
Exemptions	Property owned by individual debtors that the Bankruptcy Code or state law permits the debtor to keep from unsecured creditors.
Insider	Any relative of the debtor or of a general partner, a partnership in which the debtor is a general partner, a general partner of the debtor, or a corporation of which the debtor is an officer, director, or person in control.
Plan	A debtor's detailed description of how the debtor proposes to pay the creditor's claims over a period of time.
Preference or preferential debt payment	A debt payment made to a creditor in the 90 days prior to when a debtor files bankruptcy (or within one year, if the creditor was an insider) that gives the creditor more than the creditor would receive in a Chapter 7 case.
Priority	A statutory ranking of unsecured claims that determines the order in which they will be paid, if not enough money is available to pay all of them in full.
Proof of claim	A written statement and verified documentation filed by a creditor that describes the reasons why the debtor owes the creditor money.
Secured creditor	A creditor holding a claim against the debtor who has the right to take and hold or sell certain property in partial or complete satisfaction of the creditor's claim. Holders of secured claims usually obtain some payment in the bankruptcy; this payment is generally determined by the value of the collateral securing the claim.
Secured debt	Debt backed by a mortgage, pledge of collateral, or other lien. (Examples include mortgages and deeds of trust, as well as tax liens.)
U.S. trustee	An officer of the U.S. Justice Department responsible for supervising the administration of bankruptcy cases.
Unsecured claim	A claim or debt for which a creditor holds no assurance of payment, such as is present with a mortgage or deed of trust. It is a debt for which credit was extended solely based upon the debtor's future ability to pay. Unsecured claims have the lowest priority of repayment and are often discharged in bankruptcy.

Bankruptcy Procedures

Certain procedures must be followed pursuant to the Bankruptcy Code. Each procedure is discussed below and includes the following:

1. Bankruptcy counseling and education (if required)
2. Filing of a bankruptcy petition
3. Creation of the bankruptcy estate
4. Meeting of the creditors
5. Automatic stay of most civil actions against the debtor
6. Creditors file proofs of claim
7. Debtor may execute reaffirmation agreements
8. Distribution of property (in Chapter 7 cases)
9. Discharge of debts
10. Closing of the bankruptcy estate

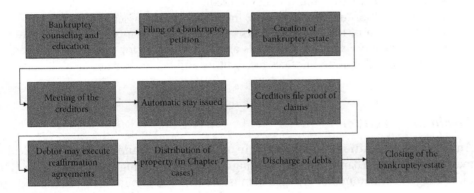

FIGURE 21.1. The Bankruptcy Procedure

Bankruptcy Counseling and Education

With a few exceptions, individual debtors who wish to file a Chapter 7 personal bankruptcy or a Chapter 13 bankruptcy must receive credit counseling by an approved credit counseling agency within 180 days before they file a bankruptcy petition. The counseling is designed to review the debtor's financial position, provide the debtor with alternatives to filing bankruptcy, and discuss budget plans.

Once a bankruptcy petition has been filed, as discussed below, the debtor must receive debtor education before his or her debts may be discharged. Debtor education assists the debtor in developing a budget, managing money, and using credit wisely. Debtor education must also be provided by a U.S. trustee–approved provider.

Filing a Bankruptcy Petition

A bankruptcy case is commenced by the filing of a voluntary or involuntary petition under a chapter of the Bankruptcy Code. The filing of the bankruptcy petition triggers several consequences, including the creation of a bankruptcy estate consisting of the debtor's property, the automatic stay (discussed below), and the creation of the preference periods for avoiding certain transactions of the debtor prior to the filing date of the petition.

Voluntary Petition

Voluntary petition
A petition filed by the insolvent debtor.

A **voluntary petition** triggers not only an automatic stay but also an automatic order for relief. An automatic stay is an injunction that automatically stops lawsuits, foreclosures, and all collection activity against the debtor from the moment a bankruptcy petition is filed. The filing date establishes the date for pre- and post-bankruptcy debts and assets. The petition includes:

- A list of all secured and unsecured creditors
- A list of all of the debtor's assets, including exempt assets
- A statement of the debtor's affairs and a schedule of income and expenses
- A schedule of executory contracts and leases; copies for trustees of filed tax returns; and required notices to creditors and tax authorities

Involuntary Petition

Involuntary petition
A petition filed by creditors of a debtor that alleges the debtor is not paying debts as they become due.

An **involuntary petition** can be filed only under Chapter 7 and Chapter 11. A debtor may be forced into a bankruptcy proceeding by creditors holding unsecured claims. The filing triggers the automatic stay against most creditor activity. In an involuntary Chapter 7 case, the debtor remains in possession of its business and property until the order for relief is entered or an interim bankruptcy trustee is appointed. The debtor has the right to contest the filing of the involuntary petition.

Creation of the Bankruptcy Estate

When a bankruptcy petition is filed, a "bankruptcy estate" is created. The bankruptcy estate includes legal and equitable interests in the debtor's property at the time of the bankruptcy filing. The Bankruptcy Code defines the property of the estate in the broadest terms possible, as "wherever located and by whomever held." The bankruptcy estate is a legal entity separate and apart from the debtor.

In most bankruptcy cases, the filing of the petition also creates an **order for relief**. The order for relief allows the case to proceed through bankruptcy.

Property Exempt from the Bankruptcy Estate

The Bankruptcy Code allows individual, not corporate, debtors to keep certain property from the bankruptcy estate. This property is called exempt property. The types of property considered outside of the bankruptcy estate is provided for by both federal and state law. States may require their citizens to use the exemptions available under the applicable state law. If the state does not have such a requirement, the debtor is free to choose between the state and federal list of exempt property. The debtor cannot mix and match between the state and federal exemptions and must choose one list of exemptions. If no dollar amount is stated, the entire asset may be exempted.

Listing all of the available exemptions is beyond the scope of this text; however, one notable exemption is the homestead exemption. A homestead exemption prevents the forced sale of a home to pay creditors if the home does not have a certain level of equity. Different jurisdictions provide different degrees of homestead protection. If the homestead's equity exceeds the homestead exemption amount, creditors may still force the sale of a residence, but the homesteader will be able to keep the protected portion from the sale proceeds. Examples of homestead provisions are as follows:

- California: $75,000 for single individuals, $100,000 for married couples, and $175,000 for people over 65 or who are legally disabled.
- Florida, Iowa, Kansas, Oklahoma, and Texas offer very broad protections to a debtor in bankruptcy. In some cases, the homestead has no dollar limit, depending on the size and location of the property.
- Federal homestead exemption: $23,675 ($47,350 if married filing jointly).

Meeting of Creditors

Once the court grants the order for relief, it schedules a meeting of creditors. This is usually scheduled between ten and 30 days after the court has granted the order for relief. At the meeting of creditors, the debtor appears and submits to questioning, under oath, by the creditors regarding the debtor's assets, finances, any transfers of property prior to bankruptcy, and so forth.

Automatic Stay

Once the bankruptcy petition is filed, an automatic stay arises. The **automatic stay** is one of the most important tools available to a debtor in bankruptcy, as it provides a period of time during which all collection activities, foreclosures, and repossessions of the debtor's property are suspended. Creditors may not pursue the debtor or the debtor's property for any debt or claim that arose before the filing of the bankruptcy petition. Criminal prosecutions against the debtor are not stayed. In addition, some personal debts continue despite the automatic stay, including child and spousal support. The stay also does not apply to lawsuits commenced against the debtor in the bankruptcy court where the debtor's bankruptcy is pending.

Automatic stay
The suspension of legal proceedings against a debtor, such as stopping a mortgage foreclosure sale.

The automatic stay prevents not only an actual foreclosure sale of any secured real property but also the following:

- The beginning of any foreclosure proceeding (such as publication or recordation of service of notice of sale)

■ The commencement or continued prosecution of a judicial (court) foreclosure action or of an action to have an independent third-party receiver appointed by the court to collect rents, issues, and profits

The bankruptcy court can penalize creditors who violate the automatic stay. The court can order the disgorgement (forced return) of the debtor's property unlawfully seized by a creditor and can award damages and attorney fees to the debtor.

In the following case, a debtor attempted to file a Chapter 13 petition moments prior to her property's foreclosure sale. The clerk did not process the filing of the petition until minutes after the sale occurred. The bankruptcy court ruled the sale void.

CASE 21.1

THE AUTOMATIC STAY BEGINS AT THE MOMENT A BANKRUPTCY PETITION IS FILED

IN RE SCHLEIER

290 B.R. 45 (2003)

United States Bankruptcy Court for the Southern District of New York

On August 31, 2001, Bank of New York ("BONY"), received a judgment of foreclosure and sale on the property of Sylvia Schleier. The foreclosure sale began at or about 9:00 a.m. on June 28, 2008, with the sale itself taking place between 9:15 and 9:20 a.m. On that same day, Schleier filed her Chapter 13 bankruptcy petition at the courthouse at or just before 9:00 a.m. Schleier presented the clerk with a skeleton petition and offered payment of the filing fee in cash. The clerk took the petition, explained that they would not accept cash payment and described to Schleier the other papers she would need to complete the filing of her petition. Following their conversation, the clerk date- and time-stamped Schleier's petition. About two months later BONY moved to vacate the automatic stay to complete the foreclosure sale. Schleier opposed the motion, and the case proceeded to trial.

Language of the Court. *Bankruptcy Courts also have held that pleadings other than petitions filed without proper filing fees will be considered "filed" as of the date the pleadings were put in the clerk's custody.*

The bankruptcy rules do not determine when a petition is filed. It requires only that a petition is accompanied by a fee. It does not mandate that a petition should not be considered filed until the fee is paid. Here, Schleier's petition was accompanied with a proffered filing fee payment. On these facts, Schleier's petition was filed when it was placed in the custody of the deputy clerk.

The burden of going forward with evidence then switched to Schleier to demonstrate that her petition was filed not at the time stamped on it, but before the foreclosure sale strike down time. Schleier presented Mr. Brandt's credible testimony and her own uncontroverted testimony to make this showing.

Mr. Brandt testified that after dropping Schleier at the Courthouse, he parked the car, entered the building and proceeded to the clerk's office arriving at 9:05 a.m. at which time he witnessed Schleier in conversation with a deputy clerk. Both Schleier's and Brandt's testimony was credible and undisputed. Accordingly, this Court finds that Schleier filed her petition at or before 9:05 a.m., at least ten minutes before the foreclosure sale strike down time.

Decision. The court found in favor of Schleier and invalidated the foreclosure sale.

FOCUS ON ETHICS

Should the law favor the debtor in these circumstances?

Relief from the Automatic Stay

Most creditor actions against a debtor are immediately and automatically stayed upon the filing of the bankruptcy petition. However, many exceptions to the automatic stay exist in which relief from the automatic stay is granted. Some of these exceptions include the following:

1. Actions to perfect a lien or security interest are taken within 30 days after the bankruptcy petition was filed.

   Example: A contractor who has not yet recorded a mechanic's lien on a property may record the lien within 30 days of an owner's filing for bankruptcy. However, the contractor is barred from filing a lawsuit to foreclose on the mechanic's lien. That action is stayed pursuant to the automatic stay.

2. A secured creditor holding a mortgage or deed of trust against the debtor's real property obtains an order from the court granting relief from the automatic stay.

In the following case, a creditor sought to have an automatic stay modified to prevent a debtor from having the rental property turned back over to him following the debtor's petition for Chapter 13 bankruptcy.

CASE 21.2

A CREDITOR CAN SEEK RELIEF FROM THE AUTOMATIC STAY WHEN A DEBTOR DOES NOT PRESENT A VIABLE PLAN TO REORGANIZE THE PROPERTY

IN RE FRANKLIN

476 B.R. 545 (2012)

United States Bankruptcy Court for the Northern District of Illinois

Dale Franklin ("Franklin") operated a rental property located in Illinois. Title to the rental property was held by Standard Bank and Trust Company of Evergreen Park as Trustee, with Franklin owning the beneficial interest in the land trust. On January 26, 2004, the Trustee executed and delivered a note to Citibank in the sum of $400,000, which was secured by a Trustee Mortgage connected to the rental property. Franklin then further secured the note by executing a personal guarantee in which he unconditionally and irrevocably guaranteed all obligations. Citibank then assigned the mortgage and note to Wells Fargo Bank, N.A. ("Wells Fargo"). Both the note and mortgage defaulted in October 2010 when Franklin failed to make monthly payments. Wells Fargo then accelerated all amounts due under the note and mortgage, demanding immediate payment. Wells Fargo filed a complaint for foreclose on the mortgage and filed an order appointing a receiver. The property was taken over by the receiver. The value of the property was assessed at $375,000. Franklin filed for Chapter 13 bankruptcy and moved to have the rental property turned back over to him by the receiver. Wells Fargo objected and sought to modify the automatic stay so that foreclosure of the property could proceed.

Language of the Court. *To be granted relief from the automatic stay, a creditor must demonstrate a lack of "adequate protection of an interest in property of such party in interest . . . the debtor does not have an equity in such property; and such property is not necessary to an effective reorganization." To defeat the motion, a debtor in Chapter 13 must have filed a "plan of reorganization that has a reasonable possibility of being confirmed within a reasonable time; or [have] commenced monthly payments" to secured creditors in amounts equal to "interest at the then applicable non-default contract rate of interest on the value of the creditor's interest in the real estate." The debtor must also show that he can adequately protect the creditor's interest.*

The Debtor has not provided adequate protection for the Creditor's interests and is unable to do so. The Mortgage and Note have been delinquent since October 2010. The amount of the arrearage owed under the Mortgage and Note at the time of the Petition is $112,969.84. Franklin has made only one monthly payment to Wells Fargo since the Petition was filed. There is a continual increase in indebtedness of Franklin to Wells Fargo in relation to the Property.

Franklin admits that he will be unable to make any payments under the mortgage and arrearage to Wells Fargo if he were brought into possession and control of the Property. Therefore, adequate protection for Wells Fargo's interests in the Property is lacking.

Franklin has not presented a viable plan to effectively reorganize the Property under Chapter 13 protection, as discussed previously. There is no evidence of efforts or plans on the part of Franklin to continue the financially sound operation established by the Receiver or to establish his own management that would enable him to meet his financial obligations under the Mortgage and Note, if the Property were turned over to him.

Decision. The court granted the creditor's motion for relief from automatic stay, allowing the creditor to proceed with foreclosure proceedings.

FOCUS ON ETHICS

In this case, did the court balance properly the competing interests of the creditor and debtor? What should the debtor have done to prevent the foreclosure?

Additional exemptions from an automatic stay include the following:

3. Any act to enforce a lien or security interest in real property, if relief from the stay was granted in a prior bankruptcy case within the last two years, provides and exemption. This provision prevents abusive serial filings of bankruptcy petitions to stop a foreclosure.
4. Actions by a commercial landlord to repossess property provide an exemption, if the lease terminated before the lessee's bankruptcy was filed.

In addition, a secured creditor can move for relief from the automatic stay for the following reasons:

■ For "cause," including lack of adequate protection, or

- If the debtor has no equity in the property and the property is not necessary for reorganization,
- Any secured lender moving for relief from stay has the burden of proving that the debtor lacks equity in the property. This requires proof of the property's value and the amount of the liens against the property. That value is usually established by the testimony of qualified appraisal experts.

Adequate protection is the relief or compensation given by a court to a secured creditor whose collateral is decreasing in value because the collateral continues to be used by the debtor or is sold during the bankruptcy case. The types of adequate protection include:

- Cash payments to the secured creditor during bankruptcy (such as continuing rent or mortgage payments)
- Additional or replacement liens (increasing the secured position of the creditor so that its position is not jeopardized)
- Other relief, which may include giving the creditor priority in the distribution of payments from the estate

The existence of an "equity cushion" may provide the secured creditor with adequate protection. An equity cushion exists when the value of the collateral is greater than the amount of the secured lender's claim plus any senior lien claims secured by the same property. It is difficult to determine what would constitute adequate protection for a secured creditor. Determining whether sufficient equity resides in the property to protect the secured creditor and prevent a foreclosure is critical in the reorganization of real estate companies.

Proof of Claim

Filing a **proof of claim** is usually a necessary step for the creditor to recover its share of the bankruptcy assets. The bankruptcy court provides the form to use to file a proof of claim.

Proof of claim
Written verification submitted by a creditor to the bankruptcy court supporting debt owed.

Two types of claims can be filed against a debtor: secured and unsecured claims. Unsecured claims are categorized as either priority claims or general unsecured claims.

Secured Claim

A secured claim is a claim secured by a valid lien on the debtor's real or personal property. Secured claims have priority over all unsecured claims in the right of payment from the bankruptcy estate, up to the amount of the claim and the value of the assets. Whether or not a creditor's claim is secured depends on the rights of the creditor under state law.

> *Example:* A debt owing to a real property lender is secured or collateralized with the property for which the debt was acquired for purchase or refinance.

Lenders usually secure the loan with a mortgage or deed of trust on the property purchased. If the mortgage or deed of trust is in proper form and is properly executed and recorded under state law, it will create a valid lien on the property. The lender will have the right to foreclose on the property if the borrower defaults. The lender's claim will qualify as a secured claim in the bankruptcy case, and the lender will be entitled to receive the value of its interest in the property before any other of the borrower's creditors receive the value of their interests.

Unsecured Claim

An unsecured claim is a claim for which no property or asset serves as collateral or security for the debt.

Filing Proof of Claims

Unsecured creditors in Chapter 7 and Chapter 13 cases must file a proof of claim with the bankruptcy court to be entitled to receive distributions at the close of the bankruptcy. In Chapter 7 or Chapter 13 proceedings, all proofs of claim must be filed within 90 days after the initial meeting of creditors. In Chapter 11 cases, a claim is deemed filed when it has been listed by the debtor in possession or the bankruptcy trustee, if the schedules filed reflect them.

Generally, Chapter 11 cases set a bar date (that is, a deadline) for the filing of proofs of claim. A proof of claim, once filed, is deemed an allowable claim of the estate unless the debtor or another party objects to the claim. A properly executed and filed proof of claim constitutes prima facie evidence of its validity. A person objecting to a claim in a bankruptcy has the duty to overcome that presumption.

Reaffirmation Agreements

Reaffirmation agreement
An agreement in which the debtor agrees to continue to pay a dischargeable debt to a creditor after the discharge in bankruptcy.

In Chapter 7 cases, a debtor may enter into a reaffirmation agreement with a creditor. A **reaffirmation agreement** is an agreement in which the debtor agrees to continue to pay a dischargeable debt to a creditor after the discharge in bankruptcy. A reaffirmation agreement must be filed with the court prior to the time at which the bankruptcy discharge is granted.

> **Example:** A debtor has an automobile that was financed with an auto loan. If the debtor wishes to continue to possess the vehicle after bankruptcy, he would enter into a reaffirmation agreement with the auto lender prior to the discharge in bankruptcy.

Distributions of Property in Chapter 7 Cases

In Chapter 7 cases, nonexempt property must be distributed to the debtor's secured and unsecured creditors pursuant to the priority set forth in the Bankruptcy Code. Secured creditors have priority over the claims of unsecured creditors.

Bankruptcy Discharge

Bankruptcy discharge
A court order that relieves a debtor from the obligation to pay for certain debts included in the bankruptcy proceeding.

A **bankruptcy discharge** releases the debtor from liability for certain specified debts. In other words, the debtor is no longer obligated to pay them. The Bankruptcy Code provides that a discharge voids any judgment against the debtor to the extent that it affects the debtor's personal liability; a discharge also stops the commencement or continuation of an action to collect or offset a debt. Debts not included in the bankruptcy, or for which a reaffirmation agreement was executed, or that cannot be discharged in bankruptcy, remain in effect after the discharge.

> *Example:* A mortgage lien that was not made unenforceable in bankruptcy remains in effect after the discharge. Thus, a secured creditor may enforce the mortgage to recover the property secured by the lien.

Chapter 7 Discharge

In a Chapter 7 bankruptcy, the debtors retain the exempt property and are discharged from liabilities, debts, and obligations that were subject to the bankruptcy proceeding.

Chapter 11 Discharge

In a Chapter 11 bankruptcy, a business entity will be discharged from its debts and liabilities that have occurred prior to the confirmation of the plan. The effect of the confirmation is to make the plan binding on all parties and to grant the debtor a discharge from those claims not provided for by the plan. Following the reorganization, the debtor is revested with all property of the estate on confirmation.

> *Example:* A real estate developer filing a Chapter 11 case would be revested in the title to all real properties held in the bankruptcy estate upon discharge.

Confirmation in Chapter 11 can occur through acceptance by a class of claims. Such acceptance requires holders of more than 50 percent of those claims and representing at least two-thirds of the dollar totals to produce to approve the plan. **Confirmation** makes the plan binding on all interested parties. Confirmation can also occur through a cramdown. If one or more classes of creditors object to the plan, the bankruptcy court can force those creditors to accept the plan through a **cramdown**. The requirements for a cramdown are:

Confirmation
Bankruptcy court approval of a plan of reorganization under Chapter 11.

Cramdown
A bankruptcy rule allowing the court to confirm a plan of reorganization over the objections of a class of creditors, subject to certain conditions.

- Acceptance by at least one class,
- A finding that the plan is fair, and
- A finding that the plan does not discriminate unfairly against any creditor classes rejecting the plan.

Chapter 13 Discharge

Chapter 13 is the simplest form of reorganization available to individuals who have debt less than certain thresholds for noncontingent, liquidated, unsecured debts and noncontingent, liquidated, secured debts.[2] In consideration of retaining nonexempt assets, the debtor must formulate a plan in which she or he is required to pay creditors not less than the value of the nonexempt assets being retained over a period of no more than five years. The debtor in a Chapter 13 case is not discharged until performance under the plan is complete.

Trustees are appointed in Chapter 13 cases, but their duties differ from those of a Chapter 7 trustee. The only property that the Chapter 13 trustee deals with is the debtor's earnings, which form the source of payments under the plan. The primary duty of the Chapter 13 trustee is to make the required disbursements to creditors and monitor the debtor's performance of the plan.

Example: A Chapter 13 debtor's proposed debt adjustment plan must provide each allowed, secured creditor with both a lien securing the claim and a proposal of future payments whose total values are not less than the claim's allowed amount. Each installment payment by the debtor must be calibrated to ensure that the creditor receives disbursements whose total present value equals or exceeds that of the allowed claim. The plan must contemplate an appropriate interest rate to address the discounted stream of deferred payments back to their present dollar value.[3]

■ ■ ■ Nondischargeable Debts in Bankruptcy

The Bankruptcy Code provides that certain debts arising from intentional or willful conduct are nondischargeable. Among them are the following:

- Loans obtained by material misrepresentations or omissions by the debtor to induce the lender to make the loan
- Claims arising from fraud, breaches of duty by a fiduciary, embezzlement, or larceny
- Claims for willful and malicious injury, including punitive damages

Other debts are nondischargeable as a matter of law including:

- Debts not listed or scheduled by the debtor in the bankruptcy, unless the creditor had actual knowledge of the bankruptcy in time to permit the timely filing of a proof of claim; however, when no assets exist that compel the filing of a proof of claim and no claim exists for nondischargeability, such unlisted or unscheduled debts are discharged
- Domestic support obligations (such as child support and spousal support)
- Student loans, in the absence of an undue hardship
- Liability for wrongful death and personal injury caused while operating a vehicle under the influence of alcohol or drugs
- Certain claims against the debtor arising from fraud while acting in a fiduciary capacity
- Claims for condominium fees, homeowners' association fees, or assessments that become due and payable post-petition
- Liability for violation of federal or state securities laws and regulations arising from or relating to the sale of a security

Debtor's Actions Barring Discharge

Sometimes a debtor's actions may bar (deny) discharge. Examples of debtor actions that bar discharge include:

- Making false representations when obtaining credit
- Transferring, concealing, removing, or destroying estate property with the intent to hinder, delay, or defraud creditors within one year before the filing date
- Falsifying, destroying, or concealing records of financial condition
- Failing to disclose all assets
- Failing to participate in the meeting of creditors
- Failing to take a credit counseling course required for personal bankruptcies (unless excused)

Revocation of Bankruptcy Discharge

A discharge can be revoked under certain circumstances. These cases often occur when the debtor has obtained the discharge fraudulently, failed to disclose that the debtor acquired or became entitled to acquire property that would constitute property of the bankruptcy estate, or committed one or several statutory acts of impropriety.

Closing of the Bankruptcy Estate

Upon the closing or dismissal of the case, the bankruptcy court continues its jurisdiction to enforce or interpret any of its orders. The bankruptcy court retains the power to reopen the case "to administer assets, to accord relief to the debtor, or for any other cause." The automatic stay terminates upon closing, except with regard to property not scheduled and not administered. Such property remains the property of the bankruptcy estate, and the debtor has no right to that property. The closing the case terminates the trustee's services.

Real Property Bankruptcy Issues

Debtors, creditors, and brokers participating in bankruptcy cases involving real property must be well versed with issues that arise during a bankruptcy proceeding. Several of the most common are now discussed.

Short Sales in Bankruptcy

The bankruptcy of a seller or buyer poses a few problems for the real estate broker. If the broker is aware of the bankruptcy process, she or he can help salvage a sale.

Where the market value of the home is less than the mortgage debt on the property, a broker will try to sell the property through a "short sale" transaction. A short sale occurs when, to facilitate a sale, the seller's mortgage lender(s) agree to accept less than what is owed on the note in exchange for releasing the seller-borrower.

Because the bankruptcy estate holds the home as an asset, the owner no longer has the ability to close easily on a short sale. An owner-seller must seek court permission to close on the short sale. This procedure may actually hurt the insolvent seller. Because bankruptcy can minimize some of the consequences of a foreclosure for a borrower and give the borrower a longer period of time to remain in his home without making rent or mortgage payments, few discharged sellers complete a closing on a post-bankruptcy short payoff transaction.

If sellers have equity in their residences when filing for bankruptcy, the automatic stay allows them and the listing brokers time to find a buyer and close. The broker must work with both the debtors' attorneys and the trustees to continue with any listing of the property. The bankruptcy court must approve the listing agreement and the commission payable upon closing.

Lien Stripping

Sometimes secured creditors have found themselves undersecured. In certain cases, the amount of a secured claim may be reduced, or stripped down, to the fair market value of the collateral as of the petition date. If the debtor is permitted to strip a secured creditor's claim down to the value of the collateral, the claim will have both a secured and an unsecured portion.

The creditor is treated as a secured creditor to the extent of the value of the collateral and as an unsecured creditor as to the balance of the debt owed; however, no lien stripping may occur in a Chapter 11 or Chapter 13 case for claims secured only by a debtor's principal residence.

Single Asset Real Estate Cases

Strict deadlines are imposed on a Chapter 11 debtor with assets consisting solely of a single parcel of real estate. This is to prevent debtors with no hope of rehabilitation from frustrating the lenders' foreclosure actions. This provision requires that such debtors be prepared for a quick-paced bankruptcy proceeding.

In a **single asset real estate case**, a creditor whose claim is secured by an interest in the real property may obtain relief from the automatic stay *unless*, within 90 days after the petition date, the debtor either (1) files a plan of reorganization that has a reasonable possibility of being confirmed within a reasonable time or (2) begins making monthly payments to the secured creditor in an amount equal to interest at the nondefault contract rate on the secured real property loan.

Many commercial real estate projects are single asset real estate cases. However, if the debtor is engaged in business that generates income from non-real estate businesses on the single parcel of real estate, bankruptcy courts often do not find that proceeding to be a single asset real estate proceeding.

> *Example:* A proceeding involving a full-service hotel with a bar and restaurant is not a single asset real estate proceeding.[4]

Beyond providing grounds for relief from stay, the plan filing deadline fast tracks a single asset real estate case. The theory underlying the law is that it should not be difficult to assess the business plan of a small real estate development and project and then present a plan for reorganization in Chapter 11.

Sale of Real Property Free and Clear of Liens

The debtor in possession or a bankruptcy trustee has the power, subject to court approval, to sell real property free and clear of all liens. This may occur if any one of the following conditions exists:

- The law allows the property to be sold.
- The debtor consents.
- The interest being released is a lien, and the sale price for the property is greater than the aggregate value of all liens on the property.
- The lien interest is in bona fide dispute.
- The creditor could be compelled to accept a monetary payment in lieu of its lien interest.

If a sale is made subject to the existing lien, the lender will want to ensure that it is aware of which liens on the property will remain on the property following the sale. In addition, a holder of a lien that is wiped out in a sale free and clear of liens must be given adequate protection. This is usually accomplished by providing that the lien attach to the sale proceeds.

Abandonment

When a debtor's property is so heavily mortgaged or encumbered that no equity exists, or if the expenses of maintaining the property may be greater than could be realized from its sale or other disposition, the court may authorize the abandonment of the property back to the debtor. This occurs only when the continuation of the property is so burdensome to the estate that it is not beneficial. Abandonment of the property results in the transfer of title to the debtor.

Example: If the property required constant, expensive dewatering due to a high underground water table, the property might be deemed abandoned.

Bad Faith Filings

When a debtor has been created for the purpose of filing a Chapter 11 case, it follows one of the classic fact patterns supporting a bad faith filing, which may compel the dismissal of the Chapter 11 proceeding. A debtor created for the purpose of filing the Chapter 11 typically shows the following characteristics:

- The debtor has only one asset, such as a tract of undeveloped or developed real property.
- A secured creditor's lien encumbers the real property.
- The debtor has little or no cash flow.
- The debtor has unsecured creditors whose claims are relatively small.
- The property has been involved in foreclosure proceedings.
- Bankruptcy offers the only possibility of forestalling loss of the real property.
- There are no employees other than the debtor's principals.
- The debtor was created on the eve of foreclosure, and the real property is transferred to that entity.

In the following case, parties suing a Chapter 11 debtor in state court filed a motion for relief from automatic stay and asserted the bankruptcy petition was a litigation tactic and thus not in good faith.

CASE 21.3

THE AUTOMATIC STAY MAY BE LIFTED WHEN THE BANKRUPTCY PETITION WAS FILED IN BAD FAITH

IN RE ALEXANDRA TRUST

526 B.R. 668 (2015)

United States Bankruptcy Court for the Northern District of Texas

Alexandra Trust ("Trust") is the debtor in this case. The Trust has no employees, but held ownership interest in various companies. One of the companies was M Street Investments, Inc. ("M Street"). M Street was at the center of an ownership dispute between the Trust and some of the company's shareholders. The shareholders filed a lawsuit to reverse transactions they claimed arose from the defendants misappropriating the majority control of the company's shares. According to the shareholders, the day before the Trust's answer to the complaint was due, the Trust filed a voluntary bankruptcy petition seeking protection under Chapter 11. The Trust filed its bankruptcy notice with the state court and asserted that an automatic stay prevented the state court action from proceeding against the Trust in state court. The shareholders filed a motion for relief from the automatic stay on the grounds that the bankruptcy petition was filed in bad faith, solely as a litigation tactic enabling the Trust ultimately to remove the case to a more favorable venue.

Language of the Court. *The shareholders allege that the Trust's bankruptcy petition was not filed in good faith, but was instead filed solely as a litigation tactic to enable the Trust to remove the action from the Mississippi state court to federal court, which is perceived as a more favorable venue. According to the shareholders, this lack of good faith constitutes "cause" to terminate the automatic stay. In its response, the Trust argues that it did file its petition in good faith, but provides no supporting facts.*

When alleging grounds to lift the automatic stay, other than for a lack of equity, the shareholders

are required to make a prima facie showing that it is entitled to relief from stay. Once the shareholders allege facts demonstrating a legal entitlement to the relief sought, the burden shifts to the Trust to prove that cause does not exist to lift the automatic stay. "In a hearing . . . (1) the party requesting such relief has the burden of proof on the issue of the Trust's equity in the property and (2) the party opposing such relief has the burden of proof on all other issues."

At the hearing, the Trust's trustee was evasive in answering questions posed by the shareholders' counsel. Even when asked by the Court to "crisply state" why the Trust filed its bankruptcy petition, the trustee had difficulty responding. He initially answered that the petition was filed on the advice of counsel, but would not articulate a substantive reason.

The record from the hearing clearly shows, and this Court finds, that the Trust had no good faith reason to file its bankruptcy petition. Rather, the bankruptcy petition was filed as a litigation tactic to gain advantage in the Mississippi Action.

Decision. The bankruptcy court granted the motion to lift the automatic stay, finding the bankruptcy petition was filed by the Trust in bad faith.

FOCUS ON ETHICS

A stay in bankruptcy is a powerful right to allow debtors time to reorganize their affairs. Are there circumstances when filing for bankruptcy would not be fair or ethical to creditors?

Avoiding Transfers

Payments made by a debtor to a creditor may be set aside and become part of the bankruptcy estate under certain situations. Payments made to a creditor within the 90-day period before a debtor files a bankruptcy petition, or payments made by a debtor to an insider within one year from filing the bankruptcy petition, are deemed **preferential transfers**. A preferential transfer is any wrongful transfer of an interest of the debtor in property. The trustee may void these preferential transfers.

    The policy underlying this power is that the debtor's assets should be equitably distributed among all creditors. In order to avoid a preferential transfer, a complaint is filed in the bankruptcy court against the third-party transferee to avoid a transfer or lien.

Preferential transfers
A wrongful transfer of the debtor's property benefiting one or more creditors allowing them to receive more than they would have otherwise received in a Chapter 7 liquidation.

Fraudulent Transfers

If the debtor transfers property with the intent to hinder, delay, or defraud a creditor, the trustee may avoid this **fraudulent transfer** if it is made within two years of the filing of the bankruptcy petition. Fraudulent transfers are determined under state law.

Fraudulent transfer
A transfer made by the debtor with the intent to hinder, delay, or defraud a creditor.

Residential and Commercial Leases

When a debtor files a bankruptcy petition, the landlord and other creditors are stayed from taking action against the property of the bankruptcy estate, including a leasehold interest. The stay continues until the property is no longer the property of the estate. Thus, a landlord or other secured party must act to exercise control of the property to protect its interest. In general, state law determines the debtor's leasehold property rights subject to the provisions of the bankruptcy code. Several issues may arise related to residential and commercial leases, as discussed below.

Security Deposits

Does an automatic stay prohibit a landlord from applying the tenant's security deposit against unpaid rent without obtaining relief from the automatic stay? The landlord is allowed to offset the delinquency with a security deposit only to address pre-petition claims for unpaid rent.

    When it comes to the application of security deposits, differences exist between commercial lessees and residential lessees. If the debtor was current under a commercial lease before the lease terminated, the landlord may have to return the entire deposit and not use it to offset the landlord's damages for lost future rent. A residential lease, on the other hand, allows the creditor to offset the delinquency with the security deposit.

Commercial Leases

Bankruptcy petitions by the landlord or tenant can severely impact the rights and obligations of the parties under a lease. The rental income from a commercial landlord may be a key asset secured by the lender in making the loan to that landlord. The parties may question whether these items are part of the bankruptcy estate and what rights the landlord and tenant have to the assets.

State law will determine what is included in the bankruptcy estate. The bankruptcy court will examine the substance of the agreement between the lender and the debtor to determine whether rents are the collateral of the creditor (that is, not part of the bankruptcy estate) or are included as property of the bankruptcy estate.

> *Example:* Hotel room charges are rents and usually collateral, but revenues from food and beverage service usually become part of the bankruptcy estate, unless the agreement provides otherwise.

Expired Commercial Leases

When a commercial lease has expired before the tenant filed a bankruptcy petition, the Bankruptcy Code allows the landlord to recover possession without seeking relief from stay. This follows from the fact that the debtor has no interest in the leasehold. The tenant may be immediately evicted.

Acceptance or Rejection of the Lease

In a Chapter 7 case involving a residential lease, the trustee must decide within 60 days after the order of relief, or a date set by the court, either to perform the lease obligations or to reject them. In a Chapter 11 or Chapter 13 proceeding, the trustee or debtor in possession generally may allow the parties to assume or reject the lease any time before confirmation of the bankruptcy plan. A creditor, however, may file a motion for a court order fixing the time within which the trustee of the debtor in possession must decide whether to assume or reject the lease.

> *Example:* A landlord may petition the court to set a date for a commercial center tenant to accept or reject the lease. The landlord must obtain a replacement tenant, and its business plans cannot be held hostage to the delayed decision making of the tenant.

Under the Bankruptcy Abuse Prevention and Consumer Protection Act of 2005 (BAPCPA), Congress created an exception to the automatic stay to allow a residential landlord to enforce a judgment for possession obtained before the tenant filed a petition for bankruptcy. Generally, if the landlord has obtained a judgment for possession before the bankruptcy that was based upon a nonmonetary default, the automatic stay will not apply. However, some states allow the tenant to remain in possession of the property if the default is cured after judgment is entered. If the judgment is based upon the default in rent payment, the tenant may be able to keep the automatic stay in effect to block eviction.

In the case of unexpired leases of commercial real property (that is, nonresidential property) under which the debtor is a lessee, these leases are deemed rejected unless assumed by the debtor at the earlier of:

- 120 days after the order of relief
- The date of entry of an order confirming a plan

Eviction

Residential tenants filing bankruptcy must disclose in their petitions whether judgment for possession of their residence has been entered. If a judgment is based on a monetary default, the exception to the stay applies automatically to allow the eviction to proceed unless the tenant files his bankruptcy petition and serves the landlord with a certification that:

- Circumstances exist under which the tenant would be entitled to cure the entire monetary default, and
- The tenant has deposited with the clerk of the court any rent that would become due in the 30 days following the filing of the bankruptcy petition.

The BAPCPA exception for terminated leases applies only to residential leases. Commercial landlords must still seek relief from the bankruptcy court before attempting to enforce any writ of possession concerning a termination of a commercial lease.

Strategies in Tenant Bankruptcy Proceedings

The lessor should pursue the following four courses of action if the lessee is in a difficult financial condition:

- Terminate the lease under state law and obtain possession of the leased premises before the bankruptcy is filed. Once the lease is terminated, there remains nothing for the debtor to cure and reinstate under state law.
- Obtain a guarantee. The landlord could secure a guarantee by a third party who is not involved with the lessee or in any operation of the business. The automatic stay does not apply to collection actions against the guarantor (unless the guarantor is also in bankruptcy).
- File an action based upon endangerment of the property or the illegal use of controlled substances on the property.
- Obtain a judgment for possession of the premises.

The automatic stay does not apply to a lessor's eviction action if the lessor obtained a judgment for possession before the bankruptcy petition was filed. The debtor tenant may obtain one 30-day stay of the eviction under limited circumstances, but the stay terminates unless the debtor/tenant cures the entire monetary default before the end of the 30-day period.

Key Terms and Concepts

- Creditor, page 538
- Debtor, page 538
- Core proceeding, page 538
- Noncore proceeding, page 539
- Chapter 7, page 539
- Chapter 11, page 539
- Chapter 13, page 540
- Bankruptcy trustee, page 540
- U.S. trustee, page 541
- Debtor in possession, page 541
- Creditor, page 541
- Voluntary petition, page 544

- Involuntary petition, page 544
- Order for relief, page 544
- Automatic stay, page 545
- Proof of claim, page 549
- Reaffirmation agreement, page 550
- Bankruptcy discharge, page 550
- Confirmation, page 551
- Cramdown, page 551
- Single asset real estate case, page 554
- Preferential transfers, page 557
- Fraudulent transfer, page 557

Chapter Summary

- Bankruptcy law is administered by the federal courts. Bankruptcies can be generally described as Chapter 7 liquidation, a reorganization under Chapter 11, or Chapter 13. Under a Chapter 7 liquidation, the petition seeks to discharge certain debts and allow the debtor to retain certain exempt property.

- A bankruptcy case is administered and heard by a bankruptcy judge who conducts core proceedings. Core proceedings are those that directly affect the reorganization or discharge of the debtor. Noncore proceedings are resolved in state or federal courts and are separate from the bankruptcy proceeding. An example is an eviction action against the debtor.

- The parties to a bankruptcy include the bankruptcy trustee, the U.S. trustee, the debtor in possession, the creditor, and the creditor committee.

- Bankruptcy usually follows a pattern in which bankruptcy counseling and education is provided (if a Chapter 7 case is sought), followed by filing a bankruptcy petition, creating a bankruptcy estate, holding a meeting of creditors,

instituting an automatic stay of most civil actions against the debtor, filing of a proof of claim, executing any reaffirmation agreements, distributing property in Chapter 7 cases, discharging debts, and then closing the bankruptcy estate.

- Upon a voluntary filing of a petition in bankruptcy, a bankruptcy estate is created. An automatic stay against collection action is triggered. Insolvency is not a prerequisite to filing a petition. A voluntary petition also results in an automatic order for relief.

- An involuntary bankruptcy proceeding can be commenced against a debtor only under Chapter 7 or Chapter 11. The petition does not result in an automatic order for relief. If the debtor does not oppose the petition, the court will enter an order for relief.

- A bankruptcy discharge releases the debtor from personal liability for certain debts. The discharge results in a permanent court order prohibiting the debtor's creditors from taking any form of collection action on discharged debts.

■ Certain property may be exempt from the bankruptcy estate. Both federal and state law describe what property may be exempted. One relevant exemption is a homestead exemption.

■ Although a debtor is not personally liable for discharged debts, a valid lien, such as a tax lien or a mortgage, that has not been avoided (set aside in the bankruptcy) will remain in effect after the bankruptcy. A secured creditor may enforce the lien to recover or sell the property secured by the lien.

■ The trustee is appointed in Chapter 7 and Chapter 13 cases; one may be appointed in a Chapter 11 proceeding. The trustee is usually elected by creditors in a Chapter 7 proceeding and is appointed by the U.S. trustee in all other cases. Broad powers are granted to the trustee. The trustee takes the place of the debtor and can assert any defense of the debtor to enforce the debtor's property rights. The trustee has priority over a secured creditor whose security interest is unperfected under state law.

■ Subject to the court's order, the debtor may continue to use, acquire, and dispose of property.

■ Under Chapter 11, the debtor has the exclusive right to file a plan of reorganization during the 120 days after the order for relief. If a trustee has been appointed, the plan may be filed at any time. A committee of unsecured creditors is appointed by the U.S. trustee. A reorganization divides creditor claims and shareholders' interests into classes. Claims in each class must be treated equally within their respective classes.

■ A secured creditor may petition the court to recognize the priority of its interest and grant relief from the automatic stay. This action will permit foreclosure of its interest.

■ Residential eviction proceedings are not stayed in cases involving continuing deterioration of the rented property or the use of controlled substances on the premises. They are also not stayed if the landlord has obtained a judgment for possession before the filing.

Chapter Problems and Assignments

1. Distinguish among Chapter 7, Chapter 11, and Chapter 13 proceedings.

2. Identify the typical events that occur in a bankruptcy proceeding.

3. What is an automatic stay? Whom does it protect and how can the automatic stay be lifted?

4. Explain why the distinction between a secured and an unsecured claim is so important when considering a creditor's rights in a bankruptcy proceeding?

5. Carter and several of his friends from law school decided to purchase a building from which to operate their law firm. They obtained a $100,000 mortgage. After they paid the principal balance of the mortgage to $80,000,

a real estate recession decreased the value of the property to $50,000. Carter and his partners file for bankruptcy to reduce the principal balance of the mortgage to the fair market value of the property. They continue to operate the business. What type of bankruptcy petition would Carter and his partners file?

6. Jackson and his wife, who file joint tax returns, file for bankruptcy protection. One of their assets is a residence. They owe $350,000 to the lender, and the home is worth $390,000. The creditors seek to have the home foreclosed and the equity used to pay debts owed to creditors. The state requires Jackson and his wife to use the federal homestead exemption. Will the property be sold?

7. In order to avoid foreclosure on her home, Staci files a bankruptcy petition. She presents her financial and tax information and a list of

creditors with their outstanding debts. The court required Staci to obtain credit counseling, and she met with a court-appointed trustee to develop a plan to repay her creditors. After court approval of the plan, Staci starts making bimonthly payments to the creditors. What type of bankruptcy proceeding did Staci file?

8. Why does the law treat orders for relief from stay differently for residential and commercial tenancies?

9. Research and identify the homestead exemption available of your state. How does the exemption in use in your state compare to the examples listed in the text? Is it more favorable or less favorable to the debtor? Does your state require a debtor to follow its law for homestead exemptions in bankruptcy proceedings?

10. Research examples of successful real estate reorganizations. As an example, General Growth Properties, a national shopping center operator, filed for bankruptcy reorganization. Explain what occurred in its bankruptcy proceedings and how successful the company has been since leaving bankruptcy. You may wish to review the price of its publicly traded common stock shares.

End Notes

1. *In re* Mantle, 153 F.3d 1082 (9th Cir. 1998).
2. Effective April 1, 2016 and valid for all of 2017 and 2018, the threshold for unsecured debt was $394,725, and the threshold for secured debts was $1,184,200. The threshold limits adjust every three years and the next adjustment will occur on April 1, 2019.
3. *Till et ux. v. SCS Credit Corp.,* 541 U.S. 465 (2004).
4. *Centofante v. CBJ Development*, 202 B.R. 467 (1996).

Chapter 22
Environmental Law in Real Estate Transactions

To waste, to destroy our natural resources, to skin and exhaust the land instead of using it so as to increase its usefulness, will result in undermining in the days of our children the very prosperity which we ought by right to hand down to them amplified and developed.
—*Theodore Roosevelt*, U.S. President, 1858-1919

Learning Objectives

1. Discuss the roles that regulatory agencies play in implementing environmental law.
2. Discuss the purpose and importance of CERCLA.
3. Describe hazardous substances most often affecting real estate.
4. Describe waste disposal sites and brownfields.

Chapter Outline

- Introduction
- Environmental Regulators
- Legislation
- Case 22.1: *Burlington Northern and Santa Fe Railway Company v. United States*
- Hazardous Substance Laws and Regulations
- Case 22.2: *Centex-Rooney Construction Co., Inc. v. Martin County*
- Water Pollution Laws and Regulations
- Solid Waste Disposal and Brownfield Sites

Opening
scenario

What are the obligations of and risks to a charitable institution when it receives potentially contaminated property as a gift? Many charitable and educational institutions receive real property from benefactors. Some of these sites may have been used for the disposal of hazardous substances, and charitable organizations are not exempt from liability as the current owner or operator of a contaminated site. In reviewing this chapter, consider the risks to such institutions of accepting and maintaining such gifts.

Introduction

Although real estate professionals are not required to possess the knowledge necessary to determine if a hazardous substance is present in a property, some level of familiarity is required. For example, a real estate professional should be aware of federal and state environmental laws and of the regulatory agencies responsible for the laws' enforcement. Such knowledge allows them to collect the necessary information on hazardous substances and provide that information to prospective buyers. Buyers can then make informed decisions on their purchases of real property, and the disclosures may protect the real estate professional from liability.

Environmental Protection Agency (EPA)
A federal agency created to protect the environment and address health concerns.

U.S. Department of Housing and Urban Development (HUD)
A cabinet department of the executive branch of the federal government supporting community development and environmental health.

U.S. Army Corps of Engineers
A federal agency responsible for public engineering, design, and construction management.

Environmental Regulators

The federal government has established several administrative agencies to enforce environmental laws and regulations. Several of the key environmental administrative agencies include: (1) the Environmental Protection Agency, (2) the U.S. Department of Housing and Urban Development, and (3) the U.S. Army Corps of Engineers.

The **Environmental Protection Agency** (EPA) is a federal agency established in 1970 to address pollution and hazardous wastes. The **U.S. Department of Housing and Urban Development** (HUD) also plays a key role in protecting the environmental health and safety of the country's citizens. Every HUD-assisted project must be examined to ensure that it does not negatively impact the surrounding environment and that the site itself will not have an adverse effect on end users. The environmental mission of the **U.S. Army Corps of Engineers** includes a duty to restore degraded ecosystems, construct sustainable facilities, regulate waterways, manage natural resources, and clean up contaminated sites from past military activities. In addition, states and local governments may have their own administrative agencies to provide oversight on environmental matters.

Legislation

Comprehensive Environmental Response, Compensation, and Liability Act (CERCLA)

A 1980 law also known as "Superfund," **CERCLA** authorized the EPA to clean up uncontrolled hazardous waste sites and force responsible parties to perform cleanups or reimburse the EPA for doing so. The law also seeks to prevent contamination of future sites by assigning liability to parties involved in some aspect of the contamination at the site. The principal federal agency involved with its enforcement is the EPA, which coordinates its work with the Army Corps of Engineers, other relevant federal land agencies, and state and local environmental agencies.

One of two possible responses follows identification of a hazardous waste site by the EPA. The first response is to remove the waste; this approach is used to handle emergency oil spills or chemical releases. **Removal actions** focus on eliminating immediate risks and ensuring public safety. The second response is remedial action, which involves management over the long term of complex contamination sites. **Remedial actions** manage releases that do not pose urgent threats to public health or the environment and do not require immediate action. Given the complexity of remedial actions, several years are often required to study the problem, develop a permanent solution, and clean up the hazardous waste.

CERCLA Liability

Through a broad definition of "hazardous substance" liability attaches to many parties. CERCLA is a strict liability law; that is, liability can be imposed upon a person for a release of hazardous substances even if that person was neither negligent nor the cause of the release. Moreover, liability may be imposed upon a party for land use operations that were lawful at the time they took place. Each party involved may be responsible for the entire cleanup. Prior federal decisions have held that since the waste continues to cause problems, the statute is not a punishment but rather a reimbursement obligation.

Who Can Be Found Liable? Potentially Responsible Parties (PRPs)

The law establishes expansive liability for many parties, including:

- *Current owners and operators of a contaminated site.* Current owners are liable even if they made no contribution to the hazardous release. Landowners who purchase a contaminated site and were aware of the condition at the time of purchase have been found liable for cleanup. This rule does not extend liability to lenders who finance the purchase of the property.
- *Past owners and operators of a contaminated site at time the pollution occurred.* These individuals will be held liable as well for any release of a toxic substance that occurred during their possession or control of the land.
- *Arrangers.* These are persons who arranged for disposal of a hazardous substance at a site.

The Comprehensive Environmental Response, Compensation, and Liability Act (CERCLA)
This law authorizes the EPA to clean up uncontrolled hazardous waste sites and force responsible parties to perform cleanups or reimburse the EPA for doing so.

Removal actions
Actions eliminating immediate risks of uncontrolled hazardous waste sites to ensure public safety.

Remedial actions
Long-term actions used to clean up sites that do not pose immediate risks to public health.

Potentially responsible party (PRP)
A party liable for the cleanup of a hazardous waste site.

■ *Transporters.* Transporters are responsible for having transported a hazardous substance to the site.

In the following case, the EPA attempted to hold a seller of toxic chemicals liable under CERCLA as an arranger.

CASE 22.1

KNOWLEDGE OF CONTINUING SPILLS WITHOUT TAKING INTENTIONAL STEPS TO DISPOSE OF HAZARDOUS WASTE DOES NOT RESULT IN ARRANGER LIABILITY

BURLINGTON NORTHERN AND SANTA FE RAILWAY COMPANY v. UNITED STATES

556 U.S. 599 (2009)

United States Supreme Court

In 1960, Brown & Bryant, Inc. ("B&B") began operating an agricultural chemical distribution business in Arvin, California. B&B later expanded onto an adjacent parcel of land owned by Burlington Northern and Santa Fe Railway Company and Union Pacific Railroad Company ("Railroads"). B&B purchased and stored various hazardous chemicals on its site, which it purchased from Shell Oil Company ("Shell"). That seller relationship to the operator, the EPA argued, made Shell an arranger and liable under CERCLA. At that time, the law was unclear as to the definition of what made someone liable as an arranger. Over time the hazardous chemicals seeped into the groundwater leading to significant soil and ground water contamination. Many of these chemical spills occurred due to equipment failures during transfer and delivery of the hazardous chemicals.

In 1989, the EPA and California's Department of Toxic Substances Control ("Agencies") exercised their CERCLA authority and spent over $8 million to clean up the site. To recover their costs, the Agencies initiated the lawsuit against Shell and the Railroads. The district court held in favor of the governments, finding both Shell and the Railroads were potentially responsible parties under CERCLA. The Railroads were held liable for 9 percent of the Governments' total response costs, and Shell was held liable for 6 percent. The Ninth Circuit Court of Appeals held that Shell as an arranger had responsibility for the disposal of hazardous substances, and it held further that Shell and the Railroads were jointly and severally liable for the Governments' clean-up costs. Shell and the Railroads appealed to the Supreme Court of the United States.

Language of the Court. *Because CERCLA does not specifically define what it means to "arrang[e] for" disposal of a hazardous substance, the phrase should be given its ordinary meaning. In common parlance, "arrange" implies action directed to a specific purpose. Thus, under the statute's plain language, an entity may qualify as an arranger when it takes intentional steps to dispose of a hazardous substance. To qualify as an arranger, Shell must have entered into hazardous waste sales with the intent that at least a portion of the product be disposed of during the transfer process by one or more of the statute's methods. The facts found by the District Court do not support such a conclusion. The evidence shows that Shell was aware that minor, accidental spills occurred during the hazardous waste transfer to B&B's storage tanks; however, it also reveals that Shell took numerous steps to encourage its distributors to reduce the likelihood of spills. Thus, Shell's mere knowledge of continuing spills and leaks is insufficient grounds for concluding that it "arranged for" hazardous waste disposal.*

The District Court reasonably apportioned the Railroads' share of the site remediation costs at 9 percent. Calculating liability based on three figures — the percentage of the total area of the facility that was owned by the Railroads, the duration of B&B's business divided by the term of the Railroads' lease, and the court's determination that only two polluting chemicals spilled on the leased parcel required remediation and that those chemicals were responsible for roughly two-thirds of the remediable site contamination — the District Court ultimately determined that the Railroads were responsible for 9 percent of the remediation costs. The District Court's detailed findings show that the primary pollution at the site was on a portion of the facility most distant from the Railroad parcel and that the hazardous-chemical spills on the Railroad parcel contributed to no more than 10 percent of the total site contamination, some of which did not require remediation. Moreover, although the evidence did not allow the District Court to calculate precisely the amount of hazardous chemicals contributed by the Railroad, the evidence showed that fewer spills occurred on the Railroad parcel and that not all of them crossed to the B&B site, where most of the contamination originated, thus supporting the conclusion that the parcel contributed only two chemicals in quantities requiring remediation.

Decision. The Supreme Court reversed the Ninth Circuit ruling holding that Shell was not an arranger under CERCLA and not liable for the contamination at the Arvin facility. It further concluded that the district court reasonably apportioned the Railroads' share of the site remediation costs at 9 percent.

FOCUS ON ETHICS

Is it ethical for Shell to escape liability because it only sold the toxic substances to the operator of the facility?

Environmental Assessments

Phase I Reports

Usually, in commercial transactions one party will obtain a Phase I Environmental Report (Phase I Report). Sometimes, these reports are known as "preliminary site assessments" and "environmental site surveys." A Phase I report provides potential or existing environmental contamination liability. In addition to site inspection by a consultant for visible evidence of signs of contamination, the report includes a review of available government lists of properties affected by toxic contamination; a review of historical documents, such as newspaper articles; and a review of the chain of title.

The decision to obtain a Phase I report is based upon the parties' knowledge about the prior history of the property's use and that of the surrounding area. Commercial lenders will require a Phase I Report, but in residential purchases, it will be the parties' decision (usually the buyer's) to obtain one.

> *Example:* If the presence of groundwater contamination on adjacent property was found, the Phase I consultant might recommend that groundwater samples be collected and tested from the property to be purchased. Similarly, asbestos samplings would be recommended if asbestos had been identified in the subject or surrounding properties.

Phase II Reports

When a Phase I report provides evidence of existence of toxic contamination, the buyer and lender will likely require a Phase II Report. In this phase, sampling and analysis of soils, groundwater, or both are performed. These tests are intended to confirm or disprove the existence of contamination disclosed in the Phase I report.

Remediation

If remediation of the subject property is required, governmental approval of the plan must be obtained. Remediation plans may include land use restrictions, which are recorded on the title to the property.

Effect upon the Parties

The risk of performing studies in advance is that the seller may have to disclose any problems found to potential buyers or a governmental agency or begin remediation sooner than desired. To avoid this risk, many sellers avoid obtaining a Phase I Report until the buyer is identified and an agreement signed.

CERCLA Defenses to Liability

To qualify for CERCLA's defenses, a prospective buyer must complete a Phase I Report consistent with the EPA's regulations requiring "all appropriate inquiries." In reviewing a Phase I Report, the buyer should consider the use of or development to be made on the property, as well as potential liability issues.

Among the most important defenses to the statute are the following four provisions of CERCLA, which may be invoked to avoid liability under CERCLA in real estate purchase and sale transactions. These are:

- *The third-party defense.* This defense applies when the landowner or PRP can show they exercised due care and that no contractual relationship existed with the third party who contaminated the property.
- *The innocent landowner defense.* Using this defense, landowners maintain they "undertook all appropriate inquiries" before purchasing the land and "had no actual or constructive knowledge" of the hazardous substance.
- *The "contiguous property owner" defense.* This defense is available to landowners who conducted all appropriate inquires and did not know that the groundwater underneath the property was contaminated by a release from an adjacent property. The landowner must have taken certain steps to show that it acted reasonably.
- *The "bona fide prospective purchaser" defense.* This defense is available if the disposal occurred before the landowner acquired the land, the landowner is not affiliated with the potentially responsible party, and the landowner has taken reasonable steps, outlined in the statute, to mitigate the contamination and cooperate with the authorities.

In addition, secured creditors may be protected from CERCLA liability. However, lenders still seek additional protections from the borrower in the form of an indemnification or other provisions. Lenders were exempted from liability as owners or operators of hazardous sites as a result of a 1996 amendment to CERCLA. This exemption will be lost if the lender "actually participate[s] in the management or operational affairs of a . . .facility."

Clean Air Act

The **Clean Air Act** was intended to protect public health and welfare from different types of air pollution caused by a variety of pollution sources. The Act's basic structure was established in 1970 to address shortcomings of earlier federal air pollution acts, and it was made subject to major revisions in 1977 and 1990. It is administered by the EPA, in coordination with state, local, and tribal governments.

The effect of this law, as amended, is to greatly expand the regulatory role of the EPA, requiring comprehensive federal and state regulations for both stationary (industrial) pollution sources and mobile sources. It also significantly expanded federal enforcement activities. The 1990 amendments addressed acid rain, ozone depletion, and toxic air pollution. It also established a national permitting program for stationary sources of air pollution.

Once intended to address common air pollution, such as dense, visible smog, the law now requires the EPA to establish national ambient air quality standards based on the latest science and requires states to adopt enforceable plans to achieve the standards. State plans also must control emissions that drift across state lines and harm air quality in downwind states. The law calls for new stationary sources to be built with the best available technology and allows less stringent standards for existing stationary sources.

Clean Air Act
An act intended to protect the public from different types of air pollution caused by a variety of pollution sources.

Hazardous Substance Laws and Regulations

Lead Paint

Lead is a highly toxic metal that was used for many years in products found in and around housing. Exposure causes such symptoms as abdominal pain, headaches, anemia, and, in severe cases, brain damage. Children, infants, and pregnant woman are more vulnerable to exposure as their growing bodies are more sensitive to the harmful effects lead exposure poses. Although banned for use in residential structures since 1978, lead-based paint is still present in millions of homes. It is often hidden under layers of new paint. Chipping or peeling lead-based paint creates a hazard.

Potential buyers and renters of property built before 1978 are required to receive certain information from the landlord, agent, or seller prior to becoming obligated to buy or rent. The purpose of this disclosure is to provide the potential buyer or renter an opportunity to conduct an independent inspection of the property. Federal law requires that individuals receive certain information before renting, buying, or renovating pre-1978 housing, including:

Lead
A highly toxic metal that was used for many years in products found in and around housing.

- ■ Sellers must disclose known information on lead-based paint or lead-based paint hazards before selling a house.
- ■ Real estate contracts must include a specific warning statement about lead-based paint.
- ■ Landlords must disclose known information on lead-based paint and lead-based paint hazards before leases take effect.

If lead-based paint is found by the tenant of a rental property, the tenant should immediately notify the landlord. If the landlord refuses to make repairs to minimize a tenant's exposure to lead, tenants can file complaints with local agencies. The following is an example from the EPA of such a disclosure form.

Disclosure of Information on Lead-Based Paint and/or Lead-Based Paint Hazards

Lead Warning Statement
Housing built before 1978 may contain lead-based paint. Lead from paint, paint chips, and dust can pose health hazards if not managed properly. Lead exposure is especially harmful to young children and pregnant women. Before renting pre-1978 housing, lessors must disclose the presence of known lead-based paint and/or lead-based paint hazards in the dwelling. Lessees must also receive a federally approved pamphlet on lead poisoning prevention.

Lessor's Disclosure

(a) Presence of lead-based paint and/or lead-based paint hazards (check (i) or (ii) below):

    (i) _____ Known lead-based paint and/or lead-based paint hazards are present in the housing (explain).

    _____

    _____

    (ii) _____ Lessor has no knowledge of lead-based paint and/or lead-based paint hazards in the housing.

(b) Records and reports available to the lessor (check (i) or (ii) below):

    (i) _____ Lessor has provided the lessee with all available records and reports pertaining to lead-based paint and/or lead-based paint hazards in the housing (list documents below).

    _____

    _____

    (ii) _____ Lessor has no reports or records pertaining to lead-based paint and/or lead-based paint hazards in the housing.

Lessee's Acknowledgment (initial)

(c) _____ Lessee has received copies of all information listed above.

(d) _____ Lessee has received the pamphlet *Protect Your Family from Lead in Your Home.*

Agent's Acknowledgment (initial)

(e) _____ Agent has informed the lessor of the lessor's obligations under 42 U.S.C. 4852d and is aware of his/her responsibility to ensure compliance.

Certification of Accuracy
The following parties have reviewed the information above and certify, to the best of their knowledge, that the information they have provided is true and accurate.

Lessor	Date	Lessor	Date
Lessee	Date	Lessee	Date
Agent	Date	Agent	Date

Exhibit 22.1. Lead-Based Paint Disclosure

Mold
A naturally occurring fungus that grows in warm, damp places and is spread by airborne spores.

Mold

Mold is a naturally occurring fungus that grows in warm, damp places and is spread by airborne spores. While there are thousands of types of mold, only a small fraction of them cause allergies or harm. Mold may affect indoor air quality, however, and exposure to mold can lead to a variety of different fungal infections and respiratory complications.

Mold is caused by high levels of humidity and excess condensation in a building, inadequate ventilation, or water intrusion through roofs, doors, and windows. Mold infestations are on the rise because buildings are increasingly tightly sealed for energy efficiency. Unfortunately, that prevents adequate ventilation to vent moisture to the exterior, facilitating the growth of mold. Many property insurers have excluded mold from their policy coverages.

Mold can be detected by stains or discolorations on walls and ceilings or through its noticeable scent. The presence of mold may sometimes be hidden, however, as the mold may be concealed behind walls, roofs, or carpeting.

In the following case, a contractor was held liable for creating conditions leading to a toxic mold infestation.

CASE 22.2

DEFECTIVE CONSTRUCTION MAY LEAD TO SUBSTANTIAL LIABILITY FROM TOXIC MOLD

CENTEX-ROONEY CONSTRUCTION CO., INC. v. MARTIN COUNTY

706 So. 2d 20 (1998)

Florida District Court of Appeal

Martin County ("County") commenced plans to construct its courthouse and constitutional office building in 1985. The plans and specifications for these buildings were completed in April 1987. The County entered into a construction management agreement with Centex-Rooney Construction, Inc. ("Centex"). Centex was the construction manager for the entire project.

Following the occupation of the courthouse in early 1989, the County began relaying several complaints to Centex regarding exterior walls and window leaks in the building as well as the presence of mold and high levels of humidity. Ultimately, Centex's own employees documented water infiltration through the building's exterior synthetic hardcoat systems (EIFS) due to defective installation, which resulted in mold growth. Investigations revealed problems with the building's heating, ventilation, and air-conditioning systems. The County received numerous complaints of health problems from the buildings' occupants as well as from visitors. The County experts tested the building and discovered the presence of two highly unusual toxigenic molds.

The County opted to evacuate the buildings in December 1992 and commenced efforts to remediate the presence of mold and excessive humidity in the buildings. During the remediation, it became apparent that 60 to 65 percent of the exterior walls of the building had visible mold growth. The County filed its lawsuit against Centex and was awarded $14,211,156 in damages. Centex appealed.

Language of the Court. *We find that the County presented sufficient evidence to meet its burden of proving that Centex's breach of its contractual responsibilities was a substantial factor in causing the County's extensive damages. First, the County proved that Centex's construction defects caused moisture problems in the buildings, resulting in extensive mold growth. Centex's own employees acknowledged that its subcontractors' defective installation of the EIFS system and windows led to extensive water infiltration and resultant mold growth. Second, the County established through expert testimony that, because of this moisture, the buildings were infested with two highly unusual toxic molds. Third, several experts attested to* the accepted scientific principle linking exposure to these two molds with health hazards. Fourth, the County established that the purpose of its ensuing remediation process was to remove the existing mold and prevent new mold growth by finding and correcting exterior wall and window leaks and other causes of excessive moisture and humidity. It was during this process that the County became aware of a myriad of previously unknown and serious structural and electrical defects, several of which contributed to the water infiltration and resulting mold infestation. Finally, the County demonstrated that these defects, caused by Centex's subcontractors, expanded the scope of the remediation process, thereby justifying the increased costs for redesign, repair, reconstruction, and relocation. Based on the foregoing, we find that the County established Centex's liability by proving that its breach of the construction management agreement was a substantial factor in causing the County's significant damages.

Decision. The court of appeal affirmed the award of damages in favor of the County.

FOCUS ON ETHICS

Given the findings of fact, was it ethical for Centex to attempt to avoid liability by its appeal?

Asbestos

Asbestos
A mineral fiber historically used in construction that is a known carcinogen causing cancer and various respiratory ailments.

Asbestos is a mineral fiber that occurs naturally in rock and soil. In the past, asbestos was frequently used in construction due to its versatility, heat resistance, and insulation capabilities. It was commonly found in many building materials, such as ceiling and floor tiles, as well as different forms of insulation.

In the 1970s the EPA began to ban asbestos-containing materials in construction. Today, asbestos is known as a carcinogen that causes asbestosis, mesothelioma, and lung cancer. Exposure to asbestos generally occurs when the asbestos-containing material is disturbed or damaged, which results in the release of asbestos fibers into the air. Prolonged exposure to asbestos can lead to serious illnesses and death.

Asbestos still appears in many buildings and products. It is not easy to determine if asbestos is present in property unless the materials are labeled. To reduce the risk of asbestos exposure, the EPA suggests having a property inspected by a trained and accredited asbestos professional for asbestos-containing material. An incorrectly performed inspection can be more hazardous than leaving the material undisturbed. Asbestos-containing material that is not damaged or disturbed should be left alone, as it is unlikely to pose any health risk.

When damaged asbestos-containing material is present in a structure, the owner has two remedies. The first option is encapsulation, which involves treating the material with a sealant that coats it, preventing release of the asbestos fibers. Another option is removal of the asbestos-containing material. Both remedies should only be performed by a trained and accredited professional, as improper removal or repair could increase the risk of asbestos exposure.

Many states require sellers to reveal the presence of asbestos in their properties on disclosure forms they supply to potential buyers. When a seller knows asbestos is present in their property but fails to make the appropriate disclosures to the buyer, the seller may be found liable to the buyer for damages suffered as result of the asbestos exposure. Many states extend this disclosure to landlords and hold landlords liable under the implied warranty of habitability for the presence of asbestos.

Sick Building Syndrome

Sick building syndrome is a general term used to describe a range of health problems caused by exposure to airborne toxins, air pollutants, and other irritants within a building when a specific source for the resulting health problems cannot be identified. The symptoms of sick building syndrome may include headache, nausea, dizziness, fatigue, and eye and skin irritations. Often these conditions are temporary, but they may cause long-term impairments to the nervous system or even cancer.

The cause of sick building syndrome has been blamed on inadequate air circulation systems, as well as chemical and biological contaminants found in carpet fibers, adhesives, and wall coverings. A study by the World Health Organization reported that up to 30 percent of new and renovated buildings worldwide generate excessive complaints related to indoor air quality. Like mold, instances of sick building syndrome can be attributed to the excessive sealing of buildings, which prevents the building from receiving adequate ventilation.

Several steps can be taken to solve or mitigate the effects of sick building syndrome. A visual inspection and a consultation with the occupant is necessary to identify the cause of the complaints and determine the most appropriate corrective actions. Inspection of the building alone may not provide the information necessary for the inspector to make a determination on the cause of the issues. Based on the potential cause, the investigator may respond in one or more ways, including:

- *Remove or modify source of pollution.* This may entail the periodic cleaning and replacement of HVAC system filters, replacement of water-stained ceiling tiles and carpets, and proper venting of emissions to the outdoors.
- *Increase ventilation and air distribution of HVAC systems.* This is a cost-effective means of reducing indoor pollutant levels. The HVAC systems should be operated to meet ventilation standards, or higher standards, to prevent sick building syndrome.
- *Clean the air.* High performance air filters should be used to capture the smaller, respirable particles not effectively captured by typical furnace filters.
- *Educate and communicate.* Building occupants, management, and maintenance personnel, if given adequate knowledge of and education about the problems, can help prevent reoccurrences.

Sick building syndrome
A term used to describe a range of health problems caused by exposure to pollutants within a building when a specific source cannot be identified.

Radon

One type of indoor air pollutant is radon. **Radon,** formed by the natural decay of radium, is a naturally occurring radioactive gas found in nearly all soils. As it radiates into a building, however, serious health problems may result. Radon is estimated to cause thousands of deaths each year.

Radon penetrates buildings through cracks or holes in the foundation. Once inside, buildings trap the radon, allowing potentially lethal levels to accumulate. The areas with the highest potential radon levels are predominately found in the Midwest and some parts of the East Coast, which contain geological formations that yield high radon levels.

Radon
A naturally occurring radioactive gas found in nearly all soils that travels through cracks in foundations of homes and causes lung cancer.

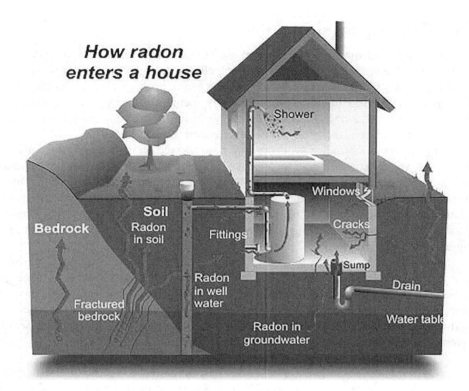

FIGURE 22.1. How Radon Enters a Home
Source: U.S. Environmental Protection Agency

Radon cannot be seen or smelled, and the only way to know the level of exposure is to test for radon inside the building. Exposure to radon is one of the leading causes of lung cancer, and it is the leading cause of lung cancer among nonsmokers. The EPA suggests that a structure be tested for radon before it is marketed for sale.

A buyer has the right to ask that a home be tested if a test has not been conducted in the last two years. The test must be conducted at the lowest living level of the home.

Example: If the buyer will be using a basement regularly, the radon test must be conducted in the basement.

If the test reveals a high level of radon, many different mitigation methods can be used, such as installation of ventilation systems and sealing cracks in the foundation. New homes can be built using radon-resistant construction techniques effective in preventing radon entry. When installed properly, these techniques help reduce indoor radon levels in homes. However, even homes built with radon-resistant techniques require periodic testing.

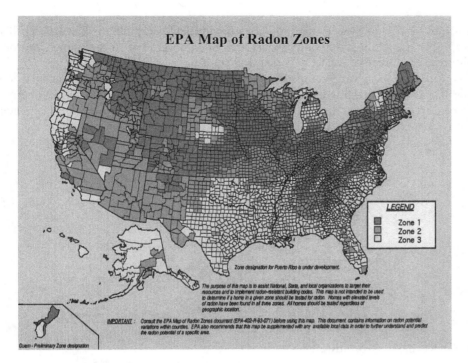

FIGURE 22.2. Radon Map
Source: U.S. Environmental Protection Agency

Carbon Monoxide

Carbon monoxide (CO) is an odorless, colorless, toxic gas. These characteristics make CO extremely dangerous. Exposure to CO can inhibit a person's ability to inhale oxygen. Exposure may result in symptoms such as headaches, dizziness, nausea, confusion, impaired vision, and poor coordination. CO poisoning can lead to death.

To reduce the risk of CO poisoning, every home should have carbon monoxide detectors on each level outside each sleeping area. These detectors should be replaced every five years. Most states have carbon monoxide detector requirements requiring installation in all single-family homes. Additionally, periodic inspection of all fuel-burning appliances, such as stoves, furnaces, fireplaces, and water heaters, is suggested.

Carbon monoxide (CO)
An odorless, colorless, toxic gas.

Water Pollution Laws and Regulations

Groundwater

Half of the United States' drinking water comes from groundwater. **Groundwater** is water found under the earth's surface. Most groundwater comes from rain and melting snow that soaks into the ground. This water fills the spaces between rocks and soils and forms the water table. Groundwater's depth below the surface, quality, and likelihood of being polluted varies from place to place. Groundwater may become polluted naturally as water moves through underground rocks and soil picking up traces of magnesium,

Groundwater
Water found under the earth's surface as a result of rain and melting snow.

calcium, and chlorides. It may also be contaminated by human activities, such as improper use and disposal of fertilizers, leaking underground storage tanks, improper disposal or storage of waste, and chemical spills.

Although the Clean Water Act and the Safe Drinking Water Act (discussed below) has provisions protecting groundwater quality, groundwater quality is primarily regulated at the local and state level. Local and state governments typically provide regulations that exceed federal requirements and address specific local conditions.

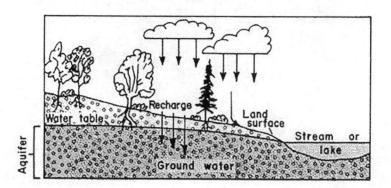

FIGURE 22.3. Groundwater

Source: U.S. Geological Survey, Department of the Interior/USGS, U.S. Geological Survey.

The Safe Drinking Water Act

Most groundwater in the United States is safe for human use. However, contaminated groundwater has been found in every state. To provide safe drinking water to all Americans, Congress passed The **Safe Drinking Water Act** (SDWA) in 1974 and amended it in 1988 and 1996. The SDWA authorizes the EPA to set national health-based standards for drinking water to protect against naturally occurring and man-made contaminants.

The law only regulates public water systems. **Public water systems** are those with at least 15 service connections or that serve at least 25 people. **Private wells**, which serve fewer than 25 individuals, are not regulated by the SDWA. The law focuses not only on the treatment of water to make it safe for consumption, it also provides source water protection and funding for water system improvements and enforces standards.

The responsibility for making sure public water systems provide safe drinking water is divided among the EPA, states, water systems, and the public. The EPA sets national standards for drinking water to protect against health risks. These standards each include requirements that water systems test for contaminants in the water to ensure the standard is achieved. The EPA also provides guidance, assistance, and public information about drinking water; collects drinking water data; and oversees state drinking water programs.

The most direct oversight of drinking water quality is conducted by each state's drinking water program. States can apply to the EPA for the authority to implement the SDWA in their jurisdiction, so long as they can show that the state will adopt standards at least as stringent as the EPA's and will ensure the water system meets these standards. All states and territories, except Wyoming and the District of Columbia, have been

Safe Drinking Water Act (SDWA)
An Act authorizing the EPA to set national health-based standards for drinking water found in public water systems.

Public water systems
Water systems with at least 15 service connections or serving at least 25 people.

Private wells
Wells serving fewer than 25 people.

granted authority. The states make sure water systems test for contaminants, review plans for water system improvements, conduct onsite inspections, and take action against water systems not meeting standards.

Multiple barriers against pollution are set up by the SDWA to ensure that drinking water is safe. Public water systems are responsible for ensuring that contaminants in tap water do not exceed the standards set by the EPA. A water supplier agency must test its water and report its results to the state. If a water system is not meeting these standards, it is the water supplier's responsibility to notify its customers.

These national drinking water standards are legally enforceable, which means that both the EPA and states can take action against water systems not meeting safety standards. The EPA and the states may issue administrative orders, take legal actions, or fine utilities.

Clean Water Act

The **Clean Water Act** (CWA) became law in 1948 as the first major U.S. law to address water pollution. It was significantly reorganized and expanded in 1972 and has been revised and modified since. The CWA establishes the basic structure for regulating discharges of pollutants into the waters of the United States and regulates the quality standards of surface waters. The CWA also assists businesses, federal facilities, and local governments by providing them with tools to help meet environmental regulatory requirements.

Since its enactment, the CWA has implemented pollution control programs and made it unlawful to discharge any pollutant into navigable waters without a permit. All point sources that discharge pollution into surface water are required to obtain a discharge permit from the National Pollution Discharge Elimination System (NPDES). The EPA works closely with state agencies to implement this system. A **point source** is pollution originating from a discernible, specific discharge point. The NPDES does not require permits for a nonpoint source of pollution. **Nonpoint sources** of pollution originate from many sources. The permit requires public hearings as well as approval from the EPA and state.

> *Example:* A point source includes a pipe, conduit, factory, or municipal wastewater treatment plant that discharges pollution, while a nonpoint source of pollution would include runoff, rainfall, or snowmelt.

When issuing a permit, the NPDES will impose restrictions and requirements on the permit holder. These limitations are based on the type of pollutant, the business industry of the discharger, the characteristics of the local watershed, and whether the discharge is from a new or existing source.

Solid Waste Disposal and Brownfield Sites

A **waste disposal site** is an area of land designated for the proper disposal of discarded or discharged material. Waste disposal sites can be of several types, with the classification of the site dependent on the type of waste disposed there.

Clean Water Act (CWA)
A statute enacted to address water pollution in the U.S.

Point source
A discernible, specific discharge point of pollution into surface waters.

Nonpoint source
A source of pollution originating from many sources.

Waste disposal site
An area of land designated for the proper disposition of discarded or discharged materials.

Landfill

Nearly everything humans do leaves behind some type of waste. In the United States, most solid waste is disposed of in landfills. A **landfill** consists of a large cavity or depression in the ground that is lined with a clay or synthetic liner to prevent any waste from leaking into the ground or water supply. Effective landfill management is important, as hazardous waste from a landfill may seep into the groundwater or release pollution into the atmosphere.

Structure of a Landfill

Landfills must include drainage systems to remove rain water that filters through the landfill waste. When water comes in contact with the buried waste, it transports chemicals in the waste to discharge points.

After waste is deposited in the landfill, a layer of topsoil is placed on top to compact the waste. This process of layering continues until the landfill is full, at which time it will be capped. **Capping** involves laying soil and grass on the top of the site to prevent erosion and improve aesthetics.

The decomposing waste creates a natural gas called methane that can be dangerous due to its explosive tendencies. To ensure these gases are not trapped in the landfill, a ventilation pipe extends from the landfill's base to collected them. The collected methane gas is used as fuel to generate electricity. These sites are monitored long the landfill closes to ensure the quality of the groundwater and proper handling of methane gas.

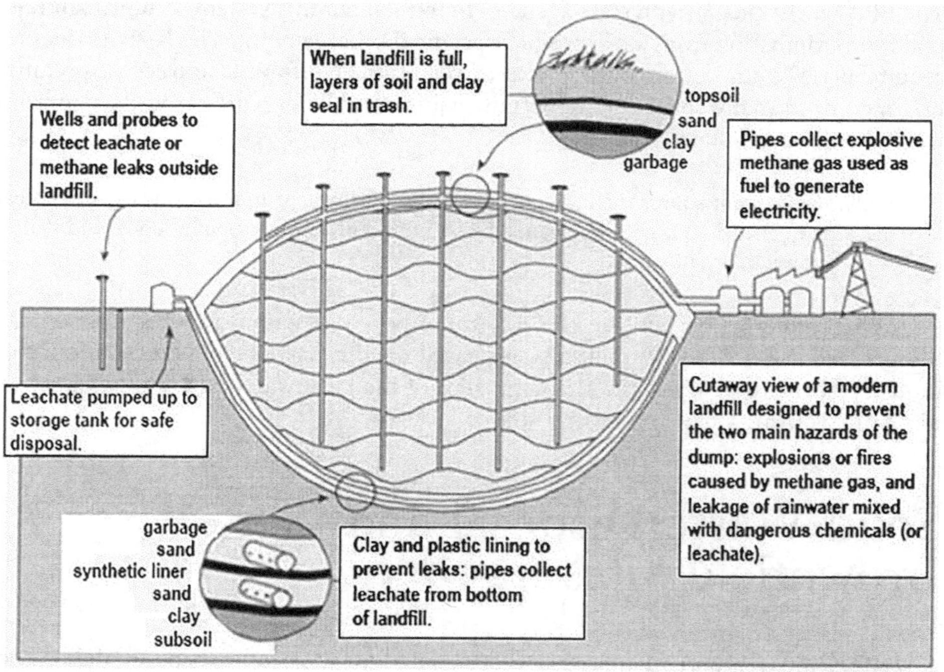

Landfill
A large cavity in the ground lined with a clay or synthetic liner to prevent waste from leaking into the ground or water supply.

Capping
The act of laying soil and grass on top of a landfill or waste disposal site to prevent erosion and improve aesthetics.

FIGURE 22.4. Landfill
Source: U.S. Environmental Protection Agency.

Location of Landfills

People do not want landfills near their residences or places of business because of potential health issues and the negative effect on property values. It is important that landfills are located, designed, and monitored in accordance with federal regulations.

Types of Landfills

Municipal Solid Waste Landfills (MSWLFs) are the most common type of landfills. MSWLFs are specifically designed to receive household waste and other types of nonhazardous material. Industrial waste landfills are designed to collect nonhazardous commercial and industrial waste, such as constructional materials. Hazardous waste landfills are facilities used specifically for the disposal of hazardous waste, and they are not used for the disposal of solid waste. These hazardous waste disposal sites are subject to stricter state and federal regulations than MSWLFs or industrial waste landfills, to minimize the risk of an accidental release of hazardous waste into the environment.

Brownfields

Brownfields are abandoned, idled, or underused properties where the presence of hazardous substances, pollutants, or contaminants has impeded redevelopment of the sites. These sites include abandoned factories and other industrial facilities, such as gas stations, oil storage facilities, dry cleaning establishments, and other businesses that handle or store hazardous substances. It is estimated that as many as 425,000 brownfields exist throughout the United States.

Brownfields
Abandoned, idled, or underused properties where the presence of hazardous substances, pollutants, or contaminants has impaired redevelopment of the sites.

An unintended consequence of CERCLA was that developers refuse to purchase and attempt to clean brownfields for fear of assuming responsibility to clean up the site. To overcome this, an amendment to CERCLA was added to protect developers and encourage them to clean up brownfields. This provision protects a bona fide prospective purchaser so long as they do not impede the performance of a response action or natural resource restoration.

The Small Business Liability Relief and Brownfields Revitalization Act was enacted to provide tools for the public and private sectors to support sustainable cleanup and reuse of brownfields. Historically, the owner or operator of the contaminated property would be held responsible for the property's cleanup. After its enactment, the act may provide a defense to CERCLA liability. Entities acquiring property and having no knowledge of the contamination at the time of purchase may be deemed innocent landowners if they made the appropriate inquiries prior to purchase. Therefore, a purchaser who did not cause or contribute to the presence of hazard substances or contaminates will not be liable for the cleanup.

According to the EPA, the brownfields projects have been very successful in revitalizing these contaminated areas. Tens of thousands of properties are enrolled in the program annually, and cleanup efforts have resulted in over 1,000,000 acres of land ready for reuse.

The positive impact of the brownfields project extends beyond environmental improvements. Another EPA study found that residential property values increased between 5 and 15.2 percent once a nearby brownfield was assessed or cleaned up. Preliminary studies have indicated a reduction in crime in these newly revitalized areas.

Underground Storage Tanks (USTs)

Underground storage tank system (UST)
A tank and any piping that has at least 10 percent of its combined volume underground.

An **underground storage tank system** (UST) is a tank and any piping connected to the tank that has at least 10 percent of its combined volume underground. Most USTs in the United States store gasoline. The danger associated with USTs is the likelihood that the tanks will leak contents into the environment.

While many leaks occur due to corrosion of the tank lining, improper installation or maintenance procedures of USTs may also cause leaks to develop. The greatest potential hazard occurs when a UST leaks petroleum or other hazardous substances and contaminates the groundwater. Tanks used to store either petroleum or certain hazardous materials are the only tanks required to comply with the federal UST regulations. These USTs are found in a variety of commercial and industrial settings as well as on military bases and at airports.

The EPA has recognized that state and local governments are in the best position to oversee USTs. Thus, regulations may vary from state to state, with some states having more stringent regulations than the federal government requirements. In an effort to remedy the potential risks associated with leaking USTs, the majority of states have instituted UST cleanup funds. These funds promote expedited cleanups and provide reimbursement to owners who undertake the cleanup process.

Key Terms and Concepts

- Environmental Protection Agency, page 564
- U.S. Department of Housing and Urban Development, page 564
- U.S. Army Corps of Engineers, page 564
- The Comprehensive Environmental Response, Compensation, and Liability Act (CERCLA), page 565
- Removal action, page 565
- Remedial action, page 565
- Potentially responsible party (PRP), page 565
- Clean Air Act, page 569
- Lead, page 569
- Mold, page 570
- Asbestos, page 572
- Sick building syndrome, page 573
- Radon, page 573
- Carbon monoxide (CO), page 575
- Groundwater, page 575
- The Safe Drinking Water Act (SDWA), page 576
- Public water system, page 576
- Private wells, page 576
- Clean Water Act (CWA), page 577
- Point source, page 577
- Nonpoint source, page 577
- Waste disposal site, page 577
- Landfill, page 578
- Capping, page 578
- Brownfields, page 579
- Underground storage tank system (UST), page 580

Chapter Summary

- Real estate professionals should be aware of federal and state environmental laws and of the regulatory agencies responsible for enforcing them.

- The federal government has established several administrative agencies to enforce environmental laws and regulations. Key environmental administrative agencies include: (1) the Environmental Protection Agency, (2) the U.S. Department of Housing and Urban Development, and (3) the U.S. Army Corps of Engineers.

- The Environmental Protection Agency is a federal agency established in 1970 to address pollution and hazardous wastes.

- The U.S. Department of Housing and Urban Development protects the environmental health and safety of the country's citizens.

- The U.S. Army Corps of Engineers' environmental mission includes a duty to restore degraded ecosystems, construct sustainable facilities, regulate waterways, manage natural resources, and clean up contaminated sites from past military activities.

- CERCLA authorizes the EPA to clean up uncontrolled hazardous waste sites and force responsible parties to perform cleanups or to reimburse the EPA for doing so.

- CERCLA is a strict liability law; that is, liability can be imposed upon a person for a release of hazardous substances even if that person was neither negligent nor the cause of the release.

- The Clean Air Act was intended to protect public health and welfare from different types of air pollution caused by a variety of pollution sources.

- Lead is a highly toxic metal that was used for many years in products found in and around housing. Exposure causes such symptoms as abdominal pain, headaches, anemia, and, in severe cases, brain damage.

- Mold is a naturally occurring fungus that grows in warm, damp places and is spread by airborne spores. Mold may affect indoor air quality, and exposure to mold can lead to a variety of fungal infections and respiratory complications.

- Asbestos is a mineral fiber occurring naturally in rock and soil. In the past, asbestos was frequently used in construction due to its versatility, heat resistance, and insulation capabilities.

- Sick building syndrome is a general term used to describe a range of health problems caused by exposure to airborne toxins, air pollutants, and other irritants in a building when a specific source for the health problems cannot be identified.

- Radon is a naturally occurring radioactive gas found in nearly all soils. Radon is emitted as a result of the natural decay of radium found within the soil.

- Carbon monoxide is an odorless, colorless, toxic gas. Exposure can inhibit a person's ability to inhale oxygen leading to symptoms such as headaches, dizziness, nausea, confusion, impaired vision, and poor coordination.

- Groundwater is water found under the earth's surface. Most groundwater comes from rain and melting snow that soaks into the ground.

- The Safe Drinking Water Act authorizes the EPA to set national health-based standards for drinking water to protect against naturally occurring and man-made contaminants.

- The Clean Water Act took effect in 1948 as the first major U.S. law to address water pollution.

- A waste disposal site is an area of land designated for the proper disposal of discarded or discharged material.

- Brownfields are abandoned, idled, or underused properties where the presence of hazardous substances, pollutants, or contaminants impedes redevelopment.

- An underground storage tank system is consists of a tank and any piping connected to it that has at least 10 percent of its combined volume underground.

Chapter Problems and Assignments

1. List the key federal administrative agencies responsible for enforcing environmental laws and regulations.

2. Distinguish between a Phase I and a Phase II environmental report.

3. Which of the following may be considered a Potentially Responsible Party under CERCLA:

   a. A transporter of a hazardous substance from one location to another
   b. The employee who arranged for the treatment or disposal of hazardous substances
   c. The former owner or operator of a facility at the time the hazardous substances were disposed of
   d. The current owner of operator of a facility

4. Braxton purchases commercial property adjacent to vacant land. Braxton had a Phase I environmental report performed that did not disclose the presence of any environmental hazards. Based on the Phase I report findings, Braxton did not order a Phase II report. After purchasing the property, hazardous waste was discovered beneath Braxton's property. The substances seeped in from the adjacent vacant site, which a few businesses had used as an illegal dumping site for hazardous substances. Does Braxton have a defense to liability under CERCLA for the presence of the hazardous waste? If so, explain it.

5. What is radon, and what makes it so dangerous?

6. Why has the presence of mold become increasingly problematic in residential and commercial buildings throughout the United States?

7. Discuss what remedies may be pursued when asbestos has been found within a structure. What if any risks are associated with these remedies?

8. Do you think the CERCLA Brownfields Program is needed? Conduct Internet research to identify such sites near where you live.

9. Research your state law on underground storage tanks. Determine if the laws of your state are more or less stringent than the requirements under the federal regulations discussed in this chapter.

10. Research your state law to determine if your state requires a seller to disclose to a buyer the presence of asbestos on the property.

Appendix

Answers to Chapter Exercises/Problems and Assignments

Chapter 1

1. Classify the property as either real or personal and as either tangible or intangible property.
    a. A single family home would be considered real, tangible property.
    b. A sofa is personal, tangible property.
    c. An air conditioning unit is real, tangible property.
    d. States vary on whether they treat mobile homes as personal or real property.
    e. A solar easement constitutes real, intangible property.
    f. Gas deposits are tangible, real property.
    g. Oil deposits themselves are tangible, while the right to come onto the land to harvest them is intangible. Likewise, once captured they become personal property.
2. Rank in order of priority the following sources of real estate law: d, a, c, b.
3. The natural rights doctrine sets forth certain rights to be inalienable, which protects an individual's rights regardless of whether there is a law enacted by the government or not. However, under the creation of law doctrine there is no particular property right unless granted by a law. Both doctrines determine the ways in which a property is owned and used.
4. Preemption
5. Ming has two options when deciding where she should file her claim against Amrit. First, Ming could ask the court to invoke *in personam* jurisdiction over Amrit by filing her claim in a New York court. This is because Amrit is present in New York. This claim should be filed in federal court because the amount in controversy exceeds $75,000 and the parties are of diverse citizenship. Ming could also file her claim in Florida federal court because the property at issue is located in Florida; this grants the Florida courts *in rem* jurisdiction over the dispute.
6. No. They do not meet the amount in controversy necessary to file in federal court. Construction R' Us is claiming $70,000 in damages, but they need to claim at least $75,000 to file in federal court. Additionally, the party they are suing would need to be a citizen of another state because the federal court also requires the parties to be diverse.
7. The trespasser's defense will be that the statute of limitations has run and therefore she cannot bring her claim of trespass.

8. The key distinctions between mediation and arbitration are that mediation is an informal process, mediators do not make factual decisions regarding liability, and mediation settlements are voluntary, while in arbitration, the arbitrator makes a finding of fact and the process is more formal. Further, if a binding arbitration decision is chosen, the decision must be enforced.
9. Calvin will need to formally petition the Supreme Court through a petition for writ of certiorari. A minimum of four of the nine justices must agree to review the case; if this occurs, the court issues a writ of certiorari and hears the case. If a writ of certiorari is denied by the Supreme Court, the decision of the lower court remains unaffected.
10. *Answers will vary.*

Chapter 2

Exercises

2.1

1. Nuisance — could be either private or public depending on how many properties are affected
2. Trespass
3. Trespass
4. Nuisance — private
5. Trespass
6. Nuisance — public
7. Nuisance — private
8. Nuisance — private
9. Trespass
10. Trespass

2.2

1. Invitee
2. Licensee
3. Licensee
4. Licensee
5. Licensee
6. Invitee
7. Invitee
8. Trespasser

Chapter Problems and Assignments

1. Yes, it is highly likely that a court would find a partially constructed home to be an attractive nuisance, especially if the construction site has various heavy equipment and unstable surfaces to climb. Owners or contractors should do their best to prevent entrance to the construction site and post warnings in order to reduce liability.
2. The oil belongs to Bruno. Under either the ownership or the non-ownership doctrine, Bruno owns the gas because he was the first to capture it.

3. Tao is liable for the damages because his excavation for his pool has resulted in the loss of lateral support for Abi's property. Since landowners are strictly liable for damages to a neighboring property, it does not matter that the excavation was reasonably performed by professionals.

4. *Answers will vary.*

5. Yes, Bonnie has a claim against Fracking, Inc. for a private nuisance because they are affecting her use and enjoyment of her property and she is the only party affected.

6. No; the only duty to Robert that Ines has is a duty to not intentionally injure. Here, there is no indication Ines was trying to injury Robert, as Ines even posted signs warning of the contaminated water.

7. It would depend upon how many farmers are seeking relief. If the group is small, the sulfur dioxide would constitute a private nuisance, and they could seek both monetary damages and an injunction. If the group of affected farmers is large, then this would constitute a public nuisance and the remedy would be limited to an injunction.

8. *Answers will vary.*

9. Yes, under these circumstances Miguel is considered an invitee as he either received an invitation to enter or remain on the property by participating in the sleep study. Therefore, the medical office building owes Miguel the duty to reasonably inspect and discover nonobvious or hidden dangerous conditions and warn against or make safe those conditions.

10. It is unnecessary because the right to exclude others from property is one of the most fundamental rights of property ownership, therefore, their intent to enter the property is not required because this would not allow landowners to properly protect their interest in their property. *As to fairness, answers will vary.*

Chapter 3

Exercise

3.1

1. License
2. Profit
3. License
4. Profit
5. Easement

Problems and Assignments

1. An affirmative easement allows the holder of the easement to use the land of another, while a negative easement prevents the servient tenement from using the land in a particular way.

2. Kyle would want the easement to be appurtenant because this way if Xavier moves, the person who buys Xavier's property will be bound by the easement. An easement in gross does not run with the land, so the subsequent purchaser is not subject to the easement limitations.

3. Chance's interest would constitute a license.
4. The four elements of an easement by necessity are:
   a. Unity of ownership of the dominant and servient estates prior to the division of the property.
   b. Severance or a division and transfer of one of the estates to another person.
   c. The easement is strictly and absolutely necessary for the benefit of either parcel.
   d. A continuing strict or absolute necessity for an easement.
5. Necessity/appurtenant
6. The purchaser of Damion's property will now have an easement appurtenant.
7. Ricardo should obtain an easement by implication because it will allow him to continue accessing the beach even though the property is being divided into two parcels. Additionally, the easement will be permanent and continue even if the easement is no longer needed, so long as the easement was reasonably necessary at the time the property was divided.
8. This is likely due to the certainty that can be provided to future property owners.
9. An easement allows the possessor of the dominant tenement to have an ownership interest, while a license provides the holder with no ownership interest.
10. One answer could be that a landowner would know that others will be similarly restricted and therefore she can protect her property interests and values accordingly. *Other answers may vary.*

Chapter 4

Exercises

4.1

1. Trade fixture
2. Personal property. The key word here is "hanging," which implies the piece of art is easily removable and not permanently fixed to the wall.
3. Fixture
4. Trade fixture if installed by the lessee for the purpose of conducting business. If installed by lessor they would be considered fixtures.
5. Fixture
6. Fixture
7. Trade fixture
8. Fixture
9. Personal property if the fridge is a standalone. However, if the fridge is built in it could be considered a fixture.
10. Fixture

4.2

1. BigMart would have priority because they possess a purchase money security interest.
2. Second Bank would have priority. Chris obtained possession of the dishwasher on November 1 and BigMart failed to timely file its financing statement.
3. BigMart, as a perfected PMSI, would still have priority. First Bank, having recorded its mortgage before Second Bank, would have priority over Second Bank.

Chapter Problems and Assignments

1. The bar installed by Haru would not be considered a fixture because the parties agreed that Haru would take it with him when he moved. When the parties have expressly agreed to the character of the property, this intention often controls whether the property is a fixture.

2. Carmen will be able to take all of these items with her when her lease expires because they are considered trade fixtures.

3. Yes, Bill is entitled to harvest the sweet corn as this is a *fructus industriales* attachment. This means that the corn was produced by human effort. A tenant who grows *fructus industriales* is entitled to the crop's harvest; this is known as an emblements.

4. In order to create a valid security interest, all of the following must occur:
   a. A written agreement recognizing the security interest is in the possession of the secured party;
   b. The value is given to the debtor; and
   c. The debtor must have rights in the collateral.

5. Banco would be paid first because this loan was secured by Hanna's home as collateral and they secured their interest first. Lendco would be paid next because this loan is secured by Hanna's car as collateral. Loanco would be paid last because they are an unsecured creditor. It does not matter that Loanco loaned money to Hanna before Lendco, because Lendco's interest is secured and Loanco's is not.

6. Banco and Lendco would want to foreclose or enforce the right to repossess the collateral so they could sell it to repay the loans given to Hanna. Loanco's loan is not attached to any collateral, therefore they would likely file a claim against Hanna and attempt to recover the debt due through a judgement.

7. Alpha, because their interest is secured and perfected, which gives them priority over the bank.

8. *Answers will vary.*

9. *Answers will vary.*

10. *Answers will vary.*

Chapter 5

Exercises

5.1

1. This is a fee simple absolute, with A possessing the present and future interest.

2. This is a fee simple determinable, with A possessing a fee simple so long as the property is used for commercial purposes. O possesses a possibility of reverter in fee simple. If the property ceases to be used for commercial purposes, the reversion to O is automatic.

3. The "provided that" language signals a fee simple determinable. A has a fee simple interest so long as the property is utilized for education purposes. O possesses a possibility of reverter in FSA. If the property ceases to be utilized for education purposes, it will automatically revert back to O.

4. The "on the condition that" language in reference to the consumption of alcohol signals a fee simple subject to a condition subsequent. A possesses a fee simple until

such time as (a) the alcohol prohibition is violated, and (b) the holder of the right of reentry (power of termination) chooses to exercise that right. While O possesses the right of reentry, the property does not automatically revert. Even if the condition is violated, A would continue to maintain her interest in Blackacre until O exercises the right of reentry.

5. The interest created here is a fee simple determinable. The language "for the time that" is not a condition subsequent that could destroy the interest but a condition required to maintain the interest. The present interest is the fee simple, which A possesses so long as the land is used for a football stadium. O possesses a future interest of a possibility of reverter in FSA

5.2

1. Present interest is a life estate in A, measured by A's life. B has a vested remainder in FSA. The remainder is guaranteed to vest upon A's death.

2. A has a life estate, measured by his own life. B's children have a contingent remainder in FSA. Contingent, because they are unascertained at the time of creation of the interest.

3. A has a life estate, measured by his own life. B's children have a vested remainder in FSA. Vested, because B already has children at the time of creation of the interest.

4. A has a life estate, measured by her own life. B has a contingent remainder subject to a condition precedent. B only takes if B survives A. O then has a reversionary interest in FSA, which would kick in only if the interest to B fails.

5. A has a defeasible life estate. She holds a life estate for her life, so long as she doesn't marry. B holds a contingent remainder subject to a condition precedent. He only receives the property if A ever marries. O has a reversionary interest in FSA, because if A dies, having never married, there would be no interest for B to take, the condition of his taking of the interest having never been met.

6. A has an executory interest in FSA. It is not a remainder, since it doesn't follow another conveyance. It is not a present interest, since it doesn't occur for ten years. O therefore holds the present interest. A's interest here is vested because it is guaranteed to occur in 10 years. Even if A dies, A's heirs would take A's interest 10 years from now.

7. The interest to A and his bodily heirs creates a fee tail. If there are no lineal heirs alive to take the interest at A's death, then the property would revert back to O in FSA. So O therefore has a reversionary interest. Note: most states would not recognize the fee tail, but would convert this interest to an FSA. The result would be that any heirs (whether lineal or not) would take A's interest upon his death, and there would be no possibility of reverter in O.

Chapter Problems and Assignments

1. a. Present: Fee Simple Determinable
      Future: Possibility of Reverter
   b. Present: Fee Simple Subject to Condition Subsequent
      Future: Right of Reentry
   c. Present and Future Interest: Fee Simple
   d. Present: Fee Simple Determinable

        Future: Possibility of Reverter

    e. Present: Fee Simple Subject to Condition Subsequent

        Future: Right of Reentry

2. The fee tail is a way of ensuring that real property will descend along bloodlines and will not be conveyed outside the family tree, whereas a fee simple may be conveyed, gifted, or sold by the holder to whomever they please.

3. Clifford's interest is a life estate *pur autre vie.*

4. a. Present: Life Estate

       Future: Contingent Remainder; B is childless and therefore they cannot be ascertained at the time of the creation of the interest.

   b. Present: Life Estate

       Future: Contingent Remainder; B will only receive an interest if she outlives A.

   c. Present: Life Estate

       Future: Vested Remainder; B is ascertained and the remainder is guaranteed to vest upon A's death.

   d. Life Estate

   e. Vested Remainder; B has children, therefore they have been ascertained and the interest is guaranteed to vest upon A's death.

5. Fee simple determinable with vested remainder.

6. It is possible that the Rule Against Perpetuities could be violated because one of Owen's grandchildren might not graduate from Highbrow until after 21 years.

7. *Answers may vary.*

8. To ensure the property is kept in good condition and the value of the property remains unimpaired.

9. The property will pass along to any heirs of the decedent or whoever the decedent conveyed the property to upon their death.

10. *Answers will vary.*

Chapter 6

Exercise

6.1

1. SE 1/4, of Section X. 160 acres.
2. E 1/2 of the NE 1/4 of Section X. 80 acres.
3. SW 1/4 of the NW 1/4 of Section X. 40 acres.
4. N 1/2 of the SW 1/4 of the NE 1/4 of Section X. 20 acres.
5. SW 1/4 of the SW 1/4 of the NE 1/4 of Section X. 10 acres.

Chapter Problems and Assignments

1. Metes and bounds
2. Plat map method
3. a. 320 acres
   b. 40 acres
   c. 80 acres
   d. 20 acres

4. A boundary survey is used to identify the boundary lines of a property, while an as-built survey provides details of the location of the improvements (roads, sewers, buildings, etc.) located within the property boundaries.

5. Monuments are objects that can be used to define either the point of beginning or the corners of a parcel. Natural monuments are those that occur naturally such as trees, streams, rivers, etc. Artificial monuments are man-made objects such as stakes, roads, fences, walls, etc.

6. The description in the deed is not valid to convey title as it fails to thoroughly and accurately describe the directions and distances, making it impossible to identify the property. For example, the description of the first tract begins at the northwest corner of Lot 196 and runs "about 8 acres to a stake." "About 8 acres" furnishes no measure for lineal measurement. The 8-acre tract might be in various shapes and forms — it could be 1680 feet to the stake, or it might be 210 feet, or some other distance.

7. This is an informal reference. Informal references are adequate to transfer the title so long as the description sufficiently identifies the land so that it cannot be confused with any other property.

8. No, corners to land boundaries are fixed by the original surveys. Mistakes made during subsequent land surveys do not adjust the land boundaries.

9. Quiet-title action or a declaratory judgment. A quiet-title action allows court to establish who has title to real property against any challenges or claims to ownership of the property. A declaratory judgment also allows the court to determine who has ownership over the land as well as set forth the parties' rights and obligations.

10. *Answers will vary.*

Chapter 7

Exercise

7.1

1. Yes, a broker has duties of loyalty and to disclose material facts to the principal. Both of those duties are potentially violated here by at least the appearance of a conflict of interest that arises as a result of the broker's brother-in-law being the purchaser of the property. It can at least be argued that his duty of loyalty (to act in good faith and with fair dealing) is called into question here. It can also be argued that by not disclosing the family relationship, the broker failed to disclose a material fact to the principal. The arrangement also at least gives rise to the possibility that the broker is serving as a dual agent.

2. Yes, the duty of care requires Bob to present all offers to the client and assist them in evaluating each offer presented. In this case, just because the two other offers are higher and the financing is secured, there may be reasons beyond what we know that might dictate the seller choosing the lower offer.

3. Yes, while this type of disclosure isn't required under state or federal law, under the circumstances, the broker had a duty to inform the prospective buyers of the fact regarding the school district. A broker may not misrepresent facts to a buyer, either

actively, or as in this case, passively. The broker knew that the home was not in the couple's school district of choice, yet failed to correct their misunderstanding.

4. Yes, this is at least a negligent nondisclosure by Bob. The facts tell us that the agent was aware of foundational problems, and those problems may or may not have caused the damage to the stucco. At the very least, the agent failed to act reasonably under the circumstances. He should have inquired further to determine if the damage to the stucco was caused by the foundation. A broker who fails to disclose the known defective conditions of a property can be held liable for the purchaser's subsequent damages.

5. Yes, if a person has died on the property in the last three years, Bob must disclose this information to the buyer.

6. Yes, Bob has likely run afoul of the state's unauthorized practice of law rules, and could have his license suspended or revoked and be sanctioned by the court. Bob's sharing of information with the prospective purchasers regarding the city zoning laws was clearly legal advice. He should have advised the prospective buyers to talk to a lawyer. Additionally, if Bob was wrong in advising the prospective buyer, and the buyers suffered a loss as a result, they would be able to bring a cause of action against him.

7. No, the courts likely would regard this statement as puffery. Although he has no other offers currently, it is not necessarily disingenuous to tell a prospective buyer that they could lose out on the property if they wait. Here, Bob never says he has an offer but rather tells the prospective purchasers that if they wait, they could lose out to other offers. This doesn't specifically imply there are currently offers on the property, but also may imply that several others are looking and very interested and may be putting an offer in soon, or that the agent anticipates that future interest in the property is likely to be strong.

Chapter Problems and Assignments

1. Ronald is an agent of Benny but is not an agent for his brother. Thus, Ronald breached his duty to Benny when he told his brother to submit a higher offer on the property.

2. a. Express authority
   b. Apparent authority
   c. Express authority
   d. Ratification

3. Upon death of the principal, if a new attorney-in-fact is selected, or if the principal becomes disabled or incapacitated (unless principal expressly granted the power of attorney to continue at the time of creation).

4. If the principal is disclosed and the agent makes an unauthorized contract, the agent is liable on the contract.

5. Both Breanne and Anthony would be liable. Anthony is liable because as the real estate broker he has a duty to supervise the salespersons and establish policies and procedures. Therefore, the broker will be liable for the acts and omissions of the salesperson.

6. Acting as a dual agent can be problematic because the broker will owe a fiduciary duty to their clients on both sides of a single transaction. This prevents them from

truly advocating for either of their clients, as they are required to remain neutral and impartial.

7. Holding brokers liable for the acts of their agents, even those in different geographical areas, is necessary to protect potential clients. This liability incentivizes brokers to take the time to properly train and supervise their salespersons. Additionally, the broker can obtain errors and omissions insurance in order to mitigate their losses resulting from liability.

8. *Answers will vary.*

9. *Answers will vary.*

10. *Answers will vary.*

Chapter 8

Exercise

8.1

1. No, a contract will not be formed if the property is destroyed prior to acceptance.

2. Probably not; there needs to be objective intent in order for the contract to be considered valid. Here, Oliva made the offer for a purpose other than to invite Noah's acceptance. However, her subjective intent is not controlling here. Instead, the court would need to consider whether a reasonable person standing in the parties' shoes would find that Oliva intended to be bound by the offer. Here, the fact that the sales price of the home was $40,000 below fair market value, coupled with Oliva's own testimony, might lead a court to conclude there was not an objective intent to form a contract. Additionally, there is no mention of a writing here, and the statute of fraud would therefore inhibit Noah from enforcing the agreement in court.

3. Yes, Logan secured Isabella's promise to keep the offer open by way of an option contract. Since the option (entered into on Monday) required Isabella to keep the offer open for a week, her attempt on Wednesday of that same week to revoke the offer was ineffective. When Logan called on Thursday to accept, that acceptance was affective to bind Isabella to the contract to purchase the condo. Again, not mentioned is whether there was a writing to this agreement. Assuming there was a written contract offer, signed by Isabella, and assuming Noah agreed to the terms of that written offer, a binding contract for the condo would have been formed. However, since Isabella gave an option to Logan, the court may estop her from denying the existence of the agreement to which the option was related.

4. No, this is a rejection and counteroffer because Mia's terms differ from the original offer, thereby not satisfying the mirror image rule.

5. No, Natalie is a minor and therefore does not have the legal capacity to enter into a contract.

6. Yes, unless they are in a state that does not recognize the partial performance of an oral contract. Mac would have to establish two of the following three elements: (1) partial or full payment of the purchase price, (2) possession of the property by the buyer, and (3) valuable improvements to the property by the purchaser. Mac is likely to prevail as she made a significant down payment of 20 percent of the purchase and she made improvements in the nature of landscaping.

Chapter Problems and Assignments

1. The elements of a valid contract are:
   a. Agreement — requires the parties' have mutual consent. This occurs when an offer is made by one party and accepted by the other party.
   b. Consideration — the bargained for exchanged given by both parties in a transaction. Both parties must give something up for what they receive in exchange.
   c. Legal capacity of the parties — both parties must be of sound mind and proper age in order to enter into a valid contract. (A person who is intoxicated does not have legal capacity.)
   d. Legal purpose — the contract cannot be for something that violates the law.
   e. Statute of Frauds — certain contracts must be evidenced by a writing or a memorandum in order to be enforceable. (The conveyance of property is subject to the statute of frauds.)
2. No, although the seller accepted the offer of $1,350,000, the seller added an additional term by requiring the closing to occur within 45 days. This does not satisfy the mirror-image rule.
3. The bank should only be held liable if the Oyers can prove that the defects in the home were latent and known to the bank.
4. Texas Incorporated will likely be able to keep the earnest money as liquidated damages but will not be able to sue Ramirez for breach of contract because Ramirez had included a financing contingency.
5. a. $10,000
   b. None
   c. Seller may obtain the earnest money deposit of $10,000.
6. Yes, because the revocation must be communicated prior to the acceptance of the offer. Here, Sophia's revocation was not received by the seller until after he had already accepted her offer.
7. The purpose of the Statute of Frauds is to eliminate uncertainty. Since real estate transactions often include various representation and warranties, it is important they are evidenced in a writing so that the rights and obligations of the parties are certain.
8. a. Yes, under misrepresentation.
   b. Yes, under undue influence.
9. *Answers will vary.*
10. *Answers will vary.*

Chapter 9

Exercises

9.1

1. Income approach
2. Income approach
3. This is a tricky one. If the property will be used for income generating purposes (i.e., a bed and breakfast), the income approach would be suitable. If a number of other comparable properties exist in the area, market approach may be suitable. Cost approach would likely not be suitable due to the adverse affect the depreciation calculation would have on the value of the property.

4. Income approach
5. Cost approach
6. Income approach

9.2

1. Yes, this is lender solicitation and it mentions a down payment percentage, thereby triggering Regulation Z.
2. Yes, "30-year fixed" is a Regulation Z trigger term, while reference to the 5 percent rate itself would not trigger Regulation Z.
3. Yes, since the amount of monthly payments is referenced, Regulation Z is triggered.
4. No, no triggering terms are referenced.
5. Yes, triggers Regulation Z by mentioning amount of down payment.

Chapter Problems and Assignments

1. Cost approach; this method should be used because there are no comparable properties in the area, therefore the market approach is not applicable. Additionally, this is not a commercial property, therefore the income approach is also not a proper method of valuation.
2. Acceleration provision
3. Adjustable rate mortgages
4. Due on sale clause
5. The Richards (the sellers) will be liable. When taking subject to a mortgage, the buyer takes title to the property, but does not become personally liable for the payment of the mortgage.
6. A mortgage is a security interest in some form of real property; this allows the lender to sue the borrower to collect against the unpaid debt, giving the lender a higher degree of protection. A deed of trust involves three parties, as there is a trustee in addition to the lender and borrower. The trustee holds the deed of trust until the obligation on the note is paid in full, then the property is conveyed.
7. In some states, there are anti-deficiency laws that do not allow for a deficiency judgement to be issued for a purchase money mortgage.
8. Brittany would prefer a mortgage because Dora would only be entitled to Brittany's payments and not the possession of the property. Dora would prefer an installment land contract because she will remain entitled to possess the property until Brittany has paid all of the purchase price.
9. *Answers will vary.*
10. *Answers will vary.*

Chapter 10

Exercise

10.1

1. C owns Blackacre because C was the first to record.
2. B owns Blackacre because B was the last bona fide purchaser.
3. A owns Blackacre because A was the first bona fide purchaser to record.

Chapter Problems and Assignments

1. The common types of deeds are:
   a. General warranty deed
   b. Special warranty deed
   c. Grant deed
   d. Deed of bargained for sale
   e. Quitclaim deed
   f. Special purpose deed
2. Actual, constructive, or inquiry notice.
3. Under a race statute, A owns Blackacre.
   Under a notice statute, C owns Blackacre.
   Under a race-notice statute, A owns Blackacre.
4. Zaiden has title to the property. Since this is a race-notice jurisdiction, the party must be both the first to record and a BFP. Here, although Declan recorded first, he is not a BFP because he knew Tana had already conveyed her property to Zaiden.
5. Yes, constructive notice arises when a search of the title records would have revealed a defect in title. All persons are deemed to have notice of what has been made part of the public records, even if they did not search for that information.
6. No, the insurance company does not have to defend Aguilar against claims that he knew about at the time he purchased the policy.
7. No, TRID does not apply to commercial properties.
8. Yes, the title company is providing something of value for referrals.
9. The Closing Disclosure needs to be provided at least three business days before the closing is consummated; therefore, the closing will occur July 11th.
10. *Answers will vary.*
11. *Answers will vary.*
12. *Answers will vary.*

Chapter 11

Chapter Problems and Assignments

1. Collection methods, judicial foreclosure, nonjudicial foreclosure, and receivership.
2. The lender may be subject to taxation on the income that results from the cancellation of indebtedness. Additionally, a bankruptcy court may find the deed to be an act of bad faith or fraudulent.
3. The advantages of this deed-in-lieu would be that it is a much quicker process than foreclosure proceedings and it allows both parties to cancel the promissory note and mortgage on the property. First Bank needs to be careful in checking the title record to ensure that there are no junior liens on the property, which would cloud the title.
4. During the statutory redemption period, Andrea has a right to repurchase the property after the foreclosure sale by paying the amount of money for which the property was sold, interest from the sale date at the mortgage's interest rate, and other costs allowed by statute. At the foreclosure sale, the purchaser will receive a certificate of sale, but not a deed. If the property is not redeemed within the statutory period, then the purchaser will get a sheriff's deed.

5. Judicial foreclosures allow for deficiency judgements to be sought by the lender against the borrower. Here, First bank would bring an action against the homeowner for the remaining $30,000 owed.
6. At the foreclosure sale, Corey will receive a certificate of sale, but not a deed. If the property is not redeemed within the statutory period, then Corey will get a sheriff's deed. The sheriff's deed provides for no representations and warranties to the quality of the title received.
7. The purpose of MERS is to expedite the transfer and securitization of mortgage loans.
8. (1) Property taxes, (2) expenses and costs of the foreclosure process, (3) second mortgage, (4) first mortgage.
9. *Answers will vary.*
10. *Answers will vary.*

Chapter 12

Chapter Problems and Assignments

1. No, joint tenancies have the right of survivorship, which transfers the decedent's interest in the property to the remaining joint tenant immediately upon death.
2. a. Tenancy in common (Lucy — 20%, Nix — 50%, Ally — 30%)
   b. Joint tenancy (Kevin, Brian, and Megan each own 33.33%)
   c. Tenancy in common (Kevin, Brian and Megan each own 33.33%)
   d. Tenancy by the entirety (Kevin and Devon each own 50%)
   e. Tenancy in common (FLG Investments and SLG Investments each own 50%)
3. No, the creditor is not able to sell the property held by Alan and Liz as tenants by the entirety. Many courts hold that the creditors of one spouse may not attach the property because it would adversely affect the interest of the other, nondebtor spouse. The underlying debt must be a joint debt in order to attach the property.
4. Yes, Mollie was about to sell her interest as a joint tenant without the consent of her sisters. This severs the joint tenancy; the new owner of Mollie's previous interest will hold their share as a tenant in common, while Annie and Maggie will remain joint tenants.
5. He can convey the property to his children. The interest that goes to his children will become a tenancy in common, while Brian and Megan will remain joint tenants.
6. Yes, in a general partnership all the partners will be liable for the negligent acts of a partner.
7. The vineyard would be considered separate property since it was acquired by inheritance. Ryan is not entitled to any interest in the vineyard.
8. Yes, many states have laws that allow a co-tenant to seek contribution from other joint tenants for repairs that are necessary to preserve the property.
9. *Answers will vary.*
10. *Answers will vary.*

Chapter 13

Chapter Problems and Assignments

1. Condominiums, townhouses, and cooperatives
2. The declaration of a condominium is a contract between the unit owners and the association that states the mutual rights and duties of the parties and establishes the individual units. The bylaws are the rules that govern the condominium association.
3. As a member of the board you could present a motion for an amendment to the bylaws to restrict the use of guest parking spaces by residents. Residents who violate this rule may be subject to fines. This power would typically be set forth in the declaration.
4. Courts have permitted the board of directors or a cooperative to deny ownership to anyone, for any reason, except if it would violate statutory or fair housing laws. Here, lawyers would not be considered a "protected class" under fair housing laws. Therefore, unless there is a state statute that prohibits a cooperative from denying a conveyance due to the buyer's occupation, the cooperative board is within its powers to deny the conveyance to Sarah.
5. The exterior of the building is part of the common area, therefore Kayla is correct in alleging the roof is the association's responsibility.
6. Yes, the association has the ability to collect a special assessment. If Elijah refuses to pay, the association may either sue or place a lien on his property, which allows the association to foreclose on Elijah's property and use to the proceeds for the dues owed.
7. If the Osbornes' use of decorations is in violation of the policies, then Curmudgeon could request that the board of directors enforce the restrictions. If the Osbornes fail to comply, they may be subjected to fines, liens, or the foreclosure of their property. The Osbornes may argue that the association has waived its enforcement ability for failure to enforce the holiday light policy in the past.
8. *Answers will vary.*
9. *Answers will vary.*
10. *Answers will vary.*

Chapter 14

Chapter Problems and Assignments

1. a. Tenancy for years — the right of possession will terminate automatically at the end of the term.
   b. Periodic tenancy — terminated by either party that gives proper and timely notice.
   c. Tenancy at will — may be terminated by either party at any time, however some states now require notice.
   d. Tenancy at sufferance — terminated by either entering into a new lease or filing an unlawful detainer lawsuit to legally evict the tenant.
2. In a gross lease, the tenant pays a fixed monthly amount. This means that the landlord will be responsible for increases in utility costs or taxes throughout the

term of the lease. A modified gross lease occurs when, in addition to a fixed monthly rate, the tenant pays for a share of the property's operating costs (utilities and taxes).

3. You will continue to remain liable to the landlord if the assignee defaults in any of the duties owed under the lease. Therefore, if the assignee fails to pay the rent, the landlord may still sue you to collect the unpaid rent.

4. Yes. The Fair Housing Act prohibits discrimination of tenants on the basis of familial status, therefore Brian has a claim against the apartment complex.

5. January 1-December 31 = tenancy for years
   January 1-March 31 (following year) = month-to-month periodic tenancy
   April 1-April 30 = month-to-month periodic tenancy
   May 1-May 4 = tenancy as sufferance

6. The landlord is not correct. The lease term is a month-to-month tenancy. A one-month tenancy does not need to be in writing to be enforceable.

7. The triple net lease provides more financial protection to the landlord than a modified gross lease. Under a triple net lease, the tenant will be responsible for all the operating costs of the property in addition to a base amount. A modified gross lease requires the tenant to pay a base amount and a portion or percentage of the operating costs.

8. Julie can claim that her landlord violated the implied warranty of habitability by not fixing her heat, thus rendering the apartment inhabitable due to the freezing conditions. Julie may either terminate the lease and abandon the premises or she can continue her lease and sue for damages. Additionally, some states may allow Julie to pay to have the heat fixed and deduct the cost from the rent she owes.

9. No, this would not constitute a constructive eviction because he was notified of potential shutting off of water for intermittent hours before signing the lease. Additionally, in order to claim constructive eviction, Jermaine must provide notice to the landlord and vacate the premises. Jermaine also would be unsuccessful under a claim for breach of the implied warranty of habitability. Although this warranty cannot be waived, under these circumstances the landlord has not failed to maintain the premise in a safe and sanitary condition as the premise is being repaired and notice was given.

10. If Alex can show that his injuries arose from Larry making a negligent repair, then Larry may be found liable for the injuries Alex obtained as a result of the faulty railing. Larry may claim that he did not know the other side of the railing was loose and therefore should not be found liable, but Alex could argue that Larry still failed to exercise reasonable care because he failed to check the entire railing of the balcony and thus was negligent.

11. Yes. The CAM provision provided for all expenses, and the landlord's ability to replace and upgrade concrete with brick and stonework would be encompassed in the CAM charges assessable to the tenants.

12. *Answers will vary.*

13. *Answers will vary.*

14. *Answers will vary.*

15. *Answers will vary.*

Chapter 15

Chapter Problems and Assignments

1. The distinction is important because an insurance agent is an agent of the insurance company, while an insurance broker is an agent of the insured. Therefore, the insured might be liable for any misrepresentations made by the broker.
2. Actual cash value
3. Fields would want to require the concert promoter to secure its own insurance policy and name Fields as an additional insured under the policy to ensure that the property is adequately protected and Fields will not have to rely on its own insurance.
4. Adoree may request the insurance agent to provide a binder. A binder is a form of temporary insurance that provides coverage under the same terms and conditions as the insurance policy that will eventually be issued to him.
5. Most insurance policies require the insured to provide notice of the loss as soon as practicable or, in other words, within a reasonable amount of time. In this situation, Jaclyn and Denae provided notice immediately after being made aware of the damage. Although it was after they returned from their six-month cruise, they still filed the claim as soon as practicable.
6. Mitchell's homeowner's insurance policy will not insure his losses from the consulting business because homeowner's insurance policies do not cover business or professional activities.
7. Yes, Large Insurance has a subrogation right against the person who vandalized the property. Subrogation allows Large Insurance to pursue the person who vandalized the property.
8. No, David does not have an insurable interest in the property.
9. Elena can sue her landlord for the loss of her personal property because of the condition of the premises. She could assert the landlord had contributed to the cause of the fire. However, in most cases Elena would bear the loss alone if cause of the fire was not foreseeable and within the knowledge of the landlord.
10. *Answers will vary.*

Chapter 16

Chapter Problems and Assignments

1. In order to adversely possess property, the possession of the property must be adverse, meaning that it is without the owner's permission and inconsistent with the true owner's legal title. The adverse possessor must have actual possession of the property; this possession must be in a manner consistent with its nature and use. The possession must also be exclusive or not shared with the legal title holder or the general public. The possession must be visible and obvious enough to put the legal owner on notice that someone is attempting to claim the property. The adverse possessor must also continuously occupy the property without significant interruption during the statutory period.
2. A taking of private property occurs where (1) the landowner is deprived of any use of the property, (2) there is a permanent physical invasion on the property, or (3) a

regulatory taking occurs that denies the landowner all economic uses of the property.

3. Yes, Ryan's refusal to allow Elliot to use the beachfront property would be adverse to Elliot's interest in the property. The adverse element is met, and as long as Ryan meets the other adverse possession requirements, he can obtain title from a tenant in common through adverse possession.

4. Yes, the Forches' possession is adverse to Omar's legal title; they have actual possession of the property as they are living in the vacation home. The Forches do not share the property with anyone else. By living in the home, their possession is visible and obvious and they have met the statutory requirement. As long as they continue to use the property as their own home for the statutory period, the Forches can successfully take title by adverse possession.

5. Kyle's sister will receive a share of the rare coin, as this does not constitute a gift. In this case, there is no actual delivery because Kyle does not surrender possession or control of the gift to his brother. Additionally, there was no constructive delivery because Kyle did not give his brother exclusive means of obtaining possession or control of the coins.

6. No, a regulatory taking occurs that denies the owner all economic uses of the property. In this case, although a regulation has resulted in the decreased value of Lance's property, it does not amount to a taking to justify eminent domain.

7. The city is correct. The term "public use" has an expansive definition. In this case, under the *Kelo* decision, although the city is gifting the property to a private party, the public may still benefit by the increased property and sales tax resulting from the developer's improvement to the property.

8. Yes, the Muchados can be forced to sell their property under eminent domain. The payment of just compensation does not have to include the emotional loss suffered. The fair market value is determined by market forces and not sentimental values.

9. *Answers will vary.*

10. *Answers will vary.*

Chapter 17

Chapter Problems and Assignments

1. Most states require the following four elements for a will to be enforceable: a writing; the testator must have capacity; the testator must sign the will; and the will must be witnessed.

2. A will dictates how property will be disposed to specific individuals at a person's death. A trust creates a legal relationship for the transfer and management of property for the beneficiaries named in a trust. The use of a trust can avoid probate and keep private the distributions found in a will.

3. The property held by Thomas in joint tenancy with Derrick will transfer to Derrick pursuant to the right of survivorship, regardless of Thomas's will.

4. Mutual wills

5. In most states, the will is revoked by physical destruction. Brad had the intent to physically revoke the will and burned a portion of it.

6. Carly will be entitled to an intestate share of the estate. State laws often provide that these pretermitted heirs will receive at least what they would have received under

intestate succession (discussed below). An exception occurs where the omission from the will was intentional and that intention is apparent upon reading the will. Here, the facts indicate that Eric did not know about Carly and therefore she was not intentionally omitted.

7. Rosita's entire estate will be distributed to her husband George

8. Under *per stirpes*, the property would be distributed as follows: 1/3 to Brent, 1/6 to Eliza, 1/6 to Fred, and 1/3 to Garrett. Under *per capita* the estate would be distributed as follows: $\frac{1}{4}$ each to Brent, Eliza, Fred, and Garrett.

9. *Answers will vary.*

10. *Answers will vary.*

Chapter 18

Chapter Problems and Assignments

1. Zoning is permissible if the zoning law promotes the health, safety, and general welfare of the people and is not arbitrary, unreasonable, or discriminatory.

2. A variance can be sought by the owner of land when they wish the land to be used in a manner inconsistent with the current zoning ordinance. Variances will be granted in exceptional cases in which the owner would suffer an undue hardship if the ordinance were enforced and the variance would not excessively disrupt the surrounding areas. Instead of a variance, the owner may obtain a conditional-use permit to provide for uses that are inconsistent to existing zoning ordinances but are either essential or desirable to the particular area.

3. Cumulative zoning

4. Incentive zoning

5. The city is correct. A nonconforming use will be lost if the nonconforming building is destroyed by fire or natural events. Even if the building is rebuilt to the same specifications as before, the prior nonconforming use may not be continued.

6. Conditional use permit

7. No, once the nonconforming use is amortized, the nonconforming use is no longer permitted. Quinn's property will need to be used for residential use.

8. Yes, Elizabeth is in violation of the homeowner's association's restrictive covenants. Northco can file a lawsuit to seek an injunction to prevent Elizabeth's violation of the CCRs. In addition, a lawsuit could also be filed for damages.

9. *Answers will vary.*

10. *Answers will vary.*

Chapter 19

Chapter Problems and Assignments

1. A tax deduction reduces taxable income, which reduce the amount of income taxes paid. A tax credit will lower the amount of taxes one is obligated to pay.

2. Government property and property that belongs certain organizations such as churches, hospitals, schools, and nonprofits are not subject to property tax.

3. The taxpayer would pay taxes of $18,000 if they received a $10,000 tax deduction. The same taxpayer would pay $10,000 if they instead received a $10,000 tax credit.

4. $375,000 — Sales Price
   ($25,000) — Selling Expenses
   ─────────────────────────────
   $350,000 = Amount Realized

   $350,000 — Amount Realized
   ($75,000) — Basis
   ─────────────────────────────
   $250,000 = Gain Realized

   Jessica will not have to pay taxes on the sale of her home because it was her personal residence for the last three years, which qualifies her for the full exclusion of $250,000.

5. Joel and Kirsten may deduct the mortgage interest from two of the residential properties from their personal tax return. In this case they will deduct the mortgage interest on the $500,000 mortgage as well as the $350,00 mortgage.

6. Yes, this qualifies as a §1031 exchange. Zachary had 45 days to identify a replacement property and did so in 30 days. Further, he had 180 days to acquire the replacement property and he did so in 75 days.

7. Garrett is entitled to deduct the interest payments from the home equity line of credit on her personal tax return.

8. No, Mack cannot deduct the home office expense. In order to deduct a home office expense where you meet with clients, the use of the home must be substantial and integral to the conduct of the business. Occasionally meeting with clients is not substantial and integral to the conduct of the business.

9. *Answers will vary.*

10. *Answers will vary.*

Chapter 20

Chapter Problems and Assignments

1. The prime contractor works directly with the owner of a project while the subcontractor is hired by the prime contractor. Usually there will only be one prime contractor on a construction project while there will be many subcontractors on a project.

2. In a fixed-price contract, the contractor agrees with the owner to build the structure for a fixed fee. If the contractor can build the project less expensively, the contractor will increase his or her profit margin. In a guaranteed maximum price contract, the owner reimburses the contractor for costs, overhead, and profit, but the owner stops making those payments once it has paid the guaranteed maximum contract price. Sometimes, a guaranteed maximum price contract allows a shared savings provision by which the contractor and the owner can share the savings of the project's cost.

3. A mechanic's lien is a lien that arises from the construction or other improvement of real estate. The mechanic's lien claimant who does not receive payment is allowed to record a lien on the title to the real property upon which work was performed and foreclose on the property to obtain payment.

4. Sam cannot sue Alicia because he was performing work as an unlicensed contractor. Many states require that the contractor be licensed at all times during the

construction project in order to recover payment for the services rendered and materials provided to the work site.

5. The Spearin doctrine is an implied warranty of the correctness of the plans and specifications provided by the owner to the contractors. The contractor will not be responsible for defects in the plan or specifications.

6. The mechanic's lien will attach to the leasehold interest only. The owner posted a notice of non-responsibility; therefore, the mechanic's lien can only attach to the leasehold interest of Bad Sports Sporting Goods.

7. A guaranteed maximum price contract with a shared savings provision.

8. Logan will obtain a performance bond to protect the owner's interest.

9. *Answers will vary.*

10. *Answers will vary.*

Chapter 21

Chapter Problems and Assignments

1. In a Chapter 7 bankruptcy proceeding, the debtors may retain exempt property and are discharged from liabilities, debts, and obligations that were subject to the bankruptcy proceeding. In a Chapter 11 bankruptcy proceeding, a business entity will be discharged from some of its debts and liabilities and will pay negotiated reduced amounts as to others that have occurred prior to the confirmation of the reorganization plan. In Chapter 13 proceedings, the debtor will be discharged of specific debts and obligations until performance is completed under the plan.

2. The typical bankruptcy procedure begins with Bankruptcy counseling and education (if a Chapter 7 bankruptcy is filed). For the other bankruptcy petitions, they begin with the filing of a bankruptcy petition that creates the bankruptcy estate and an automatic stay of all civil actions against the debtor subject to the court lifting the stay as to some lawsuits. A meeting of the creditors will then occur. After that, the creditors file proofs of claim and the debtor may execute reaffirmation agreements. The bankruptcy court will distribute property to the creditors (in Chapter 7 cases) and then discharge the debtor's debts. Once completed the bankruptcy estate is closed.

3. An automatic stay is an injunction that automatically enjoins (stops) lawsuits, foreclosures, and all collection activity against the debtor the moment a bankruptcy petition is filed. This protects the bankrupt debtor from being pursued by creditors for a period. An automatic stay can be lifted when actions to perfect a lien or security interest are taken within 30 days after the bankruptcy petition was filed or by a secured creditor holding a mortgage or deed of trust against the debtor's real property or a security interest in personal property.

4. A secured creditor may use the collateralized assets to satisfy the balance due it. The assets will be retained or sold by the creditor. A secured creditor may realize little or no payment from the bankrupt's estate in satisfaction of the balance due it.

5. Most likely, they would file a Chapter 11 bankruptcy petition. As this debt relates to business debts, they would not qualify for a Chapter 13 bankruptcy petition. A Chapter 7 bankruptcy petition would not be used because they seek to continue the operations of the business. Chapter 7 would liquidate and distribute all of the debtor's nonexempt assets.

6. The Jackson's home will not be sold due to the homestead exemption protection. The Jackson's have $40,000 in equity in the home and the federal homestead exemption is $47,350. As they do not have equity greater than $47,350, the bankruptcy court cannot use the equity in the home to satisfy the debt owed to creditors.

7. Staci has filed for Chapter 13 bankruptcy petition.

8. Under BAPCPA, Congress has sought to balance the interests of the landlord and tenant. Formerly residential tenants could enjoy prolonged periods of protection from eviction. Commercial tenants are now compelled to quickly affirm or reject the leave following the filing of a bankruptcy.

9. *Answers will vary.*

10. *Answers will vary.*

Chapter 22

Chapter Problems and Assignments

1. There are three key environmental administrative agencies responsible for enforcing laws and regulations. They include: (1) the Environmental Protection Agency, (2) the U.S. Department of Housing and Development, and (3) the U.S. Army Corps of Engineers.

2. A Phase I report provides potential or existing environmental contamination liability. The report includes: a review of available government lists of properties affected by toxic contamination; a review of historical documents such as newspaper articles; a review of the chain of title; as well as a site inspection by a consultant for visible signs of contamination. The Phase II report requires sampling and analysis of soils, groundwater, or both to be performed. It is intended to confirm the existence of contamination disclosed in the Phase I report.

3. a. Yes
   b. No
   c. Yes
   d. Yes

4. Yes. Braxton would use the innocent landowner defense under CERCLA to avoid liability. Under this defense, Braxton is required to undertake all appropriate inquiries before purchasing the land and have no actual or constructive knowledge of the hazardous substance. Braxton ordered a Phase I report that did not disclose the presence of any environmental hazards. While he didn't order the Phase II report, he did so because the Phase I report did not disclose the presence of hazards. Further, he was unaware of any environmental hazards and qualifies for this defense.

5. Radon is a naturally occurring radioactive gas that is found in nearly all soils. Radon is formed by the natural decay of radium, found within the soil. As it radiates into a building, serious health problems may result. Radon is estimated to cause thousands of deaths each year.

6. Mold infestations are on the rise because of the increased sealing of buildings for energy efficiency. Unfortunately, that prevents the building from receiving adequate ventilation to vent the moisture to the exterior, facilitating the growth of mold.

7. The owner has two remedies. The first option is encapsulation, which involves the treating of the material with a sealant that coats the material so the asbestos fibers are not released. Another option is the removal of the asbestos-containing material. Both remedies should only be performed by a trained and accredited professional, as improper removal or repair could increase the risk of asbestos exposure.

8. *Answers will vary.*

9. *Answers will vary.*

10. *Answers will vary.*

Glossary

A

Abatement   The proportional reduction in the distribution of an estate when the funds or assets are insufficient to pay all beneficiaries in full.

Absolute priority rule   Rule stipulating the order of payment wherein the first-priority debts are paid in full before any second-tier debts are paid.

Acceptance   The manifestation of assent by the offeree approving the terms of the offer.

Accretion   The process of increasing riparian land, in areas previously covered by water, by the depositing of solid materials, such as mud, sand, or sediment, so that it becomes dry land.

Acknowledged   Requirement for the signing of a will to be notarized in front of a notary public in order to be valid when a will is signed by a third party on behalf of the testator.

Acknowledgment   A declaration made before a notary public.

Action for ejectment   See *Unlawful detainer*.

Actual notice   Notice that occurs when the prospective purchaser has actual knowledge of a title defect.

Additional insured   A party unrelated to the named insured who receives the benefits of the insurance policy without having to pay the premium that the named insured pays.

Ademption   When an heir receives nothing because the testator leaves a specific devise of property and that property is no longer in the estate.

Adjudication   The legal process of resolving a dispute.

Adjustable-rate mortgage   A type of mortgage in which the interest rate and the monthly payments may be adjusted periodically to changes to a lending index agreed upon at the time the loan is made.

Administrative agencies   Agencies that have the power to enact regulations to implement legislative acts creating new law.

Administrator   A male representative of the estate appointed to administer the estate if the decedent died intestate.

Administratrix   A female representative of the estate appointed to administer the estate if the decedent died intestate.

***Ad valorem* taxes**   Taxes levied according to the value of property.

Adverse possession   A method of acquiring title by wrongfully possessing the real property of another, subject to state law requirements.

Aesthetic zoning   Regulations used to control aspects of a community's beauty.

Affirmative easement   An easement that allows the holder or owner of the dominant tenement to use the land of the servient tenement.

Agent   An individual who represents another, a principal, in dealings with third parties.

Air lot   All airspace above the imaginary 23-foot plane.

Air rights   Rights of an owner to develop the airspace located above the surface of the earth; rights which can be easements or in fee, in vertical space above the ground surface, and below navigable airspace.

Alternative dispute resolution   A nonjudicial process that seeks to resolve disputes between parties, such as mediation and arbitration.

Alternative energy   Generally, refers to electricity or any fuel other than natural gas or petroleum.

American Land Title Association   Association that issues standard policy forms for title insurers.

Amortized   The process of paying regular installments of a debt over a period of time.

Amortized loans   See *Fixed-rate mortgages.*

Apparent authority   Authority that occurs when an agent does not have authority to act on the principal's behalf, but the principal's words or conduct reasonably imply to a third party that the agent does have authority to act on the principal's behalf.

Appraise   To give an estimate of the current market value.

Arbitration   A legal proceeding in which disputes are resolved by a neutral third party appointed by the parties to make a (usually) binding and final determination.

Area variance   Variances allowing a deviation from required setbacks, structure heights, minimum lot sizes, and parking requirements.

Artificial or **man-made monuments**   Monuments formed by man, which may include stakes, roads, fences, walls, buildings, and the like.

Artificial person   A legal entity that is not a human being but is recognized in law as having legal rights and duties (such as a corporation, limited liability company, or partnership).

Asbestos   A mineral fiber historically used in construction that is a known carcinogen causing cancer and various respiratory ailments.

As-built survey   A survey providing the details of the location of improvements located within the property boundaries.

As is   When a property is sold with all known and unknown faults and defects.

Assessor parcel number   Numbers and letters assigned to a parcel of land in order to identify property for tax-assessment and collection purposes and to identify properties by real estate agents.

Assignee   A new tenant who received an assignment by an assignor.

Assignment   A transfer of a tenant's unexpired lease to a third party.

Assignor   A tenant that transfers all his or her interests under a least to a third party.

Assume an existing mortgage   When a purchaser agrees to become personally liable for an existing mortgage obligation in a real estate purchase.

Attachments   Crops, trees, bushes, and grasses attached or affixed to the land.

Attractive nuisance doctrine   Landowners will be liable for injuries caused to trespassing children if they are injured by a hazardous object or condition on the property and they were on the property because of an object or condition likely to attract children.

Automatic stay   The suspension of legal proceedings against a debtor, such as stopping a mortgage foreclosure sale.

Avulsion   The sudden and perceptible loss of or addition to land caused by the action of water or a sudden change in the bed or course of a stream.

B

Bad faith   Where the insurance company acts in a blatant and unfair manner against the insured with conduct exceeding mere negligence.

Balloon payment   A loan in which a balance remains due at the time of the loan's maturity.

Bankruptcy discharge   A court order that relieves a debtor from the obligation to pay for certain debts included in the bankruptcy proceeding.

Bankruptcy estate   An estate encompassing all legal and equitable interests in property of the debtor at the time of the filing of bankruptcy.

Bankruptcy trustee   A legal representative of the bankruptcy estate before the bankruptcy court.

Base lines   East-west latitudinal lines.

Basis   An amount representing the taxpayer's cost in acquiring an asset with adjustments to allow for changes in the condition of the asset.

Beneficiary   The lender identified in a deed of trust; the person who receives the testator's property from a will.

Bequest   A gift of personal property.

Bid   A contractor's estimated cost to construct a project.

Binder   Temporary insurance lasting until a policy is issued.

Biomass   Energy created from plants or animals and includes wood and solid waste.

Blockbusting   The illegal procedure of inducing panic among owners because of fear of minority groups moving into the neighborhood.

Bona fide purchaser   A good faith purchaser who purchases real property without notice of any prior sale by the grantor.

Boot   The receipt of cash or other consideration given to equalize the value between two properties that are exchanged.

Boundary   The dividing line between two parcels of land.

Boundary survey   A survey used to identify the boundary lines of a property.

Breach   A failure to fully perform a contract.

Brownfields   Abandoned, idled, or underused properties where the presence of hazardous substances, pollutants, or contaminants has impaired redevelopment of the sites.

Builder's risk insurance   Provides insurance for a loss or damage to a building under construction.

Bureau of Consumer Financial Protection   A federal agency that supervises all participants in the consumer-finance and mortgage arenas; regulates depository and nondepository institutions; and regulates unfair, deceptive, or abusive acts or practices in consumer products and services.

Business Judgment Rule   A rule that protects the decisions of a corporation's board of directors if a board has acted on an informed basis, in good faith, and in the honest belief that the action taken was in the best interests of the corporation and its shareholders.

Buyer agent   A real estate agent who represents the buyer of a property.

Bylaws   The rules governing the condominium association.

C

Call   A series of instructions used by metes and bounds descriptions to describe the length and direction of the boundaries of the property.

Capping   The act of laying soil and grass on top of a landfill or waste disposal site to prevent erosion and improve aesthetics.

Carbon monoxide (CO)   An odorless, colorless, toxic gas.

Caveat emptor   "Let the buyer beware."

Causa mortis **gifts**   Gifts made in contemplation of an impending death.

Certificate of sale   Document given to purchaser at a foreclosure sale certifying that, after the redemption period passed, holder received title to foreclosed property.

Certified general appraiser   An appraiser who may evaluate both residential and commercial properties of any value and complexity.

Certified residential appraiser   An appraiser who can appraise one to four residential units without regard to value or the complexity of the transaction.

CFPB   The Consumer Financial Protection Bureau is a federal agency having primary regulatory authority over consumer lending.

Chain of title   A recorded instrument found through generally accepted title searching methods. To establish constructive notice, an instrument may be required in the chain.

Change order   An amendment to a construction contract.

Chapter 7   A bankruptcy petition providing the debtor with a fresh start. The debtor's nonexempt assets are sold, and the proceeds are distributed to creditors.

Chapter 11   A bankruptcy petition allowing a debtor to restructure the debtor's finances under supervision of the bankruptcy court.

Chapter 13   A bankruptcy petition permitting the bankruptcy court to supervise the debtor's plan for repayment of unpaid debts over a period.

Check   The 24-by-24-mile area created by guide meridian lines and correction lines.

Clean Air Act   An act intended to protect the public from different types of air pollution caused by a variety of pollution sources.

Clean Water Act (CWA)   A statute enacted to address water pollution in the U.S.

Closing   The completion of all conditions in a real estate transaction necessary to convey title between the parties.

Closing disclosure   Lender's disclosure to consumer of anticipated costs and disbursements at closing.

Closing statement   A statement prepared in advance of the closing, stating the distribution of monies that will occur at the time of closing.

Cloud on title   A defect or potential defect in the owner's title arising from a lien, easement, or court order; anything of record that may affect the ability to provide marketable title.

Codicil   A revision to a will that can amend, modify, or revoke a prior will.

Color of Title   A defective legal instrument that the holder believes is effective to transfer title but cannot operate as a legal conveyance of title.

Column lot   All airspace from the surface of the earth to an imaginary plane 23 feet above the surface of the earth.

Commercial easements in gross   Easements created for a business or another money-making purpose.

Commercial general liability policy   Policy covering bodily injury, property damage, and personal injury liability arising from the operations of a business.

Commercial lease   A lease used for business or commercial purposes such a retail, restaurants, offices, or warehouses.

Commingling   Occurs when the funds of a client are mixed with the licensee's personal funds.

Commission   Compensation to a broker given by a percentage of the selling price.

Common areas   An area of common ownership within a subdivision.

Common area maintenance (CAM)   A pro rata share of costs that a tenant is required to pay for common area expenses. Frequently found in commercial leases.

Common interest communities   Communities under the control of a homeowners' association and/or a condominium association.

Common law   Nonstatutory theories developed by courts covering legal relief for one person against another.

Common law marriage   A state recognition of marital status to unmarried couples who hold themselves out to the public as if they are married.

Community property   Property acquired during marriage that is owned equally by the spouses.

Competitive market analysis (CMA)   An analysis used to estimate the sale price by adjusting the price paid for comparable properties.

Condemnation   The legal proceeding by which the government exercises its eminent-domain powers.

Conditional use permit   Allows an owner to use a property in a manner authorized by a local zoning ordinance but inconsistent with the existing zoning for the property.

Condition precedent   An event or condition that must occur before the interest becomes vested.

Condominium   A form of housing in a subdivision in which there is individual ownership of the units, but joint ownership of common areas.

Condominium hotel   The construction of a building in which a portion of the hotel is owned as condominium units but can also be utilized by the hotel for hotel guests.

Confirmation   Bankruptcy court approval of a plan of reorganization under Chapter 11.

Conforming loans   A loan that meets Fannie Mae and Freddie Mac purchase criteria in the secondary market.

Conservation easement   An easement that promotes the preservation of land and, if properly drawn, can serve as a tax-planning strategy of the grantor.

Consideration   A rule of contract law requiring an exchange of value between the parties.

Construction defect   An imperfection or shortcoming on a construction project often originating from defects in design, workmanship, and materials or from soil failures.

Construction loan   A loan that provides the financing to pay for the cost of developing and constructing an improvement on real property that often includes a sum allowing the borrower to purchase the land.

Construction manager   Prime contractor of an owner who acts as an agent.

Constructive annexation   Goods not actually annexed or fastened to the land but used in such a way or so associated with the use of the building.

Constructive delivery   A method that can be used in making gifts where the donor makes a symbolic delivery of the property to the donee; a type of delivery that is inferred from the conduct of the parties, even if the physical delivery did not take place.

Constructive eviction   A wrongful eviction in which the tenant may terminate the lease, vacate the premises, and be excused from further rent liability.

Constructive notice   A notice given by recording or occupancy; notice that arises when a search of the title records would have revealed a defect in title.

Consummation   The date on which the consumer becomes legally obligated on the loan documents.

Contingency   An event that *may* occur and that is placed in a contract to protect a party.

Contingent remainder   A remainder given to an unascertained or unidentified person or a remainder that is subject to a condition precedent.

Contract   An agreement enforceable by law.

Conventional loans   A loan made by an institutional lender that is neither guaranteed nor insured by the federal government.

Cooperating broker   A buyer's agent in transaction involving MLS-listed properties.

Cooperative A form of housing ownership where each owner owns stock with a right to occupy the unit under a proprietary lease.

Core proceedings A legal proceeding over which the bankruptcy court has jurisdiction; it is essential to the disposition of the bankruptcy estate.

Corporation A fictitious legal entity created according to statutory requirements.

Correction lines Run east-west and are placed every 24 miles from the base line.

Cost approach A method of appraisal that values the cost of the land plus the current cost to construct the property less accrued depreciation.

Cost plus contract A contract where the contractor is paid its costs plus an amount for overhead costs and profit.

Counteroffer A response to an offer containing terms that do not match the original offer.

Covenant An unconditional promise to another.

Covenants, conditions, and restrictions (CCRs) A document that regulates the uses and activities permitted on a developer's lots, recorded by the developer prior to the first sale in a development.

Covered loss An event or occurrence that triggers the duty of the insurance carrier to investigate and potentially pay an insurance claim.

Cramdown A bankruptcy rule allowing the court to confirm a plan of reorganization over the objections of a class of creditors, subject to certain restrictions.

Creation of law doctrine Property rights that are created by government action.

Credit bid Right of secured creditor to bid the amount owed to the creditor at the time of the foreclosure sale.

Creditor The lender in a credit transaction.

Creditor's committee Committee appointed by the U.S. Trustee in Chapter 11 cases that is responsible for representing the interests of the unsecured creditors.

Cumulative zoning Regulation that allows more restrictive uses that are not designated for that zone.

Curtesy A right similar to dower where a surviving husband receives a life estate interest in all of his wife's property but only if issues (children) were born from the marriage.

D

Damages Compensation for the nonbreaching party by placing the nonbreaching party in a position equivalent to the one that would have resulted if the contract had been performed.

Debtor The person who executes (signs) a note or contract and is primarily liable for repayment. The borrower in a credit transaction.

Debtor in possession The debtor in a Chapter 11 case that retains possession of its property and enjoys the same rights and powers — as well as the obligations — of a trustee in bankruptcy.

Decedent The person who dies.

Declaration of condominium   A contract between and among the unit owners and the association stating the mutual rights and duties of the parties.

Declaratory judgment   A court determination of ownership of disputed land areas in which the court determines the rights and obligations of the parties.

Deeds   Written instruments used to convey (transfer) real property.

Deed-in-lieu of foreclosure   A deed given by the borrower transferring title to the lender to satisfy a loan default.

Deed of bargain and sale   A deed that conveys real property and implies that the grantor has a claim of ownership in the property, but the grantor makes no other covenants to the grantee.

Deed of trust   A three-party instrument financing arrangement that involves a beneficiary, a trustor, and a trustee.

Default   A material breach in the borrower's promise to the lender.

Deficiency judgment   A money judgment obtained by the creditor against the borrower when the foreclosure sale does not satisfy the entire debt.

Delay damages   Damages caused by unjustifiable delay.

Deposit   An advance payment to cover certain expenses or costs that may be incurred to the landlord when the tenant vacates.

Depreciation   The gradual loss in value of property due to its deterioration and obsolescence.

Descent and distribution statute   A state statute governing how property is distributed under intestate succession.

Designated agency   An agency that occurs when different agents within the same firm are representing a buyer and a seller.

Design professionals   The architects on a project.

Devise   A gift of real property under a will.

Discovery   The process by which a party to a lawsuit gathers facts, learns of the opposing party's defenses, and prepares for trial.

Diversity of citizenship jurisdiction   A case where the amount in controversy exceeds $75,000 and all parties to the litigation are citizens of different states, or a citizen of a state and a citizen, or a subject of a foreign country.

Doctrine of correlative rights   Doctrine providing landowners a reasonable opportunity to extract a fair and reasonable share of production by preventing the destruction or recovery of mineral interest by an adjacent landowner.

Doctrine of relation back   Doctrine that states that all mechanics' liens will relate back to the period when work started, even though each individual mechanics' lien claimants' work or materials were rendered subsequent to other mechanics' lien claimants and were recorded subsequent to other liens.

Doctrine of Worthier Title   A doctrine that provides that when a grant creates a future interest in the heirs of the grantor, the future interest is void and the grantor has a reversion.

Dodd-Frank Wall Street Reform and Consumer Protection Act (Dodd-Frank)   A federal statute that covers the reform of financial institutions through the creation of several federal agencies.

Dominant tenement (dominant estate) The party whose land is benefited by an easement appurtenant.

Donee Person who receives a gift from a donor.

Donor Person who gives a gift to another.

Dower The right of a surviving wife to take a life estate in one-third of the deceased husband's real property held by the husband during marriage.

Dual agent A real estate agent who represents both the buyer and the seller in a real estate transaction.

Due process clause Part of the Fourteenth Amendment prohibiting the government from taking a person's life, liberty, or property without due process of the law.

Duress A defense asserted to the enforcement of a contract because a party was subjected to unlawful pressure or coercion to enter into the contract.

Duty of care A fiduciary duty that requires a broker to act as a reasonably competent real estate broker would act under similar circumstances.

Duty of good faith and fair dealing An implied promise that neither party will do anything to injure the other party's right to receive the rights of the agreement.

Duty of loyalty A fiduciary duty owed by an agent not to act adversely to the principal's interest.

Duty of obedience A fiduciary duty requiring a broker to obey and follow all lawful instructions and demands of the client.

Duty to defend A contractual duty obligating the insurer to provide the insured with a defense of claims typically by hiring legal counsel.

Duty to indemnify A contractual duty to pay for any loss or damage suffered by another.

E

Earnest money A buyer's initial deposit, which is often damages the seller may keep should the buyer breach the contract before the sale has closed.

Earthquake insurance Provides insurance to protect against property damage caused by an earthquake.

Easement A right of a person to use the land of another for a specific purpose.

Easement by necessity An easement recognized when an owner conveys land to another but the land conveyed has no access expect over the grantor's adjacent property or over the land of strangers.

Easement appurtenant An easement that benefits a particular parcel of land, rather than conferring a personal benefit upon the holder of the easement. The easement transfers with title of the dominant tenement.

Easements by estoppel An easement that is created when the conduct of the owner of land leads another to reasonably believe that she has an interest in the land so that she acts or does not act in reliance on that belief.

Easements by express reservation An easement that occurs when a landowner conveys property and expressly reserves an easement right across the grantee's property.

Easements by grant   Easements created by express agreement.

Easements by implication   An easement implied by a prior or preexisting use.

Easements by prescription   An easement created by continuously and in an open, notorious manner utilizing without consent the land of another for a statutorily defined period of time.

Easements in gross   An easement that benefits a person, regardless of whether that person owns any land at all.

Electronic Signatures in Global and National Commerce Act (E-SIGN)   U.S. law that allows the use of electronic signature and electronic records in commerce.

Emblements   The right to cultivate and harvest annual crops.

Eminent domain   The government's power to seize private property for public use.

Enabling statute   A state law by which the authority to control land use is delegated to local governments.

Endorsement   A written amendment to a title insurance policy modifying the policy. It may alter, enlarge, or reduce coverage.

Environmental Protection Agency (EPA)   A federal agency created to protect the environment and address health concerns.

Equal dignity rule   Requirement that the appointment of an agent for a real estate contract must be in writing to be enforceable.

Equal Protection Clause   Part of the Fourteenth Amendment requiring laws be applied and protect all persons equally.

Equity of redemption   The right of a borrower to redeem (retain) the mortgaged property before a foreclosure sale occurs.

Erosion   The gradual washing away of land bordering a stream or body of water by the water's action.

Errors and omissions insurance (E&O policies)   Insurance provided to a broker insuring the broker for breaches of fiduciary duty, negligence, misrepresentation, and other covered claims.

Escheat   A process whereby, if there are no living heirs under a state's intestacy laws, the court orders that the property be distributed to the state.

Escrow   A method of closing in which both the buyer and the seller deliver documents to an escrow agent, who holds the documents in trust for the parties until all conditions for closing are met.

Escrow agent   A person who facilitates the closing of a transaction and holds a deed in escrow until all the terms and conditions between the buyer and seller are met.

Exclusionary zoning   Regulation limiting and regulating future growth in order to preserve the historical character of the area.

Exclusive agency   An agency that provides that the broker is the exclusive agent of the seller and is entitled to a commission.

Exclusive right to sell   A listing in which the broker is granted the exclusive right to sell the property and is entitled to a commission regardless of who finds a buyer.

Exclusive use zoning   Regulation that limits property uses to those specified in the zoning ordinance.

Exculpatory clause A contract provision that relieves a party (or both parties) from liability for ordinary negligent acts.

Execute To sign a legal document.

Executory interest A future interest held by someone other than the grantor or the grantor's heirs that is triggered upon the happening of some future event.

Exempt property Certain property that the Bankruptcy Code allows individual debtors to keep.

Express authority Authority of an agent to act on behalf of the principal that may be expressly granted, orally or in writing, by a principal.

Express grants Occurs when a property owner (the grantor) grants to another the right to use a portion of the grantor's property.

Express reservation Occurs when a landowner conveys a portion of the property and expressly reserves (i.e., retains) an easement right across the grantee's property.

Extrinsic evidence Evidence that is not stated within a document but is obtained from reliable outside sources.

F

Fair Housing Act Federal law that provides everyone an equal opportunity to buy, rent, sell, and live in residential properties.

Fannie Mae (Federal National Mortgage Association) A government agency that was converted to a private profit-making corporation whose purpose is to sell commitments to lenders pledging to buy specific dollar amounts of mortgage loans within certain durations.

Federal Housing Administration A federal agency within the U.S. Department of Housing and Urban Development (HUD) that assist lenders in providing housing loans or lending opportunities for low- to moderate-income families by offering complete insurance to these lenders against the total loss arising from a foreclosure.

Federal question jurisdiction A case arising under the U.S. Constitution, treaties, or federal statutes and regulations.

Fee simple (or fee interest) Ownership that is characterized as complete and lasting until the end of time.

Fee simple defeasible Fee simple interest ownership that may be cut short by the occurrence (or nonoccurrence) of a condition, limitation, or restriction.

Fee simple determinable Ownership interest that automatically terminates upon the occurrence or nonoccurrence of some condition, limitation, or restriction.

Fee simple subject to a condition subsequent Ownership interest that is subject to a condition, and the grant generally provides that the grantor may reenter the property (take possession) and terminate the estate.

Fee tail A fee interest in which the estate must be inherited by the lineal descendants of the grantee.

Fiduciary duty A duty to act in the principal's best interest and not advance the broker's own interests.

Fiduciary relationship A relationship founded through trust and confidence from one party to another.

Fifth Amendment   No person shall be "deprived of life, liberty, or property, without due process of law; nor shall private property be taken for public use, without just compensation."

Financing statement   A legal document filed in the public records office, typically at the county level, to notify third parties of a secured party's interest in the described personal property or fixtures.

Finder   A person who brings together the buyer and seller in a real estate transaction.

Fire insurance policy   Insurance that protects real and personal property against damages resulting from a fire and certain other perils.

First mortgage   The mortgage that is recorded first in time.

Fixed price contract   A contract in which the contractor agrees with the owner to build the structure for a fixed fee, and the contractor can increase its profit margin by building the project less expensively.

Fixed-rate mortgages   Loans that have a fixed interest rate for the life of the loan.

Fixture   Personal property that has become so attached to the real property that it loses its identity as personal property and becomes real property.

Foreclosure   A procedure following a default, in which property serving as security for the loan is sold with proceeds applied to retire the debt.

Foreclosure by power of sale   A foreclosure that occurs without court involvement if the lender properly and timely gives notice of the foreclosure for the statutory periods of time.

Fourteenth Amendment   No state "shall . . . deprive any person of life, liberty, or property, without due process of law; deny to any person within its jurisdiction the equal protection of the laws."

Fraudulent transfer   A transfer made by the debtor with the intent to hinder, delay, or defraud a creditor.

Freddie Mac (Federal Home Loan Mortgage Corporation)   A secondary-market organization that issues its own securities against its own mortgage pools and guarantees that principal and interest on the mortgages within its pools are repaid in full and on time, even if the underlying mortgages are in default.

Freehold estate   An estate in which the owner has a present possessory interest in the real property.

Fructus industrials   Things produced through human effort, such as crops or fruit groves.

Fructus naturales   Things produced primarily by nature, such as forests and shrubbery.

Future interest   An interest requiring a person to wait for some event or time in the future in order to obtain possession.

G

Gain   The amount of money realized from the sale of the property in excess of the adjusted basis of the property.

General liens   Liens that arise out of actions on the part of the property owner that are unrelated to the property's ownership.

General warranty deed   A deed containing a full warranty and set of promises by the grantor to the grantee.

Geothermal   Energy created by capturing the pressurized steam and hot water under the surface of the earth.

Gift   A voluntary transfer of property without payment or the expectation of repayment.

Government survey system   See *Public Land Survey System*.

Grant deed   A deed that implies two covenants: (1) the grantor has not previously conveyed the same estate to anyone other than the grantee and (2) the property is free of encumbrances placed on it or permitted by the grantor.

Grantee   Buyer or recipient.

Grantor   Seller or donor.

Grantor-grantee index system   A system in which records are indexed and maintained alphabetically by the grantor's or the grantee's respective names.

Gross inadequacy standard   Standard that infers the inadequacy of price should be gross and the result of any mistake, accident, surprise, fraud, misconduct, or irregularity in order for the sale to be set aside.

Gross lease   A lease in which the tenant pays a fixed amount.

Groundwater   Water found under the earth's surface as a result of rain and melting snow.

Guaranteed maximum price contract   A contract in which the contractor agrees with the owner to build the structure for a guaranteed price where the contractor bears the risk in the event the project costs more than anticipated to construct.

Guide meridian lines   Run north-south and are placed every 24 miles from the principal meridian.

H

Habendum clause   Clause in a deed which sets forth the extent of ownership and any exceptions or reservations to ownership.

Holographic wills   A will that is entirely handwritten and signed by the testator.

Home equity debt   Debt secured by a mortgage on the residence for which the loan proceeds were for other than acquiring the property.

Home equity line of credit   A type of loan allowing the borrower to draw against a line of credit secured by the equity in the borrower's property.

Home equity loan   A type of second mortgage in which the borrower is able to obtain a second mortgage on the property based on the property's appreciation in value (the equity created).

Homeowner's insurance policy   Comprehensive policy covering damage to the home and the homeowner's personal property, protections against personal liability, some legal claims, and limited medical expenses for injured guests.

Homestead exemption   Exemption that prevents the forced sale of a home to pay creditors if the home does not have a certain level of equity.

Hydroelectricity   Energy created by moving water.

Hypothecated   To pledge (give as collateral) real property as security without giving up possession to guarantee the repayment of the loan.

I

Illusory promise   A promise that is not binding on a party. The party can elect to perform or not perform the promise. The resulting contract lacks consideration and is not enforceable.

Implied authority   Authority granted to an agent by the principal's actions or conduct.

Implied covenant of suitability   A covenant made by the landlord that the leased premises are free from latent defects in regard to the essential facilities needed by that commercial tenant. This implied covenant can be waived, unlike the implied warranty of habitability.

Implied periodic tenancy   A tenancy that arises when a landlord accepts rent at the beginning of a rental period.

Implied warranty of habitability   An implied warranty requiring landlords to provide premises that are habitable. Landlords warrant they will make the premises fit for habitation if they are not.

Impound account   An account kept by a lender on behalf of a borrower to pay for insurance and property taxes.

Incentive zoning   Regulations using a rewards-based system to encourage urban-development goals.

Inclusionary zoning   Regulations requiring portions of new developments to be reserved for low- to moderated-income housing.

Income approach   An appraisal method of valuation based on the property's ability to generate income.

Indexed rate   A rate tied to a cost of living index or similar index.

Industrial plant rule   Occurs when the constructive-annexation test applies to machinery in an industrial setting and the machinery is so heavy that it can no longer be regarded as movable.

Injunction   An equitable remedy by which the court prevents the party from removing the fixture; restrains the nuisance-causing activity.

***In personam* jurisdiction**   Refers to whether the court can exercise jurisdiction over the parties to a controversy.

Inquiry notice   Notice that arises when a party becomes aware, or should have become aware, of certain facts that, if investigated, would reveal the claim of another.

***In rem* jurisdiction**   Refers to the court's jurisdiction over a particular piece of property.

Installment land sale contract   A contract in which the seller provides the financing to the buyer. The seller retains title to the property until the final payment is received.

Institutional lenders   A lender that makes loans to borrowers from its own sources or those that it manages for others.

Insurable interest   A requirement that a person have a property or personal interest in the insured goods, property, or person.

Insurance   A contract that shifts the risk of loss for individuals and businesses to another in exchange for a premium payment.

Insurance agent   An agent of the insurance company, not of the applicant.

Insurance broker   The agent of the insured with regard to matters connected with the application for insurance. A broker can place insurance with a number of different insurance carriers.

Insured   The person who obtains insurance.

Insurer   The insurance company that receives payment from an insured.

Intangible property   Property interests lacking a physical form.

Integration clause   See *Merger clause.*

Intensity zoning   Regulation controlling the density and intensity of structures on land.

Intentionally misrepresents   Occurs when the broker is aware of a material fact and either intentionally misstates the fact or knowingly fails to disclose the material fact to a third party, and the third party justifiably relies on the misrepresentation.

Intentional nondisclosure   Occurs when the broker remains silent when having a duty to disclose the known material facts.

Intermediary   A nonagent broker who is employed to negotiate a transaction between the parties.

Internet listing service   An approach to real estate in which a broker typically does not maintain a traditional office and places his listings on a website.

Interstate Land Sales Full Disclosure Act   Federal law created to protect consumers from fraud and abuse in the sale or lease of unimproved land sold through interstate commerce (commerce crossing over state lines).

***Inter vivos* gifts**   Gifts made during the donor's lifetime.

***Inter vivos* trust**   A trust created during a trustor's life.

Intestate   The decedent died without a valid will at the time of death.

Intestate succession   The process of distributing property in the absence of a valid will.

Inverse condemnation   A form of disguised condemnation whereby the government obtains a benefit without having to pay the landowner for taking the owner's property.

Invitee   Persons who enter land that is generally open to the public or enters land for a business purpose.

Involuntary petition   A petition filed by creditors of a debtor that alleges the debtor is not paying the debts as they become due.

IRC Section 1031 (tax free exchange)   A deferral of the recognition of gain or loss when property held for business or commercial purposes is exchanged for like-kind property.

Irrevocable trusts   Trusts that cannot be changed or revoked during the trustor's life.

Issue   The descendants of the decedent.

J

Joint and several liability A form of unlimited liability in which each partner is liable individually for the entire partnership debt.

Joint tenancy A form of concurrent ownership in which two or more persons own equal shares of property, with the right of survivorship between the joint tenants.

Joint will A will created by two or more testators.

Judicial deed A deed that is issued as a result of a court order due to foreclosure proceedings of other forced sales.

Judicial foreclosure Foreclosure that begins with the filing and serving of a complaint (lawsuit) against persons who have an interest in the real property.

Judicial lien A lien created through a court judgment or other legal action taken by a court.

Jurisdiction The authority of a court or agency to make a legal determination over the person or property of another.

K

Kickback Anything of value (e.g., payments, commissions, fees, gifts, special privileges, etc.) received for referrals of settlement-service business.

L

Land Any unimproved real property.

Landfill A large cavity in the ground that is lined with clay or synthetic liner to prevent any waste from leaking into the ground or water supply.

Land grants Land given to settlers to establish settlements, missions, and farms.

Land-use regulation The regulation of the use of real property by both the public and private sectors.

Latent defect A defect not easily discoverable by reasonable inspection of the property.

Lateral support A requirement that landowners not damage the support of adjacent land by causing land to slip, cave in, fall, or move.

Law Complex set of laws, rules, and regulations that govern the law of real estate.

Lead A highly toxic metal that was used for many years in products found in and around housing.

Lease A contract that transfers exclusive possession of a property from one party (the landlord/lessor) to another (the tenant/lessee) for a period of time (the tenancy).

Legal duty An obligation imposed on an individual either by contract or by applicable law.

Legal right The ability to have an individual interest respected by others and enforced through court process.

Lessee A person who acquires the right to exclusively possess and use property for a duration of time.

Lessor A person who transfers the right to exclusively possess and use property for a duration of time.

License The privilege to use the land of another; usually temporary and revocable.

Licensed residential appraiser An appraiser who is qualified to appraise one- to four-unit non-complex residential properties having a transaction value of up to $1,000,000 or complex residential properties having a transaction value of up to $250,000.

Licensee A person who enters land with permission of the owner.

Lien A legal instrument by which property acts as security for the repayment of a debt.

Lien theory The process of distributing property in the absence of a valid will.

Life estate An estate in which the property is held for the duration of a person's lifetime.

Life estate *pur autre vie* An estate in which the measuring life of the estate is that of someone other than the holder of the life estate.

Life tenants The person holding the life estate interest.

Like-kind property Requirement that both the real property exchanged and the real property received must be business, trade, or investment property.

Limited common areas Areas where the use is limited to one or more owners within a subdivision.

Limited liability company (LLC) A business entity created under state law in which the owners (members) are not personally liable for the debts and obligations of the entity.

Limited partnership A partnership that has both general and limited partners.

Lineal descendants A relative in the direct line of descent of the decedent including children, grandchildren, and so on.

Liquidated damages A contract provision by which the parties agree at the time of entering into the contract the damages to be paid by a party if there is a material breach of contract.

Liquidation The conversion of nonexempt assets into cash, which is then distributed to the creditors.

Lis pendens A recorded notice of a pending lawsuit that may affect title to real property.

Listing agents Real estate agent who represents the seller of the property.

Listing agreements Written contracts between brokers and their clients.

Littoral rights Waterfront property owners' right to water from an adjacent lake, sea, or ocean.

Loan commitment A lender's promise to make a loan upon the occurrence of certain conditions.

Loan estimate Disclosures provided no later than three business days after consumer submits a loan application providing key features, costs, and risks of the mortgage for which they are applying.

Loan origination fee A fee that the borrower pays to the lender to secure the loan.

Loan servicer A company that manages the collection of payment from borrowers.

Loss The amount of money realized from the sale of the property below the adjusted basis of the property.

M

Mailbox rule   A rule in contract law that provides an acceptance is effective upon dispatch, if the requested manner of acceptance delivery was used, even if it was lost in transmission.

Maker   See *Debtor*.

Marketable record title acts   State laws that limit the look-back for examination of the public records. These acts clear the title of old defects and reduce the number of required title searches.

Marketable title   A title that is free from any unknown encumbrances or liens. Only agreed-upon encumbrances (such as real property taxes) may exist when title is conveyed, subject to certain exceptions.

Market approach   An appraisal method in which valuation is based on sale prices of similar properties.

Market value   The price agreed upon by a willing buyer and seller.

Material breach   A breach of contract where the party renders inferior performance of his duties and fails to substantially perform the contract terms.

Material fact   A fact that a reasonable person would consider important in making a decision; a fact that is important to the contract's subject matter.

Maturity date   Date of the final payment of a debt.

McCarran Ferguson Act of 1945   A federal law that delegated regulation of the insurance industry to the states.

Mechanic's lien   A specific lien recorded by a contractor, subcontractor, or material supplier for unpaid sums owed it under a construction-related contract.

Mechanic's lien release bond   A bond issued to release the lien from the title.

Mediation   A nonjudicial process in which the participants, with the help of a neutral person, attempt to reach an agreement to resolve the dispute.

Meeting of creditors   A meeting of the debtor's creditors and the debtor, where the debtor submits to questioning, under oath, by the creditors regarding the debtor's assets, finances, any transfers of property prior to bankruptcy, and so forth.

Mello-Roos assessments   See *Special assessments*.

Merger clause (integration clause)   A clause in a contract stating the parties intend the written agreement be the final and complete expression of the written contract terms.

Merger doctrine   A legal rule providing that the deed replaces all of the promises made between the buyer and seller in their purchase agreement.

Metes and bounds   A legal description that uses a series of instructions that set forth all boundary lines by describing the length and direction of the boundaries of the property.

Minor breach   A nonmaterial breach of contract by which complete performance is not rendered. The breaching party has substantially performed and the breaching party's performance deviates only slightly from the contract. Exceptions apply.

Mirror image rule   A rule in contract law requiring the offeree to accept the terms as stated in the offer.

Misrepresentation   A form of fraud arising from an intentional false representation of a material fact to another person upon which reasonable reliance is placed to that party's detriment.

Mitigation of damages   A legal doctrine requiring the nonbreaching and injured party to take reasonable steps to avoid or reduce damages.

Modified gross lease   A lease in which the tenant pays a fixed rate each month, as well as a share of other costs in the property.

Mold   A naturally occurring fungus that grows in warm, damp places and is spread by airborne spores.

Monetary damages   Money awarded to compensate for the injury or loss incurred.

Monuments   Objects used to define either the point of beginning or corners of a parcel of land.

Mortgage   A real estate security instrument. Borrower retains title but gives a lien interest and note to the lender. Also known as hypothecation.

Mortgage banker   A person who establishes a relationship with multiple lenders to offer different lending products to the mortgage banker's customers. Individuals employed as a mortgage banker are also known as mortgage loan originators.

Mortgagee   The lender or creditor in a mortgage agreement.

Mortgage Electronic Registration Systems (MERS)   A private land-title registration system created by mortgage banking companies to expedite the transfer and securitization of mortgage loans.

Mortgage insurance premium   A loan surcharge for a minimum of five years, regardless of the amount of the down payment, to reduce the risk of FHA loans to the federal government.

Mortgage loan originator   An individual who takes a residential loan application and offers or negotiates the terms of a residential mortgage loan for compensation.

Mortgagor   The owner-borrower in a mortgage agreement.

Multiple Listing Services   A network of real estate listings that provide listing brokers a larger market in which to advertise their listings.

Mutual wills   Where two or more testators execute separate wills and leave their property to each other on the condition that the surviving person, on his or her death, leaves the remaining property as agreed upon by the testators.

N

Named insured   In the event of a covered loss, the person or business receiving payment from the insurance company.

Natural monuments   Monuments formed by nature, which include mountaintops, streams, rivers, watercourses, and trees.

Natural rights doctrine   Certain individual rights may not be taken away by the government.

Navigable airspace   Airspace above the minimum safe altitude provided currently by the Federal Aviation Administration.

Navigable waters   Bodies of water that can be used for business or transportation purposes.

Negative easement   An easement that prohibits the servient tenement from some use of the land.

Negligence   Conduct falling below the standard of care for what a reasonable person would do under similar circumstances.

Net listing   A method of compensating a broker in which the broker must sell the property above a net price in order to receive any commission. Any price above the net price is the broker's commission.

No-damages-for-delay   A contract provision preventing a contractor from recovering damages for extra time spent on the project.

No deal, no commission clause   Clause that makes the closing of the deal a condition precedent to a commission.

Nonagent broker   A person who assists buyers and sellers in administrative acts to close the real estate transaction without representing the buyer or the seller.

Noncommercial easements (personal easements) in gross   Easements granted for the owner's personal use.

Nonconforming loan   A loan that fails to meet Fannie Mae and Freddie Mac purchase criteria.

Nonconforming use   A preexisting use that is allowed to continue and whose use is incompatible with current allowable uses in that zoned area.

Noncore proceedings   A legal proceeding that is not essential to the disposition of the bankruptcy estate.

Nonfreehold estate   An estate in which the tenant has a right to possess the real property but does not obtain a real property interest.

Nonownership theory   Some states treat mineral interests as migratory and flowing from one parcel of land to another. The first landowner who captures the mineral interests owns the mineral interest.

Nonpoint source   A source of pollution originating from many sources.

Nonpossessory interest   An interest in land that constitutes less than full possession or ownership of the land.

Nonrecourse obligations   A secured obligation or debt that is secured by a pledge of collateral, typically real property, but for which the borrower is not personally liable. Following the sale of the collateral due to default, the lender's payment is limited to the proceeds of the sale of collateral.

Notary public   A commissioned representative of a state that is charged with verifying the identity of the signor of the documents.

Notice of completion   A notice that construction activities have completed. This starts the time to record mechanic's liens.

Notice of non-responsibility   A notice posted by the owner in a conspicuous location on the land that shows that the owner's interest will not be affected by a tenant's improving the leasehold interest and failing to pay a subcontractor.

Notice of pending action (aka *lis pendens*)   A written notice that a lawsuit has been filed concerning real estate, involving either the title to the property or a claimed ownership interest in it. The notice is usually recorded in the land records of the county in which the property is located.

Notice statute A recording statute that provides title to the last bona fide purchaser.

Notice to owner A notice given to the owner alerting them that persons performing work on the project expect to be paid.

Novation A substitution of a new agreement or party for an existing one.

Nuisance A substantial and unreasonable interference with the use and enjoyment of another's land.

Nuisance *per se* Negligence arising from the violation of a public duty.

Nuncupative wills An oral will that is not in writing.

O

Objective intent A theory of contract law providing that the intent to be bound by an offer is determined by using a reasonable person standard and not by the party's subjective intent.

Offer An expression of intent to enter into a binding and enforceable contract that may be oral, written, or arising from a party's conduct.

Offeree The person who receives an offer to enter into a contract.

Offeror The person who makes an offer to enter into a contract.

Open listing Listing in which the owner can employ more than one broker to sell the same property.

Option contract A contract created when an offeree provides consideration to the offeror to keep an offer open for an agreed-upon time. The offeror is prevented from revoking the offer during the option period.

Order for relief A court order that allows the case to proceed through bankruptcy.

Organizational credit transactions Loans mot made to natural persons, such as loans to corporations, partnerships, churches, unions, or fraternal organizations.

Ouster A forceful removal or not allowing a co-tenant access to the premises.

Owner's Policy Title insurance that insures an owner's land interest against defect, liens, and encumbrances.

Ownership theory Some states provide, through a deed, that the owner of property owns the minerals beneath the property but can lose the interests if they are captured by adjacent landowner's through drilling.

P

Parol Evidence Rule A rule of evidence used in interpreting written contracts. The rule prevents any oral or written statements that alter, contradict, or are in addition to the terms of a written contract. Applies to prior or contemporaneous statement made at the time of entering into the contract. Exceptions apply.

Partially disclosed principal A principal whose existence is known to the third party but whose identity is not known.

Partition A legal remedy in which the court can order the division and sale of a property.

Partnership An association of two or more persons to carry on as co-owners of a business for profit.

Part performance exception   An exception to the Statute of Frauds. Allows oral real estate contracts to be enforceable if any two of the following three elements are met: (1) the purchase price has been fully or partially paid, (2) the party has received possession of the property, and/or (3) valuable improvements have been made to the property.

Patent defect   A defect that is obvious and apparent or could be discovered upon a reasonable inspection of the property.

Payee   A person who receives payment under a note or negotiable instrument (such as a check).

Payment bonds   A bond that guarantees that all claims for labor, material, equipment, and services provided to the project will be paid.

Per capita **distribution**   Form of distributing the decedent's estate in which the living lineal descendants equally share the property of the estate.

Percentage lease   A lease in which the tenant pays a fixed base rent and, in addition, pays a percentage of the revenue earned from the business.

Percolating water   Water that flows underneath the soil and is found in the pores, cracks, and spaces between rock particles.

Performance bond   A bond that ensures the project will be completed by the contracting team or by the surety in the event of a default.

Periodic tenancy   A lease that lasts for a fixed period and continues to renew for like periods until terminated.

Personal property   Property that is movable and not fixed or permanently attached to real property.

Personal representative   Gender-neutral term used to denote the person who administers the estate.

Per stirpes **distribution**   Form of distributing the decedent's estate in which surviving lineal descendants inherit through representation of their parents' inheritance share.

Petition for writ of certiorari   A petition asking the Supreme Court to hear a case.

Piggyback mortgage   A type of mortgage that occurs when a borrower takes out two mortgages for the property at the same time.

Place of public accommodation   Businesses, buildings, or facilities that are open or offer services to the general public.

Planned communities   A community developed with a common design for streets, recreational facilities, and other amenities among a mix of housing types.

Plat   A plan or map of a subdivision.

Point source   A discernible, specific discharge point of pollution into surface waters.

Points   A percentage of a loan given to the lender as additional consideration for the making of the loan. One point equals one percent of a loan.

Police power   The government's power to control the activities and rights of persons subject to its jurisdiction.

Policy limits   The amount of insurance proceeds that are payable under the policy.

Possibility of reverter   A fee simple determinable's future interest held by the grantor.

Posthumous child   A child born after the decedent's death.

Postnuptial agreements   Agreements made after a marriage that limit or waive a spouse's right to marital property.

Potentially Responsible Party (PRP)   A party who is liable for the cleanup of a hazardous waste site.

Power of attorney   The appointment of an agent by the principal to authorize the agent to act on behalf of the principal that must be signed by the principal.

Pre-workout agreement   A written agreement between the lender and borrower to permit negotiation of the loan terms while preserving the rights and remedies of each party.

Predatory lending   A term used to describe illegal and abusive lending practices (such as refinancing without any benefit to the borrower or making loans to borrowers who cannot repay the loan).

Preemption   A legal doctrine by which the laws of a higher authority displace the application of laws issued by a lower jurisdiction when the lower jurisdiction's laws conflict with those of the higher jurisdiction.

Preferential transfers   A wrongful transfer of the debtor's property benefiting one or more creditors allowing them to receive more than they would have otherwise received in a Chapter 7 liquidation.

Preliminary report   A report prepared prior to issuing a policy of title insurance showing the owner of a parcel of land, along with the liens and encumbrances on title.

Premises   The actual space or property that is to be occupied by the tenant.

Premium   The cost of insurance paid by an insured.

Prenuptial agreements   Agreements made prior to marriage between prospective spouses that limit or waive a spouse's right to marital property.

Present interest   The current ownership in property.

Pretermitted children   Children born or adopted after the execution of a will.

Primary market   Market where loans are originated, either through a broker or directly with the lender.

Prime contract   A contract between the owner and prime contractor that is created once the owner selects the prime contractor.

Prime contractor   A contractor hired directly by an owner of real property to construct an improvement to the land.

Principal   An individual who authorizes another to act on her behalf.

Principal meridian lines   North-south longitudinal lines.

Prior appropriation doctrine   The right of priority acquired on a "first in time, first in right to use water over later users."

Priority   The holder of the security interest has the right to be paid first among all creditors with respect to that collateral.

Private mortgage insurance   Insurance for lenders against foreclosure losses.

Private nuisance   Substantial and unreasonable interferences with the use and enjoyment of another's land.

Private wells   Wells serving less than 25 people.

Privity   The state of two parties being in contract with each other, which can be met by a contract, deed, will, or the laws of intestacy.

Probate   The process of a decedent's property being collected, debts and taxes paid, and the remainder of the estate being distributed.

Procuring cause   A broker who, through his efforts, laid the foundation for the negotiations resulting in a sale and may be entitled to a commission on the transaction.

Profit   The right to enter another's land and take something from it, such as timber.

Promissory note   An executed (signed) instrument acknowledging a debt and promising to pay a creditor.

Proof of claim   Written verification supporting debt owed that is submitted by a creditor to the bankruptcy court.

Property   Anything that can be owned, possessed, controlled, divided, transferred, sold, and made unavailable to others.

Property management   The administration, operation, and management of real property.

Property tax lien   A lien imposed upon real property to secure the payment of property taxes.

Proprietary lease   A lease from a cooperative to a tenant providing for the unit's occupancy.

Public Land Survey System   A method of describing property that divides land in United States down to six-mile-square townships.

Public nuisances   A substantial and unreasonable interference with the health, safety, or morals of the public.

Public use   In the context of eminent domain, any conceivable benefit to the public welfare can be deemed a public use.

Public water systems   Water systems that have at least 15 service connections or serving at least 25 people.

Purchase money mortgage   A mortgage financing the purchase a one to four unit residential property.

Purchase money security interest   A security agreement involving a creditor advancing funds for the purchase of collateral.

Q

Qualified intermediary   An entity that accepts the funds, prepares escrow for the sale, and handles the legal contracts.

Quiet title action   A legal action in which the court establishes who has title to real property against any challenges or claims to ownership of the property.

Quitclaim deed   A deed in which the grantor conveys what interest, if any, the grantor has in a specific piece of property.

R

Race-notice statute   A recording statute that states that the first bona fide purchaser to record keeps title to the property.

Race statute A recording statute that provides title to the first party to record, even if the first to record obtained his interest later in time.

Racial steering Illegal practice of directing minorities to particular areas.

Radon A naturally occurring radioactive gas found in nearly all soils that travels through cracks in the foundation of a home and causes lung cancer.

Range lines A north–south line placed every six miles from the principal meridian that creates the east or west boundary of a township.

Ratification The principal may approve, or ratify, unauthorized acts committed by the agent.

Ready, willing, and able A buyer who can purchase the property at the price stated in the listing agreement and under the terms and conditions of the listing agreement.

Reaffirmation agreement An agreement in which the debtor agrees to continue to pay a dischargeable debt to a creditor after the discharge in bankruptcy.

Real estate broker A state-licensed special agent hired by a principal for a fee to purchase or sell real estate on the principal's behalf.

Real Estate Investment Trust (REIT) A corporate entity or trust that invests in real property managed by a trustee.

Real estate licensee A person (broker or salesperson) holding a real estate license granted by the government or agency, typically the state's Department of Real Estate.

Real estate salesperson A state-licensed special agent who assists a broker in real estate transactions.

Real Estate Settlement Procedures Act (RESPA) Federal law administered by the Consumer Financial Protection Bureau charged with ensuring that consumers receive information about the cost of their mortgages and closings.

Real property The earth and all that is permanently attached and connected to it.

Reasonable conduct rule The allowance of the diversion of surface water so long as the conduct is deemed "reasonable" under the circumstances.

Reasonableness review standard A rule wherein rules adopted by the board of directors that were based on reasonable decision will be upheld.

Receiver A person appointed by the court or the parties to preserve or manage assets in a receivership.

Receivership A legal proceeding whereby a third party is assigned to preserve or manage assets.

Recording statute A state statute providing constructive notice is deemed to have been given to third parties by virtue of filing a document in the public domain.

Reformation The correction of a written legal description to conform to the original parties to the instrument.

Regulation Z Federal Reserve regulations implementing the Truth-in-Lending Act.

Regulatory Takings A government regulation that deprives the owner of all economic beneficial use of the property.

Reliction   The process of uncovering land by a permanent recession of a body of water rather than a seasonal retreat of water.

Religious Land Use and Institutionalized Persons Act   Act that gives churches and other religious facilities a way to avoid burdensome zoning restrictions on their property use.

Remainder   A future interest held in someone other than the grantor that results following the death of the life tenant.

Remedial actions   Long-term actions used to clean up sites that do not pose an immediate risk to public health.

Removal actions   Actions eliminating immediate risks of uncontrolled hazardous waste sites to ensure public safety.

Rent control   Local ordinances that can regulate and restrict a landlord's ability to increase rent and other fees.

Reorganization   A negotiation process that allows the debtor and its creditors to develop a plan for the adjustment and discharge of the debts owed by the debtor.

Rescission   Cancellation of a contract. It places the parties in their original positions prior to contract.

Reservation of rights   An insurance carrier's notification to an insured that coverage for a claim may not exist under the policy.

Reserve account   See *Impound account.*

Residential lease   A lease used for personal purposes such as an apartment or house.

Restitution   Restoration of both parties to their original positions prior to the formation of the contract.

Restrictive covenant   An unconditional promise. When recorded on title it is binding upon successor owners.

Retaliatory eviction   A wrongful eviction that occurs when the landlord retaliates against a tenant's good faith complaint.

Retention   An amount retained by the owner from monies due a contractor to ensure completion of the project. Retention is disbursed upon project completion.

Reverse mortgage   A type of mortgage for people aged 62 or older whereby the mortgagor borrows against her equity by receiving monthly payments.

Reversion   A future interest held in the grantor that results following the death of the life tenant.

Revocable trust (living trust)   A trust that can be changed or revoked at any time prior to the trustor's death.

Right of reentry, or power of termination   The future interest held by the grantor or the grantor's heirs in the event that the fee's condition is not met.

Right of removal   The right to remove fixtures in certain cases and personal property in all cases.

Right of survivorship   Upon the death of one joint tenant, the surviving joint tenants automatically receive equal shares from the deceased joint tenant.

Riparian doctrine   The right of a landowner to the reasonable use of water on, under, or adjacent to his property.

Rule Against Perpetuities   Holds that all future interests in real property must vest within 21 years after the death of someone who was alive on the effective date of the grant.

Rule in Dumpor's Case   A rule stating if a landlord consents to one assignment, it is presumed that the landlord has consented to all further assignments.

Rule in Shelley's Case   A fee simple absolute interest in which the life estate in the grantee merges with a remainder in the grantee's heirs.

Rule of Capture   Entitles an owner to the minerals that are captured and stored from a well on the owner's property, even if the gas and oil flowed to the well from beneath another's property.

Run with the land   Once created, easements automatically transfer when the property is transferred, even if the easement is not mentioned in the conveyance.

S

Safe Drinking Water Act (SDWA)   An act authorizing the EPA to set national health-based standards for drinking water found in public water systems.

Sale leaseback   A transaction in which a property owner sells the property to an investor, who then immediately leases the property back to the seller, as stated in the sales contract.

Sales-comparison approach   See *Market approach.*

Sales puffing   A statement of opinion describing the greatness of a property.

S Corporation   A small form of corporation that elects to be taxed as a partnership.

Secondary market   Market where investors (e.g., mutual funds or life-insurance companies) purchase loans made by others.

Second mortgage   The mortgage recorded next in time after a first mortgage is recorded.

Section   A one-square mile containing 640 acres.

Secured claim   A claim secured by a valid lien on the debtor's real or personal property.

Secured creditor   A creditor whose loan has collateral (e.g., real property) is used to secure the repayment of the debt in the event of a default.

Secured transaction   An agreement whereby a lender or seller retains a security interest in personal property of the debtor.

Security   A passive investment not actively managed by the investor.

Security agreement   An agreement whereby a lender or seller retains a security interest in personal property.

Security deposit   A type of deposit used to protect the landlord to cover expenses for any damage caused to the property or damages suffered because of a tenant's nonperformance of its obligations under a lease.

Security interest   An interest in property to secure a debt.

Seller's warranties policy   A policy that provides insurance to guarantee the representations made by sellers in real estate transaction contracts.

Selling expenses   Expenses involved in selling a home, such as the brokers' commissions, advertising fees, legal fees, and loan charges paid by the seller.

Selling price   The total consideration received for the sale of the home.

Separate property   Property of a spouse that does not become part of the community property.

Servicemembers Civil Relief Act (SCRA)   Federal statute that suspends temporarily judicial and administrative proceedings and transactions against servicemembers during their military service.

Servient tenement (servient estate)   The party whose land is burdened by an easement appurtenant.

Settlement agent   The person or company who causes all of the conveyance documents, mortgages, notes, and monies to be exchanged between the buyer and seller.

Settlement process   A method of closing in which both the buyer and the seller exchange documents in person.

Sheriff's deed   A deed without warranties issued to purchaser following foreclosure or tax sale.

Shock the conscience standard   As used in real estate, a manifestly and grossly unjust sales price.

Short sale   A sale that occurs when a lender allows a property to be sold for less than the current amount owed to the lender under the note and secured by a mortgage or deed of trust.

Sick building syndrome   Term used to describe a range of health problems occurring as a result of exposure to pollutants within a building when a cause for the health problems cannot be specifically identified.

Single asset real estate   A case in which a creditor whose claim is secured by an interest in the real property may obtain relief from the automatic stay unless, within 90 days after the petition date, the debtor either (1) files a plan of reorganization that has a reasonable possibility of being confirmed within a reasonable time or (2) begins making monthly payments to the secured creditor in an amount equal to interest at the nondefault contract rate on the secured real property loan.

Slander of title   Law that states that a property owner can sue a person for publishing false statements and disparaging her title in such a way that it causes damages.

Slant drilling   Angling and extending the oil or gas drill into another's property.

Solar   Energy created by capturing the radiant light and heat from the sun.

Sole proprietorship   A business entity form whereby title of property is held by an individual owner.

Spearin **doctrine**   A warranty provided by the owner promising the correctness of plans and specifications and holding that the contractor will not be responsible for defects in the plans and specifications.

Special assessments   Assessments that levy new taxes and fees that formerly were paid by local property taxes.

Special warranty deed   A warranty deed that contains the same warranties as a general warranty deed except that the covenant period is applied only to the grantor and not to all previous owners as in a general warranty deed.

Specific gift   A gift of a specific item of property in a will.

Specific liens   Liens that attach to a particular parcel of land only.

Specific performance   An equitable remedy of a court by which the court can compel a party to perform the terms of the contract.

Spot zoning   Regulation permitting a use different from those allowed in that zoned area.

Stare decisis   Latin for "to stand by the decision." A legal principal that requires a court to apply prior appellate case holdings as precedent binding on the court once certain facts have been established.

Statute   A law enacted by federal or state legislation.

Statute of Frauds   A state requirement that certain types of contracts be in writing to be enforceable.

Statute of Limitations   The maximum legal period during which a legal proceeding may be initiated, measured from date of occurrence of the event giving rise to the right to pursue the legal claim.

Statutory liens   Liens created by state statutes.

Statutory redemption period   The right of a borrower to redeem (retain) the mortgaged property after a foreclosure sale occurs within a time period established by state law.

Stop notice   A statutory remedy allowing an unpaid subcontractor or material supplier to reach the unexpended construction funds held by the owner.

Strawman   A third party that receives temporary title transfer so that the four unity requirement of joint tenancy can be met

Strict foreclosure   A foreclosure where, if the borrower does not pay within the court-designated time, the title to the property vests in the lender without any sale of the property.

Strictly liable   Liability without fault.

Subcontractor   A contractor hired by a prime contractor to perform specific construction related tasks on a construction project.

Subjacent support   A requirement that adjacent landowners preserve the support of the surface of the earth by not causing the land to subside.

Sublease   A transfer of a portion of the leasehold estate from a tenant to a third party (a subtenant).

Subprime loan   A loan made to a borrower who could not qualify for a loan from a conventional, FHA, or VA lender.

Surface waters   Waters that originate from rain, springs, or melting snow.

Surveying   The process of measuring and mapping land.

T

Tacking   If an adverse possessor has not been in possession for the statutory period, this rule allows him to add the periods of adverse use by prior adverse possessors.

Taking subject to a mortgage   When a purchaser buys real estate aware of a mortgage and makes payments on the mortgage but does not agree to become personally liable to repay the mortgage debt.

Tangible property   Property that exists in physical form.

Tax assessor   A public official who appraises all taxable properties within a jurisdiction.

Tax credit   A reduction in the amount of taxes a taxpayer is obligated to pay.

Tax deduction   A reduction to taxable income.

Tax-free exchange   See *IRC Section 1031*.

Tax lien   A lien imposed by law upon a debtor's property to secure the payment of taxes.

Tax-lien sale   A public sale of real property due to a failure to timely pay property taxes.

Tenancy   The duration of a tenant's occupancy or possession.

Tenancy at sufferance   A tenancy in which a tenant remains in possession of the property after the tenancy period has terminated without the permission of the landlord.

Tenancy at will   A lease with no stated term and no provision for the collection of rent.

Tenancy by the entirety   A form of joint tenancy limited to married couples.

Tenancy for years   An estate for a fixed and definite period of time.

Tenancy in common   A form of co-ownership of real property in which parties may hold equal or unequal shares in the land and have separate but undivided interests in the entire property as a whole.

Terrorism insurance   Insurance which protects against damages caused by terrorist activities.

Testamentary trust   A trust that takes effect upon the settlor's death.

Testate   The decedent had a valid will at the time of death.

Testator or **testatrix**   A person who makes a will.

The Comprehensive Environmental Response, Compensation, and Liability Act (CERCLA)   Also known as "Superfund," this law authorized the EPA to clean up uncontrolled hazardous waste sites and force responsible parties to perform cleanups or reimburse the EPA for doing so.

Third-party coverage   Coverage that pays third parties for damages because of the acts and omissions of the insured.

TILA-RESPA Integrated Disclosure rule   CFPB (Consumer Financial Protection Bureau) rule requiring specific loan disclosures to consumer borrowers.

Timeshare   A form of ownership characterized by a fractionalized ownership with a specified period of use.

Title   Evidence of ownership of land passed by a deed or court order.

Title abstract   A condensed chronological summary of the title's history that follows a chain of title search.

Title assurance   Third party's promise that the owner holds legal title to the property. Most commonly made by a title insurance company to a purchaser or lender.

Title closing   A method of closing in which the settlement agent arranges for the principals involved in the transaction to meet in one place where all the documents needed to transfer title and to fund the loan can be reviewed and executed.

Title commitment   An agreement by a title insurance company to issue a policy in favor of the proposed insured at the time the transaction closes. It does not represent the state of title.

Title insurance   A policy insuring against loss incurred as the result of defective title.

Title opinion   A written certificate of title opinion as to who owns the real estate, the quality of title, and exceptions, if any, to clear title for the transaction.

Title theory   A legal rule recognizing that the buyer transfers title to the real property lender during the term of the loan. Title is restored to the buyer-borrower when the obligation is paid in full.

Torrens title system   System in which a certificate and deed identify who owns the title.

Tort   Wrongful conduct that allows an injured party to sue for damages.

Townhouse   A form of housing where the houses are two or more stories with common walls, and the owner owns the land on which the unit is built.

Township   The six-mile squares created by the intersection of the range lines and township lines.

Township lines   An east–west line placed every six miles from the base line that forms the north or south boundary of a township.

Tract index system   A system in which records are indexed and summarized for each parcel of land.

Trade fixtures   Personal property installed by a business tenant used in conducting a trade or business on the premises. They are considered personal property and may be removed by the tenant.

Trainee appraiser   An appraiser who needs no experience but must be supervised by a certified residential real property appraiser or a certified general appraiser in good standing.

Transaction broker   A nonagent broker who is licensed as a facilitator to the closing of the transaction.

Transferable development rights   The sale or transfer of the right to develop property. Commonly used with the transfer of a right to build within air space.

Treaties   Agreements with foreign governments.

Trespasser   A person who enters another's land without permission.

Trespass to land   An intentional invasion of a tangible object to another's land without consent.

Triggering term   Term that includes a reference to the amount or number of monthly payments, the cash amount or percentage of down payment required, the length of the loan, or the amount of finance charges.

Triple net leases   A lease in which the tenant pays the landlord a fixed gross amount each month and also pays for the property's operating expenses (property maintenance, insurance, and property taxes).

Truth in Lending Act   Federal law requiring disclosures to consumers allowing consumers to compare loan terms and conditions by various lenders.

Trust   A legal arrangement in which one person transfers property to another to be held and used for the benefit of a third person.

Trustee   The party to a deed of trust holding (equitable) title until the underlying obligation is paid in full. Responds to demands of the beneficiary regarding enforcement of the deed of trust.

Trustor   The property owner or party to a deed of trust.

U

Umbrella policy   Liability insurance coverage that covers damages in excess of the basic liability policy that covered real or personal property. Umbrella insurance pays only where the underlying policy limits have been exhausted.

Underground storage tank system (UST)   An underground tank and any underground piping that has at least 10 percent of its combined volume underground.

Underinsurance   Occurs when the insurance policy is insufficient to cover the costs of rebuilding a home after a peril.

Underwriting   The lender's process of evaluating the credit worthiness of the prospective borrower and the suitability of the collateral.

Undisclosed principal   A principal whose existence or identity is unknown to the third party.

Undue influence   A defense asserted to the enforcement of a contract arising from the misuse of a fiduciary relationship.

Unearned fee provision   Prohibits a person from giving or accepting any part of a charge for services that are not performed.

Uniform Commercial Code   A uniform set of laws related to the sale of goods.

Uniform Partnership Act   Governing body that oversees partnerships.

Uniform Premarital Agreement Act   Act designed to create uniform governing laws regarding premarital agreements and to permit engaged couples to arrange for the disposition of their property in accordance with their personal wishes.

Uniform Probate Code   A uniform law governing inheritance and probate matters adopted in approximately one third of the states.

Uniform Residential Landlord and Tenant Act (URLTA)   A model act that has been proposed by the National Conference of Commissioners on Uniform State Laws for adoption by individual states.

Uniform Standard of Professional Appraisal Practice (USPAP)   The minimum standards of conduct for appraisals that assist in generating a certain level of trust in the appraisal process.

United States district courts   The primary trial courts of the federal court system.

Unlawful detainer   A legal proceeding a landlord must use to evict a tenant.

Unsecured claim A claim in which no property or asset serves as collateral or security for the debt.

Unsecured debt A loan that does not have some property or asset serving as collateral (i.e., security) for the debt.

Use variances Variances that allow a nonpermitted use to occur in the zoned location.

U.S. Army Corps of Engineers A federal agency responsible for public engineering, design, and construction management.

U.S. Department of Housing and Development (HUD) A cabinet department of the executive branch of the federal government supporting community development and environmental health.

U.S. trustee A federal government official who handles and supervises administrative tasks within a bankruptcy case.

Usury A rate of interest above the maximum permitted by state or federal law.

Unitization or **pooling** Limitation that prevents drillers from taking disproportionate amounts of the underground resources. The unitization of gas and oil production permits the entire field to be operated as a single entity without regard to the surface boundaries.

V

Variance An exception to the allowable uses within a zoned area.

Venue The place where a particular case should be filed or administered by a court.

Vested remainder A remainder interest provided to an ascertained or identified person or persons that does not contain a condition.

Void Contracts that have no legal affect and cannot be enforced.

Voidable Where a person can elect to perform or not perform the contract.

Voluntary liens Liens that the owner agrees to place against her title.

Voluntary payment clause If an insured fixes a problem or damage and then notifies the insurer and seeks coverage, the insurer can deny coverage.

Voluntary petition A petition filed by the insolvent debtor.

W

Waste Destruction, harm or injury caused to the use of real property by a person in possession of the property.

Waste disposal site An area of land designated for the proper disposition of discarded or discharged materials.

Watercourse A stream of water flowing in a fixed direction or course in a bed with banks. The term is applied only to inland streams such as rivers, brooks, and creeks, which are distinguished only by the water volume.

Water right The right to use water.

Will A legal instrument declaring how a person wants their property distributed upon death.

Wind energy Energy created by moving air through wind turbines.

Workout An agreement to restructure a loan.

Wraparound mortgage   A type of mortgage in which the seller keeps the existing mortgage on the property and extends to the buyer a junior mortgage that wraps around and exists in addition to a senior mortgage.

Wrongful or mistaken improver   Permits an innocent improver of the property of another to remove goods where a person acting in good faith improves the land of another.

Z

Zoning   Local regulations that regulate the use of various areas of land.

Zoning amortization provisions   Regulations that permit nonconforming uses to continue for a period of time before those uses will no longer be permitted.

Table of Cases

Principal cases are indicated by italics.

Index